ADMINISTRATIVE LAW

FOURTH EDITION

*This book is dedicated to
Professors Albert Melone and William McLauchlan,
who provided excellent role models
at crucial points in my life.*

ADMINISTRATIVE LAW

FOURTH EDITION

Steven J. Cann
Washburn University

SAGE Publications
Thousand Oaks ▪ London ▪ New Delhi

For information:

Sage Publications, Inc.
2455 Teller Road
Thousand Oaks, California 91320
E-mail: order@sagepub.com

Sage Publications Ltd.
1 Oliver's Yard
55 City Road
London EC1Y 1SP
United Kingdom

Sage Publications India Pvt. Ltd.
B-42, Panchsheel Enclave
Post Box 4109
New Delhi 110 017 India

Printed in the United States of America

Library of Congress Cataloging-in-Publication Data

Cann, Steven J.
Administrative law / Steven J. Cann.— 4th ed.
    p. cm.
Includes bibliographical references and index.
ISBN 978-1-4129-1396-6 (cloth)
    1. Administrative law—United States—Cases. 2. Administrative procedure—United States—Cases. 3. Civil service—United States—Cases. I. Title.
KF5402.A4C355 2006
342.73'06—dc22

                                    2005008160

This book is printed on acid-free paper.

08   10   9   8   7   6   5   4   3   2

Acquiring Editor:	Al Bruckner
Editorial Assistant:	MaryAnn Vail
Production Editor:	Diana E. Axelsen
Copy Editor:	Jacqueline A. Tasch
Typesetter:	C&M Digitals (P) Ltd.
Indexer:	David Luljak
Cover Designer:	Michelle Lee Kenny

CONTENTS IN BRIEF

DETAILED CONTENTS

Part II: The Administrative Process

Part III: Substantive Issues in Administrative Law

LIST OF CASES

PREFACE TO THE FOURTH EDITION

Of the courses I teach, administrative law is the most rewarding. One can readily see the fruits of one's labor as students learn about a subject that so many know so little about—the workings of bureaucracy and administrative law. Student evaluations of the course indicated satisfaction with the subject matter but dissatisfaction with the various texts that I had tried. That dissatisfaction, I believed, stemmed from the fact that many texts were written by lawyers and practitioners without an undergraduate audience in mind. The texts on the market at the time were either law school casebooks or texts with few cases in them. Law school casebooks tend to be underutilized in administrative law courses for undergraduates and master's level courses. I believe in the case method as a pedagogical approach, however, and I thought a casebook could be written that would strike a better balance in terms of the number of cases presented and that would be more student friendly than texts on the market at that time. This text, I believe, has addressed these points and offers several distinguishing features for both students and faculty.

DISTINGUISHING FEATURES OF THIS TEXT

Student-Friendly Conceptual Framework. The book is organized around a conceptual framework that contrasts democracy with the administrative state or "fourth branch of government" (significant policy making by insulated technocrats and bureaucrats), and students are already familiar with the concept of democracy.

Illustrative Cases. Each chapter begins with a scenario, or case in point, presented somewhat polemically, to pique the students' interest. These cases demonstrate an important aspect of the chapter, and often, the student is referred back to the case to illustrate concepts throughout the chapter.

Balance of Cases. Because it has been my experience that cases are an excellent pedagogical device—students enjoy reading them—this text uses cases liberally, more than do most textbooks aimed at an undergraduate or master's level audience. I have tried to find the right balance between too many cases on the one hand and too few on the other (which I find is common in many texts on the market).

More Case Content. In contrast to other texts that use cases, this book also includes more of each case so that students can better grasp what led to the lawsuit and how the Court resolved it. In addition to the introductory case in point, then, the book presents cases throughout each chapter, and chapters end with several more cases relevant to the chapter material. The cases in the middle of chapters tend to be classics or precedent-setting cases, whereas the cases ending each chapter represent more recent decisions on the same points of law.

Summary of Doctrines. Finally, I have included chapter summaries of administrative law doctrines, legal principles, and constitutional tests that students should have gleaned from the cases presented in the chapter and that they should be able to apply to the end-of-chapter cases or to hypothetical cases.

Pedagogical Design. The book is designed to be compatible with a problem-solving pedagogical approach. Questions at the end of cases query students' understanding of doctrines, principles, and constitutional tests and of whether the court applied those doctrines, principles, and tests; modified them; or ignored them. Also, the summary at the end of each chapter is compatible with a pedagogical approach that uses testing by hypothetical cases and requires students to outline.

THEORETICAL FRAMEWORK

The theoretical framework for this text is the juxtaposition of democracy and the fourth branch of government, the administrative state. Democracy is presented simply as the notion that citizens, either directly or indirectly, ought to have some influence on government policy. Each chapter, however, presents the student with examples of the administrative state—decisions and policies made by unaccountable agencies and based on the expertise of unelected individuals. Delegation of power is presented early in the text so that students become aware of the increasing abdication of congressional responsibility to agencies.

The text further argues that the president often possesses the will to control bureaucracy but lacks the raw power to do so. Congress, on the other hand, possesses the power but, generally, lacks the will to exercise it in controlling agencies. Therefore, almost by default, the task of control of the fourth branch of government falls to the courts. Administrative law is the tool at their disposal.

In the last chapter of the book, the student is asked to analyze whether courts are well-suited to this task and whether, on the whole, courts have been successful. As former Secretary of Labor Robert Reich has indicated, volumes have been written about the inconsistency of judicial review and democracy, but almost nothing has been written about the inconsistency between the administrative state and democracy.

AUDIENCE

This book was written for undergraduate students in administrative law at the junior or senior level. It would also be appropriate for master's of public administration courses because even at the graduate level, a law school casebook is underused. Because the text includes more cases, and more of each case, compared with typical casebooks not intended for law schools, it should be suitable for a number of prelaw courses.

CONTENT

Part I of the text consists of four chapters establishing the theoretical context. Chapter 1 combines a description of what agencies do and how they do it with a discussion of democracy. Chapter 2 provides a discussion of the ways in which the president attempts to control bureaucracy, beginning with an analysis of the president's constitutional Article II powers and including an analysis of the presidential appointment and removal powers. Here, the discussion focuses on presidential frustration with appointees and the concept of captivity. Cases are presented and discussed relative to executive removal. The chapter also analyzes other traditional modes of executive control, including a discussion of the concept of the administrative presidency. I argue that although the Constitution fails to provide the president with the raw power necessary to control bureaucracy, Congress has delegated its power to control bureaucracy to the White House staff. Still, whether a given president will use that delegated power depends on the partisanship of the chief executive. The presidential style of Clinton is contrasted with that of Reagan and both Bushes. President Clinton embraced bureaucracy as a policy-making ally whereas his Republican counterparts were hostile to bureaucracy and tried to control agency rule making.

Chapter 3 provides a similar analysis of Congress, demonstrating that Congress clearly possesses the raw power to control agency behavior. However, because of constituency service, "cozy" or "iron" triangles, interest group money and elections, and dependency on agencies for information, Congress generally lacks the will to exercise genuine control over bureaucracy. That is, whereas Congress has little or no incentive to play the watch-dog role or to engage in effective oversight, there are many disincentives.

Chapter 4 explores the impediments to judicial control of bureaucracy. It covers the topics of reviewability, exhaustion, primary jurisdiction, ripeness and finality, and standing and concludes with a discussion of the scope of review that courts can apply to different types of agency action.

The administrative process is the subject matter of Part II. Chapter 5 presents a discussion of bureaucracy and information. It analyzes how agencies get information and what they do with it once they have it. Chapter 6 explores informal agency decision making and subsequent judicial review. Chapter 7 provides an analysis of agency rule making and adjudication.

Part III of the text includes three chapters analyzing specific problems of administrative law. The law of public employment, discussed in Chapter 8, begins this section. This chapter offers an analysis of the law of public employment in education. Students will readily grasp the concept of a property interest with tenure as an example. The discussion then extrapolates to public employment more generally. The last part of Chapter 8 deals with discrimination in public employment. Chapter 9 covers due process of law in contexts other than public employment, and Chapter 10 presents the legal liability of government and individual government employees.

The final chapter summarizes the cases and material from the perspective of judicial control of agencies. Finally, students are exposed to modern examples of agency decision making that are not inconsistent with the concept of popular control. Agency decision making through the socialization of conflict rather than the privatization of decision making is analyzed.

ACKNOWLEDGMENTS

This book would not have been possible without the support of and partial funding from Washburn University. Covering the various editions of this book, Washburn has provided both large and small grants that paid for salaries, paper, floppy disks, postage, and other expenses. The university also awarded me sabbatical leaves, which provided the time necessary to complete the initial and subsequent editions of the book. Besides time and money, a third ingredient—the support of others—contributed to the completion of this text. Of support, I had an abundance. My secretary, Cathy Tunnell, typed and edited tirelessly, overcoming a number of obstacles to the task. I received invaluable support from my law student research assistant, Duane Rogers; my undergraduate research assistants, Tim Merchant and Shawn Beatty; my proofreader, Junie Davis; the staff of the Washburn University Law School Library; and the computer center. My colleagues in the Political Science Department provided valuable input and support. Drs. David Freeman, Marvin Heath, Loran Smith, and Mark Peterson provided helpful suggestions, most of which are included in the book. Of course, the final product would not have been possible without the help of my editors at Sage and their editorial staff. Finally, my wife, Rita, not only provided support and understanding but read most of the chapters as they were written. She may never take a class in administrative law, but she agrees that the subject is much more interesting than the usual images of administrative law connote.

HIGHLIGHTS OF RECENT EDITIONS

The third edition (2002) featured expanded discussions of standing to sue administrative agencies, warrantless administrative searches and the special needs doctrine, state action relative to the Fourteenth Amendment's due process and equal protection clauses, invasion of privacy under the Freedom of Information Act, and sexual harassment. New cases included in that edition that are also in the Fourth Edition are *Clinton v. City of New York,* 1998 (line item veto is unconstitutional), *FDA v. Brown & Williamson,* 2000 (the Food and Drug Administration is without the jurisdiction to regulate tobacco products), *FEC v. Akins,* 1998 (an interest group had standing to challenge the Federal Election Commission's decision that another interest group is not a "political committee" and hence does not have to disclose membership, contributions, and expenditures), *California Dental Association v. FTC,* 1999 (the Federal Trade Commission does have the jurisdiction to regulate nonprofit associations, but the Court of Appeals did not apply a sufficient level of review to the agency's decision finding the dental association engaged in restraint of trade), *Ferguson v. City of Charleston,* 2001 (warrantless screening of pregnant women's urine by a public entity held not to fall under the special needs doctrine so the searches violate the Fourth Amendment), *Department of Commerce v. United States House of Representatives,* 2000 (continuing saga of the fight over the counting in the census where the Census Bureau was forbidden to use sampling to conduct the census), *Gilbert v. Homar,* 1997 (predeprivation hearings restricted to employment termination and not required for employee discipline), and *West v. Gibson,* 1999 (the Equal Employment Opportunity Commission's power to impose compensatory damages on other federal agencies for violations of the Civil Rights Act of 1964 held not to violate sovereign immunity).

HIGHLIGHTS OF THE FOURTH EDITION

The Administrative Presidency. This edition features an expanded discussion of how President George W. Bush achieved the administrative presidency (the ability of the White House to exercise control of agency rule making and other activity). The Office of Information and Regulatory Affairs (OIRA) within the Office of Management and Budget (OMB) has set up a system that allows consumer-citizens to challenge existing agency rules and allows the OIRA to screen and approve or disapprove of agency-proposed rules. The discussion points out that President Clinton had the same power but lacked the ideology to apply it. There is a discussion about executive manipulation of the laws juxtaposed with the constitutional requirement that the president faithfully execute the laws (can President George W. Bush constitutionally act to dirty the air under the Clean Air Act?). Consequently, OIRA manipulation of agency rules has not been particularly successful in Court. In apparent recognition of this, with the exception of the Environmental Protection Agency (EPA), the OIRA shows greater deference to independent regulatory agencies than to Cabinet agencies.

Guidance Legislation and Congressional Control of Agencies. Congressional attempts to pass legislation that would impose rule-making restraints on all agencies (guidance legislation) ultimately failed, and the failure is chronicled. The status quo is that Congress has delegated the power to manipulate agency rules to OIRA, but that power only extends to certain subject matter (paperwork reduction, small business, major economic impact). The agencies maintain the authority to determine when their rules affect that subject matter. Conservative Republicans are not happy with this state of affairs.

Junk Science. This edition features a discussion about the conflict involving the quality of data that agencies gather and its use in the application of expertise. This discussion appears in both the chapter on the presidency and the chapter on Congress. Congress added a rider on a budget bill that is now referred to as the Data Quality Act; it imposes certain standards and procedures on agencies in terms of their use of information and data. Actually, it delegates the power to impose those things to OIRA. The discussion of junk science spills over into Chapter 4 because there is a real question about whether reports issued by agencies and the data that justify them are reviewable in court. That is because court review of agency action is limited to "final agency action," and the Supreme Court has yet to decide whether agency reports and agency gathering of data are "final"; the circuit courts are split. The reason that the discussion on the quality of data that agencies gather, use, and disseminate crops up in three chapters is because it goes to the vary essence of the administrative state (policy making based on expertise). The question of who controls the quality of that data, the agencies or the current occupant of the White House, is essential to questions about the democratic character of our system.

Freedom of Information Act. The agencies' refusal to release requested information is discussed. The law is quite clear: Agencies will release information unless it is covered by one of the exceptions. By now, there have been enough cases so that court interpretation of the exceptions is also quite clear. It turns out that the president can manipulate agency behavior to favor either release or expanded secrecy by having the attorney general manipulate the standard at which the Justice Department will defend agencies, should they get sued for not releasing requested information.

The Census. The Supreme Court settled the debate over whether the census will be taken by an actual count or by a sampling procedure, and that issue seems to be dead until Democrats control both the presidency and Congress. That has not ended the conflict, however. The Supreme Court and Congress settled the limited issue of taking the census for the purposes of determining how many representatives each state shall have. However, the census is also used to draw district lines for both congressional and state legislative districts and for the distribution of federal funds back to the states. It turns out that the Census Bureau took both an actual count and a sampled count for the 2000 census. The Bush administration refused to release numbers from the sampled census, prompting a Freedom of Information suit and suits to compel the use of sampled figures for both congressional districting and the distribution of federal funds.

Liberty Interests. The Supreme Court has been fairly rigid about not creating new liberty interests under the due process clause, and typically, civil liberties plaintiffs do not fare well before the Court's conservative majority. However, two cases that went "the other way" got attention from the national press. One case is *Lawrence v. Texas* (2003), where the Court held that the sodomy law of Texas (and presumably of other states as well) violates the right to privacy. The other case was *Hamdi v. Rumsfeld* (2004), which held that an "enemy combatant" held for more than 2 years by the military after capture in Afghanistan had a due process right to force the government to prove his status as an enemy combatant.

Sovereign Immunity. The Fourth Edition has an expanded discussion of sovereign immunity, especially as it relates to administrative law and the application of the Supreme Court's recent Eleventh Amendment jurisprudence.

The Federal Tort Claims Act and the Discretionary Function Exception. There is expanded discussion on the discretionary function exception and the fact that the Court has narrowed it to the point where there is no longer (if there ever was) a distinction between acts of discretion with policy implications and discretionary acts that simply implement policy.

Ergonomics Regulation. One of the themes of this book is that we should not expect the judicial branch to deliver us from the administrative state. The argument is made that the political branches of government that must periodically stand before us for election should exercise significant control over bureaucratic behavior. As you read the Fourth Edition, you should come to understand that the political branches of American government have enacted about as much control as we shall ever get. The final case-in-point in the summary chapter documents the case of the Occupational Safety and Health Administration (OSHA) and ergonomic regulation. Here, OSHA promulgated one of the most sweeping rules in the history of the administrative state. Ultimately, Congress passed a congressional review resolution forbidding the existence of any agency rules in the area of ergonomics. That resolution was presented to President Bush, who enthusiastically signed it into law. Apparently undaunted by the actions of lesser branches of government, OSHA has adopted "voluntary" ergonomic guidelines, conducted thousands of inspections under the auspices of the guidelines, and issued citations for infractions.

NEW CASES IN THE FOURTH EDITION

Whitman v. American Trucking Association, 2001. The case involves the EPA's enforcement of the Clean Air Act; it is the Supreme Court's most recent delegation of power case. Indeed, a federal district court found the delegation to be unconstitutional. It is the first case discussed in the text, as the case-in-point for Chapter 1, which is appropriate because it has several administrative law issues that must be resolved.

Tozzi v. Department of Health and Human Services (HHS), 2001. In this case, HHS moved a chemical up from merely being suspected of causing cancer to being a known carcinogen, and it was sued. The plaintiff in the case challenged the science that the agency relied on in changing the chemical's designation, and he also challenged the actual decision as being arbitrary. This is one of the "junk science" cases.

Norton v. Southern Utah Wilderness Alliance, 2004. President Bush's secretary of the interior made a decision to allow off-road vehicles in wilderness areas, and she was sued to compel her to take action to protect wilderness areas from off-road vehicles.

National Archives and Records Administration v. Favish, 2004. Much intrigue and speculation surrounded the apparent suicide of President Clinton's vice counsel, Vincent Foster. The president's attorney was found dead on a park bench in Washington, D.C. Because the park bench was on national park property, the National Park Service investigated the incident. This case involves a Freedom of Information request for certain photographs in the government's possession and, of course, a government refusal to disclose the photographs.

Cheney v. United States District Court, 2004. The Cheney in the case name is, in fact, the vice president of the United States. He was in charge of a planning committee that was to plot an energy policy for the Bush administration. There were charges that private individuals with a stake in the outcome were invited to these meetings (most notably, Ken Lay of Enron). This is not really a Freedom of Information Act case, but it does involve a citizen request for information about the meetings and the vice president's refusal to supply the requested material. The vice president is suing a District Court because the Court ordered him to turn over the material.

Office of Personnel Management v. Richmond, 1990. This is the Supreme Court's most recent estoppel case. A citizen was receiving disability payments. The particular government disability program had an income cap, and the citizen was aware of the existence of a cap but was uncertain as to the exact amount. Presented with an opportunity to work some overtime, he did what most of us would do—he asked the government agency what the limit was. He was given incorrect and outdated information, and of course, he lost his disability.

Pennsylvania State Police v. Suders, 2004. This is the Supreme Court's most recent sexual harassment case. Under a certain set of circumstances, an employer can be held liable for sexual harassment committed by an employee. Sometimes, the employer can raise what is called an affirmative defense (e.g., the employer was aware of the possibility of the situation and took reasonable steps to prevent the situation). Where there is "tangible employment action" (the recipient of the harassment is fired, transferred, demoted, etc.), the employer cannot raise an affirmative defense. This case decides whether a constructive discharge (due to the harassment, the employee had no choice but to quit) constitutes "tangible employment action."

Federal Maritime Commission v. South Carolina State Ports Authority, 2002. This is the Supreme Court's most recent Eleventh Amendment case. A ship company asked a state agency for a berth at the Charleston harbor for a gambling cruise ship. Although the state agency gave berths to other ships that provide gambling when out to sea, it denied this one and gave the reason that gambling violates state public policy. The ship company alleges that this behavior violates a congressional maritime law and brought a complaint to the Federal Maritime Commission for a hearing on the issue. The question is whether the South Carolina Ports Authority is protected by sovereign immunity and the Eleventh Amendment from having to defend itself before a federal agency.

United States v. Gaubert, 1991. This is the Supreme Court's most recent pronouncement on the discretionary function exception in the Federal Tort Claims Act. A federal agency took control of a fiscally healthy financial institution and got involved in the day-to-day management (the plaintiff would say mismanagement) of the institution, and eventually, the institution became insolvent. The plaintiff, who was a principal officer in the institution and lost a substantial amount of money, is suing the agency under the Federal Tort Claims Act. The question is whether the day-to-day management actions of the agency fall under the discretionary function exception of that Act.

Correctional Services Corporation v. Malesko, 2001. Correctional Services Corporation is a private company that contracts with the federal government to run halfway houses (for parolees from prison). An employee's reckless disregard caused the plaintiff to have another heart attack. The plaintiff is suing the company under a *Bivins* theory (individual federal employees are liable for constitutional torts against citizens). There is no question about whether the company is a "state actor" (a private entity that acts "as though" it is the government); the question is whether a *Bivens* action can be maintained against a private company acting as a state actor.

Legal Lingo

L awyers do not write in common English. Legal writing makes heavy use of Latin and has a unique way of citing references. As a layperson venturing into the legal world, you will need help. There are any number of good, cheap, paperback legal dictionaries on the market, and you should not attempt to take a substantive legal course (constitutional law, administrative law, etc.) without one.

In any case, for those who will begin to read the first chapter of this book prior to obtaining a law dictionary or supplement, it will be helpful to know that legal citations always consist of three essential elements: the volume number, the reference material, and the page number. Some examples are listed below:

1. The citation 440 U.S. 472 (1979) means that you will find a case (*National Muffler Dealer's Association, Inc. v. U.S.*) in volume 440 of the *United States Supreme Court Reports* (official reporter of U.S. Supreme Court decisions) on page 472, followed by the year. F.Supp 2d is the reporter for U.S. district court cases, and F.3d is the reporter for U.S. Circuit Court of Appeals cases.

2. 5 U.S.C. 551 means Title 5 of the *United States Code* (laws of the federal government), Chapter 551 (the Administrative Procedure Act of 1946). U.S.C.A. stands for *United States Code Annotated* (*annotated* means that case citations have been included where courts have interpreted the statute).

3. 36 Fed. Reg. 22906 means Volume 36 of the *Federal Register* (publication of federal agencies' rules and proposed rules) on page 22906. This is a rule requiring passive restraint in autos.

4. 29 C.F.R. 17 means Title 29 of the *Code of Federal Regulations,* Chapter 17. The *Federal Register* is sometimes hard to use because it is a weekly publication that informs interested parties of rules, regulations, or standards that nearly all of the federal agencies have promulgated that week, and it also provides notice of proposed rules, regulations, or standards on which the various agencies are about to hold hearings. Hence, it is best used on a weekly basis by those who are regulated by agencies or who have business before an agency to keep up on what the agency is about to do and what it has done. All of these weekly rules are compiled by subject matter in the C.F.R.; so Title 29, for example, deals

with labor, and Chapter 17 is the beginning of 1,600 pages of rules, regulations, and standards adopted by OSHA.

Most cases come to the U.S. Supreme Court through a *writ of certiorari* ("cert."), which is a form of appeal allowing the higher court to exercise discretion regarding whether to hear the appeal. If the Court decides to hear the appeal, it will issue a writ of cert. requesting the record from the lower court.

Once the Supreme Court decides a case, it has several options. First, it can *affirm* the lower court decision, which means the lower court's (or agency's) interpretation and/or decision was correct. Second, it can (but rarely does) *overrule* a lower federal court; that is, the Court rejects a particular interpretation and, generally, adopts a new interpretation as precedent. Third, the Court can *reverse* (set aside) a lower court decision. For a federal court or federal agency, the Court could (but again rarely does) reverse the court or agency decision and make the final decision itself. More frequently, however, the Court will reverse a state supreme court, lower federal court, or federal agency decision or interpretation and remand the case to the lower court or agency for a decision not inconsistent with the Supreme Court's interpretation.

Today, students can access legal sources through the Internet. If your college or university subscribes to *Lexis* or *West Law,* you can get the full text of the cases in the book as well as access to the *Federal Register,* the *Code of Federal Regulations,* and the *United States Code.* If you do not have access to either of these legal databases, you may find the following Web sites helpful:

For the federal government's Web site: http:/firstgov.gov

For the *Federal Register,* official site: http://www.nara.gov/fedreg/index.html

From this site, you can access the C.F.R., a link to public participation in rule making, and individual agency e-rule-making Web sites.

For the Code of Federal Regulations: http://www.access.gpo.gov/nara/cfr/index.html

To access legal news and search areas of the law: http://www.law.cornell.edu or http://www.findlaw.com

PART I

POLITICS, DEMOCRACY, AND BUREAUCRACY

1

DEMOCRACY AND BUREAUCRACY

Case in Point:
Whitman v. American Trucking Association
531 U.S. 457 (2001)

America has a remarkably strong and stable economy. Economists debate about why our economy is so much stronger than others, but many believe that our reliance on the free market has something to do with it. We are, perhaps, the most capitalistic country in the world, which means that we rely on the free market to an extent that other countries do not. That means that market forces (supply, demand, and price) drive most economic decisions in America. That is not true in the rest of the industrialized world, where governments rather than [as well as?] markets make significant economic decisions.

From a public administration perspective, the free market, wonderful though it may be, is not without its flaws. The particular flaw that will concern us in the discussion of the *American Trucking Association* case is market failure. Market failure occurs when the market provides no incentive to incur added expenses to cover costs associated with second-order consequences of doing business. Pollution is the classic example of market failure. If you own a business and your business produces a harmful by-product, your choices are simple and few: (a) you can dump the by-product into the river or on the land or (b) you can incur the added expense of disposing of it safely and properly. Choice A will not affect your profits but has adverse consequences for who live near the business or downstream from it. In the free market system, however, there is absolutely no incentive for Choice B. Indeed, if you exercise Choice B and your competitors do not, the market will actually punish you for having made a "bad" economic decision. One reason for government involvement and regulation of the economy is to force businesses into Choice B.

The Cuyahoga River runs through downtown Cleveland, Ohio, and on the morning of June 22, 1969, the river caught fire.[1] That happened because all the businesses along its banks and all who navigated it exercised Choice A. Although the 1969 fire was neither the first nor the worst fire on the Cuyahoga, this one was covered by the national media; most Americans were aware of it and bothered by the concept of a fire burning on top of a body of water. The river fire was one of the events that pressured Congress to pass the Clean Water Act in 1971. The case in point, *Whitman v. American Trucking Association,* involves the Clean Air Act rather than water, but the principle is the same. Government regulation was thought necessary because the market offered no incentive not to pollute the air we breathe.

The original Clean Air Act was entitled the Air Pollution Control Act of 1955. It has been amended and revised several times. It is a complex and lengthy law, but it works like this: Congress has required that certain pollutants be controlled; Congress delegated the power to the Environmental Protection Agency (EPA) to set standards for those pollutants, and these were called national ambient air quality standards (NAAQS); those states that meet the NAAQS need do nothing but maintain their compliance; those states that do not meet the NAAQS are called nonattainment areas, and they must submit plans to the EPA to come into compliance within a certain number of years. Finally, the EPA director is required to reevaluate each NAAQS every five years and "make such revisions . . . as may be appropriate."

In 1997, President Bill Clinton's EPA director conducted the required reevaluation and revised the NAAQS for particulate matter and ozone downward, reducing human exposure to both. Solid particles and liquid droplets in the air are what constitutes particulate matter. When the particulate matter is large enough for the naked eye to see, it is called smog, but most frequently, it is too small to see. Combustion is the primary source of particulate matter, whether it comes from gas-burning engines or firewood; the result is all sorts of respiratory problems, including "heightened risk of premature death." Indeed, the EPA believes that ozone is—and particulate matter may be—*nonthreshold pollutants,*[2] pollutants that cause adverse health effects at any atmospheric concentration above 0.

Ozone, by contrast, is a colorless, odorless gas that forms when other atmospheric pollutants react in the presence of sunlight. Ozone is beneficial high up in the atmosphere but bad at a level where we can breathe it; it causes all of the same respiratory ailments that particulate matter does.

One of the problems created by the EPA's revision of the NAAQS for particulate matter and ozone was that several of the states that had been in compliance under the old NAAQS would now be classified as nonattainment areas. They would need to make their air cleaner, which would mean imposing additional environmental costs on businesses in those states. The ink could hardly have been dry on the new NAAQS when the EPA was sued by a whole host of plaintiffs, including business associations, individual businesses, individuals, congressmen, and states, who thought the new standards were too stringent. Environmental groups sued, too, and they thought the new standards were not stringent enough.

The American Trucking Association and other plaintiffs alleged the following: that Congress violated the Constitution when it gave too much discretion to the EPA to set the NAAQS; that the Clean Air Act required the EPA to consider the costs of compliance associated with lower NAAQS, but the agency did not consider such costs; and that the EPA made a legal error in its interpretation of the Clean Air Act. The lower court found that Congress had indeed violated the Constitution in its delegation of power to the EPA and sent the case back to the EPA with orders to fix the NAAQS-setting process so as to eliminate the breadth of the delegation of power. For its part, the EPA appealed to the Supreme Court, arguing that the lower court lacked jurisdiction over the case. The EPA alleged that the case was not ripe (a legal concept that means a suit was brought too early, before anyone was hurt, and hence, the suit is speculative). The EPA also argued that the NAAQS were not final yet, and "final agency action" is required by a different statute before parties can sue a federal agency.

Over the years, courts have developed numerous decision rules, sometimes called precedent, doctrines, or constitutional tests, to help resolve the conflicts between agencies and citizens. Applying those doctrines and legal tests to the issues in the *American Trucking* case, the Supreme Court decided: the delegation of power was constitutional; the EPA was forbidden by congressional intent from considering the costs of compliance when setting the NAAQS; the case was ripe (not filed too early); and the agency's action was final, so the lower court did have jurisdiction. The final issue in the case involved the EPA's interpretation of two apparently conflicting subparts of the Clean Air Act. Basically, the EPA interpreted the Act in a manner that gave the agency considerable discretion in implementing the revised NAAQS, but the Court said the EPA's interpretation was not rational.

The *American Trucking Association* case is a good example of administrative law. Typically, the legislative branch authorizes an executive branch agency to take some action. When the agency takes action, it adversely affects individuals or businesses, and the adversely affected parties sue the agency. The judicial branch is left to clean up the mess.

As you read this text, you will learn administrative law by reading Supreme Court cases. For example, you will read the *American Trucking* case in Chapter 3, where you will learn about delegation of power to agencies. You will read the cases because that is where you will find the doctrines and decision rules that make up the common law body of administrative law. This book is not just about administrative law. It is also a book about democracy. In a democracy, public policy is supposed to be made by individuals whom the voters can hold responsible in an election. Is that how you would describe what happened with clean air?

Questions

1. Ultimately, in the *American Trucking* case, who will decide whether more states and businesses within those states will be required to spend additional billions of dollars to make the air cleaner? Did Congress make the decision? Did unelected bureaucrats make the decision? Did an unelected, job-for-life Supreme Court make the decision?

2. If you are not certain who is responsible for the policy, what does that say about the shape of your democracy?

3. If it seems plausible to you that either the bureaucracy or the Court ultimately made the policy, what does that say to you about your democracy?

4. The issue regarding whether the EPA should consider the costs of complying with more restrictive standards was an important one for the business and state plaintiffs. Do you think it would be a good idea for agencies to be forced to consider the costs of the rules they are about to make? Congress mandated in the Clean Air Act that the EPA "must set primary NAAQS . . . which are requisite to protect the public health—with an adequate margin of safety." If Congress had also mandated that the agency consider the costs of compliance with those NAAQS, then Congress would be delegating to bureaucrats the power to decide between industry profits and the public health. Sometimes, societies must make decisions like that. Who do you think should make such decisions; politicians who will cast their vote based on their desire to be reelected or experts within the agencies, who will base their decision on science and empirical data but who are not accountable to those who must live with the decision?

DEMOCRACY

If you are like most Americans, you assume that you live in a democracy, but you probably cannot define what that means. Try to define democracy, being concise and definite about what the term means.

Chances are, you did one of two things: (a) you went back to Abraham Lincoln and said, "government of the people, by the people, for the people," or (b) you tried to define it in terms of a process (elections, political parties, etc.). Without belaboring the point, let us consider these typical responses.

Government of the People

It is difficult to imagine what Lincoln had in mind when he said "of the people," but we can put the rest of his phrase to a commonsense test. Presumably, "by the people" means some variant of "the people govern." When was the last time you governed? When was the last time you had significant input into a government policy? When was the last time you had *any* input into a government policy? When was the last time anyone you know had any input into a government policy?

You may be saying to yourself, "But people can't really govern. We elect representatives to do that for us." True enough. When was the last time you called your senator or went to Washington, D.C., to see your senator about an issue of concern to you? When was the last time you provided governmental input to any of the following elected officials: U.S. representative, county commissioner, city council person, mayor, governor, U.S. president? If you have provided such input, do you think it was a significant force in shaping policy? The notion "by the people" is too simplistic to describe what part (if any) the American people play in shaping policy.

The concept "for the people" could be difficult to deal with because it would seem possible to govern "for the people" by doing the opposite of what the people want (assuming one could ever assess what the people want). Let us, for now, assume that Lincoln was getting at the notion of governmental responsiveness to citizens' demands. In the late 1970s, more than 75 percent of all Americans opposed a Panama Canal Treaty, but we got one. For the past 30 years, 65 percent or more of Americans have favored stronger gun control and doing away with the electoral college.[3] More recently, 63 percent of Americans did not want the House of Representatives to impeach President Clinton, but he was impeached anyway.[4] During the last several years of the Clinton presidency, the federal government had budget surpluses. Surveys indicated that Americans generally supported using budget surpluses to pay down the debt and shore up education, Medicare, and social security rather than "giving it back" in the form of tax cuts, but Congress passed tax cuts.[5] In the case of gun control, a small minority has been able to thwart a policy the vast majority favors. In the case of the electoral college, although proposed constitutional changes have been introduced in Congress, none has passed. Although there is some empirical evidence of association between public opinion and public policy,[6] we can say that often in the United States, the people do not get the policies they want. Indeed, the founding fathers invented or refined several ingenious devices whose purposes were to thwart government responsiveness to the demands of the masses (for instance, state legislative election of U.S. senators, the electoral college, federalism, and separation of powers—including a judicial branch that later became armed with judicial review). Even conceding that Lincoln's phrase "of the people, by the people, for the people" was an accurate description of

American democracy in 1860 (which is doubtful), it does not describe what happens in America today.

Democracy as a Process

If you defined democracy by referring to elections and competing political parties, bear in mind that many very authoritarian regimes in the world today have elections and competing parties (e.g., El Salvador, Iran, Nicaragua, and South Korea).

DEMOCRACY DEFINED

One could take a semester-long course about notions and definitions of democracy, but for our purposes, let us simply say that democracy is a form of government in which people have some influence over the policies that affect their lives. Democracy is not an absolute concept in the sense that either you have it or you do not. Rather, it is a continuum, with some countries having a lot of it, and some countries having not very much or none at all.

It can be argued, for example, that many parliamentary systems are very democratic because the political parties take divergent and clearly identifiable stands on issues and possess the party discipline to enact their platforms into law. Hence, when a voter votes for a candidate who says, "If elected, I will help my political party bring about X, Y, and Z," that voter has significant influence if his or her party wins a majority of seats in Parliament because the party will enact policies X, Y, and Z. But in the United States, due to separation of powers, federalism, and weakened political parties, even on those rare occasions when a politician or political party takes a definite and clear stand on a policy issue, the result is not predictable. To cite a popular example, look at what happened in 1988 when candidate George Bush said, "Read my lips. No new taxes." In 1992, it may have cost him reelection when, as President Bush, he was forced to accept a budget compromise containing a significant tax increase.

In any case, although we may not be the most democratic country in the world, we are certainly not the least democratic. If we can agree that a democracy is a form of government in which the people can have an impact on policies that affect their lives, a short discussion addressing how the people do that is in order.

Once a polity gets beyond a certain size (say several hundred), it becomes impossible for all the people to debate and vote on policies. According to the 2000 census, there are more than 281.4 million people in the United States,[7] so it is unlikely that everyone could have input on public policy. A republic is a democratic form of government in which people elect representatives to act for them. Political scientists use the term *linkages* to describe the devices that link the people to their representatives. Those linkages are public opinion, political parties, voting, elections, and interest groups. So, in theory at least, the people influence policy indirectly by the use of linkages with their representatives—who, presumably, reflect constituency demands in debate and votes on policies.

DEMOCRACY AND BUREAUCRACY

How democratic would you think our government was if it were true that 90 percent of the laws that regulate everyday life were made by unelected, politically insulated, job-secure, career bureaucrats?[8] What if it were true that the policy-making or legislative branch of government (at any level—federal, state, county, or city) passed only broad and vague legislation and then delegated the power to agencies to adopt standards, rules, and policies to fill in the gaps and holes, leaving those agencies with a tremendous amount of discretion? The notion of policy making by agencies and bureaucracies rather than by popularly elected (and accountable) representatives is referred to as "the administrative state" or the fourth branch of government.[9]

Specifically, the term *administrative state* connotes policy making by bureaucratic or agency expertise, and the term *fourth branch* simply means bureaucracy as an organization or structure. The latter, however, implies more than a bureaucracy. It implies a bureaucracy coequal with the presidency, Congress, and the courts, and it assumes the policy-making aspect of the administrative state. Apparently, the term *fourth branch* was coined by Justice Robert Jackson in a 1951 case.

> The rise of administrative bodies probably has been the most significant legal trend of the last century, and perhaps more values today are affected by their decisions than by those of all the courts, review of administrative decisions apart. Administrative actions also have begun to have important consequences on personal rights (*United States v. Spector,* 343 U.S. 169). They have become a veritable fourth branch of the government, which has disrupted our three-branch legal theories much as the concept of a fourth dimension unsettles our three-dimensional thinking.
>
> Courts have differed in assigning a place to these seemingly necessary bodies in our constitutional system. Administrative agencies have been called quasi-legislative, quasi-executive, or quasi-judicial, as the occasion required, to validate their functions within the separation-of-powers scheme of the Constitution. The mere retreat to the qualifying *quasi* implicitly confesses that all recognized classifications have broken down; *quasi* is a smooth cover that we draw over our confusion, as we might use a counterpane to conceal a disordered bed.[10]

We used to believe that the legislative branch was the policy-making branch, and the executive branch simply implemented the policy. The concept of the administrative state implies that the old distinction between policy making and the administration of those policies no longer exists. In the modern, complex, postindustrial world, policies are initiated, formulated, promulgated, and modified by technocratic experts who hold mid- to high-level positions in America's bureaucracies (federal, state, and local). The same agencies that make the policies also implement them. Pursuant to implementing their own policies, agencies also investigate infractions of those policies and adjudicate those infractions. The agencies can also impose sanctions. Although there may be academic squabbles over the degree of power that bureaucracies have acquired, there is virtually no disagreement over the fact that the old dichotomy between policy making and policy implementation is gone and that administrative agencies now perform both functions, fused into one institution.

It is a reflection of the administrative state that Congress passed a complex, confusing, and conflicting law to reduce the pollution in the air we breathe. Congress then delegated to the experts in the EPA the power to set the specific standards regarding how much of which pollutants is acceptable. Finally, Congress left it up to the states to decide how to reach the levels set by the EPA. State legislatures are charged with setting broad policies, such as deciding to burn cleaner fuels (that is why gas costs more in California) or requiring the application of pollution abatement technology. The legislature then delegates the power to state agencies to decide how to reach those goals.

Does the existence of the administrative state mean that there is no democracy? Not necessarily. If it were true that popularly elected officials exercise considerable control over agencies, then the elements of democracy as we have defined them and outlined them would still exist. In Chapters 2 and 3, the argument will be made that neither the chief executive (specifically the president, but governors and mayors as well) nor legislative bodies (Congress, state legislatures, or city councils) effectively control agencies. What all of this has to do with administrative law is that, almost by default, the job of attempting to control agencies has fallen to the courts, and administrative law is the tool that courts use. After readers have digested the cases, concepts, and discussions presented throughout this book, they should be able to reach their own conclusions regarding the state of democracy in America. For now, we need to understand the rise of the administrative state.

FROM GEORGE WASHINGTON TO THE ADMINISTRATIVE STATE

The U.S. polity was founded on certain basic principles, with others evolving early on to form a theoretical framework. The essential components of that framework were as follows: *limited government, negative freedom,* and *laissez-faire economics.* In limited government, the powers of government are restricted or limited. Devices such as a written constitution with a Bill of Rights, the separation of powers, and federalism limit governmental power, which is supposed to be limited to the protection of life, liberty, or property. This is the notion that "the government that governs least governs best." Negative freedom is "freedom from." A citizen is free to the degree that no other citizen or government interferes with his or her activity.[11] According to this concept, people are expected to reach their fullest potential where government does not interfere with individual initiative but simply limits itself to the protection of life, certain liberties, and the ability to accumulate and hold on to wealth. Thus, where the exercise of governmental power is limited to the protection of life, liberty, or property, citizens are truly free. In 1776, Adam Smith published *The Wealth of Nations* and articulated the notion of laissez-faire economics, that government should stay out of the economy and allow the free market to determine economic policy. Laissez-faire fits hand in glove with the two other concepts, negative freedom and limited government, and they became the foundational ideology of America.

Although early America had problems such as poverty, poor health, and poor housing, governing elites did not consider the exercise of governmental power to be a proper tool for addressing these problems. In the early 1800s, the United States had a rural population with an agrarian/cottage industry economy. The process of industrialization brings urbanization, and urbanization exacerbates problems such as poverty, poor housing, poor health, crime, hunger, malnutrition, sewage disposal, and alienation, to list just a few. A government based on concepts such as limited government, negative freedom, and laissez-faire economics (and eventually social Darwinism) is not an instrument for dealing with such problems.

Eventually, political and social movements began to espouse different positions that challenged the older theoretical framework. Farmers and merchants in the West began to demand that government regulate the rates that businesses charged (railroads and grain elevators, for example). Other segments of society began to demand that government take some action to deter child labor and that government take responsibility for educating children. Some demanded that women be allowed to vote. Still others demanded that government take responsibility for a wholesome and edible food supply and that government regulate monopolies. Labor unions began to demand that government pass laws regulating the conditions under which laborers worked. The terms that we use to identify the philosophy that encompasses these calls to government action are *positive freedom* and *positive government.* If negative freedom is "freedom from," then positive freedom is "freedom to." Positive freedom is the notion that some individuals cannot achieve their fullest potential without help and that help generally will come from government. Positive government is the idea that government has a positive role to play in the economy and in people's lives and that it should not be limited to simply protecting life, liberty, and property.[12]

The socialist and labor movements had then-German Chancellor Otto von Bismarck so concerned for the future of capitalism that in the 1880s, Germany adopted a social security and national health care system. The British followed suit some 20 years later. In the United States, the federal government's response to progressive pressure was antitrust legislation and the Federal Trade Commission (FTC). Income taxes and the Federal Reserve Bank were responses to erratic business cycles. Twice, the federal government passed laws against child labor (as did many of the states), but the Supreme Court declared them unconstitutional. This period in American constitutional law brought heavy criticism upon the Court. Many accused the Justices of the Supreme Court of engaging in judicial activism, or substituting their personal policy preferences for those passed by the legislative branch, not because of a constitutional defect but because they personally disagreed with the particular policies.

Although it is something of an oversimplification, it can be said that these two philosophies—positive and negative government—came to a head, after more than 50 years of conflict, in the election of 1932. The philosophy of positive freedom and positive government won out. Although Franklin D. Roosevelt never used the terms, the first hundred days of his first administration and the era referred to as the New Deal were the epitome of positive freedom and positive government. Shortly after FDR became president, a new economic theory, compatible with positive freedom and positive government, gained credence. That theory was Keynesian economics (that government can and should manipulate the demand for goods and services by manipulation of the money supply to lessen the effects of the cycle of inflation and recession/depression). The new public philosophy of positive government, positive freedom, and Keynesian economics replaced the old philosophy of negative freedom, limited government, and *laissez-faire* economics. This is not to say that what I have termed the "old" philosophy has disappeared. Indeed, these two philosophies form the underpinnings of the two major political parties in America today. Republicans generally believe in individual initiative rather than government programs to solve problems (negative freedom). They believe in less governmental regulation of the economy and prefer the free market to government action (laissez-faire). Finally, Republicans prefer the federal government to be smaller and more limited in scope and power (limited government). Democrats, on the other hand, generally look to government to solve problems (positive freedom). Democrats are somewhat skeptical of the free market and want it regulated (Keynesian economics). Finally, Democrats believe that the exercise of government power should not be restricted (limited) to the protection of life, liberty, or property rights (positive government). If government is going to play a large part in things such as retirement, health care, college education, housing, unemployment, job training, a clean and safe environment, automobile safety and efficiency, and so on, then government is going to need to rely on expertise to help it deliver services or implement programs (to set NAAQS, for example). The experts are the public servants who serve in agencies, constituting the situation we have described as the administrative state.

The growth of bureaucracy in the United States closely parallels historical developments. As you would expect from a government founded on the principles of negative freedom and limited government, Washington's administration had only a small bureaucracy: the Department of State, the Department of Treasury, the Post Office, the Department of War, and an Office of the Attorney General. One of the early additional departments was the Army Corps of Engineers (1802), which was created to enhance the flow of commerce through the country. It assisted in projects to make the inland waterways navigable. Another early agency was the Patent Office, which was made a federal bureau in 1803; it is necessary in a capitalistic society to protect ideas and inventions as a society begins to industrialize. Several Cabinet agencies were created after the Civil War, and a few of the first regulatory agencies were created in the clash between the status quo (limited government, negative freedom, and laissez-faire economics) and the progressive movement (positive government and positive freedom). The following is a list of agencies with their dates of creation:

Department of the Interior, 1849

Department of Agriculture, 1862

Department of Commerce and Labor, 1903

Interstate Commerce Commission, 1887

Food and Drug Administration, 1906

Federal Trade Commission, 1914

After the election of Franklin Roosevelt, a host of agencies were created to help the government deliver services:

Federal Communications Commission, 1934

Securities and Exchange Commission, 1934

National Labor Relations Board, 1935

Social Security Board, 1935

National Mediation Board, 1934

Federal Deposit Insurance Corporation, 1933

Federal Home Loan Bank, 1932

Tennessee Valley Authority, 1933

During World War II, federal bureaucracies nearly ran the country. They did everything from rationing commodities such as gas, butter, and rubber tires to controlling rent prices throughout the whole country.

Recall that this chapter began with a discussion of America's reliance on the free market, market failures, and a government policy to protect the environment. If air, water, drivers, workers, and so on are to be protected, then government must do it because the market will not. More agencies were created in the 1960s and 1970s to help with market failures and with new problems that the government decided to tackle. These agencies are as follows:

Department of Housing and Urban Development, 1965

Department of Transportation, 1966

Peace Corps, 1961

Equal Employment Opportunity Commission, 1964

Environmental Protection Agency, 1970

Occupational Safety and Health Administration, 1970

AMTRAK, 1970

Federal Election Commission, 1971

Commodity Futures Trading Commission, 1974

National Transportation Safety Board, 1976

Federal Mine Safety and Health Review Commission, 1977

Department of Energy, 1977

Department of Education, 1979

Early in the 21st century, the federal bureaucracy, displayed in Figure 1.1, has grown to 2.7 million employees (but that is down from 3.1 million in 1990), and it consists of the following: (a) an Executive Office of the President, established in 1939, with about 1,500 employees spread among 10 or 11 offices and agencies, including the Office of Management and Budget, the National Security Council, the Council of Economic Advisors, and the Office of the Vice President (this segment of the bureaucracy is referred to as a *staff agency* as opposed to a *line agency*; staff agencies have no formal administrative functions, their sole function being to advise the president);[13] (b) 15 Cabinet-level agencies, which employ about 1.6 million people; and (c) 50 or so independent agencies, government corporations, and independent regulatory commissions, hereafter referred to collectively as independent regulatory agencies, which employ slightly more than a million workers.[14] Actually, despite the addition of new agencies and departments, the size of the federal government (in terms of employees) has grown steadily but slowly since the mid-20th century and has actually declined during the decade of the 1990s. The explosive bureaucratic growth has been at the state and local levels. In 1980, the federal bureaucracy had about 2,898,000 employees. By 1998, there were only 2,783,000 federal employees, a decrease of 4 percent. State and local bureaucracies, in contrast, grew by 26 percent over the same time period, from 13.3 million employees in 1980 to 16.7 million employees in 1998.[15] In spite of the clear empirical evidence cited above, showing a reduction in the size of the federal government of 115,000 employees, those statistics are somewhat slippery. The reader should not assume that the work that used to be done by the 115,000 federal employees who are no longer there has been abandoned. What has been happening at both the state and federal levels of government are processes referred to as downsizing, outsourcing, and privatization. What those now-absent federal employees used to do is now being done by private entities that contract with government. Paul Light has estimated that

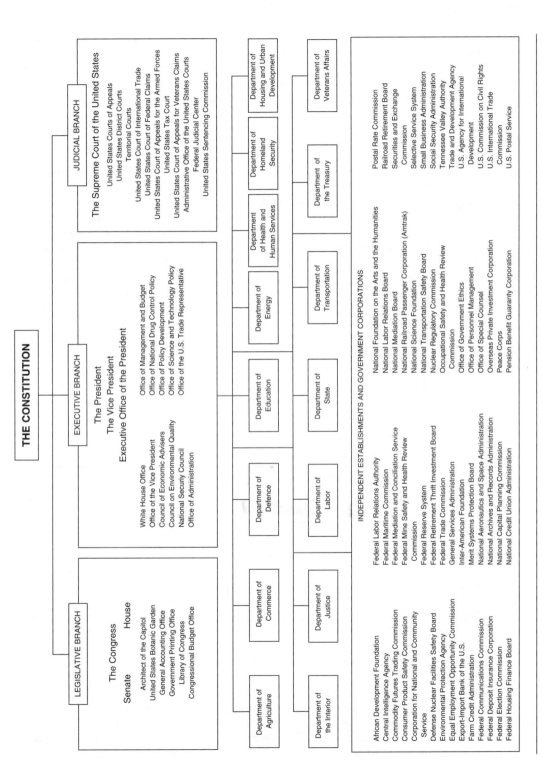

Figure 1.1 The Government of the United States

Source: 2003 United States Government Manual, p. 22

if you add to the current 2.7 million federal employees: 5.6 million who receive paychecks through federal contracts, 2.4 million who are employed through federal grants, 4.6 million state and local employees whose jobs were created through federal mandates, 1.5 million in the uniformed military, and the 850,000 Postal Service employees, you have a federal workforce of almost 17 million. The era of big government is definitely not over![16]

WHAT ADMINISTRATIVE AGENCIES DO

Most people are aware that there is a bureaucracy and that it is large, but they probably cannot explain with much accuracy what it is that bureaucracies do. Stated very simply, agencies (bureaucracies) do everything that all three branches of government do. They make laws (called rules), sometimes they set standards (NAAQS), they investigate infractions of those rules, they hold trials to adjudicate infractions of those rules, and they impose sanctions for violations of the rules. Agencies also provide services: They deliver mail, keep our national parks, maintain veterans hospitals and services, provide disaster relief, issue food stamps, and provide for social security. Agencies perform functions as well. For example, bureaus collect revenue and supervise and fund the building of our interstate highway system. One agency, the National Aeronautics and Space Administration (NASA), even sent humans to the moon and brought them back to Earth. Providing some evidence that what agencies do actually works, between 1970 and 1995, the incidence of smog dropped by a third, even though the number of autos on the road increased by 85 percent.[17] In 1972, only a third of all bodies of water in America were safe for swimming and fishing; by 1995, nearly two thirds were safe. The motor vehicle death rate dropped from 26.8 percent in 1970 to 15 percent in 1999. The number of workers killed on the job dropped 11 percent in the five years between 1997 and 2002. The infant mortality rate declined by 2 percent during the decade of the 1990s.

Basic to an understanding of agencies is the knowledge that Congress (or the state legislature) is the ultimate source of power. Congress decides whether to create an agency, where it will be located, how long it will live, how much money it will have, and, perhaps most important, how much authority it will have and how that authority will be exercised. The term used for this is *enabling legislation.* If a legal question arises concerning an agency's exercise of authority, the courts first look to the Constitution (as it did in *American Trucking* and found the delegation of power to the EPA constitutional). If there is no conflict with the Constitution, the courts look at the enabling legislation to see if they can discern legislative intent (this is also what the Court did in *American Trucking).* Hence, the first principle of administrative law is this: *Always look to the enabling legislation.*

Frequently, Congress creates agencies to deal with pressing problems of the day. Early in this century, progressive pressure forced Congress to attack the problem of monopolies, which posed a threat to free trade and the market. Congress reacted by passing the Clayton Act in 1914, which made illegal certain business practices recognized as instruments of monopolies. At the same time, Congress passed the Federal Trade Commission Act, which created the FTC and gave it the task of prohibiting "unfair methods of competition" and "unfair or deceptive acts or practices"[18] in interstate commerce. How was the FTC to accomplish this task? Remember that in 1914, the dominant philosophical framework was still a combination of negative freedom, limited government, and laissez-faire economics and that the notion of an FTC is not compatible with those concepts. It could be argued that although Congress succumbed to progressive pressure to attack monopolies by legislation, Congress was not truly ready to attack the problem by creating an agency with the power to control monopolies. Hence, the FTC was not initially given the power to promulgate rules (that did not come until the early 1970s), nor was it given the power to impose sanctions (it still does not possess such power).[19] The FTC was given the power to issue cease and desist orders for "deceptive trade practices" listed elsewhere in legislation. If a company chose not to comply with the cease and desist order, then all the FTC could do was to file a suit in federal district court. Today, of course, that means backlog and delay for FTC cease and desist orders.

Many of the agencies created more recently, however, are provided with a more impressive array of powers than Congress initially provided for the FTC. By the late 1960s, industrial accidents were a leading cause of death in the United States, so again Congress responded to pressure for federal help in the form of the Occupational Safety and Health Act of 1970. The goal of the Act was to reduce the incidence of fatal industrial accidents and to reduce the number of serious industrial accidents. To accomplish this, Congress created the Occupational Safety and Health Administration (OSHA), which describes its duties and responsibilities as follows:

> Develops and promulgates occupational safety and health standards; develops and issues regulations; conducts investigations and inspections to determine the status of compliance with safety and health standards and regulations; and issues citations and proposes penalties for noncompliance with safety and health standards and regulations.[20]

These powers and duties are typical of most regulatory agencies and even of many Cabinet-level agencies at the federal, state, and local levels of government. The enabling legislation creating OSHA is about 17 pages long. The agency has produced 1,658 pages of rules, regulations, and safety standards.[21] Charles Goodsell, a leading advocate for bureaucracy, said,

> It is in bureaucracy that all the necessary elements for collective social action are brought together—legal authority, public resources, professional expertise, institutional knowledge, and a sense of mission in behalf of all citizens . . . Unlike the policy-making activity of elected officials, this work by bureaucrats is undramatic, hidden, ongoing, and persistent. It is through bureaucracy, directly or indirectly, that much of America's collective action takes place. Without it, our nation's widespread accomplishments in recent decades would not have been achieved.[22]

Look again at Figure 1.1 and carefully read the names of the line agencies (Cabinet level departments and independent regulatory agencies). It will be clear in most cases that the agencies were created to meet a particular problem or to perform a fairly obvious set of tasks. So what agencies do is attempt to accomplish goals given to them by Congress (e.g., to reduce pollution, to reduce traffic fatalities and industrial fatalities, or to control monopolies) or to accomplish their own goals as implied from congressional direction. Most, but not all, agencies attempt to accomplish those goals by promulgating rules and standards (Chapter 7), investigating infractions of those rules (Chapter 5), adjudicating infractions of those rules (Chapter 7), and, often, imposing sanctions for infractions of those rules. Kenneth Culp Davis, perhaps the foremost authority on administrative law, had this to say about the pervasiveness of public administration in 1958:

The average person is much more directly and much more frequently affected by the administrative process than by the judicial process. The ordinary person probably regards the judicial process as somewhat remote from his [or her] own problems; a large portion of all people go through life without ever being a party to a lawsuit. But the administrative process affects nearly everyone in many ways nearly every day. The pervasiveness of the effects of the administrative process on the average person can quickly be appreciated by running over a few samples of what the administrative process protects against: excessive prices of electricity, gas, telephone, and other utility services; unreasonableness in rates, schedules, and services of airlines, railroads, street cars, and buses; disregard for the public interest in radio and television and chaotic conditions for broadcasting; unwholesome meat and poultry; adulteration in food; fraud and inadequate disclosure in sale of securities; physically unsafe locomotives, ships, airplanes, bridges, elevators; unfair labor practices by either employers or unions; false advertising and other unfair or deceptive practices; inadequate safety appliances; uncompensated injuries related to employment; cessation of income during temporary unemployment; subminimum wages; poverty in old age; industrial plants in residential areas; loss of bank deposits; and (perhaps) undue inflation or deflation. Probably the list could be expanded to a thousand or more items that we are accustomed to take for granted.

The volume of the legislative output of federal agencies far exceeds the volume of the legislative output of Congress. The *Code of Federal Regulations* is considerably larger than United States Code. The *Federal Register,* the accumulation of less than one-quarter of a century, fills much more shelf space than the Statutes at Large, the accumulation of nearly a century and three-quarters.[23]

Although not many used the term in 1958, the fourth branch or administrative state was a reality even then. If democracy is a system in which citizens have some input into policies that affect them, and if increasingly, those decisions are made by bureaucrats rather than by elected officials, then there could be a problem with our democracy. If the president or Congress exercises sufficient control over agencies, then the existence of the administrative state should not be a threat to democracy. An examination of presidential and congressional control of agencies follows in the next two chapters. Before turning our attention to subsequent chapters, however, the student should attempt to ascertain what principles or concepts can be drawn from the case, *Whitman v. American Trucking Association,* presented at the beginning of the chapter. For instance, consider the following:

1. Agencies do, in fact, make rules (or set standards) that have significant impact on people's lives, and those rules have the force and effect of law. (The administrative state is a reality.)

2. Often, presidential control over agencies is marginal. Although we do not know it for a fact, it is a safe bet that President George W. Bush does not like the revised NAAQS and most likely, his EPA director, Christine Todd Whitman, did not like them either, yet they could not change them and were forced to go to court to defend them (and they won in court, securing the more stringent NAAQS).

3. One should always look to the enabling legislation, because Congress determines what agencies do and how they must proceed. Indeed, two of the issues in the case dealt with what Congress intended for the agencies to do.

4. The courts are the final arbiters in conflicts involving public administration.

SUMMARY

In an attempt to keep things simple but realistic, we have defined democracy as a system in which people have some influence over policies that affect their lives. It is recognized that frequently, bureaucratic agencies make policies that affect people's lives (the administrative state). If, however, popularly elected officials, such as the president and members of Congress, exercise sufficient control over agency policy making, then the administrative state is not inconsistent with democracy.

NOTES

1. For information on the river fire, visit www.cwru.edu/artsci/engl/marling/60s/pages/richoux.

2. A fairly detailed discussion of particulate matter and ozone can be found in the case that was remanded back to the circuit court from the Supreme Court; all of the scientific material on particulate matter and ozone come from *American Trucking Association v. EPA* 283 F.3d 355, 359 (2002).

3. Robert Weissberg, *Public Opinion and Popular Government* (Englewood Cliffs, NJ: Prentice Hall, 1976), 126–32.

4. Gallup poll (www.gallup.com/poll/releases/pr981212.asp).

5. Gallup poll (www.gallup.com/poll/indicators/indtaxes.asp).

6. Robert Erikson, Norman Luttberg, and Kent Tedin, *American Public Opinion: Its Origins, Content and Impact,* 3d ed. (New York: Macmillan, 1988), 348–51.

7. U.S. Census Bureau, *Statistical Abstract of the United States: 2000,* 123rd ed., (Washington, D. C., 2003), Table 1, p. 8.

8. Kenneth Warren, *Administrative Law in the Political System,* 2d ed. (St. Paul, MN: West, 1988), p. 108.

9. See Frederic C. Mosher, *Democracy and the Public Service,* 2d ed. (New York: Oxford University Press, 1982), 83–109; David H. Rosenbloom, "The Evolution of the Administrative State and Transformations of Administrative Law," in *Handbook of Regulation and Administrative Law*, ed. David H. Rosenbloom and Richard D. Schwartz (New York: Marcel Dekker, Inc., 1994), 3–36; David H. Rosenbloom, "Retrofitting the Administrative State to the Constitution: Congress and the Judiciary's Twentieth Century Progress," 60 *Public Administration Review* 39–46 (January/February 2000); Emmette Redford, *Democracy in the Administrative State* (New York: Oxford University Press, 1969); Dwight Waldo, *The Administrative State* (New York: The Ronald Press Co., 1948).

10. *Federal Trade Commission v. Ruberoid Co.,* 343 U.S. 470, 487 (1951) (Justice Jackson dissenting). See also Kenneth J. Meier, *Politics and Bureaucracy: Policymaking in the Fourth Branch of Government* (North Scituate, MA: Duxbury, 1979); and Peter Strauss, "The Place of Agencies in Government: Separation of Powers and the Fourth Branch," 84 *Columbia Law Review* 574 (1984).

11. Sir Isaiah Berlin, "Two Concepts of Liberty," in *Four Essays on Liberty* (New York: Oxford University Press, 1969), 122–34.

12. Ibid.

13. One reason the Iran-Contra affair was such a fiasco was that a staff agency (the National Security Council) that is not empowered to accomplish anything assumed the task of selling arms to the enemy and sending the profits to Central America in violation of an act of Congress, whereas line agencies (the Department of State and the Department of Defense), given the authority to sell arms and conduct foreign policy, opposed the scheme.

14. U.S. Bureau of the Census, *Statistical Abstract of the United States: 2000,* 123rd ed. (Washington, D.C.: Government Printing Office, 2003), Table 500, p. 337.

15. U.S. Bureau of the Census, *Statistical Abstract of the United States: 1999,* 119th ed. (Washington, D. C.: Government Printing Office, 1999), Table 534, p. 338.

16. Paul Light, *The True Size of Government* (Washington, D.C.: Brookings Institution Press, 1999), 1–9.

17. The facts on pollution, auto and job safety, and infant mortality are in Charles Goodsell, *The Case for Bureaucracy* (Washington, D.C.: C.Q.

Press, 2004), p. 40. See also John E. Schwarz, *America's Hidden Success: A Reassessment of Public Policy from Kennedy to Reagan* (New York: Norton, 1988), Chapter 2.

18. *United States Government Manual 1991/92* (Washington, D.C.: Office of the Federal Registrar, National Archives and Records Administration, 1991), p. 600.

19. See, generally, 15 U.S.C. 45. The rule-making power is granted in 15 U.S.C. 57a.

20. *U.S. Government Manual 1991/92,* p. 418.

21. 29 C.F.R. 17.

22. Goodsell, *The Case for Bureaucracy,* pp. 39 and 41.

23. Kenneth Culp Davis, *Administrative Law Treatise,* Vol. 1 (St. Paul, MN: West, 1958), pp. 7, 8.

2

EXECUTIVE CONTROL
OF BUREAUCRACY

From Chapter 1, you learned that Congress passes broad and vague pieces of legislation and delegates the power to agencies to write rules, regulations, and standards that provide teeth to the legislation. Congress passes about 250 pieces of legislation a year (it has averaged 288 public laws per year over a 22-year period from 1975 to 1996).[1] The bureaucracy, however, adopts nearly 4,000 rules in a year, filling 19,233 single-spaced pages in the *Federal Register*, and it has been estimated that the number of federal bureaucrats writing rules has grown to 122,000.[2]

One primary objective for a chief executive in gaining control over bureaucracy is to somehow control the rule-making power of the agencies. Although the president is the titular head of the federal bureaucracy, it is Congress that creates agencies, gives them the rule-making power, and commands them to make rules enforcing legislation. Hence, it is not at all clear whether the president has the constitutional authority to control the rule-making power of agencies. This might be the case because Article II of the Constitution (the executive branch) commands that the president "shall take care that the laws be *faithfully* executed" (the emphasis is mine). If Congress passes a law that mandates clean air or worker safety and orders agencies to adopt rules or standards to achieve those results, it is not clear that a president could interfere with that agency's task. Nor is it clear whether a subsequent Congress could delegate that power to the president. The fact that it may be unconstitutional for presidents to control agency rule making mandated by Congress has not stopped modern presidents from attempting to find a way to do it. A more precise history of these attempts will be presented later in this chapter, but for now, it is enough to know that Presidents Nixon, Ford, Carter, Reagan, and both Bushes (hereafter, George Herbert Walker Bush will be referred to as Bush 41 and George W. Bush will be referred to as Bush 43) have used the Office of Management and Budget (OMB) to exercise control over agency rule making.

It is difficult to make blanket statements about executive control of bureaucracy that apply to the executive branch of government throughout the various levels of federalism. Gubernatorial power to control agencies varies depending on state constitutions and the strength of statewide political party organizations. Counties rarely have chief executives, and a mayor's power to control bureaucracy will depend on the type of city government (some mayors are truly strong while others are legally figureheads). It is even difficult to make summary statements about the president's ability to control bureaucratic rule making because some presidents are not concerned about it whereas others are absolutely obsessed with it.

Whether a president possesses the will to control agency rule making or is unconcerned with it depends on the party affiliation of the particular president. In Chapter 1, you read that Republicans generally lean toward limited government and negative freedom, and prefer the free market to government regulation. For example, whereas Congress has averaged 288 public laws per year, in the first full year of recent Republican control of Congress—1995—the Republicans enacted only 88 public bills into law. Democrats have a propensity to believe in positive freedom (individuals can reach their fullest potential through government help), positive government, and government regulation of the economy. Hence, Republican presidents will be likely to want to control agency rule making (President Bush 41 tried to stop it altogether). Democratic presidents will see the bureaucracy as their partner in positive government and be less inclined to attempt to control agency rule making. By way of an example, during the Clinton presidency, Bill Clinton (through Vice President Gore) encouraged creative agency rule making through a policy called reinventing government. At the same time, the Republican-controlled Congress passes laws to tighten control of agency rule making (see, e.g., the Small Business Regulatory Enforcement Fairness Act of 1996).[3] Later in this chapter, we will examine the extent to which President Clinton and Vice President Gore did in fact reinvent government, but the focus of this chapter is presidential control of agencies so we will concentrate on presidents who tried to do just that.

President Reagan was famous for saying that "government is not the solution for problems, government *is* the problem." He and his successor, Bush 41, tried in many ways to control agency rule making. To appreciate the difficulty presidents have in attempting to control bureaucracy, consider what happened to President Reagan. On the day he was inaugurated in January 1981, two agency rules were making their way through the administrative process, and both were philosophically distasteful to President Reagan and nearly every one else in his administration. One was the passive restraint rule from the Department of Transportation (DOT). It would require passive restraints in all vehicles manufactured or imported in the United States after 1984. The other rule was one promulgated by the Department of Energy (DOE), and it would impose minimum energy efficiency standards on all home electrical appliances manufactured or sold in the United States.[4]

Both of these rules are the kind of government regulation of business that economic conservatives (mostly Republicans) dislike. They dislike such rules because they supplement government planning for market-driven decisions about the supply and demand for goods and services. President Reagan, his chief of staff, his OMB director, and his secretaries of energy and transportation all disliked these rules and wanted to stop them from taking effect. They wanted to stop these rules because they believed that if drivers as consumers wanted to pay extra for safer cars, then market demand would cause auto manufacturers to meet that demand. The same would be true for energy-efficient home appliances: If consumers wanted them, manufacturers would supply them. President Reagan ordered his secretary of transportation to rescind the passive restraint rule, but the rescission order was overturned by the Supreme Court so the passive restraint requirement is the law today. If you have been in a store that sells home appliances lately, you may have noticed a bright yellow tag on appliances that says something like this: "This appliance meets or exceeds minimum federal efficiency standards." Score two for the bureaucracy and zero for President Reagan.

The case-in-point below involves another example of an agency rule that began under President Reagan (that he disapproved of and tried to kill) and ultimately survived a court challenge during the presidency of Bush 41. However, once the Republicans gained control of Congress, they passed a law that undid the Supreme Court's decision. This is an interesting case-in-point because it shows the political nature of the interplay among the presidency, Cabinet appointees, the courts, the Congress, the bureaucracy, and interest groups.

Case in Point:
DOLE V. UNITED STEELWORKERS OF AMERICA
494 U.S. 26 (1990)

President Reagan issued Executive Order 12291, which required all agency heads to submit proposed rules with an estimated cost to the economy of $100 million or more to the OMB for a cost-benefit analysis prior to beginning the rule-making process.[5] Bear in mind that the OMB is a staff agency, not a line agency, and because its sole legal function is to advise the president, the OMB cannot forbid the promulgation of an agency rule or standard. However, because the OMB is so close to the president and the president's advisers, OMB disapproval of a proposed rule or standard is tantamount to presidential disapproval (even though the president may not actually be cognizant of all that is going on). Those agency heads or department heads whose jobs depend on continued presidential support are likely to reach a compromise with the OMB.

Presidents Reagan and Bush 41 relied heavily on the Paperwork Reduction Act of 1980 for the statutory authority allowing the OMB to impose its will on agency rule making. The Paperwork Reduction Act was passed to reduce the amount of required paperwork. The administrator of the Occupational Safety and Health Administration (OSHA, an agency within the Department of Labor) proposed a rule called the *hazard communication standard,* which originally was intended to require all employers to warn their workers about exposure to hazardous substances on the job. Neither President Reagan, the president's chief of staff, the secretary of labor, nor the director of the OMB wanted to impose the hazard communication standard on business. When the proposed rule was submitted to the OMB as required by Executive Order 12291, the OMB objected, and subsequent to negotiations, OSHA limited the rule to apply only to manufacturing industries. A group of consumer-oriented interest groups and labor unions successfully challenged the narrower rule in court in 1983 and won. The Court forced OSHA to adopt a new rule that would apply to all work sites in all sections of the economy. The new rule was sent back to the OMB, which again voiced objections, and negotiations between the OMB and OSHA in 1987 produced another modified rule that would not apply to the construction industry. The rule adopted in 1987 was immediately challenged in the courts by the United Steelworkers Union and one of Ralph Nader's organizations. In 1990, the U.S. Supreme Court ruled in *Dole* that the OMB lacked the statutory authority under the Paperwork Reduction Act to block this and other agency rules or standards.[6]

The Court determined that the legislative purpose of the Paperwork Reduction Act was to reduce paperwork that citizens and businesses had to produce for the federal government. Because the hazard communication standard would produce paperwork intended for workers and not the government, the Paperwork Reduction Act could not supply the statutory authority to require OMB review of agency rules. Since the Constitution does not confer OMB review authority on the president, and Congress did not authorize such review in the Paperwork Reduction Act, the president is without the power to require OMB review of agency rules like this one.

One of the items in the Republican Party's Contract With America (widely acclaimed as being responsible for the Republican Party capturing control of Congress in the 1994 elections) was to amend the Paperwork Reduction Act. While Republicans did not campaign on the issue, the reason they wanted to amend the Act was to undo or reverse the Supreme Court's decision in the *Dole* case. They hoped this would provide a future Republican president with the statutory authority to block agency rules.

The Paperwork Reduction Act of 1995 is one of the few parts of the Contract With America that actually passed both Houses of Congress and was signed by President Clinton to become law. Actually, the Paperwork Act referred to in the case in point above expired, so Congress passed a new one. The Act sets year-by-year targets for the federal government to reduce paperwork. It makes the Act applicable to all federal paperwork requirements (addressing the narrow interpretation given to the original Act by the court), and it authorizes a bureau within the OMB, the Office of Information and Regulatory Affairs, to exercise control over agency rules with paperwork implications. This effectively undid the Supreme Court's decision in the *Dole* case and restored presidential control of agency rule making (at least with respect to paperwork) to the pre-*Dole* state of affairs.

Déjà vu all over again! In 1966, Congress passed a law to reduce traffic accidents and the deaths and injuries that result from them. The law delegated to the secretary of transportation the power and obligation to set auto safety standards. Since 1980, the secretary has delegated the standard-setting responsibility to the director of the National Highway Traffic Safety Administration (NHTSA, an agency within the DOT). In 1981, the NHTSA began the process of adopting rules (standards) that would require autos to be equipped with devices that would measure the pressure in tires. Underinflated tires are one of the major causes of auto accidents. Basically, the NHTSA determined that the existing technology was either too expensive or too ineffective and terminated the rule-making process without making a rule.[7] In the late 1990s, the national media began reporting on numerous accidents caused by tread separation involving Bridgestone/Firestone tires that had been installed on Ford Explorers. There were lawsuits, NHTSA opened hearings, and in 2000, under severe pressure, Ford recalled 14 million tires on its Explorers. Later that same year, Congress passed the Transportation Recall Enhancement Accountability and Documentation Act (the TREAD Act), which gave NHTSA a year to adopt a rule requiring a "warning system in new motor vehicles to indicate to the operator when a tire is significantly underinflated."

By the time the NHTSA initiated this new round of hearings on tire pressure monitoring systems, the technology had come a long way since the 1981 hearings. At the dawn of the 21st century, tire pressure monitoring falls into two broad categories: direct or indirect systems. Direct systems, as the name suggests, have a sensor in each wheel that measures the pressure in each tire and indicates to the driver which tire is under- or overinflated. Indirect systems are installed along with antilock brake systems and measure the rotation speed of each wheel. As a tire deflates, the rotation speed of the wheel increases. Indirect systems calculate a ratio by comparing wheel speeds on a diagonal (e.g., right-front and left-rear). If the ratio deviates from a set range, a warning light lets the driver know a tire is under- or overinflated, but the system cannot specify which tire. Indirect systems are cheaper and less expensive to install, as they mesh with the installation of antilock brakes. However, because indirect systems calculate a ratio using pairs of tires, they are only effective if a single tire deflates at a time. If two or more tires deflate at the same time, indirect systems would not catch the problem. The NHTSA estimates that indirect systems would miss 50 percent of the incidents of tire deflation. The rule proposed by the NHTSA had a phase-in period requiring increasing numbers of autos to be fitted with tire pressure monitoring systems until 2006, when all new autos would require them. During the phase-in period, automakers could choose to install either the direct or indirect systems, but by 2006, direct systems would be required. This proposed rule next went to the Office of Information and Regulatory Affairs within OMB during the Bush 43 administration, and that office rejected the rule. The OMB told NHTSA to rewrite the rule, giving equal weight to both types of systems. Because NHTSA estimates that direct systems would prevent 50 more deaths and in excess of 3,500 more injuries a year than indirect systems, the NHTSA balked. Ultimately, the NHTSA produced a final rule that would allow the choice during the phase-in period but fell silent on a long-term tire pressure monitoring system in favor of a new round of hearings. Perhaps the NHTSA was hoping either new technology or a Democratic administration would save it from being forced to promulgate a rule it did not want. As soon as the tire pressure rule was published, the DOT got sued by Public Citizen (Ralph Nader's organization) and other public safety interest groups. Unfortunately for the clarity of the Constitution, lawyers for the plaintiff did not attack OMB's role in agency rule making. Rather, they alleged that NHTSA violated the TREAD Act when it adopted a rule that would miss 50 percent of the potential accidents. They also argued that the agency's rule was arbitrary and capricious (an administrative law concept you will become familiar with in Chapter 4). The U.S. Circuit Court of Appeals agreed with those who had challenged the rule on both counts. The court voided the tire pressure rule and ordered the agency to come up with a new rule that would leave out the indirect option. The agency decided not to appeal to the Supreme Court.

Questions

1. Do you think Congress is capable of establishing national ambient air quality standards (NAAQS) or hazard communication standards or choosing between tire pressure monitoring systems? Do such decisions require political considerations, or do they simply involve the application of expertise?
2. If Congress passes a law to protect workers on the job or drivers from accidents, should the president (through OMB) be able to interfere?
3. Do you think Presidents Bush 41 and 43 were faithfully executing the Occupational Safety and Health Act and the TREAD Act?

Why the President Cannot Control Bureaucracy

All modern presidents, from Franklin Roosevelt to the present, are said to have complained that their worst problem was not the Soviets, not the opposition party, but, rather, the very bureaucracy the president is supposed to be in charge of. Speculating about General Eisenhower's transformation into President Eisenhower, his predecessor, Harry Truman, is reported to have said, "He'll sit here [Truman would tap his desk for emphasis], and he'll say, 'Do this! Do that!' *And nothing will happen.* Poor Ike—it won't be like the Army. He'll find it very frustrating."[8]

Truman also said, "I sit here all day trying to persuade people to do the things they ought to have sense enough to do without my persuading them. . . . that's all the powers of the President amount to."[9] An aide to President Eisenhower said, "The President still feels that when he's decided something, that *ought* to be the end of it . . . and when it comes back undone or done wrong he tends to react with shocked surprise."[10]

President Lyndon Johnson is supposed to have once said that the only power he had was nuclear, and he could not use it.[11] More recently, President Jimmy Carter complained, "I can't even get a damn mouse out of my office." Apparently, the president's request to remove the mouse got lost in a bureaucratic turf battle between the Department of the Interior, which has jurisdiction over the White House grounds, and the General Services Administration, which has jurisdiction over the White House building (which, of course, sits on the White House grounds).[12]

The public statements of presidential candidate Ross Perot in the 1992 election campaign epitomize typical American ignorance about presidential power. He said, "It's time to pick up the shovel and clean out the barn." The implication was that if Ross Perot got elected president, he would see to it that American government would work again. At the root of the problem of presidential control over bureaucracy is the fact that the founding fathers did not provide the office of the presidency with either the tools or processes to "pick up the shovel and clean out the barn."

Most modern Republican presidents have possessed the will to control bureaucracy; they simply have lacked the power to actually do it. Although Mr. Perot should have known better, there seems to be a widespread misconception about the office of the presidency, especially among younger generations, who grew up getting their news from television. It may be that it is simply easier to cover the president than it is to cover 535 members of Congress or even, say, 20 or so congressional leaders, but for whatever reason, the media spend an inordinate amount of air time covering the president. Perhaps, this has led people to believe that the office is more powerful than it really is.

Constitutional Powers

It is instructive to examine the list of presidential powers.

1. Article I, Section 7, while not using the term *veto,* says that the president can either sign or return (i.e., veto) a bill to Congress. The veto described in Article I of the Constitution makes a chief executive choose between accepting and rejecting a bill in its entirety (even if it is a good bill with objectionable parts). This has allowed Congress to play a game called attaching riders. A rider the president would oppose may be added to a bill working its way through Congress when the president is known to support the bill. Members of Congress may also attach an amendment the president likes to a bill the president is known to oppose and would veto if it were presented to him or her on its own. Hence, it is called a rider. Most of the states' governors can exercise a *line item veto* that allows them to strike parts (lines) in a budget bill or a tax bill. Only a few governors enjoy an *amendatory veto,* which is just like a line item veto except it is not limited to budget or tax bills. Republicans made the line item veto one of the planks in their Contract With America in the 1994 election. A bill authorizing the presidential use of the line item veto was passed and signed into law by President Bill Clinton, but its first use drew a lawsuit and the Supreme Court declared it unconstitutional. See *Clinton v. New York,* 524 U.S. 417, 1998 at the end of this chapter.

2. Article 2, Section 1, provides that executive power be vested in the president. You will see shortly that this section does not provide a residual of executive power for the president to use.

3. Article 2, Section 2, names the president commander-in-chief and gives him power to do the following:

    a. require written opinions from department heads (this is the only reference in the Constitution to the bureaucracy)

    b. grant reprieves and pardons

    c. make appointments (with advice and consent of the Senate)

    d. make treaties (with advice and consent of the Senate)

    e. make appointments during congressional recess; Democrats in the 108th Congress have frustrated several of President Bush 43's appointments by filibustering them. The president has had to make liberal use of this provision, including the recess appointment of Justice Antonin Scalia's son.

4. Article 2, Section 3, says that the president may do the following:

    a. inform Congress of the state of the union

    b. recommend legislation to Congress

    c. on extraordinary occasion convene Congress

    d. adjourn Congress, should both houses disagree on adjournment

    e. receive ambassadors

    f. take care that the laws be faithfully executed

These are not the powers of the most powerful executive in the world today. Indeed, those who wrote the Constitution did not intend for the office to be powerful. They intended the president to have only enough power to carry out the wishes of Congress (to see to it that laws are faithfully executed).

Extraconstitutional Powers

It is true, however, that the presidency is more powerful today than the preceding list suggests. That is because Supreme Court decisions have provided the presidency with enormous power in the area of foreign policy. By a combination of historical use and Court decisions, there are also extraconstitutional powers, such as impoundment, executive agreements, executive privilege, and delegation of power.

To understand presidential power today is to recognize a bifurcated presidency: one presidency that, in foreign affairs, is quite powerful and another presidency that, in domestic affairs, requires action by Congress in nearly every situation and hence is significantly weaker.

The Supreme Court recognized and sanctioned a notion referred to as the *sole organ theory* in cases such as *United States v. Curtis-Wright Export Corporation*, 299 U.S. 304 (1936) and *United States v. Belmont*, 301 U.S. 324 (1937). The sole organ theory is the concept that foreign policy must be conducted by one office occupied by one recognizable individual with the authority to speak for the whole nation. Hence, there is no room for 50 individual states to have a voice in foreign affairs, nor is there any room for shared power with 535 members of Congress. In the *Curtis-Wright* case, the Supreme Court said:

> In this vast external realm [foreign policy] with its important, complicated, delicate and manifold problems, the President alone has the power to speak or listen as a representative of the nation. He *makes* treaties with the advice and consent of the Senate; but he alone negotiates. Into the field of negotiation the Senate cannot intrude; and Congress itself is powerless to invade it.[13]

In the *Belmont* case, the Court sanctioned the practice of executive agreements (legally binding agreements between the president and other heads of state that do not need senatorial approval and hence circumvent the treaty provision in Article II of the Constitution). Finally, Congress has delegated some of its foreign policy powers to the president. For example, in the War Powers Resolution of 1973, Congress delegated to the president its power to declare war, and in the *Curtis-Wright* case, Congress delegated its power to enact embargoes.

The cumulative effect of congressional delegations, executive· agreements, and Supreme Court decisions supportive of the sole organ theory renders presidential power almost unchecked in the area of foreign policy. By way of example, Congress had tried to control and limit the use of executive agreements to no avail, so, in 1972, they passed a law requiring that the president notify them of each executive agreement (Case-Zablocki Act, 1 U.S.C. sec. 112b). Modern presidents routinely ignore this law with no consequences, legal, political, or otherwise.[14]

Presidential power on the domestic side is a wholly different story. As you can see from the preceding list of presidential powers, no domestic power is granted solely to the president (except for the pardon power). Again, the extraconstitutional powers of impoundment, executive privilege, and delegation of power have rendered the presidency, on the domestic side, more powerful than the list of constitutional powers suggests.

Impoundment is the idea that the president can simply refuse to spend money that has been appropriated by Congress. Generally, when presidential impoundments are challenged in court, the president loses. Congress has attempted to regulate presidential impoundment through the Congressional Budget and Impoundment Control Act of 1974. However, the president today still manages to impound nearly $12 billion annually.[15]

Executive privilege means that to enhance presidential decision making, the president (and his advisers) may withhold information from Congress and even sometimes from a court of law. The concept will be explored more fully in Chapter 5 in a discussion of the Freedom of Information Act, but suffice it to say here that executive privilege increases power in the White House to the degree that power is defined as information and its control. Should you be skeptical about the power that accumulates with the ability to manipulate information, consider the 2003 war in Iraq. The war was justified based on a new foreign policy called preemption. The idea is that a sovereign is authorized to use force to prevent imminent harm from another sovereign who represents a threat. President Bush 43 was able to sell the American public and Congress on the magnitude of the threat from Iraq, which later turned out to be nonexistent.

Delegation of power is a concept you have already been exposed to, but it has not been defined for you. Delegation of power is a topic central to the next chapter on congressional control of agencies. It is simply an instance in which Congress entrusts its constitutional

Article I, Section 8, powers to the executive branch. For example, when Congress makes the decision to reduce traffic fatalities, industrial fatalities, or smog, it assigns its law-making power to an agency so that the agency can "faithfully execute the law." When Congress delegates its power to the president, the power of the presidency is enhanced. However, Congress rarely assigns its power directly to the president. Instead, it generally transfers its power to an executive agency (e.g., OSHA, the Environmental Protection Agency (EPA), or the DOT). The degree to which the president can control agencies is the degree to which presidential power is increased via delegation of power. From the examples of tire pressure monitoring systems and the hazard communication standard, you should begin to understand that presidential control of agencies is slippery at best. Richard Neustadt, perhaps the foremost authority on the presidency, argues that presidential power amounts to the power to persuade.[16] This is particularly true on the domestic side.

In the famous *Steel Seizure*[17] case, the Supreme Court addressed an exercise of presidential power that was domestic but had serious foreign policy implications. During the Korean War, the steel workers union threatened to strike the industry, which had refused to bargain in good faith.[18] President Truman and executive officials tried to get the two sides to settle, but to no avail. With a strike against the entire steel industry scheduled for midnight on April 9, 1952 (a time when the Korean War was not going well for us), President Truman ordered Secretary of Commerce Charles Sawyer to seize the steel mills and keep them operating. Youngstown Sheet and Tube Co. and other steel mills filed suit, and a little less than two months later, the Supreme Court declared Truman's seizure to be unconstitutional. Although the case is fascinating and important, Justice Jackson's concurring opinion has the greatest lasting significance. Jackson's opinion in the case is important because the modern Supreme Court relies on it when it is called on to assess particular issues of presidential power. Justice Jackson said that presidential power falls into the following three categories:[19]

1. When the president acts pursuant to a congressional delegation of power, the president's power is at a maximum because the president is using all of the power of the executive branch plus all of the power of Congress.

2. When a president acts and Congress has said nothing on the subject, the president must rely on the powers of Article II of the Constitution to justify the action.

3. When presidential action is "incompatible with the expressed or implied will of Congress, his power is at its lowest ebb."[20]

To emphasize the point, Congress, in the steel seizure scenario, had not forbidden the president from nationalizing or seizing companies. However, a bill had been introduced to grant the president the power to seize important industries during World War II, and this bill died in committee. The Court considered the bill's demise to be the "implied will of Congress" and, therefore, decided that the president had acted counter to congressional will. His power was at its lowest ebb, and the action could not be justified by Article II of the Constitution. Hence, the presidential action was unconstitutional.

THE TOOLS OF PRESIDENTIAL CONTROL

As indicated earlier, modern presidents have had the will and, perhaps, a strong desire to control bureaucracy but have not met with a good deal of success because the raw power (the ability to make one do that which one does not want to do) is not there. Any standard

U.S. government textbook will provide a list of tools that presidents use in attempting to control agencies.[21] Those tools are appointments, removal, reorganization, executive orders, the budget, and OMB screening of proposed agency rules. Finally, the concept of the administrative presidency will be analyzed.

Presidential Appointments

A president can potentially appoint more than 1,300 officials, appointments requiring senatorial approval.[22] Some of these positions are policy-making positions (Cabinet secretaries, for example), and some are judges, U.S. attorneys, ambassadors, and so on. With many of these appointments, the president's choices are constrained by the concept of *senatorial courtesy*. Senatorial courtesy requires the president to appoint the choice of the senior senator of the president's party from the state where the vacant seat occurs. Presidential failure to do so is likely to result in the Senate's refusal to confirm. The president is also able to make another 1,140 bureaucratic appointments.[23]

The common assumption might be that when the president can appoint his or her own choice to head an agency, then presidential control over that agency is enhanced. To test this presumption, assume that you have been appointed by your longtime friend and political associate, the governor, to a seat on the Public Utilities Commission. In several weeks, you will be expected to vote on a proposal by the major electrical utility company in your state to raise its rates by 35 percent. The utility company has produced a three-volume report with facts, figures, and charts documenting rising costs, rising overhead, and dwindling revenues. A local consumer group has produced a similar document, showing that the utility made some poor investments and simply wants to recoup losses at the consumer's expense. Repeated attempts to discuss this with your old friend, the governor, have failed, due to your inability to get past the appointments secretary and chief of staff. How will you vote? How and where will you get independent information to help you cast an intelligent vote? The answer is the same for you as it is for the director of the EPA or the secretary of labor or transportation. Both you and the secretaries will turn to the technical experts who work for the respective agencies and the Public Utilities Commission (mid-level bureaucrats).

The preceding scenario introduces the concept of *captivity*. Because presidential appointees average less than two years in a position and frequently are unfamiliar with the agency or department they are appointed to head, political appointees often become the captives of the mid-level career bureaucrats who have been in the agency for decades. These bureaucrats possess expertise on which the appointee comes to depend. They also have more political influence and clout than the appointee because they have spent years cultivating a political base with members of Congress and also with powerful interest groups who have a vested interest in what happens at the agency.[24] Perhaps, the following quotations will provide the reader with a real grasp of some of the problems presidents have with appointees:

> In a real sense, delegation of authority to an operating manager of an entirely unfamiliar field [i.e., secretary delegates to the bureaucrat] means that the secretary serves the bureau chief rather than vice versa.[25]

> [The secretary's] judgement on budget items is, of course, the most important decision he will make in his term of office and is the decision he is usually least well-equipped to make intelligently.[26]

The President's title, "Chief Executive," is a misnomer. More accurately the president can be described as a "Nonexecutive Chief" for the White House is far from being the command center of the executive branch. Although the president appoints the heads of great operating departments and agencies, the principal resources upon which they depend . . . are derived from Acts of Congress. Programs and policies, to the extent that they are implemented, are carried out by tenured civil servants, who were on the job before the incumbent president arrived and who will remain there after he leaves.[27]

The single most powerful figure in the great pyramid is the bureau chief, who in many substantive ways can frustrate the president's purposes when they diverge from his own. He cultivates ties with pressure groups whose interests his organization serves and [with] the congressional committees that provide him with money and authority. Congressional committees and subcommittees welcome his attentions since all are united in a common purpose, protecting the integrity of the bureau's functions. Presidents sometimes feel so remote from the bureaus that they lose sight of their responsibility to oversee them.[28]

Candidate Ronald Reagan said that if elected, he would bring about "a new structuring of the presidential Cabinet that will make Cabinet officers the managers of the national administration—not captives of the bureaucracy or special interests they are supposed to direct."[29]

Presidents Nixon, Ford, and Carter tried to get agencies to move in particular directions and met with little success. Presidents Reagan and Bush 41 tried to get the bureaucracy to stop moving at all. Although it is fair to say that Reagan enjoyed somewhat more success than either his predecessors or Bush 41, he was not entirely successful either.[30] The cases discussed so far, *American Trucking Association, Dole,* and the tire pressure rule, are examples in which presidents and their appointed secretaries were unable to stop rules promulgated by bureaucrats. The mere fact that a president appoints a department head whose job security depends on presidential goodwill is not sufficient to enhance presidential control over agencies. Furthermore, the process of confirming a presidential appointee from either political party has become so cumbersome and lengthy and exposes the appointee to such risk that it is increasingly difficult to find good potential appointees willing to go through the process. That has produced an appointment process that favors Washington insiders who already possess an independent base of political support. That means that future presidential appointees will be more independent of the president who appointed them.[31]

Presidential Removal

Although the Constitution clearly rests the appointment power in the president with senatorial consent, the document is silent on the question of the president's power to remove those he or she has appointed. One might logically assume that because Article II of the Constitution places executive power in the president, the president's ability to remove those who serve in the executive branch would be somewhat unrestricted. Presidential removal power, however, is not that clear and to understand it, we must examine several Supreme Court cases on the subject.

In 1876, Congress passed an act providing for four-year terms for first-, second-, and third-class postmasters and further provided that such postmasters would be appointed and *removed* by the president with the *consent of the Senate.* In 1920, President Wilson (or perhaps Mrs. Wilson, as the President had suffered a stroke and reportedly was not in charge) ordered the postmaster general to fire a first-class postmaster in Portland (Mr. Myers). However, there was no senatorial consent to this firing. Although Mr. Myers died, his wife, as administratrix of his estate, sued to recover lost salary. In *Myers v. United States*, 272 U.S. 52 (1926), the Supreme Court said that the portion of the Act of 1876 requiring senatorial consent to presidential removal decisions was unconstitutional. The Court reasoned that without the absolute and unrestrained power to remove those the president has appointed, a president would be unable to (a) exercise executive power or (b) faithfully execute the laws of the United States as required by Article II of the Constitution.

Nine years later, however, the question came before the Court again. This time President Franklin Roosevelt fired William Humphrey, who had been appointed to a seven-year term on the Federal Trade Commission (FTC) by President Herbert Hoover. Actually, FDR asked Humphrey to resign, saying that it was no reflection on Mr. Humphrey personally or his performance as a commissioner but that there were deep ideological differences between FDR and Mr. Humphrey regarding what the FTC should be doing. When Humphrey refused to resign, FDR fired him. The problem this time was that the Federal Trade Commission Act specifies that commissioners may be removed only for "inefficiency, neglect of duty or malfeasance in office." Because, by the president's own admission, Humphrey met none of the criteria for removal, Humphrey sued. Curiously enough, before the case could be settled, Humphrey (like Myers) died. Hence, the case is entitled *Humphrey's Executor v. United States*, 295 U.S. 602 (1935). Two constitutional issues were before the Supreme Court: first, whether the language in the section limiting removal of commissioners to cases including specific cause was intended to limit the president's power of removal and, second, if so, is that part of the Act constitutional? The Court answered in the affirmative on both issues. Congress can restrict the power of the president to removal for cause, and that restriction is a constitutional prerogative of Congress.

The Court said that whether the president's power of removal under the executive power in Article II of the Constitution can be restricted by Congress depends on the nature of the office involved. On the one hand, some offices are political and may involve policy making. Such offices are meant to fall under executive control, and in those instances, Congress cannot restrict presidential removal power. On the other hand, some offices perform a function that is not political, executive, or policy oriented but, rather, is simply to enforce or implement the law through quasi-judicial or quasi-legislative procedures. The latter offices have as their basis expertise rather than politics and were intended from their creation to be politically independent. To these types of offices, the president's removal power does not extend absolutely, and it may be restricted as in the case here involving the FTC.

> The commission [FTC] is to be non-partisan; and must . . . act with impartiality. It is charged with the enforcement of no policy except the policy of the law. Its duties are neither political nor executive, but predominantly quasi-judicial and quasi-legislative. Like the ICC [Interstate Commerce Commission], its members are called upon to exercise the trained judgement of a body of experts "appointed by law and informed by experience." [32]

The Role of Law

You are about to read the first case from Supreme Court records presented in this text, but before you do, you need to think about what the Supreme Court does when it decides a case. The main function of the Supreme Court is to resolve issues of constitutional law so that citizens and officials will understand what can and cannot be done under the Constitution or the laws of Congress. Questions such as the following are classic: Does the Constitution forbid capital punishment? abortion? separate schools for black students and white students? Generally, when the Court answers these questions, it establishes a *doctrine*, a legal principle or rule that will guide behavior in the future in situations involving similar facts.

Students are not exposed to all of the cases in an area of law in a text such as this but, rather, to the ones that establish doctrines or legal tests. Often, the text will present a recent or interesting case so the reader can see how (or whether) the Court applied the doctrine. What would you say is the doctrine in the *Myers* case? Can you identify a doctrine for the *Humphrey* case? Do you believe the Court overruled the *Myers* doctrine in the *Humphrey* case?

If you said that the doctrine from the *Myers* case was something like, "the President's removal power is absolute," you would be right. The doctrine from the *Humphrey* case is a bit more complicated: The president's removal power is absolute for those offices that are political or executive in nature. Removal power can be restricted for those offices that Congress intended to be free from political control and those offices that perform quasi-judicial or quasi-legislative functions. The Court did not overrule *Myers* in *Humphrey* but, rather, modified it to restrict the area of unbridled presidential removal. For the case that follows (and those throughout the text), think about the following:

1. What is the doctrine or test or rule of law that the court uses to resolve this dispute?

2. Ask yourself whether the Court followed existing doctrine or whether it created a new doctrine or test.

3. Do you understand why the Court decided the case the way it did?

Wiener v. United States
357 U.S. 349 (1958)

Justice Frankfurter delivered the opinion for a unanimous Court.

This is a suit for back pay, based on petitioner's alleged illegal removal as a member of the War Claims Commission. The facts are not in dispute. By the War Claims Act of 1948, Congress established that Commission with "jurisdiction to receive and adjudicate according to law" claims for compensating internees, prisoners of war, and religious organizations, who suffered personal injury or property damage at the hands of the enemy in connection with World War II. The Commission was to be composed of three persons, at least two of whom were to be

members of the bar, to be appointed by the President, by and with the advice and consent of the Senate. The Commission was to wind up its affairs not later than three years after the expiration of the time for filing claims, originally limited to two years but extended by successive legislation first to March 1, 1951, and later to March 31, 1952. This limit on the Commission's life was the mode by which the tenure of the Commissioners was defined, and Congress made no provision for removal of a Commissioner.

Having been duly nominated by President Truman, the petitioner was confirmed on June 2, 1950, and took office on June 8, following. On his refusal to heed a request for his resignation, he was, on December 10, 1953, removed by President Eisenhower in the following terms: "I regard it as in the national interest to complete the administration of the War Claims Act of 1948, as amended, with personnel of my own selection." The following day, the President made recess appointments to the Commission, including petitioner's post. After Congress assembled, the President, on February 15, 1954, sent the names of the new appointees to the Senate. The Senate had not confirmed these nominations when the Commission was abolished, July 1, 1954. Thereupon, petitioner brought this proceeding in the Court of Claims for recovery of his salary as a War Claims Commissioner from December 10, 1953, the day of his removal by the President, to June 30, 1954, the last day of the Commission's existence. A divided Court of Claims dismissed the petition, 142 F.Supp. 910. We brought the case here because it presents a variant of the constitutional issue decided in *Humphrey's Executor v. United States*. Controversy pertaining to the scope and limits of the President's power of removal fills a thick chapter of our political and judicial history. The long stretches of its history, beginning with the very first Congress, with early echoes in the Reports of this Court, were laboriously traversed in *Myers v. United States* and need not be retraced. President Roosevelt's reliance upon the pronouncements of the Court in that case in removing a member of the Federal Trade Commission on the ground that "the aims and purposes of the Administration with respect to the work of the Commission can be carried out most effectively with personnel of my own selection" reflected contemporaneous professional opinion regarding the significance of the *Myers* decision. Speaking through a Chief Justice who himself had been President, the Court did not restrict itself to the immediate issue before it, the President's inherent power to remove a postmaster, obviously an executive official. As of set purpose and not by way of parenthetic casualness, the Court announced that the President had inherent constitutional power of removal also of officials who have "duties of a quasi-judicial character. . . whose decisions after hearing affect interests of individuals, the discharge of which the President cannot in a particular case properly influence or control." This view of presidential power was deemed to flow from his "constitutional duty of seeing that the laws be faithfully executed." The assumption was short-lived that the *Myers* case recognized the President's inherent constitutional power to remove officials, no matter what the relation of the executive to the discharge of their duties and no matter what restrictions Congress may have imposed regarding the nature of their tenure. The versatility of circumstances often mocks a natural desire for definitiveness. Within less than ten years, a unanimous Court, in *Humphrey's Executor v. United States*, narrowly confined the scope of the *Myers* decision to include only "all purely executive officers." The Court explicitly "disapproved" the expressions in *Myers* supporting the President's inherent constitutional power to remove members of quasi-judicial bodies. Congress had given members of the Federal Trade Commission a seven-year term and also provided for the removal of a Commissioner by the President for inefficiency, neglect of duty, or malfeasance in office. In the present case, Congress provided for a tenure defined by the relatively short period of time during which the War Claims Commission was to operate—that is, it was to wind up not later than three years after the expiration of the time for filing of claims. But nothing was said in the Act about removal. . . . And what is the essence of the decision in *Humphrey's* case? It drew a sharp line of cleavage between officials who were part of the Executive establishment and were thus removable by virtue of the President's constitutional powers, and those who are members of a body "to exercise its judgment without the leave or hindrance of any other official or any department of the government," as to whom a power of removal exists only if Congress may fairly be said to have conferred it. This sharp differentiation derives from the difference in functions between those who are part of the Executive establishment and those whose tasks require absolute freedom from Executive interference. "For it is quite evident," again to quote *Humphrey's Executor*, "that one who holds his office only during the pleasure of another cannot be depended upon to maintain an attitude of independence against the latter's will."

Thus, the most reliable factor for drawing an inference regarding the President's power of removal in our case is the nature of the function that Congress vested in the War Claims Commission. The Commission was established as an adjudicating body with all the paraphernalia by which legal claims are put to the test of proof, with finality of determination "not subject to review by any other official of the United States or by any court by mandamus or otherwise." The final form of the legislation, as we have seen, left the widened range of claims to be determined by adjudication.

Congress could, of course, have given jurisdiction over these claims to the District Courts or to the Court of Claims. The fact that it chose to establish a Commission to "adjudicate according to law" the classes of claims defined in the statute did not alter the intrinsic judicial character of the task with which the Commission was charged. The claims were to be "adjudicated according to law," that is, on the merits of each claim, supported by evidence and governing legal considerations, by a body that was "entirely free from the control or coercive influence, direct or indirect," of either the Executive or the Congress. If, as one must take for granted, the War Claims Act precluded the President from influencing the Commission in passing on a particular claim, *a fortiori* must it be inferred that Congress did not wish to have hang over the Commission the Damocles' sword of removal by the President for no reason other than that he preferred to have on that Commission men of his own choosing. . . . Judging the matter in all the nakedness in which it is presented, namely, the claim that the President could remove a member of an adjudicatory body like the War Claims Commission merely because he wanted his own appointees on such a Commission, we are compelled to conclude that no such power is given to the President directly by the Constitution, and none is impliedly conferred upon him by statute simply because Congress said nothing about it. The philosophy of *Humphrey's Executor*, in its explicit language as well as its implications, precludes such a claim.

The judgment is reversed.

Questions

1. Do you believe that the Court created a new doctrine in this case, or did it simply apply the existing law?
2. Wiener won this case (and Eisenhower lost). Can you explain why?

The problem with the Court's doctrine regarding presidential removal is that it rests on a simplistic notion that there is a clear and distinct dichotomy between policy making on the one hand and simple administration of those policies on the other. We know from our discussion in Chapter 1 that the dichotomy no longer exists. The doctrine in *Humphrey* survived for more than 50 years until the Court decided *Morrison v. Olson*, 487 U.S. 654 (1988), which is included at the end of this chapter. The point relative to a discussion of presidential removal power is that as a tool of presidential control over administrative agencies, removal power is not always effective—or even available. The *Morrison* case further erodes presidential power in the area of both appointment and removal.

Executive Reorganization

Executive reorganization refers to presidential efforts to shift, combine, or eliminate agencies. All agencies are created and funded by Congress, not the president; therefore, the president lacks the power or authority to modify the jurisdiction or organizational structure of any Cabinet-level bureau or independent regulatory agency. Indeed, under the Reorganization Act, the president may submit a reorganization plan to Congress transferring functions among agencies. Only if Congress endorses the plan within 90 days does it become effective (a process that is now constitutionally suspect; see Chapter 3). This is how the EPA was created in 1970.[33] The president does, however, possess the power to reorganize the staff agencies, the Executive Office of the President. Look again at Figure 1.1. The president may do this without congressional interference, but, of course, a congressional appropriation would be required to continue to operate any reorganized staff agency. In terms of the president's control over agency activity, the "power to reorganize" is not a power at all. The president's ability to reorganize departments depends, as Neustadt said about 30 years ago,[34] on the president's ability to persuade Congress and the heads of agencies involved to do it. In 1980, as a presidential candidate, Ronald Reagan made it a campaign promise to get rid of the Departments of Education and Energy. The astute reader will notice that those two agencies still exist today, as healthy as they ever were.

As a presidential candidate, Bush 43 argued that faith-based organizations ought to be able to receive federal funds to help them defray the cost of some of the social services they provide (where private organizations help the poor, government does not have to). As president, Bush 43 submitted legislation to Congress to get official recognition for an agency called the Office of Faith-Based Initiatives. The legislation is still tied up in Congress, but President Bush 43 was able to create the office and place it within the Executive Office of the President.

Shortly after America was attacked on September 11, 2001, several legislators, most notably Senator Joseph Lieberman (D-Connecticut), called for the creation of a Cabinet-level Department of Homeland Security. President Bush 43 initially opposed the idea of a department at all, then, after accepting the idea, placed it in the Executive Office of the President and did not want a Cabinet agency. As discussed in Chapter 1, executive office agencies are staff agencies as opposed to line agencies, and their sole function is to advise the president. Their virtue from a presidential perspective is that the president has absolute control and to create them, remove them, or reorganize them does not require congressional action. As an executive office agency without the power to compel action, Homeland Security could not do much, so Bush 43 submitted his own legislation to create a Cabinet-level agency. The president's version of a homeland security bill differed from Senator Lieberman's, and the creation of the Cabinet agency of homeland security languished in Congress for more than a year. The fight primarily was over employment rights of what would be the office's new employees. The president's plan, supported by Republicans, would have removed civil service protection from homeland security employees, and the Democrats were reluctant to compromise on that issue.[35] The eventual creation of the Cabinet-level agency was accomplished by combining several existing agencies. It constitutes the largest federal government reorganization since the creation of the Defense Department in the 1940s. The Department of Homeland Security has 170,000 employees.

Executive Orders

The president has the ability to issue executive orders. The Constitution does not give the president a policy-making role. Hence, the most effective executive orders are the ones that execute congressional legislation. President Reagan's Executive Order 12291 (referred to in the *Dole* case at the beginning of this chapter) required all executive agencies to submit significant proposed rules to the OMB and, "to the extent permitted by law," not to issue rules at all unless the benefits outweighed the costs. Furthermore, it required agencies to prepare an impact analysis of their proposed rules, regulations, or standards. This executive order was not issued pursuant to any congressional action and therefore rested solely for its legal authority on Article II of the Constitution vesting executive power in the president. The phrase, "to the extent permitted by law," suggests that when a conflict arises between an agency attempting to fulfill congressional mandates and Executive Order 12291, the executive order must give way. Congress has, for example, forbidden OSHA to use a cost-benefit analysis in creating safety standards.[36] Therefore, OSHA not only need not, but literally could not comply with Executive Order 12291. In *Environmental Defense Fund [EDF] v. Thomas,* 627 F.Supp. 566 (D.D.C. 1986), a federal district court in Washington, D.C., held that an OMB review of cost-benefit impact analysis cannot be used to keep agencies from complying with statutory deadlines.[37] Recall from the discussion of NAAQS in Chapter 1 that the air quality standards had been set by the EPA under Clinton, and congressional language in the Clean Air Act leaves no room for a cost-benefit analysis in setting NAAQS. The Bush 43 administration requires a cost-benefit analysis from agencies prior to adopting rules.

Much publicity and fanfare accompanied President Bush 41's executive order placing a moratorium on all federal agency rules and regulations for 90 days so that existing rules, regulations, and standards could be reviewed.[38] The theory was that those regulations not meeting President Bush's approval would be eliminated. However, an agency must conduct a notice and hearing process before rescinding a rule. Therefore, it was not certain that those rules President Bush 41 (actually a committee of his advisers headed by Vice President Dan Quayle) disapproved of would be eliminated. Furthermore, we know from the *EDF v. Thomas* case just cited that the moratorium executive order cannot be used to delay statutory deadlines. Finally, the weight of constitutional evidence suggests that the moratorium cannot interfere with agencies promulgating regulations in compliance with a congressional mandate. Indeed, by the administration's own admission, rules required by statute and those likely to benefit the economy would be exempt from the moratorium.[39] What's left? The point is that executive orders are a tool for presidential management, but they are most effective when "taking care that the laws be faithfully executed."

The Budget

To evaluate presidential control of agencies via the budget, the reader needs to understand the broad contours of the budget process. By June, the president has developed economic assumptions about the fiscal year to begin in October of the next year. He or she has decided what the total spending will be, estimated revenues, and speculated as to the size of the deficit or surplus. All of this is done with the help of the OMB, which then transmits this information to the various bureaus and agencies. They are given spending targets and have until September to submit a proposed agency budget to the OMB. At that point, the OMB may or may not modify agency-proposed budgets. The OMB holds budget hearings with the various agencies during the fall, and between December and February, the OMB, the White House staff, and the president develop the president's budget, which will be submitted to Congress in February.

Congress has its own counterpart to the OMB called the Congressional Budget Office (CBO), which does its own analysis of the economy, as well as projected revenues and deficits. Based on the findings of the CBO, the OMB, and the president's proposed budget,

Congress passes a budget resolution, which is a spending limit for the coming fiscal year. This is done by April 15. Next, the House and Senate appropriations committees decide how much to spend on specific programs and how much to give to individual agencies (the congressional side of the budget process is dealt with in more detail in the next chapter).

There is a procedure called *sequester*, in which the OMB issues a report that indicates whether spending limits have been exceeded and makes recommendations to withhold funds in specific areas to meet the spending limits. The president must then sequester the funds identified by the OMB.[40]

It is the president's budget, in the sense that if that budget calls for $2.4 trillion in spending, Congress will pass a budget for that total, but Congress frequently changes the amounts *within* the budget from the president's proposals. Given that the OMB and its director are close to the president and given the OMB's role in setting agency budgets, it is fair to say that the president exerts significant control over agencies in terms of spending limits. Agencies have a good deal of latitude about how they spend within their budgets, but whether an agency will grow and prosper and start new programs or whether it will simply maintain or even suffer cuts seems to be determined by the OMB in close collusion with the White House staff. In the past, when presidents (or their budget directors) cut an agency's budget, it was not unheard of for the bureau chief to go to Congress to get the cuts restored. President Reagan's first budget director, David Stockman, put a stop to that practice. He let it be known that bureau chiefs who did not preach the administration's line before congressional committees would be transferred to Butte, Montana, or would be required to submit status reports every Monday, Wednesday, and Friday and so on. More recent budget directors have continued the practice but more subtly. Ours is, however, a government of checks and balances, and Congress fought back against budget directors who dealt too high-handedly with bureau chiefs who Congress (and interest groups) had come to know and respect. When Congress threatened to cut the budget of the OMB under Reagan, the budget director backed off.

Generally, more recent presidents (especially Reagan and Bush 41 and 43) have been able to exercise more control over agencies through the budget than have their predecessors. That is because the OMB has become so centralized and influential, not only in the budget process but also in other aspects involving agencies.

The Administrative Presidency

The fact that the OMB has become so involved in the daily lives of agencies is a natural consequence of a quest on behalf of successive presidents to find some way to control the rule-making activity of agencies. The quest started with President Richard Nixon, and the concept is called *the administrative presidency*.[41]

When President Nixon was elected in 1968, he had an agenda he wanted to fulfill. He tried to accomplish his goals by submitting legislation to Congress, but his administration was not particularly successful at dealing with Congress. After two years, he decided to try to accomplish his goals by using the bureaucracy rather than by going through Congress, and he quickly discovered that the chief executive (or nonexecutive chief) does not control the bureaucracy. He was reelected in 1972 with a resolve to find out how to control agencies, but Watergate unfolded before he could accomplish much.

The reasons why presidents could not control agencies in Nixon's day are as follows:

- Mid- and high-level bureaucrats who controlled power and authority (and information and expertise) within bureaucracies were protected by civil service laws (now the Office of Personnel Management), and it was almost impossible to fire them; this was the essence of the controversy surrounding the creation of the Department of Homeland Security.
- Presidential appointees quickly became the captives of the agencies they were supposed to run and soon displayed more allegiance to the agency than to the president.
- Probably because of the first two reasons, the president had no control at all over agency promulgation of rules, regulations, and standards; agency rules are the essence of the administrative state, and it is crucial for a president who would control agencies to control agency rule making.
- The president had little control over agency budgets because when the president proposed to cut an agency's budget, the bureau chief, who was protected by civil service laws, could simply go to Congress and get the budget restored.

The key to the administrative presidency, then, is to find ways to counter the effects of civil service protection for high-level bureaucrats, counter the effects of captivity, control agency rule making, and gain budgetary control over the agencies. Typically, presidents tried to do this by issuing executive orders. President Nixon required the EPA to conduct Quality of Life Reviews before promulgating a rule.[42] President Gerald Ford required "inflationary impact analysis" of major rules. President Carter required major regulations to undergo an "economic impact analysis" by the Council on Wage and Price Stability, which at the time was a staff agency in the Executive Office. The term *major* or *significant rule* means a rule with a certain economic impact on society (typically today, that level is $100 million). President Carter also was able to pass a bill creating the Senior Executive Service (SES).[43] The SES is a modification of the civil service system. Under the system created by Carter, high-level bureaucrats, those who head bureaus or agencies, are given the choice of remaining under the protection of civil service laws or choosing to enter the SES. If they choose SES, they forfeit civil service job protection in favor of higher pay, which would more closely approximate private industry salaries for positions of similar responsibility. Today, about 95 percent of those eligible for the SES have taken the opportunity. The effect of the SES is to give the president more control over the professional bureaucrats who promulgate rules. President Reagan, you may recall from the case in point, issued Executive Order 12291, which required OMB review of all major rules and required every agency to prepare a cost-benefit analysis before issuing rules. Furthermore, the executive order forbid (to the extent permitted by law) any agency from producing a rule if its benefits did not clearly outweigh the costs. To counter captivity, Reagan's political appointments to agencies were based not on patronage, management skill, or administrative experience but rather on ideology. No one would be appointed to a position within an agency who did not believe that the federal government was bloated and needed to pare back. Because these appointees did not care whether they got along with their professional colleagues in the agency, or indeed, whether the business of the agency got done, the problem of captivity was pretty well solved. Reagan was also able to make effective use of OMB to exert influence over agency budgets. Hence, Reagan achieved the administrative presidency. Bush 41 inherited an administrative presidency, but having spent his whole career in the federal government, he was too much of a professional to base appointments on ideology so captivity crept back in. Also, having lost the statutory authority to require OMB review of rules in the *Dole* case, he saw the administrative presidency slip away. The process of OMB review of agency rules was revived under Clinton, primarily because Congress revised the Paperwork Reduction Act. Clinton, however, was not much interested in controlling the substance of agency rules.

Thanks to Republican control of both houses of Congress, Bush 43 has an administrative presidency. He exercises more control over agencies than any of his recent predecessors. This is the case because Congress has vested OMB with the power to check agency rules through a number of laws, and Bush 43 is disposed to use that authority. The Paperwork Reduction Act of 1995 provides the OMB with the authority to influence agency rules with paperwork implications. The Act requires agencies to perform cost-benefit analysis and a regulatory impact analysis prior to rule making. The Unfunded Mandates Reform Act requires agencies to perform similar analyses if rule-making activity involves unfunded mandates. *An unfunded mandate* exists when a higher level of government requires a lower level of government to perform a task but does not send money to pay the costs. When the Brady Bill required local police departments to perform background checks on those who wanted to purchase guns, the cost of that background search was not reimbursed by the federal government. This is an example of an unfunded mandate. Both the Regulatory Flexibility Act and the Small Business Regulatory Enforcement and Fairness Act authorized OMB review of agency activity that has an impact on small businesses, small or rural governments, and other small entities.[44] The Bush 43 administration oversees agency activity on two fronts, review of already existing rules and review of proposed rules.

Review of Already Existing Rules

As the Bush 43 administration began to establish itself, the President's chief of staff issued a memo freezing 371 rules that had been proposed by the Clinton Administration but were not final yet.[45] The Office of Information and Regulatory Affairs (OIRA) is the agency within OMB that controls the regulatory activity of federal agencies. Through notice in the *Federal Register* and via its Web site, the OIRA has requested that citizens and groups affected by agency rules submit proposals or nominations to add, strengthen, modify, or rescind specific existing agency rules. In 2001, the administration received only 71 nominations.[46] In the second year of the Bush 43 administration, OIRA received 1,700 comments on rules from businesses, trade associations, academic institutions, think tanks, nonprofit agencies, and government agencies. This input resulted in OIRA action on 316 rules involving 26 agencies. About half of the citizen suggestions requested changes to existing or proposed rules. About 8 percent requested rescinding rules, and a quarter requested new or more stringent rules. The OIRA sends what it considers to be significant requests back to the agency, and ultimately, OIRA and the agency negotiate the disposition of the request on a rule. However, OIRA insists that the final decision on a nominated rule lies with the agency, given "their resources, statutory mandate, and priorities."[47]

Review of Agency Proposals for New Rules

When agencies propose rules, there are two stages of OIRA review, the proposal stage and the final stage. The OIRA has 90 days to review proposed rules and another 90 days to review final rules.[48] Agencies submit rule-making proposals to OIRA along with all required reports and analyses (cost-benefit, regulatory impact, small business, etc.). There is an initial OIRA review and typically negotiations between OIRA and the agency. Once OIRA is satisfied with a proposed rule, the agency may begin the rule-making procedure (which you will read about in Chapter 7). Having held public hearings on a proposed rule and presumably modified the rule according to input from the hearings, the agency can now draft a final rule, which will again go to OIRA before it can actually become a rule with the force and effect of law. At this second OIRA review, the agency may simply decide to withdraw the rule, OIRA may sign off on it, or OIRA can veto it by refusing to sign off and sending the rule back to the agency.

The conflict involved in this process is that OIRA represents the president. As the CEO of the federal government, the president should have some control over what underlings do. The agencies, however, as well as being underlings to the CEO, are creatures of Congress, frequently ordered by legislation to accomplish certain tasks (clean the air or reduce industrial or traffic accidents). The Constitution gives the president no policy-making role. That is given exclusively to Congress. Consequently, agencies are not totally bound by orders or suggestions from OIRA or negotiations they conduct. Remember that OIRA ordered NHTSA to produce a final tire pressure monitoring rule that would give equal weight to both direct and indirect systems, but the agency's final rule did not do that. Recall as well, that the Court ordered NHTSA to produce a final rule that would contradict what the White House wanted.

What follows are a few samples of agency rule making that was influenced by OIRA.

• An agency called the Access Board was created to make rules regarding access for citizens with disabilities. The Access Board proposed rules for access in hotels and telephone booths. After industry representatives visited with OMB, the proposed rules were held up and modified.[49]

• The administration forced the EPA to adopt revised *new source review standards.* These rules dictate when power plants and refineries must invest in new equipment to reduce air pollution. The revised Bush 43 administration rules will give plants more discretion in deciding whether modifications to the plant will require pollution upgrades. Environmental interest groups warned that the EPA is forbidden by the Clean Air Act from adopting a rule that will produce dirtier air.[50]

• The EPA proposed a rule limiting the sulfur emissions from nonroad vehicles but revised the rule to a more lax standard after discussions with OMB and industry officials.[51]

• The White House required the EPA to soften its rules regulating mercury.[52]

• The EPA was forced, apparently against its will, to downplay the risks from asbestos in the air around Manhattan after the September 11, 2001, attack.[53] Just prior to the September 11 attack, the EPA was about to issue an emergency announcement regarding asbestos fibers at dangerous levels in the insulation in millions of homes, but the White House ordered the EPA not to make the announcement.[54]

• The Department of Housing and Urban Development (HUD) proposed a rule that would have more tightly regulated what lending institutions can charge regarding the closing costs of a home loan. The agency was forced to withdraw its proposed rule.[55]

- The Securities and Exchange Commission (SEC) adopted a rule requiring mutual funds to disclose to their investors the complete proxy voting record of the fund. As this rule will increase paperwork, the agency would have had to justify the increase, and the rule would have gone through OIRA review twice. It is unlikely that the Bush 43 administration is pleased or supports this rule. However, because the SEC is an independent regulatory agency, the OMB assumed the SEC would not be bound by OIRA orders or input.[56]

It should be obvious that one agency frequently taken to the woodshed by the Bush 43 Administration is the EPA. One of the reasons for White House attention is that the EPA relies on science to a degree that many other agencies do not. One of the hottest current issues in the administrative process is what is referred to as "junk science." Junk science is a concept that suggests that sometimes when agencies make decisions based on facts or science, the science or facts relied on may be suspect. This criticism most commonly comes from parties who are regulated by agencies and who are forced to make capital expenditures to comply with agency rules or standards. The claim that agencies rely on junk science has been made frequently and loudly by the business community. As Bush 43 has a business community orientation (as well as a business campaign finance base), he likewise has a distrust of the facts and figures relied on by the regulators. That distrust is reflected in OIRA as it reviews agency rules. What makes the junk science issue explosive is that Congress added a rider to a massive budget bill at the end of the 2000 session that requires agencies to assure the quality of the data on which they rely.[57] There were no hearings on the rider, nor was it debated.

The rider is referred to as the Information Quality Act or the Data Quality Act (DQA). The DQA is tied to the Paperwork Reduction Act of 1995 and applies wherever there are paperwork implications. The DQA ordered the director of OMB to issue guidelines within a year that would ensure the "quality, objectivity, utility, and integrity" of information agencies use, rely on, and disseminate. In addition, each agency is supposed to issue its own guidelines, with two goals. First, they are to establish a procedure or mechanism for assuring the quality of information or data. Second, the guidelines are to establish a procedure ensuring that those affected by agency action can obtain the data, challenge its accuracy, and force the agency to correct information if it is inaccurate or fails to meet scientific standards. The OMB and OIRA have issued many guidelines and directives to agencies regarding the DQA. One OMB directive that has received considerable attention is one that requires agencies to rely on studies or information that have been peer reviewed and can be replicated. Peer review is a concept that connotes that experts in the field have reviewed a piece of research and have found it acceptable. Replication means that if a study is repeated, the results should be the same. Typically, before your professor can get an article published, the proposed article must be reviewed by experts in the discipline. The White House does not want agencies to make decisions based on studies or science unless the study or science has been peer-reviewed first.[58] Several but not all federal agencies use scientific panels to review data, studies, and statistics before the agency takes action based on them. The science underlying the setting of the NAAQS promulgated by the EPA, for example, was reviewed by a panel of scientific experts. However, now, the OMB has issued new guidelines for the establishment of peer review panels. The guidelines look with disfavor on agencies using academics who have received agency grants but fall silent on the use of industry (regulated) scientists for the panels. The White House retains the final say on peer review panel personnel. This has put the scientific community, those who live by the scientific method, in the awkward position of protesting the concept of peer review. The scientific community fears that the White House will politicize the use of scientific data and that Bush 43 will use peer review to delay and curtail rules and regulations that are necessary to protect the public health and safety.

Indeed, another OMB proposal would provide the OIRA with a veto power over agency emergency announcements.[59] Agencies warn the public of emergencies such as an outbreak of mad cow disease or anthrax or a nuclear power accident. The Bush 43 Administration wants control over these emergency declarations on the theory that if the warnings are based on suspect science, industries could suffer serious financial harm.

The White House under Bush 43 has achieved a level of control over agencies that is unprecedented. The OIRA monitors agency cost-benefit analysis, regulatory impact analysis, the quality of the data and science, and the substance of the proposed rules, and it can approve or veto agency rules. The White House has also instigated a process where the regulated can nominate existing rules for modification and rescission. However, when an agency proposes a rule that is the result of a direct delegation of power from Congress, it appears as though the agency need not cave in to OMB demands. It also appears as though OMB pays more deference to independent regulatory agencies than it does to Cabinet-level agencies, as evidenced by the SEC mutual fund proxy rule. The conflict involving the agencies' place in the separation of powers struggle is a legal problem. Although a congressional delegation of power may insulate an agency from forced compliance with OIRA orders, as a political matter, the agency that refuses to cooperate may find itself without recourse when it comes to the budget process.

Finally, the Bush 43 Administration has been able to influence agency budgets more than his predecessors.[60] President Bush 43 reorganized the budget, which used to be based on governmental functions or policy areas such as national defense or entitlement. Now it is organized by agency, and each agency is required to assess its performance in a number of areas. The OMB reviews and scores each agency's assessments and performance toward its goals as well as performance toward standards set by the president. Budget decisions are based on OMB evaluation of agency performance.

There is no doubt that Bush 43 has achieved the administrative presidency. He controls the substance of agency action. He even controls the information agencies can use. The administrative presidency has not fared so well in court, however. Bush 43 was forced to defend Clinton era air quality standards in court, standards that were presumably more stringent than Bush 43 would have liked. After the White House forced the NHTSA to modify its tire pressure rule, a court rejected OMB's modifications. In another case, a conservative interest group challenged a decision by the Department of Health and Human Services (HHS). Again in a Clinton era decision, HHS decided to upgrade dioxin from a "reasonably anticipated human carcinogen" to a "known human carcinogen." The legal attack was on the science the agency used in its decision, but the court of appeals sided with the agency.[61]

The Need for a Court Decision on Presidential Control of Agencies

One day, the Supreme Court will need to settle the separation of power issue over control of bureaucracy. As the policy-making branch of government, Congress clearly can create agencies and enlist their help in seeing that policy is executed. From the next chapter, you will learn that Congress can delegate some legislative power to the executive branch. It is also clear that the Constitution vests the president with executive power (although the Supreme Court has avoided defining that concept), and it is his or her job to administer legislative policy. What is not constitutionally clear is whether a president who disagrees with congressional policy can modify the policy through administrative tools. President Bush 43 has been able to modify policy via OIRA review, but when challenged in the courts, he has been less successful. What is even less clear is whether Congress can delegate virtual law-making authority to the presidency. This is what Congress has done with the Paperwork Reduction Act of 1995, the DQA, and other legislation vesting power in OMB. Going back to Chapter 1, the essential difference between Republicans and Democrats is their view of the role of government. Republicans have a restrictive view of what the federal government should do whereas the Democratic perspective is more expansive. All of the policies discussed in the first two chapters—clean air, worker safety, and traffic safety— were adopted by overwhelming Democratic majorities in both houses of Congress. Republican support for those policies is lukewarm at best. Rather than antagonize voters by undoing the former Democratic policies, the Republican majorities in Congress are pursuing a different strategy. The Republicans have been delegating sufficient power to the White House to allow a president to modify the Democratic policies. With the election of Bush 43, there is a president with a free market orientation and the will to use the congressional authorizations to modify the law. One day, the Supreme Court will be forced to take a case where the issue will be whether Congress can delegate sufficient legislative power to the president so the president can virtually change the law.

Presidents Who Do Not Possess the Will to Control Agencies

This chapter began with the proposition that presidents may have the will to control the fourth branch but lack the power. Some presidents possess more will to control agencies than do others. President Nixon was paranoid about it, President Reagan was committed to it, and President Bush 41 tried to continue in the Reagan mold but was not enough of an ideologue to avoid captivity problems and suffered some setbacks (e.g., the *Dole* decision). President Clinton was not concerned about controlling agency regulations. On September 30, 1993, he rescinded the Reagan era executive orders that imposed White House micromanagement on agencies. However, he issued his own executive orders, which imposed cost-benefit analysis and OIRA review of major rules, but White House review of agency rules under Clinton was more benign that it was under Reagan or Bush 41.[62]

Presidents like Clinton, who believe in positive government, are not threatened by agency rule making because bureaucracy is the tool of positive government. Presidents who are less enthusiastic about positive government have more reason to try to inhibit agency rule making.

It is instructive to compare recent Republican presidents with Clinton regarding their approach to dealing with bureaucracy. Whereas Reagan and Bush 41 tried to limit the rule-making authority of agencies, Clinton tried to reinvent agencies. The discussion above describes the Reagan/Bush 41 and 43 attempts to control agencies. Let us now turn attention to President Clinton's efforts to reinvent government (actually, the effort is more closely associated with Vice President Gore).

National Performance Review or reinventing government has its most recent expression in Osborne and Gaebler, *Reinventing Government: How the Entrepreneurial Spirit Is Transforming the Public Sector.*[63] The concept of reinventing government connotes decentralizing decision making within agencies and encouraging employee input and employee empowerment (empowering employees at the citizen-contact level to make decisions rather than deferring the decision up the hierarchy of the organization). Reinventing government also implies cutting red tape and strategic planning. Strategic planning would force agencies to adopt goals and plans for meeting those goals. The plans should include measurable outcomes so the agency, the president, the Congress, and the people can assess how close each agency comes to meeting its goals and objectives. Finally, reinvention implies that government agencies treat their citizen-clients as consumers rather than as subjects.[64]

Moving from the theoretical to real-life politics, the reinventing government movement is manifested in the Government Performance and Results Act of 1993 (GPRA).[65] GPRA imposes strategic planning on all agencies, requires the adoption of performance plans, and makes agencies submit performance reports to the president and Congress (the reports are supposed to assess the agency's progress toward goal achievement during the past fiscal year). The Act allows agencies to request a variance from existing procedure to encourage agency flexibility and initiative, establishes pilot projects, and ties the performance of agencies to their budget requests.

On signing GPRA into law, President Clinton said, "Injecting competition and market forces into the delivery of these services will reduce duplication, lower overhead costs, and better serve the American People."[66] Clinton followed up the legislation with Executive Order 12862, "Setting Customer Standards," which requires all agencies to identify their customers, find out what they want, and develop customer standards.[67] The Clinton Administration claimed the following successes from reinventing government:

> Eliminated 250 outdated government programs and 16,000 pages of regulations; cut more than 640,000 pages of internal rules; reduced the federal budget by more than $137 billion; established nearly 4,000 customer service standards; gave out more than 1,000 "Hammer Awards" to teams of federal workers; and cut more than 350,000 employees—resulting in the smallest federal government on a percentage basis since the 1930s.[68]

Evaluation of the success of GPRA by those with less of a vested interest is only now beginning to emerge because agencies were given seven years to comply; hence, fiscal year 2000 was the first one under full compliance. However, academic analysis of reinvention efforts shows mixed results.[69]

Summary

Depending on ideology and partisanship, many modern presidents possess the will to control agencies but lack the constitutional authority to do so effectively. The Constitution makes control of the bureaucracy a shared power between the executive and Congress, but clearly, Congress possesses the lion's share of the power. Recently, Congress has delegated some of that power to the White House.

Presidents do have at their disposal tools that at first glance would appear to provide the executive branch with control over agencies, but after closer examination, these tools seem to be flawed. Recent presidents exercise more control over agencies than did their predecessors, going back to the point in history where civil service became the law (1883). This increased presidential control is due to the SES, to the increased role of the OMB in the daily activities of agencies, and to congressional delegations of authority to OMB and OIRA. It remains to be seen whether the Supreme Court will sanction further OMB modification of public policy or the delegation of power that allows it.

1. *Dole v. United Steelworkers,* which disallowed OMB authority over agency rule-making has been undone by the Paperwork Reduction Act of 1995 and other legislation vesting review authority over agency rules in the presidency.

2. Where Congress attempts to place restrictions on the president's removal power, the test is whether those restrictions are of such a nature that they impede the president's ability to perform his or her constitutional duties—that is, to exercise executive power and see that the laws are faithfully executed (*Morrison v. Olson*).

END-OF-CHAPTER CASES

Dole v. United Steelworkers of America
494 U.S. 26 (1990)

Justice Brennan delivered the opinion of the Court, joined by Justices Marshall, Blackmun, Stevens, O'Connor, Scalia, and Kennedy. Justice White dissented, joined by Chief Justice Rehnquist.

Among the regulatory tools available to government agencies charged with protecting public health and safety are rules which require regulated entities to disclose information directly to employees, consumers, or others. Disclosure rules protect by providing access to information about what dangers exist and how these dangers can be avoided. Today we decide whether the Office of Management and Budget (OMB) has the authority under the Paperwork Reduction Act of 1980 (Act), 44 U.S.C. § 3501, to review such regulations.

I

In 1983, pursuant to the Occupational Safety and Health Act of 1970 (OSH Act), which authorizes the Department of Labor (DOL) to set health and safety standards for workplaces, DOL promulgated a Hazard Communications Standard. 29 C.F.R. § 1910 (1984). The Standard imposed various requirements on manufacturers aimed at ensuring that their employees were informed of the potential hazards posed by chemicals found at their workplace.

Specifically, the Standard required chemical manufacturers to label containers of hazardous chemicals with appropriate warnings. "Downstream" manufacturers—commercial purchasers who used the chemicals in their manufacturing plants—were obliged to keep the original labels intact or else transfer the information onto any substitute containers. The Standard also required chemical manufacturers to provide "material safety data sheets" to downstream manufacturers. The data sheets were to list the physical characteristics and hazards of each chemical, the symptoms caused by overexposure, and any pre-existing medical conditions aggravated by exposure. In addition, the data sheets were to recommend safety precautions and first aid and emergency procedures in case of overexposure and provide a source for additional information. Both chemical manufacturers and downstream manufacturers were required to make the data sheets available to their employees and to provide training on the dangers of the particular hazardous chemicals found at each workplace.

Respondent United Steelworkers of America, among others, challenged the Standard in the Court of Appeals for the Third Circuit. That court held that the Occupational Safety and Health Administration (OSHA) had not adequately explained why the regulation was limited to the manufacturing sector, in view of the OSH Act's clear directive that, to the extent feasible, OSHA is to ensure that no employee suffers material impairment of health from toxic or other harmful agents. The court directed OSHA either to apply the hazard standard rules to workplaces in other sectors or to state reasons why such application would not be feasible. *United Steelworkers of America v. Auchter,* 763 F.2d 728, 739 (CA3 1985).

When DOL responded by initiating an entirely new rulemaking proceeding, the union and its copetitioners sought enforcement of the earlier order. The Third Circuit Court of Appeals directed DOL, under threat of contempt, to publish in the Federal Register within 60 days either a hazard communication standard applicable to all workers covered by the OSH Act or a statement of reasons why such a standard was not feasible on the basis of the existing record, as to each category of excluded workers. *United Steelworkers of America v. Pendergrass,* 819 F.2d 1263, 1270 (CA3 1987).

DOL complied by issuing a revised Hazard Communications Standard that applied to worksites in all sectors of the economy. At the same time, DOL submitted the Standard to OMB for review of any paperwork requirements. After holding a public hearing, OMB approved all but three of its provisions. OMB rejected a requirement that employees who work at multi-employer sites (such as construction sites) be provided with data sheets describing the hazardous substances to which they were likely to be exposed, through the activities of any of the companies working at the same site. The provision permitted employers either to exchange data sheets and make them available at their home offices or to maintain all relevant data sheets at a central location on the worksite. OMB also disapproved a provision exempting consumer products used in the workplace in the same manner, and resulting in the same frequency and duration of exposure, as in normal consumer use. Finally, OMB vetoed an exemption for drugs sold in solid, final form for direct administration to patients. OMB disapproved these provisions based on its determination that the requirements were not necessary to protect employees. OMB's objection to the exemptions was that they were too narrow, and that the Standard, therefore, applied to situations in which disclosure did not benefit employees. DOL disagreed with OMB's assessment, but it published notice that the three

provisions were withdrawn. DOL added its reasons for believing that the provisions were necessary, proposed that they be retained, and invited public comment.

The union and its copetitioners responded by filing a motion for further relief with the Third Circuit. That court ordered DOL to reinstate the OMB-disapproved provisions. The court reasoned that the provisions represented good faith compliance by DOL with the court's prior orders, that OMB lacked authority under the Paperwork Reduction Act to disapprove the provisions, and that, therefore, DOL had no legitimate basis for withdrawing them.

The United States sought review in this Court. We granted *certiorari* to answer the important question whether the Paperwork Reduction Act authorizes OMB to review and countermand agency regulations mandating disclosure by regulated entities directly to third parties. We hold that the Paperwork Reduction Act does not give OMB that authority, and therefore affirm.

II

The Paperwork Reduction Act was enacted in response to one of the less auspicious aspects of the enormous growth of our federal bureaucracy: its seemingly insatiable appetite for data. Outcries from small businesses, individuals, and state and local governments, that they were being buried under demands for paperwork, led Congress to institute controls. Congress designated OMB the overseer of other agencies with respect to paperwork and set forth a comprehensive scheme designed to reduce the paperwork burden. The Act charges OMB with developing uniform policies for efficient information processing, storage, and transmittal systems, both within and among agencies. OMB is directed to reduce federal collection of all information by set percentages, establish a Federal Information Locator System, and develop and implement procedures for guarding the privacy of those providing confidential information. The Act prohibits any federal agency from adopting regulations which impose paperwork requirements on the public unless the information is not available to the agency from another source within the Federal Government, and the agency must formulate a plan for tabulating the information in a useful manner.

Agencies are also required to minimize the burden on the public to the extent practicable. In addition, the Act institutes a second layer of review by OMB for new paperwork requirements. After an agency has satisfied itself that an instrument for collecting information—termed an "information collection request"—is needed, the agency must submit the request to OMB for approval. If OMB disapproves the request, the agency may not collect the information . . .

The promulgation of a disclosure rule is a final agency action that represents a substantive regulatory choice. An agency charged with protecting employees from hazardous chemicals has a variety of regulatory weapons from which to choose: It can ban the chemical altogether; it can mandate specified safety measures, such as gloves or goggles; or it can require labels or other warnings alerting users to dangers and recommended precautions. An agency chooses to impose a warning requirement because it believes that such a requirement is the least intrusive measure that will sufficiently protect the public, not because the measure is a means of acquiring information useful in performing some other agency function.

Petitioner submits that the provisions requiring labeling and employee training are "reporting requirements" and that the provision requiring accessible data sheets containing health and safety information is a "recordkeeping requirement." We believe, however, that the language, structure, and purpose of the Paperwork Reduction Act reveal that petitioner's position is untenable because Congress did not intend the Act to encompass these or any other third-party disclosure rules.

On a pure question of statutory construction, our first job is to try to determine congressional intent, using traditional tools of statutory construction. . . . Petitioner's interpretation of "obtaining or soliciting facts by an agency through . . . reporting or recordkeeping requirements" is not the most natural reading of this language. The common-sense view of "obtaining or soliciting facts by an agency" is that the phrase refers to an agency's efforts to gather facts for its own use and that Congress used the

word "solicit" in addition to the word "obtain" in order to cover information requests that rely on the voluntary cooperation of information suppliers as well as rules which make compliance mandatory. Similarly, data sheets consisting of advisory material on health and safety do not fall within the normal meaning of "records," and a government-imposed reporting requirement customarily requires reports to be made to the government, not training and labels to be given to someone else altogether.

That a more limited reading of the phrase "reporting and recordkeeping requirement" was intended derives some further support from the words surrounding it. The traditional canon of construction, *noscitur a sociis,* dictates that "words grouped in a list should be given related meaning." The other examples listed in the definitions of "information collection request" and "collection of information" are forms for communicating information to the party requesting that information. If "reporting and recordkeeping requirement" is understood to be analogous to the examples surrounding it, the phrase would comprise only rules requiring information to be sent or made available to a federal agency, not disclosure rules.

The same conclusion is produced by a consideration of the object and structure of the Act as a whole. Particularly useful is the provision detailing Congress' purposes in enacting the statute. The Act declares that its purposes are: "(1) to minimize the Federal paperwork burden for individuals, small businesses, State and local governments, and other persons; (2) to minimize the cost to the Federal Government of collecting, maintaining, using, and disseminating information; (3) to maximize the usefulness of information collected, maintained, and disseminated by the Federal Government; (4) to coordinate, integrate, and, to the extent practicable and appropriate, make uniform Federal information policies and practices; (5) to ensure that automatic data processing, telecommunications, and other information technologies are acquired and used by the Federal Government in a manner which improves service delivery and program management, increases productivity, improves the quality of decision-making, reduces waste and fraud, and wherever practicable and appropriate, reduces the information processing burden for the Federal Government and for persons who provide information to and for the Federal Government; and (6) to ensure that the collection, maintenance, use, and dissemination of information by the Federal Government is consistent with applicable laws relating to confidentiality, including . . . the Privacy Act." Disclosure rules present none of the problems Congress sought to solve through the Paperwork Reduction Act, and none of Congress' enumerated purposes would be served by subjecting disclosure rules to the provisions of the Act.

III

For the foregoing reasons, we find that the terms "collection of information" and "information collection request," when considered in light of the language and structure of the Act as a whole, refer solely to the collection of information by, or for the use of, a federal agency; they cannot reasonably be interpreted to cover rules mandating disclosure of information to a third party. Because we find that the statute, as a whole, clearly expresses Congress' intention, we decline to defer to OMB's interpretation. *Chevron U.S.A. Inc. v. Natural Resources Defense Council, Inc.,* 467 U.S. 837 (1984) ("If the intent of Congress is clear, that is the end of the matter"). We affirm the judgment of the Third Circuit insofar as it held that the Paperwork Reduction Act does not give OMB the authority to review agency rules mandating disclosure by regulated entities to third parties.

It is so ordered.

Morrison v. Olson
487 U.S. 654 (1988)

Chief Justice Rehnquist delivered the opinion of the Court, joined by Justices Brennan, White, Marshall, Blackmun, Stevens, and O'Connor. Justice Scalia dissented, and Justice Kennedy did not participate.

This case presents us with a challenge to the independent counsel provisions of the Ethics in Government Act of 1978. We hold today that these provisions of the Act do not violate the Appointments Clause of the Constitution or the limitations of Article III, nor do they impermissibly interfere with the President's authority under Article II in violation of the constitutional principle of separation of powers.

I

Briefly stated, Title VI of the Ethics in Government Act allows for the appointment of an "independent counsel" to investigate and, if appropriate, prosecute certain high-ranking Government officials for violations of federal criminal laws. The Act requires the Attorney General, upon receipt of information that he determines is "sufficient to constitute grounds to investigate whether any person [covered by the Act] may have violated any Federal criminal law," to conduct a preliminary investigation of the matter. When the Attorney General has completed this investigation, or 90 days has elapsed, he is required to report to a special court (the Special Division) created by the Act "for the purpose of appointing independent counsels." If the Attorney General determines that "there are no reasonable grounds to believe that further investigation is warranted," then he must notify the Special Division of this result. In such a case, "the division of the court shall have no power to appoint an independent counsel." If, however, the Attorney General has determined that there are "reasonable grounds to believe that further investigation or prosecution is warranted," then he "shall apply to the division of the court for the appointment of an independent counsel." The Attorney General's application to the court "shall contain sufficient information to assist the [court] in selecting an independent counsel and in defining that independent counsel's prosecutorial jurisdiction." § 592(d).

Upon receiving this application, the Special Division "shall appoint an appropriate independent counsel and shall define that independent counsel's prosecutorial jurisdiction." With respect to all matters within the independent counsel's jurisdiction, the Act grants the counsel "full power and independent authority to exercise all investigative and prosecutorial functions and powers of the Department of Justice, the Attorney General, and any other officer or employee of the Department of Justice." The functions of the independent counsel include conducting grand jury proceedings and other investigations, participating in civil and criminal court proceedings and litigation, and appealing any decision in any case in which the counsel participates in an official capacity.

. . . The counsel's powers include "initiating and conducting prosecutions in any court of competent jurisdiction, framing and signing indictments, filing informations, and handling all aspects of any case, in the name of the United States." The counsel may appoint employees, may request and obtain assistance from the Department of Justice, and may accept referral of matters from the Attorney General if the matter falls within the counsel's jurisdiction as defined by the Special Division. Two statutory provisions govern the length of an independent counsel's tenure in office. The first defines the procedure for removing an independent counsel. Section 596(a)(1) provides: "An independent counsel appointed under this chapter may be removed from office, other than by impeachment and conviction, only by the personal action of the Attorney General and only for good cause, physical disability, mental incapacity, or any other condition that substantially impairs the performance of such independent counsel's duties." If an independent counsel is removed pursuant to this section, the Attorney General is required to submit a report to both the Special Division and the Judiciary Committees of the Senate and the House "specifying the facts found and the ultimate grounds for such removal." Under the current version of the Act, an independent counsel can obtain judicial review of the Attorney General's action by filing a civil action in the United States District Court for the District of Columbia.

Members of the Special Division "may not hear or determine any such civil action or any appeal of a decision in any such civil action." The reviewing court is authorized to grant reinstatement or "other appropriate relief." Under the Act as originally enacted, an independent counsel who was removed could obtain judicial review of the Attorney General's decision in a civil action commenced before the Special Division. If the removal was "based on error of law or fact," the court could order "reinstatement or other appropriate relief." 28 U.S.C. § 596(a)(3).

The other provision governing the tenure of the independent counsel defines the procedures for "terminating" the counsel's office. Under § 596(b)(1), the office of an independent counsel terminates when he or she notifies the Attorney General that he or she has completed or substantially completed any investigations or prosecutions undertaken pursuant to the Act. In addition, the Special Division, acting either on its own or on the suggestion of the Attorney General, may terminate the office of an independent counsel at any time if it finds that "the investigation of all matters within the prosecutorial jurisdiction of such independent counsel . . . have been completed or so substantially completed that it would be appropriate for the Department of Justice to complete such investigations and prosecutions."

. . . Finally, the Act provides for Congressional oversight of the activities of independent counsel. The proceedings in this case provide an example of how the Act works in practice. In 1982, two Subcommittees of the House of Representatives issued subpoenas directing the Environmental Protection Agency (EPA) to produce certain documents relating to the efforts of the EPA and the Land and Natural Resources Division of the Justice Department to enforce the "Superfund Law." At that time, appellee Olson was the Assistant Attorney General for the Office of Legal Counsel (OLC), appellee Schmults was Deputy Attorney General, and appellee Dinkins was the Assistant Attorney General for the Land and Natural Resources Division. Acting on the advice of the Justice Department, the President ordered the Administrator of the EPA to invoke executive privilege to withhold certain of the documents on the ground that they contained "enforcement sensitive information." The Administrator obeyed this order and withheld the documents. In response, the House voted to hold the Administrator in contempt, after which the Administrator and the United States together filed a lawsuit against the House. The conflict abated in March 1983, when the administration agreed to give the House Subcommittees limited access to the documents. The following year, the House Judiciary Committee began an investigation into the Justice Department's role in the controversy over the EPA documents. During this investigation, appellee Olson testified before a House Subcommittee on March 10, 1983.

Both before and after that testimony, the Department complied with several Committee requests to produce certain documents. Other documents were at first withheld, although these documents were eventually disclosed by the Department after the Committee learned of their existence. In 1985, the majority members of the Judiciary Committee published a lengthy report on the Committee's investigation. *Report on Investigation of the Role of the Department of Justice in the Withholding of Environmental Protection Agency Documents from Congress* in 1982-83, H.R.Rep. No. 99-435 (1985). The report not only criticized various officials in the Department of Justice for their role in the EPA executive privilege dispute, but it also suggested that appellee Olson had given false and misleading testimony to the Subcommittee on March 10, 1983, and that appellees Schmults and Dinkins had wrongfully withheld certain documents from the Committee, thus obstructing the Committee's investigation. The Chairman of the Judiciary Committee forwarded a copy of the report to the Attorney General with a request . . . that he seek the appointment of an independent counsel to investigate the allegations against Olson, Schmults, and Dinkins.

The Attorney General directed the Public Integrity Section of the Criminal Division to conduct a preliminary investigation. The Section's report concluded that the appointment of an independent counsel was warranted to investigate the Committee's allegations with respect to all three appellees. After consulting with other Department officials, however, the Attorney General chose to apply to the Special Division for the appointment of an independent counsel solely with respect to appellee Olson. The Attorney General accordingly requested appointment of an independent counsel to investigate whether Olson's March 10, 1983, testimony "regarding the completeness of [OLC's] response to the Judiciary Committee's request for OLC documents, and regarding his knowledge of EPA's willingness to turn over certain disputed documents to Congress, violated . . . any provision of federal criminal law." The Attorney General also requested that the independent counsel have authority to investigate "any other matter related to that allegation." On April 23, 1986, the Special Division appointed James C. McKay as independent counsel to investigate "whether the testimony of . . . Olson and his revision of such testimony on March 10, 1983, violated . . . any provision of federal law." The court also ordered that the independent counsel "shall have jurisdiction to investigate any other allegation of evidence of violation of any Federal criminal law by Theodore Olson developed during investigations, by the Independent Counsel, referred to earlier, and connected with or arising out of that investigation, and Independent Counsel shall have jurisdiction to prosecute for any such violation." McKay later resigned as independent counsel, and on May 29, 1986, the Division appointed appellant Morrison as his replacement, with the same jurisdiction.

In January 1987, appellant asked the Attorney General to refer to her as "related matters" the Committee's allegations against appellees Schmults and Dinkins. The Attorney General refused to refer the matters, concluding that his decision not to request the appointment of an independent counsel in regard to those matters was final. Appellant then asked the Special Division to order that the matters be referred to her. On April 2, 1987, the Division ruled that the Attorney General's decision not to seek appointment of an independent counsel with respect to Schmults and Dinkins was final and unreviewable and that therefore the court had no authority to make the requested referral. *In re Olson*, 260 U.S.App.D.C. 168, 818 F.2d 34. The court ruled, however, that its original grant of jurisdiction to appellant was broad enough to permit inquiry into whether Olson may have conspired with others, including Schmults and Dinkins, to obstruct the Committee's investigation.

Following this ruling, in May and June 1987, appellant caused a grand jury to issue and serve subpoenas *ad testificandum* and *duces tecum* on appellees. All three appellees moved to quash the subpoenas, claiming, among other things, that the independent counsel provisions of the Act were unconstitutional and that appellant accordingly had no authority to proceed. On July 20, 1987, the District Court upheld the constitutionality of the Act and denied the motions to quash. *In re Sealed Case*, 665 F.Supp. 56 (DC). The court subsequently ordered that appellees be held in contempt for continuing to refuse to comply with the subpoenas. The court stayed the effect of its contempt orders pending expedited appeal.

III

The Appointments Clause of Article II reads as follows: "[The President] shall nominate, and by and with the Advice and Consent of the Senate, shall appoint Ambassadors, other public Ministers and Consuls, Judges of the Supreme Court, and all other Officers of the United States, whose Appointments are not herein otherwise provided for, and which shall be established by Law: but the Congress may by Law vest the Appointment of such inferior Officers, as they think proper, in the President alone, in the Courts of Law, or in the Heads of Departments." The parties do not dispute that "[t]he Constitution for purposes of appointment . . . divides all its officers into two classes." As we stated in *Buckley v. Valeo*, 424 U.S. 1, 132 (1976): "[P]rincipal officers are selected by the President with the advice and consent of the Senate. Inferior officers Congress may allow to be appointed by the President alone, by the heads of departments, or by the Judiciary." The initial question is, accordingly, whether appellant is an "inferior" or a "principal" officer. If she is the latter, as the Court of Appeals concluded, then the Act is in violation of the Appointments Clause. First, appellant is subject to removal by a higher Executive Branch official.

Although appellant may not be "subordinate" to the Attorney General (and the President) insofar as she possesses a degree of independent discretion to exercise the powers delegated to her under the Act, the fact that she can be removed by the Attorney General indicates that she is to some degree "inferior" in rank and authority.

Second, appellant is empowered by the Act to perform only certain, limited duties. An independent counsel's role is restricted primarily to investigation and, if appropriate, prosecution for certain federal crimes. Admittedly, the Act delegates to appellant "full power and independent authority to exercise all investigative and prosecutorial functions and powers of the Department of Justice," but this grant of authority does not include any authority to formulate policy for the Government or the Executive Branch, nor does it give appellant any administrative duties outside of those necessary to operate her office. The Act specifically provides that in policy matters appellant is to comply to the extent possible with the policies of the Department.

Third, appellant's office is limited in jurisdiction. Not only is the Act itself restricted in applicability to certain federal officials suspected of certain serious federal crimes, but an independent counsel can only act within the scope of the jurisdiction that has been granted by the Special Division pursuant to a request by the Attorney General.

Finally, appellant's office is limited in tenure. There is concededly no time limit on the appointment of a particular counsel. Nonetheless, the office of independent counsel is "temporary" in the sense that an independent counsel is appointed essentially to accomplish a single task, and when that task is over the office is terminated, either by the counsel herself or by action of the Special Division. Unlike other prosecutors, appellant has no ongoing responsibilities that extend beyond the accomplishment of the mission that she was appointed for and authorized by the Special Division to undertake. In our view, these factors relating to the "ideas of tenure, duration . . . and duties" of the independent counsel are sufficient to establish that appellant is an "inferior" officer in the constitutional sense. . . . This does not, however, end our inquiry under the Appointments Clause. Appellees argue that even if appellant is an "inferior" officer, the Clause does not empower Congress to place the power to appoint such an officer outside the Executive Branch. They contend that the Clause does not contemplate congressional authorization of "interbranch appointments," in which an officer of one branch is appointed by officers of another branch. The relevant language of the Appointments Clause is worth repeating. It reads: ". . . but the Congress may by Law vest the Appointment of such inferior Officers, as they think proper, in the President alone, in the courts of Law, or in the Heads of Departments." On its face, the language of this "excepting clause" admits of no limitation on interbranch appointments. Indeed, the inclusion of "as they think proper" seems clearly to give Congress significant discretion to determine whether it is "proper" to vest the appointment of, for example, executive officials in the "courts of Law."

V

We now turn to consider whether the Act is invalid under the constitutional principle of separation of powers. Two related issues must be addressed: The first is whether the provision of the Act restricting the Attorney General's power to remove the independent counsel to only those instances in which he can show "good cause," taken by itself, impermissibly interferes with the President's exercise of his constitutionally appointed functions. The second is whether, taken as a whole, the Act violates the separation of powers by reducing the President's ability to control the prosecutorial powers wielded by the independent counsel.

Two Terms ago we had occasion to consider whether it was consistent with the separation of powers for Congress to pass a statute that authorized a Government official who is removable only by Congress to participate in what we found to be "executive powers." *Bowsher v. Synar*, 478 U.S. 714, 730 (1986). We held in *Bowsher* that "Congress cannot reserve for itself the power of removal of an officer charged with the execution of the laws except by impeachment." . . . Our present considered view is that the determination of whether the Constitution allows Congress

to impose a "good cause"-type restriction on the President's power to remove an official cannot be made to turn on whether or not that official is classified as "purely executive." The analysis contained in our removal cases is designed not to define rigid categories of those officials who may or may not be removed at will by the President, but to ensure that Congress does not interfere with the President's exercise of the "executive power" and his constitutionally appointed duty to "take care that the laws be faithfully executed" under Article II. . . . The real question is whether the removal restrictions are of such a nature that they impede the President's ability to perform his constitutional duty, and the functions of the officials in question must be analyzed in that light. . . .

Considering for the moment the "good cause" removal provision in isolation from the other parts of the Act at issue in this case, we cannot say that the imposition of a "good cause" standard for removal by itself unduly trammels on executive authority. There is no real dispute that the functions performed by the independent counsel are "executive" in the sense that they are law enforcement functions that typically have been undertaken by officials within the Executive Branch. As we noted earlier, however, the independent counsel is an inferior officer under the Appointments Clause, with limited jurisdiction and tenure and lacking policymaking or significant administrative authority. Here, as with the provision of the Act conferring the appointment authority of the independent counsel on the special court, the congressional determination to limit the removal power of the Attorney General was essential, in the view of Congress, to establish the necessary independence of the office. We do not think that this limitation as it presently stands sufficiently deprives the President of control over the independent counsel to interfere impermissibly with his constitutional obligation to ensure the faithful execution of the laws.

VI

In sum, we conclude today that it does not violate the Appointments Clause for Congress to vest the appointment of independent counsel in the Special Division; that the powers exercised by the Special Division under the Act do not violate Article III; and that the Act does not violate the separation-of-powers principle by impermissibly interfering with the functions of the Executive Branch. The decision of the Court of Appeals is therefore Reversed.

Justice Scalia, dissenting

I will not discuss at any length why the restrictions upon the removal of the independent counsel also violate our established precedent dealing with that specific subject. For most of it, I simply refer the reader to the scholarly opinion of Judge Silberman for the Court of Appeals below. See *In re Sealed Case,* 267 U.S.App.D.C. 178, 838 F.2d 476 (1988). I cannot avoid commenting, however, about the essence of what the Court has done to our removal jurisprudence today.

There is, of course, no provision in the Constitution stating who may remove executive officers, except the provisions for removal by impeachment. Before the present decision it was established, however, (1) that the President's power to remove principal officers who exercise purely executive powers could not be restricted, see *Myers v. United States,* 272 U.S. 52 (1926), and (2) that his power to remove inferior officers who exercise purely executive powers, and whose appointment Congress had removed from the usual procedure of Presidential appointment with Senate consent, could be restricted, at least where the appointment had been made by an officer of the Executive Branch. The Court could have resolved the removal power issue in this case by simply relying upon its erroneous conclusion that the independent counsel was an inferior officer, and then extending our holding that the removal of inferior officers appointed by the Executive can be restricted to a new holding that even the removal of inferior officers appointed by the courts can be restricted. That would in my view be a considerable and unjustified extension, giving the Executive full discretion in neither the selection nor the removal of a purely executive officer. The course the Court has chosen, however, is even worse.

Since our 1935 decision in *Humphrey's Executor v. United States,* 295 U.S. 602—which was considered by many at the time the product of an activist, anti-New Deal Court bent on reducing the power of President Franklin Roosevelt—it has been established that the line of permissible restriction upon removal of principal officers lies at the point at which the powers exercised by those officers are no longer purely executive. Thus, removal restrictions have been generally regarded as lawful for so-called "independent regulatory agencies," such as the Federal Trade Commission, the Interstate Commerce Commission, and the Consumer Product Safety Commission, which engage substantially in what has been called the "quasi-legislative activity" of rulemaking, and for members of Article I courts, such as the Court of Military Appeals, who engage in the "quasi-judicial" function of adjudication.

It has often been observed, correctly in my view, that the line between "purely executive" functions and "quasi-legislative" or "quasi-judicial" functions is not a clear one or even a rational one. But at least it permitted the identification of certain officers, and certain agencies, whose functions were entirely within the control of the President. Congress had to be aware of that restriction in its legislation. Today, however, *Humphrey's Executor* is swept into the dustbin of repudiated constitutional principles. "[O]ur present considered view," the Court says, "is that the determination of whether the Constitution allows Congress to impose a 'good cause'-type restriction on the President's power to remove an official cannot be made to turn on whether or not that official is classified as 'purely executive.'" What *Humphrey's Executor* (and presumably *Myers*) really means, we are now told, is not that there are any "rigid categories of those officials who may or may not be removed at will by the President," but simply that Congress cannot "interfere with the President's exercise of the 'executive power' and his constitutionally appointed duty to 'take care that the laws be faithfully executed.'" One can hardly grieve for the shoddy treatment given today to *Humphrey's Executor,* which, after all, accorded the same indignity (with much less justification)

to Chief Justice Taft's opinion 10 years earlier in *Myers v. United States*—gutting, in six quick pages devoid of textual or historical precedent for the novel principle it set forth, a carefully researched and reasoned 70-page opinion.

It is in fact comforting to witness the reality that he who lives by the *ipse dixit* dies by the *ipse dixit*. But one must grieve for the Constitution. *Humphrey's Executor* at least had the decency formally to observe the constitutional principle that the President had to be the repository of all executive power, which, as *Myers* carefully explained, necessarily means that he must be able to discharge those who do not perform executive functions according to his liking. As we noted in *Bowsher,* once an officer is appointed "'it is only the authority that can remove him, and not the authority that appointed him, that he must fear and, in the performance of his functions, obey.'" By contrast, "our present considered view" is simply that any executive officer's removal can be restricted, so long as the President remains "able to accomplish his constitutional role." There are now no lines. If the removal of a prosecutor, the virtual embodiment of the power to "take care that the laws be faithfully executed," can be restricted, what officer's removal cannot? This is an open invitation for Congress to experiment. What about a special Assistant Secretary of State, with responsibility for one very narrow area of foreign policy, who would not only have to be confirmed by the Senate but could also be removed only pursuant to certain carefully designed restrictions? Could this possibly render the President "[un]able to accomplish his constitutional role"? Or a special Assistant Secretary of Defense for Procurement? The possibilities are endless, and the Court does not understand what the separation of powers, what "[a]mbition . . . counteract[ing] ambition," is all about, if it does not expect Congress to try them.

As far as I can discern from the Court's opinion, it is now open season upon the President's removal power for all executive officers, with not even the superficially principled restriction of *Humphrey's Executor* as cover. The Court essentially says to the President: "Trust us. We will make sure that you are able to accomplish your constitutional role." I think the Constitution gives the President—and the people—more protection than that.

Clinton v. City of New York
524 U.S. 417 (1998)

Justice Stevens delivered the opinion of the Court, joined by Chief Justice Rehnquist, and Justices Souter, Thomas, and Ginsburg. Justice Kennedy concurred. Justice Scalia joined by O'Connor concurred in part and dissented in part. Justice Breyer dissented.

The Line Item Veto Act (Act), 2 U.S.C. § 691, was enacted in April 1996 and became effective on January 1, 1997. The following day, six Members of Congress who had voted against the Act brought suit in the District Court for the District of Columbia challenging its constitutionality. On April 10, 1997, the District Court entered an order holding that the Act is unconstitutional. *Byrd v. Raines,* 956 F. Supp. 25. In obedience to the statutory direction to allow a direct, expedited appeal to this Court, we promptly noted probable jurisdiction and expedited review, 520 U.S. 1194 (1997). We determined, however, that the Members of Congress did not have standing to sue because they had not "alleged a sufficiently concrete injury to have established Article III standing," *Raines v. Byrd,* 521 U.S. 811 (1997), thus, "in . . . light of [the] overriding and time-honored concern about keeping the Judiciary's power within its proper constitutional sphere," we remanded the case to the District Court with instructions to dismiss the complaint for lack of jurisdiction.

Less than two months after our decision in that case, the President exercised his authority to cancel one provision in the Balanced Budget Act of 1997, Pub. L. 105-33, and two provisions in the Taxpayer Relief Act of 1997, Pub. L. 105-34. Appellees, claiming that they had been injured by two of those cancellations, filed these cases in the District Court. That Court again held the statute invalid, 985 F. Supp. 168, 177-182 (1998), and we again expedited our review. We now hold that these appellees have standing to challenge the constitutionality of the Act and, reaching the merits, we agree that the cancellation procedures set forth in the Act violate the Presentment Clause, Art. I, § 7, cl. 2, of the Constitution. We begin by reviewing the canceled items that are at issue in these cases.

Section 4722(c) of the Balanced Budget Act

Title XIX of the Social Security Act, 79 Stat. 343, as amended, authorizes the Federal Government to transfer huge sums of money to the States to help finance medical care for the indigent. See 42 U.S.C. § 1396d(b). In 1991, Congress directed that those federal subsidies be reduced by the amount of certain taxes levied by the States on health care providers. In 1994, the Department of Health and Human Services (HHS) notified the State of New York that 15 of its taxes were covered by the 1991 Act, and that as of June 30, 1994, the statute therefore required New York to return $955 million to the United States. The notice advised the State that it could apply for a waiver on certain statutory grounds. New York did request a waiver for those tax programs, as well as for a number of others, but HHS has not formally acted on any of those waiver requests. New York has estimated that the amount at issue for the period from October 1992 through March 1997 is as high as $2.6 billion.

Because HHS had not taken any action on the waiver requests, New York turned to Congress for relief. On August 5, 1997, Congress enacted a law that resolved the issue in New York's favor. Section 4722(c) of the Balanced Budget Act of 1997 identifies the disputed taxes and provides that they "are deemed to be permissible health care related taxes and in compliance with the requirements" of the relevant provisions of the 1991 statute.

On August 11, 1997, the President sent identical notices to the Senate and to the House of Representatives canceling "one item of new direct spending," specifying § 4722(c) as that item, and stating that he had determined that "this cancellation will reduce the Federal budget deficit." He explained that § 4722(c) would have permitted New York "to continue relying upon impermissible provider taxes to finance its Medicaid program" and that "this preferential treatment would have increased Medicaid costs, would have treated New York differently from all other States, and would have established a costly precedent for other States to request comparable treatment."

Section 968 of the Taxpayer Relief Act

A person who realizes a profit from the sale of securities is generally subject to a capital gains tax. Under existing law, however, an ordinary business corporation can acquire a corporation, including a food processing or refining company, in a merger or stock-for-stock transaction in which no gain is recognized to the seller, see 26 U.S.C. § § 354(a), 368(a); the seller's tax payment, therefore, is deferred. If, however, the purchaser is a farmers' cooperative, the parties cannot structure such a transaction because the stock of the cooperative may be held only by its members, see 26 U.S.C. § 521(b)(2); thus, a seller dealing with a farmers' cooperative cannot obtain the benefits of tax deferral.

In § 968 of the Taxpayer Relief Act of 1997, Congress amended § 1042 of the Internal Revenue Code to permit owners of certain food refiners and processors to defer the recognition of gain if they sell their stock to eligible farmers' cooperatives. The purpose of the amendment, as repeatedly explained by its sponsors, was "to facilitate the transfer of refiners and processors to farmers' cooperatives." The amendment to § 1042 was one of the 79 "limited tax benefits" authorized by the Taxpayer Relief Act of 1997 and specifically identified in Title XVII of that Act as "subject to [the] line item veto."

On the same date that he canceled the "item of new direct spending" involving New York's health care programs, the President also canceled this limited tax benefit. In his explanation of that action, the President endorsed the objective of encouraging "value-added farming through the purchase by farmers' cooperatives of refiners or processors of agricultural goods," but concluded that the provision lacked safeguards and also "failed to target its benefits to small-and-medium-size cooperatives."

II

Appellees filed two separate actions against the President and other federal officials challenging these two cancellations. The plaintiffs in the first case are the City of New York, two hospital associations, one hospital, and two unions representing health care employees. The plaintiffs in the second are a farmers' cooperative consisting of about 30 potato growers in Idaho and an individual farmer who is a member and officer of the cooperative. The District Court consolidated the two cases and determined that at least one of the plaintiffs in each had standing under Article III of the Constitution. . . .

IV

The Line Item Veto Act gives the President the power to "cancel in whole" three types of provisions that have been signed into law: "(1) any dollar amount of discretionary budget authority; (2) any item of new direct spending; or (3) any limited tax benefit." 2 U.S.C. § 691(a) (1994 ed., Supp. II). It is undisputed that the New York case involves an "item of new direct spending" and that the Snake River case involves a "limited tax benefit" as those terms are defined in the Act. It is also undisputed that each of those provisions had been signed into law pursuant to Article I, § 7, of the Constitution before it was canceled.

The Act requires the President to adhere to precise procedures whenever he exercises his cancellation authority. In identifying items for cancellation he must consider the legislative history, the purposes, and other relevant information about the items. He must determine, with respect to each cancellation, that it will "(i) reduce the Federal budget deficit; (ii) not impair any essential Government functions; and (iii) not harm the national interest." § 691(a)(A). Moreover, he must transmit a special message to Congress notifying it of each cancellation within five calendar days (excluding Sundays) after the enactment of the canceled provision. It

is undisputed that the President meticulously followed these procedures in these cases.

A cancellation takes effect upon receipt by Congress of the special message from the President. If, however, a "disapproval bill" pertaining to a special message is enacted into law, the cancellations set forth in that message become "null and void." The Act sets forth a detailed expedited procedure for the consideration of a "disapproval bill," but no such bill was passed for either of the cancellations involved in these cases. A majority vote of both Houses is sufficient to enact a disapproval bill. The Act does not grant the President the authority to cancel a disapproval bill, but he does, of course, retain his constitutional authority to veto such a bill.

The effect of a cancellation is plainly stated in § 691e, which defines the principal terms used in the Act. With respect to both an item of new direct spending and a limited tax benefit, the cancellation prevents the item "from having legal force or effect." 2 U.S.C. § § 691e(4)(B)-(C). Thus, under the plain text of the statute, the two actions of the President that are challenged in these cases prevented one section of the Balanced Budget Act of 1997 and one section of the Taxpayer Relief Act of 1997 "from having legal force or effect." The remaining provisions of those statutes, with the exception of the second canceled item in the latter, continue to have the same force and effect as they had when signed into law.

In both legal and practical effect, the President has amended two Acts of Congress by repealing a portion of each. "Repeal of statutes, no less than enactment, must conform with Art. I." *INS v. Chadha,* 462 U.S. 919, 954, (1983). There is no provision in the Constitution that authorizes the President to enact, to amend, or to repeal statutes. Both Article I and Article II assign responsibilities to the President that directly relate to the lawmaking process, but neither addresses the issue presented by these cases. The President "shall from time to time give to the Congress Information on the State of the Union, and recommend to their Consideration such Measures as he shall judge necessary and expedient . . . " Art. II, § 3. Thus, he may initiate and influence legislative proposals. Moreover, after a bill has passed both

Houses of Congress, but "before it becomes a Law," it must be presented to the President. If he approves it, "he shall sign it, but if not he shall return it, with his Objections to that House in which it shall have originated, who shall enter the Objections at large on their Journal, and proceed to reconsider it." Art. I, § 7, cl. 2. His "return" of a bill, which is usually described as a "veto," is subject to being overridden by a two-thirds vote in each House.

There are important differences between the President's "return" of a bill pursuant to Article I, § 7, and the exercise of the President's cancellation authority pursuant to the Line Item Veto Act. The constitutional return takes place before the bill becomes law; the statutory cancellation occurs after the bill becomes law. The constitutional return is of the entire bill; the statutory cancellation is of only a part. Although the Constitution expressly authorizes the President to play a role in the process of enacting statutes, it is silent on the subject of unilateral Presidential action that either repeals or amends parts of duly enacted statutes.

There are powerful reasons for construing constitutional silence on this profoundly important issue as equivalent to an express prohibition. The procedures governing the enactment of statutes set forth in the text of Article I were the product of the great debates and compromises that produced the Constitution itself. Familiar historical materials provide abundant support for the conclusion that the power to enact statutes may only "be exercised in accord with a single, finely wrought and exhaustively considered, procedure." *Chadha,* 462 U.S. at 951. Our first President understood the text of the Presentment Clause as requiring that he either "approve all the parts of a Bill, or reject it *in toto.*" What has emerged in these cases from the President's exercise of his statutory cancellation powers, however, are truncated versions of two bills that passed both Houses of Congress. They are not the product of the "finely wrought" procedure that the Framers designed. . . .

V

The Government advances two related arguments to support its position that despite the unambiguous provisions of the Act, cancellations do not amend or repeal properly enacted statutes in violation of the Presentment Clause. First, relying primarily on *Field v. Clark,* 143 U.S. 649 (1892), the Government contends that the cancellations were merely exercises of discretionary authority granted to the President by the Balanced Budget Act and the Taxpayer Relief Act read in light of the previously enacted Line Item Veto Act. Second, the Government submits that the substance of the authority to cancel tax and spending items "is, in practical effect, no more and no less than the power to 'decline to spend' specified sums of money, or to 'decline to implement' specified tax measures." *Brief for Appellants* 40. Neither argument is persuasive.

In *Field v. Clark,* the Court upheld the constitutionality of the Tariff Act of 1890. That statute contained a "free list" of almost 300 specific articles that were exempted from import duties "unless otherwise specially provided for in this act." Section 3 was a special provision that directed the President to suspend that exemption for sugar, molasses, coffee, tea, and hides "whenever, and so often" as he should be satisfied that any country producing and exporting those products imposed duties on the agricultural products of the United States that he deemed to be "reciprocally unequal and unreasonable." quoted in *Field,* 143 U.S. at 680. The section then specified the duties to be imposed on those products during any such suspension. . . .

This passage [omitted here from above] identifies three critical differences between the power to suspend the exemption from import duties and the power to cancel portions of a duly enacted statute. First, the exercise of the suspension power was contingent upon a condition that did not exist when the Tariff Act was passed: the imposition of "reciprocally unequal and unreasonable" import duties by other countries. In contrast, the exercise of the cancellation power within five days after the enactment of the Balanced Budget and Tax Reform Acts necessarily was based on the same conditions that Congress evaluated when it passed those statutes. Second, under the Tariff Act, when the President determined that the contingency had arisen, he had a duty to suspend; in contrast, while it is true that the President was required by the Act to make three determinations before he canceled a provision, those determinations did not qualify his discretion to cancel or not to cancel. Finally, whenever the President suspended an exemption under the Tariff Act, he was executing the policy that Congress had embodied in the statute. In contrast, whenever the President cancels an item of new direct spending or a limited tax benefit, he is rejecting the policy judgment made by Congress and relying on his own policy judgment. Thus, the conclusion in *Field v. Clark* that the suspensions mandated by the Tariff Act were not exercises of legislative power does not undermine our opinion that cancellations pursuant to the Line Item Veto Act are the functional equivalent of partial repeals of Acts of Congress that fail to satisfy Article I, § 7.

The Government's reliance upon other tariff and import statutes, discussed in *Field,* that contain provisions similar to the one challenged in *Field* is unavailing for the same reasons. Some of those statutes authorized the President to "suspend and discontinue" statutory duties upon his determination that discriminatory duties imposed by other nations had been abolished. . . .

The cited statutes all relate to foreign trade, and this Court has recognized that in the foreign affairs arena, the President has "a degree of discretion and freedom from statutory restriction which would not be admissible were domestic affairs alone involved." *United States v. Curtiss-Wright Export Corp.,* 299 U.S. 304, 320 (1936). "Moreover, he, not Congress, has the better opportunity of knowing the conditions which prevail in foreign countries." Ibid. More important, when enacting the statutes discussed in *Field,* Congress itself made the decision to suspend or repeal the particular provisions at issue upon the occurrence of particular events subsequent to enactment, and it left only the determination of whether such events occurred up to the President. The Line Item Veto Act authorizes the President himself to effect the repeal of laws, for his own policy reasons, without observing the procedures set out in Article I, § 7. The fact that Congress intended such a result is of no moment. Although Congress presumably anticipated that the President might cancel some of the items in the Balanced Budget Act and in the Taxpayer Relief Act, Congress cannot alter the procedures set out in Article I, § 7, without amending the Constitution.

Neither are we persuaded by the Government's contention that the President's authority to cancel new direct spending and tax benefit items is no greater than his traditional authority to decline to spend appropriated funds. The Government has reviewed in some detail the series of statutes in which Congress has given the Executive broad discretion over the expenditure of appropriated funds. For example, the First Congress appropriated "sums not exceeding" specified amounts to be spent on various Government operations. In those statutes, as in later years, the President was given wide discretion with respect to both the amounts to be spent and how the money would be allocated among different functions. It is argued that the Line Item Veto Act merely confers comparable discretionary authority over the expenditure of appropriated funds. The critical difference between this statute and all of its predecessors, however, is that unlike any of them, this Act gives the President the unilateral power to change the text of duly enacted statutes. None of the Act's predecessors could even arguably have been construed to authorize such a change.

VI

Although they are implicit in what we have already written, the profound importance of these cases makes it appropriate to emphasize three points.

First, we express no opinion about the wisdom of the procedures authorized by the Line Item Veto Act. Many members of both major political parties who have served in the Legislative and the Executive Branches have long advocated the enactment of such procedures for the purpose of "ensuring greater fiscal accountability in Washington." H. R. Conf. Rep. 104-491, p. 15 (1996). The text of the Act was itself the product of much debate and deliberation in both Houses of Congress, and that precise text was signed into law by the President. We do not lightly conclude that their action was unauthorized by the Constitution. We have, however, twice had full argument and briefing on the question and have concluded that our duty is clear.

Second, although appellees challenge the validity of the Act on alternative grounds, the only issue we address concerns the "finely wrought" procedure commanded by the Constitution. *Chadha,* 462 U.S. at 951. We have been favored with extensive debate about the scope of Congress' power to delegate law-making authority, or its functional equivalent, to the President. The excellent briefs filed by the parties and their *amici curiae* have provided us with valuable historical information that illuminates the delegation issue but does not really bear on the narrow issue that is dispositive of these cases. Thus, because we conclude that the Act's cancellation provisions violate Article I, § 7, of the Constitution, we find it unnecessary to consider the District Court's alternative holding that the Act "impermissibly disrupts the balance of powers among the three branches of government."

Third, our decision rests on the narrow ground that the procedures authorized by the Line Item Veto Act are not authorized by the Constitution. The Balanced Budget Act of 1997 is a 500-page document that became Public Law 105-33 after three procedural steps were taken: (1) a bill containing its exact text was approved by a majority of the Members of the House of Representatives; (2) the Senate approved precisely the same text; and (3) that text was signed into law by the President. The Constitution explicitly requires that each of those three steps be taken before a bill may "become a law." Art. I, § 7. If one paragraph of that text had been omitted at any one of those three stages, Public Law 105-33 would not have been validly enacted. If the Line Item Veto Act were valid, it would authorize the President to create a different law—one whose text was not voted on by either House of Congress or presented to the President for signature. Something that might be known as "Public Law 105-33 as modified by the President" may or may not be desirable, but it is surely not a document that may "become a law" pursuant to the procedures designed by the Framers of Article I, § 7, of the Constitution.

If there is to be a new procedure in which the President will play a different role in determining the final text of what may "become a law," such change must come not by legislation but through the amendment procedures set forth in Article V of the Constitution. Cf. *U.S. Term Limits, Inc. v. Thornton,* 514 U.S. 779, 837 (1995).

The judgment of the District Court is affirmed. It is so ordered. . . .

Justice Breyer, with whom Justice O'Connor and Justice Scalia join as to Part III, dissenting.

I

I agree with the Court that the parties have standing, but I do not agree with its ultimate conclusion. In my view the Line Item Veto Act does not violate any specific textual constitutional command, nor does it violate any implicit Separation of Powers principle. Consequently, I believe that the Act is constitutional.

II

I approach the constitutional question before us with three general considerations in mind. First, the Act represents a legislative effort to provide the President with the power to give effect to some, but not to all, of the expenditure and revenue-diminishing provisions contained in a single massive appropriations bill. And this objective is constitutionally proper. . . .

Second, the case in part requires us to focus upon the Constitution's generally phrased structural provisions, provisions that delegate all "legislative" power to Congress and vest all "executive" power in the President. The Court, when applying these provisions, has interpreted them generously in terms of the institutional arrangements that they permit. . . .

Third, we need not here referee a dispute among the other two branches. . . .

III

The Court believes that the Act violates the literal text of the Constitution. A simple syllogism captures its basic reasoning:

Major Premise: The Constitution sets forth an exclusive method for enacting, repealing, or amending laws.

Minor Premise: The Act authorizes the President to "repeal or amend" laws in a different way, namely by announcing a cancellation of a portion of a previously enacted law.

Conclusion: The Act is inconsistent with the Constitution.

I find this syllogism unconvincing, however, because its Minor Premise is faulty. When the President "canceled" the two appropriation measures now before us, he did not repeal any law nor did he amend any law. He simply followed the law, leaving the statutes, as they are literally written, intact.

To understand why one cannot say, literally speaking, that the President has repealed or amended any law, imagine how the provisions of law before us might have been, but were not, written. Imagine that the canceled New York health care tax provision at issue here, Pub. L. 105-33, § 4722(c), had instead said the following:

Section One. Taxes . . . that were collected by the State of New York from a health care provider before June 1, 1997, and for which a waiver of provisions [requiring payment] have been sought . . . are deemed to be permissible health care related taxes . . . provided however that the President may prevent the just-mentioned provision from having legal force or effect if he determines x, y, and z. (Assume x, y, and z to be the same determinations required by the Line Item Veto Act).

Whatever a person might say, or think, about the constitutionality of this imaginary law, there is one thing the English language would prevent one from saying. One could not say that a President who "prevents" the deeming language from "having legal force or effect," see 2 U.S.C. § 691e(4)(B), has either repealed or amended this particular hypothetical statute. Rather, the President has followed that law to the letter. He has exercised the power it explicitly delegates to him. He has executed the law, not repealed it.

It could make no significant difference to this linguistic point were the italicized proviso to appear, not as part of what I have called

Section One, but, instead, at the bottom of the statute page, say referenced by an asterisk, with a statement that it applies to every spending provision in the act next to which a similar asterisk appears. And that being so, it could make no difference if that proviso appeared, instead, in a different, earlier-enacted law, along with legal language that makes it applicable to every future spending provision picked out according to a specified formula. See, e.g., Balanced Budget and Emergency Deficit Control Act of 1985 (Gramm-Rudman-Hollings Act), Pub. L. 99-177, 2 U.S.C. § 901 (enforcing strict spending and deficit-neutrality limits on future appropriations statutes); see also 1 U.S.C. § 1 (in "any Act of Congress" singular words include plural, and vice versa) (emphasis added).

But, of course, this last-mentioned possibility is this very case. The earlier law, namely, the Line Item Veto Act, says that "the President may . . . prevent such [future] budget authority from having legal force or effect." 2 U.S.C. § § 691(a). Its definitional sections make clear that it applies to the 1997 New York health care provision, just as they give a special legal meaning to the word "cancel." For that reason, one cannot dispose of this case through a purely literal analysis as the majority does. Literally speaking, the President has not "repealed" or "amended" anything. He has simply executed a power conferred upon him by Congress, which power is contained in laws that were enacted in compliance with the exclusive method set forth in the Constitution. See *Field v. Clark,* 143 U.S. 649, 693 (1892) (President's power to raise tariff rates "was a part of the law itself, as it left the hands of Congress" [emphasis added]).

Nor can one dismiss this literal compliance as some kind of formal quibble, as if it were somehow "obvious" that what the President has done "amounts to," "comes close to," or is "analogous to" the repeal or amendment of a previously enacted law. That is because the power the Act grants the President (to render designated appropriations items without "legal force or effect") also "amounts to," "comes close to," or is "analogous to" a different legal animal, the delegation of a power to choose one legal path as opposed to another, such as a power to appoint.

To take a simple example, a legal document, say a will or a trust instrument, might grant a beneficiary the power (a) to appoint property "to Jones for his life, remainder to Smith for 10 years so long as Smith . . . etc., and then to Brown," or (b) to appoint the same property "to Black and the heirs of his body," or (c) not to exercise the power of appointment at all. To choose the second or third of these alternatives prevents from taking effect the legal consequences that flow from the first alternative, which the legal instrument describes in detail. Any such choice, made in the exercise of a delegated power, renders that first alternative language without "legal force or effect." But such a choice does not "repeal" or "amend" either that language or the document itself. The will or trust instrument, in delegating the power of appointment, has not delegated a power to amend or to repeal the instrument; to the contrary, it requires the delegated power to be exercised in accordance with the instrument's terms.

The trust example is useful not merely because of its simplicity, but also because it illustrates the logic that must apply when a power to execute is conferred, not by a private trust document, but by a federal statute. This is not the first time that Congress has delegated to the President or to others this kind of power—a contingent power to deny effect to certain statutory language. See, e.g., Pub. L. 95-384, § 13(a), 92 Stat. 737 ("Section 620(x) of the Foreign Assistance Act of 1961 shall be of no further force and effect upon the President's determination and certification to the Congress that the resumption of full military cooperation with Turkey is in the national interest of the United States and [other criteria]") (emphasis added); 28 U.S.C. § 2072 (Supreme Court is authorized to promulgate rules of practice and procedure in federal courts, and "all laws in conflict with such rules shall be of no further force and effect"). . . .

All of these examples, like the Act, delegate a power to take action that will render statutory provisions "without force or effect." Every one of these examples, like the present Act, delegates the power to choose between alternatives, each of which the statute spells out in some detail. None of these examples delegates a power to "repeal" or "amend" a statute, or to "make" a new law. Nor does the Act. Rather, the delegated power to nullify statutory language was itself created and defined by Congress, and included in the statute books on an equal footing with (indeed, as a component part of) the sections that are potentially subject to nullification. As a Pennsylvania court put the matter more than a century ago: "The legislature cannot delegate its power to make a law; but it can make a law to delegate a power." *Locke's Appeal,* 72 Pa. 491, 498 (1873). . . .

As much as the Court goes on about Art. I, § 7, therefore, that provision does not demand the result the Court reaches. It no more categorically prohibits the Executive reduction of congressional dispositions in the course of implementing statutes that authorize such reduction, than it categorically prohibits the Executive augmentation of congressional dispositions in the course of implementing statutes that authorize such augmentation—generally known as substantive rulemaking. There are, to be sure, limits upon the former just as there are limits upon the latter—and I am prepared to acknowledge that the limits upon the former may be much more severe. Those limits are established, however, not by some categorical prohibition of Art. I, § 7, which our cases conclusively disprove, but by what has come to be known as the doctrine of unconstitutional delegation of legislative authority: When authorized Executive reduction or augmentation is allowed to go too far, it usurps the nondelegable function of Congress and violates the separation of powers. The short of the matter is this: Had the Line Item Veto Act authorized the President to "decline to spend" any item of spending contained in the Balanced Budget Act of 1997, there is not the slightest doubt that authorization would have been constitutional. What the Line Item Veto Act does instead—authorizing the President to "cancel" an item of spending— is technically different. But the technical difference does not relate to the technicalities of the Presentment Clause, which have been fully complied with; and the doctrine of unconstitutional delegation, which is at issue here, is preeminently not a doctrine of technicalities. The title of the Line Item Veto Act, which was perhaps designed to simplify for public comprehension, or perhaps merely to comply with the terms of a campaign pledge, has succeeded in faking out the Supreme Court. The President's action it authorizes in fact is not a line-item veto and thus does not offend Art. I, § 7; and insofar as the substance of that action is concerned, it is no different from what Congress has permitted the President to do since the formation of the Union.

IV

I would hold that the President's cancellation of § 4722(c) of the Balanced Budget Act as an item of direct spending does not violate the Constitution. Because I find no party before us who has standing to challenge the President's cancellation of § 968 of the Taxpayer Relief Act, I do not reach the question whether that violates the Constitution.

For the foregoing reasons, I respectfully dissent.

NOTES

1. Congressional Quarterly, Inc., 9 *Congress and the Nation 1993-1996* 14 (Washington, D.C.: C.Q. Press, 1996).

2. Bill Walsh, "Unelected Make the Laws: Agencies' Rules far Outnumber Congresses," *The New Orleans Times-Picayune* [national edition], August 7, 2003, p. 10; Robert Pear, "Aids Urge Bush to Impose Moratorium on Regulations," *The New York Times* [national edition], January 21, 1992, p. A1; David Rosenbaum and Keith Schneider, "Bush Is Extending Regulatory Freeze with a Fanfare," *The New York Times* [national edition], April 29, 1992, p. A1.

3. 5 USCS 601. See also David H. Rosenbloom, "Retrofitting the Administrative State to the Constitution: Congress and the Judiciary's Twentieth Century Progress," 60 *Public Administration Review* 39 (January/February 2000).

4. Lief H. Carter and Christine B. Harrington, *Administrative Law and Politics,* 2d ed. (New York: Harper Collins, 1991), 40–41.

5. David Rosenbloom, *Public Administration: Understanding Management, Politics and the Law in the Public Sector*, 2d ed. (New York: Random House, 1989), 378–79.

6. This information comes from Linda Greenhouse, "High Court Decides Budget Office Exceeded Power in Blocking Rules," *The New York Times* [national edition], February 22, 1990, p. A1. However, the actual case of *Dole v. Steel Workers of America* appears at the end of the chapter.

7. The material on the tire pressure issue comes from *Public Citizen v. Mineta,* 340 F.3d. 39,42-52 (Second Circuit, 2003); Miles Moore, "Tire Pressure Monitoring Rule Overturned by Court, NHTSA Mulls Review, Appeal," *Tire Business*, August 18, 2003, p. 1; "NHTSA Will Try Again: Agency to Rewrite Tire Pressure Monitoring Rule," *Tire Business,* October 13, 2003, p. 3.

8. Richard E. Neustadt, *Presidential Power: The Politics of Leadership From FDR to Carter* (New York: John Wiley, 1980), p. 9.

9. Ibid.

10. Ibid.

11. Alan Gitelson, Robert Dudley, and Melvin Dubnic, *American Government,* 2d ed. (Boston: Houghton Mifflin, 1991), p. 313.

12. Rosenbloom, *Public Administration,* p. 54.

13. *United States v. Curtis-Wright Export Corp.,* 299 U.S. 304, 319 (1936).

14. Arthur Miller, *Presidential Power: In a Nutshell* (St. Paul, MN: West, 1977), 141–42.

15. Ibid., 257–59.

16. Neustadt, *Presidential Power.*

17. *Youngstown Sheet and Tube Co. v. Sawyer,* 343 U.S. 579 (1952).

18. Alan F. Westin, *The Anatomy of a Constitutional Law Case: Youngstown Sheet and Tube v. Sawyer* (New York: Macmillan, 1958), 2–6, 14–16.

19. *Youngstown Sheet and Tube Co. v. Sawyer,* 343 U.S. 579, 634–55 (1952) (Jackson, J. concurring).

20. *Youngstown Sheet and Tube Co. v. Sawyer,* 343 U.S. 579, 637 (1952).

21. For example, see Susan Welch, John Gruhl, Michael Steinman, and John Comer, *American Government,* 3d ed. (St. Paul, MN: West, 1990), 389–94.

22. Ibid., p. 389.

23. Ibid.

24. Rosenbloom, *Public Administration,* 48–61.

25. Ibid., p. 60.

26. Ibid.

27. Louis Koenig, *The Chief Executive,* 5th ed. (New York: Harcourt, Brace, Jovanovich, 1986), p. 175.

28. Ibid., p. 177.

29. Richard Nathan, "The Reagan Presidency in Domestic Affairs," in *The Reagan Presidency: An Early Assessment,* ed. Fred Greenstein (Baltimore: Johns Hopkins University Press, 1983), p. 71.

30. See, generally, Richard Nathan, *The Administrative Presidency* (New York: John Wiley, 1983).

31. Jennifer Miller, "Presidential Appointees Face Weak Process," 23 *PA Times* 1 (June 2000).

32. *Humphrey's Executor v. United States,* 295 U.S. 602, 624 (1935).

33. Earnest Gellhorn and Ronald Levin, *Administrative Law and Process: In a Nutshell* (St. Paul, MN: West, 1990), 61–62.

34. Neustadt, *Presidential Power.*

35. The material on the office/Department of Homeland Security comes from David Firestone, "Security Agency, Yes, but Whose Version?" *The New York Times,* August 4, 2002, http://www.nytimes.com/2002/08/04/politics/04SECU.html.

36. Gellhorn and Levin, *Administrative Law and Process,* p. 65.

37. Ibid.

38. Pear, "Aids Urge Bush"; Rosenbaum and Schneider, "Bush Is Extending Regulatory Freeze."

39. Pear, "Aids Urge Bush."

40. Information on the budget process was taken from John Harrigan, *Politics and the American Future,* 3d ed. (New York: McGraw-Hill, 1992), 333–42; but for a thorough treatment of the subject, see Aaron Wildavsky, *The New Politics of the Budgetary Process* (New York: Harper Collins, 1991).

41. See, generally, Nathan, *Administrative Presidency.*

42. The material on executive orders and agencies comes from Fred Anderson et al., "Regulatory Improvement Legislation: Risk Assessment, Cost-Benefit Analysis, and Judicial Review," 11 *Duke Environmental Law and Policy Forum* 89, 94–96 (2000).

43. The material on the Senior Executive Service comes from James W. Fesler and Donald F. Kettl, *The Politics of the Administrative Process* (Chatham, NJ: Chatham House, 1991), 158–75.

44. The material on the procedure for OIRA review of agency rules comes from the prepared remarks of The Honorable John Graham, Administrator of the Office of Information and Regulatory Affairs, regarding his testimony before The House Small Business Committee, hearings on Real Estate Settlement Procedure Act regulations, 6 January, 2004.

45. Zachary Cole, "Bush Seeks Sweeping Overhaul of Federal Rules: Health Regulation, Environmental Protection among Hundreds of Targets," *The San Francisco Chronicle,* December 22, 2002, p. A1.

46. The material on citizen nomination of rules for change comes from Cindy Skrzycki, "267 Rules Up for Review: Referendum Names Environmental, Auto Standards," *The Washington Post,* December 19, 2002, p. E1.

47. Rob Grover, "Complaints Trigger Request to Review a Host of Rules," *The American Banker,* December 31, 2002, p. 4.

48. Graham, prepared remarks.

49. Michael S. Gerber, "Industries Lobby to Change ADA," *The Hill,* January 10, 2004, p. 16.

50. Eric Painin, "Senators to Subpoena White House: Documents on Air Pollution Regulation Sought," *The Washington Post,* January 24, 2002, p. A2.

51. Maureen Lorenzetti, "White House Reviewing EPA Nonroad, Low-Sulpher Diesel Plan," *Oil and Gas Journal,* March 24, 2003, p. 34.

52. Jennifer Lee, "White House Minimizes the Risks of Mercury in Proposed Rules, Scientists say," *The New York Times,* April 7, 2004, p. A16.

53. John W. Dean, *Worse than Watergate: The Secret Presidency of George W. Bush* (New York: Little, Brown, 2004), 162–63.

54. Ibid.

55. Jennifer Bayot, "Revised Rules on Mortgages Are Scuttled," *The New York Times.* March 23, 2004, p. C1.

56. "Mutual Fund Charge SEC Proxy Rule Violates Paperwork Reduction Law: Urge Withdrawal," 30 *Securities Week* 9, March 24, 2003.

57. The Information on the DQA comes from James W. Conrad, Jr., "Information Disclosures by Government: Data Quality and Security Concerns: The Information Quality Act–Antiregulatory Costs of Mythic Proportions?" 12 *Kansas Journal of Law and Public Policy* 521 (2003); and Michelle V.

Lacko, "The Data Quality Act: Prologue to a Farce or a Tragedy?" 53 *Emory Law Journal* 305 (2004).

58. The information on junk science and peer review comes from Rick Weiss, "Peer Review Plan Draws Criticism: Under Bush Proposal, OMB Would Evaluate Science Before Rules Take Effect," *The Washington Post,* January 15, 2004, p. A19; Adrianne Appel, "Federal 'Junk Science' Rule Draws Fire: Academics Say it Stifles Research," *Boston Globe,* December 23, 2003, Health Science Section. p. C4.

59. Andrew Schneider, "White House Seeks Control on Health, Safety Issues: Agency Wants Final Say on Release of Emergency Declarations," *St. Louis Post-Dispatch,* January 11, 2004, p. A1.

60. Information on the Bush 43 budget process comes from John Kamensky, "Bush Reformats Federal Budget: Performance Based Format Reminiscent of Approach in Texas," 25 *PA Times* 1, March 2002.

61. *Tozzi v. U.S. Department of Health and Human Services,* 271 F. 3d. 301 (D.C. Circuit, 2001).

62. Steven Croley, "White House Review of Agency Rulemaking: An Empirical Investigation," 70 *University of Chicago Law Review* 821, 824–27 (2003); John Cushman, Jr., "President Moves to Loosen Grip of White House on Regulations," *The New York Times* [national edition], October 1, 1993, p. A16.

63. David E. Osborne and Ted Gaebler, *Reinventing Government: How the Entrepreneurial Spirit Is Transforming the Public Sector* (Reading, Mass.: Addison Wesley, 1992).

64. See generally Osborne and Gaebler, *Reinventing Government*; Susan Kallam, *Reinventing Government: Will Efforts to Improve Government Pay Off?* (Washington, D.C.: C.Q. Press, 1995); Gary D. Libecap, *Reinventing Government and the Problem of Democracy* (Greenwich, Conn.: JAI Press, 1996); Hindy Lauer Schachter, *Reinventing Government or Reinventing Ourselves: The Role of Citizen Owners in Making a Better Government* (Albany: State University of New York Press, 1997); Reinventing Government: Using New Technology to Improve Service and Cut Costs: Hearings before the Subcommittee on Regulation and Government Information of the Committee on Governmental Affairs. 103rd Congress, 1st session, December 2, 1993 (Washington, D.C.: Government Printing Office, 1994).

65. GPRA actually amends various parts of the U.S. Code, but it starts at 5 USC 306. GPRA was accompanied by three other pieces of reinventing legislation: The Federal Crop Insurance Reform and Department of Agriculture Act of 1994, The Government Management Reform Act of 1994, and The Federal Acquisition Streamlining Act of 1994. See also, Paul Light, *Tides of Reform* (New Haven, Conn.: Yale University Press, 1997), 39–43.

66. Light, *Tides of Reform,* 40–41.

67. Michael Milakovich, "The Best in the Business: Improving Customer Service in Government," 22 *PA Times* 1 (June 1999).

68. Ibid.

69. Thomas J. Hennessey, "Reinventing Government: Does Leadership Make the Difference?" 58(6) *Public Administration Review* 522 (1998); Donald Kittl, *Reinventing Government: A Five-Year Report Card* (Washington D.C.: Brookings Institute, 1998); Milakovich, "The Best in the Business"; Light, *Tides of Reform* 179–215; Leslie Lenkowsky and James L. Perry, "Reinventing Government: The Case of National Service," 60 *Public Administration Review* 298 (July/August 2000); Beryl A. Radin, "The Government Performance and Results Act (GPRA): Hydra-Headed Monster or Flexible Management Tool?" 58 *Public Administration Review* 307 (July/August 1998); Bruce Reinhart, *In the Middle of a Muddle: How **NOT** to Reinvent Government* (Vienna, Va.: Manta Press, 1999); James R. Thompson, "Reinventing as Reform: Assessing the National Performance Review," 60 *Public Administration Review* 508 (November/December 2000).

3

LEGISLATIVE CONTROL OF BUREAUCRACY

I n Chapter 1, you were introduced to the concept of the administrative state. That is, we live in a political system where many significant policy decisions are made by bureaucrats applying expertise rather than by elected representatives who stand accountable to the public for the decisions. This raises potential problems for the state of our democracy. If no elected body or official can control or be held accountable for the bureaucratic policies, then can we say we live in a democracy? You have started to get a feel for the kinds of policies made by bureaucrats. The Environmental Protection Agency (EPA) set stiffer air quality standards, the Department of Energy (DOE) adopted minimum energy efficiency standards for home appliances, the Occupational Safety and Health Administration (OSHA) promulgated the hazardous communication standard, and the Department of Transportation (DOT) attempted to adopt a rule about tire pressure monitoring devices. Later in this chapter, you will read a case that has become known as the Benzene Case. In that case, the secretary of labor was urged by the OSHA director to promulgate a safety standard that would have lowered the allowable parts per million (ppm) of benzene in the workplace from 10 ppm to 1 ppm. At an initial investment of $266 million and recurring annual costs of $34 million to the petroleum refining industry,[1] this decision by the Department of Labor (DOL) would have affected both the supply and the cost of gasoline. Although it took a concurring opinion by Chief Justice William Rehnquist to adequately frame the issue in the Benzene Case, Congress had effectively delegated to OSHA (and hence to the DOL) the power to choose between workers' health and industry profits. In an advanced and complex society like ours, hard decisions like that often need to be made. In a democracy, however, hard decisions like that should be made by someone whom the voting public can reward or punish for the decision. Neither the director of OSHA nor the secretary of labor stands before the American public for election.

In Chapter 2, the argument was made that the Constitution does not supply the office of the president with sufficient power to control agency rule making. The subject of this chapter is the ability of the legislative branch to control bureaucracy. The Benzene Case involved a congressional delegation of power (Congress gave away its Article I, Section 8, power to OSHA). In the case-in-point, below, we will revisit the *American Trucking Association* case from Chapter 1 with particular attention to the delegation of power.

What Congress gives, Congress can take away. Or can it? By now, you are familiar with the concept of delegation of power. That is, Congress makes a decision to deal with an issue or problem (cleaner air or worker or traffic safety) and delegates its power to an agency so that the agency can use its expertise to attack the problem. Democratic theory, however, demands that Congress keep track of what the agency is doing and maintain sufficient leverage so that agency rules, regulations, or standards are consistent with legislative intent. There are two ways Congress could do that. First, Congress could exert more control on the front side of the issue by being more specific about what it wants the agency to do. Second, it could maintain control on the back side by exercising some sort of veto or modifying agency rules. Congress pursued the latter strategy by delegating the power to the president via the Office of Management and Budget (OMB) and the Office of Information and Regulatory Affairs (OIRA) to modify agency rules, but there are still unresolved constitutional problems with that approach, as discussed in Chapter 2. Congress also tried the back side policy with a concept called a legislative veto. A legislative veto provision allows a committee or a subcommittee of Congress a period of time to review agency rules. Legislative vetoes provide that either house of the legislature can pass a resolution undoing an agency rule, regulation, or standard. Legislative vetoes will normally be found in the enabling legislation. Since 1932, Congress has attached a legislative veto to nearly 200 pieces of legislation,[2] and legislative vetoes are common with state legislatures as well. In 1983, the Supreme Court ruled that legislative vetoes as practiced were unconstitutional. Basically, the Court said that when Congress vetoed an agency rule, it was making a policy decision, and the Constitution is explicit about the policy-making process. It requires bicameralism (both houses must pass identical bills) and presentment (to the President for signature or veto). Under the legislative veto process, agency rules were vetoed by only one house of Congress and were not sent to the president. Congress has cured the procedural defects and now calls such action *congressional review* but has only used it once. Congressional review will be discussed later in this chapter, but for now, we turn attention to the issue at the front side of the problem, delegation of power.

Case in Point:
Whitman v. American Trucking Association
531 U.S. 457 (2001)

In case you need more background than is provided here, you may wish to return to the case in point in Chapter 1. Once Congress decided that a federal policy to make the air cleaner was necessary, it passed the Clean Air Act (CAA). The Act identifies certain pollutants and mandates that those pollutants be controlled (particulate matter and ozone in this particular case). The CAA delegates to the EPA the power to set standards for control of the pollutants, and these are called *national ambient air quality standards* (NAAQS). Once the EPA sets the standards, it needs to review them every five years; compliance is left to the states with EPA oversight. In this case, the EPA reviewed the standards and, in 1997, revised them. The revised particulate matter and ozone standards are what caused the lawsuits.

There were four administrative law issues in this case, which appears at the end of the chapter. We will discuss only two of them, both related to the congressional delegation of power to the EPA. The first issue is whether the EPA is required to consider what it will cost to comply with tighter standards, that is, whether the EPA should modify standards that it may be considering because of the costs of compliance. The second issue is whether Congress unconstitutionally delegated legislative power to the EPA in passing the CAA.

Here is the exact language Congress used in delegating the authority to the EPA to set NAAQS. The quote is from Justice Scalia's majority opinion in the *American Trucking Association* case.

Section 109(b)(1) of the CAA instructs the EPA to set "ambient air quality standards the attainment and maintenance of which, in the judgement of the administrator, based on [the] criteria [documents of section 108] and allowing an adequate margin of safety, are requisite to protect the public health."[3]

From the language above, is it clear to you that Congress did not intend for the EPA to consider the costs of compliance when it sets the air quality standards? Does the language use the word *costs*? Can we or should we assume that Congress meant for the EPA to consider costs but for some reason failed to mention it? Given that the CAA has been amended several times, it is probably safe to assume that if Congress intended for the EPA to consider costs, it had plenty of opportunity to say so. Would it be consistent with democracy if unelected, life-tenured judges could simply insert language into a public law? In any case, the Court, by consulting dictionary definitions of *requisite* and *public health,* and by a reading of the language above—"set standards the attainment . . . of which. . . allowing for an adequate margin of safety, are requisite to protect the public health"—decided that the EPA was forbidden to consider the costs.

The second issue in the case is whether the language cited above constitutes an unconstitutional delegation of legislative power to an executive agency. A delegation of power occurs if Congress gave some of its Article I, section 8, powers to the executive branch. That would theoretically be forbidden for two reasons. First, we elect representatives to enact public policy on our behalf. If our elected representatives surrender that power to someone else who does not stand for election (the directors of EPA, OMB, or OIRA, for example), that would threaten our representative democracy. Second, the Constitution is fairly explicit about who should do what. Article I begins: "All legislative powers herein granted shall be vested in a Congress." Article II starts: "The executive power shall be vested in a President," and Article III: "The judicial power. . . shall be vested in one supreme Court." There are no ands, ifs, or buts. Congress may not give away its legislative power. The Supreme Court has created a delegation doctrine that you will read about in more detail shortly. The doctrine says that Congress cannot give away its legislative power, but it can confer decision-making authority on agencies. However, when it does that, the transferred authority must be accompanied by intelligible principles that limit the decision-making authority of the person authorized to act. The question in this case is whether the language discussed above provides sufficient guidelines and intelligible principles that limit the EPA's authority. The court of appeals thought that the statutory language was sufficient, but the EPA's interpretation of that language crossed the line drawn by the delegation doctrine. The Supreme Court ruled that the delegation of power to the EPA met the terms of the delegation doctrine.

Questions

1. Do you think the language used in the CAA sufficiently limits the EPA's discretion in setting air quality standards?
2. Given the technical nature of setting air quality standards, would it be possible for Congress to be more specific?

LEGISLATIVE CONTROL OF AGENCIES

What was said of presidential control of agencies in the last chapter can be turned on its head for congressional control. If the president possesses the will to control agencies but lacks the power and authority to do so, Congress does possess the power but generally lacks the will to exercise it. Congress rarely exercises truly effective control over agencies. Occasionally, however, when an agency has gone "too far" and upset powerful constituents and interest groups, Congress can and will pull on the reins and control that agency.

In 1964, the Federal Trade Commission (FTC) promulgated a rule that would have required cigarette manufacturers to print a label on the package to the effect that smoking causes death.[4] The rule would have also banned all cigarette advertising that might lead the public to believe that smoking "promotes good health or physical well-being."[5]

When the rule was promulgated, 50 million Americans smoked 549 billion cigarettes per year for an annual per capita consumption of 4,345 cigarettes. Smokers spent $20 billion on tobacco products, and tobacco was grown in 23 states (so 46 senators were upset by the proposed rule). The tobacco industry employed 2 million people, paid $22 billion in taxes, and spent billions on advertising (tobacco ads accounted for 10 percent to 20 percent of all advertising revenues).[6] The tobacco industry felt sufficiently threatened to have industry presidents, lobbyists, and members of the Tobacco Institute travel to Washington to see what Congress was going to do about this "problem." Congressional reaction was swift and effective (two characteristics not particularly associated with congressional action). Congress passed, and President Johnson signed, the Cigarette Labeling and Advertising Act of 1965. Packaged as a health and truth-in-advertising measure, the Act did require a warning to be printed on cigarette packages. The Act also, however, stripped the FTC of its rule-making power in the area of cigarette advertising for four years (the original bill called for a permanent ban) and banned smoking rule promulgation by any other federal agency (the Federal Communications Commission [FCC] was also considering action). The Act by Congress constitutes what is called *federal preemption,* which means that the states were preempted from passing any kind of warning label law (and several states were considering doing just that).[7] The label that was required by Congress in the 1965 Act was mild and certainly did not mention death. It read: "Caution: Cigarette Smoking May Be Hazardous to Your Health." By contrast, these were the proposed labels that the FTC considered in its 1964 rule-making procedure:

CAUTION—CIGARETTE SMOKING IS A HEALTH HAZARD: The surgeon general's advisory committee has found that "cigarette smoking contributes to mortality from specific diseases and to the overall death rate."

CAUTION: Smoking is dangerous to health. It may cause death from cancer and other diseases.

After passage of the 1965 Act, the FTC was forced to rescind its label warning. To ensure peace of mind for important constituents, Congress, in 1970, passed another act continuing the ban on FTC rule making in the cigarette area for two more years.[8] Furthermore, Congress required the FTC to provide six months' advance notice of "any plans it might have . . . to adopt a trade regulation rule affecting cigarettes."[9] It also required the FTC to submit supporting evidence for any such proposed rule along with the notice.

After the FTC promulgated rules unfavorable to other industries—pharmaceutical companies, the insurance industry, used car dealers, undertakers, and TV advertising aimed at children—Congress reacted even more harshly than it had in the cigarette controversy,[10] with proposed legislation to do away with the FTC, budget cuts, and legislative vetoes. Congress took away rule-making jurisdiction again, this time with regard to the funeral industry and children's TV advertising. The FTC was forbidden to investigate certain areas (agricultural cooperatives) and is now required to engage in cost-benefit analysis (by Congress, as well as by the OMB) before it proposes a rule.[11]

By the mid 1970s, Congress, in unrelated legislation, transferred jurisdiction to regulate hazardous substances from the Food and Drug Administration (FDA) to the Consumer Product Safety Commission, and the American Public Health Association petitioned the Commission to hold hearings to regulate cigarettes and the tobacco industry.[12] The Commission being a newer agency and not wanting to begin its bureaucratic life by incurring the kind of congressional wrath that the FTC had suffered, decided that it did not have the jurisdiction to regulate the tobacco industry. The Public Health Association promptly sued the Commission, and the Court ordered the Commission to reexamine its position on the question of jurisdiction over tobacco products.[13] Realizing that another agency was about to take on tobacco, Congress quickly removed the threat by passing legislation that removed the Consumer Product Safety Commission's jurisdiction over tobacco and tobacco products.[14]

The astute reader will recognize that the tobacco issue did not end in the 1970s. Indeed, it simply moved to a different agency and ultimately to the courts. In 1996, the FDA held public hearings on proposed rules to regulate the access of minors to tobacco products. Having received 700,000 submissions from those hearings, the FDA concluded that nicotine was a drug under the definition of the Food, Drug, and Cosmetic Act (i.e., it affects the structure and/or function of the body). The FDA also concluded that cigarettes and smokeless tobacco products were delivery devices for the drug nicotine. From this conclusion, the FDA promulgated several rules that would limit tobacco availability to minors. The FDA was quickly sued by Brown & Williamson and other tobacco companies. Ultimately, the Supreme Court decided that the FDA lacked the jurisdiction to regulate tobacco products because the Food, Drug, and Cosmetic Act authorizes the FDA to regulate products to ensure that those products are "safe and effective" for their intended use.[15] In its assertion of jurisdiction over tobacco products, the FDA declared tobacco to be "the single leading cause of preventable death in the United States,"[16] and therefore, *a fortiori* tobacco cannot be safe. The FDA cannot regulate an unsafe product, so if it wants jurisdiction over tobacco products, then it must ban the sale. You will read the tobacco case at the end of this chapter.

By 1998, the tobacco companies settled with several of the states who sued them to recoup Medicare costs associated with smoking. In the settlement, the tobacco companies agreed to restrict tobacco sales and advertisements to minors in many of the ways that the FDA had proposed. One of the points you may come to appreciate as you work your way through this book is that the American political system is porous. People who disagree with a policy—if they have sufficient resources—can turn to the legislative branch, then to the agency with jurisdiction (or perhaps more than one agency), and finally, to the courts. The attorney general of Massachusetts believed there were holes in the 1998 settlement agreement with the tobacco companies. Pursuant to the attorney general's power to adopt rules to prevent unfair or deceptive trade practices, rules were promulgated that restricted the sale and advertisement of tobacco products to minors. The attorney general was sued by tobacco maker Lorillard, and the Supreme Court found that most of the Massachusetts regulations were either preempted by the 1965 federal legislation or violated the First Amendment, freedom of speech (advertising as a form of speech receives some constitutional protection).[17]

The point of the tobacco discussion is to demonstrate that when Congress chooses to do so, it possesses the power and authority to control agencies. The operative phrase in the sentence above is "when it chooses." Generally, it does not.

Subgovernments

The case of the FTC is unique, for no other federal agency has been singled out and treated so harshly by Congress. Both the CIA and the FBI have been criticized for intelligence failures leading up to September 11, but congressional action seems to be oriented toward fixing what went wrong rather than punishment, as was the case with the FTC. The FTC, despite being one of the oldest regulatory agencies in government, had stepped on the toes of powerful interests and had little or no support from members of Congress or nontobacco interest groups. Much more typical of the relationship between agencies and Congress are subgovernments. *Subgovernments* is a term used to describe policy making by a small and intimate triad of government agencies, interest groups, and congressional subcommittees. The following are several of the better known subgovernments:

Department of Agriculture (USDA), House and Senate subcommittees on agriculture, and farm interest groups (e.g., Tobacco Growers Association, American Dairy Association)

The procurement office of the Pentagon, House and Senate appropriations subcommittees on defense, defense contractors

Department of Veterans Affairs, House and Senate veterans affairs subcommittees, veterans' organizations (e.g., Veterans of Foreign Wars, American Legion, Disabled American Veterans)

Federal Maritime Commission, merchant marine and fisheries subcommittees of the house, merchant marine companies and their trade association[18]

These are subgovernments because they "effectively make most of the routine decisions in a given substantive area of policy."[19] They have been referred to as *iron triangles,* but I prefer the more descriptive term *cozy triangles* (see Figure 3.1).

Some of the coziest triangles are those between the Agricultural Stabilization and Conservation Service and the Commodity Credit Corporation in the USDA, the House and Senate subcommittees on particular commodities (tobacco, wheat, cotton, soybeans, peanuts, etc.), and various interest groups (e.g., National Cotton Council, Soybean Council

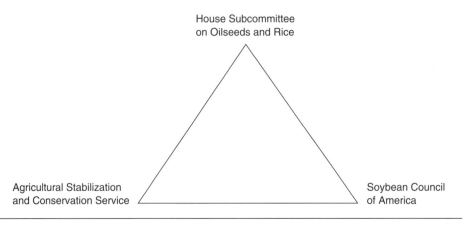

Figure 3.1   Cozy Triangles

of America, Tobacco Institute, National Association of Wheat Growers). These agricultural cozy triangles have quietly produced an array of government benefits, such as price supports for each crop. Among them are:

> Price support loans [mandated loan rates for commodities grown by farmers who can use their crop as collateral and default if the market price is lower than the loan rate]; acreage and production controls [to keep supplies low and prices up]; mandated target price levels [these generate deficiency income support payments to farmers when market prices fall below target levels]; . . . marketing orders, storage facilities, tax breaks, agricultural research and development, low interest loans.[20]

In some cases (peanuts and hops), a licensing system ensures that only a privileged few can grow the crop.[21] Some, but not all of the agricultural subsidies mentioned above were abolished by Republican majorities in Congress after the 1994 elections, but they demonstrate how a good deal of public policy gets made in America.

The triangles are cozy because the relationship within them is symbiotic; that is, each member of the triangle gets something it needs from other members. The agency gets appropriations and new programs from the subcommittee. The subcommittee gets support and information from the agency. The interest groups get policies and benefits from both the subcommittee and the agency (broad policy from Congress and favorable implementation rules from the agency). The subcommittee gets support, information, and campaign contributions for its members from the interest groups. Meanwhile, the agency gets information and support from the interest groups before Congress and those outside the triangle (the OMB, for example). The relationships between individuals who work together in the triangle are often personal: Those who represent the three sides of the triangle tend to enjoy longevity in office and come to know each other well.

The relationships between the partners in the triangle are, as the name suggests, not antagonistic. Rather, they are friendly, cooperative relationships from which all parties benefit. Cozy triangles often exist where the agency or bureau is involved in implementing distributive policies that affect a relatively small number of people. Consequently, they tend to enjoy low visibility and do not gain public attention.

The problem for the FTC in 1964, when it attempted to require the warning label on cigarettes, was that it ran smack into the tobacco cozy triangle and had no triangular relationship of its own for support. Not all substantive policy areas have triangles, and because there is no coordination between triangles, we often end up with Kafka-like situations. For example, the federal government provides generous price supports for tobacco and low excise taxes on cigarettes, on the one hand, but on the other hand, the cozy triangle involving the health care industry has seen government spending rise to $5 billion a year on cancer research and health problems caused by smoking.[22] This may seem irrational, but if one understands that a good deal of policy gets made in separate and distinct subgovernments, it makes perfect sense. Each of the triangles (tobacco and health care) is doing what it does best—and doing it very efficiently.

The relationships in these triangles are so cozy that triangles have been referred to as "incest groups."[23] The point is that all of the players know each other so well that no part of the triangle is likely to take action that would disturb the equilibrium. Consequently, there is no reason for Congress to exercise its power to control the agencies. Indeed, the existence of triangles often makes it difficult for congressional subcommittees to exercise truly effective and legitimate oversight of the agencies in their triangle.

Whether there are triangular relationships or not, many agencies have clients instead of cozy triangular partners. These clients often are powerful and not shy about protecting their own interests by lobbying Congress on behalf of "their agency." The FDA was willing to take on tobacco in 1996 because a head administrator was on a mission against cigarettes, and a powerful health care community clientele was equally committed against tobacco.

It is testimony to the strength of triangular and client relationships with agencies that the Departments of Education and Energy are still alive and well today and apparently are not endangered in spite of over two decades of attack by Republican presidents and presidential candidates and more recently by Republican majorities in Congress. An even better testimony to the staying power of agencies is the National Endowment for the Arts. Even though the agency's budget is less than a pittance of the whole federal budget (it is even a pittance of just the discretionary funding portion of the budget), the agency became the symbolic whipping boy of former Speaker of the House of Representatives Newt Gingrich, the House Republican leadership, and the Republican majorities in Congress, who got elected in 1994 by displaying the will to control bureaucracy.

The National Endowment for the Arts clients are not powerful like the tobacco lobby, and they could not stop the Republican Congress from cutting the agency's budget by 40 percent in 1995. The Republicans promised a "phase out" of the agency by fiscal year 1996, but the agency is making a comeback. It is still funded at reduced levels, but the Republican leadership had to admit that it lacked the votes to kill the agency. Indeed, *The New York Times* headline introducing one story says, "House Panel Praises Endowment for the Arts."[24]

The agencies that were selected by Congress for extinction (Departments of Education and Energy and the National Endowment for the Arts) are joined in notoriety by two other agencies: the Federal Legal Services Corporation (you might know it locally as Legal Aid) and the Bureau of Alcohol, Tobacco, and Firearms (ATF). The Departments of Education and Energy were never seriously threatened. Their clients are too powerful for Congress to attack them successfully. The other three agencies however, National Endowment for the Arts, ATF, and Legal Aid, were seriously threatened by Congress.[25] The distinguishing feature of each agency is its weakness in terms of client support. The ATF not only lacks a client base for support but also has a very powerful enemy in the National Rifle Association, which constantly lobbies Congress for its demise. The important point to note, however, is that although Congress possesses the power to extinguish each of these agencies, they are still alive today; crippled perhaps, but alive nonetheless. Congress possessed the power to destroy these agencies but could not muster the will to get it done. The ATF is now part of the Department of Homeland Security.

Reelection and Constituency Service

The second reason Congress rarely chooses to exercise its control over agencies is simply because bureaucrats and their agencies help legislators get reelected. The concept is called casework or constituency service. Although average citizens may assume that they sent their senator or representative off to Washington to legislate and conduct the nation's business, those citizens would be wrong. Members of Congress perform three tasks: "lawmaking, pork-barreling, and casework."[26] Members of Congress spend the least amount of time doing what you would most expect them to do—making laws. They spend a bit more time pork barreling and as much time (and resources) on casework as they do on the other two things put together.[27]

Constituency service simply means that the legislator, who will sometime during the fiscal year vote on the agencies' budgets and programs, runs interference for constituents who are having trouble with a federal agency. The congressperson might get requests for help with social security problems, veterans benefits, unemployment compensation, the Small Business Administration, the Internal Revenue Service, or immigration problems.[28] Casework helps senators and representatives get reelected because, except for casework, the effects of congressional action are not readily noticeable to the average constituent. How the senator voted on a particular bill or issue generally has little immediate effect on the constituent (who, by the way, is nearly always ignorant of how the senator voted or even that a vote was taken). Although the effects of pork barreling are somewhat more noticeable, many constituents may not be aware that the senator's efforts resulted in the post office building they are standing in or that the senator got the money for the dam that created the lake where the constituent can go fishing or boating.

Most constituents, however, have, through casual conversation with a neighbor or family member, heard something similar to this: "So and so was having trouble with the VA, so he called Senator X's office, and within a week the VA was taking care of him."

Americans generally show low levels of support for Congress but high levels of support for their own representative. Less than 20 percent give Congress a high approval rating but you would have to go back to the 1982 election to find an election year where less than 90 percent of House incumbents won.[29] According to Susan Welch et al., "Members [of Congress] who served in the 1987–89 Congress were as likely to be absent from the 1989–90 Congress because they died as because they were defeated."[30] Constituents may not like Congress as an institution, but they sure do like their representative—and the reason is constituency service. Senators and representatives are aware of this. Most members of their staff, both in Washington, D.C., and at home, are assigned to casework.

As with triangles, notice the symbiotic relationship in casework. The legislator needs the bureaucrat because the bureaucrat has the information, expertise, and ability to solve the legislator's (i.e., constituent's) problem. The bureaucrat needs the legislator's support for his or her budget and for the program's growth or maintenance (this becomes especially crucial when the bureaucrat's own president is attempting to slash the bureau's funding). Good results with congressional casework can help the bureaucrat protect both budget and programs from the OMB and the White House without publicly appearing to oppose the administration. Although bureaucrats are aware of the need for such political trade-offs, they are not as happy about playing the casework game as they are about triangular relationships. That is because when an agency has to put daily business on hold to take care of a particular senator's problem, the service to thousands gets held up for the sake of one.

Pork Barrel Projects

Pork barrel projects accomplish much the same thing as casework does for Congress. The spending of several million federal dollars for a post office, military installation, dam, or water project benefits any local economy. Whether pork barrel money actually translates into votes the way casework does is debatable, but the politicians believe that it does. From the viewpoint of the agency, pork barreling promotes a better relationship than does casework because casework interferes with the agency mission whereas pork barreling means growth and more money for the agency (another dam for the Army Corps). Passage of the line item veto was meant to help control federal spending by providing the president with a tool to attack pork barrel spending.[31]

Unfortunately for the FTC, it has no triangular relationship, it cannot help Congress with casework, and it is not in a position to help a representative bring home the pork, so it was very vulnerable when it took on powerful interests. Congress does have the power and tools to control bureaucracy, but because of cozy triangles, dependency on bureaucrats for constituency service, and the need to "bring home the bacon," Congress rarely finds it necessary to use those tools in any effective way.

TOOLS OF CONGRESSIONAL CONTROL OF BUREAUCRACY

As it does with the presidency, any standard text lists the tools of congressional control: the power to (a) create and organize, (b) control budgets, (c) investigate agency activity, and (d) pass guidance legislation.[32]

The Power to Create and Organize Agencies

Here, it *is* true that what Congress gives, it can (if it chooses) take away. The example of the FTC should make that clear. Congress rarely gets to the point where it has to take something away, because Congress often exercises caution in creating an agency. In the enabling legislation, Congress decides several crucial things for an agency. First, it decides the jurisdiction of the agency. In the case of the FTC, Congress later restricted the agency's jurisdiction several times. Second, Congress decides whether the agency will have the power to make rules. Remember from Chapter 1 that the FTC was not originally given the power to make rules; it could only issue cease and desist orders and had no power to enforce those. Even if an agency is given the power to promulgate rules, Congress can make it easy or difficult for the agency to make those rules. The FDA, too, has the potential to step on the toes of powerful interests Congress would prefer to protect. Therefore, in establishing the FDA, Congress gave the agency the power to make rules, but also made it difficult to do so.

There are basically two ways for agencies to make rules. One is the rule promulgation procedure already referred to in earlier chapters. Here, an agency announces in the *Federal Register* that it is proposing to make a rule, announces a time and place for a hearing, receives input, and makes a decision. These decisions are called *rules,* and they have the force and effect of law. The hearing resembles a city council hearing or a meeting of student government. Agencies can also make decisions or policy by going through a quasi-judicial hearing that looks every bit like a trial. These decisions are called *orders,* and they also have the force and effect of law. Congress provided the FDA with only the quasi-judicial procedure, which is a clumsy, time-consuming, and haphazard way of making policy. As a somewhat famous example, the FDA discovered that the peanut content in peanut butter varied widely among brands, so in 1959, the agency decided to standardize the peanuts in peanut butter at 90 percent. The two major brands at the time contained only 87 percent peanuts, so the Peanut Butter Manufacturer's Association decided to fight the agency. The quasi-judicial hearing regarding whether peanut butter should be required to contain 90 percent peanuts started in 1959 and continued until 1966. The agency issued a final order in 1968; the record from the adjudicatory hearing over 3 percent peanuts ran 7,736 pages of testimony—much of it irrelevant to the issue. The agency's order was challenged and upheld in the courts in 1970.[33]

Congress also decides whether agencies will have the power to issue subpoenas, whether they will have the power to issue cease and desist orders, and whether they will be able to back them up. The degree to which an agency is likely to be successful in terms of accomplishing legislative goals depends to a large degree on whether or not Congress intends for it to be successful, as seen by the powers given to the agency in the enabling legislation.

Clearly, Congress did not originally intend for either the FTC or the FDA to be very successful. Congress is more likely to restrict the powers of an agency in the enabling legislation than to rein in an agency later by restricting jurisdiction or rule-making ability.

Congressional creation of agencies is sometimes messy. Shortly after the September 11 attack, President Bush 43 created the Office of Homeland Security, placing it in the White House. Concerned that the director would lack sufficient authority to make the homeland safer,[34] Congress held hearings and wanted to question the director, but Bush 43 refused to allow him to testify. Eventually, Bush 43 came to accept that the agency needed to have Cabinet-level status with legal authority and a budget (and perhaps the muscle to compel intelligence agencies to talk to each other and share information). The Bush proposal was submitted to Congress in the early summer of 2002 and was quickly passed by the Republican-controlled House. There was pressure to establish the department by the anniversary of 9/11, but the Senate was controlled by Democrats who did not like the Bush 43 proposal. The conflict involved the Bush proposal to remove civil service protection from the homeland security workers. The Democrats had enough votes to pass their version of homeland security, but the Republicans filibustered the Democratic bill. As it takes 60 votes to cut off debate (and end a filibuster) in the Senate and the Democrats did not have them, it became obvious that there would not be a homeland security department by September 11, 2002. During the midterm elections, President Bush 43 campaigned on national security and accused the Democrats of being more concerned about protecting the interests of organized labor than protecting homeland security. The Republicans won back control of the Senate again in the election, and the lame duck Congress passed the president's version of a bill creating the Department of Homeland Security.

The Power to Control Agency Budgets

The Constitution gives Congress the power to tax and spend, and clearly, the power to control agency budgets rests here. To understand congressional budgeting and agencies, one must have a passing familiarity with the following concepts: incrementalism, budget authorization, and budget appropriation.

Businesses or institutions smaller than the federal government often tie budget decisions to goals. If a business wants to increase sales, then additional resources go to the sales department. To increase production, one might hire additional help. The federal government does not do budgeting this way. (Indeed, this type of budgeting was forced on government in the 1960s but did not work.) Federal budget decisions are based on incrementalism, a process in which this year's budget is simply last year's budget plus inflation and plus, perhaps, a new program or two. There is not a lot of soul-searching or analysis either within agencies or Congress when it comes to putting together the next year's budget. The Clinton-Gore administration intended to change incremental budgeting with its efforts at "reinventing government" and the Government Performance and Results Act. President Bush 43 has used that Act effectively to enforce goal-oriented budgeting.

Congress has divided its budget process into a bifurcated system of authorizations and appropriations. An *authorization* is the legal authority to spend, whereas an *appropriation* is the actual giving of the money. Authorizations are done by the standing committees. For example, the House Agricultural Committee will authorize the USDA to spend a certain amount during the fiscal year. It will also hold hearings on new programs the USDA may be contemplating. It is the standing committees (and their subcommittees) that form the cozy triangles with agencies and interest groups.

Each house of Congress has an appropriations committee, and it is there that agencies are actually provided with an appropriation for the fiscal year. Because the appropriations committees are supposed to abide by a spending ceiling recommended by Congress earlier in the year, appropriations are often smaller than authorizations. According to Fenno, appropriations committees are expected to be the fiscal watchdogs and to cut appropriations. Therefore, authorizations always come in high.[35] Appropriations committees are not actually involved in cozy triangles, but members and their staff maintain regular and close contact with agencies. Under normal circumstances, an agency would prepare a budget that would request an amount of money equal to what the agency had last year plus inflation. The director of the OMB might recommend small cuts, and the agency would try to negotiate with the OMB. If the agency were unsuccessful with the OMB, it would submit its slightly lower request to the standing committee for the authorization. Assuming a fairly cozy triangular relationship, the standing committee might restore the OMB cuts. The appropriations committee might cut the authorization slightly but perhaps not as much as the OMB. The agency would then end up with not as much as it wanted but more than the president wanted it to have. Finally, there may be the sequester procedure or even a presidential impoundment. The budgeting process is accomplished through a seemingly interminable series of hearings in the authorization subcommittee, the authorization committee, the appropriations subcommittees, and the full committee. Bureaucrats who testify at these hearings are questioned about programs, effectiveness, and expectations for the agency.

Each appropriations committee has 13 subcommittees, and agencies can be affected by events either at the full committee or the subcommittee; in addition, individual members may attach riders from the floor. In 2000, a USDA appropriations bill stripped an undersecretary of his supervisory control over the Forest Service and the Natural Resources Conservation Service.[36] Apparently, there had been a series of clashes between the Republican members of the committee and the Democratic Clinton appointee. Congress can restrict an agency's use of funds and curtail or enhance programs. In short, Congress can do whatever it wants to do. Davidson and Oleszek argue that the appropriations process is where the most effective legislative oversight of agencies takes place.[37]

The Power to Investigate Agency Activity

A good deal of what Congress does is called *legislative oversight,* and the name implies that Congress is aware of what agencies are doing. Hence, it sounds as if the popularly elected officials are controlling the bureaucracy. Actually, the authorization process referred to earlier is a form of legislative oversight, but cozy triangles and constituency service often inhibit effective oversight of this nature. When Congress restricted FTC's activity, that too was a form of legislative oversight. The kind of oversight that citizens hear the most about is when an agency is called before Congress to explain "administrative irregularities,"[38] such as the purchase of a $300 toilet seat by the Air Force (which the agency apparently explained to congressional satisfaction).

Some of the famous congressional investigations of agency action are: Teapot Dome; Watergate; Iran-Contra; the Branch-Dividian fire in Waco, Texas; the Firestone tire/Ford SUV problem (discussed in Chapter 2); the Columbia space shuttle disaster; the intelligence failures prior to September 11; and misinformation regarding weapons of mass destruction as a justification for war on Iraq in 2003.

An initial observation one could make is that many of these irregularities come to the attention of the press first and to Congress after the fact. In many instances, Congress is clearly not aware of what the agencies are doing or failing to do. Such oversight is done to show the people that Congress is attempting to control the situation and, it is hoped, to avoid a repeat performance. While congressional investigations occur after the fact, they do inform the public about what government is up to and, in some cases, spawn legislation. This happened after hearings on the collapse of Enron, for example.

Any standing committee has the power to investigate an agency it has jurisdiction over, but Congress has deemed it necessary to create special committees (Government Operations in the House and Governmental Affairs in the Senate) to investigate agencies. Although Government Operations Committee investigations often get good press, they are not effective in terms of controlling agencies. The Government Operations Committee exercises ineffective control because it lacks a significant legislative function (it writes reports, but it does not propose legislation), because members also sit on other standing committees (cozy triangles again), and, finally, because standing committees actually threaten the investigating committees so that the latter back off.[39]

Guidance Legislation

Guidance legislation is a term given to legislation that applies to all agencies as opposed to enabling legislation, which is agency specific. Examples are the Pendleton Act, the Administrative Procedure Act, the Hatch Act, the Freedom of Information Act (FOIA), the Sunshine Act, and the Government Performance and Results Act.

The Pendleton Act is what you would recognize as the Civil Service Act, and it depoliticized and professionalized bureaucracy. The federal government now operates under the Civil Service Reform Act of 1978. You will come to know the Administrative Procedure Act well by the time you have finished this course. It is the major legislation that controls and standardizes agency procedure and court review of agency action. The Hatch Act forbids federal employees from contributing money or taking an active part in federal election campaigns. Both FOIA and the Sunshine Act are amendments to the Administrative Procedure Act, but they allow citizens to access the information that agencies have (FOIA) and to force government policy making to be conducted in open hearings (Sunshine Act). The Government Performance and Results Act was discussed in some detail in Chapter 2. It is the embodiment of reinventing government, and it forces strategic planning on all agencies. Not that long ago, cozy triangles did their work in closed committee hearings and behind the closed doors of administrative agencies; they were not compelled to release pertinent information to the public. The Sunshine Act was passed in 1976 and the FOIA in 1966. Generally, guidance legislation has been beneficial in a democratic context, for it has reduced agency discretion and imposed regularized congressional control.

DELEGATION OF POWER

"Congressional power, like chastity is never lost, rarely taken by force, and almost always given away."[40] As with presidential removal, the Constitution does not address the problem of Congress' giving away its Article I, Section 8, powers. This is probably because the men who drafted the Constitution had all read John Locke, who argued that elected representatives should never give their power to anyone or anything (i.e., another institution). The reason is simple. If the citizens elect the representatives and the representatives make the policy, then the people, judging the policies, can hold the representatives accountable. If the representatives have given their power to someone else who does not stand for election, then the people lose accountability and, therefore, democracy. Because the Constitution does not address the question of delegation of power, that question is left to the courts. Early justices of the Supreme Court also read John Locke, and they articulated a theory of jurisprudence that would become known as the *nondelegation doctrine*. That doctrine says it is unconstitutional for the legislature to delegate its power.

As you will see from the following case, although the Supreme Court said the words *nondelegation doctrine*, it allowed delegation almost from the beginning. The modern problem in terms of delegation of power is not *whether* Congress should delegate its power but, rather, *how* Congress should delegate its power.

Hampton v. United States
276 U.S. 394 (1928)

Chief Justice Taft delivered the opinion for a unanimous Court.

J. W. Hampton, Jr., & Co. made an importation into New York of barium dioxide which the collector of customs assessed at the dutiable rate of six cents per pound. This was two cents per pound more than that fixed by statute. The rate was raised by the collector by virtue of the proclamation of the President, issued under, and by authority of, section 315 of title 3 of the Tariff Act of September 21, 1922, which is the so-called flexible tariff provision. Protest was made and an appeal was taken. . . . The case came on for hearing before the United States Customs Court. A majority held the act constitutional. Thereafter the case was appealed to the United States Court of Customs Appeals.

On the 16th day of October, 1926, the Attorney General certified that in his opinion the case was of such importance as to render expedient its review by this Court.

. . . The pertinent part of the Tariff Act says that in order to regulate the foreign commerce of the United States and to put into force and effect the policy of the Congress by this act intended, whenever the President, upon investigation of the differences in costs of production of articles wholly or in part the growth or product of the United States and of like or similar articles wholly or in part the growth or product of competing foreign countries, shall find it thereby shown that the duties fixed in this act do not equalize the said differences in costs of production in the United States and the principal competing country he shall, by such investigation, ascertain said differences and determine and proclaim the changes in classifications or increases or decreases in any rate of duty provided in this act shown by said ascertained differences in such costs of production necessary to equalize the same. The President issued his proclamation May 19, 1924. " . . . Now, therefore, I, Calvin Coolidge, President of the United States of America, do hereby determine and proclaim that the increase in rate of duty provided in said act shown by said ascertained differences in said costs of production necessary to equalize the same is as follows: 'An increase in said duty on barium dioxide (within the limit of total increase provided for in said act) from 4 cents per pound to 6 cents per pound.'"

. . . The issue here is as to the constitutionality of section 315, upon which depends the authority for the proclamation of the President and for two of the six cents per pound duty collected from the petitioner. The contention of the taxpayers is twofold—first, they argue that the section is invalid in that it is a delegation to the President of the legislative power, which by article 1, § 1 of the Constitution, is vested in Congress, the power being that declared in section 8 of article 1, that the Congress shall have power to lay and collect taxes, duties, imposts, and excises. Their second objection is that, as section 315 was enacted with the avowed intent and for the purpose of protecting the industries of the United States, it is invalid because the Constitution gives power to lay such taxes only for revenue.

[1] First. It seems clear what Congress intended by section 315. Its plan was to secure by law the imposition of customs duties on articles of imported merchandise which should equal the difference between the cost of producing in a foreign country the articles in question and laying them down for sale in the United States, and the cost of producing and selling like or similar articles in the United States, so that the duties not only secure revenue, but at the same time enable domestic producers to compete on terms of equality with foreign producers in the markets of the United States. It may be that it is difficult to fix with exactness this difference, but the difference which is sought in the statute is perfectly clear and perfectly intelligible. Because of the difficulty in practically determining what that difference is, Congress seems to have doubted that the information in its possession was such as to enable it to make the adjustment accurately, and also to have apprehended that with changing conditions the difference might vary in such a way that some readjustments would be necessary to give effect to the principle on which the statute proceeds. To avoid such difficulties, Congress adopted in section 315 the method of describing with clearness what its policy and plan was and then authorizing a member of the executive branch to carry out its policy and plan and to find the changing difference from time to time and to make the adjustments necessary to conform the duties to the standard underlying that policy and plan.

. . . Our Federal Constitution and state Constitutions of this country divide the governmental power into three branches. The first is the legislative, the second is the executive, and the third is the judicial, and the rule is that in the actual administration of the government Congress or the Legislature should exercise the legislative power, the President or the state executive, the Governor, the executive power, and the courts or the judiciary the judicial power, and in carrying out that constitutional division into three branches it is a breach of the national fundamental law if Congress gives up its legislative power and transfers it to the

President, or to the judicial branch, or if by law it attempts to invest itself or its members with either executive power or judicial power. This is not to say that the three branches are not co-ordinate parts of one government and that each in the field of its duties may not invoke the action of the two other branches in so far as the action invoked shall not be an assumption of the constitutional field of action of another branch. In determining what it may do in seeking assistance from another branch, the extent and character of that assistance must be fixed according to common sense and the inherent necessities of the governmental co-ordination.

. . . As Judge Ranney, of the Ohio Supreme Court in Cincinnati, said in such a case: "The true distinction, therefore, is, between the delegation of power to make the law, which necessarily involves a discretion as to what it shall be, and conferring an authority or discretion as to its execution, to be exercised under and in pursuance of the law. The first cannot be done; to the latter no valid objection can be made." Again, one of the great functions conferred on Congress by the Federal Constitution is the regulation of interstate commerce and rates to be exacted by interstate carriers for the passenger and merchandise traffic. The rates to be fixed are myriad. If Congress were to be required to fix every rate, it would be impossible to exercise the power at all. Therefore, common sense requires that in the fixing of such rates Congress may provide a Commission, as it does, called the Interstate Commerce Commission, to fix those rates, after hearing evidence and argument concerning them from interested parties, all in accord with a general rule that Congress first lays down that rates shall be just and reasonable considering the service given and not discriminatory. As said by this Court in *Interstate Commerce Commission v. Goodrich Transit Co.,* 224 U.S. 194, "The Congress may not delegate its purely legislative power to a commission, but, having laid down the general rules of action under which a commission shall proceed, it may require of that commission the application of such rules to particular situations and the investigation of facts, with a view to making orders in a particular matter within the rules laid down by the Congress."

. . . It is conceded by counsel that Congress may use executive officers in the application and enforcement of a policy declared in law by Congress and authorize such officers in the application of the congressional declaration to enforce it by regulation equivalent to law. But it is said that this never has been permitted to be done where Congress has exercised the power to levy taxes and fix customs duties. The authorities make no such distinction. The same principle that permits Congress to exercise its rate-making power in interstate commerce by declaring the rule which shall prevail in the legislative fixing of rates, and enables it to remit to a rate-making body created in accordance with its provisions the fixing of such rates, justifies a similar provision for the fixing of customs duties on imported merchandise. *If Congress shall lay down by legislative act an intelligible principle to which the person or body authorized to fix such rates is directed to conform, such legislative action is not a forbidden delegation of legislative power* [italics added]. If it is thought wise to vary the customs duties according to changing conditions of production at home and abroad, it may authorize the Chief Executive to carry out this purpose, with the advisory assistance of a Tariff Commission appointed under congressional authority. This conclusion is amply sustained by a case in which there was no advisory commission furnished the President—a case to which this Court gave the fullest consideration nearly 40 years ago. In *Marshall Field & Co. v. Clark,* 143 U.S. 649, the third section of the Act of October 1890 contained this provision: "That with a view to secure reciprocal trade with countries producing the following articles, and for this purpose, on and after the first day of January, eighteen hundred and ninety-two, whenever, and so often as the President shall be satisfied that the government of any country producing and exporting sugars, molasses, coffee, tea and hides, raw and uncured, or any of such articles, imposes duties or other exactions upon the agricultural or other products of the United States, which in view of the free introduction of such sugar, molasses, coffee, tea, and hides into the United States he may deem to be reciprocally unequal and unreasonable, he shall have the power and it shall be his duty to suspend, by proclamation to that effect, the provisions of this act relating to the free introduction of such sugar, molasses, coffee, tea, and hides, the production of such country, for such time as he shall deem just, and in such case and during such suspension duties shall be lived, collected, and paid upon sugar, molasses, coffee, tea, and hides, the product of or exported from such designated country as follows, namely."

Then followed certain rates of duty to be imposed. It was contended that this section delegated to the President both legislative and treaty-making powers and was unconstitutional. After an examination of all the authorities, the Court said that, while Congress could not delegate legislative power to the President, this act did not in any real sense invest the President with the power of legislation, because nothing involving the [expediency] or just operation of such legislation was left to the determination of the President; that the legislative power was exercised when Congress declared that the suspension should take effect upon a named contingency. What the President was required to do was merely in execution of the act of Congress.

It was not the making of law. He was the mere agent of the lawmaking department to ascertain and declare the event upon which its expressed will was to take effect.

[2] Second . . . It is contended that the only power of Congress in the levying of customs duties is to create revenue, and that it is unconstitutional to frame the customs duties with any other view than that of revenue raising. As we said in the Child Labor Tax Case, "Taxes are occasionally imposed in the discretion of the Legislature on proper subjects with the primary motive of obtaining revenue from them and with the incidental motive of discouraging them by making their continuance onerous. They do not lose their character as taxes because of the incidental motive." And so here the fact that Congress declares that one of its motives in fixing the rates of duty is so to fix them that they shall encourage the industries of this country in the competition with producers in other countries in the sale of goods in this country cannot invalidate a revenue act so framed. Section 315 and its provisions are within the power of Congress.

The judgment of the Court of Customs Appeals is affirmed.

Question

It is obvious in the *Hampton* case that the Court will allow congressional delegations of power under certain circumstances. Those circumstances constitute the Court doctrine of the constitutional test for when a delegation of power is constitutional. Can you state that doctrine?

The Court Applies the *Hampton* Test

The *Hampton* case was decided in 1928, and seven years later, the Court struck down two congressional delegations of power. In *Panama Refining Company v. Ryan*, 293 U.S. 388 (1935), the Court declared the following delegation of power to be unconstitutional:

Section 9 (c) of the National Industrial Recovery Act says: The President is authorized to prohibit the transportation in interstate and foreign commerce of petroleum and the products thereof produced or withdrawn from storage in excess of the amount permitted to be produced or withdrawn from storage by any state law or valid regulation or order prescribed thereunder. . . . Any violation of any order of the President issued under the provisions of this subsection shall be punishable by fine of not to exceed $1,000, or imprisonment for not to exceed six months, or both.

From the delegation just quoted, the president delegated to the secretary of the interior the power to promulgate rules to prohibit the interstate shipment of "hot oil" (oil produced and sold in violation of production quotas). The secretary's rule required petroleum producers to file, under oath, a monthly report of their production. The rule also required buyers of petroleum to file similar reports. The Court said that Congress had failed to provide "intelligible standards or principles" or guidelines with the delegation so that administrative discretion could be held in check.

Five months later, the Court held Section 3 of the National Industrial Recovery Act to be unconstitutional in a famous case called the Sick Chicken Case, *Schechter Poultry Corporation v. United States,* 295 U.S. 495 (1935). Section 3 of the Recovery Act authorized the president to approve Codes of Fair Competition. One of the codes he approved was called the Live Poultry Code, and he approved it by issuing an executive order. The constitutional problem with the delegation of power here was that Congress had authorized *private* trade associations to create codes of fair competition for their own industry and present them to the president for his authorization. The Act did specify a few things the president had to be assured of before he authorized the code, but the real problem here was not simply the absence of "intelligible standards"; it was a delegation of legislative power to private business groups.

What is now called the *delegation doctrine* says that congressional delegations of power are constitutional so long as they are accompanied by sufficient standards or guidelines so that the executive branch's exercise of legislative power is not unbridled and that, rather, the exercise of such power is channeled and controlled by Congress. The Court has declared that the best way for Congress to channel and control the administrative exercise of legislative power is for the delegation of power to be accompanied by "intelligible standards or principles or guidelines."

The Benzene Case, which follows, is notable for Justice Rehnquist's concurring opinion. How well do you think the Court applied the Delegation Doctrine to OSHA's regulation of benzene?

Industrial Union Department AFL-CIO v. American Petroleum Institute (The Benzene Case)
448 U.S. 607 (1980)

Justice Stevens announced the judgment of the Court and delivered the opinion. Chief Justice Burger concurred, as did Justices Stewart, Powell, and Rehnquist. Justice Marshall's dissent was joined by Justices Brennan, White, and Blackmun.

The Occupational Safety and Health Act of 1970 (Act), 84 Stat. 1590, 29 U.S.C. § 651 et seq.,

was enacted for the purpose of ensuring safe and healthful working conditions for every working man and woman in the Nation. This litigation concerns a standard promulgated by the Secretary of Labor to regulate occupational exposure to benzene, a substance which has been shown to cause cancer at high exposure levels. The principal question is whether such a showing is a sufficient basis for a standard that places the most stringent limitation on exposure to benzene that is technologically and economically possible.

The Act delegates broad authority to the Secretary to promulgate different kinds of standards. The basic definition of an "occupational safety and health standard" is found in § 3(8), which provides: "The term 'occupational safety and health standard' means a standard which requires conditions, or the adoption or use of one or more practices, means, methods, operations, or processes, reasonably necessary or appropriate to provide safe or healthful employment and places of employment." Where toxic materials or harmful physical agents are concerned, a standard must also comply with § 6(b)(5), which provides: "The Secretary, in promulgating standards dealing with toxic materials or harmful physical agents under this subsection, shall set the standard which most adequately assures, to the extent feasible, on the basis of the best available evidence, that no employee will suffer material impairment of health or functional capacity even if such employee has regular exposure to the hazard dealt with by such standard for the period of his working life. Development of standards under this subsection shall be based upon research, demonstrations, experiments, and such other information as may be appropriate. In addition to the attainment of the highest degree of health and safety protection for the employee, other considerations shall be the latest available scientific data in the field, the feasibility of the standards, and experience gained under this and other health and safety laws."

* * *

Wherever the toxic material to be regulated is a carcinogen, the Secretary has taken the position that no safe exposure level can be determined and that § 6(b)(5) requires him to set an exposure limit at the lowest technologically feasible level that will not impair the viability of the industries regulated. In this case, after having determined that there is a causal connection between benzene and leukemia (a cancer of the white blood cells), the Secretary set an exposure limit on airborne concentrations

of benzene of one part benzene per million parts of air (1 ppm), regulated dermal and eye contact with solutions containing benzene, and imposed complex monitoring and medical testing requirements on employers whose workplaces contain 0.5 ppm or more of benzene. . . . On pre-enforcement review . . . the United States Court of Appeals for the Fifth Circuit held the regulation invalid. *American Petroleum Institute v. OSHA*, 581 F.2d 493 (1978). The court concluded that the Occupational Safety and Health Administration (OSHA) had exceeded its standard-setting authority because it had not shown that the new benzene exposure limit was "reasonably necessary or appropriate to provide safe or healthful employment" as required by § 3(8), and because § 6(b)(5) does "not give OSHA the unbridled discretion to adopt standards designed to create absolutely risk-free workplaces regardless of costs." Reaching the two provisions together, the Fifth Circuit held that the Secretary was under a duty to determine whether the benefits expected from the new standard bore a reasonable relationship to the costs that it imposed. The court noted that OSHA had made an estimate of the costs of compliance, but that the record lacked substantial evidence of any discernible benefits. . . .

[1] We agree with the Fifth Circuit's holding that § 3(8) requires the Secretary to find, as a threshold matter, that the toxic substance in question poses a significant health risk in the workplace and that a new, lower standard is therefore "reasonably necessary or appropriate to provide safe or healthful employment and places of employment." Unless and until such a finding is made, it is not necessary to address the further question whether the Court of Appeals correctly held that there must be a reasonable correlation between costs and benefits, or whether, as the federal parties argue, the Secretary is then required by § 6(b)(5) to promulgate a standard that goes as far as technologically and economically possible to eliminate the risk.

Because these are unusually important cases of first impression, we have reviewed the record with special care. In this opinion, we (1) describe the benzene standard, (2) analyze the Agency's rationale for imposing a 1 ppm exposure limit, (3) discuss the controlling legal issues, and (4) comment briefly on the dermal contact limitation.

I

Benzene is a familiar and important commodity. It is a colorless, aromatic liquid that evaporates rapidly under ordinary atmospheric conditions. Approximately 11 billion pounds of benzene were produced in the United States in 1976. Ninety-four percent of that total was produced by the petroleum and petrochemical industries, with the remainder produced by the steel industry as a byproduct of coking operations. Benzene is used in manufacturing a variety of products including motor fuels (which may contain as much as 2% benzene), solvents, detergents, pesticides, and other organic chemicals. 43 Fed.Reg. 5918 (1978).

The entire population of the United States is exposed to small quantities of benzene, ranging from a few parts per billion to 0.5 ppm, in the ambient air. Over one million workers are subject to additional low-level exposures as a consequence of their employment. The majority of these employees work in gasoline service stations, benzene production (petroleum refineries and coking operations), chemical processing, benzene transportation, rubber manufacturing, and laboratory operations. . . .

Benzene is a toxic substance. Although it could conceivably cause harm to a person who swallowed or touched it, the principal risk of harm comes from inhalation of benzene vapors. When these vapors are inhaled, the benzene diffuses through the lungs and is quickly absorbed into the blood. Exposure to high concentrations produces an almost immediate effect on the central nervous system. Inhalation of concentrations of 20,000 ppm can be fatal within minutes; exposures in the range of 250 to 500 ppm can cause vertigo, nausea, and other symptoms of mild poisoning. Persistent exposures at levels above 25–40 ppm may lead to blood deficiencies and diseases of the blood-forming organs, including aplastic anemia, which is generally fatal.

Industrial health experts have long been aware that exposure to benzene may lead to various types of nonmalignant diseases. By 1948 the evidence connecting high levels of benzene to serious blood disorders had become so strong that the Commonwealth of Massachusetts imposed a 35 ppm limitation on workplaces within its jurisdiction. In 1969 the American National Standards Institute (ANSI) adopted a national consensus standard of 10 ppm averaged over an 8-hour period with a ceiling concentration of 25 ppm for 10-minute periods or a maximum peak concentration of 50 ppm. Id., at 5919. In 1971, after the Occupational Safety and Health Act was passed, the Secretary adopted this consensus standard as the federal standard. . . . The final standard was issued on February 10, 1978.

In its final form, the benzene standard is designed to protect workers from whatever hazards are associated with low-level benzene exposures by requiring employers to monitor workplaces to determine the level of exposure, to provide medical examinations when the level rises above 0.5 ppm, and to institute whatever engineering or other controls are necessary to keep exposures at or below 1 ppm. . . . As presently formulated, the benzene standard is an expensive way of providing some additional protection for a relatively small number of employees. According to OSHA's figures, the standard will require capital investments in engineering controls of approximately $266 million, first-year operating costs (for monitoring, medical testing, employee training, and respirators) of $187 million to $205 million, and recurring annual costs of approximately $34 million. The figures outlined in OSHA's explanation of the costs of compliance to various industries indicate that only 35,000 employees would gain any benefit from the regulation in terms of a reduction in their exposure to benzene. Over two-thirds of these workers (24,450) are employed in the rubber-manufacturing industry. Compliance costs in that industry are estimated to be rather low, with no capital costs and initial operating expenses estimated at only $34 million ($1,390 per employee); recurring annual costs would also be rather low, totaling less than $1 million. By contrast, the segment of the petroleum refining industry that produces benzene would be required to incur $24 million in capital costs and $600,000 in first-year operating expenses to provide additional protection for 300 workers ($82,000 per employee), while the petrochemical industry would be required to incur $20.9 million in capital costs and $1 million in initial operating expenses for the benefit of 552 employees ($39,675 per employee). . . .

[3] Any discussion of the 1 ppm exposure limit must, of course, begin with the Agency's rationale for imposing that limit. The written explanation of the standard fills 184 pages of the printed appendix. Much of it is devoted to a discussion of the voluminous evidence of the adverse effects of exposure to benzene at levels of concentration well above 10 ppm.

OSHA did not state, however, that the nonmalignant effects of benzene exposure justified a reduction in the permissible exposure limit to 1 ppm. In the end OSHA's rationale for lowering the permissible exposure limit to 1 ppm was based, not on any finding that leukemia has ever been caused by exposure to 10 ppm of benzene and that it will not be caused by exposure to 1 ppm, but rather on a series of assumptions indicating that some leukemias might result from exposure to 10 ppm and that the number of cases might be reduced by reducing the exposure level to 1 ppm.

In light of the Agency's disavowal of any ability to determine the numbers of employees likely to be adversely affected by exposures of 10 ppm, the Court of Appeals held this finding to be unsupported by the record.

[5] If the purpose of the statute were to eliminate completely and with absolute certainty any risk of serious harm, we would agree that it would be proper for the Secretary to interpret §§ 3(8) and 6(b)(5) in this fashion. But we think it is clear that the statute was not designed to require employers to provide absolutely risk-free workplaces whenever it is technologically feasible to do so, so long as the cost is not great enough to destroy an entire industry. Rather, both the language and structure of the Act, as well as its legislative history, indicate that it was intended to require the elimination, as far as feasible, of significant risks of harm.

[6] By empowering the Secretary to promulgate standards that are "reasonably necessary or appropriate to provide safe or healthful employment and places of employment," the Act implies that, before promulgating any standard, the Secretary must make a finding that the workplaces in question are not safe. But "safe" is not the equivalent of "risk-free." There are many activities that we engage in every day—such as driving a car or even breathing city air—that entail some risk of accident or material health impairment; nevertheless, few people would consider these activities "unsafe." Similarly, a workplace can hardly be considered "unsafe" unless it threatens the workers with a significant risk of harm.

[7] [8] Therefore, before he can promulgate any permanent health or safety standard, the Secretary is required to make a threshold finding that a place of employment is unsafe—in the sense that significant risks are present and can be eliminated or lessened by a change in practices.

[10] In this case the record makes it perfectly clear that the Secretary relied squarely on a special policy for carcinogens that imposed the burden on industry of proving the existence of a safe level of exposure, thereby avoiding the Secretary's threshold responsibility of establishing the need for more stringent standards. In so interpreting his statutory authority, the Secretary exceeded his power. . . .

The judgment of the Court of Appeals remanding the petition for review to the Secretary for further proceedings is affirmed.

It is so ordered.

Justice Rehnquist, concurring in the judgment

The statutory provision at the center of the present controversy, § 6(b)(5) of the Occupational Safety and Health Act of 1970, states, in relevant part, that the Secretary of Labor " . . . in promulgating standards dealing with toxic materials or harmful physical agents . . . shall set the standard which most adequately assures, to the extent feasible, on the basis of the best available evidence, that no employee will suffer material impairment of health or functional capacity even if such employee has regular exposure to the hazard dealt with by such standard for the period of his working life." According to the Secretary, who is one of the petitioners herein, § 6(b)(5) imposes upon him an absolute duty, in regulating harmful substances like benzene for which no safe level is known, to set the standard for permissible exposure at the lowest level that "can be achieved at bearable cost with available technology." . . .

Respondents reply that § 6(b)(5) must be read in light of another provision in the same Act, § 3(8), which . . . requires the Secretary to demonstrate that any particular health standard is justifiable on the basis of a rough balancing of costs and benefits. In considering these alternative interpretations, my colleagues manifest a good deal of uncertainty, and ultimately divide over whether the Secretary produced sufficient evidence that the proposed standard for benzene will result in any appreciable benefits at all. This uncertainty, I would suggest, is eminently justified, since I believe that this litigation presents the Court with what has to be one of the most difficult issues that could confront a decisionmaker: whether the statistical possibility of future deaths should ever be disregarded in light of the economic costs of preventing those deaths. . . . Congress, the governmental body best suited and most obligated to make the choice confronting us in this litigation, has improperly delegated that choice to the Secretary of Labor and, derivatively, to this Court. . . . In his Second Treatise of Civil Government, published in 1690, John Locke wrote that "[t]he . . . legislative can have no power to transfer their authority of making laws and place it in other hands." . . . The rule against delegation of legislative power is not, however, so cardinal of principle as to allow for no exception. . . .

This Court also has recognized that a hermetic sealing-off of the three branches of government from one another could easily frustrate the establishment of a National Government capable of effectively exercising the substantive powers granted to the various branches by the Constitution. . . . Later decisions that have upheld congressional delegations of authority to the Executive Branch have done so largely on the theory that Congress may wish to exercise its authority in a particular field, but because the field is sufficiently technical, the ground to

be covered sufficiently large, and the Members of Congress themselves not necessarily expert in the area in which they choose to legislate, the most that may be asked under the separation-of-powers doctrine is that Congress lay down the general policy and standards that animate the law, leaving the agency to refine those standards, "fill in the blanks," or apply the standards to particular cases.

These decisions, to my mind, simply illustrate the above-quoted principle stated more than 50 years ago by Mr. Chief Justice Taft that delegations of legislative authority must be judged "according to common sense and the inherent necessities of the governmental co-ordination."

Viewing the legislation at issue here in light of these principles, I believe that it fails to pass muster. . . . In drafting § 6(b)(5), Congress was faced with a clear, if difficult, choice between balancing statistical lives and industrial resources or authorizing the Secretary to elevate human life above all concerns save massive dislocation in an affected industry. That Congress recognized the difficulty of this choice is clear. . . . That Congress chose, intentionally or unintentionally, to pass this difficult choice on to the Secretary is evident from the spectral quality of the standard it selected and is capsulized in Senator Saxbe's unfulfilled promise that "the terms that we are passing back and forth are going to have to be identified."

As formulated and enforced by this Court, the nondelegation doctrine serves three important functions. First, and most abstractly, it ensures to the extent consistent with orderly governmental administration that important choices of social policy are made by Congress, the branch of our Government most responsive to the popular will. See *Arizona v. California*, 373 U.S. 546, 626 (Harlan, J., dissenting in part); *United States v. Robel*, 389 U.S. 258, 276 (1967) (Brennan, J., concurring in result). Second, the doctrine guarantees that, to the extent Congress finds it necessary to delegate authority, it provides the recipient of that authority with an "intelligible principle" to guide the exercise of the delegated discretion. See *J. W. Hampton & Co. v. United States*, 276 U.S., at 409 (1928); *Panama Refining Co. v. Ryan*, 293 U.S., at 430. Third, and derivative of the second, the doctrine ensures that courts charged with reviewing the exercise of delegated legislative discretion will be able to test that exercise against ascertainable standards. See *Arizona v. California,* supra, 373 U.S., at 626 (Harlan, J., dissenting in part); *American Power & Light Co. v. SEC,* supra, at 106.

I believe the legislation at issue here fails on all three counts. The decision whether the law of diminishing returns should have any place in the regulation of toxic substances is quintessentially one of legislative policy. For Congress to pass that decision on to the Secretary in the manner it did violates, in my mind, John Locke's caveat—reflected in the cases cited earlier in this opinion—that legislatures are to make laws, not legislators. Nor, as I think the prior discussion amply demonstrates, do the provisions at issue or their legislative history provide the Secretary with any guidance that might lead him to his somewhat tentative conclusion that he must eliminate exposure to benzene as far as technologically and economically possible. Finally, I would suggest that the standard of "feasibility" renders meaningful judicial review impossible. . . . A number of observers have suggested that this Court should once more take up its burden of ensuring that Congress does not unnecessarily delegate important choices of social policy to politically unresponsive administrators. Other observers, as might be imagined, have disagreed. . . .

If we are ever to reshoulder the burden of ensuring that Congress itself make the critical policy decisions, these are surely the cases in which to do it. It is difficult to imagine a more obvious example of Congress simply avoiding a choice which was both fundamental for purposes of the statute and yet politically so divisive that the necessary decision or compromise was difficult, if not impossible, to hammer out in the legislative forge. Far from detracting from the substantive authority of Congress, a declaration that the first sentence of § 6(b)(5) of the Occupational Safety and Health Act constitutes an invalid delegation to the Secretary of Labor would preserve the authority of Congress. If Congress wishes to legislate in an area which it has not previously sought to enter, it will in today's political world undoubtedly run into opposition no matter how the legislation is formulated. But that is the very essence of legislative authority under our system. It is the hard choices, and not the filling in of the blanks, which must be made by the elected representatives of the people. When fundamental policy decisions underlying important legislation about to be enacted are to be made, the buck stops with Congress and the president insofar as he exercises his constitutional role in the legislative process.

I would invalidate the first sentence of § 6(b)(5) of the Occupational Safety and Health Act of 1970 as it applies to any toxic substance or harmful physical agent for which a safe level, that is, a level at which "no employee will suffer material impairment of health or functional capacity even if such employee has regular exposure to [that hazard] for the period of his working life," is, according to the Secretary, unknown or otherwise "infeasible." Absent further congressional action, the Secretary would then have to choose, when acting pursuant to § 6(b)(5), between setting a safe standard or setting no standard at all. Accordingly, for the reasons stated above, I concur in the judgment of the Court affirming the judgment of the Court of Appeals.

Questions

1. Did the Court declare Section 6(b)(5) of the Occupational Safety and Health Act to be an unconstitutional delegation of power?
2. Can you synthesize Justice Rehnquist's argument into a short paragraph? Do you agree with him? Why?

Since the two cases in 1935, the Supreme Court has not declared a congressional delegation of power to be unconstitutional, and it has reviewed some broad and sweeping delegations. See whether you believe that the following delegations of power supply sufficient guidelines so that they channel administrative discretion.

1. A price control administrator is delegated the power to "set generally fair and equitable prices."[41]

2. The Securities and Exchange Commission (SEC) is delegated the power "to prevent an unfair or inequitable distribution of voting power among security holders."[42]

3. The Federal Power Commission (FPC) is delegated the power "to determine just and reasonable rates."[43]

4. The Federal Communications Commission (FCC) is delegated the power to grant broadcast licenses "as the public interest, convenience, or necessity require."[44]

5. The secretary of every federal department is delegated the power "to determine when excessive profits have been realized" and to renegotiate federal contracts with those who realized such profits.[45]

There may be reasons for Congress to give away so much unregulated power. Justice Rehnquist refers to some of those reasons in the Benzene Case: Increasing problems require more areas for regulation; the areas in need of regulation are increasingly technical, and Congress lacks the expertise to be precise in its language; and the subject matter to be regulated may be too broad for Congress to be specific. The point of Justice Rehnquist's concurring opinion, however, is that what was delegated to OSHA was the power to decide which is more important: the life of a worker or industry profits. When Congress, which *is* constitutionally empowered to make such decisions or value judgments, passes this power on to an unelected bureaucrat, the citizens have lost significant control of their democracy. Justice Rehnquist is not the only one to argue that the U.S. Supreme Court should continue to declare each and every overly broad, vague, and loose delegation of congressional power to be unconstitutional.[46]

Situations like this do not develop independently of historical context. Congress has delegated its power to the executive branch almost from the beginning.[47] Initially, the federal government was small and operated under an ideology (negative freedom, limited government, and laissez-faire economics) that restricted governmental activity. Therefore, Congress felt no particular need to go to great lengths to keep an eye on the bureaucracy. With the onset of the Progressive Era and the realignment of the 1930s, however, Congress began to enact distributive, redistributive, and regulatory policies,[48] which often require congressional reliance on expertise. This had two consequences: First, it changed the political nature of Congress. As constituents came to rely on entitlements and to expect other benefits, such as pork barrel projects, elected representatives had to spend more time on casework, pork barrel legislation, and building relationships with bureaucrats. Second, because legislative politics had changed, institutional processes changed, too, so that cozy triangles developed, legislative oversight became important, and Congress started to think of ways to control agency rule making.

Control of Agencies by Legislative Veto and Congressional Review

The material at the beginning of this chapter introduced you to the concept of a legislative veto. This gets at the notion of congressional control on the back side of the regulatory process so that Congress (rather than the President) controls the substance of agency rules or standards. The Congressional veto was declared unconstitutional in 1983. The Republican-controlled Congress has replaced it with a concept called *congressional review*. In 1996, Congress passed the Small Business Regulatory Enforcement Fairness Act (SBREFA), also called the Congressional Review Act. It requires that proposed rules that would have a major impact on several aspects of society be submitted to the appropriate committee or subcommittee of Congress and to the General Accounting Office (GAO) before they can take effect. Congress has 60 days to act on the proposed rule. The proposed rule can be "disapproved"—that is, vetoed—by a joint resolution of Congress (bicameralism). The disapproval resolution, however, must be presented to the president for a signature or a veto. A presidential veto can be overridden by the process in Article I of the Constitution. If an agency's proposed rule is successfully disapproved with a presidential signature, that rule cannot be reissued without specific legislation allowing it.[49] Basically, Congress says, "We do not want an agency rule that does X." Hence, it would take new congressional legislation approving X before there could be agency activity in the area of X. This process appears to cure the constitutional defects the Supreme Court found with congressional vetoes (bicameralism and presentment). What goes to Congress in the congressional review process is a proposed rule as opposed to the final rule that was involved in the legislative veto. The difference is that a final rule has the force and effect of law; it is a policy, and to change a policy requires the legislative process as outlined in Article I of the Constitution. A proposal, however, is just that—a wish—and it does not necessarily require bicameralism and presentment to change it.

Having created congressional review in 1996, Congress never used it because the Republicans in Congress knew that as long as Clinton was the president, he would veto their resolutions. When an agency promulgates a rule, it first announces a proposed rule and then holds public hearings on that proposal. Having considered the public input on the proposed rule, the agency will issue a final rule, but it will not have the force and effect of law until after it has been published for 60 days. Four days before President Clinton left office, OSHA published its final version of ergonomics rules.[50] Ergonomics is an applied science aiming to design an environment that is safe for people; bad ergonomics leads to repetitive stress syndrome or injuries caused by the performance of repetitive tasks; the medical name for these problems is musculoskeletal disorders. The fight over OSHA's adoption of the ergonomics rules was bitter, and the proposed rules were vigorously opposed by businesses, their lobbyists, and Republicans in Congress, but there was support from labor unions and consumer and health organizations. President Bush 43 could hardly have warmed up the chair in the Oval Office before Congress started to review the ergonomics rules. A joint resolution of disapproval was passed by both houses of Congress and signed into law by President Bush 43. When this edition was going to press, this had been the only use of congressional review. Should you believe that was the end of ergonomics regulation, you perhaps do not appreciate the resiliency of agencies and the complexity of the administrative state. OSHA has reissued new ergonomics "voluntary guidelines" and announced an enforcement policy. The enabling legislation to reduce workplace injuries prohibits creating a "recognized" hazard in the workplace and OSHA has been using that authority to inspect and issue citations for ergonomics violations.

Early in the 21st century, conservative Republicans in Congress are pushing for more congressional control over agency rules. The House majority leader complained that in the midst of a conservative, business-oriented administration, with Republicans in control of both houses of Congress, agencies nevertheless produced "64,431 pages of regulations to tell us how we should live."[51] Conservatives are calling for Congress to review all agency rule proposals, not just major ones or ones that affect small business. The major complaint seems to be that the congressional review process gives wide discretion to the agencies to determine which rules will have a major impact.

Republican Majorities and the Will to Control Bureaucracy

Since the realigning election of 1932 (referred to in Chapter 1), the Democratic Party has pretty much controlled both houses of Congress, especially the House of Representatives. The Republicans took control of both houses in the off-year election of 1946 but lost them to the Democrats again in the 1948 election. With the election of Eisenhower in 1952, the Republicans took control of both Houses again but lost them in the next election in 1954. The House stayed under Democratic control for the next 40 years until 1994. The Senate was also controlled by Democrats except for six years of Republican control between 1980 and 1986. In the off-year election of 1994, Representative Newt Gingrich masterminded a brilliant electoral mobilization and was responsible for a Republican gain of 52 seats and the first Republican majority in the House in four decades. Republicans also took control of the Senate. Newt Gingrich recruited a conservative group of candidates to run in that election, and he rallied them and mobilized Republican voters around a device called the Contract With America.

The Contract With America and accompanying campaign rhetoric was an attack on the government status quo, and a good deal of it was aimed at Congress' partner in sin, the bureaucracy. The 52 Republican freshmen elected in 1994 were committed to the free market, individual responsibility, and a smaller (less active) federal government, so it is certainly true that they were possessed of more of a will to control bureaucracy than are more moderate Republicans and most Democrats. It is also true that it takes 218 votes in the House and 51 in the Senate to exercise more control over agencies, and the 1994 Republican freshman class and its leadership were not able to muster the required votes either to pass legislation or to pass it over a presidential veto. Very little of the Contract With America ever made it into law.

The Contract With America was in reality only a promise to bring certain legislation to the floor of the House for a vote within the first hundred days of new Republican control of the House, and in that sense, the Contract was met. Most of the legislation that made up the Contract With America passed in the House. A good deal of it languished and died in the Republican-controlled Senate. Some of it got vetoed by President Clinton, and some of it was declared unconstitutional by the Supreme Court. The following is an account of what happened to Contract legislation that relates to bureaucracy. Welfare reform (i.e., Aid to Families with Dependent Children, as opposed to the hundreds of other welfare programs) passed, but it has not affected the size or scope of the Department of Health and Human Services (HHS). Some, but not all, agricultural subsidies were legislated out of existence. The line item veto was passed but declared unconstitutional. Legislation was passed that prohibits unfunded mandates and that could inhibit agency growth by reducing agency proposals for new programs or regulations.

One of the sections of the Contract, entitled "Roll Back Government Regulations," had three specific legislative proposals. One proposal was the banning of unfunded mandates discussed above. Another proposal was the Paperwork Reduction Act discussed in Chapter 2. The final proposal would impose cost-benefit and risk assessment analysis on all federal agencies before they could propose rules, regulations, or standards. This legislation also included a requirement that any agency action that reduced the value of property would require just compensation.

Legislative action to control bureaucracy will sound familiar to you from the discussion in Chapter 2 on OMB/OIRA review of agency rules. The basic difference is that Congress could not accomplish it, while the White House has. The first year Republicans had control of both houses (1995), the House passed what was described as a wide-ranging bill that would have required all agencies to use cost-benefit analysis and risk analysis. Risk analysis would require the EPA, for example, to assess the risks to the public health at higher and lower ozone levels and make that information available to interested parties. The bill also allowed adversely affected parties to petition the agency to modify or revoke rules or standards. Finally, the bill made it easier for injured parties to sue an agency[52] (at the same time, as you will learn in Chapter 4, the five conservative Republican members of the Supreme Court were making it more difficult for injured parties to sue agencies). Another bill would have required all agencies to review all existing rules within seven years and remove those that were "unnecessary, outdated, or overly burdensome." This bill would also have negated any new regulation that had not gone through the above-mentioned review within three years of adoption.[53] There was also legislation to undo a small part of the Superfund legislation, to modify the Endangered Species Act to allow more liberal compensation for those whose property was affected by the Act, and to require cost-benefit analysis of the Safe Drinking Water Act.[54] All of these efforts either did not pass the House or died in the Senate. The broader regulatory reform bill died in the Senate after it was filibustered three different times and the Republicans did not have the votes to cut off debate. What did pass from the Contract in 1995 was the Paperwork Reduction Act and unfunded mandates legislation, which causes agencies to take special precautions if rules implicate unfunded mandates. The Republicans cut the budgets of the EPA and other selected agencies, sometimes by as much as 24 percent. Republican budget cuts met with Clinton vetoes several times, and the budget battle eventually shut down the federal government as it ran out of money to function.

The new conservative Republican majorities took a public relations beating over the budget battle and what was seen as attacks on the environment and public health.[55] They also suffered electoral losses in the 1996 election. They decided to soften their approach to regulatory reform and offered a more lenient measure that would have required cost-benefit and risk analysis on major bills, peer review, and judicial review of the cost-benefit and risk analyses.[56] This bill had been modified from the previous one in negotiations with the Clinton Administration to avoid a veto and to satisfy Democratic opposition.[57] However, because of the modifications to a softer bill, it lost the support of conservative Republicans, and liberal Democrats still opposed it. The bill never came up for a vote in the Senate and was not introduced in the House. The Republicans took another beating in the 1998 election and now seem to be content with having delegated the power to control the content of agency rules to the White House. There has also been an increase in bureaucracy bashing on the floors of Congress and in Republican speeches.[58] There is an occasional agency-specific attack, and Congress did pass the Data Quality Act (which ensures peer review) as a rider. However, as noted above, the Republican leadership is still pushing for tighter congressional control of agency regulatory activity. The leadership is unhappy because the acts delegating the power to review agency rules to OMB leave discretion with the agencies to determine what a major rule is, what has paperwork implications, and what affects small businesses. The conservative Republicans also do not trust the agencies in their performance of cost-benefit analysis.

Finally, regarding the legislative will to control agencies, remember that such will is closely tied to reelection fortunes. The basic reason that Congress has failed to exercise control over agencies is because the incumbents have come to depend on bureaucrats and their clients in cozy triangles, in providing constituency service, and in bringing home the bacon. None of these things became extinct with the election of Republican majorities in 1994. Especially with the demise of the push for term limits, look for incumbents to spend most of their time raising reelection money, taking care of constituents, and pork barreling, along with continuing dependency on agency expertise.

The basic premise—that both Republicans and Democrats in Congress depend on agencies and bureaucrats for constituency service and pork barreling—is true. It is true because the primary goal of incumbent senators and representatives is to get reelected, and that applies to Republicans and Democrats alike. Reelection depends on constituency service and pork, and both of those require good relations with bureaucrats. However, what was said about the differences between Republican and Democratic presidents in Chapter 2 is also true regarding which party controls Congress. Republicans have more of a will to control bureaucracy than Democrats do. While the Republican majorities in Congress have lacked the votes to shut down certain agencies and more tightly control bureaucracy, they have made some efforts.

Finally, if Congress wants to favor an agency, it can do that as well. Congress has toughened immigration laws to make deportation easier and given the Immigration and Naturalization Service (INS) the budget and mandate to deport illegal immigrants. In 1998, Congress earmarked $1 billion for the detention and deportation of immigrants. Generous budgets have transformed the INS into the largest federal law enforcement agency, with 15,000 officers. Prior to the change in the law, most deportations involved people who got arrested for crimes and then were deported. Today, that is no longer the case. In 1997, the INS set a goal of deporting 93,000 people, but it surpassed its goal by deporting 114,000 people. Spurred by such success, INS increased its 1998 goal to 127,000 deportations, and it exceeded that goal as well by deporting 169,000 people.[59] The INS was moved into the Department of Homeland Security.

SUMMARY

1. *Five ways for Congress to control agencies.* Although it appears that the White House exercises more control over agencies than Congress does, that is only because Congress has delegated that power away. We can only count on executive control of agencies if a Republican is in the White House. Congress clearly possesses the power to control agencies, but even with Republican majorities in Congress, legislation to control agencies, for the most part, has not passed. Congress can exercise power over agencies in five ways: First, Congress can amend a specific agency's enabling legislation. This action becomes less likely as agencies accumulate powerful clientele and more likely when agencies acquire powerful enemies (ATF, Legal Aid, EPA). Second, Congress can exercise absolute

control through the budget. This appears to be only theoretically true, however. The fact is that when conservative Republicans controlled Congress, the executive branch, and even the judicial branch, the National Endowment for the Arts and Legal Aid survived. They are wounded perhaps, but there is no evidence of their imminent demise. Third, Congress could exert more control by passing narrower and tighter delegations of power. For the reasons articulated by Chief Justice Rehnquist in his concurring opinion in the Benzene Case, this is not a likely scenario either. There also appears to be political payoff for Congress to assign broad and sweeping power to agencies and then go home around election time and blame bureaucrats for all that is wrong with America. Fourth, Congress controls the substance of agency rules through the congressional review process. There is little need to exercise it with Bush 43 in the White House, and when a Democrat is in the White House, Republicans in Congress would need veto-proof majorities to be able to exercise it. Finally, Congress could pass guidance legislation such as a regulatory improvement act. As the recent history of such an effort shows, this is not a strong possibility either. Republicans would need to increase their majorities in the Senate enough to avoid a filibuster and would also need a Republican in the White House.

2. *Delegation of power.* Congress is not supposed to delegate its raw legislative power to anyone. Where Congress enlists the help of the executive branch by delegating authority, that delegation is supposed to be accompanied by intelligible principles and standards.

3. *Congressional review.* The process involved in congressional review appears to have cured the constitutional defects of the old legislative veto.

END-OF-CHAPTER CASES

Immigration and Naturalization Service v. Chadha
462 U.S. 919 (1983)

Chief Justice Burger delivered the opinion of the Court, joined by Justices Brennan, Marshall, Blackmun, Stevens, and O'Connor. Justice Powell concurred, and Justices White and Rehnquist were in dissent.

We granted certiorari in Nos. 80–2170 and 80–2171 and postponed consideration of the question of jurisdiction in No. 80–1832. Each presents a challenge to the constitutionality of the provision in the Immigration and Nationality Act, authorizing one House of Congress, by resolution, to invalidate the decision of the Executive Branch, pursuant to authority delegated by Congress to the Attorney General of the

United States, to allow a particular deportable alien to remain in the United States.

I

Chadha is an East Indian who was born in Kenya and holds a British passport. He was lawfully admitted to the United States in 1966 on a nonimmigrant student visa. His visa expired on June 30, 1972. On October 11, 1973, the District Director of the Immigration and Naturalization Service ordered Chadha to show cause why he should not be deported for having "remained in the United States for a longer time than permitted." . . . A deportation hearing was held before an immigration judge on

January 11, 1974. Chadha conceded that he was deportable for overstaying his visa and the hearing was adjourned to enable him to file an application for suspension of deportation under § 244(a)(1) of the Act, Section 244(a)(1) provides: "[a] As hereinafter prescribed in this section, the Attorney General may, in his discretion, suspend deportation and adjust the status to that of an alien lawfully admitted for permanent residence, in the case of an alien who applies to the Attorney General for suspension of deportation and—(1) is deportable under any law of the United States except the provisions specified in paragraph (2) of this subsection; has been physically present in the United States for a continuous period of not less than seven years immediately preceding the date of such application, and proves that during all of such period he was and is a person of good moral character; and is a person whose deportation would, in the opinion of the Attorney General, result in extreme hardship to the alien or to his spouse, parent, or child, who is a citizen of the United States or an alien lawfully admitted for permanent residence."

After Chadha submitted his application for suspension of deportation, the deportation hearing was resumed on February 7, 1974. On the basis of evidence adduced at the hearing, affidavits submitted with the application, and the results of a character investigation conducted by the INS, the immigration judge, on June 25, 1974, ordered that Chadha's deportation be suspended. The immigration judge found that Chadha met the requirements of § 244(a)(1): he had resided continuously in the United States for over seven years, was of good moral character, and would suffer "extreme hardship" if deported. Pursuant to § 244(c)(1) of the Act, the immigration judge suspended Chadha's deportation and a report of the suspension was transmitted to Congress. Once the Attorney General's recommendation for suspension of Chadha's deportation was conveyed to Congress, Congress had the power under § 244(c)(2) of the Act to veto the Attorney General's determination that Chadha should not be deported.

The June 25, 1974, order of the immigration judge suspending Chadha's deportation remained outstanding as a valid order for a year and a half. For reasons not disclosed by the record, Congress did not exercise the veto authority reserved to it under § 244(c)(2) until the first session of the 94th Congress. This was the final session in which Congress, pursuant to § 244(c)(2), could act to veto the Attorney General's determination that Chadha should not be deported. The session ended on December 19, 1975. Absent Congressional action, Chadha's deportation proceedings would have been cancelled after this date and his status adjusted to that of a permanent resident alien.

On December 12, 1975, Representative Eilberg, Chairman of the Judiciary Subcommittee on Immigration, Citizenship, and International Law, introduced a resolution opposing "the granting of permanent residence in the United States to [six] aliens," including Chadha. The resolution was referred to the House Committee on the Judiciary. On December 16, 1975, the resolution was discharged from further consideration by the House Committee on the Judiciary and submitted to the House of Representatives for a vote. The resolution had not been printed and was not made available to other Members of the House prior to or at the time it was voted on. So far as the record before us shows, the House consideration of the resolution was based on Representative Eilberg's statement from the floor that "[i]t was the feeling of the committee, after reviewing 340 cases, that the aliens contained in the resolution [Chadha and five others] did not meet these statutory requirements, particularly as it relates to hardship; and it is the opinion of the committee that their deportation should not be suspended." The resolution was passed without debate or recorded vote. Since the House action was pursuant to § 244(c)(2), the resolution was not treated as an Article I legislative act; it was not submitted to the Senate or presented to the President for his action.

After the House veto of the Attorney General's decision to allow Chadha to remain in the United States, the immigration judge reopened the deportation proceedings to implement the House order deporting Chadha.

Chadha moved to terminate the proceedings on the ground that § 244(c)(2) is unconstitutional. The immigration judge held that he had no authority to rule on the constitutional validity of § 244(c)(2). On November 8, 1976, Chadha was ordered deported pursuant to the House action.

III

A

We turn now to the question whether action of one House of Congress under § 244(c)(2) violates strictures of the Constitution. We begin, of course, with the presumption that the challenged statute is valid. Justice White undertakes to make a case for the proposition that the one-House veto is a useful "political invention," and we need not challenge that assertion. We can even concede this utilitarian argument although the long range political wisdom of this "invention" is arguable. It has been vigorously debated and it is instructive to compare the views of the protagonists. . . . But policy arguments supporting even useful "political inventions" are subject to the demands of the Constitution which defines powers and, with respect to this subject, sets out just how those powers are to be exercised. Explicit and unambiguous provisions of the Constitution prescribe and define the respective functions of the Congress and of the Executive in the legislative process. Since the precise terms of those familiar provisions are critical to the resolution of this case, we set them out verbatim.

Art. I provides: "All legislative Powers herein granted shall be vested in a Congress of the United States, which shall consist of a Senate and a House of Representatives." Art. I, § 1. "Every Bill which shall have passed the House of Representatives and the Senate, shall, before it becomes a Law, be presented to the President of the United States." Art. I, § 7, cl. 2. "Every Order, Resolution, or Vote to which the Concurrence of the Senate and House of Representatives may be necessary (except on a question of Adjournment) shall be presented to the President of the United States; and before the Same shall take Effect, shall be approved by him, or being disapproved by him, shall be repassed by two thirds of the Senate and House of Representatives, according to the Rules and Limitations prescribed in the Case of a Bill." Art. I, § 7, cl. 3.

These provisions of Art. I are integral parts of the constitutional design for the separation of powers. We have recently noted that "[t]he principle of separation of powers was not simply an abstract generalization in the minds of the Framers: it was woven into the documents that they drafted in Philadelphia in the summer of 1787." Just as we relied on the textual provision of Art. II, § 2, cl. 2, to vindicate the principle of separation of powers in *Buckley,* we find that the purposes underlying the Presentment Clauses, and the bicameral requirement of Art. I, guide our resolution of the important question presented in this case. The very structure of the articles delegating and separating powers under Arts. I, II, and III exemplify the concept of separation of powers and we now turn to Art. I.

B

The Presentment Clauses

The records of the Constitutional Convention reveal that the requirement that all legislation be presented to the President before becoming law was uniformly accepted by the Framers. Presentment to the President and the Presidential veto were considered so imperative that the draftsmen took special pains to assure that these requirements could not be circumvented. The President's role in the lawmaking process also reflects the Framers' careful efforts to check whatever propensity a particular Congress might have to enact oppressive, improvident, or ill-considered measures.

C

Bicameralism

The bicameral requirement of Art. I, §§ 1, 7 was of scarcely less concern to the Framers than was the Presidential veto and indeed the two concepts are interdependent. By providing that no law could take effect without the concurrence of the prescribed majority of the Members of both Houses, the Framers reemphasized their belief, already remarked upon in connection with the Presentment Clauses, that legislation should not be enacted unless it has been carefully and fully considered by the Nation's elected officials.

Finally, we see that when the Framers intended to authorize either House of Congress to act alone and outside of its prescribed bicameral legislative role, they narrowly and precisely defined the procedure for such action. There are but four provisions in the Constitution, explicit and unambiguous, by which one House may act alone with the unreviewable force of law, not subject to the President's veto: (a) The House of Representatives alone was given the power to initiate impeachments. Art. I, § 2, cl. 6; (b) The Senate alone was given the power to conduct trials following impeachment on charges initiated by the House and to convict following trial. Art. I, § 3, cl. 5; (c) The Senate alone was given final unreviewable power to approve or to disapprove presidential appointments. Art. II, § 2, cl. 2; (d) The Senate alone was given unreviewable power to ratify treaties negotiated by the President. Art. II, § 2, cl. 2. Clearly, when the Draftsmen sought to confer special powers on one House, independent of the other House, or of the President, they did so in explicit, unambiguous terms. These carefully defined exceptions from presentment and bicameralism underscore the difference between the legislative functions of Congress and other unilateral but important and binding one-House acts provided for in the Constitution. These exceptions are narrow, explicit, and separately justified; none of them authorize the action challenged here. On the contrary, they provide further support for the conclusion that Congressional authority is not to be implied and for the conclusion that the veto provided for in § 244(c)(2) is not authorized by the constitutional design of the powers of the Legislative Branch.

Since it is clear that the action by the House under § 244(c)(2) was not within any of the express constitutional exceptions authorizing one House to act alone, and equally clear that it was an exercise of legislative power, that action was subject to the standards prescribed in Article I. The bicameral requirement, the Presentment Clauses, the President's veto, and Congress' power to override a veto were intended to erect enduring checks on each Branch and to protect the people from the improvident exercise of power by mandating certain prescribed steps. To preserve those checks, and maintain the separation of powers, the carefully defined limits on the power of each Branch must not be eroded. To accomplish what has been attempted by one House of Congress in this case requires action in conformity with the express procedures of the Constitution's prescription for legislative action: passage by a majority of both Houses and presentment to the President.

IV

We hold that the Congressional veto provision in § 244(c)(2) is severable from the Act and that it is unconstitutional. Accordingly, the judgment of the Court of Appeals is Affirmed.

Justice White, dissenting

Today the Court not only invalidates § 244(c)(2) of the Immigration and Nationality Act, but also sounds the death knell for nearly 200 other statutory provisions in which Congress has reserved a "legislative veto." For this reason, the Court's decision is of surpassing importance. And it is for this reason that the Court would have been well-advised to decide the case, if possible, on the narrower grounds of separation of powers, leaving for full consideration the constitutionality of other congressional review statutes operating on such varied matters as war powers and agency rulemaking, some of which concern the independent regulatory agencies. The prominence of the legislative veto mechanism in our contemporary political system and its importance to Congress can hardly be overstated. It has become a central means by which Congress secures the accountability of executive and independent agencies. Without the legislative veto, Congress is faced with a Hobson's choice: either to refrain from delegating the necessary authority, leaving itself with a hopeless task of writing laws with the requisite specificity to cover endless special circumstances across the entire policy landscape, or in the alternative, to abdicate its law-making function to the executive branch and independent agencies. To choose the former leaves major national problems unresolved; to opt for the latter risks unaccountable policy making by those not elected to fill that role. Accordingly, over the past five decades, the legislative veto has been placed in nearly 200 statutes. The device is known in every field of governmental concern: reorganization, budgets, foreign affairs, war powers, and regulation of trade, safety, energy, the environment, and the economy.

The wisdom and the constitutionality of these broad delegations are matters that still have not been put to rest. But for present purposes, these cases establish that by virtue of congressional delegation, legislative power can be exercised by independent agencies and Executive departments without the passage of new legislation. For some time, the sheer amount of law—the substantive rules that regulate private conduct and direct the operation of government—made by the agencies has far outnumbered the lawmaking engaged in by Congress through the traditional process. There is no question but that agency rulemaking is lawmaking in any functional or realistic sense of the term. The Administrative Procedure Act, provides that a "rule" is an agency statement "designed to implement, interpret, or prescribe law or policy." When agencies are authorized to prescribe law through substantive rulemaking, the administrator's regulation is not only due deference, but is accorded "legislative effect." These regulations bind courts and officers of the federal government, may pre-empt state law, and grant rights to and impose obligations on the public. In sum, they have the force

of law. If Congress may delegate lawmaking power to independent and executive agencies, it is most difficult to understand Article I as forbidding Congress from also reserving a check on legislative power for itself. Absent the veto, the agencies receiving delegations of legislative or quasi-legislative power may issue regulations having the force of law without bicameral approval and without the President's signature.

It is thus not apparent why the reservation of a veto over the exercise of that legislative power must be subject to a more exacting test. In both cases, it is enough that the initial statutory authorizations comply with the Article I requirements. I do not suggest that all legislative vetoes are necessarily consistent with separation of powers principles. A legislative check on an inherently executive function, for example that of initiating prosecutions, poses an entirely different question. But the legislative veto device here—and in many other settings—is far from an instance of legislative tyranny over the Executive. It is a necessary check on the unavoidably expanding power of the agencies, both executive and independent, as they engage in exercising authority delegated by Congress.

V

I regret that I am in disagreement with my colleagues on the fundamental questions that this case presents. But even more I regret the destructive scope of the Court's holding. It reflects a profoundly different conception of the Constitution than that held by the Courts which sanctioned the modern administrative state. Today's decision strikes down in one fell swoop provisions in more laws enacted by Congress than the Court has cumulatively invalidated in its history. I fear it will now be more difficult "to insure that the fundamental policy decisions in our society will be made not by an appointed official but by the body immediately responsible to the people." I must dissent.

Food and Drug Administration v. Brown and Williamson Corp.
529 U.S. 120 (2000)

Justice O'Connor delivered the opinion of the Court, in which Chief Justice Rehnquist and Justices Scalia, Kennedy, and Thomas joined. Justice Breyer filed a dissenting opinion, in which Justices Stevens, Souter, and Ginsburg joined.

I

The Food, Drug, and Cosmetic Act (FDCA) grants the FDA, as the designee of the Secretary of Health and Human Services, the authority to regulate, among other items, "drugs" and "devices." See 21 U.S.C. §§ 321(g)-(h). The Act defines "drug" to include "articles (other than food) intended to affect the structure or any function of the body." It defines "device," in part, as "an instrument, apparatus, implement, machine, contrivance, . . . or other similar or related article, including any component, part, or accessory, which is . . .. intended to affect the structure or any function of the body." The Act also grants the FDA the authority to regulate so-called "combination products," which "constitute a combination of a drug, device, or biologic product." The FDA has construed this provision as giving it the discretion to regulate combination products as drugs, as devices, or as both. See 61 Fed. Reg. 44400 (1996).

On August 11, 1995, the FDA published a proposed rule concerning the sale of cigarettes and smokeless tobacco to children and adolescents. 60 Fed. Reg. 41314-41787. The rule, which included several restrictions on the sale, distribution, and advertisement of tobacco products, was designed to reduce the availability and attractiveness of tobacco products to young people. A public comment period followed, during which the FDA received over 700,000 submissions, more than "at any other time in its history on any other subject." 61 Fed. Reg. 44418 (1996).

On August 28, 1996, the FDA issued a final rule entitled "Regulations Restricting the Sale and Distribution of Cigarettes and Smokeless Tobacco to Protect Children and Adolescents." The FDA determined that nicotine is a "drug" and that cigarettes and smokeless tobacco are "drug delivery devices," and therefore it had jurisdiction under the FDCA to regulate tobacco products as customarily marketed—that is, without manufacturer claims of therapeutic benefit. First, the FDA found that tobacco products "'affect the structure or any function of the body'" because nicotine "has significant pharmacological effects." Specifically, nicotine "exerts psychoactive, or mood-altering, effects on the brain" that cause and sustain addiction, have both tranquilizing and stimulating effects, and control weight. Second, the FDA determined that these effects were "intended" under the FDCA because they "are so widely known and foreseeable that [they] may be deemed to have been intended by the manufacturers"; consumers use tobacco products "predominantly or nearly exclusively" to obtain these effects, and the statements, research, and actions of manufacturers revealed that they "have 'designed' cigarettes to provide pharmacologically active doses of nicotine to consumers." Finally, the agency concluded that cigarettes and smokeless tobacco are "combination products" because, in addition to containing nicotine, they include device components that deliver a controlled amount of nicotine to the body. Having resolved the jurisdictional question, the FDA next explained the policy justifications for its regulations, detailing the deleterious health effects associated with tobacco use. It found that tobacco consumption was "the single leading cause of preventable death in the United States." According to the FDA, "more than 400,000 people die each year from tobacco-related illnesses, such as cancer, respiratory illnesses, and heart disease." The agency also determined that the only way to reduce the amount of tobacco-related illness and mortality was to reduce the level of addiction, a goal that could be accomplished only by preventing children and adolescents from starting to use tobacco. The FDA found that 82% of adult smokers had their first cigarette before the age of 18, and more than half had already become regular smokers by that age. It also found that children were beginning to smoke at a younger age, that the prevalence of youth smoking had recently increased, and that similar problems existed with respect to smokeless tobacco. The FDA accordingly concluded that if "the number of children and adolescents who begin tobacco use can be substantially diminished, tobacco-related illness can be correspondingly reduced because data suggest that anyone who does not begin smoking in childhood or adolescence is unlikely ever to begin."

Based on these findings, the FDA promulgated regulations concerning tobacco products' promotion, labeling, and accessibility to children and adolescents. The access regulations prohibit the sale of cigarettes or smokeless tobacco to persons younger than 18; require retailers to verify through photo identification the age of all purchasers younger than 27; prohibit the sale of cigarettes in quantities smaller than 20; prohibit the distribution of free samples; and prohibit sales through self-service displays and vending machines except in adult-only locations. The promotion regulations require that any print advertising appear in a black-and-white, text-only format unless the publication in which it appears is read almost exclusively by adults; prohibit outdoor advertising within 1,000 feet of any public playground or school; prohibit the distribution of any promotional items, such as T-shirts or hats, bearing the manufacturer's brand name; and prohibit a manufacturer from sponsoring any athletic, musical, artistic, or other social or cultural event using its brand name. The labeling regulation requires that the statement, "A Nicotine-Delivery Device for Persons 18 or Older," appear on all tobacco product packages.

The FDA promulgated these regulations pursuant to its authority to regulate "restricted devices." The FDA construed giving it the discretion to regulate "combination products" using the Act's drug authorities, device authorities, or both, depending on "how the public health goals of the act can be best accomplished." Given the greater flexibility in the FDCA for the regulation of devices, the FDA determined that "the device authorities provide the most appropriate basis for regulating cigarettes and smokeless tobacco." The agency may "require that a device be restricted to sale, distribution, or use . . . upon such other conditions as [the FDA] may prescribe in such regulation, if, because of its potentiality for harmful effect or the collateral measures necessary to its use, [the FDA] determines that there cannot otherwise be reasonable assurance of its safety and effectiveness." The FDA reasoned that its regulations fell within the authority granted . . . because they related to the sale or distribution of tobacco products and were necessary for providing a reasonable assurance of safety. Respondents, a group of tobacco manufacturers, retailers, and advertisers, filed suit in United States District Court for the Middle District of North Carolina challenging the regulations. . . .

II

The FDA's assertion of jurisdiction to regulate tobacco products is founded on its conclusions that nicotine is a "drug" and that cigarettes and smokeless tobacco are "drug delivery devices." Again, the FDA found that tobacco products are "intended" to deliver the pharmacological effects of satisfying addiction, stimulation and tranquilization, and weight control because those effects are foreseeable to any reasonable manufacturer, consumers use tobacco products to obtain those effects, and tobacco manufacturers have designed their products to produce those effects. As an initial matter, respondents take issue with the FDA's reading of "intended," arguing that it is a term of art that refers exclusively to claims made by the manufacturer or vendor about the product. See Brief for Respondent Brown & Williamson Tobacco Corp. That is, a product is not a drug or device under the FDCA unless the manufacturer or vendor makes some express claim concerning the product's therapeutic benefits. We need not resolve this question, however, because assuming, *arguendo,* that a product can be "intended to affect the structure or any function of the body" absent claims of therapeutic or medical benefit, the FDA's claim to jurisdiction contravenes the clear intent of Congress.

A threshold issue is the appropriate framework for analyzing the FDA's assertion of authority to regulate tobacco products. Because this case involves an administrative agency's construction of a statute that it administers, our analysis is governed by *Chevron U.S.A. Inc. v. Natural Resources Defense Council, Inc.,* 467 U.S. 837 (1984). Under *Chevron,* a reviewing court must first ask "whether Congress has directly spoken to the precise question at issue." If Congress has done so, the inquiry is at an end; the court "must give effect to the unambiguously expressed intent of Congress." But if Congress has not specifically addressed the question, a reviewing court must respect the agency's construction of the statute so long as it is permissible. Such deference is justified because "the responsibilities for assessing the wisdom of such policy choices and resolving the struggle between competing views of the public interest are not judicial ones," Chevron, *supra,* at 866, and because of the agency's greater familiarity with the ever-changing facts and circumstances surrounding the subjects regulated, see *Rust v. Sullivan,* 500 U.S. 173 (1991).

In determining whether Congress has specifically addressed the question at issue, a reviewing court should not confine itself to examining a particular statutory provision in isolation. The meaning—or ambiguity—of certain words or phrases may only become evident when placed in context. See *Brown v. Gardner,* 513 U.S. 115,118 (1994).

("Ambiguity is a creature not of definitional possibilities but of statutory context"). It is a "fundamental canon of statutory construction that the words of a statute must be read in their context and with a view to their place in the overall statutory scheme." A court must therefore interpret the statute "as a symmetrical and coherent regulatory scheme," *Gustafson v. Alloyd Co.,* 513 U.S. 561, 569 (1995) and "fit, if possible, all parts into an harmonious whole."

Similarly, the meaning of one statute may be affected by other Acts, particularly where Congress has spoken subsequently and more specifically to the topic at hand. In addition, we must be guided to a degree by common sense as to the manner in which Congress is likely to delegate a policy decision of such economic and political magnitude to an administrative agency. With these principles in mind, we find that Congress has directly spoken to the issue here and precluded the FDA's jurisdiction to regulate tobacco products.

A

Viewing the FDCA as a whole, it is evident that one of the Act's core objectives is to ensure that any product regulated by the FDA is "safe" and "effective" for its intended use. . . . This essential purpose pervades the FDCA. . . . The FDCA requires premarket approval of any new drug, with some limited exceptions, and states that the FDA "shall issue an order refusing to approve the application" of a new drug if it is not safe and effective for its intended purpose. If the FDA discovers after approval that a drug is unsafe or ineffective, it "shall, after due notice and opportunity for hearing to the applicant, withdraw approval" of the drug. The Act also requires the FDA to classify all devices into one of three categories. Regardless of which category the FDA chooses, there must be a "reasonable assurance of the safety and effectiveness of the device." Even the "restricted device" provision pursuant to which the FDA promulgated the regulations at issue here authorizes the agency to place conditions on the sale or distribution of a device specifically when "there cannot otherwise be reasonable assurance of its safety and effectiveness." Thus, the Act generally requires the FDA to prevent the marketing of any drug or device where the "potential for inflicting death or physical injury is not offset by the possibility of therapeutic benefit."

In its rule making proceeding, the FDA quite exhaustively documented that "tobacco products are unsafe," "dangerous," and "cause great pain and suffering from illness." 61 Fed. Reg. 44412 (1996). It found that the consumption of tobacco products "presents extraordinary health risks" and that "tobacco use is the single leading cause of preventable death in the United States." Id., at 44398. It stated that "more than 400,000 people die each year from tobacco-related illnesses, such as cancer, respiratory illnesses, and heart disease, often suffering long and painful deaths" and that "tobacco alone kills more people each year in the United States than acquired immunodeficiency syndrome (AIDS), car accidents, alcohol, homicides, illegal drugs, suicides, and fires, combined." Indeed, the FDA characterized smoking as "a pediatric disease," because "one out of every three young people who become regular smokers . . . will die prematurely as a result."

These findings logically imply that, if tobacco products were "devices" under the FDCA, the FDA would be required to remove them from the market. Consider, first, the FDCA's provisions concerning the misbranding of drugs or devices. The Act prohibits "the introduction or delivery for introduction into interstate commerce of any food, drug, device, or cosmetic that is adultered or misbranded." In light of the FDA's findings, two distinct FDCA provisions would render cigarettes and smokeless tobacco misbranded devices. First, § 352(j) deems a drug or device misbranded "if it is dangerous to health when used in the dosage or manner, or with the frequency or duration prescribed, recommended, or suggested in the labeling thereof." The FDA's findings make clear that tobacco products are "dangerous to health" when used in the manner prescribed. Second, a drug or device is misbranded under the Act "unless its labeling bears . . . adequate directions for use . . . in such manner and form, as are necessary for the protection of users," except where such directions are "not necessary for the protection of the public health." § 352(f)(1). Given the FDA's conclusions concerning the health consequences of tobacco use, there are no directions that could adequately protect consumers. That is, there are no directions that could make tobacco products safe for obtaining their intended effects. Thus, were tobacco products within the FDA's jurisdiction, the Act would deem them misbranded devices

that could not be introduced into interstate commerce. Contrary to the dissent's contention, the Act admits no remedial discretion once it is evident that the device is misbranded.

Second, the FDCA requires the FDA to place all devices that it regulates into one of three classifications. The agency relies on a device's classification in determining the degree of control and regulation necessary to ensure that there is "a reasonable assurance of safety and effectiveness." 61 Fed. Reg. 44412 (1996). The FDA has yet to classify tobacco products. Instead, the regulations at issue here represent so-called "general controls," which the Act entitles the agency to impose in advance of classification. Although the FDCA prescribes no deadline for device classification, the FDA has stated that it will classify tobacco products "in a future rulemaking" as required by the Act. Given the FDA's findings regarding the health consequences of tobacco use, the agency would have to place cigarettes and smokeless tobacco in Class III because, even after the application of the Act's available controls, they would "present a potential unreasonable risk of illness or injury." 21 U.S.C. § 360c(a)(1)(C). As Class III devices, tobacco products would be subject to the FDCA's premarket approval process. Under these provisions, the FDA would be prohibited from approving an application for premarket approval without "a showing of reasonable assurance that such device is safe under the conditions of use prescribed, recommended, or suggested on the labeling thereof." In view of the FDA's conclusions regarding the health effects of tobacco use, the agency would have no basis for finding any such reasonable assurance of safety. Thus, once the FDA fulfilled its statutory obligation to classify tobacco products, it could not allow them to be marketed. . . .

Congress, however, has foreclosed the removal of tobacco products from the market. A provision of the United States Code currently in force states that "the marketing of tobacco constitutes one of the greatest basic industries of the United States with ramifying activities which directly affect interstate and foreign commerce at every point, and stable conditions therein are necessary to the general welfare."

More importantly, Congress has directly addressed the problem of tobacco and health through legislation on six occasions since 1965. See Federal Cigarette Labeling and Advertising Act (FCLAA). . . . When Congress enacted these statutes, the adverse health consequences of tobacco use were well known, as were nicotine's pharmacological effects. . . . Nonetheless, Congress stopped well short of ordering a ban.

Instead, it has generally regulated the labeling and advertisement of tobacco products, expressly providing that it is the policy of Congress that "commerce and the national economy may be . . . protected to the maximum extent consistent with" consumers "being adequately informed about any adverse health effects." Congress' decisions to regulate labeling and advertising and to adopt the express policy of protecting "commerce and the national economy . . . to the maximum extent" reveal its intent that tobacco products remain on the market. Indeed, the collective premise of these statutes is that cigarettes and smokeless tobacco will continue to be sold in the United States. A ban of tobacco products by the FDA would therefore plainly contradict congressional policy.

The FDA apparently recognized this dilemma and concluded, somewhat ironically, that tobacco products are actually "safe" within the meaning of the FDCA. In promulgating its regulations, the agency conceded that "tobacco products are unsafe, as that term is conventionally understood." 61 Fed. Reg. 44412 (1996). Nonetheless, the FDA reasoned that, in determining whether a device is safe under the Act, it must consider "not only the risks presented by a product but also any of the countervailing effects of use of that product, including the consequences of not permitting the product to be marketed."

Applying this standard, the FDA found that, because of the high level of addiction among tobacco users, a ban would likely be "dangerous." In particular, current tobacco users could suffer from extreme withdrawal, the health care system and available pharmaceuticals might not be able to meet the treatment demands of those suffering from withdrawal, and a black

market offering cigarettes even more dangerous than those currently sold legally would likely develop. Ibid. The FDA therefore concluded that "while taking cigarettes and smokeless tobacco off the market could prevent some people from becoming addicted and reduce death and disease for others, the record does not establish that such a ban is the appropriate public health response under the act."

It may well be, as the FDA asserts, that "these factors must be considered when developing a regulatory scheme that achieves the best public health result for these products." But the FDA's judgment that leaving tobacco products on the market "is more effective in achieving public health goals than a ban," ibid., is no substitute for the specific safety determinations required by the FDCA's various operative provisions. Several provisions in the Act require the FDA to determine that the product itself is safe as used by consumers. That is, the product's probable therapeutic benefits must outweigh its risk of harm. See United States v. Rutherford, 442 U.S. at 555 ("The Commissioner generally considers a drug safe when the expected therapeutic gain justifies the risk entailed by its use"). . . .

Considering the FDCA as a whole, it is clear that Congress intended to exclude tobacco products from the FDA's jurisdiction. A fundamental precept of the FDCA is that any product regulated by the FDA—but not banned—must be safe for its intended use. Various provisions of the Act make clear that this refers to the safety of using the product to obtain its intended effects, not the public health ramifications of alternative administrative actions by the FDA. That is, the FDA must determine that there is a reasonable assurance that the product's therapeutic benefits outweigh the risk of harm to the consumer. According to this standard, the FDA has concluded that, although tobacco products might be effective in delivering certain pharmacological effects, they are "unsafe" and "dangerous" when used for these purposes. Consequently, if tobacco products were within the FDA's jurisdiction, the Act would require the FDA to remove them from the market entirely. But a ban would contradict Congress' clear intent as expressed in its more recent, tobacco-specific legislation. The inescapable conclusion is that there is no room for tobacco products within the FDCA's regulatory scheme. If they cannot be used safely for any therapeutic purpose, and yet they cannot be banned, they simply do not fit. . . .

Taken together, these actions by Congress over the past 35 years preclude an interpretation of the FDCA that grants the FDA jurisdiction to regulate tobacco products. We do not rely on Congress' failure to act—its consideration and rejection of bills that would have given the FDA this authority—in reaching this conclusion. Indeed, this is not a case of simple inaction by Congress that purportedly represents its acquiescence in an agency's position. To the contrary, Congress has enacted several statutes addressing the particular subject of tobacco and health, creating a distinct regulatory scheme for cigarettes and smokeless tobacco. In doing so, Congress has been aware of tobacco's health hazards and its pharmacological effects. It has also enacted this legislation against the background of the FDA repeatedly and consistently asserting that it lacks jurisdiction under the FDCA to regulate tobacco products as customarily marketed. Further, Congress has persistently acted to preclude a meaningful role for any administrative agency in making policy on the subject of tobacco and health. Moreover, the substance of Congress' regulatory scheme is, in an important respect, incompatible with FDA jurisdiction. Although the supervision of product labeling to protect consumer health is a substantial component of the FDA's regulation of drugs and devices, see 21 U.S.C. § 352 (1994 ed. and Supp. III), the FCLAA and the CSTHEA explicitly prohibit any federal agency from imposing any health-related labeling requirements on cigarettes or smokeless tobacco products.

Under these circumstances, it is clear that Congress' tobacco-specific legislation has effectively ratified the FDA's previous position that it lacks jurisdiction to regulate tobacco. As in *Bob Jones Univ. v. United States*, 461 U.S. 574 (1983), "it is hardly conceivable that Congress—and in this setting, any Member of Congress—was not abundantly aware of what was going on."

Congress has affirmatively acted to address the issue of tobacco and health, relying on the representations of the FDA that it had no authority to regulate tobacco. It has created a distinct scheme to regulate the sale of tobacco products, focused on labeling and advertising, and premised on the belief that the FDA lacks such jurisdiction under the FDCA. As a result, Congress' tobacco-specific statutes preclude the FDA from regulating tobacco products as customarily marketed. . . .

Finally, our inquiry into whether Congress has directly spoken to the precise question at issue is shaped, at least in some measure, by the nature of the question presented. Deference under *Chevron* to an agency's construction of a statute that it administers is premised on the theory that a statute's ambiguity constitutes an implicit delegation from Congress to the agency to fill in the statutory gaps. See *Chevron*, 467 U.S. at 844. In extraordinary cases, however, there may be reason to hesitate before concluding that Congress has intended such an implicit delegation. Cf. Breyer, Judicial Review of Questions of Law and Policy, 38 *Admin. L. Rev.* 363, 370 (1986) ("A court may also ask whether the legal question is an important one. Congress is more likely to have focused upon, and answered, major questions, while leaving interstitial matters to answer themselves in the course of the statute's daily administration").

This is hardly an ordinary case. Contrary to its representations to Congress since 1914, the FDA has now asserted jurisdiction to regulate an industry constituting a significant portion of the American economy. In fact, the FDA contends that, were it to determine that tobacco products provide no "reasonable assurance of safety," it would have the authority to ban cigarettes and smokeless tobacco entirely. Owing to its unique place in American history and society, tobacco has its own unique political history. Congress, for better or for worse, has created a distinct regulatory scheme for tobacco products, squarely rejected proposals to give the FDA jurisdiction over tobacco, and repeatedly acted to preclude any agency from exercising significant policymaking authority in the area. Given this history and the breadth of the authority that the FDA has asserted, we are obliged to defer not to the agency's expansive construction of the statute, but to Congress' consistent judgment to deny the FDA this power. . . . we are confident that Congress could not have intended to delegate a decision of such economic and political significance to an agency in so cryptic a fashion. To find that the FDA has the authority to regulate tobacco products, one must not only adopt an extremely strained understanding of "safety" as it is used throughout the Act—a concept central to the FDCA's regulatory scheme—but also ignore the plain implication of Congress' subsequent tobacco-specific legislation. It is therefore clear, based on the FDCA's overall regulatory scheme and the subsequent tobacco legislation, that Congress has directly spoken to the question at issue and precluded the FDA from regulating tobacco products.

. . . For these reasons, the judgment of the Court of Appeals for the Fourth Circuit is affirmed.

It is so ordered.

Christine Todd Whitman, Administrator of Environmental Protection Agency, et al. v. American Trucking Associations, Inc., et al.
531 U.S. 457 (2001)

Justice Scalia delivered the opinion of the Court. There were four issues, and some were unanimous, but Justices Thomas, Breyer, and Stevens filed concurring opinions. Justice Souter joined the concurring opinion of Justice Stevens.

These cases present the following questions: (1) Whether § 109(b)(1) of the Clean Air Act (CAA) delegates legislative power to the Administrator of the Environmental Protection Agency (EPA). (2) Whether the Administrator may consider the costs of implementation in setting national ambient air quality standards (NAAQS) under § 109(b)(1). (3) Whether the Court of Appeals had jurisdiction to review the EPA's interpretation of Part D of Title I of the CAA, 42 U.S.C. §§ 7501-7515, with respect to implementing the revised ozone NAAQS. (4) If so, whether the EPA's interpretation of that part was permissible.

I

Section 109(a) of the CAA, 42 U.S.C. § 7409(a) requires the Administrator of the EPA to promulgate NAAQS for each air pollutant for which "air quality criteria" have been issued under § 108, 42 U.S.C. § 7408. Once a NAAQS has been promulgated, the Administrator must review the standard (and the criteria on which it is based) "at five-year intervals" and make "such revisions . . . as may be appropriate." These cases arose when, on July 18, 1997, the Administrator revised the NAAQS for particulate matter (PM) and ozone. American Trucking Associations, Inc., and its co-respondents in No. 99-1257 which include, in addition to other private companies, the States of Michigan, Ohio, and West Virginia, challenged the new standards in the Court of Appeals for the District of Columbia Circuit.

The District of Columbia Circuit accepted some of the challenges and rejected others. It agreed with the respondents that § 109(b)(1) delegated legislative power to the Administrator in contravention of the United States Constitution, Art. I, § 1, because it found that the EPA had interpreted the statute to provide no "intelligible principle" to guide the agency's exercise of authority. *American Trucking Assns., Inc. v. EPA,* 175 F.3d 1027, 1034 (1999). The court thought, however, that the EPA could perhaps avoid the unconstitutional delegation by adopting a restrictive construction of § 109(b)(1), so instead of declaring the section unconstitutional the court remanded the NAAQS to the agency. On the second issue that the Court of Appeals addressed, it unanimously rejected respondents' argument that the court should depart from the rule of *Lead Industries Assn., Inc. v. EPA*, 647 F.2d 1130, 1148 (CADC 1980), that the EPA may not consider the cost of implementing a NAAQS in setting the initial standard. . . .

II

In *Lead Industries Assn., Inc. v. EPA, supra,* at 1148, the District of Columbia Circuit held that "economic considerations [may] play no part in the promulgation of ambient air quality standards under Section 109" of the CAA. In the present cases, the court adhered to that holding as it had done on many other occasions. . . . Respondents argue that these decisions are incorrect. We disagree; and since the first step in assessing whether a statute delegates legislative power is to determine what authority the statute confers, we address that issue of interpretation first and reach respondents' constitutional arguments in Part III, infra.

Section 109(b)(1) instructs the EPA to set primary ambient air quality standards "the attainment and maintenance of which . . . are requisite to protect the public health" with "an adequate margin of safety." Were it not for the hundreds of pages of briefing respondents have submitted on the issue, one would have thought it fairly clear that this text does not permit the EPA to consider costs in setting the standards. The language, as one scholar has noted, "is absolute." D. Currie, "Air Pollution: Federal Law and Analysis" 4-15 (1981). The EPA, "based on" the information about health effects contained in the technical "criteria" documents compiled under § 108(a)(2), is to identify the maximum airborne concentration of a pollutant that the public health can tolerate, decrease the concentration to provide an "adequate" margin of safety, and set the standard at that level. Nowhere are the costs of achieving such a standard made part of that initial calculation.

Against this most natural of readings, respondents make a lengthy, spirited, but ultimately unsuccessful attack. They begin with the object of § 109(b)(1)'s focus, the "public health." When the term first appeared in federal clean air legislation—in the Act of July 14,

1955 (1955 Act), which expressed "recognition of the dangers to the public health" from air pollution—its ordinary meaning was "the health of the community." *Webster's New International Dictionary* 2005 (2d ed. 1950). Respondents argue, however, that § 109(b)(1), as added by the Clean Air Amendments of 1970 (1970 Act), meant to use the term's secondary meaning: "the ways and means of conserving the health of the members of a community, as by preventive medicine, organized care of the sick, etc." Ibid. Words that can have more than one meaning are given content, however, by their surroundings, *FDA v. Brown & Williamson Tobacco Corp.*, 529 U.S. 120, 132-133, and in the context of § 109(b)(1) this second definition makes no sense. Congress could not have meant to instruct the Administrator to set NAAQS at a level "requisite to protect" "the art and science dealing with the protection and improvement of community health." *Webster's Third New International Dictionary* 1836 (1981). We therefore revert to the primary definition of the term: the health of the public.

Even so, respondents argue, many more factors than air pollution affect public health. In particular, the economic cost of implementing a very stringent standard might produce health losses sufficient to offset the health gains achieved in cleaning the air—for example, by closing down whole industries and thereby impoverishing the workers and consumers dependent upon those industries. That is unquestionably true, and Congress was unquestionably aware of it. Thus, Congress had commissioned in the Air Quality Act of 1967 (1967 Act) "a detailed estimate of the cost of carrying out the provisions of this Act; a comprehensive study of the cost of program implementation by affected units of government; and a comprehensive study of the economic impact of air quality standards on the Nation's industries, communities, and other contributing sources of pollution." The 1970 Congress, armed with the results of this study, not only anticipated that compliance costs could injure the public health, but provided for that precise exigency. Section 110(f)(1) of the CAA permitted the Administrator to waive the compliance deadline for stationary sources if, inter alia, sufficient control measures were simply unavailable and "the continued operation of such sources is essential . . . to the public health or welfare." Other provisions explicitly permitted or required economic costs to be taken into account in implementing the air quality standards. Section 111(b)(1)(B), for example, commanded the Administrator to set "standards of performance" for certain new sources of emissions that as specified in § 111(a)(1) were to "reflect the degree of emission limitation achievable through the application of the best system of emission reduction which (taking into account the cost of achieving such reduction) the Administrator determines has been adequately demonstrated." Section 202(a)(2) prescribed that emissions standards for automobiles could take effect only "after such period as the Administrator finds necessary to permit the development and application of the requisite technology, giving appropriate consideration to the cost of compliance within such period." . . . Subsequent amendments to the CAA have added many more provisions directing, in explicit language, that the Administrator consider costs in performing various duties. See, e.g., 42 U.S.C. § 7545(k)(1) (reformulate gasoline to "require the greatest reduction in emissions . . . taking into consideration the cost of achieving such emissions reductions") . . .

Accordingly, to prevail in their present challenge, respondents must show a textual commitment of authority to the EPA to consider costs in setting NAAQS under § 109(b)(1). And because § 109(b)(1) and the NAAQS for which it provides are the engine that drives nearly all of Title I of the CAA, that textual commitment must be a clear one. Congress, we have held, does not alter the fundamental details of a regulatory scheme in vague terms or ancillary provisions— it does not, one might say, hide elephants in mouseholes. . . . Respondents' textual arguments ultimately founder upon this principle.

Their first claim is that § 109(b)(1)'s terms "adequate margin" and "requisite" leave room to pad health effects with cost concerns. Just as we found it "highly unlikely that Congress would leave the determination of whether an industry will be entirely, or even substantially, rate-regulated to agency discretion—and even

more unlikely that it would achieve that through such a subtle device as permission to 'modify' rate-filing requirements," so also we find it implausible that Congress would give to the EPA through these modest words the power to determine whether implementation costs should moderate national air quality standards.

The same defect inheres in respondents' next two arguments: that while the Administrator's judgment about what is requisite to protect the public health must be "based on [the] criteria" documents developed under § 108(a)(2), it need not be based solely on those criteria; and that those criteria themselves, while they must include "effects on public health or welfare which may be expected from the presence of such pollutant in the ambient air," are not necessarily limited to those effects. Even if we were to concede those premises, we still would not conclude that one of the unenumerated factors that the agency can consider in developing and applying the criteria is cost of implementation. That factor is both so indirectly related to public health and so full of potential for canceling the conclusions drawn from direct health effects that it would surely have been expressly mentioned in §§ 108 and 109 had Congress meant it to be considered. Yet while those provisions describe in detail how the health effects of pollutants in the ambient air are to be calculated and given effect, they say not a word about costs.

Respondents point, finally, to a number of provisions in the CAA that do require attainment cost data to be generated. Section 108(b)(1), for example, instructs the Administrator to "issue to the States," simultaneously with the criteria documents, "information on air pollution control techniques, which information shall include data relating to the cost of installation and operation." 42 U.S.C. § 7408 (b)(l). And § 109 (d)(2)(C)(iv) requires the Clean Air Scientific Advisory Committee to "advise the Administrator of any adverse public health, welfare, social, economic, or energy effects which may result from various strategies for attainment and maintenance."

Respondents argue that these provisions make no sense unless costs are to be considered in setting the NAAQS. That is not so. These provisions enable the Administrator to assist the

States in carrying out their statutory role as primary implementers of the NAAQS. It is to the States that the Act assigns initial and primary responsibility for deciding what emissions reductions will be required from which sources. It would be impossible to perform that task intelligently without considering which abatement technologies are most efficient, and most economically feasible—which is why we have said that "the most important forum for consideration of claims of economic and technological infeasibility is before the state agency formulating the implementation plan." Thus, federal clean air legislation has, from the very beginning, directed federal agencies to develop and transmit implementation data, including cost data, to the States. That Congress chose to carry forward this research program to assist States in choosing the means through which they would implement the standards is perfectly sensible, and has no bearing upon whether cost considerations are to be taken into account in formulating the standards.

It should be clear from what we have said that the canon requiring texts to be so construed as to avoid serious constitutional problems has no application here. No matter how severe the constitutional doubt, courts may choose only between reasonably available interpretations of a text. The text of § 109(b), interpreted in its statutory and historical context and with appreciation for its importance to the CAA as a whole, unambiguously bars cost considerations from the NAAQS-setting process, and thus ends the matter for us as well as the EPA. We therefore affirm the judgment of the Court of Appeals on this point.

III

Section 109(b)(1) of the CAA instructs the EPA to set "ambient air quality standards the attainment and maintenance of which in the judgment of the Administrator, based on [the] criteria [documents of § 108] and allowing an adequate margin of safety, are requisite to protect the public health." 42 U.S.C. § 7409(b)(1). The Court of Appeals held that this section as interpreted by the Administrator did not provide an "intelligible principle" to guide the EPA's exercise of authority in setting NAAQS. "[The] EPA," it said, "lacked any determinate criteria for drawing lines. It has failed to state intelligibly how much is too much." The court hence found that the EPA's interpretation (but not the statute itself) violated the nondelegation doctrine. We disagree.

In a delegation challenge, the constitutional question is whether the statute has delegated legislative power to the agency. Article I, § 1, of the Constitution vests "all legislative Powers herein granted . . . in a Congress of the United States." This text permits no delegation of those powers, and so we repeatedly have said that when Congress confers decision making authority upon agencies Congress must "lay down by legislative act an intelligible principle to which the person or body authorized to [act] is directed to conform." *J. W. Hampton, Jr., & Co. v. United States,* 276 U.S. 394, 409 (1928). We have never suggested that an agency can cure an unlawful delegation of legislative power by adopting in its discretion a limiting construction of the statute. . . . The idea that an agency can cure an unconstitutionally standardless delegation of power by declining to exercise some of that power seems to us internally contradictory. The very choice of which portion of the power to exercise—that is to say, the prescription of the standard that Congress had omitted—would itself be an exercise of the forbidden legislative authority. Whether the statute delegates legislative power is a question for the courts, and an agency's voluntary self-denial has no bearing upon the answer.

We agree with the Solicitor General that the text of § 109 (b)(1) of the CAA at a minimum requires that "for a discrete set of pollutants and based on published air quality criteria that reflect the latest scientific knowledge, [the] EPA must establish uniform national standards at a level that is requisite to protect public health from the adverse effects of the pollutant in the ambient air." Requisite, in turn, "means sufficient, but not more than necessary." These limits on the EPA's discretion are strikingly similar to the ones we approved in *Touby v. United States,* 500 U.S. 160 (1991), which permitted the Attorney General to designate a drug as a controlled substance for purposes of criminal drug enforcement if doing so was "'necessary to avoid an imminent hazard to the public safety.'" They also resemble the Occupational Safety and Health Act provision requiring the agency to "'set the standard which most adequately assures, to the extent feasible, on the basis of the best available evidence, that no employee will suffer any impairment of health'"—which the Court upheld in *Industrial Union Dept., AFL-CIO v. American Petroleum Institute,* 448 U.S. 607, 646 (1980) and which even then Justice Rehnquist, who alone in that case thought the statute violated the nondelegation doctrine (opinion concurring in judgment), would have upheld if, like the statute here, it did not permit economic costs to be considered.

The scope of discretion § 109(b)(1) allows is in fact well within the outer limits of our nondelegation precedents. In the history of the Court we have found the requisite "intelligible principle" lacking in only two statutes, one of which provided literally no guidance for the exercise of discretion, and the other of which conferred authority to regulate the entire economy on the basis of no more precise a standard than stimulating the economy by assuring "fair competition." See *Panama Refining Co. v. Ryan,* 293 U.S. 388 (1935); *A. L. A. Schechter Poultry Corp. v. United States,* 295 U.S. 495 (1935). We have, on the other hand, upheld the validity of § 11(b)(2) of the Public Utility Holding Company Act of 1935, which gave the Securities and Exchange Commission authority to modify the structure of holding company systems so as to ensure that they are not "unduly or unnecessarily complicated" and do not "unfairly or inequitably distribute voting power among security holders." *American Power & Light Co. v. SEC,* 329 U.S. 90, 104 (1946). We have approved the wartime conferral of agency power to fix the prices of commodities at a level that "'will be generally fair and equitable and will effectuate the [in some respects conflicting] purposes of the Act.'" *Yakus v. United States,* 321 U.S. 414, 420, 423-426 (1944). And we have found an "intelligible principle" in various statutes authorizing regulation in the "public interest." See, e.g., *National Broadcasting Co. v. United States,* 319 U.S. 190, 225-226 (1943). . . . In short,

we have "almost never felt qualified to second-guess Congress regarding the permissible degree of policy judgment that can be left to those executing or applying the law."

It is true enough that the degree of agency discretion that is acceptable varies according to the scope of the power congressionally conferred. . . . While Congress need not provide any direction to the EPA regarding the manner in which it is to define "country elevators," which are to be exempt from new-stationary-source regulations governing grain elevators, it must provide substantial guidance on setting air standards that affect the entire national economy. But even in sweeping regulatory schemes we have never demanded, as the Court of Appeals did here, that statutes provide a "determinate criterion" for saying "how much [of the regulated harm] is too much."

In *Touby,* for example, we did not require the statute to decree how "imminent" was too imminent, or how "necessary" was necessary enough, or even—most relevant here—how "hazardous" was too hazardous. Similarly, the statute at issue in *Lichter* authorized agencies to recoup "excess profits" paid under wartime Government contracts, yet we did not insist that Congress specify how much profit was too much. 334 U.S. at 783-786. It is therefore not conclusive for delegation purposes that, as respondents argue, ozone and particulate matter are "nonthreshold" pollutants that inflict a continuum of adverse health effects at any airborne concentration greater than zero, and hence require the EPA to make judgments of degree. "[A] certain degree of discretion, and thus of lawmaking, inheres in most executive or judicial action."

Section 109(b)(1) of the CAA, which to repeat we interpret as requiring the EPA to set air quality standards at the level that is "requisite"—that is, not lower or higher than is necessary—to protect the public health with an adequate margin of safety, fits comfortably within the scope of discretion permitted by our precedent.

We therefore reverse the judgment of the Court of Appeals remanding for reinterpretation that would avoid a supposed delegation of legislative power. It will remain for the Court of Appeals—on the remand that we direct for other reasons—to dispose of any other pre-served challenge to the NAAQS under the judicial-review provisions contained in 42 U.S.C.§ 7607(d)(9). . . .

Justice Thomas, concurring.

I agree with the majority that § 109's directive to the agency is no less an "intelligible principle" than a host of other directives that we have approved. I also agree that the Court of Appeals' remand to the agency to make its own corrective interpretation does not accord with our understanding of the delegation issue. I write separately, however, to express my concern that there may nevertheless be a genuine constitutional problem with § 109, a problem which the parties did not address.

The parties to this case who briefed the constitutional issue wrangled over constitutional doctrine with barely a nod to the text of the Constitution. Although this Court since 1928 has treated the "intelligible principle" requirement as the only constitutional limit on congressional grants of power to administrative agencies, . . . the Constitution does not speak of "intelligible principles." Rather, it speaks in much simpler terms: "All legislative Powers herein granted shall be vested in a Congress." U.S. Const., Art. 1, § 1. I am not convinced that the intelligible principle doctrine serves to prevent all cessions of legislative power. I believe that there are cases in which the principle is intelligible and yet the significance of the delegated decision is simply too great for the decision to be called anything other than "legislative."

As it is, none of the parties to this case has examined the text of the Constitution or asked us to reconsider our precedents on cessions of legislative power. On a future day, however, I would be willing to address the question whether our delegation jurisprudence has strayed too far from our Founders' understanding of separation of powers. . . .

NOTES

1. *Industrial Union Department, AFL-CIO v. American Petroleum Institute,* 488 U.S. 607, 628–29 (1980).

2. Craig Ducat and Harold Chase, *Constitutional Interpretations,* 4th ed. (St. Paul, Minn.: West, 1988), p. 185.

3. *Whitman v. American Trucking Association,* 531 U.S. 457,472 (2001).

4. The material on the FTC and the smoking rule comes from A. Lee Fritschler, *Smoking and Politics: Policy Making and the Federal Bureaucracy,* 4th ed. (Englewood Cliffs, N.J.: Prentice Hall, 1989), p. 72.

5. Ibid., p. 73.

6. Ibid., pp. 6, 18.

7. Ibid., pp. 96–97.

8. The Cigarette Labeling and Advertising Act of 1970, 15 U.S.C. 1331.

9. Fritschler, *Smoking and Politics,* p. 95.

10. Ibid.

11. Ibid., p. 96.

12. *Food and Drug Administration v. Brown and Williamson Tobacco Co.,* 529 U.S. 120 (2000).

13. Ibid.

14. Ibid.

15. Ibid., p. 1301.

16. Ibid., p. 1298.

17. *Lorillard v. Reilley,* 533 U.S. 525 (2001).

18. The material on subgovernments comes from Randal B. Ripley and Grace A. Franklin, *Congress, the Bureaucracy, and Public Policy,* 4th ed. (Chicago: Dorsey Press, 1987).

19. Ibid., p. 8.

20. Ibid., p. 114.

21. Congressional Quarterly, Inc., *The Washington Lobby,* 4th ed. (Washington, D.C.: Congressional Quarterly Press, 1982), 25–27.

22. Ripley and Franklin, *Congress, the Bureaucracy, and Public Policy,* 116–18.

23. Ibid., p. 10.

24. Judith Miller, *The New York Times,* March 14, 1997, p. A13.

25. Fox Butterfield, "Limits on Power and Zeal Hamper Firearms Agency," *The New York Times,* July 22, 1999, p. A1; Linda Greenhouse, "Weighing Restrictions on Legal Aid for the Poor," *The New York Times,* April 4, 2000, p. A14.

26. Morris P. Fiorina, *Congress: Keystone of the Washington Establishment* (New Haven, Conn.: Yale University Press, 1977), p. 41.

27. Fiorina, *Congress,* 41–49. See also James Boyd, "'Legislate? Who Me?': What Happens to a Senator's Day," in *Inside the System,* 4th ed., ed. Charles Peters and Nicholas Lemann (New York: Holt, Rinehart & Winston, 1979), 99–107.

28. Roger Davidson and Walter Oleszek, *Congress and Its Members,* 9th ed. (Washington, D.C.: Congressional Quarterly Press, 2004), 141–43.

29. Susan Welch, John Gruhl, John Comer, Susan M. Rigdon, and Jan Vermeer, *Understanding American Government,* 5th ed. (Belmont, Calif.: Wadsworth, 1999), 271–79.

30. Susan Wilch, John Gruhl, Michael Steinman, and John Comer, *American Government,* 3rd ed. (St. Paul, Minn.: West, 1990), p. 338.

31. On pork-barrel spending and agencies, see Davidson and Oleszek, *Congress and Its Members,* 336–37; and Brian Kelly, *Adventures in PorkLand: How Washington Wastes Your Money and Why They Won't Stop* (New York: Villard Books, 1992).

32. Kenneth Warren, *Administrative Law in the Political System,* 2d ed. (St. Paul, Minn.: West, 1988), p. 172.

33. Robert Hamilton, "Rulemaking on a Record by the FDA," 50 *Texas Law Review* 1132 (1972); the court case affirming the FDA's decision is *Corn Products Co. v. FDA,* 427 F.2d 511 (3rd Cir.) (1970).

34. The material on the creation of the Department of Homeland Security comes from Davidson and Oleszek, *Congress and Its Members,* 322–24.

35. Richard F. Fenno, Jr., *Congressmen in Committees* (Boston: Little, Brown, 1973), 193–202, esp. 193–94.

36. Davidson and Oleszek, *Congress and Its Members,* p. 340.

37. Ibid.

38. Warren, *Administrative Law,* p. 184.

39. Ibid., 184–87.

40. David B. Frohnmayer, "The Separation of Powers: An Essay on the Vitality of a Constitutional Idea," 52 *Oregon Law Review* 220 (1973).

41. *Yakus v. United States,* 321 U.S. 414, 426 (1944).

42. *American Power and Light Company v. Securities and Exchange Commission,* 329 U.S. 90, 105 (1946).

43. *Federal Power Commission v. Hope Natural Gas Company,* 320 U.S. 591, 600 (1944).

44. *National Broadcasting Company v. United States,* 319 U.S. 190, 225–26 (1943).

45. *Lichter v. United States,* 334 U.S. 742 (1948). Delegations cited in notes 41–45 are the Court's own list in *Mistretta v. United States,* 488 U.S. 361, 373–74 (1988).

46. Theodore J. Lowi, *The End of Liberalism: Ideology, Policy, and the Crisis of Public Authority* (New York: Norton, 1969), Chapter 10.

47. See "The Brig Aurora," 7 *Cranch* 382 (1813). Power was delegated to the president to determine whether Britain or France violated the neutrality of U.S. commerce, and if they had not, then sections of an expired 1809 act would be revived; *Field v. Clark,* 143 U.S. 649 (1892) delegated the power to the president to determine whether agricultural products from specific countries were being imported into the United States at a disadvantage to U.S. agriculture. If the president found that to be the case, he or she could raise the tariff on the product from a specific country; as a result of *United States v. Grimoud,* 220 U.S. 506 (1911), the secretary of agriculture was delegated the power to make rules necessary to protect the public forests.

48. Ripley and Franklin, *Congress, the Bureaucracy,* 21–28.

49. The material on congressional review comes from: David H. Rosenbloom, "Retrofitting the Administrative State to the Constitution: Congress and the Judiciary's Twentieth Century Progress," 60 *Public Administration Review* 41–42 (January/February, 2000). David Rosenbloom and Robert Kravchuk, *Public Administration: Understanding Management, Politics, and Law in the Public Sector* (New York: McGraw-Hill, 2005), 83–84; Davidson and Oleszek, *Congress and Its Members,* p. 334.

50. The information on ergonomics rules comes from Charles Morgan, "OSHA Ergonomic Guidelines: After Repeal of a Far-Reaching Rule, the Agency Has Issued a New Plan and Engaged in Targeted Enforcement," *The National Law Journal,* January 12, 2004, p. 17.

51. The material on more extensive congressional review comes from Bob Cusack, "DeLay Seeks Major Overhaul of Federal Regulatory System," *The Hill,* May 27, 2003; http://www.usnewswire.com; "GOP Pushes for Regulatory Reforms: Congressional Review Gets Support from Think Tanks," *The Hill,* July 8, 2003, p. 11.

52. *Congressional Quarterly* 2159 (July 22, 1995).

53. Ibid., p. 2162.

54. 54(3) *Congressional Quarterly* (January 20, 1996), p. 152.

55. 54(45) *Congressional Quarterly* (November 9, 1996), p. 3309.

56. 55(35) *Congressional Quarterly* (September 6, 1997), p. 2076.

57. For an excellent analysis of both executive and legislative branch efforts to control agencies see, Fred Anderson et al., "Regulatory Improvement Legislation: Risk Assessment, Cost-Benefit Analysis, and Judicial Review," 11 *Duke Environmental Law and Policy Forum* 89, 94–102.

58. Thad Hall, "Live Bureaucrats and Dead Public Servants: How People in Government Are Discussed on the Floor of the House," 62 (2) *Public Administration Review* 242 (March/April 2002); "Research Finds Congress Guilty of Bureaucrat Bashing," 25(4) *PA Times* 1 (April 2002).

59. Mirta Ojito, "Change in Laws Sets Off Big Wave of Deportations," *The New York Times,* December 15, 1998, p. A1.

4

CONTROL OF AGENCIES BY DEFAULT

The Courts and Administrative Law

So far, Chapter 1 introduced you to the concept of the administrative state and raised questions about democratic accountability. In Chapter 2, the argument was made that the president (especially Republican presidents) may possess the will to control agency rule making, but the office simply lacks the raw constitutional power to do so. In Chapter 3, you learned that although Congress possesses the power to control agency rule making, it generally lacks the will to exercise that power. As with presidents, Republican majorities in Congress may be possessed of more of a will to control bureaucracy than Democrats, but they have not had the votes to exercise that control. Congress made some earnest attempts to try to pass broad regulatory reform legislation as guidance legislation between 1995 and 1999 but did not have the votes to get it passed. Congress did adopt congressional review but, except for ergonomics regulation, has not used it. Congress seems content with occasional agency-specific attacks, having delegated the power to control agency activity to the White House, and with verbal assaults on bureaucracy on the House and Senate floors. The basic problem with delegating control to the Office of Management and Budget (OMB) is that it only works when there is a Republican in the White House. If a Democrat is president when Republicans control Congress, the latter could try to impose congressional review, but achieving their goal is unlikely unless the Republicans have veto-proof majorities.

If any branch of government is going to exercise control over the administrative state, perhaps that task will fall to the courts. To the extent that courts attempt to exercise control over agencies, administrative law is the tool they use. If we must look to the judicial branch for control over the administrative state, then democracy is in trouble because the judicial branch of government (especially at the federal level but in some states, too) is an undemocratic institution. Federal judges are appointed for a life term (literally a job for life) by design so they will have the institutional freedom to interpret the Constitution without fear of political or partisan reprisal. If, by default, control of one undemocratic institution (the administrative state) falls to another undemocratic institution (the judicial branch), how democratic can our system be?

IMPEDIMENTS TO JUDICIAL CONTROL OF AGENCIES

Not only is the federal judicial branch an undemocratic institution, but for a number of reasons, courts are particularly unsuited to play a watchdog role over agencies:

1. *Judicial temperament.* Judges are first of all lawyers, and they all learned the law by examination of precedent. Judicial decision making is dependent on past decisions. Most judges, whether elected or not, see the courts as a conflict resolution institution rather than a policy-making institution.[1]

2. *Deference to expertise.* Throughout the remainder of this book, you will read case after case in which the courts have deferred to agency expertise. That is because courts, judges, lawyers, and juries are not particularly suited to resolve conflicts concerning the optimum parts per million (PPM) of benzene in the air in the workplace, PPM of ozone or particulate matter in the air, the uses of embryonic research, or the availability of genetically altered foods in the food supply. Questions like these are why the administrative state is a reality. Although it may not necessarily reflect judicial deference to agency expertise, research demonstrates that several of the current Supreme Court justices frequently decide in favor of the agencies. A 1990 study (that would not have included Justices Thomas, Ginsburg, or Breyer) indicates that during the 1986–87 term, the Supreme Court sided with the agencies more than 70 percent of the time.[2] Table 4.1 presents a list of current justices of the Supreme Court who were on the Court during the 1986 term; their votes siding with agencies are expressed as a percentage of all administrative law cases in which they participated.

3. *Passive decision making.* Refer again to the case of *Clinton v. New York* at the end of Chapter 2, the line item veto case in which six Supreme Court justices said the line item veto was unconstitutional. Those six justices probably knew it was unconstitutional when Congress passed the Act, but they had to wait for someone to challenge the Act in court before they could decide on the case. Courts are passive decision makers. That means judges must wait for a proper lawsuit before they can exercise decision-making authority. That is not true of the other two branches of government, the legislative and the executive.

4. *Constraints on judicial power.* Besides having to wait before they can act, judges also encounter institutional constraints on their exercise of judicial power. Courts must be certain that various threshold criteria are met before they can decide a case. The field of administrative law has even more threshold criteria to be met than other areas of the law. The remainder of this chapter is an examination of those constraints.

Table 4.1   Sitting Members of the U.S. Supreme Court and Percentage of Administrative
Law Cases in Which They Supported the Agency (1986–87)

O'Connor	76.6%
Rehnquist	72.3%
Scalia	67.4%
Stevens	63.8%
Kennedy	62.5%

NOTE: The other current Supreme Court justices had not been appointed when the study was done.

SOURCE: Richard A. Brisbin, Jr., "The Conservatism of Antonin Scalia," 105 *Political Science Quarterly* 13 (Spring 1990).

Case in Point:
Steel Company, aka Chicago Steel and Pickling Co. v. Citizens for a Better Environment (CBE)
523 U.S. 88 (1998)

The Emergency Planning and Community Right to Know Act of 1986 (EPCRA) establishes a framework of state, regional, and local agencies designed to inform the public about the presence of hazardous and toxic chemicals. It also provides for an emergency response in the event of a health-threatening release of toxic chemicals. The law accomplishes its goal of informing the public by requiring businesses that use hazardous and toxic chemicals to submit annual reports of such use to the Environmental Protection Agency (EPA), as well as to state and local agencies. Hence, the public will know which hazardous materials are "in the area" in company inventories and be apprised of the nature, quantity, and disposal method of toxic chemicals. The EPCRA reporting requirements went into effect in 1988. EPCRA can be enforced in many ways: The EPA can seek criminal, civil, or administrative penalties for reporting violations; state governments can seek civil penalties or equity relief in the form of injunctions; or this statute, like many others, authorizes a private citizen to sue as a means of enforcement. "Any person may commence a civil action on his own behalf against . . . an owner or operator of a facility for failure, among other things" to submit the proper reports. As a prerequisite for filing a citizen suit, the potential plaintiff must notify the EPA, state and local agencies, and the alleged violator 60 days before commencing the suit. The citizen suit will not be allowed to proceed if either the EPA or state or local governments plan legal action against the alleged violator.

Chicago Steel had hazardous material in its inventory and was disposing of toxic chemicals, making the company subject to EPCRA reporting requirements. Citizens for a Better Environment (CBE) is an environmental watchdog group, or as the Court described it, "an association of individuals interested in environmental protection." Chicago Steel ignored the EPCRA reporting requirements until it got caught by CBE. On receiving the 60-day notice of intent to file a citizens enforcement suit, Chicago Steel filed all the required reports with all the relevant agencies. The EPA decided not to bring any legal or administrative action. The state of Illinois also decided not to sue, so CBE filed its citizen suit when the 60-day waiting period expired. Chicago Steel filed motions to dismiss the suit.

This is a unique and complex case that resulted in a unanimous Supreme Court decision. But the 9 to 0 decision had a majority opinion of only three. Justice Scalia wrote the Court opinion, joined by Justices Rehnquist and Thomas. Justices O'Connor and Breyer joined part of Scalia's opinion and concurred with the rest of it. Justice O'Connor wrote a concurring opinion that was joined in part by Justice Kennedy. Justice Breyer wrote a concurring opinion, and Justice Stevens wrote a concurring opinion that was joined in part by Souter and Ginsburg. Two questions were before the Court: (1) Does EPCRA authorize suit for "purely historical violations" of the reporting requirement? Because Chicago Steel was absolutely current in compliance with reporting requirements when the suit was filed, the alleged (and admitted) violations were purely historical. The answer to this legal question is not obvious from the language in the statute, and reasonable people can disagree. (2) The second legal question involves one of those constraints on the exercise of judicial power mentioned above. The question was whether CBE has standing to bring this suit.

As you will read shortly in this chapter, there are several impediments to the exercise of judicial power. A plaintiff in any suit must offer proof that there is a real (not hypothetical) conflict between the parties, that the suit is timely, that the court has jurisdiction, and that the plaintiff is the proper party to bring the suit. The concept of standing is the later question (is the plaintiff the proper party to file this suit?). The Court has developed several tests for standing depending on the type of legal action. The standing test at issue in this case is a three-pronged test: (1) injury in fact, (2) traceability, and (3) redressability. Injury in fact means whether the plaintiff has suffered a demonstrable injury. Traceability gets at causality. It asks whether the injuries suffered by the plaintiff are fairly traceable to the actions of the defendant. Redressability gets at remedies. Every lawsuit must ask the court for a remedy or remedies to compensate the plaintiff for the injuries caused by the defendant. Redressability addresses the issue of whether the plaintiff's injuries can be redressed (remedied) by a favorable court decision. If a favorable court decision will not be of help, then you should not be in court. The plaintiff bears the burden of proving that all three elements of the standing test have been met.

Do you think the CBE has standing to sue Chicago Steel? Before you say, "I don't see an injury," you should know that legal injuries do not necessarily have to be economic. Indeed, even aesthetic injuries have been litigated. CBE says it reports to its members, the public, and the media about the storage and release of toxic materials. It seeks to reduce hazardous and toxic materials in the environment, and it promotes enforcement of environmental laws. CBE says that when companies like Chicago Steel flagrantly violate toxic reporting requirements and hide the presence of hazardous and toxic materials from the public, CBE is prohibited from doing what it exists to do, and its members cannot be accurately informed. Realizing that for fiscal and political reasons the EPA and state governments might not effectively enforce EPCRA, Congress authorized citizen suits for just such a purpose.

Now do you think CBE has standing to sue Chicago Steel? Do you think the Supreme Court said CBE could sue Chicago Steel? Do you think the Supreme Court would allow a business to flagrantly violate the law and get away with it? The Court decided that CBE did not have standing to sue Chicago Steel. The Court was not certain whether there was an injury in fact: "(this Court has) not had occasion to decide whether being deprived of information that is supposed to be disclosed . . . is a concrete injury in fact." The Court passed on the injury question saying that CBE lacked redressability.

In its suit, CBE asked the court to declare the company to be in violation of EPCRA. The company admits it. There is no controversy over this, and such a declaration will not help CBE. CBE asked for fines of $25,000 a day for two violations during the period the company was in violation ($25,000 a day times two for several years). However, by statute, if the money was awarded by the court, it would go into the U.S. Treasury, not into CBE coffers. CBE asked the Court to authorize CBE inspections of the company's records and its facilities, but because CBE failed to allege that the company would violate EPCRA in the future, this would amount to inspection for past violations that everyone admits took place.

Finally, CBE asked the Court for reimbursements for investigative costs (what it cost CBE to find out about the company's lawlessness). CBE also asked to be reimbursed for reasonable attorney fees. However, according to Justice Scalia,

> A plaintiff cannot achieve standing to litigate a substantive issue by bringing suit for the costs of bringing the suit. The litigation must give the plaintiff some other benefit besides reimbursement of costs that are a by-product of the litigation itself . . . CBE finds itself, in other words, impaled upon the horns of a dilemma: for the expenses to be reimbursable under the statute, they must be costs of litigation; but reimbursement of the costs of litigation cannot alone support standing.[3]

Even if the Court granted CBE everything it asked for in its suit, CBE would be no better off than it was before the suit. Hence, there is no redressability. If a favorable decision will not help CBE, then CBE should not be in court.

CBE could not sue, so Chicago Steel did indeed get away with flagrantly breaking the law. The point is that there are institutional constraints on the exercise of judicial power, and standing is only one of them.

General Constraints on the Exercise of Judicial Power

Jurisdiction

Before a court can hear a case, it must have the power to resolve that particular conflict. That power is called jurisdiction, and it is conferred on courts by constitutions (state or federal) or by legislatures (state or federal).

Article III of the federal Constitution, for instance, confers the jurisdiction on federal courts to hear cases or controversies involving conflicts that may arise under either the Constitution or laws of the federal government. It goes on to give Congress the power to set jurisdiction for federal courts for cases they can hear on review (called *appellate jurisdiction*). Jurisdiction can be a complicated concept, and in some cases, the issue before the court is whether the court has jurisdiction to hear the case. Not only do courts need to have jurisdiction over a conflict to resolve it, but agencies can only act within the jurisdiction given them by Congress. In the Tobacco Case *(Food and Drug Administration v. Brown and Williamson Corp,* 529 U.S. 120 [2000]*)* at the end of the last chapter, the question was whether the FDA had the jurisdiction to regulate tobacco products. When the California Dental Association prohibited advertising for discount dental services and advertising about the quality of dental care, the Federal Trade Commission (FTC) filed a complaint in federal court alleging restraint of trade by prohibiting truthful and nondeceptive advertising. One of the legal issues in the case was whether the FTC has the jurisdiction to regulate a nonprofit professional association. As is often the case, the answer to that question is not obvious by the language in the statute, but the Supreme Court decided that the FTC did have the jurisdiction.[4] A more dramatic example of an agency found to be acting beyond its jurisdiction can be found in *Bowen v. American Hospital Association.*[5] Apparently, one way for parents, doctors, and hospitals to deal with severely deformed babies is to simply withhold food and life-sustaining treatment. When the Department of Health and Human Services (HHS) documented the extent of such inaction, it adopted regulations that would forbid the practice in any medical facility that received federal money. The HHS said it got the authority (read jurisdiction) to adopt the regulations from Section 504 of the Rehabilitation Act of 1973. That section reads in pertinent part, "No otherwise qualified handicapped individual . . . shall, solely by reason of his handicap, be excluded from the participation in, be denied the benefits of, or be subject to discrimination under any program or activity receiving Federal financial assistance." When HHS got sued by the American Hospital Association, the American Medical Association, and others, the Supreme Court said that HHS lacked the jurisdiction to adopt the regulations. When President Clinton dropped Major Goldsmith from the rolls of the Air Force, the major appealed to the Court of Appeals for the Armed Forces (CAAF). The CAAF issued an injunction against the president, but the Supreme Court said that the CAAF lacked jurisdiction to hear the case.[6] The Illinois Council on Long Term Care, Inc., sued the secretary of health and human services, Donna Shalala, in Federal District Court, alleging that certain Medicare regulations violated the Constitution. However, Congress has established a special internal appeals process for social security and Medicare problems, and the Supreme Court found that the district court was without jurisdiction to hear the case.[7] So, one of the first hurdles in a lawsuit is whether the court has jurisdiction to hear the dispute. In a civil lawsuit, the plaintiff has the burden of establishing that the court has jurisdiction over the subject matter of the lawsuit, that it has jurisdiction over both of the parties to the suit, and in some cases, that the court has jurisdiction over property that may be involved in the suit. In the administrative law context, jurisdictional questions are more common where the question is whether an agency acted within its jurisdiction. Generally, federal courts have jurisdiction when one sues an agency. That is because agencies nearly always act pursuant to a federal law; thus, the issue becomes what is referred to as a federal question, and that gives federal courts jurisdiction.

Standing

You are already somewhat familiar with the issue of standing because of the Case-in-Point. Standing is the concept that limits who can sue. Generally, one cannot sue the government or a government actor unless the plaintiff is the one who suffered an injury as a result of that government action. How the courts define or interpret the concept of standing is important. The narrower the interpretation, the smaller the class of people who can use the courts for redress of an administrative decision or action.

In administrative law, court interpretations about who is a proper party to challenge an administrative action were at first very narrow and constrictive. The U.S. Supreme Court broadened the concept of standing in the late 1960s and into the 1970s, but as evidenced by the CBE Case and the Lujan Case, which you will read shortly, the Rehnquist Court seems to be in the process of narrowing the concept of standing again.

Prior to broadening the concept of standing, the courts applied a test referred to as the *legal interest test.* This meant that an administrative action could not be challenged unless the challenger could show a legally protected interest had been adversely affected. The simple fact that the challenger suffered economic loss because of an administrative action was not enough by itself. That economic loss had to be covered by an existing legal right, such as contract law (breach of contract), property law, probate law, tort law, and so on.

The case that rejected the legal interest test and broadened the class of people who could challenge administrative action was *Association of Data Processing Service Organizations v. Camp,* 397 U.S. 159 (1970). In this case, Mr. Camp, the comptroller of the currency, promulgated the following rule: "Incidental to its banking services, a national bank may make available its data processing equipment or perform data processing services on such equipment for other banks and bank customers." The plaintiff in this case is a trade association of data processing companies that provide data processing services to businesses. Assume for the moment that the businesses and corporations making up the Association of Data Processing Service Organizations control 75 to 90 percent of the market that supplies data processing to businesses. If the national banks are allowed to enter that market, they will cut into the profits of the businesses belonging to the trade association. That reduction of profit is the very definition of economic injury, especially in light of the fact that Section 4 of the Bank Service Corporation Act says, "No bank service corporation may . . . engage in any activity other than the performance of banking services for banks."

Despite the fact that the Administrative Procedure Act grants standing to challenge an administrative action to a person "aggrieved by agency action within the meaning of a relevant statute" (see Section 702 of the Administrative Procedure Act in Appendix A), the district court dismissed the suit, saying the Association of Data Processing Service Organizations lacked standing to challenge the comptroller's action. The district court said (and the circuit court of appeals affirmed) that "a Plaintiff may challenge an alleged illegal competition when as complainant it pursues—1) a legal interest by reason of public . . . charter or contract . . . 2) a legal interest by reason of statutory protection."[8] Because in this case there was no breach of contract or a statute that conferred a special privilege on the data processors, the lower federal courts, following precedent, dismissed the suit. The Supreme Court reversed, creating a two-pronged test for standing to challenge administrative action.

Subsequent to the *Camp* decision, to establish standing, a plaintiff or petitioner needed only to show the following:

1. injury in fact;

2. that the action complained of is arguably under the zone of interest meant to be protected by a particular statute.

The first prong, injury in fact, means that people challenging an administrative action needed only to show that the action or decision caused them some definable injury, economic or otherwise (aesthetic, conservational, or maybe even recreational), and it need not be tied to a legal right or interest.

The second prong of the test is tied to the Administrative Procedure Act, which confers standing on people aggrieved by agency action "*within the meaning of a relevant statute* [italics added]." That is, people challenging agency action must argue (a) that they have suffered some demonstrable injury from agency action, and (b) that the agency action falls under a statute that arguably protects the plaintiff from such action. To apply the first part of the test in this case, the injury in fact is lost profits and, indeed, a lost contract.

The petitioners not only allege that competition by national banks in the business of providing data processing services might entail some future loss of profits for the petitioners, they also allege that respondent American National Bank and Trust was performing or preparing to perform such services for two customers for whom petitioner, Data Systems, Inc., had previously agreed or negotiated to perform such services.[9]

Regarding the second part of the test, the agency action arguably falls under the zone of interest meant to protect the person challenging the agency action, because in this case, the plaintiffs contend the Bank Services Corporation Act strictly limits banks to banking. Hence, arguably, the Act should protect them from the comptroller's policy.

Question

1. What result do you get when you apply the two-pronged test to what you know about the CBE case?

Lujan v. Defenders of Wildlife
504 U.S. 555(1992)

Defenders of Wildlife (DOW) is suing Secretary of the Interior Lujan for a declaratory judgment against a rule promulgated by the Department of Interior (DOI) in 1986. The suit also asks the court to require the Secretary to promulgate a new rule. The Endangered Species Act of 1973 delegates primary enforcement to the DOI. The law requires the Secretary to identify endangered species and their habitat. Further the law requires that all other federal agencies consult with the Secretary prior to taking any action that might adversely impact an endangered species or its habitat. In 1979 DOI promulgated a rule extending the consultation requirement to actions contemplated by federal agencies to be taken overseas. In 1986 the Reagan administration promulgated the rule challenged here that restricts the consultation provision to domestic situations (i.e., not to overseas actions). The crux of the Plaintiff's (DOW) argument is that the Agency for International Development (AID) loaned funds to Egypt and Sri Lanka for water projects that will negatively impact on the habitats of elephants, leopards, and crocodiles (all endangered species) and that AID did so without consulting with the Secretary of Interior. Such consultation would have been required prior to the 1986 change in the requirement.

The opinion was written by Justice Scalia and joined by Justices White and Thomas and Chief Justice Rehnquist. Concurring opinions were by Justice Kennedy, joined by Justices Souter and Stevens; Justice Blackmun joined by Justice O'Connor dissented.

This case involves a challenge to a rule promulgated by the Secretary of the Interior interpreting § 7 of the Endangered Species Act of 1973 (ESA), 87 Stat. 884, in such fashion as to render it applicable only to actions within the United States or on the high seas. The preliminary issue, and the only one we reach, is whether respondents here, plaintiffs below, have standing to seek judicial review of the rule.

I

The ESA, as amended, seeks to protect species of animals against threats to their continuing existence caused by man. The ESA instructs the

Secretary of the Interior to promulgate by regulation a list of those species which are either endangered or threatened under enumerated criteria, and to define the critical habitat of these species.

In 1978, the Fish and Wildlife Service (FWS) and the National Marine Fisheries Service (NMFS), on behalf of the Secretary of the Interior and the Secretary of Commerce respectively, promulgated a joint regulation stating that the obligations imposed by § 7(a)(2) extend to actions taken in foreign nations. The next year, however, the Interior Department began to reexamine its position. A revised joint regulation, reinterpreting 7(a)(2) to require consultation only for actions taken in the United States or on the high seas, was proposed in 1983, 48 Fed.Reg., and promulgated in 1986, 50 CFR 402.01 (1991).

Shortly thereafter, respondents, organizations dedicated to wildlife conservation and other environmental causes, filed this action against the Secretary of the Interior, seeking a declaratory judgment that the new regulation is in error as to the geographic scope of § 7(a)(2) and an injunction requiring the Secretary to promulgate a new regulation restoring the initial interpretation. The District Court granted the Secretary's motion to dismiss for lack of standing. *Defenders of Wildlife v. Hodel,* 658 F.Supp. 43 (Minn.1987). The Court of Appeals for the Eighth Circuit reversed by a divided vote. *Defenders of Wildlife v. Hodel,* 851 F.2d 1035 (1988). On remand, the Secretary moved for summary judgment on the standing issue, and respondents moved for summary judgment on the merits. The District Court denied the Secretary's motion, on the ground that the Eighth Circuit had already determined the standing question in this case; it granted respondents' merits motion and ordered the Secretary to publish a revised regulation. *Defenders of Wildlife v. Hodel,* 707 F.Supp. 1082 (Minn.1989). The Eighth Circuit affirmed. 911 F.2d 117 (1990). We granted certiorari. . . .

[3][4] Over the years, our cases have established that the irreducible constitutional minimum of standing contains three elements. First, the plaintiff must have suffered an "injury in fact"—an invasion of a legally protected interest which is (a) concrete and particularized, . . . and

(b) "actual or imminent, not 'conjectural' or 'hypothetical.'" Second, there must be a causal connection between the injury and the conduct complained of—the injury has to be "fairly . . . trace[able] to the challenged action of the defendant, and not . . . th[e] result [of] the independent action of some third party not before the court." *Simon v. Eastern Ky. Welfare Rights Organization,* 426 U.S. 26, 41–42 (1976). Third, it must be "likely," as opposed to merely "speculative," that the injury will be "redressed by a favorable decision."

[5][6][7] The party invoking federal jurisdiction bears the burden of establishing these elements. Since they are not mere pleading requirements but rather an indispensable part of the plaintiff's case, each element must be supported in the same way as any other matter on which the plaintiff bears the burden of proof, i.e., with the manner and degree of evidence required at the successive stages of the litigation. . . .

[8] When the suit is one challenging the legality of government action or inaction, the nature and extent of facts that must be averred (at the summary judgment stage) or proved (at the trial stage) in order to establish standing depends considerably upon whether the plaintiff is himself an object of the action (or forgone action) at issue. If he is, there is ordinarily little question that the action or inaction has caused him injury and that a judgment preventing or requiring the action will redress it. When, however, as in this case, a plaintiff's asserted injury arises from the government's allegedly unlawful regulation (or lack of regulation) of someone else, much more is needed. In that circumstance, causation and redressability ordinarily hinge on the response of the regulated (or regulable) third party to the government action or inaction—and perhaps on the response of others as well. The existence of one or more of the essential elements of standing "depends on the unfettered choices made by independent actors not before the courts and whose exercise of broad and legitimate discretion the courts cannot presume either to control or to predict," also *Simon,* supra, 426 U.S., at 41–42, and it becomes the burden of the plaintiff to adduce facts showing that those choices have been or

will be made in such manner as to produce causation and permit redressability of injury.

A

[9][10] Respondents' claim to injury is that the lack of consultation with respect to certain funded activities abroad "increas[es] the rate of extinction of endangered and threatened species." Of course, the desire to use or observe an animal species, even for purely esthetic purposes, is undeniably a cognizable interest for purpose of standing. "But the 'injury in fact' test requires more than an injury to a cognizable interest. It requires that the party seeking review be himself among the injured." To survive the Secretary's summary judgment motion, respondents had to submit affidavits or other evidence showing, through specific facts, not only that listed species were in fact being threatened by funded activities abroad, but also that one or more of respondents' members would thereby be "directly" affected apart from their "'special interest' in th[e] subject." See generally *Hunt v. Washington State Apple Advertising Comm'n,* 432 U.S. 333, 343,(1977).

[11][12] With respect to this aspect of the case, the Court of Appeals focused on the affidavits of two Defenders' members—Joyce Kelly and Amy Skilbred. Ms. Kelly stated that she traveled to Egypt in 1986 and "observed the traditional habitat of the endangered Nile crocodile there and intend[s] to do so again, and hope[s] to observe the crocodile directly," and that she "will suffer harm in fact as the result of [the] American . . . role . . . in overseeing the rehabilitation of the Aswan High Dam on the Nile . . . and [in] develop [ing] . . . Egypt's . . . Master Water Plan." Ms. Skilbred averred that she traveled to Sri Lanka in 1981 and "observed th[e] habitat" of "endangered species such as the Asian elephant and the leopard" at what is now the site of the Mahaweli project funded by the Agency for International Development (AID), although she "was unable to see any of the endangered species"; "this development project," she continued, "will seriously reduce endangered, threatened, and endemic species habitat including areas that I visited . . . [which] may severely shorten the future of these species"; that threat, she concluded, harmed her because

she "intend[s] to return to Sri Lanka in the future and hope[s] to be more fortunate in spotting at least the endangered elephant and leopard." When Ms. Skilbred was asked at a subsequent deposition if and when she had any plans to return to Sri Lanka, she reiterated that "I intend to go back to Sri Lanka," but confessed that she had no current plans: "I don't know [when]. There is a civil war going on right now. I don't know. Not next year, I will say. In the future."

We shall assume for the sake of argument that these affidavits contain facts showing that certain agency-funded projects threaten listed species—though that is questionable. They plainly contain no facts, however, showing how damage to the species will produce "imminent" injury to Mses. Kelly and Skilbred. That the women "had visited" the areas of the projects before the projects commenced proves nothing. As we have said in a related context, "Past exposure to illegal conduct does not in itself show a present case or controversy regarding injunctive relief . . . if unaccompanied by any continuing, present adverse effects." *Lyons,* 461 U.S., at 102, 103. And the affiants' profession of an "inten[t]" to return to the places they had visited before— where they will presumably, this time, be deprived of the opportunity to observe animals of the endangered species—is simply not enough. Such "some day" intentions—without any description of concrete plans, or indeed even any specification of when the some day will be—do not support a finding of the "actual or imminent" injury that our cases require.

Besides relying upon the Kelly and Skilbred affidavits, respondents propose a series of novel standing theories. The first, inelegantly styled "ecosystem nexus," proposes that any person who uses any part of a "contiguous ecosystem" adversely affected by a funded activity has standing even if the activity is located a great distance away. This approach, as the Court of Appeals correctly observed, is inconsistent with our opinion in *National Wildlife Federation,* which held that a plaintiff claiming injury from environmental damage must use the area affected by the challenged activity and not an area roughly "in the vicinity" of it.

[14] Respondents' other theories are called, alas, the "animal nexus" approach, whereby

anyone who has an interest in studying or seeing the endangered animals anywhere on the globe has standing; and the "vocational nexus" approach, under which anyone with a professional interest in such animals can sue. Under these theories, anyone who goes to see Asian elephants in the Bronx Zoo, and anyone who is a keeper of Asian elephants in the Bronx Zoo, has standing to sue because the Director of the Agency for International Development (AID) did not consult with the Secretary regarding the AID-funded project in Sri Lanka. This is beyond all reason.

B

Besides failing to show injury, respondents failed to demonstrate redressability. Instead of attacking the separate decisions to fund particular projects allegedly causing them harm, respondents chose to challenge a more generalized level of Government action (rules regarding consultation), the invalidation of which would affect all overseas projects. This programmatic approach has obvious practical advantages, but also obvious difficulties insofar as proof of causation or redressability is concerned. As we have said in another context, "suits challenging, not specifically identifiable Government violations of law, but the particular programs agencies establish to carry out their legal obligations . . . [are], even when premised on allegations of several instances of violations of law, . . . rarely if ever appropriate for federal-court adjudication." *Allen,* 468 U.S., at 759-760.

[15] The most obvious problem in the present case is redressability. Since the agencies funding the projects were not parties to the case, the District Court could accord relief only against the Secretary: He could be ordered to revise his regulation to require consultation for foreign projects. But this would not remedy respondents' alleged injury unless the funding agencies were bound by the Secretary's regulation, which is very much an open question.

The short of the matter is that redress of the only injury in fact respondents complain of requires action (termination of funding until consultation) by the individual funding agencies; and any relief the District Court could

have provided in this suit against the Secretary was not likely to produce that action.

[17] A further impediment to redressability is the fact that the agencies generally supply only a fraction of the funding for a foreign project. AID, for example, has provided less than 10% of the funding for the Mahaweli project. Respondents have produced nothing to indicate that the projects they have named will either be suspended, or do less harm to listed species, if that fraction is eliminated. . . .

[19] We have consistently held that a plaintiff raising only a generally available grievance about government—claiming only harm to his and every citizen's interest in proper application of the Constitution and laws, and seeking relief that no more directly and tangibly benefits him than it does the public at large—does not state an Article III case or controversy.

* * *

We hold that respondents lack standing to bring this action and that the Court of Appeals erred in denying the summary judgment motion filed by the United States. The opinion of the Court of Appeals is hereby reversed, and the cause is remanded for proceedings consistent with this opinion.

It is so ordered.

Justice Blackmun, with whom Justice O'Connor joins, dissenting.

I part company with the Court in this case in two respects. First, I believe that respondents have raised genuine issues of fact—sufficient to survive summary judgment—both as to injury and as to redressability. Second, I question the Court's breadth of language in rejecting standing for "procedural" injuries. I fear the Court seeks to impose fresh limitations on the constitutional authority of Congress to allow citizen suits in the federal courts for injuries deemed "procedural" in nature. I dissent.

I

Article III of the Constitution confines the federal courts to adjudication of actual "Cases" and "Controversies." To ensure the presence of a "case" or "controversy," this Court has held that Article III requires, as an irreducible minimum, that a plaintiff allege (1) an injury that is (2) "fairly traceable to the defendant's allegedly unlawful conduct" and that is (3) "likely to be redressed by the requested relief." *Allen v. Wright,* 468 U.S. 737, 751 (1984).

A

To survive petitioner's motion for summary judgment on standing, respondents need not prove that they are actually or imminently harmed. They need show only a "genuine issue" of material fact as to standing. Fed.Rule Civ.Proc. 56(c). This is not a heavy burden. A "genuine issue" exists so long as "the evidence is such that a reasonable jury could return a verdict for the nonmoving party." *Anderson v. Liberty Lobby, Inc.,* 477 U.S. 242, 248 (1986). This Court's "function is not [it]self to weigh the evidence and determine the truth of the matter but to determine whether there is a genuine issue for trial." . . .

I think a reasonable finder of fact could conclude from the information in the affidavits and deposition testimony that either Kelly or Skilbred will soon return to the project sites, thereby satisfying the "actual or imminent" injury standard. . . .

I fear the Court's demand for detailed descriptions of future conduct will do little to weed out those who are genuinely harmed from those who are not. More likely, it will resurrect a code-pleading formalism in federal court summary judgment practice, as federal courts, newly doubting their jurisdiction, will demand more and more particularized showings of future harm. Just to survive summary judgment, for example, a property owner claiming a decline in the value of his property from governmental action might have to specify the exact date he intends to sell his property and show that there is a market for the property, lest it be surmised he might not sell again. A nurse turned down for a job on grounds of her race had better be prepared to show on what date she was prepared to start work, that she had arranged day care for her child, and that she would not have accepted work at another hospital instead. And a Federal Tort Claims Act plaintiff alleging loss of consortium should make sure to furnish this Court with a "description of concrete plans" for her nightly schedule of attempted activities. . . .

I find myself unable to agree with the plurality's analysis of redressability, based as it is on its invitation of executive lawlessness, ignorance of principles of collateral estoppel, unfounded assumptions about causation, and erroneous conclusions about what the record does not say. In my view, respondents have satisfactorily shown a genuine issue of fact as to whether their injury would likely be redressed by a decision in their favor. . . .

In conclusion, I cannot join the Court on what amounts to a slash-and-burn expedition through the law of environmental standing. In my view, "[t]he very essence of civil liberty certainly consists in the right of every individual to claim the protection of the laws, whenever he receives an injury." *Marbury v. Madison,* 1 Cranch 137, 163, 2 L.Ed. 60 (1803).

I dissent.

Questions

1. The Court does not resolve the legal dispute in *Lujan* the same way it resolved standing in *Camp.* Does the Court offer an explanation of why it did not apply the precedent from *Camp?*
2. Can you find any mention of the "zone of interest" mentioned in the *Lujan* case?
3. What result do you think you would get in *Lujan* if the zone of interest test were applied?

Compare the results in *Lujan* and *Chicago Steel* with *Bennett v. Spear,* 520 U.S. 154 (1997). In *Bennett,* the U.S. Fish and Wildlife Service issued a biological opinion that claimed that long-term operation of the Klamath project would jeopardize the existence of two species of fish on the endangered species list. The Klamath project is a federal Bureau of Reclamation project in California and Oregon consisting of lakes, rivers, dams, and irrigation canals. The biological opinion said that maintaining minimum water levels in two of the lakes would solve the problem. When the Bureau of Reclamation notified the Fish and Wildlife Service and the public that it would operate the Klamath project in accordance with the biological opinion, two ranchers and two irrigation districts sued. Plaintiffs alleged that the mandated lake levels would adversely affect their use of water from the project and that the lake levels set by the Fish and Wildlife Service are not necessary to protect the fish. They attack the procedure used to support the biological opinion as well as its substance. Plaintiffs are suing the secretary of interior and certain Fish and Wildlife Service officials, and they are suing under a citizen-suit provision in the Endangered Species Act, just like the one CBE tried to use. The district court dismissed the suit saying that only plaintiffs with an interest in protecting endangered species fall under the zone of interest protected by the Act. The court of appeals affirmed, but the Supreme Court reversed and found standing. The Court said that the zone of interest protected by the Endangered Species Act is not limited to environmentalists and, furthermore, the plaintiffs demonstrated an injury in fact, traceability, and redressability.

Two variables are at work in these standing cases. The first variable is a constitutional separation of power variable that the courts have imposed to restrict the use of the judicial branch as a vehicle for those who would change public policy simply because they disagree with the policy. The courts refer to this standing aspect as *prudential standing.* The second variable relates to the parties involved in the dispute that the Court has been asked to resolve. One cannot sue on behalf of another person, and the plaintiff must be the injured party.

In a typical case, an agency has taken some action that adversely affects a business, corporation, industry, interest group, or individual. In Chapter 1, for example when the director of the EPA set new air quality standards that reduced the allowable PPM of certain pollutants, not only were individual businesses affected but so were industries and states. The same can be said for Secretary Dole's decision to restrict the effectiveness of the hazard communication standard. Workers who would not receive the warnings were adversely affected. Ditto for the secretary of labor's decision to reduce the PPM of benzene in the air from 10 to 1, which adversely affected petroleum producers' profits.

In situations like these, standing is not difficult because there is an obvious injury in fact and the injured party can show that a particular statute (or constitutional or common law provision) arguably protects them from the actions the agency has taken (i.e., the zone of interest test). The zone of interest test is meant to ensure that ordinary citizens like you and I do not attempt to use the judicial branch to change those public policies with which we disagree (we should use the legislative branch). However, those who are specifically injured by government action (the automobile industry, construction workers, and petroleum producers) do have standing to challenge the policy in court.

Less frequently, however, government action has affected an intervening or third party and that party's action theoretically adversely affects an injured party. The injured party then sues the government agency that started the chain reaction. Such was the case in *Lujan* (and also in *L.A. v. Lyons,* which appears at the end of this chapter).

The Defenders of Wildlife in the *Lujan* case are concerned with the actions of Egypt and Sri Lanka and only more remotely with AID and DOI. Basically, plaintiffs in such situations must argue that the government action (or inaction) caused another party to take some action (or inaction) that adversely affects the plaintiffs. In these third-party standing cases, the Court has created a three-pronged test:

1. Is there injury in fact?

2. Is the injury to the plaintiff fairly traceable to the defendant (i.e. the agency)?

3. If the Court were to grant the plaintiff the remedy requested, would that redress the plaintiffs' injury?

You are already familiar with the first prong, injury in fact. The second prong is referred to as *traceability,* a concept that relates to causality. That is, did the actions of the agency cause the harm to the plaintiffs? In *Lujan,* the Defenders of Wildlife cannot show that the threat to crocodiles, elephants, and leopards is caused by the failure of the DOI to review overseas projects for Endangered Species Act implications. Their injury was not fairly traceable to the DOI.

The third prong of the test, referred to as *redressability,* asks whether the courts can solve the plaintiff's problem. Although the Defenders of Wildlife had traceability problems in their suit against DOI, the Court concentrated on the redressability problem. To understand redressability, you have to know what remedy the plaintiffs have requested. The Defenders of Wildlife were asking the Court to reverse a DOI rule restricting the department's consultation under the Endangered Species Act to domestic projects. Even if the Court were to order Interior to consult on overseas projects related to endangered species, that would not necessarily prevent Egypt and Sri Lanka from proceeding with the projects that threaten crocodiles and elephants and leopards. Hence, according to the Court, Defenders of Wildlife cannot show redressability and lack standing to sue the DOI. Similarly, CBE could not show an injury or redressability in the *Chicago Steel* case. Given what you know about standing, do you think the following plaintiffs have standing to sue?

The mother of an illegitimate child sued a Texas prosecutor and the child's father. Texas had a law that made it a misdemeanor for "any person" to desert, neglect, or fail to provide support and maintenance to his or her child. The law imposed a two-year sentence on anyone convicted. The Texas courts, however, interpreted the law so that it only applied to the parents of children born while the parents were married (Texas imposed no legal duty on parents to support their illegitimate children). The mother in this case sued to require the prosecutor, who had otherwise refused following the Texas courts' interpretation, to prosecute the father for nonsupport. She also asked the federal court to impose reasonable child support on the father. Does she have standing? This 1973 case was an early case articulating the concept of redressability. What does the mother want? She wants child support. What will the mother get if the Court forces the prosecutor and Texas to prosecute the father? She will get the father thrown in jail for two years, but she will not get what she really wants—child support. She is asking the federal courts to force Texas to apply the law equally to the parents of illegitimate and legitimate children. She lacks standing because of redressability.[10]

The Internal Revenue Service (IRS) at one point in time had a rule that required a hospital seeking status as a charitable organization to provide service to those who cannot pay, "to the extent of its financial ability to do so." Status as a charitable organization is desirable because donations and gifts are tax deductible, and that, of course, encourages donations and gifts. When the IRS changed the rule so that hospitals could have charitable status without having to service the poor, the Eastern Kentucky Welfare Rights Organization sued. The plaintiff organization represents poor people and was able to prove that some members were denied hospital care because of their inability to pay. The hospitals that denied service received charitable status from the IRS. Plaintiffs challenged the revised IRS rule on charitable status, alleging that the new rule caused harm. Do you think the welfare rights organization has standing to sue the IRS? What injury has been suffered? The injury is denied medical care. Who caused that injury? The hospital caused it. This is a traceability case. Can you say that, absent the turnabout by the IRS, the individuals who were denied medical service would have received it? The Supreme Court said that the welfare rights organization lacks standing because it cannot show that the injury is fairly traceable to the actions of the IRS.[11] This case was decided in 1976, three years after the Texas case regarding child support.

In 1984, the IRS got sued again in *Allan v. Wright.*[12] This time Black parents who live in the South sued the IRS because it granted tax-exempt status to private schools that discriminate on the basis of race. Laws forbid such discrimination, and even the IRS at the time had a rule that required tax-exempt organizations not to discriminate on the basis of race. The parents, the Wrights, sued to force the IRS to abide by its rule of nondiscrimination. Although the IRS had a rule forbidding discrimination by tax-exempt organizations, it also had a policy that tax-exempt schools merely had to produce a policy statement of nondiscrimination as proof; whether or not the policy statement ever got implemented was not a matter of concern for the IRS. The Wrights attacked this policy in court. The Wrights never attempted to enroll their children in any of these private academies because the private schools were not accepting the applications of Black children. The Wrights sued alleging that their children's constitutionally protected right to attend racially integrated schools was thwarted by the IRS's implementation policy, which encourages white flight from the public schools to private academies. Do you think the Wrights had standing? Do you think this case is similar to the welfare rights case and to *Lujan?* The problem the Wrights faced is that, like poor people in need of medical care and the Defenders of Wildlife, their injury was caused by the private academies (or hospitals or Sri Lanka and Egypt) and not necessarily by agency action. Indeed, the Supreme Court was even at a loss to find that the Wrights had suffered any injury at all.

The *Lujan* case followed on the heels of *Allen v. Wright et al.* At least through *Lujan* in 1990, the Court applied the three-pronged test only in cases where a third party allegedly caused injury, but the plaintiffs were suing an agency. As you can tell from the *Chicago Steel* case, the Court now uses the three-pronged test in all situations, even where one private individual sues another private entity and the suit is specifically authorized by Congress (CBE sues Chicago Steel).

The case of the *Federal Election Commission v. Akins* at the end of this chapter is a good one because the Court applies both standing tests, the zone of interest test and the three-pronged test. The *Akins* case involves a group of voters who are opposed to the political activities of the American Israel Public Affairs Committee (AIPAC). The voters asked the Federal Election Commission (FEC) to find that AIPAC was a "political Committee" under the Federal Election Campaign Act of 1971. Such a finding would mean AIPAC had to disclose its membership list, contributions, and expenditures. The FEC found that AIPAC was not a political committee under the Act, and the voters challenged that decision in court. To find out whether the voters have standing, you will have to read the case.

Although this is an oversimplification, restricting access to the courts is generally based on a conservative, judicial self-restraint notion, and allowing broader access to the courts is a liberal or judicial activism notion. Currently, a majority of the Supreme Court justices could be called conservative. They were appointed by Presidents Nixon, Reagan, and Bush (Rehnquist, O'Connor, Scalia, Kennedy, and Thomas), and they have used the added concepts of traceability and redressability to restrict plaintiffs' ability to gain standing to challenge government action. Do not be lulled into the belief that concepts like traceability and redressability are neutral and objective criteria. Most of the Supreme Court decisions related to standing inspired spirited dissents. It appears to be true that environmentalist and civil rights plaintiffs have a difficult time meeting the three-pronged test requirements before the current Supreme Court.

Compare the results in *Northeastern Florida Chapter of the Associated General Contractors of America v. City of Jacksonville* (1993)[13] with *Allen v. Wright.* The City of Jacksonville had a minority business set-aside program (10 percent of all city contracts had to be let to minority businesses). The plaintiff is an association that represents contractors in Jacksonville who never bothered to bid on the contracts in question. They did not bid because they believed the contracts would be awarded to minority businesses. The Wrights never tried to enroll their children in the private academies. They did not attempt to enroll because private academies in the South are the modern vehicle for avoiding the requirements of *Brown v. Board of Education* and are not interested in the applications of Black children. While the Court was at a loss to find an injury, traceability, or redressability in *Allen,* it had no difficulty finding all three for the contractors. Indeed, Chief Justice Rehnquist has defined the jurisprudence of strict constructionism as voting against the defendant in criminal cases and against the plaintiff in civil rights cases,[14] regardless of the issues or the facts.

Timing Constraints

Two concepts are related to the timing of a lawsuit: ripeness and mootness. *Ripeness* means the plaintiff tried to file the suit too soon (before it was ripe for a judicial determination). *Mootness* occurs when the conflict that spurred the lawsuit no longer exists between the parties.

Ripeness

Ripeness in administrative law is not a frequent issue. Ripeness problems are somewhat checked in administrative law by two other concepts you will be introduced to shortly, namely exhaustion and primary jurisdiction. Exhaustion requires a potential plaintiff against an agency to try to resolve the dispute within the agency. Primary jurisdiction means that if a potential plaintiff has a choice between suing the agency in court or pursuing an appeal process within the agency, the plaintiff must go through the agency first. Hence, a person in conflict with an agency rarely turns to the courts before the conflict is ripe. You will occasionally come across the term *finality* in the cases you will read. That means you cannot challenge an agency action until the action is final. Finality is associated with ripeness because it means that the ultimate person within the agency must have decided on the issue before it can be ripe for judicial review. For example, prior to the 1990 census, the director of the Bureau of the Census decided to take the census with the help of sampling techniques. Ultimately, however, the secretary of commerce, who is the boss of the Census Bureau director, decided against using sampling to take the census. Finality was the secretary's decision, and the census bureau could not be sued over its decision to sample until the secretary acted.

Ripeness problems often occur when a plaintiff's injuries are in the future and speculative. For example, in 1940, Congress passed the Hatch Act, which forbids federal executive branch employees from campaigning in federal elections. At the time, the union representing federal workers sued the Civil Service Commission, seeking to have the Hatch Act declared unconstitutional as a violation of their freedoms of association and expression. In the complaint, the federal employees contended that they would like to engage in campaign activity but were afraid of arrest and loss of employment. The case was dismissed by the Supreme Court on the basis of ripeness. No one had been arrested, no one had been fired, and no one had engaged in illegal activity; the Civil Service Commission had taken no action against the plaintiffs. According to the Court, the injury was hypothetical, and the case was dismissed for want of a ripe controversy.[15]

In a similar case, the Immigration and Naturalization Service (INS) promulgated a rule that said the agency would treat resident aliens returning to the United States from outside the country as aliens attempting to enter the first time. This rule would potentially have had the most adverse impact on fishermen who travel to Alaska every year during the summer on commercial fishing boats. Their union sued the INS challenging the rule. The fishermen argued that some of them might not be allowed to reenter the country if the rule were allowed to stand. The suit was dismissed on ripeness grounds. The injury (potential inability of some resident aliens to return to the United States) was too speculative and hypothetical.[16] The most recent administrative law ripeness case involves the National Park Service and those who contract with it for concessions in our national parks.[17] The Contract Dispute Act (CDA) requires those who have contract disputes with the federal government to go through a certain procedure. The Act requires one or two attempts to settle within the agency and then allows for an appeal to the federal courts. In 1998, Congress passed the National Parks Omnibus Management Act. The Act establishes a management program for concessions in the national parks and delegates the power to promulgate rules for implementation to DOI. The DOI subdelegated the rule-making power to the National Park Service, which began to promulgate rules. In one of the rules it adopted, a concession contract was interpreted in such a way that the contracts would not fall under the Contract Dispute Act. A trade association that represented a concessioner in the national parks sued the National Park Service. As there was no contract in dispute yet under the new rules, the Supreme Court dismissed the suit for lack of ripeness.

The concept of speculative injury means that people need not wait for actual injury to occur before they can sue an agency. If agency action will cause imminent injury, the case is considered to be ripe. The Court said that the potential injury in the two cases above was "too remote" for judicial determination. For the classic administrative law ripeness case, see *Abbott Laboratories v. Gardner* 387, U.S. 136 (1967).

Mootness

Mootness is the opposite of ripeness. If a conflict has already been resolved by the time it gets to an appellate court, it may be moot, and the suit may be dismissed. The classic example of a mootness case (although it was not an administrative law case) is *DeFunis v. Odegaard*.[18] This was one of the early reverse discrimination cases. DeFunis was denied admission to law school while certain minority applicants who had lower admission statistics than his were admitted. He sued under the equal protection clause of the Fourteenth

Amendment, and a local judge issued an order forcing the law school to admit DeFunis until the courts could resolve the legal issue. By the time the case got to the Supreme Court, DeFunis had graduated from the law school and was a practicing attorney. There was no longer a legal conflict between DeFunis and the law school, so the case was dismissed as moot.

CONSTRAINTS ON THE EXERCISE OF JUDICIAL POWER THAT ARE UNIQUE TO ADMINISTRATIVE LAW

Reviewability

As indicated earlier, the Constitution gives Congress the power to set the jurisdiction of federal courts in terms of the questions it can hear acting as a reviewing court, that is, as a court reviewing the decision of a lower court (or administrative agency) rather than acting as a trial court. Indeed, the ability to manipulate federal courts' appellate jurisdiction is a powerful tool in the check and balance system that Congress uses to check the courts. During the Civil War, for example, Congress withdrew federal court jurisdiction to review habeas corpus petitions from prisoners convicted by military tribunals (*Ex Parte McCardle*, 74 U.S. [7 Wall.] 506 [1869]). More recently, Congress limited federal court review of habeas corpus petitions from state prisoners on death row; see the Antiterrorism and Effective Death Penalty Act of 1996.[19]

In the context of administrative law, the decisions of administrative agencies were once covered by a common law presumption of unreviewability. That is, it was considered "mischief" for the courts to interfere with the performance of executive functions.[20] Only if Congress specifically authorized judicial review of an agency's action would the courts grant review. In Chapter 7 of the Administrative Procedure Act (see Appendix A), Congress specifically authorized judicial review of nearly all federal agencies' decisions: "A person suffering legal wrong because of agency action, or adversely affected or aggrieved by agency action . . . is entitled to judicial review thereof."[21]

Today, then, nearly all federal agency decisions are reviewable, but it is important to remember that this is the case only because Congress has said so. Indeed, that same section of the Administrative Procedure Act exempts from judicial review two situations: (a) those in which Congress has precluded judicial review by statute and (b) those in which agency action is committed to agency discretion by law.

The first of these exceptions is referred to as *statutory preclusion of judicial review*. The most often cited and litigated example of this preclusion involved the Veterans Administration (VA). In passing the Veterans Benefits Act of 1957, Congress said, "The decisions of the administrator on any question of law or fact . . . providing benefits for veterans and their dependents or survivors shall be final . . . and no . . . court of the United States shall have the power or jurisdiction to review any such decision."[22]

Despite the clarity of the language in the Veterans Benefits Act, the courts have found instances in which preclusion of review does not apply, and the courts have reviewed VA actions. Where a decision allegedly violated the free-exercise clause of the Constitution, the Court said statutory preclusion of judicial review did not apply (*Johnson v. Robinson*, 415 U.S. 361 [1974]). In that case, Robinson, a conscientious objector who served his time in alternate service as required by the draft laws, argued that the VA's decision to deny him benefits violated his free exercise of religion. While Congress can preclude judicial review of normal VA benefit denials, it cannot preclude judicial review of benefit denials that are alleged to violate the Constitution. Only the courts can judge constitutional claims. In a more recent case, the Court decided that the statutory preclusion of review did not apply where a decision of the VA ran counter to another congressional act that applied to all federal agencies.

Traynor v. Turnage
485 U.S. 535 (1988)

Traynor and other petitioners in this case are honorably discharged veterans who have not exhausted their education assistance benefits from the VA within ten years following their discharge. In passing the "GI Bill," Congress mandated that benefits must be used within ten years of discharge. Veterans may obtain an extension beyond the ten-year limit, however, if they were prevented from using the benefits "by a physical or mental disorder which was not the result of (their) own willful misconduct" (38 U.S.C. Sec 1662 [a] [1]).

Traynor, a recovering alcoholic, did not use his benefits within the ten-year limit due to his earlier alcoholism. Turnage, the administrator of the VA, enforced the agency's interpretation that "primary" alcoholism (alcoholism unrelated to an underlying psychiatric disorder) is "willful mis-conduct" and denied Traynor's application for a waiver from the ten-year limit.

Traynor argued that the VA's decision is prohibited by the Rehabilitation Act of 1973, which forbids federal agencies from discriminating against handicapped persons solely on the basis of the handicap (and alcoholism is considered to be a handicap).

The VA argued that the administrator's decisions "on questions of law or fact . . . providing benefits . . . shall be final . . . and no court of the U.S. shall have the power to review any such decision."

The district court held that judicial review was not foreclosed and invalidated the VA's interpretation relating to primary alcoholism as violating the Rehabilitation Act. The circuit court of appeals agreed on the question of reviewability but found the VA's interpretation relating to primary alcoholism to be rational and reasonable and not in conflict with the Rehabilitation Act.

Justice White wrote the opinion, joined by Justices Rehnquist, O'Connor, and Stevens and joined in part by Justices Brennan, Marshall, and Blackmun. Justices Scalia and Kennedy took no part in the decision.

We must first consider whether 211(a)'s bar against judicial review of "the decisions of the Administrator on any question of law or fact under any law administered by the Veterans' Administration providing benefits for veterans" extends to petitioner's claim that the Veterans'

Administration regulation defining primary alcoholism as "willful misconduct" discriminates against handicapped persons in violation of the Rehabilitation Act. We have repeatedly acknowledged "the strong presumption that Congress intends judicial review of administrative action." *Bowen v. Michigan Academy of Family Physicians,* 476 U.S. 667, 670 (1986); see also *Dunlop v. Bachowski,* 421 U.S. 560, 567 (1975); *Barlow v. Collins,* 397 U.S. 159, 166–167 (1970). The presumption in favor of judicial review may be overcome "only upon a showing of 'clear and convincing evidence' of a contrary legislative intent." *Abbott Laboratories v. Gardner,* 387 U.S. 136, 141 (1967) (citations omitted). We look to such evidence as "'specific language or specific legislative history that is a reliable indicator of congressional intent,' or a specific congressional intent to preclude judicial review that is 'fairly discernible in the detail of the legislative scheme.'" *Bowen v. Michigan Academy of Family Physicians,* supra, at 673.

In *Johnson v. Robison,* supra, we held that the federal courts could entertain constitutional challenges to veterans' benefits legislation. We determined that "neither the text nor the scant legislative history of 211(a)" provided the requisite "clear and convincing" evidence of congressional intent to foreclose judicial review of challenges to the constitutionality of a law administered by the Veterans' Administration. 415 U.S., at 373–374. In that case, we reasoned that "the prohibitions [of 211(a)] would appear to be aimed at review only of those decisions of law or fact that arise in the administration by the Veterans' Administration of a statute providing benefits for veterans." 415 U.S., at 367. The questions of law presented in that case, however, arose under the Constitution rather than under the veterans' benefits statute and concerned whether there was a valid law on the subject for the Veterans' Administration to execute. We went on to conclude that the principal purposes of 211(a)—"(1) to insure that veterans' benefits claims will not burden the courts and the Veterans' Administration with expensive and time-consuming litigation, and (2) to insure that the technical and complex determinations and applications of Veterans' Administration policy connected with veterans' benefits decisions will be adequately and uniformly made," Id., at 370—would not be frustrated if federal courts were permitted to exercise jurisdiction over constitutional challenges to the very statute that was sought to be enforced. We noted that such challenges "cannot be expected to burden the courts by their volume, nor do they involve technical consideration of Veterans' Administration policy." Id., at 373.

The text and legislative history of 211(a) likewise provide no clear and convincing evidence of any congressional intent to preclude a suit claiming that 504 of the Rehabilitation Act,

a statute applicable to all federal agencies, has invalidated an otherwise valid regulation issued by the Veterans' Administration and purporting to have the force of law. Section 211(a) insulates from review decisions of law and fact "under any law administered by the Veterans' Administration," that is, decisions made in interpreting or applying a particular provision of that statute to a particular set of facts. Id., at 367. But the cases now before us involve the issue whether the law sought to be administered is valid in light of a subsequent statute whose enforcement is not the exclusive domain of the Veterans' Administration. There is no claim that the regulation at issue is inconsistent with the statute under which it was issued; and there is no challenge to the Veterans' Administration's construction of any statute dealing with veterans' benefits, except to the extent that its construction may be affected by the Rehabilitation Act. Nor is there any reason to believe that the Veterans' Administration has any special expertise in assessing the validity of its regulations construing veterans' benefits statutes under a later-passed statute of general application.

Permitting these cases to go forward will not undermine the purposes of 211(a) any more than did the result in *Johnson.* It cannot be assumed that the availability of the federal courts to decide whether there is some fundamental inconsistency between the Veterans' Administration's construction of veterans' benefits statutes, as reflected in the regulation at issue here, and the admonitions of the Rehabilitation Act will enmesh the courts in "the technical and complex determinations and applications of Veterans' Administration policy connected with veterans' benefits decisions" or "burden the courts and the Veterans' Administration with expensive and time-consuming litigation." Id., at 370. Of course, if experience proves otherwise, the Veterans' Administration is fully capable of seeking appropriate relief from Congress. Accordingly, we conclude that the question whether a Veterans' Administration regulation violates the Rehabilitation Act is not foreclosed from judicial review by 211(a). We therefore turn to the merits of petitioners' Rehabilitation Act claim.

III

... It is thus clear that the 1977 legislation precluded an extension of time to a veteran who had not pursued his education because of primary alcoholism. If Congress had intended instead that primary alcoholism not be deemed "willful mis-conduct" for purposes of 1662(a)(1), as it had been deemed for purposes of other veterans' benefits statutes, Congress most certainly would have said so.

Petitioners, however, perceive an inconsistency between 504 and the conclusive presumption that alcoholism not motivated by mental illness is necessarily "willful." They contend that 504 mandates an individualized determination of "willfulness" with respect to each veteran who claims to have been disabled by alcoholism. It would arguably be inconsistent with 504 for Congress to distinguish between categories of disabled veterans according to generalized determinations that lack any substantial basis. If primary alcoholism is not always "willful," as that term has been defined by Congress and the Veterans' Administration, some veterans denied benefits may well be excluded solely on the basis of their disability. We are unable to conclude that Congress failed to act in accordance with 504 in this instance, however, given what the District of Columbia Circuit accurately characterized as "a substantial body of medical literature that even contests the proposition that alcoholism is a disease, much less that it is a disease for which the victim bears no responsibility." 792 F.2d, at 200–201. Indeed, even among many who consider alcoholism a "disease" to which its victims are genetically predisposed, the consumption of alcohol is not regarded as wholly involuntary. See Fingarette, The Perils of Powell: In Search of a Factual Foundation for the "Disease Concept of Alcoholism," 83 Harv. L. Rev. 793, 802–808 (1970). As we see it, 504 does not demand inquiry into whether factors other than mental illness rendered an individual veteran's drinking so entirely beyond his control as to negate any degree of "willfulness" where Congress and the Veterans' Administration have reasonably determined for purposes of the veterans' benefits statutes that no such factors exist.

In sum, we hold that a construction of 1662(a)(1) that reflects the original congressional intent that primary alcoholics not be excused from the 10-year delimiting period for utilizing "G. I. Bill" benefits is not inconsistent with the prohibition on discrimination against the handicapped contained in 504 of the Rehabilitation Act. Accordingly, since we "are not at liberty to pick and choose among congressional enactments ... when two statutes are capable of co-existence," *Morton v. Mancari*, 417 U.S., at 551, we must conclude that the earlier, more specific provisions of 1662(a)(1) were neither expressly nor implicitly repealed by the later, more general provisions of 504.

This litigation does not require the Court to decide whether alcoholism is a disease whose course its victims cannot control. It is not our role to resolve this medical issue on which the authorities remain sharply divided. Our task is to decide whether Congress intended, in enacting 504 of the Rehabilitation Act, to reject the position taken on the issue by the Veterans' Administration and by Congress itself only one year earlier. In our view it is by no means clear that 504 and the characterization of primary alcoholism as a willfully incurred disability are in irreconcilable conflict.

If petitioners and their proponents continue to believe that this position is erroneous, their arguments are better presented to Congress than to the courts ...

Questions

1. The court does review the VA decision; can you explain why?
2. Are there similarities between the reason for reviewing this VA decision and the decision in *Robinson*?

In 1988, as Congress moved the VA from an independent agency to a Cabinet-level agency, it also modified the preclusion of review so that now most (but still not all) of the rulings of the VA are reviewable.

In the fall of 1996, Congress revised the Immigration and Naturalization Act in an attempt to restrict immigration into the United States. In doing so, the conservative Republican majorities believed that the INS would be a better watchdog over immigration policy than the "liberal" courts. Congress made INS immigration decisions unreviewable by the courts in the area of the granting of political asylum. Fortunately for Francisco Lucas Rodriguez-Roman, his case was reviewed by the federal court before the new immigration law went into effect. Mr. Rodriguez so hated the Castro regime that he gave up a career as a teacher to join the merchant marine with the hope that some day he could jump ship in America. This he did, but the INS judge denied him political asylum and ordered him deported to face "harsh if not fatal punishment." The INS judge compared Mr. Rodriguez's desertion to that of Pvt. Eddie Slovik during WW II (Slovik was the only American soldier executed for desertion in WW II). The court reviewing the INS deportation of Mr. Rodriguez reversed the holding that harsh punishment does provide grounds for asylum. At least one member of the court pointed out that had the Rodriguez case hit the courts a few months later after the new immigration bill, Mr. Rodriguez would be on his way back to Cuba because the INS decision would be unreviewable. According to the judge, that surely was not a result intended by the bill's sponsor, Rep. Lamar Smith (R-Texas), who was adamant about denying court review of INS asylum decisions.[23]

If you will turn to the Administrative Procedure Act in Appendix A at the back of your book, you will notice that Sections 564–570 deal with a procedure called *negotiated rule-making* (Neg-Reg), which will be discussed in Chapter 7. For now, however, if you read the first two lines under section 570, which is titled *Judicial Review,* you will see that Congress has exercised statutory preclusion of judicial review for negotiated rules. If you return to the first case in this book in Chapter 2, *Weiner v. U.S.,* you will see that the decisions of the War Claims Commission were precluded from judicial review.

The second exception to general reviewability of agency actions is "agency action committed to agency discretion by law," and this is likely to be confusing. Prior to the Administrative Procedure Act of 1946, most administrative decisions were considered to be unreviewable. For the most part, Congress intended to change that with the passage of the Act. It declared that, with two exceptions, all actions and decisions of federal agencies are subject to judicial review in federal court. First, Congress meant to exempt from judicial review the decisions of agencies for which Congress specifically excluded review in the enabling legislation, such as the VA, War Claims Commission, or negotiated rules. Second, Congress (apparently) intended to exempt another category of agency decisions, but the best description they could come up with was "where agency action is committed to agency discretion by law."

You may be thinking to yourself, "Well, that doesn't mean much to me, but surely a judge, trained in the law, will understand what Congress meant." You would be wrong. There are not many cases in which courts have had to interpret this clause, but where courts have had to deal with it, the judges have been forced to "guess at its meaning and differ as to its application." Justice Souter's opinion in the case below discusses some of the past decisions in this area.

Lincoln v. Vigil
508 U.S. 182 (1993)

Justice Souter delivered the unanimous opinion of the Court.

For several years in the late 1970s and early 1980s, the Indian Health Service provided diagnostic and treatment services, referred to collectively as the Indian Children's Program, to handicapped Indian children in the Southwest. In 1985, the Service decided to reallocate the Program's resources to a nationwide effort to assist such children. We hold that the Service's decision to discontinue the Program was "committed to agency discretion by law" and therefore not subject to judicial review under the Administrative Procedure Act, 5 U.S.C. § 701(a)(2) and that the Service's exercise of that discretion was not subject to the notice-and-comment rulemaking requirements imposed by § 553.

I

The Indian Health Service, an agency within the Public Health Service of the Department of Health and Human Services, provides health care for some 1.5 million American Indian and Alaska Native people . . . The Service receives yearly lump-sum appropriations from Congress and expends the funds under authority of the Snyder Act, 25 U.S.C. § 13, and the Indian Health Care Improvement Act, 25 U.S.C. § 1601. So far as it concerns us here, the Snyder Act authorizes the Service to "expend such moneys as Congress may from time to time appropriate, for the benefit, care, and assistance of the Indians," for the "relief of distress and conservation of health." The Improvement Act authorizes expenditures for Indian mental-health care, and specifically for "therapeutic and residential treatment centers" . . .

This case concerns a collection of related services, commonly known as the Indian Children's Program, that the Service provided from 1978 to 1985. In the words of the Court of Appeals, a "clou[d of] bureaucratic haze" obscures the history of the Program, . . . which seems to have grown out of a plan "to establish therapeutic and residential treatment centers for disturbed Indian children." These centers were to be established under a "major cooperative care agreement" between the Service and the Bureau of Indian Affairs and would have provided such children "with intensive care in a residential setting."

Congress never expressly appropriated funds for these centers. In 1978, however, the Service allocated approximately $292,000 from its fiscal year 1978 appropriation to its office in Albuquerque, New Mexico, for the planning and development of a pilot project for handicapped Indian children, which became known as the Indian Children's Program. The pilot project apparently convinced the Service that a building was needed, and, in 1979, the Service requested $3.5 million from Congress to construct a diagnostic and treatment center for handicapped Indian children. . . . The appropriation for fiscal year 1980 did not expressly provide the requested funds, however, and legislative reports indicated only that Congress had increased the Service's funding by $300,000 for nationwide expansion and development of the Program in coordination with the Bureau.

Plans for a national program to be managed jointly by the Service and the Bureau were never fulfilled, however, and the Program continued simply as an offering of the Service's Albuquerque office, from which the Program's staff of 11 to 16 employees would make monthly visits to Indian communities in New Mexico and Southern Colorado and on the Navajo and Hopi Reservations. The Program's staff provided "diagnostic, evaluation, treatment planning and followup services" for Indian children with emotional, educational, physical, or mental handicaps. "For parents, community groups, school personnel and health care personnel," the staff provided training in child development, prevention of handicapping conditions, and care of the handicapped child." Congress never authorized or appropriated monies expressly for the Program, and the Service continued to pay for its regional activities out of annual lump-sum appropriations from 1980 to 1985, during which period the Service repeatedly apprised Congress of the Program's continuing operation.

Nevertheless, the Service had not abandoned the proposal for a nationwide treatment program, and in June 1985 it notified those who referred patients to the Program that it was "re-evaluating [the Program's] purpose . . . as a national mental health program for Indian children and adolescents." In August 1985, the Service determined that Program staff hitherto assigned to provide direct clinical services should be reassigned as consultants to other nationwide Service programs, and discontinued the direct clinical services to Indian children in the Southwest. The Service announced its decision in a memorandum, dated August 21, 1985, addressed to Service offices and Program referral sources . . .

The Service invited public "input" during this "difficult transition," and explained that the reallocation of resources had been "motivated by our goal of increased mental health services for all Indian [c]hildren." Ibid. [FN2]

Respondents, handicapped Indian children eligible to receive services through the Program, subsequently brought this action for declaratory and injunctive relief against petitioners, the Director of the Service and others (collectively, the Service) in the United States District Court for the District of New Mexico. Respondents alleged, inter alia, that the Service's decision to discontinue direct clinical services violated the federal trust responsibility to Indians, the Snyder Act, the Improvement Act, the Administrative Procedure Act, various agency regulations, and the Fifth Amendment's Due Process Clause.

II

First is the question whether it was error for the Court of Appeals to hold the substance of the Service's decision to terminate the Program reviewable under the APA. The Act provides that "[a] person suffering legal wrong because of agency action, or adversely affected or aggrieved by agency action within the meaning of a relevant statute, is entitled to judicial review thereof," and we have read the Act as embodying a "basic presumption of judicial review." *Abbott Laboratories v. Gardner*, 387 U.S. 136. This is "just" a presumption, however, *Block v. Community Nutrition Institute*, 467 U.S. 340 (1984), and under § 701(a)(2) agency action is not subject to judicial review "to the extent that" such action "is committed to agency discretion by law." As we explained in *Heckler v. Chaney*, 470 U.S. 821 (1985), § 701(a)(2) makes it clear that "review is not to be had" in those rare circumstances where the relevant statute "is drawn so that a court would have no meaningful standard against which to judge the agency's exercise of discretion." "In such a case, the statute ('law') can be taken to have 'committed' the decisionmaking to the agency's judgment absolutely." *Heckler*, supra, at 830.

Over the years, we have read § 701(a)(2) to preclude judicial review of certain categories of administrative decisions that courts traditionally have regarded as "committed to agency discretion" . . . In *Heckler* itself, we held an agency's decision not to institute enforcement proceedings to be presumptively unreviewable under § 701(a)(2). An agency's "decision not to enforce often involves a complicated balancing of a number of factors which are peculiarly within its expertise," ibid., and for this and other good reasons, we concluded, "such a decision has traditionally been 'committed to agency discretion.' " Similarly, in *ICC v. Locomotive Engineers*, 482 U.S. 270 (1987), we held that § 701(a)(2) precludes judicial review of another type of administrative decision traditionally left to agency discretion, an agency's refusal to grant reconsideration of an action because of material error. In so holding, we emphasized "the impossibility of devising an adequate standard of review for such agency action." Ibid. Finally, . . . 701(a)(2) precludes judicial review of a decision by the Director of

Central Intelligence to terminate an employee in the interests of national security, an area of executive action "in which courts have long been hesitant to intrude."

The allocation of funds from a lump-sum appropriation is another administrative decision traditionally regarded as committed to agency discretion. After all, the very point of a lump-sum appropriation is to give an agency the capacity to adapt to changing circumstances and meet its statutory responsibilities in what it sees as the most effective or desirable way. See *International Union, United Automobile, Aerospace & Agricultural Implement Workers of America v. Donovan*, 746 F.2d 855, 861 (1984) (Scalia, J.) ("A lump-sum appropriation leaves it to the recipient agency (as a matter of law, at least) to distribute the funds among some or all of the permissible objects as it sees fit"). For this reason, a fundamental principle of appropriations law is that where "Congress merely appropriates lump-sum amounts without statutorily restricting what can be done with those funds, a clear inference arises that it does not intend to impose legally binding restrictions, and indicia in committee reports and other legislative history as to how the funds should or are expected to be spent do not establish any legal requirements on" the agency. . . . *American Hospital Assn. v. NLRB*, 111 S.Ct. 1539 (1991) (statements in committee reports do not have the force of law). Put another way, a lump-sum appropriation reflects a congressional recognition that an agency must be allowed "flexibility to shift . . . funds within a particular . . . appropriation account so that" the agency "can make necessary adjustments for 'unforeseen developments'" and "'changing requirements.'"

[2] Like the decision against instituting enforcement proceedings, then, an agency's allocation of funds from a lump-sum appropriation requires "a complicated balancing of a number of factors which are peculiarly within its expertise": whether its "resources are best spent" on one program or another; whether it "is likely to succeed" in fulfilling its statutory mandate; whether a particular program "best fits the agency's overall policies"; and, "indeed,

whether the agency has enough resources" to fund a program "at all." *Heckler,* 470 U.S., at 831. As in *Heckler,* so here, the "agency is far better equipped than the courts to deal with the many variables involved in the proper ordering of its priorities." Of course, an agency is not free simply to disregard statutory responsibilities: Congress may always circumscribe agency discretion to allocate resources by putting restrictions in the operative statutes (though not, as we have seen, just in the legislative history).

And, of course, we hardly need to note that an agency's decision to ignore congressional expectations may expose it to grave political consequences. But as long as the agency allocates funds from a lump-sum appropriation to meet permissible statutory objectives, § 701(a)(2) gives the courts no leave to intrude. "[T]o [that] extent," the decision to allocate funds "is committed to agency discretion by law."

[3] The Service's decision to discontinue the Program is accordingly unreviewable under § 701(a)(2). As the Court of Appeals recognized the appropriations Acts for the relevant period do not so much as mention the Program, and both the Snyder Act and the Improvement Act likewise speak about Indian health only in general terms. It is true that the Service repeatedly apprised Congress of the Program's continued operation, but, as we have explained, these representations do not translate through the medium of legislative history into legally binding obligations. The reallocation of agency resources to assist handicapped Indian children nationwide clearly falls within the Service's statutory mandate to provide health care to Indian people, and respondents, indeed, do not seriously contend otherwise. The decision to terminate the Program was committed to the Service's discretion.

IV

The judgment of the Court of Appeals is reversed, and the case is remanded for further proceedings consistent with this opinion.

It is so ordered.

Questions

1. The agency's decision to terminate the program was not reviewable. Can you explain why?
2. Justice Souter lists several kinds of decisions that are not reviewable because they are committed to agency discretion by law. Can you pick them out?

In the *Lincoln* case above, the Court finds that the agency action is unreviewable because it is committed to agency discretion by law. In the case below, the secretary of transportation argues that his decision is unreviewable, but the Court finds that it is reviewable. See if you can find another category of agency decisions that are not reviewable as committed to agency discretion.

Citizens to Preserve Overton Park v. Volpe
401 U.S. 402 (1971)

In 1968, the secretary of transportation announced that he agreed with local Memphis officials that a six-lane federal highway would have to be routed through Overton Park. In 1969, the secretary approved the authorizations of federal highway funds for the highway through the park. Neither the announcement nor the decision was accompanied by a statement of reasons or findings of fact or an explanation.

Citizens to Preserve Overton Park sued the secretary to enjoin the release of federal monies on the basis of section 4 of the Department of Transportation Act of 1966, 49 U.S.C. 1653, and section 138 of the Federal-Aid Highway Act of 1968, 23 U.S.C. 138. They forbid the authorization of federal funds for highways through public parks if a "feasible and prudent" alternate route exists. If the secretary finds that no feasible and prudent alternate route exists, then the secretary may release funds only after "all possible planning to minimize harm" to the park.

Both the district and circuit courts would have dismissed the suit against the secretary of transportation (Volpe) on a technicality. The Supreme Court merely said that the two lower courts were wrong to dismiss the case and sent it back for trial to the district court. In their dissent, Justices Black and Brennan argued that the secretary of transportation had abused his power and the whole affair should be sent back to him for hearings and a new decision (i.e., they would void the secretary's decision rather than overruling the lower courts on technical points of law).

Justice Marshall wrote the opinion, joined by Chief Justice Burger and Justices Harlan, Stewart, White, and Blackmun. Justice Black dissented, joined by Justice Brennan. Justice Douglas did not participate.

A threshold question—whether petitioners are entitled to any judicial review—is easily answered. Section 701 of the Administrative Procedure Act, 5 U.S.C. 701, provides that the action of "each authority of the Government of the United States," which includes the Department of Transportation, is subject to judicial review except where there is a statutory prohibition on review or where "agency action is committed to agency discretion by law." In this case, there is no indication that Congress sought to prohibit judicial review and there is most certainly no "showing of 'clear and convincing evidence' of a . . . legislative intent" to restrict access to judicial review. Similarly, the Secretary's decision here does not fall within the exception for action "committed to agency discretion." This is a very narrow exception. Berger, Administrative Arbitrariness and Judicial Review, 65 *Col. L. Rev.* 55 (1965). The legislative history of the Administrative Procedure Act indicates that it is applicable in those rare instances where "statutes are drawn in such broad terms that in a given case there is no law to apply." Section 4 (f) of the Department of Transportation Act and 138 of the Federal-Aid Highway Act are clear and specific directives. Both the Department of Transportation Act and the Federal-Aid Highway Act provide that the Secretary "shall not approve any program or project" that requires the use of any public park land "unless (1) there is no feasible and prudent alternative to the use of such land, and (2) such program includes all possible planning to minimize harm to such park. . . ." 23 U.S.C. 138 49 U.S.C. 1653 (f). This language is a plain and explicit bar to the use of federal funds for construction of highways through parks—only the most unusual situations are exempted.

Despite the clarity of the statutory language, respondents argue that the Secretary has wide discretion. They recognize that the requirement that there be no "feasible" alternative route admits of little administrative discretion. For this exemption to apply the Secretary must find that as a matter of sound engineering it would not be feasible to build the highway along any other route. Respondents argue, however, that the requirement that there be no other "prudent" route requires the Secretary to engage in a wide-ranging balancing of competing interests.

They contend that the Secretary should weigh the detriment resulting from the destruction of park land against the cost of other routes, safety considerations, and other factors, and determine on the basis of the importance that he attaches to these other factors whether, on balance, alternative feasible routes would be "prudent." But no such wide-ranging endeavor was intended.

It is obvious that in most cases considerations of cost, directness of route, and community disruption will indicate that park land should be used for highway construction whenever possible. Although it may be necessary to transfer funds from one jurisdiction to another, there will always be a smaller outlay required from the public purse when park land is used since the public already owns the land and there will be no need to pay for right-of-way. And since people do not live or work in parks, if a highway is built on park land no one will have to leave his home or give up his business. Such factors are common to substantially all highway construction.

Thus, if Congress intended these factors to be on an equal footing with preservation of park land there would have been no need for the statutes. Congress clearly did not intend that cost and disruption of the community were to be ignored by the Secretary. But the very existence of the statutes indicates that protection of park land was to be given paramount importance. The few green havens that are public parks were not to be lost unless there were truly unusual factors present in a particular case or the cost or community disruption resulting from alternative routes reached extraordinary magnitudes. If the statutes are to have any meaning, the Secretary cannot approve the destruction of park land unless he finds that alternative routes present unique problems.

Plainly, there is "law to apply" and thus the exemption for action "committed to agency discretion" is inapplicable. But the existence of judicial review is only the start: the standard for review must also be determined.

The student should not be overly concerned that the Court's attempt to clarify the "committed to agency discretion" clause may not have been much help. It is easier to describe certain situations where agency action is committed to agency discretion by law than it is to define the concept. Here is the laundry list:

1. When there is no meaningful standard against which to judge the agency's action

2. When there is no law to apply to the agency's action (from *Overton Park*)

3. When an agency decides not to institute enforcement proceedings

4. When an agency refuses to grant a reconsideration hearing after a final decision

5. When an agency uses funds appropriated from Congress as a lump-sum (from *Lincoln*)

6. When agency decisions involve national security or defense issues

In a recent case, the CIA director fired an employee because the employee was a homosexual. The statutory authority used by the director says, "the Director . . . may, in his discretion, terminate the employment of any officer or employee of the agency *whenever he shall deem such termination necessary or advisable in the interest of the United States* [the emphasis is mine]." The terminated employee sued the director on two fronts: First, he alleged the director abused his discretion under the Act (firing for sexual orientation is not in the interests of the United States) and, second, he alleged a constitutional due process violation in that he was fired without a hearing. The Court said that the director's firing decision under the Act was committed to agency discretion by law and not reviewable. As was the case in the *Robinson* case, the constitutional claim was reviewable.[24] What is important to grasp here is that reviewability of agency action is granted by legislation and that, generally, Congress intended to extend judicial review to most agency actions. There are two exceptions. The first exception is where Congress specifically forbids judicial review for a particular agency or a particular kind of action. The second exception is a nebulous category of actions referred to as "actions committed to agency discretion," a category that is hard to define and little used.

For an interesting case dealing with both standing and action committed to agency discretion by law, see *Dalton v. Specter*, 511 U.S. 642 (1994). In this case, Senator Arlen Specter (R-Pennsylvania) challenged the closure of the Philadelphia Naval Shipyard under the 1990 Defense Base Closure and Realignment Act. The majority of the court found that the senator lacked standing under the Administrative Procedure Act and that President Clinton's acceptance of Closure Commission recommendations was action committed to the President and, hence, was not reviewable. In a concurring opinion, four justices thought that base closure decisions precluded judicial review by statute.

Reviewability of Cost/Benefit Analysis, Risk Analysis, and Science

One of the hottest areas of academic debate in administrative law is whether and to what extent the science and data used by agencies is reviewable in court. Recall from the material in Chapter 2 that Congress passed (as a rider to a budget bill) the Data Quality Act. Because it was a rider, there is no legislative history, no committee hearings, no floor debate, and so on. The Act delegates legislative power to the White House, actually to the OMB, which subdelegates it to the Office of Information and Regulatory Affairs, which issues guidelines for all agencies on the use of data and science. Each agency, then, is to adopt its own specific guidelines and procedures for making its data and science available to the public. The public and regulated parties are to be able to access an agency's data or science and challenge it. Furthermore, by other legislation, nearly all agencies (but the White House is mostly concerned with the environment and health areas) are required to engage in cost/benefit or risk analysis prior to adopting rules. A major issue is whether an agency's cost/benefit analysis, the science on which it relies, or any agency decision not to rectify challenged science is reviewable. The issue is open because agency action is generally not reviewable unless it is final. The concept of finality means that the head of an agency has made a final decision or an agency's proposed rule has become a final rule with the force and effect of law. Typically, an agency's cost/benefit or risk analysis is done prior to proposing the rule (if the benefits do not outweigh the costs, there is no sense proposing the rule).

The question of whether a court can review agency science is debatable because, as indicated above, Congress has not addressed the issue. Neither has the Supreme Court. Indeed, there is little case law on the subject and the circuits appear to be in conflict.

Although the Supreme Court has not addressed that specific issue, it has decided a case that involved the quality of the science placed in evidence at trial. In 1993, the Court decided *Daubert v. Merrell Dow Pharmaceuticals,*[25] in which the parents of minor children who were born with defects sued the manufacturer of the prescription drug Bendectin. The plaintiffs alleged that the mothers took the drug during pregnancy, and it caused the deformities. The drug company moved to dismiss the case, arguing that no epidemiological (human statistical) studies demonstrated a statistically significant association between Bendectin and birth defects. The phrase *statistically significant association* means the probability that two variables vary together is not due to chance (the ingestion of Bendectin, together with the presence of birth defects, either is or is not due to chance). The plaintiffs relied on test-tube and live-animal studies, pharmacological studies of drugs with similar properties, and reanalysis or recalculation of previously published epidemiological studies.

The trial judge sided with the drug company and dismissed the suit. The judge concluded that epidemiological evidence was the most reliable. Therefore, the live-animal, test-tube, and pharmacological evidence was inadmissible. The recalculated epidemiological evidence was inadmissible as well because it was not peer reviewed. The court of appeals agreed, but the Supreme Court reversed. Actually, the issue in the case was a narrow one: What is the proper standard for the admission of expert testimony under federal rules of evidence? The Court said that scientific evidence must be both relevant and reliable. Reliability means that it is based on scientific validity. Validity in scientific parlance means that a measure measures what it is supposed to measure.[26] The Supreme Court reversed the lower courts because they had applied the wrong standard. It was possible that some of the excluded testimony was both relevant and reliable. This is the only Supreme Court case to examine judicial review of science, but its relevance to administrative law may be tenuous. *Daubert* was a tort case, and other than the federal rules of evidence, there was no statutory law to compound things. Two circuit courts have decided administrative law cases that are on point and have reached somewhat different conclusions.

In a 2002 case,[27] the EPA issued a report in 1993 entitled *Respiratory Health Effects of Passive Smoking: Lung Cancer and Other Disorders.* The report categorized secondhand smoke (environmental tobacco smoke) as a Group A (known human) carcinogen responsible for 3,000 nonsmoker deaths a year. Nearly all of the American tobacco companies sued. The tobacco plaintiffs alleged a number of problems with the EPA's procedure, studies, and the report. They argued that the EPA exceeded its jurisdiction and violated some statutory restrictions on investigating tobacco products. They accused the EPA of not following the proper procedure, and they said the decision making was not reasoned (as required by the Administrative Procedure Act) because of the faulty science and scientific procedures. The trial judge decided in favor of the tobacco companies and vacated the EPA's report. Although the trial judge was overruled by the circuit court, what he concluded about the EPA's behavior is instructive because it echoes what the business community has been arguing for years about overburdensome bureaucratic rules and the "junk science" on which they are based.

In this case, the court said the EPA publicly committed to a conclusion before research had begun; excluded industry by violating the Act's procedural requirements; adjusted established procedure and scientific norms to validate the agency's public conclusion; and aggressively used the Act's authority to disseminate findings to establish a de facto regulatory scheme intended to restrict plaintiff's products and to influence public opinion. On conducting the secondhand smoke risk assessment, the EPA disregarded information and made findings on selected information; did not disseminate significant epidemiological information; deviated from its own risk assessment guidelines; failed to disclose important findings and reasoning; and left significant questions without answers. The EPA's conduct left substantial holes in the administrative record. While so doing, the EPA produced limited evidence, then claimed the weight of the agency's research evidence demonstrated that secondhand smoke causes cancer.[28]

The circuit court, however, found that the report was not a final agency action and neither it nor the science/procedure that produced it was reviewable under the Administrative Procedure Act. The EPA report was produced pursuant to a mandate from a law called the Radon Research Act, which orders the EPA to establish a research program for radon gas and indoor air quality. It also instructs the EPA to coordinate such research at the federal, state, local, and private level. Furthermore, the EPA is directed to disseminate the research findings. You will notice from the above description of the Radon Research Act that it does not authorize the EPA to take any regulatory action. The EPA is simply to conduct, coordinate, and disseminate research. Citing both *Bennett v. Spear* and *Dalton v. Specter,* the Court found that the agency action (issuing the report) had "no direct and appreciable legal consequences" on either the plaintiffs or anyone else. Hence, it is not a "final agency action" so the report is unreviewable.[29]

The second case is slightly different because the agency action affected other federal and state agencies, which then caused private citizens to react: It did have a legal effect. The case is *Tozzi v. HHS* (2001),[30] and it was mentioned in the discussion of junk science in Chapter 2; it appears at the end of this chapter. In the *Tozzi* case, the Department of Health and Human Services moved a chemical (dioxin) from one category to another, from "reasonably anticipated to cause cancer" to "a known carcinogen" and published it as such in the *Federal Register.* Once it was published in the *Federal Register* as a known carcinogen, the Occupational Safety and Health Administration (OSHA) included it in its hazardous communication standards, which caused businesses that use it to warn employees about it. That is a legal effect, and the Court said the agency action was reviewable. The *Tozzi* case at the end of the chapter is a good one because Jim Tozzi, a former member of the U.S. House of Representatives, is one of the leaders of the antiregulation forces. He is responsible for the attachment of the Data Quality Act as a rider, and he is the name associated with the concept of junk science.[31] The case is interesting because the Court analyzes the quality of peer review and the science the agency used.

Exhaustion

If people believe they have been or are about to be injured by administrative action, they cannot turn to the courts for help until they have gone through all the available channels within the agency. That is, they must *exhaust* all legal remedies within the agency.

Every agency has published procedural rules for clients of the agency to follow in trying to redress an adverse agency decision or other agency action. For example, if people believe they are eligible for veterans benefits, Social Security, or a tax exemption, they can apply to the VA or Social Security Administration or, in the latter case, simply claim the exemption on a tax return. If the claim is denied in any of those situations, the procedure to follow is similar for anyone wishing to challenge that denial. First, appeal the initial denial decision to the supervisor of the clerk who processed the application and determined that it did not qualify for the benefit (or tax exemption). Most often, the supervisor will support the position of the clerk. Next, appeal to the supervisor's supervisor, who will most likely be the director of the local office. If that appeal is unsuccessful, appeal the decision of the local director to the regional office. If the decision from the regional office is still adverse, some agencies require (allow) an appeal to the head of the agency for a final agency decision, which can then (and only then) be challenged in the courts. That is the concept of exhaustion, and under normal circumstances, a federal court will simply not entertain a suit by a plaintiff who has not exhausted all avenues of appeal available within the agency. Virtually all states use the concept of exhaustion, but there are myriad differences between states in terms of exceptions allowed so that a potential plaintiff can "short circuit" exhaustion.

In a recent exhaustion case, a prison inmate claimed that prison guards assaulted him; tightened and twisted handcuffs, which caused injury; withheld medical treatment for the injured wrists; and threw cleaning fluid in his face.[32] He wanted money damages for violation of his constitutional right to be free from cruel and unusual punishment. Congress passed the Prison Litigation Reform Act of 1995, which in pertinent part required prison inmates to exhaust internal prison remedies before suing over prison conditions. The prison in question had an inmate grievance procedure with a hearing and two stages of appeal, but even if an inmate was successful in pursuing a grievance, money damages were not available as a remedy. Booth, the inmate, filed a grievance and had the hearing but skipped the appeals because he could not obtain the money damages even if he won. He sued instead. The Supreme Court said it was proper to dismiss his suit for failure to exhaust available remedies, even if the remedy he sought was not available through the agency procedure.

Primary Jurisdiction

When a question could be handled by either a court of law or an administrative agency, the court should normally decline to exercise jurisdiction until the administrative agency has had the opportunity to deal with the issue first. This is the concept of *primary jurisdiction,* and it generally requires a party in conflict with an agency to go through the agency first rather than turning to the courts.

For example, between 1944 and 1950, the Army contracted with the Bangor and Sea Board Railroad and with the Western Pacific to transport bomb casings filled with napalm. The railroads billed the Army at a first-class rate for carrying "incendiary bombs," but the Army paid at the lower, fifth-class rate for carrying "gasoline in steel drums." The railroads here have two choices. They can sue in a federal court of claims, or they can bring their case to the Interstate Commerce Commission (ICC).

In fact, the railroads chose the court of claims, which decided in their favor. However, on appeal, the Supreme Court said that "the question of tariff construction, as well as the reasonableness of the tariff . . . are within the exclusive primary jurisdiction of the ICC." The Court vacated the decision of the court of claims and mandated that the issue be dealt with first by the ICC.[33] Following is one of the most famous primary jurisdiction cases, in which Allegheny Airlines had the misfortune of bumping consumer activist Ralph Nader from one of its flights.

Nader v. Allegheny Airlines, Incorporated
426 U.S. 290 (1976)

Justice Powell delivered the opinion, joined by a unanimous court (Burger, Brennan, Stewart, White, Marshall, Blackmun, Rehnquist, and Stevens).

I

The facts are not contested. Petitioner agreed to make several appearances in Connecticut on April 28, 1972, in support of the fundraising efforts of the Connecticut Citizen Action Group (CCAG), a nonprofit public interest organization. His two principal appearances were to be at a noon rally in Hartford and a later address at the Storrs campus of the University of Connecticut. On April 25, petitioner reserved a seat on respondent's flight 864 for April 28. The flight was scheduled to leave Washington, D.C., at 10:15 a.m. and to arrive in Hartford at 11:15 a.m. Petitioner's ticket was purchased from a travel agency on the morning of the flight. It indicated, by the standard "OK" notation, that the reservation was confirmed.

Petitioner arrived at the boarding and check-in area approximately five minutes before the scheduled departure time. He was informed that all seats on the flight were occupied and that he, like several other passengers who had arrived shortly before him, could not be accommodated. Explaining that he had to arrive in Hartford in time for the noon rally, petitioner asked respondent's agent to determine whether any standby passengers had been allowed to board by mistake or whether anyone already on board would voluntarily give up his or her seat. Both requests were refused. In accordance with respondent's practice, petitioner was offered alternative transportation by air taxi to Philadelphia, where connections could be made with an Allegheny flight scheduled to arrive in Hartford at 12:15 p.m. Fearing that the Philadelphia connection, which allowed only 10 minutes between planes, was too close, petitioner rejected this offer and elected to fly to Boston, where he was met by a CCAG staff member who drove him to Storrs.

Both parties agree that petitioner's reservation was not honored because respondent had accepted more reservations for flight 864 than it could in fact accommodate. One hour prior to the flight, 107 reservations had been confirmed for the 100 seats actually available. Such overbooking is a common industry practice, designed to ensure that each flight leaves with as few empty seats as possible despite the large number of "no-shows"—reservation-holding passengers who do not appear at flight time. By the use of statistical studies of no-show patterns on specific flights, the airlines attempt to predict the appropriate number of reservations necessary to fill each flight. In this way, they attempt to ensure the most efficient use of aircraft while preserving a flexible booking system that permits passengers to cancel and change reservations without notice or penalty. At times the practice of overbooking results in oversales, which occur when more reservation-holding passengers than can be accommodated actually appear to board the flight. When this occurs, some passengers must be denied boarding ("bumped"). The chance that any particular passenger will be bumped is so negligible that few prospective passengers aware of the possibility would give it a second thought.

In April 1972, the month in which petitioner's reservation was dishonored, 6.7 confirmed passengers per 10,000 enplanements were denied boarding on domestic flights. For all domestic airlines, oversales resulted in bumping an average of 5.4 passengers per 10,000 enplanements in 1972, and 4.6 per 10,000 enplanements in 1973. In domestic operations respondent oversold 6.3 seats per 10,000 enplanements in 1972 and 4.5 seats per 10,000 enplanements in 1973. Thus, based on the 1972 experience of all domestic airlines, there was only slightly more than one chance in 2,000 that any particular passenger would be bumped on a given flight. Nevertheless, the total number of confirmed ticket holders denied seats is quite substantial, numbering over 82,000 passengers in 1972 and about 76,000 in 1973.

The only issue before us concerns the Court of Appeals' disposition on the merits of petitioner's claim of fraudulent misrepresentation. Although the court rejected respondent's argument that the existence of the Board's cease-and-desist power under 411 of the Act eliminates all private remedies for common-law torts arising from unfair or deceptive practices by regulated carriers, it held that a determination by the Board that a practice is not deceptive within the meaning of 411 would, as a matter of law, preclude a common-law tort action seeking damages for injuries caused by that practice. Therefore, the court held that the Board must be allowed to determine in the first instance whether the challenged practice (in this case, the alleged failure to disclose the practice of overbooking) falls within the ambit of 411. The court took judicial notice that a rule-making proceeding concerning possible changes in reservation practices in response to the 1973–1974 fuel crisis was already underway and that a challenge to the carriers' overbooking practices had been raised by an intervenor in that proceeding. The District Court was instructed to stay further action on petitioner's misrepresentation claim pending the outcome of the rule-making proceeding. The Court of Appeals characterized its holding as "but another application of the principles of primary jurisdiction, a doctrine whose purpose is the coordination of the workings of agency and court," 512 F.2d, at 544.

The question before us, then, is whether the Board must be given an opportunity to determine whether respondent's alleged failure to disclose its practice of deliberate overbooking is a deceptive practice under 411 before petitioner's common-law action is allowed to proceed. The decision of the Court of Appeals requires the District Court to stay the action brought by petitioner in order to give the Board an opportunity to resolve the question. If the Board were to find that there had been no violation of 411, respondent would be immunized from common-law liability.

The doctrine of primary jurisdiction is concerned with promoting proper relationships between the courts and administrative agencies charged with particular regulatory duties. The doctrine has been applied, for example, when an action otherwise within the jurisdiction of the court raises a question of the validity of a rate or practice included in a tariff filed with an agency, e.g., *Danna v. Air France*, 463 F.2d 407 (CA2 1972); *Southwestern Sugar & Molasses Co. v. River Terminals Corp.*, 360 U.S. 411, 417–418 (1959), particularly when the issue involves technical questions of fact uniquely within the expertise and experience of an agency—such as matters turning on an assessment of industry conditions, e.g., *United States v. Western Pacific R. Co.*, supra, at 66–67. In this case, however, considerations of uniformity in regulation and of technical expertise do not call for prior reference to the Board.

Petitioner seeks damages for respondent's failure to disclose its overbooking practices. He makes no challenge to any provision in the tariff, and indeed there is no tariff provision or Board regulation applicable to disclosure practices. Petitioner also makes no challenge, comparable to those made in *Southwestern Sugar & Molasses Co. v. River Terminals Corp.,* supra, and *Lichten v. Eastern Airlines, Inc.,* 189 F.2d 939 (CA2 1951), to limitations on common-law damages imposed through exculpatory clauses included in a tariff. Referral of the misrepresentation issue to the Board cannot be justified by the interest in informing the court's ultimate decision with "the expert and specialized knowledge," *United States v. Western Pacific R. Co.,* supra, at 64, of the Board. The action brought by petitioner does not turn on a determination of the reasonableness of a challenged practice— a determination that could be facilitated by

an informed evaluation of the economics or technology of the regulated industry. The standards to be applied in an action for fraudulent misrepresentation are within the conventional competence of the courts, and the judgment of a technically expert body is not likely to be helpful in the application of these standards to the facts of this case.

III

We conclude that petitioner's tort action should not be stayed pending reference to the Board and accordingly the decision of the Court of Appeals on this issue is reversed. The Court of Appeals did not address the question whether petitioner had introduced sufficient evidence to sustain his claim. We remand the case for consideration of that question and for further proceedings consistent with this opinion.

Question

1. This case and previous cases make it clear that courts do not always have to defer to agencies in cases like this. Can you list the two situations that need to exist before primary jurisdiction comes into play? Try to answer this question from the case before checking the summary section at the end of the chapter.

For a more recent primary jurisdiction case, see *Marquez v. Screen Actors Guild,* 525 U.S. 33 (1998). Naomi Marquez was an actress who won a part in a television show. The Screen Actors Guild had a union security clause with the production company. Such a clause prohibits the company from hiring actors unless they belong to the union. If they do not belong, the would-be actors are given a specific amount of time to join the union. Ms. Marquez failed to join the union by the time the company was ready to film, so they hired another actress. The plaintiff sued the union in federal district court, claiming that the union committed what is called an *unfair representation,* a claim that would have been appropriately heard in federal district court. The union, however, claimed that what the actress was complaining about was an *unfair labor practice,* and such a claim would fall within the primary jurisdiction of the National Labor Relations Board (NLRB). The Supreme Court agreed that it was an issue of whether the union engaged in an unfair labor practice; hence, the district court did not have jurisdiction to hear the case until the NLRB decided the issue first.

An individual who has been adversely affected by a federal agency action or decision and who wants to sue must demonstrate (a) that the court has jurisdiction to hear the case, (b) that the individual has standing to challenge the administrative decision or action, (c) that the case is ripe and not moot, (d) that the agency's action is reviewable, (e) that the individual has exhausted all administrative remedies available within the agency, and (f) that primary jurisdiction problems are not involved. If all of those barriers are overcome, the individual may challenge the agency action in court. The question to which we now turn our attention is this: Once a court has decided to review agency action, how closely should the court examine the agency behavior? This is referred to as the *scope of review.*

Section 706 of the Administrative Procedures Act, entitled *Scope of Review,* authorized courts reviewing agency action to take two kinds of action. First, in Section 706 [1] (B) courts can compel agency action if an agency has illegally refused to act (see *Heckler v. Chaney* below and *Norton v. Southern Utah Wilderness Alliance* at the end of this chapter) or if an agency has unreasonably delayed action (meant to provide a remedy against agency foot-dragging). Second, courts can void or reverse the following kinds of agency action: unconstitutional agency action, Section 706 [2] (B); agency action contrary to federal law or beyond the jurisdiction of an agency, Section 706 [2] (C); agency action in violation of procedure, Section 706 [2] (D); agency action that is arbitrary, capricious, or an abuse of discretion, Section 706 [2] (A) (this is what you will shortly come to know as the "arbitrary or capricious scope of review of agency decisions"); agency decisions not supported by substantial evidence in the record, Section 706 [2] (E) (this is what you will come to refer as the substantial evidence test); and finally, agency action found to be unwarranted by the facts after a trial *de novo* by reviewing court, Section 706 [2] (F).

Court Review of Agency Foot-Dragging and Inaction

The language of Section 706 (1) makes it clear that Congress intended to authorize courts to compel agencies to act in cases of bureaucratic recalcitrance. However, typically, courts show tremendous deference toward agency excuses for inaction. This deference is explained by the Court in the case that follows.

Heckler v. Chaney
470 U.S. 821 (1985)

Justice Rehnquist wrote the opinion, joined by a unanimous court (Burger, White, Blackmun, Powell, Stewart, and O'Connor). Justices Brennan and Marshall concurred.

I

Respondents have been sentenced to death by lethal injection of drugs under the laws of the States of Oklahoma and Texas. Those States, and several others, have recently adopted this method for carrying out the capital sentence. Respondents first petitioned the FDA, claiming that the drugs used by the States for this purpose, although approved by the FDA for the medical purposes stated on their labels, were not approved for use in human executions. They alleged that the drugs had not been tested for the purpose for which they were to be used, and that, given that the drugs would likely be administered by untrained personnel, it was also likely that the drugs would not induce the quick and painless death intended. They urged that use of these drugs for human execution was the "unapproved use of an approved drug" and constituted a violation of the Act's prohibitions against "misbranding." They also suggested that the FDA's requirements for approval of "new drugs" applied, since these drugs were now being used for a new purpose. Accordingly, respondents claimed that the FDA was required to approve the drugs as "safe and effective" for human execution before they could be distributed in interstate commerce. See 21 U.S.C. 355. They therefore requested the FDA to take various investigatory and enforcement actions to prevent these perceived violations; they requested the FDA to affix warnings to the labels of all the drugs stating that they were unapproved and unsafe for human execution, to send statements to the drug manufacturers and prison administrators stating that the drugs should not be so used, and to adopt procedures for seizing the drugs from state prisons and to recommend the prosecution of all those in the chain of distribution who knowingly distribute or purchase the drugs with intent to use them for human execution. The FDA Commissioner responded, refusing to take the requested actions. The Commissioner first detailed his disagreement with respondents' understanding of the scope of FDA jurisdiction over the unapproved use of approved drugs for human execution, concluding that FDA jurisdiction in the area was generally unclear but in any event should not be exercised to interfere with this particular aspect of state criminal justice systems. He went on to state:

"Were FDA clearly to have jurisdiction in the area, moreover, we believe we would be authorized to decline to exercise it under our inherent discretion to decline to pursue certain enforcement matters. The unapproved use of approved drugs is an area in which the case law is far from uniform. Generally, enforcement proceedings in this area are initiated only when there is a serious danger to the public health or a blatant scheme to defraud. We cannot conclude that those dangers are present under State lethal injection laws, which are duly authorized statutory enactments in furtherance of proper State functions. . . ."

II

Respondents then filed the instant suit in the United States District Court for the District of Columbia, claiming the same violations of the FDCA and asking that the FDA be required to take the same enforcement actions requested in the prior petition. Jurisdiction was grounded in the general federal-question jurisdiction statute, 28 U.S.C. 1331, and review of the agency action was sought under the judicial review provisions of the APA, 5 U.S.C. 701–706. The District Court granted summary judgment for petitioner. It began with the proposition that "decisions of executive departments and agencies to refrain from instituting investigative and enforcement proceedings are essentially unreviewable by the courts." The court then cited case law stating that nothing in the FDCA indicated an intent to circumscribe the FDA's enforcement discretion or to make it reviewable. A divided panel of the Court of Appeals for the District of Columbia Circuit reversed. The majority began by discussing the FDA's jurisdiction over the unapproved use of approved drugs for human execution, and concluded that the FDA did have jurisdiction over such a use. The court then addressed the Government's assertion of unreviewable discretion to refuse enforcement action. The APA's comprehensive provisions for judicial review of "agency actions" are contained in 5 U.S.C. 701–706. Any person "adversely affected or aggrieved" by agency action, including a "failure to act," is entitled to "judicial review thereof," as long as the action is a "final agency action for which there is no other adequate remedy in a court." The standards to be applied on review are governed by the provisions of 706. But before any review at all may be had, a party must first clear the hurdle of 701(a). That section provides that the chapter on judicial review "applies, according to the provisions thereof, except to the extent that—(1) statutes preclude judicial review; or (2) agency action is committed to agency discretion by law." Petitioner urges that the decision of the FDA to refuse enforcement is an action "committed to agency discretion by law" under 701(a)(2).

This Court has not had occasion to interpret this second exception in 701(a) in any great detail. To this point our analysis does not differ significantly from that of the Court of Appeals. That court purported to apply the "no law to apply" standard of *Overton Park*. We disagree, however, with that court's insistence that the "narrow construction" of (a)(2) required application of a presumption of reviewability even to an agency's decision not to undertake certain enforcement actions. Here we think the Court of Appeals broke with tradition, case law, and sound reasoning.

Overton Park did not involve an agency's refusal to take requested enforcement action. It involved an affirmative act of approval under a statute that set clear guidelines for determining when such approval should be given. Refusals to take enforcement steps generally involve precisely the opposite situation, and in that situation we think the presumption is that judicial review is not available. This Court has recognized on several occasions over many years that an agency's decision not to prosecute or enforce, whether through civil or criminal process, is a decision generally committed to an agency's absolute discretion. See *United States v. Batchelder*, 442 U.S. 114, 123–124 (1979); *United States v. Nixon*, 418 U.S. 683, 693 (1974); *Vaca v. Sipes*, 386 U.S. 171, 182 (1967); *Confiscation Cases*, 7 Wall. 454 (1869). This recognition of the existence of discretion is attributable in no small part to the general unsuitability for judicial review of agency decisions to refuse enforcement.

The reasons for this general unsuitability are many. First, an agency decision not to enforce often involves a complicated balancing of a number of factors which are peculiarly within its expertise. Thus, the agency must not only assess whether a violation has occurred, but whether agency resources are best spent on this violation or another, whether the agency is likely to succeed if it acts, whether the particular enforcement action requested best fits the agency's overall policies, and, indeed, whether the agency has enough resources to undertake the action at all. An agency generally cannot act against each technical violation of the statute it is charged with enforcing. The agency is far better equipped than the courts to deal with the many variables involved in the proper ordering of its priorities. Similar concerns animate the principles of administrative law that courts generally will defer to an agency's construction of the statute it is charged with implementing, and to the procedures it adopts for implementing that statute. See *Vermont Yankee Nuclear Power Corp. v. Natural Resources Defense Council, Inc.*, 435 U.S. 519, 543 (1978); *Train v. Natural Resources Defense Council, Inc.*, 421 U.S. 60, 87 (1975).

In addition to these administrative concerns, we note that when an agency refuses to act it generally does not exercise its coercive power over an individual's liberty or property rights, and thus does not infringe upon areas that courts often are called upon to protect. Similarly, when an agency does act to enforce, that action itself provides a focus for judicial review, inasmuch as the agency must have exercised its power in some manner. The action at least can be reviewed to determine whether the agency exceeded its statutory powers. See, e.g., *FTC v. Klesner*, 280 U.S. 19 (1929). Finally, we recognize that an agency's refusal to institute proceedings shares to some extent the characteristics of the decision of a prosecutor in the Executive Branch not to indict—a decision which has long been regarded as the special province of the Executive Branch, inasmuch as it is the Executive who is charged by the Constitution to "take Care that the Laws be faithfully executed." U.S. Const., Art. II, 3.

We of course only list the above concerns to facilitate understanding of our conclusion that an agency's decision not to take enforcement action should be presumed immune from judicial review under 701(a)(2). For good reasons, such a decision has traditionally been "committed to agency discretion," and we believe that the Congress enacting the APA did not intend to alter that tradition. In so stating, we emphasize that the decision is only presumptively unreviewable; the presumption may be rebutted where the substantive statute has provided guidelines for the agency to follow in exercising its enforcement powers. Thus, in establishing this presumption in the APA, Congress did not set agencies free to disregard legislative direction in the statutory scheme that the agency administers. Congress may limit an agency's exercise of enforcement power if it wishes, either by setting substantive priorities, or by otherwise circumscribing an agency's power to discriminate among issues or cases it will pursue. The FDA's decision not to take the enforcement actions requested by respondents is therefore not subject to judicial review under the APA. The general exception to reviewability provided by 701(a)(2) for action "committed to agency discretion" remains a narrow one, see *Citizens to Preserve Overton Park v. Volpe,* 401 U.S. 402 (1971), but within that exception are included agency refusals to institute investigative or enforcement proceedings, unless Congress has indicated otherwise.

In so holding, we essentially leave to Congress, and not to the courts, the decision as to whether an agency's refusal to institute proceedings should be judicially reviewable. No colorable claim is made in this case that the agency's refusal to institute proceedings violated any constitutional rights of respondents, and we do not address the issue that would be raised in such a case. *Johnson v. Robison,* 415 U.S. 361, 366 (1974); *Yick Wo v. Hopkins,* 118 U.S. 356, 372–374 (1886). The fact that the drugs involved in this case are ultimately to be used in imposing the death penalty must not lead this Court or other courts to import profound differences of opinion over the meaning of the Eighth Amendment to the United States Constitution into the domain of administrative law.

The judgment of the Court of Appeals is Reversed.

The Law/Fact Distinction

As indicated in Chapter 1, agencies frequently interpret law. In making decisions or taking action, there is almost always a statute involved and usually an agency interpretation of that statute. The agency generally applies its interpretation of the statute to factual situations and makes a decision or takes some action (or refuses to act). In reviewing each agency action, courts show less deference to an agency's interpretation of the law than they do to an agency's determination of facts. This is because courts are just as well-suited to interpret law as agencies are; hence, any reason such as expertise for court deference to agencies disappears.

The *law/fact distinction* addresses the notion that courts will exercise stringent judicial review of agency action on questions of laws: Does the agency action violate a provision of the Constitution or some other federal law? Is the agency's interpretation of the law consistent with congressional intent? Has the agency attempted to take some action that is beyond its jurisdiction? However, the courts will show considerable deference to an agency's finding of fact: Were the employee's injuries work related? Does the applicant meet the requirements for a license or requested benefits? Did management engage in an unfair labor practice?

Court Review of Agency Action

If a challenged agency action survives court review of the questions of law involved, review will move to scrutiny of the agency decision, rule, or action. Here, court interpretations of Section 706 of the Administrative Procedure Act have established three standards of court review. The three standards of the scope of review are referred to as (a) the arbitrary and capricious standard, (b) the substantial evidence test, and (c) *de novo* review. The legal term *de novo* means "completely new from the start,"[34] so *de novo* review of agency action would require a whole new trial on the issue or action. This type of court review of agency action is rare, but Section 552(B) of the Administrative Procedure Act (in Appendix A) requires *de novo* court review of an agency's decision to withhold information under the Freedom of Information Act. The *Overton Park* case was presented earlier in this chapter. Two legal issues were considered: whether the secretary of transportation's decision was reviewable (the Court said it was) and what standard of review should the Court apply to the Secretary's decision? That part of the *Overton Park* case will be presented shortly.

Substantial evidence review of agency action is, by practice, limited to review of decisions, orders, or agency action that comes about as the result of a quasi-judicial hearing. The "substantial evidence test" means the reviewing court should examine the full record to be satisfied that there is substantial evidence in the record to support the decision of the agency. This test is similar to the kind of review appellate courts should apply when reviewing the decision of a trial court. The two interesting cases presented next are illustrative of court attempts to apply the substantial evidence test.

State Employees' Retirement System v. Industrial Accident Commission
217 P.2D 992 (1950)

The opinion by Justice Sparks.

This is a proceeding upon writ of review of a death benefit award made by the Industrial Accident Commission in favor of the widow and three minor children of Karl Lund, deceased. Petitioner State Employees' Retirement System seeks an annulment of the award, on the grounds that respondent commission had acted without and in excess of its powers and that the evidence was insufficient to justify the findings of fact. The decedent, Karl Lund, was employed as a game warden by the Department of Natural Resources. As such officer his duties were to enforce the provisions of the Fish and Game Code, and in so doing he had no regular or prescribed hours of duty. At times he was required to go on night patrol and to station himself in isolated areas where infractions of the Fish and Game Code might occur. An automobile equipped with a two-way radio was furnished him by his employer. The car was also so equipped that it might be converted into a bed, and it was permissible for him, while on night patrol, to sleep in the car.

On June 13, 1948, the deceased went on duty at 10 o'clock in the morning. According to

the entries in his diary he went on patrol to "Napa State Hospital, Soscal, thence to Cuttings Wharf, Brown's Valley to Oakville night patrol Trinity Road." At 2:58 p.m. on the 13th Lund reported by radio to the sheriff's office that he was in service. No further reports were received from him. On the 14th, Lund not having returned or checked in by radio, a search was made for him. At a point 16 or 18 miles from Napa, the car furnished Lund by the state was found. It was parked about 20 feet off a side road, facing into a hill. This side road was a slight distance from the Oakville-Trinity Mountain road. It was in "wild" country and where, according to Lund's superior officer, apprehensions were made of violators hunting deer at night with spotlights. About 12 feet to the rear of the state car there was another automobile parked. Investigation revealed that the interior of the state car had been converted into a bed, and on this bed were found the dead bodies of Karl Lund and of a woman, Chelsea Miami. The bodies were clad respectively only in shorts and panties and were partially covered by a blanket. The ignition switch, radio and heater of the car were all turned on and the gasoline tank was empty. All of the doors and windows were closed with the exception of one side wing-window which was slightly open. Lund's clothes, boots, and gun were in the back of the car and under the seat. The deaths were attributed by the coroner to carbon monoxide poisoning, the vapor of which apparently had infiltrated into the car from the running motor and been inhaled while the deceased were lying on the bed. Approximate time of death was fixed as between 1 and 3 a.m. of June 14th. Herminia Miami, the sister of Chelsea, testified that Chelsea had received a telephone call at their home from Lund shortly before 9 p.m.; that he had asked Chelsea to meet him, and within a few minutes after receiving the call Chelsea had changed to slacks and left in her own car.

There was no rule or regulation of the department by whom Lund was employed which prohibited any of the game wardens, while on duty, from having company. Upon the facts adduced at the hearing, summary of which has been given above, respondent Industrial Accident Commission made its finding that Karl Lund had sustained injury occurring in the course of and arising out of employment proximately causing his death from inhalation of carbon monoxide fumes. A petition for rehearing was granted by respondent commission, and after a further hearing respondent affirmed its findings of fact theretofore made.

Petitioner contends that these findings are irrational for the reason that the evidence shows that deceased met his death while on a personal adventure, and that in so doing he had deviated from the scope of his employment and from his duties as fish and game warden. In reviewing the evidence we are not permitted to substitute our views for those of the commission and annul an award unless there is no substantial evidence to support the findings and order. On the contrary, we are required to indulge all reasonable inferences which may be drawn legitimately from the facts in order to support the findings of the commission, and in doing so all that is required is reasonable probability; not absolute certainty. It is the duty of a reviewing court to search the record to discover whether the evidence is reasonably susceptible of the inferences drawn by the commission in support of its conclusion, and upon favorable

discovery to affirm the award. Neither may the award be annulled because there are two conclusions which fairly may be drawn from the evidence, both of which are reasonable, the one sustaining and the other opposing the right to compensation. Nor may an award be rejected solely on the basis of moral or ethical considerations. Measured by these rules we note in reviewing the record the following facts and circumstances in support of respondent's findings: That Lund, as a fish and game warden, had no regular or fixed hours of employment; that frequently he did patrol duty at night for the purpose of intercepting violators of the fish and game laws; that the last entry in his diary sets forth his itinerary for the 13th and concludes, "to Oakville night patrol Trinity Road"; that his diary also discloses that he had been on night patrol on the preceding evening. His death having occurred between 1 and 3 a.m. does not therefore justify any conclusion that it happened outside of the hours of his employment. As to the place of his death, the evidence shows that he had stationed himself in a territory which was under surveillance for the illegal spotlight killing of deer. The two-way radio with which the car was equipped was turned on so that Lund could not only have received messages from headquarters, but if need be could have sent them. While on such duty he was not only permitted to, but it was contemplated that he could convert the car into a bed (for it was so equipped), and that he might retire thereon or sleep.

There was no rule that forbade his having company while on duty. The testimony of Captain Shea in this regard is as follows: "[Mr. Faulkner] Q. . . . Now, would you—is there any order or rule or regulation of the department that prohibits you, while you're sitting there in your car or stationed in your car or in bed in your car, from talking to anybody that comes along? A. Definitely not. Q. Is there any rule or regulation prohibiting that person from getting into the car and sitting down with you, having a smoke or a chat? A. No, there isn't. Q. Is there any rule or regulation of the department that prohibits you or any of the men, any of the game wardens, from—while on duty—from talking or entertaining or enjoying the company of other people? A. No, there's no regulation to that effect. Q. No rule against it? A. No rule against it." And finally, his death was occasioned from carbon monoxide poisoning from the use of equipment furnished him by his employer. From this and other facts and circumstances in the record, we cannot say there was not substantial evidence to support the findings of the commission, or that the findings were irrational. In doing so we are well aware of the contrary inferences which might have been drawn from the same set of facts. The secluded spot in a remote area could have been selected by Lund for its advantages as a rendezvous in which to conduct an illicit love affair. The manner in which the cars were parked, the state of partial dishabille in which the bodies were found, the fact that Lund had divested himself of his uniform and placed his gun and boots underneath the seat, all are circumstances from which the trier of facts might have reasonably concluded that he had either abandoned or deviated from his duty. However, as stated above, it is not our province to resolve these facts or to substitute our own views for those of the commission. Lund, while acting in the scope of his employment, was permitted to drive to isolated spots where game violators might be found. It was a matter of discretion with him whether or not at such times he converted the car into a bed and slept. In so doing he was acting within the course of his employment. There was no rule which forbade him from having company while on duty, and the presence of a woman in the car with him does not necessarily compel a conclusion that he had thereby either abandoned his employment or deviated therefrom. There being a choice between two inferences reasonably deducible from the evidence, we cannot say that the commission acted without or in excess of its powers or that its findings of fact were unreasonable. The award is affirmed. Adams, P. J., and Peek, J., concurred.

United States ex rel. Exarchou v. Murff
265 F.2D 504 (1959)

George Exarchou entered the United States illegally in 1945. In 1949, the Immigration and Naturalization Service (INS) determined that he was deportable, but he petitioned the INS for eligibility for a discretionary grant of voluntary departure (which would allow him to reenter the United States legally at a later date). The INS found him to be qualified for a voluntary departure, but then it further recommended that his deportation be suspended. By 1953, Congress failed to pass a resolution approving the recommended suspension of deportation, so the INS again granted him permission to voluntarily depart the United States.

Just prior to his departure, however, his case was reopened at the INS by a letter written by his estranged wife. In the letter she charged him with infidelity and requested that her petitions of support on his behalf be withdrawn. A special inquiry officer conducted an investigation and found that in 1954 shortly after separation from his wife, Exarchou lived with a divorcée, her two children, and her mother. The inquiry officer found that Exarchou had engaged in adultery and hence was not of "good moral character," and that consequently he was not eligible for voluntary departure. The inquiry officer sent these findings to the INS, which then reversed its earlier position recommending voluntary departure. At a hearing in 1956, where Exarchou was again requesting voluntary departure and asking the INS to reconsider its findings, the testimony (and hence the written record) consisted of the following witnesses and their testimony:

Mr. Exarchou testified that his relationship with the divorcée was totally platonic and not adulterous, that they occasionally went dancing but nothing else, that he paid her rent, that he slept on the living room sofa and she slept in her bedroom on the second floor with her seven-year-old son, that the other two bedrooms were occupied by the divorcée's mother and her college-aged son.

The divorced woman in question was called to the stand, but she refused to testify based on her Fifth Amendment right against self-incrimination.

The estranged wife did not testify. In a hearing like this, the petitioner (Mr. Exarchou) has the burden of proving his good moral character. The INS found he failed to carry that burden and ordered him deported. That decision was sustained by the district court and was appealed to the circuit court.

The opinion of the court is by Chief Judge Clark.

As the Service concedes, no inference may be legally drawn from the refusal of the woman at whose home Exarchou briefly resided in 1954 to testify. *United States v. Maloney*, 2 Cir., 262 F.2d 535, 537. Actually the record indicates that avoidance of embarrassment was probably a stronger factor in her refusal than fear of self-incrimination. She had remarried by the time of the hearing and stated frankly that she was annoyed at being drawn into the proceedings and had sought and obtained advice as to means—which she took—to eliminate herself from a dispute in which she had no concern or interest. Exarchou's first wife did not testify at all after a hearing in 1954, nor was her actual testimony adverse then. Her only adverse comments were contained in her rambling, accusatory letter written when domestic ties between them were strained. Even if we overlook its hearsay quality we do not believe weight should attach to a letter written under such circumstances.

Hence the Service was thrown back completely on Exarchou's own testimony as to his conduct during the period in question. Perhaps the most doubtful fact here was the amount of money he admitted to having paid the woman, more than would be a reasonable rent under the circumstances. But he seems generally to have been free with his money. Beyond this his denials of adulterous conduct were steady, persistent, and unshaken. They would appear consistent with the surrounding facts and circumstances he disclosed. It is of course true that questions of a witness' credibility must be left to the administrative fact finder. Here, however, the Special Inquiry Officer's report demonstrates an incredulity not of the witness, but of the story itself.[1]

The Officer simply did not believe it possible that a man who behaved like relator (Exarchou) could not have been committing adultery. We do not think this finding of impossibility accords with the facts of human life. Moreover, we are disturbed by the insistence in the decision upon the appearance of good moral character. The statute makes good character itself, not a reputation for it, the finding necessary to the Service's decision. Thus we cannot accept the Service's alternative conclusion that, even if Exarchou truthfully described his conduct, "a married man is not free to carry on such a relationship and still be considered one of good character." We conclude only that Exarchou has sustained his burden of establishing good moral character under 19(c) of the Immigration Act of 1917 and is entitled to further consideration of his application.

---

[1] "I think I can best sum up my impressions of the respondent by saying that he tells an interesting, almost fantastic, story. Certainly not one that I consider credible. In fact, I do not believe it. The respondent would have me believe that he continued this so-called platonic relationship with this woman out of the goodness of his heart and out of his sympathy for her at a time when he was admittedly separated from his own wife. Even were it the truth, and as I say I do not believe it, it seems to me that a married man is not free to carry on such a relationship and still be considered one of good character. The mores of our times may well be most liberal but I do not think they have reached that degree of liberality as yet."

Question

1. For both preceding cases list the evidence in the record on a sheet of paper. Do it in columns so that you can clearly see the evidence in support of a board's decision and the evidence that does not support the decision. In either case, can you conclude that the reviewing court was in error?

If de novo review is rarely used and substantial evidence applies only in those situations in which agency action resulted from a quasi-judicial hearing, then the final standard of review, the arbitrary and capricious standard, must apply to all other agency decisions and actions (and inaction, when it is reviewed). This standard of review applies to court review of agency rule promulgation or quasi-legislative decision making. It also applies to more informal agency decisions or action, such as Secretary Volpe's decision to approve federal highway funds for a highway through Overton Park. Section 706 (2) (a) of the Administrative Procedure Act authorizes courts to void those actions of agencies that are found to be arbitrary or capricious. That is what the trial judge did with the EPA report on second-hand smoke. He voided the report because he thought the agency's manipulation of science produced an arbitrary decision that secondhand smoke is a known carcinogen. Unfortunately, describing what the arbitrary and capricious standard applies to is easier than describing the standard and how it is applied. You are already familiar with the *Overton Park* case presented earlier. What follows is that part of the *Overton Park* decision relating to the scope of review of the secretary's decision.

Citizens to Preserve Overton Park v. Volpe
401 U.S. 402 (1971)

[The facts in this case appear earlier in this chapter.]

. . . Scrutiny of the facts does not end, however, with the determination that the Secretary has acted within the scope of his statutory authority. Section 706 (2) (A) requires a finding that the actual choice made was not "arbitrary, capricious, an abuse of discretion, or otherwise not in accordance with law." 5 U.S.C. 706 (2) (A). To make this finding the court must consider whether the decision was based on a consideration of the relevant factors and whether there has been a clear error of judgment. Although this inquiry into the facts is to be searching and careful, the ultimate standard of review is a

narrow one. The court is not empowered to substitute its judgment for that of the agency. The administrative record is not, however, before us. The lower courts based their review on the litigation affidavits that were presented. These affidavits were merely "post hoc" rationalizations, *Burlington Truck Lines v. United States*, 371 U.S. 156, 168–169 (1962), which have traditionally been found to be an inadequate basis for review. And they clearly do not constitute the "whole record" compiled by the agency: the basis for review required by 706 of the Administrative Procedure Act.

Thus it is necessary to remand this case to the District Court for plenary review of the Secretary's decision. That review is to be based on the full administrative record that was before the Secretary at the time he made his decision. But since the bare record may not disclose the factors that were considered or the Secretary's construction of the evidence it may be necessary for the District Court to require some explanation in order to determine if the Secretary acted within the scope of his authority and if the Secretary's action was justifiable under the applicable standard. The court may require the administrative officials who participated in the decision to give testimony explaining their action. Of course, such inquiry into the mental processes of administrative decisionmakers is usually to be avoided. *United States v. Morgan,* 313 U.S. 409, 422 (1941). And where there are administrative findings that were made at the same time as the decision, as was the case in *Morgan,* there must be a strong showing of bad faith or improper behavior before such inquiry may be made. But here there are no such formal findings and it may be that the only way there can be effective judicial review is by examining the decisionmakers themselves. See *Shaughnessy v. Accardi,* 349 U.S. 280 (1955).

The District Court is not, however, required to make such an inquiry. It may be that the Secretary can prepare formal findings including the information required by DOT Order 5610.1 that will provide an adequate explanation for his action. Such an explanation will, to some extent, be a "post hoc rationalization" and thus must be viewed critically. If the District Court decides that additional explanation is necessary, that court should consider which method will prove the most expeditious so that full review may be had as soon as possible.

Reversed and remanded.

Questions

1. Succinctly state the precise disposition of this case.
2. What will happen next?
3. In your opinion, was the secretary's decision arbitrary? Why?
4. Did the Supreme Court find the secretary's decision to be arbitrary?

Because of the decision in the *Overton Park* case and others like it, agency decision makers in today's world do not make decisions without at least some kind of paper trail, such as a written explanation for the decision. In informal rule making under Section 553 of the Administrative Procedure Act, there is somewhat of a record for a reviewing court to review, and, indeed, Subsection C of 553 requires the agency to "adopt a concise general statement of their (the rules') basis and purpose." However, the record generated by the notice and comment hearing is "indistinguishable . . . from [materials collected in] the proceedings before a legislative committee hearing on a proposed bill—letters, telegrams, and written statements from proponents and opponents, including occasional oral testimony not subject to adversary cross-examination."[35]

The point is that a court reviewing the record of an agency's decision arrived at through a 553 rule-making procedure is in exactly the same position as a court reviewing a legislative decision. The judge must be careful that he or she is not simply substituting his or her policy preferences for the preferences of the legislature (or administrative agency).

Occasionally, courts reviewing agency action will apply a standard of review that is different from what is required in the Administrative Procedure Act. For the past three decades, when the Census Bureau prepared to take the census, it considered using sampling techniques. The Bureau did this because the census, as it has traditionally been conducted, undercounts the population. Those who do not get counted are disproportionately poor, urban, and people of color. The use of sampling would fix this problem. This is important because the census determines the number of representatives each state will have in Congress. It also determines how much federal money will be returned to the states under various programs, but the constitutional purpose for the census is to determine representation. Prior to the 1990 census, the director of the Bureau of the Census decided to use sampling, but his decision was vetoed by his boss, the secretary of commerce. Parties that would have benefited from the use of sampling sued the secretary. The circuit court of appeals reviewing the secretary's decision said that because congressional districts must come as close as possible to "one person-one vote," the secretary could not justify any procedure that did not come as close as possible to numerical accuracy. Hence, the secretary would be forced to use sampling. The court had applied a higher standard of review than is required under the Administrative Procedure Act. It applied a "strict scrutiny" standard of review that accompanies litigation involving the right to vote. The Supreme Court reversed and said the secretary's decision was not arbitrary or capricious under the appropriate standard of review required by the Administrative Procedure Act and allowed the secretary's decision to stand.[36]

In another case, the Nuclear Regulatory Commission (NRC) was sued over its decision to approve the construction of a nuclear plant. An appeals court applied a standard of review more rigorous than the arbitrary standard required by the Administrative Procedure Act. The Supreme Court reversed the appeals court.[37]

The *California Dental Association* case was discussed above briefly and is presented at the end of this chapter. In that case, the FTC decided that because the dental association restricted truthful advertising, it had unlawfully restrained trade. That decision received what is called "quick look" review by the court of appeals, which sustained the FTC decision. The Supreme Court said quick-look review was insufficient and sent the case back for review on the substantial evidence standard. The point is that the Administrative Procedure Act specifies substantial evidence review for quasi-judicial decisions and the arbitrary and capricious standard for all others, and appeals courts are often reversed if they apply a standard either too high or too low.

SUMMARY

1. *Jurisdiction.* This is the power of a court to resolve a dispute. Because federal courts have jurisdiction over any case or controversy under the laws or statutes of the United States and because all administrative actions are taken pursuant to congressional statute, federal courts have jurisdiction over conflicts arising under federal agencies. Normally, jurisdiction questions involve whether the agency overstepped its jurisdictional mandate from Congress.

2. *Standing.* This involves a determination of who is the proper party to challenge an administrative action. The court has created a two-pronged test for standing to challenge an administrative decision: (a) Can the plaintiff demonstrate an identifiable injury? (b) Is the agency action complained of arguably under the zone of interest meant to be protected by a particular statute? This test applied in those situations where agency action directly affected an individual, business, or group. The Court now applies a three-pronged test: injury in fact, traceability, and redressability. This test is most appropriate where government action has caused an intervening party to act, and the third party's action has allegedly caused injury to a plaintiff, who now sues the government. It should be clear, however that

without so much as a whisper about overruling precedent (the zone of interest test), the Court has moved to the three-pronged test in all situations. Indeed, in some cases, the Court uses both tests as it did in *FEC v. Akins,* which appears at the end of this chapter.

3. *Ripeness.* An injury cannot be too hypothetical or too far off in the future. There must either be a documentable injury, or injury must be imminent.

4. *Mootness.* The conflict that led to the lawsuit in the first place cannot already be resolved.

5. *Reviewability.* This is a legislative grant of authority to courts to review agency action. First, at the federal level prior to enactment of the Administrative Procedure Act (1947), there was a common law presumption that courts could not review the actions of administrative agencies unless the enabling legislation specifically provided for court review. In most states, there was also a presumption of unreviewability, which, at some levels in some states, still exists today due to a lack of legislation extending judicial review to all agency actions. Second, the intent and plain meaning of the Act is to extend court review to virtually all agency actions at the federal level with two exceptions: (a) cases in which Congress has forbidden court review for a specific agency and (b) a nebulous category of supposedly unreviewable situations in which the agency action is "committed to agency discretion by law."

6. *Exhaustion.* Before people can sue an agency in court, they must first have exhausted all avenues of appeal within the agency.

7. *Primary jurisdiction.* Within the federal system, in those situations in which people are in conflict with an agency, they can either exhaust remedies within the agency or turn to the courts. Two situations require the courts to defer to the agency first: (a) if the conflict involves subject matter that requires one uniform national standard (ICC rates, for example) and (b) if, for resolution, the subject matter requires agency expertise that courts are unlikely to possess.

8. *Scope of review.* There are, for all practical purposes, two standards of review that courts apply in reviewing agency activity: (a) The substantial evidence test applies to agency decisions, orders, or rulings that are made via a quasi-judicial procedure. (b) The arbitrary and capricious test applies to all other agency activity.

END-OF-CHAPTER CASES

City of Los Angeles v. Lyons
461 U.S. 55 (1983)

[The following facts of the case are taken from Justice Marshall's dissent.]

Respondent Adolph Lyons is a 24-year-old Negro male who resides in Los Angeles. According to the uncontradicted evidence in the record, at about 2 a.m. on October 6, 1976, Lyons was pulled over to the curb by two officers of the Los Angeles Police Department (LAPD) for a traffic infraction because one of his taillights was burned out. The officers greeted him with drawn revolvers as he exited from his car. Lyons was told to face his car and spread his legs. He did so. He was then ordered to clasp his hands and put them on top of his head. He again complied. After one of the officers completed a patdown search, Lyons dropped his hands, but was ordered to place them back above his head, and one of the officers grabbed Lyons' hands and slammed them onto his head. Lyons complained about the pain caused by the ring of keys he was holding in his hand. Within 5 to 10 seconds, the officer began to choke Lyons by applying a forearm against his throat. As Lyons struggled for air, the officer handcuffed him, but continued to apply the chokehold until he blacked out. When Lyons regained consciousness, he was lying face down on the ground, choking, gasping for air, and spitting up blood and dirt. He had urinated and defecated. He was issued a traffic citation and released.

Opinion by Justice White joined by Chief Justice Burger and Justices Powell, Rehnquist, and O'Connor. Justices Marshall, Brennan, Blackmun, and Stevens dissented.

It goes without saying that those who seek to invoke the jurisdiction of the federal courts must satisfy the threshold requirement imposed by Art. III of the Constitution by alleging an actual case or controversy. *Flast v. Cohen,* 392 U.S. 83, 94–101 (1968); *Jenkins v. McKeithen,* 395 U.S. 411, 421–425 (1969). Plaintiffs must demonstrate a "personal stake in the outcome" in order to "assure that concrete adverseness which sharpens the presentation of issues" necessary for the proper resolution of constitutional questions. *Baker v. Carr,* 369 U.S. 186, 204 (1962). Abstract injury is not enough. The plaintiff must show that he "has sustained or is immediately in danger of sustaining some direct injury" as the result of the challenged official conduct and the injury or threat of injury must be both "real and immediate," not "conjectural" or "hypothetical." See, e.g., *Golden v. Zwickler,* 394 U.S. 103, 109–110 (1969). . . .

In *O'Shea v. Littleton,* 414 U.S. 488 (1974), we dealt with a case brought by a class of plaintiffs claiming that they had been subjected to discriminatory enforcement of the criminal law. Among other things, a county magistrate and judge were accused of discriminatory conduct in various respects, such as sentencing members of plaintiff's class more harshly than other defendants. The Court of Appeals reversed the dismissal of the suit by the District Court, ruling that if the allegations were proved, an appropriate injunction could be entered.

We reversed for failure of the complaint to allege a case or controversy. Although it was claimed in that case that particular members of the plaintiff class had actually suffered from the alleged unconstitutional practices, we observed that "[p]ast exposure to illegal conduct does not in itself show a present case or controversy regarding injunctive relief . . . if unaccompanied by any continuing, present adverse effects." Past wrongs were evidence bearing on "whether there is a real and immediate threat of repeated injury." But the prospect of future injury rested "on the likelihood that [plaintiffs] will again be arrested for and charged with violations of the criminal law and will again be subjected to bond proceedings, trial, or sentencing before petitioners." The most that could be said for plaintiffs' standing was "that if [plaintiffs] proceed to violate an unchallenged law and if they are charged, held to answer, and tried in any proceedings before petitioners, they will be subjected to the discriminatory practices that petitioners are alleged to have followed." We could not find a case or controversy in those circumstances: the threat to the plaintiffs was not "sufficiently real and immediate to show an existing controversy simply because they anticipate violating lawful criminal statutes and being tried for their offenses. . . ." It was to be assumed "that [plaintiffs] will conduct their activities within the law and so avoid prosecution and conviction as well as exposure to the challenged course of conduct said to be followed by petitioners."

Another relevant decision for present purposes is *Rizzo v. Goode,* 423 U.S. 362 (1976), a case in which plaintiffs alleged widespread illegal and unconstitutional police conduct aimed at minority citizens and against city residents in general. The Court reiterated the holding in *O'Shea* that past wrongs do not in themselves amount to that real and immediate threat of

If it happened in past it
. . . never happen again

injury necessary to make out a case or controversy. The claim of injury rested upon "what one of a small, unnamed minority of policemen might do to them in the future because of that unknown policeman's perception" of departmental procedures. This hypothesis was "even more attenuated than those allegations of future injury found insufficient in *O'Shea* to warrant [the] invocation of federal jurisdiction." The Court also held that plaintiffs' showing at trial of a relatively few instances of violations by individual police officers, without any showing of a deliberate policy on behalf of the named defendants, did not provide a basis for equitable relief.

No extension of *O'Shea* and *Rizzo* is necessary to hold that respondent Lyons has failed to demonstrate a case or controversy with the City that would justify the equitable relief sought. Lyons' standing to seek the injunction requested depended on whether he was likely to suffer future injury from the use of the chokeholds by police officers. Count V of the complaint alleged the traffic stop and choking incident five months before. That Lyons may have been illegally choked by the police on October 6, 1976, while presumably affording Lyons standing to claim damages against the individual officers and perhaps against the City, does nothing to establish a real and immediate threat that he would again be stopped for a traffic violation, or for any other offense, by an officer or officers who would illegally choke him into unconsciousness without any provocation or resistance on his part. The additional allegation in the complaint that the police in Los Angeles routinely apply chokeholds in situations where they are not threatened by the use of deadly force falls far short of the allegations that would be necessary to establish a case or controversy between these parties.

In order to establish an actual controversy in this case, Lyons would have had not only to allege that he would have another encounter with the police but also to make the incredible assertion either, (1) that all police officers in Los Angeles always choke any citizen with whom they happen to have an encounter, whether for the purpose of arrest, issuing a citation, or for questioning, or (2) that the City ordered or authorized police officers to act in such manner. Although Count V alleged that the City authorized the use of the control holds in situations where deadly force was not threatened, it did not indicate why Lyons might be realistically threatened by police officers who acted within the strictures of the City's policy. If, for example, choke holds were authorized to be used only to counter resistance to an arrest by a suspect, or to thwart an effort to escape, any future threat to Lyons from the City's policy or from the conduct of police officers would be no more real than the possibility that he would again have an encounter with the police and that either he would illegally resist arrest or detention or the officers would disobey their instructions and again render him unconscious without any provocation.

Lyons fares no better if it be assumed that his pending damages suit affords him Art. III standing to seek an injunction as a remedy for the claim arising out of the October 1976 events. The equitable remedy is unavailable absent a showing of irreparable injury, a requirement that cannot be met where there is no showing of any real or immediate threat that the plaintiff will be wronged again—a "likelihood of substantial and immediate irreparable injury." *O'Shea v. Littleton,* 414 U.S., at 502. The speculative nature of Lyons' claim of future injury requires a finding that this prerequisite of equitable relief has not been fulfilled.

Nor will the injury that Lyons allegedly suffered in 1976 go unrecompensed; for that injury, he has an adequate remedy at law. Contrary to the view of the Court of Appeals, it is not at all "difficult" under our holding "to see how anyone can ever challenge police or similar administrative practices." 615 F.2d, at 1250. The legality of the violence to which Lyons claims he was once subjected is at issue in his suit for damages and can be determined there.

Absent a sufficient likelihood that he will again be wronged in a similar way, Lyons is no more entitled to an injunction than any other citizen of Los Angeles; and a federal court may not entertain a claim by any or all citizens who no more than assert that certain practices of law enforcement officers are unconstitutional. Cf. *Warth v. Seldin,* 422 U.S. 490 (1975); *Schlesinger v. Reservists to Stop the War,* 418 U.S. 208 (1974); *United States v. Richardson,* 418 U.S. 166 (1974). This is not to suggest that such undifferentiated claims should not be taken seriously by local authorities.

Indeed, the interest of an alert and interested citizen is an essential element of an effective and fair government, whether on the local, state, or national level. A federal court, however, is not the proper forum to press such claims unless the requirements for entry and the prerequisites for injunctive relief are satisfied.

Federal Election Commission v. Akins
524 U.S. 11 (1998)

Justice Breyer delivered the opinion of the Court, in which Chief Justice Rehnquist and Justices Stevens, Kennedy, Souter, and Ginsburg joined. Justice Scalia filed a dissenting opinion, in which Justices O'Connor and Thomas joined.

The Federal Election Commission (FEC) has determined that the American Israel Public Affairs Committee (AIPAC) is not a "political committee" as defined by the Federal Election Campaign Act of 1971, 86 Stat. 11, as amended, 2 U.S.C. § 431(4) (FECA), and, for that reason, the Commission has refused to require AIPAC to make disclosures regarding its membership, contributions, and expenditures that FECA would otherwise require. We hold that respondents, a group of voters, have standing to challenge the Commission's determination in court, and we remand this case for further proceedings.

I

In light of our disposition of this case, we believe it necessary to describe its procedural background in some detail. As commonly understood, the Federal Election Campaign Act seeks to remedy any actual or perceived corruption of the political process in several important ways.

The Act imposes limits upon the amounts that individuals, corporations, "political committees"

(including political action committees), and political parties can contribute to a candidate for federal political office. The Act also imposes limits on the amount these individuals or entities can spend in coordination with a candidate. (It treats these expenditures as "contributions to" a candidate for purposes of the Act.). As originally written, the Act set limits upon the total amount that a candidate could spend of his own money, and upon the amounts that other individuals, corporations, and "political committees" could spend independent of a candidate—though the Court found that certain of these last-mentioned limitations violated the First Amendment. *Buckley v. Valeo,* 424 U.S. 1, 39-59. . . .

This case concerns requirements in the Act that extend beyond these better-known contribution and expenditure limitations. In particular the Act imposes extensive recordkeeping and disclosure requirements upon groups that fall within the Act's definition of a "political committee."

Those groups must register with the FEC, appoint a treasurer, keep names and addresses of contributors, track the amount and purpose of disbursements, and file complex FEC reports that include lists of donors giving in excess of $200 per year (often, these donors may be the group's members), contributions, expenditures, and any other disbursements irrespective of their purposes.

The Act's use of the word "political committee" calls to mind the term "political action committee," or "PAC," a term that normally refers to organizations that corporations or trade unions might establish for the purpose of making contributions or expenditures that the Act would otherwise prohibit. But, in fact, the Act's term "political committee" has a much broader scope. The Act states that a "political committee" includes "any committee, club, association or other group of persons which receives" more than $1,000 in "contributions" or "which makes" more than $1,000 in "expenditures" in any given year.

This broad definition, however, is less universally encompassing than at first it may seem, for later definitional subsections limit its scope. The Act defines the key terms "contribution" and "expenditure" as covering only those contributions and expenditures that are made "for the purpose of influencing any election for Federal office."

Moreover, the Act sets forth detailed categories of disbursements, loans, and assistance-in-kind that do not count as a "contribution" or an "expenditure," even when made for election-related purposes. In particular, assistance given to help a particular candidate will not count toward the $1,000 "expenditure" ceiling that qualifies an organization as a "political committee" if it takes the form of a "communication" by an organization "to its members"—as long as the organization at issue is a "membership organization or corporation" and it is not "organized primarily for the purpose of influencing the nomination . . . or election, of any individual."

This case arises out of an effort by respondents, a group of voters with views often opposed to those of AIPAC, to persuade the FEC to treat AIPAC as a "political committee." Respondents filed a complaint with the FEC, stating that AIPAC had made more than $1,000 in qualifying "expenditures" per year, and thereby became a "political committee." They added that AIPAC had violated the FEC provisions requiring "political committees" to register and to make public the information about members, contributions, and expenditures to which we have just referred. Respondents also claimed that AIPAC had violated § 441b of FECA, which prohibits corporate campaign "contributions" and "expenditures." They asked the FEC to find that AIPAC had violated the Act, and, among other things, to order AIPAC to make public the information that FECA demands of a "political committee."

AIPAC asked the FEC to dismiss the complaint. AIPAC described itself as an issue-oriented organization that seeks to maintain friendship and promote goodwill between the United States and Israel. AIPAC conceded that it lobbies elected officials and disseminates information about candidates for public office. But in responding to the § 441b charge, AIPAC denied that it had made the kinds of "expenditures" that matter for FECA purposes (i.e., the kinds of election-related expenditures that corporations cannot make, and which count as the kind of expenditures that, when they exceed $1,000, qualify a group as a "political committee").

To put the matter more specifically: AIPAC focused on certain "expenditures" that respondents had claimed were election-related, such as the costs of meetings with candidates, the introduction of AIPAC members to candidates, and the distribution of candidate position papers. AIPAC said that its spending on such activities, even if election-related, fell within a relevant exception. They amounted, said AIPAC, to communications by a membership organization with its members, which the Act exempts from its definition of "expenditures," In AIPAC's view, these communications therefore did not violate (the) corporate expenditure prohibition. (And, if AIPAC was right, those expenditures would not count towards the $1,000 ceiling on "expenditures" that might transform an ordinary issue-related group into a "political committee.")

The FEC's General Counsel concluded that, between 1983 and 1988, AIPAC had indeed funded communications of the sort described. The General Counsel said that those expenditures were campaign related, in that they amounted to advocating the election or defeat of particular candidates. He added that these expenditures were "likely to have crossed the $1,000 threshold." At the same time, the FEC closed the door to AIPAC's invocation of the "communications" exception. The FEC said that, although it was a "close question," these expenditures were not membership communications, because that exception applies to a membership organization's communications with its members, and most of the persons who belonged to AIPAC did not qualify as "members" for purposes of the Act.

Still, given the closeness of the issue, the FEC exercised its discretion and decided not to proceed further with respect to the claimed "corporate contribution" violation.

The FEC's determination that many of the persons who belonged to AIPAC were not "members" effectively foreclosed any claim that AIPAC's communications did not count as "expenditures" for purposes of determining whether it was a "political committee." Since AIPAC's activities fell outside the "membership communications" exception, AIPAC could not invoke that exception as a way of escaping the scope of the Act's term "political committee" and the Act's disclosure provisions, which that definition triggers.

The FEC nonetheless held that AIPAC was not subject to the disclosure requirements, but for a different reason. In the FEC's view, the Act's definition of "political committee" includes only those organizations that have as a "major purpose" the nomination or election of candidates. Cf. *Buckley v. Valeo,* 424 U.S. at 79. AIPAC, it added, was fundamentally an issue-oriented lobbying organization, not campaign-related organization, and hence AIPAC fell outside the definition of a "political committee" regardless. The FEC consequently dismissed respondents' complaint.

Respondents filed a petition in Federal District Court seeking review of the FEC's determination dismissing their complaint.

The District Court granted summary judgment for the FEC, and a divided panel of the Court of Appeals affirmed, 66 F.3d 348 (CADC 1995). The *en banc* Court of Appeals reversed, however, on the ground that the FEC's "major purpose" test improperly interpreted the Act's definition of a "political committee." 101 F.3d 731 (CADC 1997). We granted the Government's petition for *certiorari,* which contained the following two questions:

"1. Whether respondents had standing to challenge the Federal Election Commission's decision not to bring an enforcement action in this case."

"2. Whether an organization that spends more than $1,000 on contributions or coordinated expenditures in a calendar year, but is neither controlled by a candidate nor has its major purpose the nomination or election of candidates, is a 'political committee' within the meaning of the [Act]."

We shall answer the first of these questions, but not the second.

II

The Solicitor General argues that respondents lack standing to challenge the FEC's decision not to proceed against AIPAC. He claims that they have failed to satisfy the "prudential" standing requirements upon which this Court has insisted. See, e.g., *Association of Data Processing Service Organizations, Inc. v. Camp,* 397 U.S. 150, 153 (1970) (Data Processing). He adds that respondents have not shown that they "suffer injury in fact," that their injury is "fairly traceable" to the FEC's decision, or that a judicial decision in their favor would "redress" the injury. E.g., *Bennett v. Spear,* 520 U.S. 154, 1997 (1997); *Lujan v. Defenders of Wildlife,* 504 U.S. 555 (1992).

In his view, respondents' District Court petition consequently failed to meet Article III's demand for a "case" or "controversy."

We do not agree with the FEC's "prudential standing" claim. Congress has specifically provided in FECA that "any person who believes a violation of this Act . . . has occurred, may file a complaint with the Commission." § 437g(a)(1). It has added that "any party aggrieved by an order of the Commission dismissing a complaint filed by such party . . . may file a petition" in district court seeking review of that dismissal. § 437g(8)(A). History associates the word "aggrieved" with a congressional intent to cast the standing net broadly—beyond the common-law interests and substantive statutory rights upon which "prudential" standing traditionally rested. *Scripps-Howard Radio, Inc. v. FCC,* 316 U.S. 4 (1942); *FCC v. Sanders Brothers Radio Station,* 309 U.S. 470 (1940); *Office of Communication of the United Church of Christ v. FCC,* 359 F.2d 994 (CADC 1966)

(Burger, J.); *Associated Industries of New York State v. Ickes,* 134 F.2d 694 (1943) (Frank, J.). Cf. Administrative Procedure Act, 5 U.S.C. § 702 (stating that those "suffering legal wrong" or "adversely affected or aggrieved . . . within the meaning of a relevant statute" may seek judicial review of agency action).

Moreover, prudential standing is satisfied when the injury asserted by a plaintiff "arguably [falls] within the zone of interests to be protected or regulated by the statute . . . in question." NCUA, Data Processing, supra, at 153. The injury of which respondents complain—their failure to obtain relevant information—is injury of a kind that FECA seeks to address. *Buckley,* 424 U.S. at 66-67 ("political committees" must disclose contributors and disbursements to help voters understand who provides which candidates with financial support). We have found nothing in the Act that suggests Congress intended to exclude voters from the benefits of these provisions, or otherwise to restrict standing, say, to political parties, candidates, or their committees.

Given the language of the statute and the nature of the injury, we conclude that Congress, intending to protect voters such as respondents from suffering the kind of injury here at issue, intended to authorize this kind of suit. Consequently, respondents satisfy "prudential" standing requirements. . . .

Nor do we agree with the FEC or the dissent that Congress lacks the constitutional power to authorize federal courts to adjudicate this lawsuit. Article III, of course, limits Congress' grant of judicial power to "cases" or "controversies." That limitation means that respondents must show, among other things, an "injury in fact"—a requirement that helps assure that courts will not "pass upon . . . abstract, intellectual problems," but adjudicate "concrete, living contests between adversaries."

. . . In our view, respondents here have suffered a genuine "injury in fact." The "injury in fact" that respondents have suffered consists of their inability to obtain information—lists of AIPAC donors (who are, according to AIPAC, its members) and campaign-related contributions and expenditures—that, on respondents' view of the law, the statute requires that AIPAC make

public. There is no reason to doubt their claim that the information would help them (and others to whom they would communicate it) to evaluate candidates for public office, especially candidates who received assistance from AIPAC, and to evaluate the role that AIPAC's financial assistance might play in a specific election. Respondents' injury consequently seems concrete and particular. Indeed, this Court has previously held that a plaintiff suffers an "injury in fact" when the plaintiff fails to obtain information which must be publicly disclosed pursuant to a statute. *Public Citizen v. Department of Justice,* 491 U.S. 440, 449 (1989) (failure to obtain information subject to disclosure under Federal Advisory Committee Act "constitutes a sufficiently distinct injury to provide standing to sue"). See also *Havens Realty Corp. v. Coleman,* 455 U.S. 363, 373-374 (1982) (deprivation of information about housing availability constitutes "specific injury" permitting standing). . . .

Thus respondents' "injury in fact" is "fairly traceable" to the FEC's decision not to issue its complaint, even though the FEC might reach the same result exercising its discretionary powers lawfully. For similar reasons, the courts in this case can "redress" respondents' "injury in fact." Finally, the FEC argues that we should deny respondents standing because this case involves an agency's decision not to undertake an enforcement action—an area generally not subject to judicial review.

In *Heckler,* this Court noted that agency enforcement decisions "have traditionally been 'committed to agency discretion,'" and concluded that Congress did not intend to alter that tradition in enacting the APA. *Heckler,* 470 U.S. 821 at 832, 5 U.S.C. § 701(a) (courts will not review agency actions where "statutes preclude judicial review," or where the "agency action is committed to agency discretion by law"). We deal here with a statute that explicitly indicates the contrary. . . .

In sum, respondents, as voters, have satisfied both prudential and constitutional standing requirements. They may bring this petition for a declaration that the FEC's dismissal of their complaint was unlawful. . . .

The upshot, in our view, is that we should permit the FEC to address, in the first instance, the issue presented by Question Two. We can thereby take advantage of the relevant agency's expertise, by allowing it to develop a more precise rule that may dispose of this case, or at a minimum, will aid the Court in reaching a more informed conclusion. In our view, the FEC should proceed to determine whether or not AIPAC's expenditures qualify as "membership communications," and thereby fall outside the scope of "expenditures" that could qualify it as a "political committee." If the FEC decides that despite its new rules, the communications here do not qualify for this exception, then the lower courts, in reconsidering respondents' arguments,

can still evaluate the significance of the communicative context in which the case arises. If, on the other hand, the FEC decides that AIPAC's activities fall within the "membership communications" exception, the matter will become moot.

For these reasons, the decision of the Court of Appeals is vacated, and the case is remanded for further proceedings consistent with this opinion.

It is so ordered.

Author's Note: Justice Scalia's dissent argues that this is an action to require an agency to enforce and as such is not reviewable. Whether to begin enforcement proceedings is an action committed to agency discretion by law according to *Heckler V. Chaney.*

Tozzi v. U. S. Department of Health and Human Services 271 F. 3d 301 (D.C. Circuit 2001)

Opinion delivered by Judge Tatel, after hearing with Senior Circuit Judges Silberman and Williams.

Acting pursuant to a provision of the Public Health Service Act that requires the Secretary of Health and Human Services to publish a list of substances "known" or "reasonably anticipated to be" human carcinogens, the Secretary upgraded the chemical dioxin from the "reasonably anticipated" to the "known" category. A manufacturer of products that release dioxin when incinerated, together with others allegedly affected by the upgrade, argue that the Secretary, in violation of HHS regulations, acted without sufficient epidemiological evidence that dioxin is a known human carcinogen. Although we reject the Secretary's arguments that the manufacturer lacks standing and that the upgrade decision is unreviewable, we agree with the district court that, given the deference owed an agency's interpretation of its own regulations, the Secretary acted neither arbitrarily nor capriciously.

I

In 1978, Congress amended the Public Health Service Act to require the Secretary of Health, Education, and Welfare, now Health and Human Services, to publish a list of known and suspected carcinogens. . . . Entitled the Report on Carcinogens, the list is prepared biennially by the Department's National Toxicology Program ("NTP"). Although HHS does not regulate substances based upon their inclusion in the Report, a listing—or in some instances an upgrade—may trigger obligations under other agency regulations. For example, OSHA's Hazard Communication Standard requires manufacturers to label as a carcinogen every substance listed in the Report. . . . A listing can also trigger obligations under state regulations.

Before the Secretary may list (or delist) a substance, the substance undergoes a multi-step review process. See HHS Eighth Report on Carcinogens (1998). Acting on recommendations from the scientific community, the NTP begins by publishing in the Federal Register a list of substances that the agency believes merit consideration. At about the same time, an NTP committee, the Report on Carcinogens Review Committee, reviews the scientific literature and prepares a background document discussing the literature and recommending substances for listing. These recommendations, together with the background document and any public comments received in response to the Federal Register notice, are sent to two peer review committees: the NTP's Interagency Working Group (a committee composed of scientists from several federal agencies) and a subcommittee of the NTP's Board of Scientific Counselors (a chartered advisory committee). The subcommittee holds public hearings and receives written comments. Then, the subcommittee and the Working Group make formal recommendations to the NTP Executive Committee, which in turn makes a recommendation to the NTP Director. After independently evaluating the Executive Committee's recommendation, the Director submits a final draft of the Report to the Secretary. If the Secretary approves the Report, a notice is published in the Federal Register identifying all newly listed (or delisted) substances classifying them as either "known" or "reasonably anticipated to be" human carcinogens, and announcing the availability of the latest Report. Of significance to this case, the Secretary may not move substances from one category to the other without going through the same formal review process.

The Secretary has issued "criteria" for classifying substances as "known" or "reasonably anticipated to be" human carcinogens. As originally issued in 1982, the criteria provided:

Known to be Carcinogens:

There is sufficient evidence of carcinogenicity from studies in humans which indicates a causal relationship between the agent and human cancer.

Reasonably Anticipated to be a Human Carcinogen:

A. There is limited evidence of carcinogenicity from studies in humans, which indicates that causal interpretation is credible, but that the alternative explanations, such as chance, bias or confounding, could not adequately be excluded, or

B. There is sufficient evidence of carcinogenicity from studies in experimental animals which indicates that there is an increased incidence of malignant tumors: (a) in multiple species or strains, or (b) in multiple experiments (preferably with different routes of administration or using different dose levels), or (c) to an unusual degree with regard to incidence, site or type of tumor, or age at onset. Additional evidence may be provided by data concerning dose-response effects, as well as information on mutagenicity or chemical structure.

Eighth Report

The parties agree that under these criteria only epidemiological studies were considered when placing a substance in the first category. Many in the scientific community, however, began to urge revision of the criteria to provide for broader consideration of "mechanistic" evidence—that is, evidence of the actual biochemical processes by which a substance causes cancer. In response, the Secretary published revised criteria in 1996. Because the differences between these criteria and the 1982 version are central to this case, we quote the new version in full:

Known to be a Human Carcinogen:

There is sufficient evidence of carcinogenicity from studies in humans which indicates a causal relationship between exposure to the agent, substance or mixture and human cancer.

Reasonably Anticipated to be a Human Carcinogen:

There is limited evidence of carcinogenicity from studies in humans, which indicates that causal interpretation is credible, but that alternative explanations, such as chance, bias or confounding, could not adequately be excluded; or

There is sufficient evidence of carcinogenicity from studies in experimental animals which indicates that there is an increased incidence of malignant and/or combined benign and malignant tumors: (a) in multiple species or at multiple tissue sites, or (b) by multiple routes of exposure, or (c) to an unusual degree with regard to incidence, site or type of tumor, or age at onset; or

There is less than sufficient evidence of carcinogenicity in humans or laboratory animals; however, the agent belongs to a well defined structurally-related class of substances whose members are listed in a previous Annual or Biennial Report on Carcinogens as either known to be human carcinogen, or reasonably anticipated to be human carcinogen or there is convincing relevant information that the agent acts through mechanisms indicating it would likely cause cancer in humans.

Conclusions regarding carcinogenicity in humans or experimental animals are based on scientific judgment, with consideration given to all relevant information. Relevant information includes but is not limited to dose response, route of exposure, chemical structure, metabolism, pharmacokinetics, sensitive subpopulations, genetic effects, or other data relating to mechanism of action or factors that may be unique to a given substance. For example, there may be substances for which there is evidence of carcinogenicity in laboratory animals but there are compelling data indicating that the agent acts through mechanisms which do not operate in humans and would therefore not reasonably be anticipated to cause cancer in humans.

The precise question before us is whether the final, unindented paragraph modifies both categories (as the Secretary interprets it) or only the "reasonably anticipated" category (as appellants claim).

This case involves the Secretary's decision to upgrade dioxin from the "reasonably anticipated" to the "known" category. A colorless, needle-shaped chemical not commercially produced, dioxin is released as a by-product of paper and pulp bleaching. Dioxin is also emitted during incineration of chlorine-containing materials, such as polyvinyl chloride ("PVC") plastic. Incineration of hospital waste, which usually contains PVC plastic, produces large quantities of dioxin.

Chemically stable, dioxin persists in the environment for long periods of time. Because dioxin settles into soil and water, it ends up in animal fatty tissue and eventually meat and dairy products. According to the Ninth Report, human exposure occurs in several ways:

Food is the major source (> 90%) of human exposure to [dioxin] . . . Other pathways of exposure include inhalation of [dioxin] from municipal, medical, and industrial waste incinerators and other incineration and combustion processes . . . and ingestion of drinking water (0.01% of the daily intake).

Most people have some level of dioxin in their tissues.

The Secretary originally listed dioxin in the "reasonably anticipated" category. See Ninth Report supra. In 1997, however, the International Agency for Research on Cancer ("IARC"), a division of the World Health Organization that has its own carcinogen classification scheme, upgraded dioxin to its highest category based on "limited" epidemiological evidence and "strong" evidence that dioxin acts "through a relevant mechanism of carcinogenicity." In response, the NTP proposed upgrading dioxin to the "known" category. After approval by the Report on Carcinogens Review Committee, the proposed listing was forwarded to the Working Group and the subcommittee of the Board of Scientific Counselors. The Working Group approved the upgrade, and after notice and public comment, so did the Board. The draft background document relied on both epidemiological and mechanistic evidence:

[Dioxin] is known to be a human carcinogen based on several types of evidence:

Human studies have found an association between dioxin exposure and cancer mortality with respect to all cancers combined, non-Hodgkin's lymphoma, and lung cancer;

Studies in experimental animals have shown that [dioxin] induces benign and malignant neoplasms at multiple issue [sic] sites in multiple species;

A compelling body of evidence indicates a basic similarity in the mechanism of induction of animal and human tissue biochemical and toxicological responses to [dioxin] at comparable doses and tissue levels.

Following the Board's approval, Jim Tozzi, a "regulatory consultant" and an appellant in this case, sent a letter to the NTP Director stating that the Secretary may not list substances in the known category without "sufficient" evidence from epidemiological studies. Tozzi also complained that "too much was crammed into too little time" and that the NTP failed to provide certain "key" documents to the public. Responding to Tozzi's letter and conceding that "review had been inadequate," the NTP Director announced a "re-review" of dioxin "including another open, public review by the NTP Board Subcommittee." At the same time, the Director emphasized his belief that "the criteria [had been] appropriately applied." After the additional round of notice and comment, the Board of Scientific Counselors voted against the upgrade, but both the NTP Executive Committee and the NTP Director approved it. Concurring with the Director, the Secretary listed dioxin in the Ninth Report as a known carcinogen.

Tozzi, together with Brevet Industries, a manufacturer of disposable plastic connectors used during open heart surgery, the Empire State Restaurant & Tavern Association, and Greenbaum & Gilhooleys, a New York restaurant, then filed suit in the United States District Court for the District of Columbia pursuant to the Administrative Procedure Act, 5 U.S.C. 702-706, claiming that the Secretary acted arbitrarily and capriciously by upgrading dioxin without sufficient epidemiological evidence that it causes cancer in humans. Finding the Secretary's interpretation of the criteria "eminently reasonable," the district court granted summary judgment for the Department. See *Tozzi v. United States Dep't of Health and Human Servs.,* 180 F. Supp. 2d 1, 2000.

II

We begin with two threshold issues. The Department argues that none of the appellants has standing to challenge the dioxin upgrade and that, in any case, listing decisions are unreviewable. We consider each argument in turn.

Standing

To have Article III standing, a plaintiff must demonstrate an "actual or immediate" "injury-in-fact" that is "fairly traceable" to the challenged conduct and "likely" to be "redressed by a favorable decision." *Lujan v. Defenders of Wildlife,* 504 U.S. 555, 560–61 (1992). The plaintiff's allegations must not be purely "speculative—the ultimate label for injuries too implausible to support standing." Applying this standard, the district court found that Brevet had standing.

The Department first argues that Brevet has failed to show actual or immediate injury. We disagree. According to an affidavit submitted by Brevet's president, over ninety-five percent of the company's sales depend on the continued use of PVC plastic by the medical establishment. The president also states that health care companies, pressured by environmental groups, have expressed concern over the dioxin hazards associated with incineration of PVC medical supplies; that some municipalities have adopted resolutions calling for the phasing out of all, or nearly all, PVC containing products, including medical supplies; and that Brevet's "profits, reputation and goodwill" would be adversely affected if an "authoritative U.S. government agency issued and widely disseminated a report implying . . . that Brevet's products are responsible for introducing a known human carcinogen into the environment."

Record evidence supports Brevet's claims. Three California municipalities—San Francisco, Oakland and Berkeley—adopted resolutions forcefully calling for health care institutions to eliminate their use of PVC plastic. . . . Supporting Brevet's claim that environmental groups are pressuring healthcare providers to reduce or eliminate the use of PVC plastic, record evidence demonstrates that Tenet Healthcare Corporation, which annually purchases over three billion dollars worth of medical supplies, has announced that it will seek to purchase PVC-free products. Other Brevet customers (actual and potential) including Baxter International, Universal Health Services, Kaiser

Permanente and Catholic Healthcare West have announced similar . . . moves. We thus think it not at all speculative . . . to expect that Brevet, a company whose revenues depend almost entirely on the continued use of PVC plastic in the medical industry, will experience reduced profits.

The Department next argues that even if Brevet's profits were to decline, that injury would not be "fairly traceable" to the dioxin upgrade. *Lujan,* 504 U.S. at 590. The Department points out that the anti-dioxin movement predates the listing process. It also claims that pressure on government agencies to regulate dioxin and on healthcare companies to reduce the use of PVC products will continue whether or not dioxin remains listed as a known human carcinogen.

Even if the Department's claims were true, we disagree that Brevet has failed to show that its injury is fairly traceable to the dioxin upgrade. . . . Where, as here, the alleged injury flows not directly from the challenged agency action, but rather from independent actions of third parties, we have required only a showing that "the agency action is at least a substantial factor motivating the third parties' actions." . . .

Applying this standard to the facts of this case, we have little doubt that the dioxin upgrade will represent a "substantial factor" in the decisions of state and local agencies to regulate products containing dioxin or of healthcare companies to reduce or end purchases of PVC plastics. . . .

Equally without merit is the Department's contention that even assuming a likely injury fairly traceable to the dioxin upgrade, Brevet's injury is not "redressable." *Lujan,* 504 U.S. at 561. While it may be true, as the Department insists, that municipalities and healthcare providers will not reverse decisions to limit PVC use, we do not agree that "Brevet's alleged future harm could not be redressed by a decision of this Court." . . . Thus, were we to set aside the Secretary's upgrade decision, dioxin activists could no longer point to an authoritative determination by the United States government that dioxin is "known" to cause cancer in humans. . . .

Reviewability

Reviewability under the APA hinges upon whether the listing has "legal effect, which in turn is a function of the agency's intention to bind either itself or regulated parties." *Kennecott Utah Copper Corp. v. United States Dep't of Interior,* 319 U.S. App. D.C. 128, 88 F.3d 1191, 1223 (D.C. Cir. 1996). In making this determination, we have sometimes looked to "the agency's own characterization of its action" and to "publication or the lack thereof in the Federal Register or the Code of Federal Regulations." Where the agency characterizes its action as non-binding or does not publish in the Federal Register, we have found the action unreviewable.

Seizing upon these two indicia of unreviewability, the Department argues that the listing is unreviewable. It points out that the Report's preamble states that it is "for informational purposes only" and that the Secretary never published the entire report in the Federal Register. Taken alone, the characterization of the Report as informational might well support a conclusion that the Report has no "legal effect." Additional considerations, however, lead us to conclude otherwise.

To begin with, although the final Report was not published in the Federal Register, the Secretary did publish a notice proposing a dioxin upgrade and, once finalized, a summary of the decision. Equally important, even though the Secretary takes no action pursuant to a listing, the contention that a listing has no "binding effect" is inaccurate: Listing a substance as a human carcinogen triggers obligations under OSHA, Department of Labor and state regulations. Additional evidence of a listing's "legal effect" comes from the fact that in order to remove a substance from either category, the Secretary must undertake the same elaborate procedure—including notice and comment—required for an initial listing.

Having found that Brevet has standing and that the listing is reviewable, we turn to the merits.

III

Brevet argues that by upgrading dioxin on the basis of mechanistic rather than epidemiological evidence, the Secretary acted arbitrarily and capriciously. According to Brevet, the criteria's final paragraph, which permits the use of mechanistic evidence, applies only to the "reasonably anticipated" category, leaving unaffected the traditional understanding that the Secretary may list a substance in the "known" category only if there is "sufficient" evidence from epidemiological studies. Interpreting the criteria differently, the Department insists that the last paragraph applies to both categories, thus permitting reliance on mechanistic evidence when classifying substances as known carcinogens. In support of this interpretation, the Department points out that the version appearing in the published Report, quoted in full earlier in this opinion, shows the last paragraph with wider margins than the preceding paragraphs.

Because Brevet challenges the Secretary's interpretation of an HHS regulation (Brevet nowhere argues that the criteria are not a regulation), we owe the Secretary "substantial deference." We need not find that the agency's construction is the only possible one, or even the one that the court would have adopted in the first instance. Indeed, we give the agency's interpretation "controlling weight," unless an "alternative reading is compelled by the regulation's plain language or by other indications of the Secretary's intent at the time of the regulation's promulgation." Brevet falls far short of meeting this highly deferential standard.

For one thing, not only does the absence of indentation support the Secretary's interpretation, but Brevet points to no textual evidence demonstrating that the last paragraph applies only to the "reasonably anticipated" category. Brevet argues that the Secretary's interpretation completely defeats language in the "known" category, which the company says requires "studies in humans" (meaning, according to Brevet, exclusively epidemiology) that are "sufficient" to "indicate a causal relationship" between the substance and cancer. Thus, Brevet says, a substance that fails that test cannot be classified as such. At most, however, Brevet has shown an inconsistency between the criteria's formatting (the absence of indentation) and the "known" category's text, in which case we would defer to the Secretary's resolution of the contradiction. . . .

Brevet next argues that "contemporaneous evidence" indicates that the Secretary had no intention of broadening the "known" criteria through the 1996 revisions. In support of this argument, Brevet points to a press release issued by the Secretary's Office on the day the revised criteria were published and to an article in *Environmental Health Perspectives,* the NTP's official newsletter, both of which state that the criteria for listing in the "known" category remain "unchanged." We see nothing in either document demonstrating that the interpretation the Department offers here "marks a departure from [the Secretary's] stated prior understanding in enacting the regulation." Although portions of the press release quote the Secretary, the statement that the criteria for the "known" category remain unchanged was not a quotation, nor does anything in the record indicate that the Secretary or any official with authority to interpret the criteria authorized the statement. In addition to suffering from the same defect, the newsletter is at best ambiguous. Although saying that the 1996 criteria for the "known" category are substantively unchanged, the newsletter, after quoting the criteria's final paragraph in full, states that "the last factor is especially important" for the reasonably anticipated to be a human carcinogen category. The phrase "especially important" suggests that the final paragraph applies to the "known" category as well.

The decision of the district court is affirmed. So ordered.

California Dental Association v. Federal Trade Commission
526 U.S. 756 (1999)

Justice Souter delivered the opinion for a unanimous Court with respect to Parts I and II, and the opinion of the Court with respect to Part III, in which Chief Justice Rehnquist and Justices O'Connor, Scalia, and Thomas joined. Justice Breyer filed an opinion concurring in part and dissenting in part, in which Justices Stevens, Kennedy, and Ginsburg joined.

There are two issues in this case: whether the jurisdiction of the Federal Trade Commission extends to the California Dental Association (CDA), a nonprofit professional association, and whether a "quick look" sufficed to justify finding that certain advertising restrictions adopted by the CDA violated the antitrust laws. We hold that the Commission's jurisdiction under the Federal Trade Commission Act (FTC Act) extends to an association that, like the CDA, provides substantial economic benefit to its for-profit members, but that where, as here, any anticompetitive effects of given restraints are far from intuitively obvious, the rule of reason demands a more thorough enquiry into the consequences of those restraints than the Court of Appeals performed.

The CDA is a voluntary nonprofit association of local dental societies to which some 19,000 dentists belong, including about three-quarters of those practicing in the State. The CDA is exempt from federal income tax under 26 U.S.C. § 501(c)(6), covering "business leagues, chambers of commerce, real-estate boards, [and] boards of trade," although it has for-profit subsidiaries that give its members advantageous access to various sorts of insurance, including liability coverage, and to financing for their real estate, equipment, cars, and patients' bills. The CDA lobbies and litigates in its members' interests and conducts marketing and public relations campaigns for their benefit.

The dentists who belong to the CDA through these associations agree to abide by a Code of Ethics (Code) including the following:

"Although any dentist may advertise, no dentist shall advertise or solicit patients in any form of communication in a manner that is false or misleading in any material respect. In order to properly serve the public, dentists should represent themselves in a manner that contributes to the esteem of the public. Dentists should not misrepresent their training and competence in any way that would be false or misleading in any material respect."

The CDA has issued a number of advisory opinions interpreting this section, and through separate advertising guidelines intended to help members comply with the Code and with state law the CDA has advised its dentists of disclosures they must make under state law when engaging in discount advertising:

"Any communication or advertisement which refers to the cost of dental services shall be exact, without omissions, and shall make each service clearly identifiable, without the use of such phrases as 'as low as,' 'and up,' 'lowest prices,' or words or phrases of similar import.

"Any advertisement which refers to the cost of dental services and uses words of comparison or relativity—for example, 'low fees'—must be based on verifiable data substantiating the comparison or statement of relativity. The burden shall be on the dentist who advertises in such terms to establish the accuracy of the comparison or statement of relativity."

"Advertising claims as to the quality of services are not susceptible to measurement or verification; accordingly, such claims are likely to be false or misleading in any material respect."

Responsibility for enforcing the Code rests in the first instance with the local dental societies, to which applicants for CDA membership must submit copies of their own advertisements and those of their employers or referral services to assure compliance with the Code. The local societies also actively seek information about potential Code violations by applicants or CDA members. Applicants who refuse to withdraw or revise objectionable advertisements may be denied membership; and members who, after a hearing, remain similarly recalcitrant are subject to censure, suspension, or expulsion from the CDA.

The Commission brought a complaint against the CDA, alleging that it applied its guidelines so as to restrict truthful, nondeceptive advertising, and so violated § 5 of the FTC Act, 15 U.S.C. § 45.

The complaint alleged that the CDA had unreasonably restricted two types of advertising: price advertising, particularly discounted fees, and advertising relating to the quality of dental services. An Administrative Law Judge (ALJ) held the Commission to have jurisdiction over the CDA, which, the ALJ noted, had itself "stated that a selection of its programs and services has a potential value to members of between $22,739 and $65,127," 121 F.T.C. at 207. He found that, although there had been no proof that the CDA exerted market power, no such proof was required to establish an antitrust violation under *In re Mass. Bd. of Registration in Optometry*, 110 F.T.C. 549 (1988), since the CDA had unreasonably prevented members and potential members from using truthful, nondeceptive advertising, all to the detriment of both dentists and consumers of dental services. He accordingly found a violation of § 5 of the FTC Act. 121 F.T.C. at 272- 273.

The Commission adopted the factual findings of the ALJ except for his conclusion that the CDA lacked market power, with which the Commission disagreed. The Commission treated the CDA's restrictions on discount advertising as illegal per se. 128 F.3d at 725. In the alternative, the Commission held the price advertising (as well as the nonprice) restrictions to be violations of the Sherman and FTC Acts under an abbreviated rule-of-reason analysis. One Commissioner concurred separately, arguing that the Commission should have applied the Mass Bd. standard, not the per se analysis, to the limitations on price advertising. Another Commissioner dissented, finding the evidence insufficient to show either that the restrictions had an anticompetitive effect under the rule of reason, or that the CDA had market power.

The Court of Appeals for the Ninth Circuit affirmed, sustaining the Commission's assertion of jurisdiction over the CDA and its ultimate conclusion on the merits. 128 F.3d at 730. The court thought it error for the Commission to have applied per se analysis to the price advertising restrictions, finding analysis under the rule of reason required for all the restrictions. But the Court of Appeals went on to explain that the Commission had properly "applied an abbreviated, or 'quick look,' rule of reason analysis designed for restraints that are not per se unlawful but are sufficiently anticompetitive on their face that they do not require a full-blown rule of reason inquiry. See *National Collegiate Athletic Assn. v. Board of Regents of Univ. of Okla.*, 468 U.S. 85 (1984)]" . . .

The Court of Appeals thought truncated rule-of-reason analysis to be in order for several reasons. As for the restrictions on discount advertising, they "amounted in practice to a fairly 'naked' restraint on price competition itself." The CDA's procompetitive justification, that the restrictions encouraged disclosure and prevented false and misleading advertising, carried little weight because "it is simply infeasible to disclose all of the information that is required," 128 F.3d at 728, and "the record provides no evidence that the rule has in fact led to increased disclosure and transparency of dental pricing," ibid. As to non-price advertising restrictions, the court said that "these restrictions are in effect a form of output limitation, as they restrict the supply of information about individual dentists' services. See *Areeda & Hovenkamp*, Antitrust Law P1505 at 693-694 (Supp. 1997) . . . The restrictions may also affect output more directly, as quality and comfort advertising may induce some customers to obtain nonemergency care when they might not otherwise do so. . . . Under these circumstances, we think that the restriction is a sufficiently naked restraint on output to justify quick look analysis." Ibid.

The Court of Appeals went on to hold that the Commission's findings with respect to the CDA's agreement and intent to restrain trade, as well as on the effect of the restrictions and the existence of market power, were all supported by substantial evidence. 128 F.3d at 728-730.

In dissent, Judge Real took the position that the Commission's jurisdiction did not cover the CDA as a nonprofit professional association engaging in no commercial operations. 128 F.3d at 730. But even assuming jurisdiction, he argued, full-bore rule-of-reason analysis was called for, since the disclosure requirements were not naked restraints and neither fixed prices nor banned nondeceptive advertising. 128 F.3d at 730-731.

We granted *certiorari* to resolve conflicts among the Circuits on the Commission's jurisdiction over a nonprofit professional association and the occasions for abbreviated rule-of-reason analysis.We now vacate the judgment of the Court of Appeals and remand.

II

The FTC Act gives the Commission authority over "persons, partnerships, or corporations," 15 U.S.C. § 45(a)(2), and defines "corporation" to include "any company . . . or association, incorporated or unincorporated, without shares of capital or capital stock or certificates of interest, except partnerships, which is organized to carry on business for its own profit or that of its members." Although the Circuits have not agreed on the precise extent of this definition, the Commission has long held that some circumstances give it jurisdiction over an entity that seeks no profit for itself. While the Commission has claimed to have jurisdiction over a nonprofit entity if a substantial part of its total activities provide pecuniary benefits to its members, see *In re American Medical Assn.,* 94 F.T.C. 701, 983-984 (1980), respondent now advances the slightly different formulation that the Commission has jurisdiction "over anticompetitive practices by nonprofit associations whose activities provide substantial economic benefits to their for-profit members' businesses." Respondent urges deference to this interpretation of the Commission's jurisdiction as reasonable. Brief for Respondent 25–26 (citing *Chevron U.S.A. Inc. v. Natural Resources Defense Council, Inc.,* 467 U.S. 837 (1984); *Mississippi Power & Light Co. v. Mississippi ex rel. Moore,* 487 U.S. 354 (1988). But we have no occasion to review the call for deference here, the interpretation urged in respondent's brief being clearly the better reading of the statute under ordinary principles of construction. . . .

Just as the FTC Act does not require that a supporting organization must devote itself entirely to its members' profits, neither does the Act say anything about how much of the entity's activities must go to raising the members' bottom lines. There is accordingly no apparent reason to let the statute's application turn on meeting some threshold percentage of activity for this purpose, or even satisfying a softer formulation calling for a substantial part of the nonprofit entity's total activities to be aimed at its members' pecuniary benefit. To be sure, proximate relation to lucre must appear; the FTC Act does not cover all membership organizations of profit-making corporations without more, and an organization devoted solely to professional education may lie outside the FTC Act's jurisdictional reach, even though the quality of professional services ultimately affects the profits of those who deliver them.

There is no line drawing exercise in this case, however, where the CDA's contributions to the profits of its individual members are proximate and apparent. Through for-profit subsidiaries, the CDA provides advantageous insurance and preferential financing arrangements for its members, and it engages in lobbying, litigation, marketing, and public relations for the benefit of its members' interests. This congeries of activities confers far more than *de minimis* or merely presumed economic benefits on CDA members; the economic benefits conferred upon the CDA's profit-seeking professionals plainly fall within the object of enhancing its members' "profit," which the FTC Act makes the jurisdictional touchstone. There is no difficulty in concluding that the Commission has jurisdiction over the CDA. . . .

III

The Court of Appeals treated as distinct questions the sufficiency of the analysis of anticompetitive effects and the substantiality of the evidence supporting the Commission's conclusions. Because we decide that the Court of Appeals erred when it held as a matter of law that quick-look analysis was appropriate (with the consequence that the Commission's abbreviated analysis and conclusion were sustainable), we do not reach the question of the substantiality of the evidence supporting the Commission's conclusion.

In *National Collegiate Athletic Assn. v. Board of Regents of Univ. of Okla.,* 468 U.S. 85 (1984), we held that a "naked restraint on price and output requires some competitive justification even in the absence of a detailed market analysis." Elsewhere, we held that "no elaborate industry analysis is required to demonstrate the anticompetitive character of" horizontal agreements among competitors to refuse to discuss prices, *National Soc. of Professional Engineers v. United States,* 435 U.S. 679, 692 (1978), or to withhold a particular desired service, *FTC v. Indiana Federation of Dentists,* 476 U.S. 447, 459 (1986) (quoting *National Soc. of Professional Engineers,* supra, at 692). In each of these cases, which have formed the basis for what has come to be called abbreviated or "quick-look" analysis under the rule of reason, an observer with even a rudimentary understanding of economics could conclude that the arrangements in question would have an anticompetitive effect on customers and markets. In *National Collegiate Athletic Assn.,* the league's television plan expressly limited output (the number of games that could be televised) and fixed a minimum price. 468 U.S. at 99-100. In *National Soc. of Professional Engineers,* the restraint was "an absolute ban on competitive bidding." 435 U.S. at 692. In *Indiana Federation of Dentists,* the restraint was "a horizontal agreement among the participating dentists to withhold from their customers a particular service that they desire." 476 U.S. at 459. As in such cases, quick-look analysis carries the day when the great likelihood of anticompetitive effects can easily be ascertained. . . .

The case before us, however, fails to present a situation in which the likelihood of anticompetitive effects is comparably obvious. Even on Justice Breyer's view that bars on truthful and verifiable price and quality advertising are prima facie anticompetitive (opinion concurring in part and dissenting in part) and place the burden of procompetitive justification on those who agree to adopt them, the very issue at the threshold of this case is whether professional price and quality advertising is sufficiently verifiable in theory and in fact to fall within such a general rule. Ultimately our disagreement with Justice Breyer turns on our different responses to this issue. Whereas he accepts, as the Ninth Circuit seems to have done, that the restrictions here were like restrictions on advertisement of price and quality generally, it seems to us that the CDA's advertising restrictions might plausibly be thought to have a net procompetitive effect, or possibly no effect at all on competition. The restrictions on both discount and nondiscount advertising are, at least on their face, designed to avoid false or deceptive advertising in a market characterized by striking disparities between the information available to the professional and the patient. . . .

In a market for professional services, in which advertising is relatively rare and the comparability of service packages not easily established, the difficulty for customers or potential competitors to get and verify information about the price and availability of services magnifies the dangers to competition associated with misleading advertising. What is more, the quality of professional services tends to resist either calibration or monitoring by individual patients or clients, partly because of the specialized knowledge required to evaluate the services, and partly because of the difficulty in determining whether, and the degree to which, an outcome is attributable to the quality of services (like a poor job of tooth-filling) or to something else (like a very tough walnut). . . .

The existence of such significant challenges to informed decisionmaking by the customer for professional services immediately suggests that advertising restrictions arguably protecting patients from misleading or irrelevant advertising call for more than cursory treatment as obviously comparable to classic horizontal agreements to limit output or price competition.

The explanation proffered by the Court of Appeals for the likely anticompetitive effect of the CDA's restrictions on discount advertising began with the unexceptionable statements that "price advertising is fundamental to price competition," 128 F.3d at 727, and that "restrictions on the ability to advertise prices normally make it more difficult for consumers to find a lower price and for dentists to compete on the basis of price," ibid. The court then acknowledged that, according to the CDA, the restrictions nonetheless furthered the "legitimate, indeed procompetitive, goal of preventing false and misleading price advertising." 128 F.3d at 728. The Court of Appeals might, at this juncture, have recognized that the restrictions at issue here are very far from a total ban on price or discount advertising, and might have considered the possibility that the particular restrictions on professional advertising could have different effects from those "normally" found in the commercial world, even to the point of promoting competition by reducing the occurrence of unverifiable and misleading across-the-board discount advertising. Instead, the Court of Appeals confined itself to the brief assertion that the "CDA's disclosure requirements appear to prohibit across-the-board discounts because it is simply infeasible to disclose all of the information that is required," ibid., followed by the observation that "the record provides no evidence that the rule has in fact led to increased disclosure and transparency of dental pricing." . . .

Whether advertisements that announced discounts for, say, first-time customers, would be less effective at conveying information relevant to competition if they listed the original and discounted prices for checkups, X-rays, and fillings, than they would be if they simply specified a percentage discount across the board, seems to us a question susceptible to empirical but not a priori analysis. In a suspicious world, the discipline of specific example may well be a necessary condition of plausibility for professional claims that for all practical purposes defy comparison shopping. It is also possible in principle that, even if across-the-board discount advertisements were more effective in drawing customers in the short run, the recurrence of some measure of intentional or accidental misstatement due to the breadth of their claims might leak out over time to make potential patients skeptical of any

such across-the-board advertising, so undercutting the method's effectiveness. Cf. Akerlof, 84 Q. J. Econ., at 495 (explaining that "dishonest dealings tend to drive honest dealings out of the market"). It might be, too, that across-the-board discount advertisements would continue to attract business indefinitely, but might work precisely because they were misleading customers, and thus just because their effect would be anticompetitive, not procompetitive. Put another way, the CDA's rule appears to reflect the prediction that any costs to competition associated with the elimination of across-the-board advertising will be outweighed by gains to consumer information (and hence competition) created by discount advertising that is exact, accurate, and more easily verifiable (at least by regulators). As a matter of economics this view may or may not be correct, but it is not implausible, and neither a court nor the Commission may initially dismiss it as presumptively wrong. . . .

The question is not whether the universe of possible advertisements has been limited (as assuredly it has), but whether the limitation on advertisements obviously tends to limit the total delivery of dental services. The court came closest to addressing this latter question when it went on to assert that limiting advertisements regarding quality and safety "prevents dentists from fully describing the package of services they offer," 128 F.3d at 728, adding that "the restrictions may also affect output more directly, as quality and comfort advertising may induce some customers to obtain nonemergency care when they might not otherwise do so," ibid. This suggestion about output is also puzzling. If quality advertising actually induces some patients to obtain more care than they would in its absence, then restricting such advertising would reduce the demand for dental services, not the supply; and it is of course the producers' supply of a good in relation to demand that is normally relevant in determining whether a producer-imposed output limitation has the anticompetitive effect of artificially raising prices. . . .

The point is not that the CDA's restrictions necessarily have the procompetitive effect claimed by the CDA; it is possible that banning quality claims might have no effect at all on competitiveness if, for example, many dentists made very much the same sort of claims.

And it is also of course possible that the restrictions might in the final analysis be anti-competitive. The point, rather, is that the plausibility of competing claims about the effects of the professional advertising restrictions rules out the indulgently abbreviated review to which the Commission's order was treated. The obvious anticompetitive effect that triggers abbreviated analysis has not been shown. . . .

As the circumstances here demonstrate, there is generally no categorical line to be drawn between restraints that give rise to an intuitively obvious inference of anticompetitive effect and those that call for more detailed treatment. What is required, rather, is an enquiry meet for the case, looking to the circumstances, details, and logic of a restraint. The object is to see whether the experience of the market has been so clear, or necessarily will be, that a confident conclusion about the principal tendency of a restriction will follow from a quick (or at least quicker) look, in place of a more sedulous one. And of course what we see may vary over time, if rule-of-reason analyses in case after case reach identical conclusions. For now, at least, a less quick look was required for the initial assessment of the tendency of these professional advertising restrictions. Because the Court of Appeals did not scrutinize the assumption of relative anticompetitive tendencies, we vacate the judgment and remand the case for a fuller consideration of the issue.

Norton, Secretary of the Interior, v. Southern Utah Wilderness Alliance 124 S. Ct. 2373 (2004)

Justice Scalia delivered the opinion for a unanimous Court.

In this case, we must decide whether the authority of a federal court under the Administrative Procedure Act (APA) to "compel agency action unlawfully withheld or unreasonably delayed," 5 U.S.C. § 706(1), extends to the review of the United States Bureau of Land Management's stewardship of public lands under certain statutory provisions and its own planning documents.

I

Almost half the State of Utah, about 23 million acres, is federal land administered by the Bureau of Land Management (BLM), an agency within the Department of Interior. For nearly 30 years, BLM's management of public lands has been governed by the Federal Land Policy and Management Act of 1976 (FLPMA), 43 U.S.C. § 1701 which "established a policy in favor of retaining public lands for multiple use management." "Multiple use management" is a deceptively simple term that describes the enormously complicated task of striking a balance among the many competing "uses to which land can be put, including, but not limited to, recreation, range, timber, minerals, watershed, wildlife and fish, and [uses serving] natural scenic, scientific and historical values." A second management goal, "sustained yield," requires BLM to control depleting uses over time, so as to ensure a high level of valuable uses in the future. To these ends, FLPMA establishes a dual regime of inventory and planning. Sections 1711 and 1712, respectively, provide for a comprehensive, ongoing inventory of federal lands, and for a land use planning process that "projects" "present and future use," given the lands' inventoried characteristics.

Of course not all uses are compatible. Congress made the judgment that some lands should be set aside as wilderness at the expense of commercial and recreational uses.

A pre-FLPMA enactment, the Wilderness Act of 1964, provides that designated wilderness areas, subject to certain exceptions, "shall [have] no commercial enterprise and no permanent road," no motorized vehicles, and no manmade structures. The designation of a wilderness area can be made only by Act of Congress.

Pursuant to § 1782, the Secretary of the Interior has identified so-called "wilderness study areas" (WSAs), roadless lands of 5,000 acres or more that possess "wilderness characteristics," as determined in the Secretary's land inventory. As the name suggests, WSAs (as well as certain wild lands identified prior to the passage of FLPMA) have been subjected to further examination and public comment in order to evaluate their suitability for designation as wilderness. In 1991, out of 3.3 million acres in Utah that had been identified for study, 2 million were recommended as suitable for wilderness designation. This recommendation was forwarded to Congress, which has not yet acted upon it. Until Congress acts one way or the other, FLPMA provides that "the Secretary shall continue to manage such lands . . . in a manner so as not to impair the suitability of such areas for preservation as wilderness." This nonimpairment mandate applies to all WSAs identified under § 1782, including lands considered unsuitable by the Secretary.

Aside from identification of WSAs, the main tool that BLM employs to balance wilderness protection against other uses is a land use plan—what BLM regulations call a "resource management plan." 43 CFR § 1601.0-5(k) (2003). Land use plans, adopted after notice and comment, are "designed to guide and control future management actions." Generally, a land use plan describes, for a particular area, allowable uses, goals for future condition of the land, and specific next steps. Under FLPMA, "the Secretary shall manage the public lands under principles of multiple use and sustained yield, in accordance with the land use plans . . . when they are available."

Protection of wilderness has come into increasing conflict with another element of multiple use, recreational use of so-called off-road vehicles (ORVs), which include vehicles primarily designed for off-road use, such as lightweight, four-wheel "all-terrain vehicles," and vehicles capable of such use, such as sport utility vehicles. According to the United States Forest Service's most recent estimates, some 42 million Americans participate in off-road travel each year, more than double the number two decades ago. H. Cordell, *Outdoor Recreation for 21st Century America* 40 (2004). United States sales of all-terrain vehicles alone have roughly doubled in the past five years, reaching almost 900,000 in 2003. See Tanz, "Making Tracks, Making Enemies," *N. Y. Times,* Jan. 2, 2004, p. F1, col. 5. . . . The use of ORVs on federal land has negative environmental consequences, including soil disruption and compaction, harassment of animals, and annoyance of wilderness lovers. Thus, BLM faces a classic land use dilemma of sharply inconsistent uses, in a context of scarce resources and congressional silence with respect to wilderness designation.

In 1999, respondents Southern Utah Wilderness Alliance and other organizations (collectively SUWA) filed this action in the United States District Court for Utah against petitioners BLM, its Director, and the Secretary. In its second amended complaint, SUWA sought declaratory and injunctive relief for BLM's failure to act to protect public lands in Utah from damage caused by ORV use. SUWA made three claims that are relevant here: (1) that BLM had violated its nonimpairment obligation under § 1782(a) by allowing degradation in certain WSAs; (2) that BLM had failed to implement provisions in its land use plans relating to ORV use; (3) that BLM had failed to take a "hard look" at whether, pursuant to the National Environmental Policy Act of 1969 (NEPA), 42 U.S.C. § 4321, it should undertake supplemental environmental analyses for areas in which ORV use had increased. SUWA contended that it could sue to remedy these three failures to act pursuant to the APA's provision of a cause of action to "compel agency action unlawfully withheld or unreasonably delayed." 5 U.S.C. § 706(1).

The District Court entered a dismissal with respect to the three claims. A divided panel of the Tenth Circuit reversed. 301 F.3d 1217 (2002).

II

All three claims at issue here involve assertions that BLM failed to take action with respect to ORV use that it was required to take. Failures to act are sometimes remediable under the APA, but not always. We begin by considering what limits the APA places upon judicial review of agency inaction.

The APA authorizes suit by "[a] person suffering legal wrong because of agency action, or adversely affected or aggrieved by agency action within the meaning of a relevant statute." 5 U.S.C. § 702. Where no other statute provides a private right of action, the "agency action" complained of must be "final agency action." "Agency action" is defined in § 551(13) to include "the whole or a part of an agency rule, order, license, sanction, relief, or the equivalent or denial thereof, or failure to act." The APA provides relief for a failure to act in § 706(1): "The reviewing court shall . . . compel agency action unlawfully withheld or unreasonably delayed."

Sections 702, 704, and 706(1) all insist upon an "agency action," either as the action complained of (in §§ 702 and 704 or as the action to be compelled (in § 706(1)). The definition of that term begins with a list of five categories of decisions made or outcomes implemented by an agency—"agency rule, order, license, sanction [or] relief." All of those categories involve circumscribed, discrete agency actions, as their definitions make clear: "an agency statement of . . . future effect designed to implement, interpret, or prescribe law or policy" (rule); "a final disposition . . . in a matter other than rule making" (order); a "permit . . . or other form of permission" (license); a "prohibition . . . or taking [of] other compulsory or restrictive action" (sanction); or a "grant of money, assistance, license, authority," etc., or "recognition of a claim, right, immunity," etc., or "taking of other action on the application or petition of, and beneficial to, a person" (relief).

The terms following those five categories of agency action are not defined in the APA: "or the equivalent or denial thereof, or failure to act." But an "equivalent . . . thereof" must also be discrete (or it would not be equivalent), and a "denial thereof" must be the denial of a discrete listed action (and perhaps denial of a discrete equivalent).

The final term in the definition, "failure to act," is in our view properly understood as a failure to take an agency action—that is, a failure to take one of the agency actions (including their equivalents) earlier defined in § 551(13). Moreover, even without this equation of "act" with "agency action" the interpretive canon of *ejusdem generis* would attribute to the last item ("failure to act") the same characteristic of discreteness shared by all the preceding items. . . . A "failure to act" is not the same thing as a "denial." The latter is the agency's act of saying no to a request; the former is simply the omission of an action without formally rejecting a request—for example, the failure to promulgate a rule or take some decision by a statutory deadline. The important point is that a "failure to act" is properly understood to be limited, as are the other items in § 551(13), to a discrete action.

A second point central to the analysis of the present case is that the only agency action that can be compelled under the APA is action legally required. This limitation appears in § 706(1)'s authorization for courts to "compel agency action unlawfully withheld." . . . As described in the Attorney General's Manual on the APA, a document whose reasoning we have often found persuasive, . . . § 706(1) empowers a court only to compel an agency "to perform a ministerial or non-discretionary act," or "to take action upon a matter, without directing how it shall act." *Attorney General's Manual on the Administrative Procedure Act* 108 (1947).

Thus, a claim under § 706(1) can proceed only where a plaintiff asserts that an agency failed to take a discrete agency action that it is required to take. These limitations rule out several kinds of challenges. The limitation to discrete agency action precludes the kind of broad programmatic attack we rejected in *Lujan v. Nat'l Wildlife Fed'n*, 497 U.S. 871 (1990). There we considered a challenge to BLM's land withdrawal review program, couched as unlawful agency "action" that the plaintiffs wished to have "set aside" under § 706(2). We concluded that the program was not an "agency action":

"Respondent cannot seek wholesale improvement of this program by court decree, rather than in the offices of the Department or the halls of Congress, where programmatic improvements are normally made. Under the terms of the APA, respondent must direct its attack against some particular 'agency action' that causes it harm."

The plaintiffs in *National Wildlife Federation* would have fared no better if they had characterized the agency's alleged "failure to revise land use plans in proper fashion" and "failure to consider multiple use," in terms of "agency action unlawfully withheld" under § 706(1), rather than agency action "not in accordance with law" under § 706(2).

The limitation to required agency action rules out judicial direction of even discrete agency action that is not demanded by law (which includes, of course, agency regulations that have the force of law). Thus, when an agency is compelled by law to act within a certain time period, but the manner of its action is left to the agency's discretion, a court can compel the agency to act, but has no power to specify what the action must be. For example, 47 U.S.C. § 251(d)(1), which required the Federal Communications Commission "to establish regulations to implement" interconnection requirements "within 6 months" of the date of enactment of the Telecommunications Act of 1996, would have supported a judicial decree under the APA requiring the prompt issuance of regulations, but not a judicial decree setting forth the content of those regulations.

III

A

With these principles in mind, we turn to SUWA's first claim, that by permitting ORV use in certain WSAs, BLM violated its mandate to "continue to manage [WSAs] . . . in a manner so as not to impair the suitability of such areas for preservation as wilderness," SUWA relies not only upon § 1782(c) but also upon a provision of BLM's Interim Management Policy for Lands Under Wilderness Review, which interprets the nonimpairment mandate to require BLM to manage WSAs so as to prevent them from being "degraded so far, compared with the area's values for other purposes, as to significantly constrain the Congress's prerogative to either designate [it] as wilderness or release it for other uses."

Section 1782(c) is mandatory as to the object to be achieved, but it leaves BLM a great deal of discretion in deciding how to achieve it. It assuredly does not mandate, with the clarity necessary to support judicial action under § 706(1), the total exclusion of ORV use.

SUWA argues that § 1782 does contain a categorical imperative, namely the command to comply with the nonimpairment mandate. It contends that a federal court could simply enter a general order compelling compliance with that mandate, without suggesting any particular manner of compliance. It relies upon the language from the Attorney General's Manual quoted earlier, that a court can "take action upon a matter, without directing how [the agency] shall act," and upon language in a case cited by the Manual noting that "mandamus will lie . . . even though the act required involves the exercise of judgment and discretion." *Safeway Stores v. Brown,* 138 F.2d 278, 280. The action referred to in these excerpts, however, is discrete agency action, as we have discussed above. General deficiencies in compliance, unlike the failure to issue a ruling that was discussed in *Safeway Stores,* lack the specificity requisite for agency action.

The principal purpose of the APA limitations we have discussed—and of the traditional limitations upon mandamus from which they were derived—is to protect agencies from undue judicial interference with their lawful discretion, and to avoid judicial entanglement in abstract policy disagreements which courts lack both expertise and information to resolve. If courts were empowered to enter general orders compelling compliance with broad statutory mandates, they would necessarily be empowered, as well, to determine whether compliance was achieved—which would mean that it would ultimately become the task of the supervising court, rather than the agency, to work out compliance with the broad statutory mandate, injecting the judge into day-to-day agency management. To take just a few examples from federal resources management, a plaintiff might allege that the Secretary had failed to "manage wild free-roaming horses and burros in a manner that is designed to achieve and maintain a thriving natural ecological balance," or to "manage the [New Orleans Jazz National] Historical Park in such a manner as will preserve and perpetuate knowledge and understanding of the history of jazz," or to "manage the [Steens Mountain] Cooperative Management and Protection Area for the benefit of present and future generations." The prospect of pervasive oversight by federal courts over the manner and pace of agency compliance with such congressional directives is not contemplated by the APA.

B

SUWA's second claim is that BLM failed to comply with certain provisions in its land use plans, thus contravening the requirement that "the Secretary shall manage the public lands . . . in accordance with the land use plans when they are available." The relevant count in SUWA's second amended complaint alleged that BLM had violated a variety of commitments in its land use plans, but over the course of the litigation these have been reduced to two, one relating to the 1991 resource management plan for the San Rafael area, and the other to various aspects of the 1990 ORV implementation plan for the Henry Mountains area. . . .

The statutory directive that BLM manage "in accordance with" land use plans, and the regulatory requirement that authorizations and actions "conform to" those plans, prevent BLM from taking actions inconsistent with the provisions of a land use plan. Unless and until the plan is amended, such actions can be set aside as contrary to law pursuant to 5 U.S.C. § 706(2). The claim presently under discussion, however, would have us go further, and conclude that a statement in a plan that BLM "will" take this, that, or the other action, is a binding commitment that can be compelled under § 706(1). In our view it is not—at least absent clear indication of binding commitment in the terms of the plan.

FLPMA describes land use plans as tools by which "present and future use is projected." 43 U.S.C. § 1701(a)(2). The implementing regulations make clear that land use plans are a preliminary step in the overall process of managing public lands—"designed to guide and control future management actions and the development of subsequent, more detailed and limited scope plans for resources and uses." The statute and regulations confirm that a land use plan is not ordinarily the medium for affirmative decisions that implement the agency's "projections." Title 43 U.S.C. § 1712(e) provides that "the Secretary may issue management decisions to implement land use plans"—the decisions, that is, are distinct from the plan itself, picking up the same theme; the regulation defining a land use plan declares that a plan "is not a final implementation decision on actions which require further specific plans, process steps, or decisions under specific provisions of law and regulations." The BLM's *Land Use Planning Handbook* specifies that land use plans are normally not used to make site-specific implementation decisions. . . .

Quite unlike a specific statutory command requiring an agency to promulgate regulations by a certain date, a land use plan is generally a statement of priorities; it guides and constrains actions, but does not (at least in the usual case) prescribe them. It would be unreasonable to think that either Congress or the agency intended otherwise, since land use plans nationwide would commit the agency to actions far in the future, for which funds have not yet been appropriated. Some plans make explicit that implementation of their programmatic content is subject to budgetary constraints. While the Henry Mountains plan does not contain such a specification, we think it must reasonably be implied. A statement by BLM about what it plans to do, at some point, provided it has the funds and there are not more pressing priorities, cannot be plucked out of context and made a basis for suit under § 706(1).

We therefore hold that the Henry Mountains plan's statements to the effect that BLM will conduct "use supervision and monitoring" in designated areas—like other "will do" projections of agency action set forth in land use plans—are not a legally binding commitment enforceable under § 706(1). That being so, we find it unnecessary to consider whether the action envisioned by the statements is sufficiently discrete to be amenable to compulsion under the APA.

IV

Finally, we turn to SUWA's contention that BLM failed to fulfill certain obligations under NEPA. Before addressing whether a NEPA-required duty is actionable under the APA, we must decide whether NEPA creates an obligation in the first place. NEPA requires a federal agency to prepare an environmental impact statement (EIS) as part of any "proposals for legislation and other major Federal actions significantly affecting the quality of the human environment." 42 U.S.C. sec.4332(2)(c). Often an initial EIS is sufficient, but in certain circumstances an EIS must be supplemented. See *Marsh v. Oregon Natural Resources Council,* 490 U.S. 360, 370-374 (1989). A regulation of the Council on Environmental Quality requires supplementation where "there are significant new circumstances or information relevant to environmental concerns and bearing on the proposed action or its impacts." In *Marsh,* we interpreted § 4332 in light of this regulation to require an agency to take a "hard look" at the new information to assess whether supplementation might be necessary.

SUWA argues that evidence of increased ORV use is "significant new circumstances or information" that requires a "hard look." We disagree. As we noted in *Marsh,* supplementation is necessary only if "there remains 'major Federal action' to occur," as that term is used in § 4332(2)(C). 490 U.S., at 374. In *Marsh,* that condition was met: the dam construction project that gave rise to environmental review was not yet completed. Here, by contrast, although the "approval of a [land use plan]" is a "major Federal action" requiring an EIS, that action is completed when the plan is approved. The land use plan is the "proposed action" contemplated by the regulation. There is no ongoing "major Federal action" that could require supplementation (though BLM is required to perform additional NEPA analysis if a plan is amended or revised).

The judgement of the Court of Appeals is reversed, and the case is remanded for further proceedings consistent with this opinion.

It is so ordered.

NOTES

1. But for a different view, see, Malcolm M. Feeley and Edward L. Rubin, *Judicial Policy Making in the Modern State: How the Courts Reformed America's Prisons* (New York: Cambridge University Press, 2000).

2. Richard A. Brisbin, Jr., "The Conservatism of Antonin Scalia," 105 *Political Science Quarterly* 13 (Spring 1990).

3. *Steel Company v. Citizens for a Better Environment,* 523 U.S. 88,107–8 (1998).

4. *California Dental Association v. Federal Trade Commission,* 526 U.S. 757 (1999).

5. *Bowen v. American Hospital Association,* 476 U.S. 610 (1986).

6. *Clinton v. Goldsmith,* 526 U.S. 529 (1999).

7. *Shalala v. Illinois Council on Long Term Care, Inc.,* 120 S.Ct. 1738 (2000).

8. *Association of Data Processing Service Organizations v. Camp,* 397 U.S. 150, 152 (1970).

9. Ibid.

10. *Linda R. S. v. Richard D.,* 410 U.S. 614 (1973).

11. *Simon v. Eastern Kentucky Welfare Rights Organization,* 426 U.S. 26 (1976).

12. *Allen v. Wright et al.,* 468 U.S. 737 (1984).

13. 508 U.S. 656 (1993).

14. John Dean, *The Rehnquist Choice: The Untold Story of the Nixon Appointment That Redefined the Supreme Court* (New York: The Free Press, 2001), p. 16.

15. *United Public Workers v. Mitchell,* 330 U.S. 75 (1947).

16. *International Longshoremen's & Warehousemen's Union v. Boyd,* 347 U.S. 222 (1954).

17. *National Park Hospitality Association v. Department of Interior,* 538 U.S. 803 (2003).

18. 416 U.S. 312 (1974).

19. Lee Epstein and Thomas Walker, *Constitutional Law for a Changing America: Rights, Liberties, and Justice,* 3d ed. (Washington, D.C.: Congressional Quarterly Press, 1998), p. 62.

20. *Decatur v. Paulding,* 39 U.S. 497, 516 (1840).

21. 5 U.S.C. 702.

22. 38 U.S.C. 211(a).

23. Anthony Lewis, *The New York Times,* 11 November 1996, p. A11.

24. *Webster v. Doe,* 486 U.S. 592 (1988).

25. 509 U.S. 579 (1993).

26. Susan Welch and John Comer, *Quantitative Methods for Public Administration: Techniques and Applications,* 3d ed. (Mason, Ohio: South-Western, Thompson Learning, 2001), 41–43.

27. *Flue-Cured Tobacco Cooperative Stabilization Corporation v. the Environmental Protection Agency,* 313 F. 3rd. 852 (Fourth Cir., 2002).

28. *Flue-Cured Tobacco v. EPA,* 4 F. Supp 2d. 435, 465–66 (1998*).*

29. *Flue-Cured Tobacco v. EPA,* 313 F. 3rd. 852, 859.

30. *Tozzi v. U.S. Department of Health and Human* Services, 271 F. 3rd. 301 (D.C. Cir., 2001).

31. Michelle Laco, "The Data Quality Act: Prologue to a Farce or a Tragedy?" 53 *Emory Law Journal* 305, 307 (Winter 2004); see also, Wendy Wagner, "Science in the Regulatory Process: Reclaiming the Debate over the Role of Science in Public Health and Environment Regulation," 66 *Law and Contemporary Problems* 63 (Fall 2003); Thomas McGarity, "Science in the Regulatory Process: On the Prospect of '*Daubertizing'* Judicial Review of Risk Assessment," 66 *Law and Contemporary Problems* 155 (Fall 2003).

32. *Booth v. Churner,* 532 U.S. 731 (2001).

33. *United States v. Western Pacific Railroad Company,* 352 U.S. 59 (1956).

34. Daniel Oran, *Oran's Dictionary of the Law* (St. Paul, Minn.: West, 1983), p. 116.

35. Ernest Gellhorn and Ronald Levin, *Administrative Law and Process: In a Nutshell* (St. Paul, Minn.: West, 1990), p. 110.

36. *Wisconsin v. New York,* 517 U.S. 1 (1996).

37. *Vermont Yankee Nuclear Power Corporation v. Natural Resources Defense Council,* 435 U.S. 519 (1978).

PART II

THE ADMINISTRATIVE PROCESS

5

The Government and Information

Section A: Collecting Information

Case in Point:
Marshall v. Barlow's, Incorporated
436 U.S. 307 (1978)

In the mid-1970s, Mr. Bill Barlow owned and operated a small plumbing and air conditioning shop in Pocatello, Idaho. One day, an Occupational Safety and Health Administration (OSHA) inspector showed up at Barlow's shop and informed Barlow that he wanted to inspect Barlow's shop for violations of OSHA rules and regulations. Barlow asked whether OSHA had received complaints about working conditions in his shop. The inspector told Barlow that no complaints had been lodged but that Barlow's shop had simply "turned up" on the agency's list. The inspector again asked Barlow for permission to enter the back shop to conduct the inspection. As a member of the John Birch Society, Mr. Barlow believed that government, generally, and particularly a federal administrative agency, is forbidden by the Fourth Amendment of the Constitution from entering his business without a warrant. When Mr. Barlow inquired whether the OSHA inspector had a warrant, the inspector indicated that no warrant was required because Congress had authorized warrantless inspections of businesses to enforce OSHA rules and regulations.

Mr. Barlow refused to allow the OSHA inspector into the back shop, and, subsequently, the secretary of labor filed suit in Idaho Federal District Court to compel Barlow to admit the inspector. The court issued the order, and when an OSHA inspector showed up again at Barlow's shop armed with a court order but still without a warrant, Barlow again refused to allow the inspector into his shop. At this point, Mr. Barlow went to the Idaho Federal District Court to get an injunction preventing OSHA from searching his shop without a warrant. Barlow won his case at the district court, and the secretary of labor appealed.

The Fourth Amendment reads as follows:

The right of the people to be secure in their persons, houses, papers, and effects, against unreasonable searches and seizures, shall not be violated, and no warrant shall issue, but upon probable cause, supported by oath or affirmation, and particularly describing the place to be searched, and the persons or things to be seized.

Notice that what the amendment forbids is unreasonable searches and seizures, but it does not define for us what an unreasonable search or seizure is. The task of deciding what constitutes an unreasonable search has fallen to the U.S. Supreme Court, and the Court has said that warrantless searches and seizures are unreasonable. This is what has come to be known as the warrant requirement: To meet the dictates of the Fourth Amendment, a search must be accompanied by a warrant. No sooner did the Court establish the warrant requirement than it began to create exceptions to it. Those exceptions are referred to as *exigent circumstances* and are generally created in those situations in which requiring a warrant would be impractical. For example, probable cause to stop an automobile may provide the legal authority to search the car without a warrant. Border searches, consent, plain view, and hot pursuit are some other situations in which the Court has created exceptions to the warrant requirement.

The question in the *Barlow* case is whether administrative searches that do not result in criminal charges are to be another exception to the warrant requirement. It would be helpful at this point to reflect on some history. One impetus for the Fourth Amendment was the hatred that businessmen of the former colonies held for the *general warrant,* a procedure that authorized officers of the king to conduct so-called fishing expeditions. That is, the British officer would search a business (or house) without any evidence of wrongdoing just to see whether colonists were complying with certain tax measures. That is why the Fourth Amendment is so specific at the point where it says, "no warrant shall issue."

The Court had decided cases on both sides of the question of whether administrative searches require a warrant. In 1967, the Court decided two cases that could support Mr. Barlow's position. In *Camara v. Municipal Court,* 387 U.S. 523 (1967), the Court said that a San Francisco public health inspector would need a warrant to inspect an apartment leased by Camara (the property was not supposed to be used as a personal dwelling, but allegedly it was). Similarly, the Court said the Seattle Fire Department would need a warrant to conduct an inspection of a warehouse during a routine canvass of businesses for compliance with the city fire code (*See v. Seattle,* 387 U.S. 541 [1967]).

In contrast, the Court said no warrant was required to inspect a firearms business (*United States v. Biswell,* 406 U.S. 311 [1972]) or a liquor establishment (*Colonnade Catering Corporation v. United States,* 397 U.S. 72 [1970]). The Court reasoned that these were "pervasively regulated businesses" that had been subject to "close governmental supervision and inspection" for a long period of time. Furthermore, both businesses had contracted with the federal government and hence fell under a 1936 Act[1] that authorizes warrantless inspections for compliance with minimum wage and hour provisions. Barlow's case was similar to *Biswell* and *Colonnade* in that a congressional act had authorized OSHA's warrantless searches.

Questions

1. Given what you know of the *Barlow* case, how do you think the Supreme Court decided? Why?
2. Barlow owned a small business and had perhaps six or seven employees. How is it that his business fell under the jurisdiction of OSHA? Is every business in the United States subject to the federal government's jurisdiction here? Where is the line drawn?
3. Barlow used to speak in my classes when I taught in Pocatello, and he indicated that it cost $60,000 in legal fees to get his case to the Supreme Court (and he got to skip the Circuit Court of Appeals). Barlow did not have that kind of money. How do you suppose "little people" like Barlow get their cases to the Supreme Court?

GOVERNMENT'S NEED FOR INFORMATION

Toward the end of Chapter 3, the point was made that as the United States began to reject the ideology of negative freedom, limited government, and laissez-faire economics and embrace a newer ideology of positive freedom, positive government, and Keynesian economics, the government became increasingly more involved in distributive, redistributive, and regulatory policy. Distributive policies are those that attempt to encourage private activity, often using subsidies or tax incentives.[2] It is in the area of distributive policies that cozy triangles occur most frequently. Both the triangle that provides subsidies to tobacco growers and the triangle providing research funds to fight cancer are examples of distributive policies. The federal tax deduction for interest on a home mortgage and property tax is also an example of distributive policy.

As the name implies, *redistributive* policies attempt to "manipulate the allocation of wealth, property, rights, or some other value among social classes or racial groups in society."[3] A reduction in the rate at which capital gains are taxed would be redistributive from the bottom to the top, whereas programs such as Aid to Families with Dependent Children (AFDC), legal aid, food stamps, and affirmative action are examples of redistributive policies in the other direction.

Regulatory policies can attempt to regulate competition, primarily because of scarce resources (the licensing of businesses that use air waves and interstate common carriers), or they can regulate in the interest of protecting the public (consumer and environmental laws).

Whether a specific policy involves an agricultural subsidy, a tax incentive, the regulation of an industry, protection of the environment, or provision of an entitlement program, you can see that Congress needs to rely on the expertise of agencies. Those agencies need to collect and use information. The agencies need information to make the rules necessary to implement the policy, to assess the execution of the policy, and to ensure compliance with the policy. Gellhorn and Levin have stated the problem simply: "Good decisions require good data."[4]

Primarily, federal agencies (state and local agencies as well) acquire information in these three ways: (a) by requiring regulated parties to maintain records and make the records available for agency inspection or to submit periodic reports; (b) by subpoenaing information from businesses, individuals, or other parties; (c) by conducting physical inspections of businesses or property (as in the *Barlow* case).

Requiring Regulated Parties to Keep Records

Agencies acquire the power to compel information from private parties in two ways. First, occasionally, Congress will specify that power in legislation. The Fair Labor Standards Act, the federal minimum wage and hour law, requires those businesses that fall under the Act's jurisdiction (e.g., those involved in interstate commerce) to keep records relating to hourly pay and overtime. The Act further authorizes the secretary of labor (or designate) to enforce provisions of the Act by examining those records. Second, if a statute does not specifically require private parties to maintain records for agency inspection, that power can be inferred from the delegation of power. In that case, the agency will generally go through the public notice and comment procedure (see Chapter 7) to notify regulated parties that it will require them to keep certain information.

What constitutional problem do you think might arise when the government says, "We want you to keep records about *X*, and an agency will look at your records. If we find you are not in compliance with *X*, we will fine you." Potentially, the Fifth Amendment protects individuals from incriminating themselves where government has accused them of wrongdoing. During World War II, the Price Control Act established price controls on many crucial commodities. It required retailers to maintain sales records for inspection by the price control administrator. As suggested in the case that follows, Shapiro was suspected of selling goods at prices above the set level. The Price Control Administration requested his sales receipts, and he refused.

Shapiro v. United States
335 U.S. 1 (1948)

Chief Justice Vinson delivered the opinion of the Court, joined by Justices Black, Reed, Douglas, and Burton. Justices Frankfurter, Jackson, Rutledge, and Murphy dissented.

Petitioner was tried on charges of having made tie-in sales in violation of regulations under the Emergency Price Control. A plea in bar, claiming immunity from prosecution based on § 202(g) of the Act, was overruled by the trial judge; judgment of conviction followed and was affirmed on appeal, 159 F.2d 890. A contrary conclusion was reached by the district judge in *United States v. Hoffman*, 335 U.S. 77. Because this conflict involves an important question of

statutory construction, these cases were brought here and heard together. Additional minor considerations involved in the Hoffman case are dealt with in a separate opinion. . . .

The petitioner, a wholesaler of fruit and produce, on September 29, 1944, was served with a *subpoena duces tecum* and *ad testificandum* issued, by the Price Administrator, under authority of the Emergency Price Control Act. The subpoena directed petitioner to appear before designated enforcement attorneys of the Office of Price Administration and to produce "all duplicate sales invoices, sales books, ledgers, inventory records, contracts and records relating to the sale of all commodities from September 1st, 1944, to September 28,

1944." In compliance with the subpoena, petitioner appeared and, after being sworn, was requested to turn over the subpoenaed records. Petitioner's counsel inquired whether petitioner was being granted immunity "as to any and all matters for information obtained as a result of the investigation and examination of these records." The presiding official stated that the "witness is entitled to whatever immunity which flows as a matter of law from the production of these books and records which are required to be kept." Petitioner thereupon produced the records, but claimed constitutional privilege. . . . The plea in bar alleged that the name of the purchaser in the transactions involved in the information appeared in the subpoenaed sales invoices and other similar documents. And it was alleged that the Office of Price Administration had used the name and other unspecified leads obtained from these documents to search out evidence of the violations, which had occurred in the preceding year.

The Circuit Court of Appeals ruled that the records which petitioner was compelled to produce were records required to be kept by a valid regulation under the Price Control Act; that thereby they became public documents, as to which no constitutional privilege against self-incrimination attaches; that accordingly the immunity of § 202(g) did not extend to the production of these records and the plea in bar was properly overruled by the trial court.

It should be observed at the outset that the decision in the instant case turns on the construction of a compulsory testimony-immunity provision which incorporates by reference the Compulsory Testimony Act of 1893. This provision, in conjunction with broad record-keeping requirements, has been included not merely in a temporary wartime measure, but also, in substantially the same terms, in virtually all of the major regulatory enactments of the Federal Government. . . . In adopting the language used in the earlier act, Congress "must be considered to have adopted also the construction given by this Court to such language, and made it a part of the enactment." That judicial construction is made up of the doctrines enunciated by this Court in spelling out the non-privileged status

of records validly required by law to be kept, in *Wilson v. United States,* 221 U.S. 361, and the inapplicability of immunity provisions to non-privileged documents, in *Heike v. United States,* 227 U.S. 131. . . .

In view of the clear rationale in *Wilson,* taken together with the ruling in *Heike* as to how statutory immunity provisos should be construed, the conclusion seems inevitable that Congress must have intended the immunity proviso in the Price Control Act to be coterminous with what would otherwise have been the constitutional privilege of petitioner in the case at bar. Since he could assert no valid privilege as to the required records here in question, he was entitled to no immunity under the statute thus viewed. . . .

It may be assumed at the outset that there are limits which the government cannot constitutionally exceed in requiring the keeping of records which may be inspected by an administrative agency and may be used in prosecuting statutory violations committed by the record-keeper himself. But no serious misgiving that those bounds have been overstepped would appear to be evoked when there is a sufficient relation between the activity sought to be regulated and the public concern so that the government can constitutionally regulate or forbid the basic activity concerned, and can constitutionally require the keeping of particular records, subject to inspection by the Administrator.

It is not questioned here that Congress has constitutional authority to prescribe commodity prices as a war emergency measure, and that the licensing and record-keeping requirements of the Price Control Act represent a legitimate exercise of that power. Accordingly, the principle enunciated in the *Wilson* case, and reaffirmed as recently as the *Davis* case, is clearly applicable here: namely, that the privilege which exists as to private papers cannot be maintained in relation to "records required by law to be kept in order that there may be suitable information of transactions which are the appropriate subjects of governmental regulation, and the enforcement of restrictions validly established." Even the dissenting Justices in the *Davis* case conceded that "there is an important difference in the constitutional protection afforded their possessors between papers exclusively private and documents having public aspects," a difference whose essence is that the latter papers, "once they have been legally obtained, are available as evidence." In the case at bar, it cannot be doubted that the sales record which petitioner was required to keep as a licensee under the Price Control Act has "public aspects." Nor can there be any doubt that when it was obtained by the Administrator through the use of subpoena, as authorized specifically by § 202(b) of the statute, it was "legally obtained" and hence "available as evidence."

The record involved in the case at bar was a sales record required to be maintained under an appropriate regulation, its relevance to the lawful purpose of the Administrator is unquestioned, and the transaction which it recorded was one in which the petitioner could lawfully engage solely by virtue of the license granted to him under the statute.

In the view that we have taken of the case, we find it unnecessary to consider the additional contention by the government that, in any event, no immunity attaches to the production of the books by the petitioner because the connection between the books and the evidence produced at the trial was too tenuous to justify the claim.

For the foregoing reasons, the judgment of the Circuit Court of Appeals is affirmed.

Question

1. The Court resolves difficult issues by what is called a *balancing test;* that is, the Court will balance the interest of the parties to see which interest outweighs the other. That is what the Court did in this case. Can you articulate the two interests? Which interest won? Why?

The Court has decided many cases in the area of the Fifth Amendment's self-incrimination clause since 1948, although relatively few of them have involved administrative law. The Court has restricted the concept of self-incrimination so that it applies only to individuals and not to businesses. It applies only in cases in which criminal charges could result and hence does not apply in civil actions such as administrative law. Finally, self-incrimination applies only to oral testimony. It does not apply to physical evidence, such as records or test results. Therefore, the Court today rarely has occasion to apply the self-incrimination clause in this area of administrative law.

You will probably notice as you read administrative law cases that there is a propensity on behalf of the courts to show deference toward agency expertise. That deference is apparent in cases involving agency acquisition of information. If the courts do not interfere with congressional attempts to acquire information, why should the courts be any more prone to interfere with Congress' expert delegate (i.e., bureaucracy)? See, for example, *Superior Oil Company v. Federal Energy Regulatory Commission,* 563 F.2d. 191 (1977), and *In Re Federal Trade Commission Line of Business Report,* 595 F 2d 685 (D.C. Cir., 1978).

Administrative Subpoenas

Sometimes agencies need information that is readily available, sometimes they require specific types of information to be made available (as in the preceding cases), and sometimes they need additional information that a private party may be unwilling to surrender. In these latter situations, agencies have the power to subpoena the desired information. A subpoena is a court's order for a person to appear in court and testify or perhaps to bring documents. It differs from a warrant in that a subpoena can be challenged prior to execution, whereas a warrant can be challenged only after the fact. For example, if a court issued a subpoena to a physician, the doctor's lawyer might be able to challenge the subpoena on the grounds of privileged information (doctor/client privilege) and perhaps get the subpoena quashed. In the public administration context, a subpoena is an order by an agency to appear before the agency or, more typically, to bring certain documents to the agency. Another difference between a warrant and a subpoena is that the Fourth Amendment specifies that a warrant can be issued based only on probable cause. But what if an administrative agency wants to go on a "fishing expedition" with a subpoena? The two cases that follow address the question of the Fourth Amendment and administrative subpoenas. They are also interesting in that they represent the two different ideologies discussed in Chapter 1.

Federal Trade Commission v. American Tobacco Company
264 U.S. 298 (1924)

Justice Holmes delivered the opinion for a unanimous Court.

[1] These are two petitions for writs of mandamus to the respective corporations respondent, manufacturers and sellers of tobacco, brought by the Federal Trade Commission under the Act of September 26, 1914, and in alleged pursuance of a resolution of the Senate passed on August 9, 1921. The purpose of the petitions is to require production of records, contracts, memoranda and correspondence for inspection and making copies. They were denied by the District Court. 283 Fed. 999. The resolution directs the Commission to investigate the tobacco situation as to domestic and export trade with particular reference to market price to producers, etc. The act directs the Commission to prevent the use of unfair methods of competition in commerce and provides for a complaint by the Commission, a hearing and a report, with an order to desist if it deems the use of a prohibited method proved. The Commission and the party concerned are both given a resort to the Circuit Court of Appeals. By section 6 the Commission shall have power (a) to gather information concerning, and to investigate the business, conduct, practices, and management of any corporation engaged in commerce, except banks and common carriers,

and its relation to other corporations and individuals; (b) to require reports and answers under oath to specific questions furnishing the Commission such information as it may require on the above subjects; . . . (d) upon the direction of the President or either House of Congress to investigate and report the facts as to alleged violation of the Anti-Trust Acts. By section 9 for the purposes of this act the Commission shall at all reasonable times have access to, for the purposes of examination, and the right to copy any documentary evidence of any corporation being investigated or proceeded against and shall have power to require by subpoena the attendance and testimony of witnesses and the production of all such documentary evidence relating to any matter under investigation. In case of disobedience an order may be obtained from a District Court. Upon application of the Attorney General the District Courts are given jurisdiction to issue writs of mandamus to require compliance with the act or any order of the commission made in pursuance thereof. The petitions are filed under this clause and the question is whether orders of the Commission to allow inspection and copies of the documents and correspondence referred to were authorized by the act.

The petitions allege that complaints have been filed with the Commission charging the respondents severally with unfair competition by regulating the prices at which their commodities should be resold. . . . There are the necessary formal allegations and a prayer that unless the accounts, books, records, documents, memoranda, contracts, papers, and correspondence of the respondents are immediately submitted for inspection and examination and for the purpose of making copies thereof, a mandamus issue requiring, in the case of the American Tobacco Company, the exhibition during business hours when the Commission's agent requests it, of all letters and telegrams received by the Company from or sent by it to all of its jobber customers, between January 1, 1921, to December 31, 1921, inclusive. In the case of the P. Lorillard Company the same requirement is made and also all letters, telegrams, or reports from or to its salesmen, or from or to all tobacco jobbers' or wholesale grocers' associations, all contracts or arrangements with such associations, and correspondence and agreements with a list of corporations named.

The mere facts of carrying on a commerce not confined within State lines and of being organized as a corporation do not make men's affairs public, as those of a railroad company now may be. *Smith v. Interstate Commerce Commission,* 245 U.S. 33. Anyone who respects the spirit as well as the letter of the Fourth Amendment would be loath to believe that Congress intended to authorize one of its subordinate agencies to sweep all our traditions into the fire . . . and to direct fishing expeditions into private papers on the possibility that they may disclose evidence of crime. We do not discuss the question whether it could do so if it tried, as nothing short of the most explicit language would induce us to attribute to Congress that intent. The interruption of business, the possible revelation of trade secrets, and the expense that compliance with the Commission's wholesale demand would cause are the least considerations. It is contrary to the first principles of justice to allow a search through all the respondents' records, relevant or irrelevant, in the hope that something will turn up. The unwillingness of this Court to sustain such a claim is shown in *Harriman v. Interstate Commerce Commission,*

211 U.S. 407, and as to correspondence, even in the case of a common carrier, in *United States v. Louisville & Nashville R. R. Co.,* 236 U.S. 318. The question is a different one where the State granting the charter gives its Commission power to inspect. . . .

[3] The right of access given by the statute is to documentary evidence—not to all documents, but to such documents as are evidence. The analogies of the law do not allow the party wanting evidence to call for all documents in order to see if they do not contain it. Some ground must be shown for supposing that the documents called for do contain it. Formerly in equity the ground must be found in admissions in the answer. We assume that the rule to be applied here is more liberal but still a ground must be laid and the ground and the demand must be reasonable. A general subpoena in the form of these petitions would be bad. Some evidence of the materiality of the papers demanded must be produced. . . . We assume for present purposes that even some part of the presumably large mass of papers relating only to intrastate business may be so connected with charges of unfair competition in interstate matters as to be relevant, but that possibility does not warrant a demand for the whole. For all that appears the corporations would have been willing to produce such papers as they conceived to be relevant to the matter in hand. If their judgment upon that matter was not final, at least some evidence must be offered to show that it was wrong. No such evidence is shown.

We have considered this case on the general claim of authority put forward by the Commission. The argument for the Government attaches some force to the investigations and proceedings upon which the Commission had entered. The investigations and complaints seem to have been only on hearsay or suspicion—but even if they were induced by substantial evidence under oath the rudimentary principles of justice that we have laid down would apply. We cannot attribute to Congress an intent to defy the Fourth Amendment or even to come so near to doing so as to raise a serious question of constitutional law.

Judgment affirmed.

Oklahoma Press Publishing Company v. Walling
327 U.S. 186 (1946)

Justice Rutledge delivered the opinion of the Court. Justice Murphy dissented, and Justice Jackson did not participate.

These cases bring for decision important questions concerning the Administrator's right to judicial enforcement of subpoenas *duces tecum* issued by him in the course of investigations conducted pursuant to § 11(a) of the Fair Labor Standards Act. . . . The subpoenas sought the production of specified records to determine whether petitioners were violating the Fair Labor Standards Act, including records relating to coverage. Petitioners, newspaper publishing corporations, maintain that the Act is not applicable to them, for constitutional and other reasons, and insist that the question of coverage must be adjudicated before the subpoenas may be enforced.

I

Coloring almost all of petitioners' position, as we understand them, is a primary misconception that the First Amendment knocks out any possible application of the Fair Labor Standards Act to the business of publishing and distributing newspapers. The argument has two prongs.

The broadside assertion that petitioners "could not be covered by the Act," for the reason that "application of this Act to its newspaper publishing business would violate its rights as guaranteed by the First Amendment," is without merit. . . . If Congress can remove obstructions to commerce by requiring publishers to bargain collectively with employees and refrain from interfering with their rights of self-organization, matters closely related to eliminating low wages and long hours, Congress likewise may strike directly at those evils when they adversely affect commerce.

II

Other questions pertain to whether enforcement of the subpoenas as directed by the Circuit Courts of Appeals will violate any of petitioners' rights secured by the Fourth Amendment and related issues concerning Congress' intent. It is claimed that enforcement would permit the Administrator to conduct general fishing expeditions into petitioners' books, records, and papers, in order to secure evidence that they have violated the Act, without a prior charge or complaint and simply to secure information upon which to base one, all allegedly in violation of the Amendment's search and seizure provisions. Supporting this is an argument that Congress did not intend such use to be made of the delegated power, which rests in part upon asserted constitutional implications, but primarily upon the reports of legislative committees, particularly in the House of Representatives, made in passing upon appropriations for years subsequent to the Act's effective date. . . . The short answer to the Fourth Amendment objections is that the records in these cases present no question of actual search and seizure, but raise only the question whether orders of court for the production of specified records have been validly made; and no sufficient showing appears to justify setting them aside. No officer or other person has sought to enter petitioners' premises against their will, to search them, or to seize or examine their books, records, or papers without their assent, otherwise than pursuant to orders of court authorized by law and made after adequate opportunity to present objections, which in fact were made. Nor has any objection been taken to the breadth of the subpoenas or to any other specific defect which would invalidate them. . . . What petitioners seek is not to prevent an unlawful search and seizure. It is rather a total immunity to the Act's provisions, applicable to all others similarly situated, requiring them to submit their pertinent records for the Administrator's inspection under every judicial safeguard, after and only after an order of court made pursuant to and in exact compliance with authority granted by Congress. This broad claim of immunity no doubt is induced by petitioners' First Amendment contentions. But beyond them it is rested also upon conceptions of the Fourth Amendment equally lacking in merit.

Petitioners' plea that the Fourth Amendment places them so far above the law that they are beyond the reach of congressional and judicial power as those powers have been exerted here only raises the ghost of controversy long since settled adversely to their claim.

Section 11(a) expressly authorizes the Administrator to "enter and inspect such places and such records (and make such transcriptions thereof), question such employees, and investigate such facts, conditions, practices, or matters as he may deem appropriate to determine whether any person has violated any provision of this Act, or which may aid in the enforcement of the provisions of this Act." The subpoena power conferred by § 9 . . . is given in aid of this investigation and, in case of disobedience, the District Courts are called upon to enforce the subpoena through their contempt powers, without express condition requiring showing of coverage. . . . In view of these provisions, with which the Administrator's action was in exact compliance, this case presents an instance of "the most explicit language" which leaves no room for questioning Congress' intent. The very purpose of the subpoena and of the order, as of the authorized investigation, is to discover and procure evidence, not to prove a pending charge or complaint, but upon which to make one if, in the Administrator's judgment, the facts thus discovered should justify doing so. . . .

III

Whatever limits there may be to congressional power to provide for the production of corporate or other business records, therefore, they are not to be found, in view of the course of prior decisions, in any such absolute or universal immunity as petitioners seek. . . . Without attempt to summarize or accurately distinguish all of the cases, the fair distillation, in so far as they apply merely to the production of corporate records and papers in response to a subpoena or order authorized by law and safeguarded by judicial sanction, seems to be that the Fifth Amendment affords no protection by virtue of the self-incrimination provision, whether for the corporation or for its officers; and the Fourth, if applicable, at the most guards against abuse only by way of too much indefiniteness or breadth in the things required to be "particularly described," if also the inquiry is one the demanding agency is authorized by law to make and the materials specified are relevant. The gist of the protection is in the requirement, expressed in terms, that the disclosure sought shall not be unreasonable.

As this has taken form in the decisions, the following specific results have been worked out. It is not necessary, as in the case of a warrant, that a specific charge or complaint of violation of law be pending or that the order be made pursuant to one. It is enough that the investigation be for a lawfully authorized purpose, within the power of Congress to command. . . . The requirement of "probable cause, supported by oath or affirmation" literally applicable in the case of a warrant is satisfied, in that of an order for production, by the court's determination that the investigation is authorized by Congress, is for a purpose Congress can order, and the documents sought are relevant to the inquiry. Beyond this the requirement of reasonableness, including particularity in "describing the place to be searched, and the persons or things to be seized," also literally applicable to warrants, comes down to specification of the documents to be produced adequate, but not excessive, for the purposes of the relevant inquiry. . . .

When these principles are applied to the facts of the present cases, it is impossible to conceive how a violation of petitioners' rights could have been involved. Both were corporations. The only records or documents sought were corporate ones. No possible element of self-incrimination was therefore presented or in fact claimed. All the records sought were relevant to the authorized inquiry, the purpose of which was to determine two issues, whether petitioners were subject to the Act and, if so, whether they were violating it. These were subjects of investigation authorized by § 11(a), the latter expressly, the former by necessary implication. It is not to be doubted that Congress could authorize investigation of these matters. In all these respects, the specifications more than meet the requirements long established by many precedents. The Administrator is authorized to enter and inspect, but the Act makes his right to do so subject in all cases to judicial supervision. Persons from whom he seeks relevant information are not required to submit to his demand, if in any respect it is unreasonable or overreaches the authority Congress has given. To it they may make "appropriate defense" surrounded by every safeguard of judicial restraint.

Nor is there room for intimation that the Administrator has proceeded in these cases in any manner contrary to petitioners' fundamental rights or otherwise than strictly according to law. It is to be remembered that petitioners' are not the only rights which may be involved or threatened with possible infringement. Their employees' rights and the public interest under the declared policy of Congress also would be affected if petitioners should enjoy the practically complete immunity they seek.

No sufficient reason was set forth in the returns or the accompanying affidavits for not enforcing the subpoenas, a burden petitioners were required to assume in order to make "appropriate defense."

Accordingly the judgments in both causes, No. 61 and No. 63, are affirmed.

Affirmed.

Justice Murphy, dissenting

It is not without difficulty that I dissent from a procedure the constitutionality of which has been established for many years. But I am unable to approve the use of non-judicial subpoenas issued by administrative agents.

Administrative law has increased greatly in the past few years and seems destined to be augmented even further in the future. But attending this growth should be a new and broader sense of responsibility on the part of administrative agencies and officials. Excessive use or abuse of authority can not only destroy man's instinct for liberty but will eventually undo the administrative processes themselves. Our history is not without a precedent of a successful revolt against a ruler who "sent hither swarms of officers to harass our people."

Perhaps we are too far removed from the experiences of the past to appreciate fully the consequences that may result from an irresponsible though well-meaning use of the subpoena power. To allow a non-judicial officer, unarmed with judicial process, to demand the books and papers of an individual is an open invitation to abuse of that power. It is no answer that the individual may refuse to produce the material demanded. Many persons have yielded solely because of the air of authority with which the demand is made, a demand that cannot be enforced without subsequent judicial aid. Many invasions of private rights thus occur without the restraining hand of the judiciary ever intervening.

Only by confining the subpoena power exclusively to the judiciary can there be any insurance against this corrosion of liberty. Statutory enforcement would not thereby be made impossible.

Indeed, it would be made easier. A people's desire to cooperate with the enforcement of a statute is in direct proportion to the respect for individual rights shown in the enforcement process. Liberty is too priceless to be forfeited through the zeal of an administrative agent.

Questions

1. What is your answer to the question whether administrative agencies may go on "fishing expeditions" with a subpoena?
2. Would the administrative state exist without this investigative tool? Is that good or bad? Why?

According to Gellhorn, Byse, and Strauss, the test that the courts apply now when a party challenges an administrative subpoena is "whether the topic to which the inquiry pertains is a topic the official has been empowered to investigate."[5] In other words, the Court will ask whether the subject matter of the subpoena is subject matter the agency has the power to investigate. In the *Oklahoma Press* case, for example, the subject matter of the subpoena was employee records, and the secretary of labor is empowered under the Fair Labor Standards Act to investigate violations of wage and hour provisions; hence, the Court will enforce the subpoena. Provided that a subpoena seeks information in an area that the agency is empowered to investigate, that it does not request privileged information, and that it is sufficiently specific, the courts will generally enforce agency subpoenas.

The fact that an agency has issued a subpoena does not necessarily mean that requested documents will be immediately forthcoming. That is because, unlike court-issued subpoenas, administrative agencies rarely have any enforcement mechanism. If an individual ignored a court-issued subpoena and failed to appear before the court at the proper time, a bench warrant would likely be issued for the subject's arrest, and contempt of court proceedings would follow. Congress has made it a federal misdemeanor to fail to comply with a subpoena issued by the Securities and Exchange Commission (SEC), but that is the exception rather than the rule. More typically, if an agency issues a subpoena and the party refuses to comply, the agency must go to federal court to obtain a court order to comply with the subpoena. At such hearings, the courts apply the test cited earlier: "whether the topic to which the inquiry pertains is a topic the official has been empowered to investigate." Frequently, a court will issue the order for compliance with the subpoena, and if the party still refuses to comply, then the agency must go back to court and instigate contempt proceedings. The problem is that a court's decision to issue a judicial order requiring compliance with an agency subpoena is an appealable decision and can be appealed to the circuit court of appeals. It could be appealed further to the U.S. Supreme Court, as the *American Tobacco* and *Oklahoma Press* cases were. The point is that, given a good enough legal division, a business or corporation could tie up compliance with an agency subpoena for years, if it so chooses.

In 2003, Congress passed the Partial-Birth Abortion Ban Act, which imposes civil and criminal penalties on physicians who perform them (in facilities that receive federal funds). The term *partial birth* is defined in the statute. The Act was quickly challenged by doctors who perform such abortions. The essence of the complaint is that the Act makes no exceptions, for example, to save the life of the mother. Several of the plaintiff doctors were also planning to testify as experts about the medical necessity of the procedure to save the life of some of the mothers. Hoping to find some evidence to discredit the doctors' testimony, former Attorney General John Ashcroft subpoenaed the medical records of women who had the procedure. These records were in the possession of various hospitals around the country, so the subpoenas were directed at the hospitals, all of whom balked at turning over the records. The attorney general went to court to obtain a court order to enforce the subpoenas. The results have been mixed in various jurisdictions. The original suit was filed in New York, and the District Court there issued an enforcement order in support of the subpoena.[6] However, district courts in Illinois and California have quashed the subpoenas. The Illinois decision was upheld by the Circuit Court.[7]

Conducting Physical Inspections

Physical inspection is an indispensable tool in an agency's arsenal for implementing laws and policies. There are fire inspections, housing code inspections, meat inspections, nuclear plant inspections, mine safety inspections, plant effluent inspections, defense plant inspections, AFDC inspections, bank inspections—the list is almost endless. To this point, we know that the Fifth Amendment's self-incrimination clause is not involved in those situations in which agencies require businesses to maintain certain records and, as a consequence of inspecting those records, may impose fines. We also know the Fourth Amendment is rarely involved where agencies issue subpoenas. The question that opened this chapter, and to which we now turn, is whether the Fourth Amendment is involved in administrative searches or physical inspections.

Marshall v. Barlow's, Incorporated
436 U.S. 307 (1978)

Justice White delivered the opinion of the Court, joined by Chief Justice Burger and Justices Brennan, Stewart, Marshall, and Powell. Justice Stevens dissented, joined by Justices Blackmun and Rehnquist.

Section 8(a) of the Occupational Safety and Health Act of 1970 (OSHA or Act) empowers agents of the Secretary of Labor (Secretary) to search the work area of any employment facility within the Act's jurisdiction. The purpose of the search is to inspect for safety hazards and violations of OSHA regulations. No search warrant or other process is expressly required under the Act. . . . On the morning of September 11, 1975, an OSHA inspector entered the customer service area of Barlow's, Inc., an electrical and plumbing installation business located in Pocatello, Idaho. The president and general manager, Ferrol G. "Bill" Barlow, was on hand; and the OSHA inspector, after showing his credentials, informed Mr. Barlow that he wished to conduct a search of the working areas of the business. Mr. Barlow inquired whether any complaint had been received about his company. The inspector answered no, but that Barlow's, Inc., had simply turned up in the agency's selection process. The inspector again asked to enter the nonpublic area of the business; Mr. Barlow's response was to inquire whether the inspector had a search warrant. The inspector had none. Thereupon, Mr. Barlow refused the inspector admission to the employee area of his business. He said he was relying on his rights as guaranteed by the Fourth Amendment

of the United States Constitution. . . . Three months later, the Secretary petitioned the United States District Court for the District of Idaho to issue an order compelling Mr. Barlow to admit the inspector. The requested order was issued on December 30, 1975, and was presented to Mr. Barlow on January 5, 1976. Mr. Barlow again refused admission, and he sought his own injunctive relief against the warrantless searches assertedly permitted by OSHA. A three-judge court was convened. On December 30, 1976, it ruled in Mr. Barlow's favor. 424 F.Supp. 437. Concluding that *Camara v. Municipal Court,* 387 U.S. 523 (1967), and *See v. City of Seattle,* 387 U.S. 541 (1967), controlled this case, the court held that the Fourth Amendment required a warrant for the type of search involved here and that the statutory authorization for warrantless inspections was unconstitutional. An injunction against searches or inspections pursuant to § 8(a) was entered. The Secretary appealed, challenging the judgment, and we noted probable jurisdiction. . . .

[1] The Warrant Clause of the Fourth Amendment protects commercial buildings as well as private homes. To hold otherwise would belie the origin of that Amendment, and the American colonial experience. An important forerunner of the first 10 Amendments to the United States Constitution, the Virginia Bill of Rights, specifically opposed "general warrants, whereby an officer or messenger may be commanded to search suspected places without evidence of a fact committed." The general warrant was a recurring point of contention

in the Colonies immediately preceding the Revolution. The particular offensiveness it engendered was acutely felt by the merchants and businessmen whose premises and products were inspected for compliance with the several parliamentary revenue measures that most irritated the colonists. "[T]he Fourth Amendment's commands grew in large measure out of the colonists' experience with the writs of assistance . . . [that] granted sweeping power to customs officials and other agents of the King to search at large for smuggled goods."

Against this background, it is untenable that the ban on warrantless searches was not intended to shield places of business as well as of residence. . . .

This Court has already held that warrantless searches are generally unreasonable, and that this rule applies to commercial premises as well as homes. In *Camara v. Municipal Court,* supra, 387 U.S., we held: "[E]xcept in certain carefully defined classes of cases, a search of private property without proper consent is 'unreasonable' unless it has been authorized by a valid search warrant." On the same day, we also ruled: "As we explained in *Camara,* a search of private houses is presumptively unreasonable if conducted without a warrant. The businessman, like the occupant of a residence, has a constitutional right to go about his business free from unreasonable official entries upon his private commercial property. The businessman, too, has that right placed in jeopardy if the decision to enter and inspect for violation of regulatory laws can be made and enforced by the inspector in the field without official authority evidenced by a warrant." These same cases also held that the Fourth Amendment prohibition against unreasonable searches protects against warrantless intrusions during civil as well as criminal investigations. The reason is found in the "basic purpose of this Amendment . . . [which] is to safeguard the privacy and security of individuals against arbitrary invasions by governmental officials." If the government intrudes on a person's property, the privacy interest suffers whether the government's motivation is to investigate violations of criminal laws or breaches of other statutory or regulatory standards. It therefore appears that unless some

recognized exception to the warrant requirement applies, *See v. City of Seattle* would require a warrant to conduct the inspection sought in this case.

The clear import of our cases is that the closely regulated industry of the type involved in *Colonnade* and *Biswell* is the exception. The Secretary would make it the rule. Invoking the Walsh-Healey Act of 1936, 41 U.S.C. § 35 et seq., the Secretary attempts to support a conclusion that all businesses involved in interstate commerce have long been subjected to close supervision of employee safety and health conditions. But the degree of federal involvement in employee working circumstances has never been of the order of specificity and pervasiveness that OSHA mandates. It is quite unconvincing to argue that the imposition of minimum wages and maximum hours on employers who contracted with the Government under the Walsh-Healey Act prepared the entirety of American interstate commerce for regulation of working conditions to the minutest detail. Nor can any but the most fictional sense of voluntary consent to later searches be found in the single fact that one conducts a business affecting interstate commerce; under current practice and law, few businesses can be conducted without having some effect on interstate commerce. . . .

Whether the Secretary proceeds to secure a warrant or other process, with or without prior notice, his entitlement to inspect will not depend on his demonstrating probable cause to believe that conditions in violation of OSHA exist on the premises. Probable cause in the criminal law sense is not required. For purposes of an administrative search such as this, probable cause justifying the issuance of a warrant may be based not only on specific evidence of an existing violation but also on a showing that "reasonable legislative or administrative standards for conducting an . . . inspection are satisfied with respect to a particular [establishment]." *Camara v. Municipal Court,* 387 U.S., at 538. A warrant showing that a specific business has been chosen for an OSHA search on the basis of a general administrative plan for the enforcement of the Act derived from neutral sources such as, for example, dispersion of employees in various types of industries across a given area, and the desired frequency of searches in any of the lesser divisions of the area, would protect an employer's Fourth Amendment rights. We doubt that the consumption of enforcement energies in the obtaining of such warrants will exceed manageable proportions. . . . Nor do we agree that the incremental protections afforded the employer's privacy by a warrant are so marginal that they fail to justify the administrative burdens that may be entailed. The authority to make warrantless searches devolves almost unbridled discretion upon executive and administrative officers, particularly those in the field, as to when to search and whom to search. A warrant, by contrast, would provide assurances from a neutral officer that the inspection is reasonable under the Constitution, is authorized by statute, and is pursuant to an administrative plan containing specific neutral criteria. Also, a warrant would then and there advise the owner of the scope and objects of the search, beyond which limits the inspector is not expected to proceed. These are important functions for a warrant to perform, functions which underlie the Court's prior decisions that the Warrant Clause applies to inspections for compliance with regulatory statutes. We conclude that the concerns expressed by the Secretary do not suffice to justify warrantless inspections under OSHA or vitiate the general constitutional requirement that for a search to be reasonable a warrant must be obtained.

III

We hold that Barlow was entitled to a declaratory judgment, that the Act is unconstitutional insofar as it purports to authorize inspections without warrant or its equivalent and to an injunction enjoining the Act's enforcement to that extent. The judgment of the District Court is therefore affirmed. So ordered.

Justice Stevens, dissenting, joined by Justices Blackmun and Rehnquist.

I

The warrant requirement is linked "textually . . . to the probable-cause concept" in the warrant clause. The routine OSHA inspections are, by definition, not based on cause to believe there is a violation on the premises to be inspected. Hence, if the inspections were measured against the requirements of the Warrant Clause, they would be automatically and unequivocally unreasonable.

Because of the acknowledged importance and reasonableness of routine inspections in the enforcement of federal regulatory statutes such as OSHA, the Court recognizes that requiring full compliance with the Warrant Clause would invalidate all such inspection programs. Yet, rather than simply analyzing such programs under the "Reasonableness" Clause of the Fourth Amendment, the Court holds the OSHA program invalid under the Warrant Clause and then avoids a blanket prohibition on all routine regulatory inspections by relying on the notion that the "probable cause" requirement in the Warrant Clause may be relaxed whenever the Court believes that the governmental need to conduct a category of "searches" outweighs the intrusion on interests protected by the Fourth Amendment.

The Court's approach disregards the plain language of the Warrant Clause and is unfaithful to the balance struck by the Framers of the Fourth Amendment. . . ."[O]ur constitutional fathers were not concerned about warrantless searches, but about overreaching warrants. It is perhaps too much to say that they feared the warrant more than the search, but it is plain enough that the warrant was the prime object of their concern. Far from looking at the warrant as a protection against unreasonable searches, they saw it as an authority for unreasonable and oppressive searches. . . ."

Since the general warrant, not the warrantless search, was the immediate evil at which the Fourth Amendment was directed, it is not surprising that the Framers placed precise limits on its issuance. The requirement that a warrant only issue on a showing of particularized probable cause was the means adopted to circumscribe the warrant power. While the subsequent course of Fourth Amendment jurisprudence in this Court emphasizes the dangers posed by warrantless searches conducted without probable cause, it is the general reasonableness standard in the first Clause, not the Warrant Clause, that the Framers adopted to limit this category of searches. It is, of course, true that the existence of a valid warrant normally satisfies the reasonableness requirement under the Fourth Amendment. But we should not dilute the requirements of the Warrant Clause in an effort to force every kind of governmental intrusion which satisfies the Fourth Amendment definition of a "search" into a judicially developed, warrant-preference scheme.

Fidelity to the original understanding of the Fourth Amendment, therefore, leads to the conclusion that the Warrant Clause has no application to routine, regulatory inspections of commercial premises. If such inspections are valid, it is because they comport with the ultimate reasonableness standard of the Fourth Amendment. If the Court were correct in its view that such inspections, if undertaken without a warrant, are unreasonable in the constitutional sense, the issuance of a "new-fangled warrant"—to use Mr. Justice Clark's characteristically expressive term—without any true showing of particularized probable cause would not be sufficient to validate them. . . . Even if a warrant requirement does not "frustrate" the legislative purpose, the Court has no authority to impose an additional burden on the Secretary unless that burden is required to protect the employer's Fourth Amendment interests. The essential function of the traditional warrant requirement is the interposition of a neutral magistrate between the citizen and the presumably zealous law enforcement officer so that there might be an objective determination of probable cause. But this purpose is not served by the newfangled inspection warrant.

What purposes, then, are served by the administrative warrant procedure? The inspection warrant purports to serve three functions: to inform the employer that the inspection is authorized by the statute, to advise him of the lawful limits of the inspection, and to assure him that the person demanding entry is an authorized inspector. An examination of these functions in the OSHA context reveals that the inspection warrant adds little to the protections already afforded by the statute and pertinent regulations, and the slight additional benefit it might provide is insufficient to identify a constitutional violation or to justify overriding Congress' judgment that the power to conduct warrantless inspections is essential. . . .

The pertinent inquiry is not whether the inspection program is authorized by a regulatory statute directed at a single industry, but whether Congress has limited the exercise of the inspection power to those commercial premises where the evils at which the statute is directed are to be found. Thus, in *Biswell*, if Congress had authorized inspections of all commercial premises as a means of restricting the illegal traffic in firearms, the Court would have found the inspection program unreasonable; the power to inspect was upheld because it was tailored to the subject matter of Congress' proper exercise of regulatory power. Similarly, OSHA is directed at health and safety hazards in the workplace, and the inspection power granted the Secretary extends only to those areas where such hazards are likely to be found. Here, as well as in *Biswell*, businesses are required to be aware of and comply with regulations governing their business activities. In both situations, the validity of the regulations depends not upon the consent of those regulated, but on the existence of a federal statute embodying a congressional determination that the public interest in the health of the Nation's work force or the limitation of illegal firearms traffic outweighs the businessman's interest in preventing a Government inspector from viewing those areas of his premises which relate to the subject matter of the regulation.

The case before us involves an attempt to conduct a warrantless search of the working area of an electrical and plumbing contractor. The statute authorizes such an inspection during reasonable hours. The inspection is limited to those areas over which Congress has exercised its proper legislative authority. The area is also one to which employees have regular access without any suggestion that the work performed or the equipment used has any special claim to confidentiality. Congress has determined that industrial safety is an urgent federal interest requiring regulation and supervision, and further, that warrantless inspections are necessary to accomplish the safety goals of the legislation. While one may question the wisdom of pervasive governmental oversight of industrial life, I decline to question Congress' judgment that the inspection power is a necessary enforcement device in achieving the goals of a valid exercise of regulatory power. . . . I respectfully dissent.

Questions

1. The state of the law prior to *Barlow* was that businesses were generally protected by the Fourth Amendment and that a warrant would be required to inspect a business unless that business was in a "pervasively regulated industry." Did the decision in *Barlow* change the state of the law?
2. Do administrative search warrants require probable cause?
3. What good does it do to require a warrant and then allow one to be issued without probable cause?

Although *Marshall v. Barlow's* is a famous administrative law case, it really set no new precedent and, in fact, followed the reasoning established in *See v. Seattle* and *Camara v. Municipal Court.* What makes the *Barlow* case unusual is the presence of a federal law authorizing warrantless searches and the fact that the Court declared that part of the law unconstitutional. Often, we assume that because judicial review exists, the Court frequently uses it to declare acts of Congress unconstitutional. The Court, however, has declared only 162 acts of Congress to be unconstitutional, although the Court has shown less deference to state legislatures (1,299 acts declared unconstitutional).[8]

As stated in the first question following the *Barlow* case, the state of the law, both before and after *Barlow,* was that warrantless administrative searches were unconstitutional except in heavily regulated (and licensed) industries. The problem is that not all situations will fit neatly into that dichotomy. For example, can a fire marshal search the scene of a burned business for evidence of arson without a warrant (*Michigan v. Tyler,* 436 U.S. 399 [1978])? Can a pollution control inspector enter business property—but not the building—and take an air sample to see if the business is in compliance with standards without a warrant (*Air Pollution Variance Board v. Western Alfalfa Corporation,* 416 U.S. 861 [1974])? Can a high school vice principal search a student's purse without a warrant (*New Jersey v. T.L.O.,* 469 U.S. 325 [1985])? Can the Environmental Protection Agency (EPA) fly over a business and use aerial photographs as a means of physical inspection without a warrant (*Dow Chemical Company v. United States,* 476 U.S. 227 [1986])? Can the Immigration and Naturalization Service (INS) conduct a "factory survey" without the warrant being specific (*INS v. Delgado,* 466 U.S. 210 [1984])? In a factory survey, INS agents block the exits of a business and walk through the plant, systematically asking questions of workers of Mexican descent about their presence in the United States and arresting those whom the agents suspect of being illegal aliens. Does the Constitution require the exclusion of admittedly illegally seized evidence by the INS at a deportation hearing (*INS v. Lopez-Mendoza,* 468 U.S. 1032 [1984])? Can a public school require drug testing through urinalysis of any student who wants to participate in sports (*Vernonia School District 47J v. Acton,* 515 U.S. 646 [1995])? Can a public hospital conduct drug tests on unsuspecting pregnant women and give some of them with positive results the following choice: face prosecution or enter a rehabilitation program (*Ferguson v. City of Charleston* (186 F 3d 469 [4th Cir. 1999])*?* The *Dow Chemical* and *Ferguson* cases appear at the end of this chapter.

The questions posed in the preceding cases do not readily fit into the "heavily regulated industry versus other businesses" dichotomy suggested by the Court's decisions. In the criminal area, one of the crucial variables regarding whether a warrant is required is the notion of an expectation of privacy. The more likely it is that the individual (or business) has a legitimate expectation of privacy, the more likely a warrant will be required. The automobile is an exception to the warrant requirement because the Court has said that individuals have less of an expectation of privacy in an auto than they do in their homes and businesses. In a 2001 case, the Supreme Court threw out a warrantless search by a Department of Interior agent who aimed a thermal-imaging device at a suspect's home. The device was used to measure heat within the home to provide evidence of a grow light. The Court said it was a search within the meaning of the Fourth Amendment, and the suspect had a reasonable expectation of privacy.[9] Pervasively regulated industries are exceptions to the warrant requirement because "certain industries have such a history of government oversight that *no reasonable expectation of privacy* could exist for a proprietor over the stock of such an enterprise. Liquor (*Colonnade*) and firearms *(Biswell)* are industries of this type [italics added]."[10]

OSHA must obtain a warrant prior to inspecting Mr. Barlow's business, because, once past the public areas of Barlow's business, Mr. Barlow has a reasonable expectation of privacy in his back shop. The Court has said that an individual has a reasonable expectation of privacy in a public telephone booth, *Katz v. United States,* 389 U.S. 347 (1967), and in a footlocker, *United States v. Chadwick,* 433 U.S. 1 (1977). Given that, do you think Dow Chemical has a reasonable expectation of privacy from aerial inspections by the EPA? Do you believe the student, T.L.O., had a reasonable expectation of privacy in her purse? In all of the cases discussed above, the searches were reasonable according to the Court and hence constitutional. In the *Lopez-Mendoza* case, the search was unconstitutional, but evidence gained from it was admitted at the deportation hearing. The case that follows presents the interesting question of whether a welfare recipient has a reasonable expectation of privacy in her own home.

Wyman v. James
400 U.S. 309 (1971)

Justice Blackmun delivered the opinion of the Court, joined by Chief Justice Burger and Justices Black, Harlan, and Stewart. Justice White concurred in part, and dissents were filed by Justices Douglas and Marshall joined by Justice Brennan.

This appeal presents the issue whether a beneficiary of the program for Aid to Families with

Dependent Children (AFDC) may refuse a home visit by the caseworker without risking the termination of benefits. . . . The District Court majority held that a mother receiving AFDC relief may refuse, without forfeiting her right to that relief, the periodic home visit which the cited New York statutes and regulations prescribe as a condition for the continuance of assistance under the program. The beneficiary's thesis, and that of the District Court majority, is that home visitation is a search and, when not consented to or when not supported by a warrant based on probable cause, violates the beneficiary's Fourth and Fourteenth Amendment rights. . . . Plaintiff Barbara James is the mother of a son, Maurice, who was born in May 1967. They reside in New York City. Mrs. James first applied for AFDC assistance shortly before Maurice's birth. A caseworker made a visit to her apartment at that time without objection. The assistance was authorized.

Two years later, on May 8, 1969, a caseworker wrote Mrs. James that she would visit her home on May 14. Upon receipt of this advice, Mrs. James telephoned the worker that, although she was willing to supply information "reasonable and relevant" to her need for public assistance, any discussion was not to take place at her home. The worker told Mrs. James that she was required by law to visit in her home and that refusal to permit the visit would result in the termination of assistance. Permission was still denied.

On May 13 the City Department of Social Services sent Mrs. James a notice of intent to discontinue assistance because of the visitation refusal. The notice advised the beneficiary of her right to a hearing before a review officer. The hearing was requested and was held on May 27. Mrs. James appeared with an attorney at that hearing. They continued to refuse permission for a worker to visit the James home, but again expressed willingness to cooperate and to permit visits elsewhere. The review officer ruled that the refusal was a proper ground for the termination of assistance. . . .

III

When a case involves a home and some type of official intrusion into that home, as this case appears to do, an immediate and natural reaction is one of concern about Fourth Amendment rights and the protection which that Amendment is intended to afford. Its emphasis indeed is upon one of the most precious aspects of personal security in the home: "The right of the people to be secure in their persons, houses, papers, and effects." This Court has characterized that right as "basic to a free society." *Wolf v. Colorado*, 338 U.S. 25 (1949); *Camara v. Municipal Court*, 387 U.S. 523 (1967). And over the years the Court consistently has been most protective of the privacy of the dwelling. In *Camara* Mr. Justice White ... went on to observe, "Nevertheless, one governing principle, justified by history and by current experience, has consistently been followed: except in certain carefully defined classes of cases, a search of private property without proper consent is 'unreasonable' unless it has been authorized by a valid search warrant." He pointed out, too, that one's Fourth Amendment protection subsists apart from his being suspected of criminal behavior.

IV

This natural and quite proper protective attitude, however, is not a factor in this case, for the seemingly obvious and simple reason that we are not concerned here with any search by the New York social service agency in the Fourth Amendment meaning of that term. It is true that the governing statute and regulations appear to make mandatory the initial home visit and the subsequent periodic "contacts" (which may include home visits) for the inception and continuance of aid. It is also true that the caseworker's posture in the home visit is perhaps, in a sense, both rehabilitative and investigative. But this latter aspect, we think, is given too broad a character and far more emphasis than it deserves if it is equated with a search in the traditional criminal law context. We note, too, that the visitation in itself is not forced or compelled, and that the beneficiary's denial of permission is not a criminal act. If consent to the visitation is withheld, no visitation takes place. The aid then never begins or merely ceases, as the case may be. There is no entry of the home and there is no search.

V

If, however, we were to assume that a caseworker's home visit, before or subsequent to the beneficiary's initial qualification for benefits, somehow (perhaps because the average beneficiary might feel she is in no position to refuse consent to the visit), and despite its interview nature, does possess some of the characteristics of a search in the traditional sense, we nevertheless conclude that the visit does not fall within the Fourth Amendment's proscription. This is because it does not descend to the level of unreasonableness.

There are a number of factors that compel us to conclude that the home visit proposed for Mrs. James is not unreasonable:

1. The public's interest in this particular segment of the area of assistance to the unfortunate is protection and aid for the dependent child whose family requires such aid for that child. The focus is on the child and, further, it is on the child who is dependent.

2. The agency, with tax funds provided from federal as well as from state sources, is fulfilling a public trust. The State, working through its qualified welfare agency, has appropriate and paramount interest and concern in seeing and assuring that the intended and proper objects of that tax-produced assistance are the ones who benefit from the aid it dispenses. Surely it is not unreasonable, in the Fourth Amendment sense or in any other sense of that term, that the State have at its command a gentle means, of limited extent and of practical and considerate application, of achieving that assurance.

3. One who dispenses purely private charity naturally has an interest in and expects to know how his charitable funds are utilized and put to work. The public, when it is the provider, rightly expects the same.

4. The home visit, it is true, is not required by federal statute or regulation. But it has been noted that the visit is "the heart of welfare administration"; that it affords "a personal, rehabilitative orientation, unlike that of most federal programs"; and that the "more pronounced service orientation" effected by Congress with the 1956 amendments to the Social Security Act "gave redoubled importance to the practice of home visiting." Mrs. James, in fact, on this record presents no specific complaint of any unreasonable intrusion of her home and nothing that supports an inference that the desired home visit had as its purpose the obtaining of information as to criminal activity. She complains of no proposed visitation at an awkward or retirement hour. She suggests no forcible entry. She refers to no snooping. She describes no impolite or reprehensible conduct of any kind. She alleges only, in general and nonspecific terms, that on previous visits and, on information and belief, on visitation at the home of other aid recipients, "questions concerning personal relationships, beliefs and behavior are raised and pressed which are unnecessary for a determination of continuing eligibility." Paradoxically, this same complaint could be made of a conference held elsewhere than in the home, and yet this is what is sought by Mrs. James. The same complaint could be made of the census taker's questions. What Mrs. James appears to want from the agency that provides her and her infant son with the necessities for life is the right to receive those necessities upon her own informational terms, to utilize the Fourth Amendment as a wedge for imposing those terms, and to avoid questions of any kind. We are not persuaded, as Mrs. James would have us be, that all information pertinent to the issue of eligibility can be obtained by the agency through an interview at a place other than the home, or, as the District Court majority suggested, by examining a lease or a birth certificate, or by periodic medical examinations, or by interviews with school personnel. Although these secondary sources might be helpful, they would not always assure verification of actual residence or of actual physical presence in the home, which are requisites for AFDC benefits, or of impending medical needs. And, of course, little children, such as Maurice James, are not yet registered in school. The visit is not one by police or uniformed authority. It is made by a caseworker of some training whose primary objective is, or should be, the welfare, not the prosecution, of the aid recipient for whom the worker has profound responsibility. It seems to us that the situation is akin to that where an Internal Revenue Service agent, in making a routine civil audit of a taxpayer's income tax return, asks that the taxpayer produce for the agent's

review some proof of a deduction the taxpayer has asserted to his benefit in the computation of his tax. If the taxpayer refuses, there is, absent fraud, only a disallowance of the claimed deduction and a consequent additional tax. The taxpayer is fully within his "rights" in refusing to produce the proof, but in maintaining and asserting those rights a tax detriment results and it is a detriment of the taxpayer's own making. So here Mrs. James has the "right" to refuse the home visit, but a consequence in the form of cessation of aid, similar to the taxpayer's resultant additional tax, flows from that refusal. The choice is entirely hers, and nothing of constitutional magnitude is involved.

Camara v. Municipal Court, 387 U.S. 523 (1967), and its companion case, *See v. City of Seattle,* 387 U.S. 541 (1967), both by a divided Court, are not inconsistent with our result here. Those cases concerned, respectively, a refusal of entry to city housing inspectors checking for a violation of a building's occupancy permit, and a refusal of entry to a fire department representative interested in compliance with a city's fire code.

In each case a majority of this Court held that the Fourth Amendment barred prosecution for refusal to permit the desired warrantless inspection. *Frank v. Maryland,* 359 U.S. 360, 79 S.Ct. 804, 3 L.Ed.2d 877 (1959), a case that reached an opposing result and that concerned a request by a health officer for entry in order to check the source of a rat infestation, was *pro tanto* overruled. Both *Frank* and *Camara* involved dwelling quarters. *See* had to do with a commercial warehouse.

But the facts of the three cases are significantly different from those before us. Each concerned a true search for violations. *Frank* was a criminal prosecution for the owner's refusal to permit entry. So, too, was *See. Camara* had to do with a writ of prohibition sought to prevent an already pending criminal prosecution. The community welfare aspects, of course, were highly important, but each case arose in a criminal context where a genuine search was denied and prosecution followed.

In contrast, Mrs. James is not being prosecuted for her refusal to permit the home visit and is not about to be so prosecuted.

VII

Our holding today does not mean, of course, that a termination of benefits upon refusal of a home visit is to be upheld against constitutional challenge under all conceivable circumstances. The early morning mass raid upon homes of welfare recipients is not unknown. See *Parrish v. Civil Service Comm.,* 425 P.2d 223 (1967); Reich, *Midnight Welfare Searches and the Social Security Act,* 72 Yale L.J. 1347 (1963). But that is not this case. Facts of that kind present another case for another day.

We therefore conclude that the home visitation as structured by the New York statutes and regulations is a reasonable administrative tool; that it serves a valid and proper administrative purpose for the dispensation of the AFDC program; that it is not an unwarranted invasion of personal privacy; and that it violates no right guaranteed by the Fourth Amendment. Reversed and remanded with directions to enter a judgment of dismissal.

It is so ordered.

Reversed and remanded with directions.

Questions

1. Do you believe that Mrs. James had a reasonable expectation of privacy?
2. Do you believe that, by accepting "welfare," one should forfeit his or her expectation of privacy?
3. Does James's expectation of privacy have anything to do with the disposition of the case? Why?

The Court has several options open to it when it hears a case involving administrative searches and physical inspections. The Court can find that no warrant is required because a heavily regulated industry is involved, as in *Donovan v. Dewey,* 452 U.S. 594 (1981), which upheld the warrantless inspection of a stone quarry, and *New York v. Burger,* 482 U.S. 691 (1987), which upheld the warrantless search of a junkyard. The Court can find, as it did in the *Wyman* case, that the inspection is not a search, or, if it is, it is a reasonable search. This is the result reached in the *Dow Chemical Co.* case, the search of the student's purse, the case of the pollution control inspector who sampled the air on the property of the alfalfa company, and the two drug-testing cases. This is also what the Court said about factory surveys by the INS. Finally, the Court can find a reasonable expectation of privacy and require a warrant as it did in the *Barlow* case. Most of the Court's recent physical inspection cases, however, allow warrantless searches rather than following the *Barlow* precedent.

The law of administrative searches may seem confusing because there is no way to tell whether the Court will apply the *Barlow* jurisprudence or the *Wyman–T.L.O.–Dow Chemical* analysis. It may be helpful to return to the case-in-point and recall that what the Fourth Amendment prohibits is *unreasonable* searches and seizures. Today, it looks like search and seizure cases fall into two broad categories: First, there are cases involving individualized suspicion relative to law enforcement. For these cases, the warrant requirement is the law. That is, as a general rule, a warrant is required for a search to be *reasonable.* However, there are some 12 or so exceptions to the warrant requirement and within those exceptions, warrantless searches are *reasonable.* Second, there is another world of searches and seizures that are often suspicionless and do not have as their goal solving or preventing crime. Most administrative searches fit into this category. Indeed, of all the cases you have been exposed to so far, the only search resulting from suspicion was the search of the student, T.L.O.'s purse.

The first variable to look at in analyzing search and seizure is the expectation of privacy. Where the expectation of privacy is high, a warrant (administrative, not criminal) will likely be required. See *Barlow.* Where there is less of an expectation of privacy, a warrant is less likely. Dow Chemical, for example had no expectation of privacy in the "open field." Ms. James may have had an expectation of privacy in her home, but remember, there was no search of her home. She refused to allow social workers to "inspect" her home so she lost her entitlement under the law.

The second variable to examine is whether the object of the search is a business in a heavily regulated industry. If so, no warrant will be required. Finally, there is another sub-category of suspicionless searches, and these fall under a doctrine called the *special needs doctrine.* As the name suggests, these warrantless searches and seizures are justified by the "special needs" of society beyond the normal need for law enforcement. This line of cases is best exemplified by, but not limited to, urine tests for drug use. When government attempts to justify a warrantless search based on special needs, a reviewing court will examine the specific context of the search and apply a balancing test. The court will balance the privacy interests of the individual against the public interest that created the special need. The Supreme Court has insisted that special needs searches will be allowed only in a limited (special) set of circumstances. Furthermore, the invasion of privacy must be minimal. Finally, if the important governmental interest advanced for the intrusion would be placed in jeopardy by requiring individualized suspicion (and hence a warrant), then these warrantless searches will be *reasonable.*[11] To see how this test applies, the Court's urine drug-testing cases are instructive. The Court has addressed the issue of warrantless, suspicionless, forced drug tests through urinalysis in six cases. In *National Treasury Employees Union v. Von Raab,* certain customs officials were required to provide urine samples for testing. The Court found that the balance tipped in favor of society's special needs for those customs agents directly involved in drug interdiction and for those agents who are required to carry firearms. The balance tipped in favor of the individuals' privacy, however, for customs officials forced to produce urine samples because they handle "classified" material. For the classified material employees, the agency was not able to justify the special need. Justice Scalia dissented as to the decision regarding the other two categories of employees because the agency had not demonstrated that drug use by its employees had been a problem. The *Von Raab* case appears below.

On the same day the Supreme Court sanctioned the urine searches for the two categories of customs employees, it also approved of urine sample searches for certain railroad employees following train wrecks. The Federal Railroad Administration convinced the Court that drug and alcohol use was a major factor in train accidents. The danger to public safety justified the special need.[12]

In 1995, the Court allowed a school district to require urine-sample drug tests of students who wanted to participate in sports. There was evidence of a significant drug problem in the high school and evidence that athletes were a source of the problem before the Court. The intrusion, while perhaps significant, was voluntary in the sense that students could choose to participate in sports (and hence submit to drug testing) or not. The balance tipped in favor of the public interest that created the special need.[13] The Court reached the same decision in a 2002 case where a school district imposed urine tests on all students who wanted to participate in any extracurricular activity.[14]

Moving from the playground to the ballot box, the State of Georgia passed a law requiring candidates for political office to submit to a drug test before their name could appear on the ballot. In *Chandler v. Miller* 520 U.S.305 (1997), the law was challenged by three Libertarian Party candidates. Because there was no evidence of problems in Georgia caused by drug-using politicians, the state was left to defend the policy as a "symbolic commitment to the struggle against drug abuse." The Court found that justification lacking to support a special need. The balance tipped in favor of individual privacy.

In 2001, the Supreme Court heard the case of *Ferguson v. City of Charlestown.* The case involves a public hospital that started screening the urine of pregnant women who met certain criteria associated with cocaine use during pregnancy. Although the women were, of course, aware that they were supplying urine for lab tests, they were not aware that their urine was being screened for cocaine use. At first, if a test showed positive, women were arrested; later, the policy was amended so that the women were given a choice: if they did not "voluntarily" enter a drug treatment program, the evidence of cocaine use would be turned over to prosecutors. In the later case, the women would be charged with delivering a controlled substance to a minor under the age of 18 (cocaine to the fetus). Several women whose urine was tested and some who were arrested are the plaintiffs in this case, and they are alleging a violation of their Fourth Amendment rights. They also allege a violation under civil rights laws because the policy impacts most heavily on women of color. Among the criteria that cause a urine sample to be tested for cocaine is late or inconsistent prenatal care, or early termination thereof. The plaintiffs allege that these criteria are more symptomatic of poverty than of drug use. The trial court found in favor of the hospital by finding that the women had given implied consent to the search. The Circuit Court affirmed, finding that the balance tipped in favor of protecting newborn infants under the special needs doctrine. There was evidence of significant increases in infant mortality and birth defects caused by women who ingested cocaine during pregnancy. In a six to three decision, the Court said that this was not a suspicionless search under the special needs doctrine. Rather, it was a suspicion-focused search for the general purpose of law enforcement. Unless there is a recognized exception to the warrant requirement in these searches, they violate the Fourth Amendment. The Court found that the plaintiffs did not consent (implicit or otherwise) to these searches, so the searches require a warrant. The women plaintiffs won. This case appears at the end of this chapter.

The Court has even applied the special needs doctrine to a law enforcement warrantless search and seizure.[15] This kind of analysis could justify the search of T.L.O.'s purse by the vice principal. Look for the Court to apply the special needs balancing approach to an increasing number of warrantless administrative searches. The *Von Raab* case is the precedent-setting special needs case and is reproduced below.

National Treasury Employees Union v. Von Raab
489 U.S. 656 (1989)

Justice Kennedy delivered the opinion of the Court, joined by Chief Justice Rehnquist and Justices White, Blackmun, and O'Connor. Justice Marshall filed a dissent, joined by Justice Brennan, and Justice Scalia dissented with Justice Stevens.

We granted *certiorari* to decide whether it violates the Fourth Amendment for the United States Customs Service to require a urinalysis test from employees who seek transfer or promotion to certain positions.

I

The United States Customs Service, a bureau of the Department of the Treasury, is the federal agency responsible for processing persons, carriers, cargo, and mail into the United States, collecting revenue from imports, and enforcing customs and related laws. An important responsibility of the Service is the interdiction and seizure of contraband, including illegal drugs. Ibid. In 1987 alone, Customs agents seized drugs with a retail value of nearly $9 billion. In the routine discharge of their duties, many Customs employees have direct contact with those who traffic in drugs for profit. Drug import operations, often directed by sophisticated criminal syndicates, may be effected by

violence or its threat. As a necessary response, many Customs operatives carry and use firearms in connection with their official duties.

In December 1985, respondent, the Commissioner of Customs, established a Drug Screening Task Force to explore the possibility of implementing a drug-screening program within the Service. After extensive research and consultation with experts in the field, the task force concluded "that drug screening through urinalysis is technologically reliable, valid and accurate." Citing this conclusion, the Commissioner announced his intention to require drug tests of employees who applied for, or occupied, certain positions within the Service. The Commissioner stated his belief that "Customs is largely drug-free," but noted also that "unfortunately no segment of society is immune from the threat of illegal drug use." Drug interdiction has become the agency's primary enforcement mission, and the Commissioner stressed that "there is no room in the Customs Service for those who break the laws prohibiting the possession and use of illegal drugs." In May 1986, the Commissioner announced implementation of the drug-testing program. Drug tests were made a condition of placement or employment for positions that meet one or more of three criteria. The first is direct involvement in drug interdiction or enforcement of related laws, an activity the Commissioner deemed fraught with obvious dangers to the mission of the agency and the lives of customs agents. The second criterion is a requirement that the incumbent carry firearms, as the Commissioner concluded that "[p]ublic safety demands that employees who carry deadly arms and are prepared to make instant life or death decisions be drug free."

The third criterion is a requirement for the incumbent to handle "classified" material, which the Commissioner determined might fall into the hands of smugglers if accessible to employees who, by reason of their own illegal drug use, are susceptible to bribery or blackmail. After an employee qualifies for a position covered by the Customs testing program, the Service advises him by letter that his final selection is contingent upon successful completion of drug screening. An independent contractor contacts the employee to fix the time and place for collecting the sample. On reporting for the test, the employee must produce photographic identification and remove any outer garments, such as a coat or a jacket, and personal belongings. The employee may produce the sample behind a partition, or in the privacy of a bathroom stall if he so chooses. To ensure against adulteration of the specimen, or substitution of a sample from another person, a monitor of the same sex as the employee remains close at hand to listen for the normal sounds of urination. Dye is added to the toilet water to prevent the employee from using the water to adulterate the sample.

Upon receiving the specimen, the monitor inspects it to ensure its proper temperature and color, places a tamper-proof custody seal over the container, and affixes an identification label indicating the date and the individual's specimen number. The employee signs a chain-of-custody form, which is initialed by the monitor, and the urine sample is placed in a plastic bag, sealed, and submitted to a laboratory. . . .

Customs employees who test positive for drugs and who can offer no satisfactory explanation are subject to dismissal from the Service. Test results may not, however, be turned over to any other agency, including criminal prosecutors, without the employee's written consent.

Petitioners, a union of federal employees and a union official, commenced this suit in the United States District Court for the Eastern District of Louisiana on behalf of current Customs Service employees who seek covered positions. Petitioners alleged that the Custom Service drug-testing program violated, *inter alia*, the Fourth Amendment. The District Court agreed. 649 F.Supp. 380 (1986). The court acknowledged "the legitimate governmental interest in a drug-free work place and work force," but concluded that "the drug testing plan constitutes an overly intrusive policy of searches and seizures without probable cause or reasonable suspicion, in violation of legitimate expectations of privacy." The court enjoined the drug-testing program, and ordered the Customs Service not to require drug tests of any applicants for covered positions.

A divided panel of the United States Court of Appeals for the Fifth Circuit vacated the injunction. 816 F.2d 170 (1987). We now affirm so much of the judgment of the Court of Appeals as upheld the testing of employees directly involved in drug interdiction or required to carry firearms. We vacate the judgment to the extent it upheld the testing of applicants for positions requiring the incumbent to handle classified materials, and remand for further proceedings.

It is clear that the Customs Service's drug-testing program is not designed to serve the ordinary needs of law enforcement. Test results may not be used in a criminal prosecution of the employee without the employee's consent. The purposes of the program are to deter drug use among those eligible for promotion to sensitive positions within the Service and to prevent the promotion of drug users to those positions. These substantial interests, no less than the Government's concern for safe rail transportation at issue in *Railway Labor Executives,* present a special need that may justify departure from the ordinary warrant and probable-cause requirements.

Furthermore, a warrant would provide little or nothing in the way of additional protection of personal privacy. A warrant serves primarily to advise the citizen that an intrusion is authorized by law and limited in its permissible scope and to interpose a neutral magistrate between the citizen and the law enforcement officer "engaged in the often competitive enterprise of ferreting out crime." But in the present context, "the circumstances justifying toxicological testing and the permissible limits of such intrusions are defined narrowly and specifically . . . , and doubtless are well known to covered employees." Under the Customs program, every employee who seeks a transfer to a covered position knows that he must take a drug test, and is likewise aware of the procedures the Service must follow in administering the test. A covered employee is simply not subject "to the discretion of the official in the field." The process becomes automatic when the employee elects to apply for, and thereafter pursue, a covered position. Because the Service does not make a discretionary determination to search based on a judgment that certain conditions are present, there are simply "no special facts for a neutral magistrate to evaluate."

We think the Government's need to conduct the suspicionless searches required by the Customs program outweighs the privacy interests of employees engaged directly in drug interdiction, and of those who otherwise are required to carry firearms.

Employees of the United States Mint, for example, should expect to be subject to certain routine personal searches when they leave the workplace every day. Similarly, those who join our military or intelligence services may not only be required to give what in other contexts might be viewed as extraordinary assurances of trustworthiness and probity, but also may expect intrusive inquiries into their physical fitness for those special positions.

We think Customs employees who are directly involved in the interdiction of illegal drugs or who are required to carry firearms in the line of duty likewise have a diminished expectation of privacy in respect to the intrusions occasioned by a urine test. Unlike most private citizens or government employees in general, employees involved in drug interdiction reasonably should expect effective inquiry into their fitness and probity. Much the same is true of employees who are required to carry firearms. Because successful performance of their duties depends uniquely on their judgment and

dexterity, these employees cannot reasonably expect to keep from the Service personal information that bears directly on their fitness. While reasonable tests designed to elicit this information doubtless infringe some privacy expectations, we do not believe these expectations outweigh the Government's compelling interests in safety and in the integrity of our borders. . . .

III

Where the Government requires its employees to produce urine samples to be analyzed for evidence of illegal drug use, the collection and subsequent chemical analysis of such samples are searches that must meet the reasonableness requirement of the Fourth Amendment. Because the testing program adopted by the Customs Service is not designed to serve the ordinary needs of law enforcement, we have balanced the public interest in the Service's testing program against the privacy concerns implicated by the tests, without reference to our usual presumption in favor of the procedures specified in the Warrant Clause, to assess whether the tests required by Customs are reasonable.

We hold that the suspicionless testing of employees who apply for promotion to positions directly involving the interdiction of illegal drugs, or to positions that require the incumbent to carry a firearm, is reasonable. The Government's compelling interests in preventing the promotion of drug users to positions where they might endanger the integrity of our Nation's borders or the life of the citizenry outweigh the privacy interests of those who seek promotion to these positions, who enjoy a diminished expectation of privacy by virtue of the special, and obvious, physical and ethical demands of those positions. We do not decide whether testing those who apply for promotion to positions where they would handle "classified" information is reasonable because we find the record inadequate for this purpose.

The judgment of the Court of Appeals for the Fifth Circuit is affirmed in part and vacated in part, and the case is remanded for further proceedings consistent with this opinion.

It is so ordered.

Justice Scalia, dissenting. Justice Stevens joined with Justice Scalia in dissenting.

The issue in this case is not whether Customs Service employees can constitutionally be denied promotion, or even dismissed, for a single instance of unlawful drug use, at home or at work. They assuredly can. The issue here is what steps can constitutionally be taken to detect such drug use. The Government asserts it can demand that employees perform "an excretory function traditionally shielded by great privacy," *Skinner v. Railway Labor Executives' Assn.,* 489 U.S., at 626, while "a monitor of the same sex . . . remains close at hand to listen for the normal sounds," and that the excretion thus produced be turned over to the Government for chemical analysis. The Court agrees that this constitutes a search for purposes of the Fourth Amendment—and I think it obvious that it is a type of search particularly destructive of privacy and offensive to personal dignity. Until today this Court had upheld a bodily search separate from arrest and without individualized suspicion of wrongdoing only with respect to prison inmates, relying upon the uniquely dangerous nature of that environment. See *Bell v. Wolfish,* 441 U.S. 520, 558–560 (1979). Today, in *Skinner,* we allow a less intrusive bodily search of railroad employees involved in train accidents. I joined the Court's opinion there because the demonstrated frequency of drug and alcohol use by the targeted class of employees, and the demonstrated connection between such use and grave harm, rendered the search a reasonable means of protecting society. I decline to join the Court's opinion in the present case because neither frequency of use nor connection to harm is demonstrated or even likely. In my view the Customs Service rules are a kind of immolation of privacy and human dignity in symbolic opposition to drug use.

The Fourth Amendment protects the "right of the people to be secure in their persons, houses, papers, and effects, against unreasonable searches and seizures." While there are some absolutes in Fourth Amendment law, as soon as those have been left behind and the question comes down to whether a particular search has been "reasonable," the answer depends largely upon the social necessity that prompts the search. What is absent in the Government's justifications—notably absent, revealingly absent, and as far as I am concerned dispositively absent—is the recitation of even a single instance in which any of the speculated horribles actually occurred: an instance, that is, in which the cause of bribe-taking, or of poor aim, or of unsympathetic law enforcement, or of compromise of classified information, was drug use. Although the Court points out that several employees have in the past been removed from the Service for accepting bribes and other integrity violations, and that at least nine officers have died in the line of duty since 1974, there is no indication whatever that these incidents were related to drug use by Service employees. Perhaps concrete evidence of the severity of a problem is unnecessary when it is so well known that courts can almost take judicial notice of it; but that is surely not the case here. The Commissioner of Customs himself has stated that he "believe[s] that Customs is largely drug-free," that "[t]he extent of illegal drug use by Customs employees was not the reason for establishing this program," and that he "hope[s] and expect[s] to receive reports of very few positive findings through drug screening." The test results have fulfilled those hopes and expectations. According to the Service's counsel, out of 3,600 employees tested, no more than 5 tested positive for drugs.

The Court's response to this lack of evidence is that "[t]here is little reason to believe that American workplaces are immune from [the] pervasive social problem" of drug abuse. Perhaps such a generalization would suffice if the workplace at issue could produce such catastrophic social harm that no risk whatever is tolerable—the secured areas of a nuclear power plant, for example, see *Rushton v. Nebraska Public Power District,* 844 F.2d 562 (CA8 1988). But if such a generalization suffices to justify demeaning bodily searches, without particularized suspicion, to guard against the bribing or blackmailing of a law enforcement agent, or the careless use of a firearm, then the Fourth Amendment has become frail protection indeed. In *Skinner, Bell, T.L.O.,* and *Martinez-Fuerte,* we took pains to establish the existence of special need for the search or seizure—a need based not upon the existence of a "pervasive social problem" combined with speculation as to the effect of that problem in the field at issue, but rather upon well known or well demonstrated evils in that field, with well known or well demonstrated consequences.

There is irony in the Government's citation, in support of its position, of Justice Brandeis' statement in *Olmstead v. United States,* 277 U.S. 438, 485 (1928) that "[f]or good or for ill, [our Government] teaches the whole people by its example." Brandeis was there dissenting from the Court's admission of evidence obtained through an unlawful Government wiretap. He was not praising the Government's example of vigor and enthusiasm in combatting crime, but condemning its example that "the end justifies the means," 277 U.S., at 485. An even more apt quotation from that famous Brandeis dissent would have been the following: "[I]t

is . . . immaterial that the intrusion was in aid of law enforcement. Experience should teach us to be most on our guard to protect liberty when the Government's purposes are beneficent. Men born to freedom are naturally alert to repel invasion of their liberty by evil-minded rulers. The greatest dangers to liberty lurk in insidious encroachment by men of zeal, well-meaning but without understanding." Those who lose because of the lack of understanding that begot the present exercise in symbolism are not just the Customs Service employees, whose dignity is thus offended, but all of us—who suffer a coarsening of our national manners that ultimately give the Fourth Amendment its content, and who become subject to the administration of federal officials whose respect for our privacy can hardly be greater than the small respect they have been taught to have for their own.

I respectfully dissent.

Before the discussion moves to what government does with the information after obtaining it, the student should be aware that agencies are not necessarily limited to the three methods discussed earlier (requiring the regulated to keep certain records, subpoena, and physical inspection). For example, you may have read in the newspaper that Sears got caught by the California Department of Consumer Affairs bilking auto repair customers. This information was obtained through a "sting" operation, in which the agency took cars in top mechanical condition to Sears Auto Centers, where investigators were overcharged an average of $223 per car.[16]

Section B: Agencies as Repositories of Information

The collection, housing, and release of information by government are important and significant aspects of the administrative state.

The way we think about information [has] changed during the past 20 years. Government information in the 1980s has become a tangible commodity with a dollar value. "Information Management" is being defined as a multi-faceted process involving the collection, processing, storage, transmission and use of information.[17]

As an undergraduate student in the early 1960s, I was continually frustrated because government conducted its business in secret and the citizenry knew only what government wanted them to know. For the most part, that has changed. It has changed because of the Freedom of Information Act (FOIA, 1966), The Privacy Act (1974), and the Open Meetings Act (1976). The FOIA[18] requires agencies to release information in their possession if another party has requested such information, unless the information is protected by an exemption under the Act. The Privacy Act,[19] better known as the Buckley Amendment, provides for an individual to access his or her records that are in an agency's possession. It allows the citizen to correct such records, and it provides the individual with a remedy of money damages in the event of unauthorized release of such information by an agency. The government in the Sunshine Act or Open Meetings Act[20] requires those agencies headed by a "collegial body" to notify the public and conduct "official agency business" in public. Again, there are exceptions.

Several federal laws focus on information. Just the ones you have been exposed to so far in this text are: FOIA, Privacy Act, Emergency Planning and Community Right to Know Act, the Paperwork Reduction Act, the Radon Research Act, and the Data Quality Act. You have read about agency action that focused on information: the hazardous communication standard and the classification of dioxin and secondhand smoke as known carcinogens. Finally, computers and the Internet are significantly impacting agencies and how they do business.[21] Today, there is a concept called E-Government. E-Government has a statutory basis in two laws: the E-Government Act of 2002[22] and the 1996 amendments to the FOIA called the Electronic Freedom of Information Act Amendments.[23] The latter moves toward Internet publication of releasable data whereas the former requires all federal agencies to create Websites and make current agency activity (procedures, policies, or proposed rules) available to the public. Not only is the agency more transparent, but agencies are required to maintain the capability to communicate and interact with citizens regarding agency business. The E-Government legislation delegates to the Office of Management and Budget (OMB) the power to oversee agency implementation of E-Government. Along with the Office of Information and Regulatory Affairs (OIRA), there is an Office of E-Government within OMB.[24]

In Chapter 2, there was a discussion of attempts by the White House to gain control over agency release of emergency information. The theory is that if an agency issued a warning based on bad science or misinformation, the business or industry affected could be permanently damaged. In the *Tozzi* case from the last chapter, the Court discussed the costs to a manufacturer of dioxin that resulted from the simple listing of a substance as a known carcinogen. When a case of Mad Cow Disease broke out in Canada eight months before the outbreak in America, the primary reaction of American officials was to close the U.S. border to Canadian cattle and to reassure the American public that our supply of beef was safe. Meat packers pressured the government to reopen the borders quickly as the increased supply of cattle from Canada reduced the price they would have to pay American cattlemen and save the industry $455 million a year.[25]

A business or individual damaged by government release of information has little legal recourse.[26] You will read in Chapter 10 about *sovereign immunity,* a concept that forbids lawsuits against government unless government consents. It has not consented to be sued over release of information. It has consented to be sued for its torts (a legal wrong done to a person or their property), but release of information, whether intentionally or by mistake, is generally not a tort (especially where the information is truthful). From Chapter 4, you learned that conflicts over information contained in government reports may not always be reviewable under the Administrative Procedure Act. There may be a recourse for release of information concerning an individual under the Privacy Act, but businesses are not covered.

By now, most states have legislation that protects against unauthorized release of information as well as laws assuring access to information in its possession, so that people who work for government agencies at any level should be familiar with administrative law regarding information. At the federal level, neither the Privacy Act nor the Sunshine Act has spawned much litigation (for an example, see *Common Cause v. NRC,* 674 F.2d 921 [D.C. Cir. 1982]), but the FOIA has been litigated a lot.

THE FREEDOM OF INFORMATION ACT

The FOIA is presented in Appendix A of this book (Section 522 of the Administrative Procedure Act), and you should read it now. According to Professor Lotte E. Feinberg,

> The FOIA uneasily rests on four broad, often incompatible premises. . . . [that] an informed electorate is essential to safeguard democracy; publicity is one of the best protections against the potential for official misconduct; privacy is a fundamental right and corresponds with a need to restrict government's intrusions into peoples lives; and secrecy is endemic to bureaucracy and perhaps facilitates organizational efficiency.[27]

In 1999, the public submitted 1,965,919 FOIA requests, and agencies processed 1,939,668 requests.[28] The FBI occasionally must call agents in from the field to help meet statutory deadlines in processing FOIA requests.

The key to understanding the litigation surrounding FOIA requests is to understand the exemptions. Although there are nine exemptions under FOIA, this discussion will concentrate on those that are most difficult to understand and that have spawned considerable litigation. Those exemptions are No. 4, the trade secrets and commercial information exemption; No. 5, the evidentiary privilege exemption; and Nos. 6 and 7, which contain language that forbids release of information that would constitute an unwarranted invasion of privacy. You will notice from your reading of the FOIA that the language favors release of information by the agency. The requester need only reasonably describe the material, and the agency is given only 20 days to identify the material and make an initial decision to either release or withhold (although an extension for an additional 10 days is possible). If the agency decision is to withhold, the requester must be informed of the reason and of the right to appeal the withholding decision to the head of the agency. The agency must identify by name the bureaucrat who made the decision to withhold. If the requester appeals to the head of the agency, that official must make a decision within 20 days. If the requester decides to appeal the agency head's decision to the federal courts, such suits are to be placed in the federal courts' expedited calendar, and the government has only 30 days to answer the requester's complaint. Attorney fees may be reimbursed for requesters who "substantially prevail" in the courts. If the agency does provide the requested material, the agency may not charge a fee that exceeds the direct costs of search and duplication. Finally, where an agency determines that some portions of a document are exempt and not releasable, the Act requires that the agency block out the exempted material and release the rest.[29] Most of the language in the FOIA, exacting agency action within specific time frames, was added by amendments in 1974 and 1976 because Congress found "foot dragging by the federal bureaucracy and difficulties in convincing the 'secrecy minded bureaucrat that public records are public property.'"[30]

Although the Act may sound clear in this description, the interpretation of it becomes political. The language in the statute changes only when Congress amends or modifies it, but the Attorney General's office is given administrative control over its enforcement within each agency.[31] Specifically, the Department of Justice is given the statutory responsibility to defend agencies when they withhold requested information and then get sued. Hence, attorneys general for different administrations manipulate the threshold for agencies to withhold requested information by manipulating the standard above which it will or will not defend an agency's refusal to release information. The Reagan Administration adopted a low threshold so that agencies could feel comfortable denying release of requested information as long as the agency had "a substantial legal basis" for the denial.[32] Anytime an agency denied requested information, the Department of Justice would defend it if the agency had a substantial legal basis for its decision. The Clinton Administration raised the standard to make it more difficult for agencies to withhold requested information. Attorney General Janet Reno adopted a "foreseeable harm" standard so the Department would only defend an agency's decision to withhold information "in those cases where the agency reasonably could foresee that disclosure would be harmful to an interest protected by an exemption."[33] The Bush 43 administration has reverted to the Reagan standard, saying it will defend any decision to withhold information unless it lacks a sound legal basis.

In creating the Department of Homeland Security, Congress created another exception to the FOIA by adding a subsection of the Homeland Security Act that has become known as the Critical Infrastructure Information Act. The Act exempts from release under FOIA information submitted to the government regarding the security of critical infrastructure and protected systems. This exemption applies only to records or information submitted to the Department of Homeland Security.[34]

Section b, Number 4, of the FOIA reads as follows: "(b) This section does not apply to matters that are . . . trade secrets and commercial or financial information obtained from a person and privileged or confidential." This means that if an agency possesses information that an individual has requested and the information constitutes a trade secret, the agency can—if it chooses—withhold the information. If it is not a trade secret but is commercial or financial information obtained from an individual or a business or corporation (i.e., not obtained from another government agency) and if the information is either privileged (attorney/client) or confidential, the agency can withhold. Most of this is not difficult to recognize. We can recognize a trade secret (usually). We do recognize commercial or financial information, and we know whether it has come from a business, individual, or corporation. The business, individual, or corporation will inform us if the information is clothed with a legally recognized privilege. The question of whether the information sought is confidential is the problem, and the case you are about to read defines the term *confidential.*

National Parks and Conservation Association v. Morton
498 F.2d 765 (1974)

The opinion is by Circuit Judge Tamm.

Appellant brought this action under the Freedom of Information Act, 5 U.S.C. 552 (1970), seeking to enjoin officials of the Department of the Interior from refusing to permit inspection and copying of certain agency records concerning concessions operated in the national parks. The district court granted summary judgment for the defendant on the ground that the information sought is exempt from disclosure under section 552(b)(4) of the Act which states: (b) This section does not apply to matters that are . . . (4) trade secrets and commercial or financial information obtained from a person and privileged or confidential. . . . In order to bring a matter (other than a trade secret) within this exemption, it must be shown that the information is (a) commercial or financial, (b) obtained from a person, and (c) privileged or confidential. Since the parties agree that the matter in question is financial information obtained from a person and that it is not privileged, the only issue on appeal is whether the information is "confidential" within the meaning of the exemption.

I

Unfortunately, the statute contains no definition of the word "confidential." In the past, our decisions concerning this exemption have been guided by the following passage from the Senate Report. . . . This exception is necessary to protect the confidentiality of information which is obtained by the Government through questionnaires or other inquiries, but which would customarily not be released to the public by the person from whom it was obtained. . . . Whether particular information would customarily be disclosed to the public by the person from whom it was obtained is not the only relevant inquiry in determining whether that information is "confidential" for purposes of section 552(b)(4). A court must also be satisfied that non-disclosure is justified by the legislative purpose which underlies the exemption. Our first task, therefore, is to ascertain the ends which Congress sought to attain in enacting the exemption for "commercial or financial" information. In general, the various exemptions included in the statute serve two interests—that of the Government in efficient operation and that of persons supplying certain kinds of information in maintaining its secrecy. The Senate Report acknowledges both of these legislative goals: . . .

The "financial information" exemption recognizes the need of government policymakers to have access to commercial and financial data. Unless persons having necessary information can be assured that it will remain confidential, they may decline to cooperate with officials

and the ability of the Government to make intelligent, well informed decisions will be impaired. This concern finds expression in the legislative history as well as the case law. . . . Apart from encouraging cooperation with the Government by persons having information useful to officials, section 552(b)(4) serves another distinct but equally important purpose. It protects persons who submit financial or commercial data to government agencies from the competitive disadvantages which would result from its publication. The need for such protection was raised several times during hearings. . . .

In each of these instances it was suggested that an exemption for "trade secrets" would avert the danger that valuable business information would be made public by agencies which had obtained it pursuant to statute or regulation. A representative of the Department of Justice endorsed this idea at length: A second problem area lies in the large body of the Government's information involving private business data and trade secrets, the disclosure of which could severely damage individual enterprise and cause widespread disruption of the channels of commerce. Much of this information is volunteered by employers, merchants, manufacturers, carriers, exporters, and other businessmen and professional people for purposes of market news services, labor and wage statistics, commercial reports, and other Government services which are considered useful to the cooperating reporters, the public, and the agencies. Perhaps the greater part of such information is exacted, by statute, in the course of necessary regulatory or other governmental functions. Again, not only as a matter of fairness, but as a matter of right, and as a matter basic to our free enterprise system, private business information should be afforded appropriate protection, at least from competitors.

A particularly significant aspect of the latter statement is its recognition of a twofold justification for the exemption of commercial material: (1) encouraging cooperation by those who are not obliged to provide information to the government and (2) protecting the rights of those who must.

II

The financial information sought by appellant consists of audits conducted upon the books of companies operating concessions in national parks, annual financial statements filed by the concessionaires with the National Park Service, and other financial information. The district court concluded that this information was of the kind "that would not generally be made available for public perusal." While we discern no error in this finding, we do not think that, by itself, it supports application of the financial information exemption. The district court must also inquire into the possibility that disclosure will harm legitimate private or governmental interests in secrecy.

On the record before us the Government has no apparent interest in preventing disclosure of the matter in question. Some, if not all, of the information is supplied to the Park Service pursuant to statute. Whether supplied pursuant to statute, regulation, or some less formal mandate, however, it is clear that disclosure of this material to the Park Service is a mandatory condition of the concessionaires' right to operate in national parks. Since the concessionaires are required to provide this financial information to the government, there is presumably no danger that public disclosure will impair the ability of the Government to obtain this information in the future.

As we have already explained, however, section 552(b)(4) may be applicable even though the Government itself has no interest in keeping the information secret. The exemption may be invoked for the benefit of the person who has provided commercial or financial information if it can be shown that public disclosure is likely to cause substantial harm to his competitive position. Appellant argues that such a showing cannot be made in this case because the concessionaires are monopolists, protected from competition during the term of their contracts and enjoying a statutory preference over other bidders at renewal time. In other words, appellant argues that disclosure cannot impair the concessionaires' competitive position because they have no competition. While this argument is very compelling, we are reluctant to accept it without first providing appellee the opportunity to develop a fuller record in the district court. It might be shown, for example, that disclosure of information about concession activities will injure the concessioner's competitive position in a nonconcession enterprise. In that case disclosure would be improper. This matter is therefore remanded to the district court for the purpose of determining whether public disclosure of the information in question poses the likelihood of substantial harm to the competitive positions of the parties from whom it has been obtained. If the district court finds in the affirmative, then the information is "confidential" within the meaning of section 552(b)(4) and exempt from disclosure. If only some parts of the information are confidential, the district court may prevent inappropriate disclosures by excising from otherwise disclosable documents any matters which are confidential in the sense that the word has been construed in this opinion.

The judgment of the district court is reversed and this matter is remanded for further proceedings consistent with this opinion.

So ordered.

Question

1. The court provides a two-pronged test for the confidentiality of requested material. First material is confidential when the person (or business) from whom it was obtained would not ordinarily release it to the public. Second, withholding of information must fit the legislative purpose for the exemption. In the preceding case, the court lists two legislative purposes for Exemption 4. Can you identify them?

Table 5.1   Decision Tree: Freedom of Information Act Exemption 4

1. Is the material a trade secret?
     YES = withhold
     NO = Go to #2

2. Is the material financial or commercial information?
     YES = Go to #3
     NO = It is not covered by this exemption; release unless covered by another exemption.

3. Was the material obtained from an individual or business?
     YES = Go to #4
     NO = If it was obtained from another agency, look to Exemption 5, but it is releasable under Exemption 4.

4. Is it privileged information (attorney/client)?
     YES = withhold
     NO = Go to #5

5. Is the material confidential?
     A. Is it the kind of information that the person who gave it to the agency would not want released to the public?
       YES = potentially confidential, proceed to B
       NO = not confidential; release
     B. If the information were withheld, would that be consistent with the legislative purpose behind the exemption?

       B-1. Would release impair the government's ability to obtain information in the future?
         YES = probably confidential, withhold
         NO = Do not release the information yet; proceed to B-2.
       B-2. Would release of the information harm the competitive position of the individual or business that provided it?
         YES = confidential; withhold
         NO = Even if the material is not the kind that the provider would release to the public, if both B-1 and B-2 are negative, then the material is releasable because to withhold would not be consistent with the reasons Congress created the exemption.

As you are confronted with situations in which commercial or financial information is sought and an agency must decide whether to release or withhold, it may help you to follow the decision tree in Table 5.1.

The case you are about to read next, *Chrysler v. Brown,* addresses the question of what happens when an agency possesses information that it clearly could withhold under Exemption 4 but chooses to release it anyway. This is a difficult and confusing case, but you will understand it better if you follow the decision tree and try to answer the following questions: (a) Why does the agency want to release exemptible information? The agency argues that it has to do so, but by what authority? (b) The Trade Secrets Act[35] makes it a crime for bureaucrats to release certain information that comes to them during the course of employment. Why cannot Chrysler use this law to stop the agency in this case from releasing information?

Chrysler v. Brown
441 U.S. 281 (1979)

Justice Rehnquist delivered the opinion for a unanimous Court, with Justice Marshall concurring.

The expanding range of federal regulatory activity and growth in the Government sector of the economy have increased federal agencies' demands for information about the activities of private individuals and corporations. These developments have paralleled a related concern about secrecy in Government and abuse of power.

The Freedom of Information Act (hereinafter FOIA) was a response to this concern, but it has also had a largely unforeseen tendency to exacerbate the uneasiness of those who comply with governmental demands for information. For under the FOIA third parties have been able to obtain Government files containing information submitted by corporations and individuals who thought that the information would be held in confidence.

This case belongs to a class that has been popularly denominated "reverse-FOIA" suits. The Chrysler Corp. (hereinafter Chrysler) seeks to enjoin agency disclosure on the grounds that it is inconsistent with the FOIA and 18 U.S.C. § 1905, a criminal statute with origins in the 19th century that proscribes disclosure of certain classes of business and personal information. We agree with the Court of Appeals for the Third Circuit that the FOIA is purely a disclosure statute and affords Chrysler no private right of action to enjoin agency disclosure. But we cannot agree with that court's conclusion that this disclosure is "authorized by law" within the meaning of § 1905. Therefore, we vacate the Court of Appeals' judgment and remand so that it can consider whether the documents at issue in this case fall within the terms of § 1905.

I

As a party to numerous Government contracts, Chrysler is required to comply with Executive Orders 11246 and 11375, which charge the Secretary of Labor with ensuring that corporations that benefit from Government contracts provide equal employment opportunity regardless of race or sex. The United States Department of Labor's Office of Federal Contract Compliance Programs (OFCCP) has promulgated regulations which require Government contractors to furnish reports and other information about their affirmative-action programs and the general composition of their work forces. . . .

Regulations promulgated by the Secretary of Labor provide for public disclosure of information from records of the OFCCP and its compliance agencies. Those regulations state that notwithstanding exemption from mandatory disclosure under the FOIA, 5 U.S.C. § 552, "records obtained or generated pursuant to Executive Order 11246 (as amended) . . . shall be made available for inspection and copying . . . if it is determined that the requested inspection or copying furthers the public interest and does not impede any of the functions of the OFCC or the Compliance Agencies except in the case of records disclosure of which is prohibited by law" . . .

It is the voluntary disclosure contemplated by this regulation, over and above that mandated by the FOIA, which is the *gravamen* of Chrysler's complaint in this case.

This controversy began on May 14, 1975, when the DLA [Defense Logistics Agency] informed Chrysler that third parties had made an FOIA request for disclosure of the 1974 AAP [affirmative action program] for Chrysler's Newark, Del., assembly plant and an October 1974 CIR [complaint investigation report] for the same facility. Nine days later, Chrysler objected to release of the requested information, relying on OFCCP's disclosure regulations and on exemptions to the FOIA. Chrysler also requested a copy of the CIR, since it had never seen it. DLA responded the following week that it had determined that the requested material was subject to disclosure under the FOIA and the OFCCP disclosure rules, and that both documents would be released five days later.

On the day the documents were to be released Chrysler filed a complaint in the United States District Court for Delaware seeking to enjoin release of the Newark documents. The District Court granted a temporary restraining order barring disclosure of the Newark documents and requiring that DLA give five days' notice to Chrysler before releasing any similar documents. Pursuant to this order, Chrysler was informed on July 1, 1975, that DLA had received a similar request for information about Chrysler's Hamtramck, Mich., plant. Chrysler amended its complaint and obtained a restraining order with regard to the Hamtramck disclosure as well.

Chrysler made three arguments in support of its prayer for an injunction: that disclosure was barred by the FOIA; that it was inconsistent with 18 U.S.C. § 1905, 42 U.S.C. § 2000e-8(e), and 44 U.S.C. § 3508, which for ease of reference will be referred to as the "confidentiality statutes"; and finally that disclosure was an abuse of agency discretion insofar as it conflicted with OFCCP rules. The District Court held that it had jurisdiction to subject the disclosure decision to review under the Administrative Procedure Act (APA). It conducted a trial de novo on all of Chrysler's claims; both sides presented extensive expert testimony during August 1975.

On April 20, 1976, the District Court issued its opinion. It held that certain of the requested information, the "manning" tables, fell within Exemption 4 of the FOIA. The District Court reasoned from this holding that the tables may or must be withheld, depending on applicable agency regulations, and that here a governing regulation required that the information be withheld. Pursuant to 5 U.S.C. § 301, the enabling statute which gives federal department heads control over department records, the Secretary of Labor has promulgated a regulation, 29 CFR § 70.21(a) (1978), stating that no officer or employee of the Department is to violate 18 U.S.C. § 1905. That section imposes criminal sanctions on Government employees who make unauthorized disclosure of certain classes of information submitted to a Government agency, including trade secrets and confidential statistical data. In essence, the District Court read § 1905 as not merely a prohibition of unauthorized disclosure of sensitive information by Government employees, but as a restriction on official agency actions taken pursuant to promulgated regulations. Both sides appealed, and the Court of Appeals for the Third Circuit vacated the District Court's judgment. Because of a conflict in the Circuits and the general importance of these "reverse-FOIA" cases, we granted *certiorari,* and now vacate the judgment of the Third Circuit and remand for further proceedings.

II

[1] We have decided a number of FOIA cases in the last few years. Although we have not had to face squarely the question whether the FOIA *ex proprio vigore* forbids governmental agencies from disclosing certain classes of information to the public, we have in the course of at least one opinion intimated an answer. We have, moreover, consistently recognized that the basic objective of the Act is disclosure. In contending that the FOIA bars disclosure of the requested equal employment opportunity information, Chrysler relies on the Act's nine exemptions and argues that they require an agency to withhold exempted material. In this case it relies specifically on Exemption 4: "(b) [FOIA] does not apply to matters that are . . . (4) trade secrets and commercial or financial information obtained from a person and privileged or confidential. . . ." Chrysler contends that the nine exemptions in general, and Exemption 4 in particular, reflect a sensitivity to the privacy interests of private individuals and nongovernmental entities. That contention may be conceded without inexorably requiring the conclusion that the exemptions impose affirmative duties on an agency to withhold information sought. In fact, that conclusion is not supported by the language, logic, or history of the Act. The organization of the Act is straightforward. Subsection (a), 5 U.S.C. § 552(a), places a general obligation on the agency to make information available to the public and

sets out specific modes of disclosure for certain classes of information.

Subsection (b), which lists the exemptions, simply states that the specified material is not subject to the disclosure obligations set out in subsection (a). By its terms, subsection (b) demarcates the agency's obligation to disclose; it does not foreclose disclosure. . . .

We simply hold here that Congress did not design the FOIA exemptions to be mandatory bars to disclosure. We therefore conclude that Congress did not limit an agency's discretion to disclose information when it enacted the FOIA. It necessarily follows that the Act does not afford Chrysler any right to enjoin agency disclosure.

III

Chrysler contends, however, that even if its suit for injunctive relief cannot be based on the FOIA, such an action can be premised on the Trade Secrets Act, 18 U.S.C. § 1905. The Act provides: "Whoever, being an officer or employee of the United States or of any department or agency thereof, publishes, divulges, discloses, or makes known in any manner or to any extent not authorized by law any information coming to him in the course of his employment or official duties or by reason of any examination or investigation made by, or return, report or record made to or filed with, such department or agency or officer or employee thereof, which information concerns or relates to the trade secrets, processes, operations, style of work, or apparatus, or to the identity, confidential statistical data, amount or source of any income, profits, losses, or expenditures of any person, firm, partnership, corporation, or association; or permits any income return or copy thereof or any book containing any abstract or particulars thereof to be seen or examined by any person except as provided by law; shall be fined not more than $1,000, or imprisoned not more than one year, or both; and shall be removed from office or employment." There are necessarily two parts to Chrysler's argument: that § 1905 is applicable to the type of disclosure threatened in this case,

and that it affords Chrysler a private right of action to obtain injunctive relief.

A

The Court of Appeals held that § 1905 was not applicable to the agency disclosure at issue here because such disclosure was "authorized by law" within the meaning of the Act. The court found the source of that authorization to be the OFCCP regulations that DLA relied on in deciding to disclose information on the Hamtramck and Newark plants. Chrysler contends here that these agency regulations are not "law" within the meaning of § 1905. . . .

In order for a regulation to have the "force and effect of law," it must have certain substantive characteristics and be the product of certain procedural requisites. The central distinction among agency regulations found in the APA is that between "substantive rules" on the one hand and "interpretative rules, general statements of policy, or rules of agency organization, procedure, or practice" on the other. A "substantive rule" is not defined in the APA, and other authoritative sources essentially offer definitions by negative inference. But in *Morton v. Ruiz,* 415 U.S. 199 (1974), we noted a characteristic inherent in the concept of a "substantive rule." We described a substantive rule—or a "legislative-type rule"—as one "affecting individual rights and obligations." This characteristic is an important touchstone for distinguishing those rules that may be "binding" or have the "force of law." That an agency regulation is "substantive," however, does not by itself give it the "force and effect of law." The legislative power of the United States is vested in the Congress, and the exercise of quasi-legislative authority by governmental departments and agencies must be rooted in a grant of such power by the Congress and subject to limitations which that body imposes. . . . Likewise the promulgation of these regulations must conform with any procedural requirements imposed by Congress. For agency discretion is limited not only by substantive, statutory grants of authority, but also by the procedural requirements which "assure fairness and mature consideration of rules of general application." The pertinent procedural limitations in this case are those found in the APA.

The regulations relied on by the respondents in this case as providing "authoriz[ation] by law" within the meaning of § 1905 certainly affect individual rights and obligations; they govern the public's right to information in records obtained under Executive Order 11246 and the confidentiality rights of those who submit information to OFCCP and its compliance agencies. It is a much closer question, however, whether they are the product of a congressional grant of legislative authority.

But in order for such regulations to have the "force and effect of law," it is necessary to establish a nexus between the regulations and some delegation of the requisite legislative authority by Congress. For purposes of this case, it is not necessary to decide whether Executive Order 11246 as amended is authorized by the Federal Property and Administrative Services Act of 1949, Titles VI and VII of the Civil Rights Act of 1964, the Equal Employment Opportunity Act of 1972, or some more general notion that the Executive can impose reasonable contractual requirements in the exercise of its procurement authority.

The pertinent inquiry is whether under any of the arguable statutory grants of authority the OFCCP disclosure regulations relied on by the respondents are reasonably within the contemplation of that grant of authority. We think that it is clear that when it enacted these statutes, Congress was not concerned with public disclosure of trade secrets or confidential business information, and, unless we were to hold that any federal statute that implies some authority to collect information must grant legislative authority to disclose that information to the public, it is simply not possible to find in these statutes a delegation of the disclosure authority asserted by the respondents here. There is also a procedural defect in the OFCCP disclosure regulations which precludes courts from affording them the force and effect of law. That defect is a lack of strict compliance with the APA. Section 4 of the APA, 5 U.S.C. § 553, specifies that an agency shall afford interested persons

general notice of proposed rule-making and an opportunity to comment before a substantive rule is promulgated. When the Secretary of Labor published the regulations pertinent in this case, he stated: "As the changes made by this document relate solely to interpretive rules, general statements of policy, and to rules of agency procedure and practice, neither notice of proposed rule making nor public participation therein is required by 5 U.S.C. 553. We need not decide whether these regulations are properly characterized as "'interpretative rules.'"

It is enough that such regulations are not properly promulgated as substantive rules, and therefore not the product of procedures which Congress prescribed as necessary prerequisites to giving a regulation the binding effect of law. An interpretative regulation or general statement of agency policy cannot be the "authoriz[ation] by law" required by § 1905. We reject, however, Chrysler's contention that the Trade Secrets Act affords a private right of action to enjoin disclosure in violation of the statute. In *Cort v. Ash,* 422 U.S. 66 (1975), we noted that this Court has rarely implied a private right of action under a criminal statute, and where it has done so "there was at least a statutory basis for inferring that a civil cause of action of some sort lay in favor of someone." Nothing in § 1905 prompts such an inference. Nor are other pertinent circumstances outlined in *Cort* present here. As our review of the legislative history of § 1905—or lack of same—might suggest, there is no indication of legislative intent to create a private right of action. Most importantly, a private right of action under § 1905 is not "necessary to make effective the congressional purpose," for we find that review of DLA's decision to disclose Chrysler's employment data is available under the APA. . . .

IV

Therefore, we conclude that DLA's decision to disclose the Chrysler reports is reviewable agency action and Chrysler is a person "adversely affected or aggrieved" within the meaning of

§ 10(a). . . . For the reasons previously stated, we believe any disclosure that violates § 1905 is "not in accordance with law" within the meaning of 5 U.S.C. § 706(2)(A). De novo review by the District Court is ordinarily not necessary to decide whether a contemplated disclosure runs afoul of § 1905. The District Court in this case concluded that disclosure of some of Chrysler's documents was barred by § 1905, but the Court of Appeals did not reach the issue. We shall therefore vacate the Court of Appeals' judgment and remand for further proceedings consistent with this opinion in order that the Court of Appeals may consider whether the contemplated disclosures would violate the prohibition of § 1905.

Since the decision regarding this substantive issue—the scope of § 1905—will necessarily have some effect on the proper form of judicial review pursuant to § 706(2), we think it unnecessary, and therefore unwise, at the present stage of this case for us to express any additional views on that issue.

Vacated and remanded.

Question

1. What did the Court decide about whether an agency may release otherwise exempt information?

Two events took place in 1987 that modify the Court's decision in *Chrysler v. Brown*. First, a D.C. Circuit Court interpreted the Trade Secrets Act to require agencies to withhold material that qualifies for a No. 4 exemption.[36] Second, President Reagan issued an executive order that requires agencies to notify a provider when an agency is considering a request to release material that qualifies for exemption. It requires the agency to permit the provider to present arguments to the agency.

Exemption 5 states: "(5) inter-agency or intra-agency memorandums or letters which would not be available by law to a party other than an agency in litigation with the agency." This means that those materials that a party suing the agency would not be able to obtain through the discovery process are exempt. The discovery process is simply an "exchange of information between sides in a lawsuit."[37] This process can be formal, controlled by an administrative law judge, or it can be less formal communication between attorneys. In any case, not all information requested by the other side in a lawsuit needs to be released. For example, some information is protected as privileged (attorney/client), and a prosecutor is not obligated to turn over to the defense information that is not material to the case (information that could influence the outcome). In terms of the FOIA, Congress apparently intended to exempt under No. 5 two kinds of privileged material. First, attorney/client work product is exempted, and second, those materials clothed with executive privilege can be withheld.

The notion of executive privilege is addressed in three other FOIA exemptions, No. 1, No. 7, and the Critical Infrastructure Information Act. Exemption 1 exempts classified material, especially in the area of defense or foreign policy. Exemption 7 is referred to as the "law enforcement exemption" and could be used, for example, to protect the identity of an informant. The Critical Infrastructure Information Act, discussed above, exempts critical infrastructure information given to the Department of Homeland Security. The executive privilege contemplated in Exemption 5 is what I will call "decisional executive privilege," in that it is meant to preserve the integrity of the decision-making process. The concept is addressed in the case you are about to read, but it is aimed at ensuring that a decision maker is presented with all options and full information before a decision is made. More accurately, executive privilege in this context means to ensure that an option, piece of advice, or information is not withheld from the decision maker's consideration out of fear that the advice will be held up to public ridicule at a later date.

National Labor Relations Board v. Sears, Roebuck & Company
421 U.S. 132 (1975)

Justice White delivered the opinion for a unanimous Court, with Chief Justice Burger concurring and Justice Powell not participating.

The National Labor Relations Board (the Board) and its General Counsel seek to set aside an order of the United States District Court directing disclosure to respondent, Sears, Roebuck & Co. (Sears), pursuant to the Freedom of Information Act, of certain memoranda, known as "Advice Memoranda" and "Appeals Memoranda," and related documents generated by the Office of the General Counsel in the course of deciding whether or not to permit the filing with the Board of unfair labor practice complaints.

The Act's background and its principal objectives are described in *EPA v. Mink*, 410 U.S. 73 (1973), and will not be repeated here. It is sufficient to note for present purposes that the Act seeks "to establish a general philosophy of full agency disclosure unless information is exempted under clearly delineated statutory language." As the Act is structured, virtually every document generated by an agency is available to the public in one form or another, unless it falls within one of the Act's nine exemptions. . . . The Act expressly states, however, that the disclosure obligation "does not apply" to those documents described in the nine enumerated exempt categories listed in § 552(b). . . .

Sears claims, and the courts below ruled, that the memoranda sought are expressions of legal and policy decisions already adopted by the agency and constitute "final opinions" and "instructions to staff that affect a member of the public," both categories being expressly disclosable under § 552(a)(2) of the Act, pursuant to its purposes to prevent the creation of "secret law." In any event, Sears claims, the memoranda are nonexempt "identifiable records" which must be disclosed under § 552(a)(3). The General Counsel, on the other hand, claims that the memoranda sought here are not final opinions under § 552(a)(2) and that even if they are "identifiable records" otherwise disclosable under § 552(a)(3), they are exempt under § 552(b), principally as "intra-agency" communications under § 552(b)(5) (Exemption 5), made in the course of formulating agency decisions on legal and policy matters.

II

This case arose in the following context. By letter dated July 14, 1971, Sears requested that the General Counsel disclose to it pursuant to the Act all Advice and Appeals Memoranda issued within the previous five years on the subjects of "the propriety of withdrawals by employers or unions from multi-employer bargaining, disputes as to commencement date of negotiations, or conflicting interpretations in any other context of the Board's Retail Associates rule." The letter also sought the subject-matter index or digest of Advice and Appeals Memoranda. The letter urged disclosure on the theory that the Advice and Appeals Memoranda are the only source of agency "law" on some issues. By letter dated July 23, 1971, the General Counsel declined Sears' disclosure request in full. The letter stated that Advice Memoranda are simply "guides for a Regional Director" and are not final; that they are exempt from disclosure under 5 U.S.C. § 552(b)(5) as "intra-agency memoranda" which reflect the thought processes of the General Counsel's staff; and that they are exempt pursuant to 5 U.S.C. § 552(b)(7) as part of the "investigative process." The letter said that Appeals Memoranda were not indexed by subject matter and, therefore, the General Counsel was "unable" to comply with Sears' request. In further explanation of his decision, with respect to Appeals Memoranda, the General Counsel wrote to Sears on August 4, 1971, and stated that Appeals Memoranda which ordered the filing of a complaint were not "final opinions." The letter further stated that those Appeals Memoranda which were "final opinions, i.e., those in which an appeal was denied" and which directed that no complaint be filed, numbered several thousand, and that in the General Counsel's view they had no precedential significance. Accordingly, if disclosable at all, they were disclosable under 5 U.S.C. § 552(a)(3) relating to "identifiable records." The General Counsel then said that Sears had failed adequately to identify the material sought and that he could not justify the expenditure of time necessary for the agency to identify them. . . .

On August 4, 1971, Sears filed a complaint pursuant to the Act seeking a declaration that the General Counsel's refusal to disclose the Advice and Appeals Memoranda and indices thereof requested by Sears violated the Act, and an injunction enjoining continued violations of the Act. On August 24, 1971, the current General Counsel took office. In order to give him time to develop his own disclosure policy, the filing of his answer was postponed until February 3, 1972. The answer denied that the Act required disclosure of any of the documents sought but referred to a letter of the same date in which the General Counsel informed Sears that he would make available the index to Advice Memoranda and also all Advice and Appeals Memoranda in cases which had been closed—either because litigation before the Board had been completed or because a decision not to file a complaint had become final.

He stated, however, that he would not disclose the memoranda in open cases; that he would, in any event, delete names of witnesses and "security sensitive" matter from the memoranda he did disclose; and that he did not consider the General Counsel's Office bound to pursue this new policy "in all instances" in the future.

Not wholly satisfied with the voluntary disclosures offered and made by the General Counsel, Sears moved for summary judgement and the General Counsel did likewise. Sears thus continued to seek memoranda in open cases. Moreover, Sears objected to the deletions in the memoranda in closed cases and asserted that many Appeals Memoranda were unintelligible because they incorporated by reference documents which were not themselves disclosed and also referred to "the circumstances of the case" which were not set out and about which Sears was ignorant. The General Counsel contended that all of the documents were exempt from disclosure as "intra-agency" memoranda within the coverage of 5 U.S.C. § 552(b)(5); and that the documents incorporated by reference were exempt from disclosure as "investigatory files" pursuant to 5 U.S.C. § 552(b) (7). The parties also did not agree as to the function of an Advice Memorandum. Sears claimed that Advice Memoranda are binding on Regional Directors. The General Counsel claimed that they are not, noting the fact that the Regional Director himself has the delegated power to issue a complaint. The District Court granted Sears' motion for summary judgment and denied that of the General Counsel. . . .

III

It is clear, and the General Counsel concedes, that Appeals and Advice Memoranda are at the least "identifiable records" which must be disclosed on demand, unless they fall within one of the Act's exempt categories. It is also clear that, if the memoranda do fall within one of the Act's exempt categories, our inquiry is at an end, for the Act "does not apply" to such documents. Thus our inquiry, strictly speaking, must be into the scope of the exemptions which the General Counsel claims to be applicable—principally Exemption 5 relating to "intra-agency memorandums." The General Counsel also concedes, however, and we hold for the reasons set forth below, that Exemption 5 does not apply to any document which falls within the meaning of the phrase "final opinion . . . made in the adjudication of cases." The General Counsel argues, therefore, as he must, that no Advice or Appeals Memorandum is a final opinion made in the adjudication of a case and that all are "intra-agency" memoranda within the coverage of Exemption 5. He bases this argument in large measure on what he claims to be his lack of adjudicative authority. It is true that the General Counsel lacks any authority finally to adjudicate an unfair labor practice claim in favor of the claimant; but he does possess the authority to adjudicate such a claim against the claimant through his power to decline to file a complaint with the Board. We hold for reasons more fully set forth below that those Advice and Appeals Memoranda which explain decisions by the General Counsel not to file a complaint are "final opinions" made in the adjudication of a case and fall outside the scope of Exemption 5; but that those Advice and Appeals Memoranda which explain decisions by the General Counsel to file a complaint and commence litigation before the Board are not "final opinions" made in the adjudication of a case and do fall within the scope of Exemption 5. . . .

A

The parties are in apparent agreement that Exemption 5 withholds from a member of the public documents which a private party could not discover in litigation with the agency. Since virtually any document not privileged may be discovered by the appropriate litigant, if it is relevant to his litigation, and since the Act clearly intended to give any member of the public as much right to disclosure as one with a special interest therein, it is reasonable to construe Exemption 5 to exempt those documents, and only those documents, normally privileged in the civil discovery context. The privileges claimed by petitioners to be relevant to this case are (i) the "generally . . . recognized" privilege for "confidential intra-agency advisory opinions . . . ," disclosure of which "would be injurious to the consultative functions of government . . ." (sometimes referred to as "executive privilege"), and (ii) the attorney-client and attorney work-product privileges generally available to all litigants. . . .

(i)

That Congress had the Government's executive privilege specifically in mind in adopting Exemption 5 is clear. The precise contours of the privilege in the context of this case are less clear, but may be gleaned from expressions of legislative purpose and the prior case law. The cases uniformly rest the privilege on the policy of protecting the "decision making processes of government agencies," and focus on documents "reflecting advisory opinions, recommendations and deliberations comprising part of a process by which governmental decisions and policies are formulated." The point, plainly made in the Senate Report, is that the "frank discussion of legal or policy matters" in writing might be inhibited if the discussion were made public; and that the "decisions" and "policies formulated" would be the poorer as a result. As a lower court has pointed out, "there are enough incentives as it is for playing it safe and listing with the wind," and as we have said in an analogous context, "[h]uman experience teaches that those who expect public dissemination of their remarks may well temper candor with a concern for appearances . . . to the detriment of the decision-making process." *United States v. Nixon,* 418 U.S. 683 (1974).

Manifestly, the ultimate purpose of this long-recognized privilege is to prevent injury to the quality of agency decisions. The quality of a particular agency decision will clearly be affected by the communications received by the decision-maker on the subject of the decision prior to the time the decision is made. However, it is difficult to see how the quality of a decision will be affected by communications with respect to the decision occurring after the decision is finally reached; and therefore equally difficult to see how the quality of the decision will be affected by forced disclosure of such communications, as long as prior communications and the ingredients of the decision-making process are not disclosed. Accordingly, the lower courts have uniformly drawn a distinction between predecisional communications, which are privileged, and communications made after the decision and designed to explain it, which are not. This distinction is supported not only by the lesser injury to the decision-making process flowing from disclosure of post-decisional communications, but also, in the case of those communications which explain the decision, by the increased public interest in knowing the basis for agency policy already adopted. The public is only marginally concerned with reasons supporting a policy which an agency has rejected, or with reasons which might have supplied, but did not supply, the basis for a policy which was actually adopted on a different ground. In contrast, the public is vitally concerned with the reasons which did supply the basis for an agency policy actually adopted. These reasons, if expressed within the agency, constitute the "working law" of the agency and have been held by the lower courts to be outside the protection of Exemption 5. . . . Exemption 5, properly construed, calls for "disclosure of all 'opinions and interpretations' which embody the agency's effective law and policy, and the withholding of all papers which reflect the agency's group thinking in the process of working out its policy and determining what its law shall be."

(ii)

It is equally clear that Congress had the attorney's work-product privilege specifically in mind when it adopted Exemption 5 and that such a privilege had been recognized in the civil discovery context by the prior case law. The Senate Report states that Exemption 5 "would include the working papers of the agency attorney and documents which would come within the attorney-client privilege if applied to private parties," and the case law clearly makes the attorney's work-product rule of *Hickman v. Taylor,* 329 U.S. 495, applicable to Government attorneys in litigation. Whatever the outer boundaries of the attorney's work-product rule are, the rule clearly applies to

memoranda prepared by an attorney in contemplation of litigation which set forth the attorney's theory of the case and his litigation strategy.

B

Applying these principles to the memoranda sought by Sears, it becomes clear that Exemption 5 does not apply to those Appeals and Advice Memoranda which conclude that no complaint should be filed and which have the effect of finally denying relief to the charging party; but that Exemption 5 does protect from disclosure those Appeals and Advice Memoranda which direct the filing of a complaint and the commencement of litigation before the Board.

(i)

Under the procedures employed by the General Counsel, Advice and Appeals Memoranda are communicated to the Regional Director after the General Counsel, through his Advice and Appeals Branches, has decided whether or not to issue a complaint; and represent an explanation to the Regional Director of a legal or policy decision already adopted by the General Counsel. In the case of decisions not to file a complaint, the memoranda effect as "final" a "disposition," as an administrative decision can—representing, as it does, an unreviewable rejection of the charge filed by the private party. Disclosure of these memoranda would not intrude on predecisional processes, and protecting them would not improve the quality of agency decisions, since when the memoranda are communicated to the Regional Director, the General Counsel has already reached his decision and the Regional Director who receives them has no decision to make—he is bound to dismiss the charge. Moreover, the General Counsel's decisions not to file complaints together with the Advice and Appeals Memoranda explaining them, are precisely the kind of agency law in which the public is so vitally interested and which Congress sought to prevent the agency from keeping secret.

(ii)

Advice and Appeals Memoranda which direct the filing of a complaint, on the other hand, fall within the coverage of Exemption 5. The filing of a complaint does not finally dispose even of the General Counsel's responsibility with respect to the case. The case will be litigated before and decided by the Board; and the General Counsel will have the responsibility of advocating the position of the charging party before the Board. The Memoranda will inexorably contain the General Counsel's theory of the case and may communicate to the Regional Director some litigation strategy or settlement advice. Since the Memoranda will also have been prepared in contemplation of the upcoming litigation, they fall squarely within Exemption 5's protection of an attorney's work product. At the same time, the public's interest in disclosure is substantially reduced by the fact, as pointed out by the ABA [American Bar Association] Committee, see supra, at 1519, that the basis for the General Counsel's legal decision will come out in the course of litigation before the Board; and that the "law" with respect to these cases will ultimately be made not by the General Counsel but by the Board or the courts.

We recognize that an Advice or Appeals Memorandum directing the filing of a complaint—although representing only a decision that a legal issue is sufficiently in doubt to warrant determination by another body—has many of the characteristics of the documents described in 5 U.S.C. § 552(a)(2). Although not a "final opinion" in the "adjudication" of a "case" because it does not effect a "final disposition," the memorandum does explain a decision already reached by the General Counsel which has real operative effect—it permits litigation before the Board; and we have indicated a reluctance to construe Exemption 5 to protect such documents. We do so in this case only because the decision-maker—the General Counsel—must become a litigating party to the case with respect to which he has made his decision. The attorney's work-product policies which Congress clearly incorporated into Exemption 5 thus come into play and lead us to hold that the Advice and Appeals Memoranda directing the filing of a complaint are exempt whether or not they are, as the District Court held, "instructions to staff that affect a member of the public." The probability that an agency employee will be inhibited from freely advising a decision-maker for fear that his advice, if adopted, will become public is slight. First, when adopted, the reasoning becomes that of the agency and becomes its responsibility to defend. Second, agency employees will generally be encouraged rather than discouraged by public knowledge that their policy suggestions have been adopted by the agency. Moreover, the public interest in knowing the reasons for a policy actually adopted by an agency supports the District Court's decision below.

Thus, we hold that, if an agency chooses expressly to adopt or incorporate by reference an intra-agency memorandum previously covered by Exemption 5 in what would otherwise be a final opinion, that memorandum may be withheld on the ground that it falls within the coverage of some exemption other than Exemption 5.

Questions

1. The purpose of the FOIA was to benefit the public. What was the purpose of Sears's FOIA request? Should the FOIA be used by lawyers as a supplement or substitute for normal discovery tools in suits with an agency?
2. It is clear from this case that not all attorney-client, interagency, or intra-agency communications will fall under Exemption 5. Can you describe which are exempt and which are not? Can you explain why?

Table 5.2   Freedom of Information Act Exemption 5 Dichotomy: Does the information predate the decision? Was the information relied on to make the decision?

	Predecisional	*Post-Decisional*
Relied on for decision	Release: Public has a right to know	Release: Not privileged
Not relied on for decision	Do not release: Privileged and covered by Exemption 5	Release: Not privileged

Students often find the question of whether material is exempt as privileged under Exemption 5 to be confusing. Bear in mind that the exemption was meant to maintain the integrity of the decision-making process. That means that a decision maker should have as much information as possible prior to making a decision. If advisors must fear that options proffered to the decision maker will show up in next week's newspaper, then they will be less likely to offer options or information. Consequently, any information that the decision maker obtains after the decision was made is releasable because to withhold it will not protect the decision-making process. It is only information in the hands of the decision maker before the decision is made that is potentially exempt from release. If the information is relied on to make the decision, then the public (requester) has a right to the information because it forms the basis of public policy. Only predecisional information, which was not used to make the decision, is exempt from release under the FOIA Exemption 5. That is because to withhold such information from public scrutiny will protect the decision-making process. You may find Table 5.2 helpful in interpreting Exemption 5 questions.

Shortly after assuming the presidency, President George W. Bush created the National Energy Policy Development Group (NEPDG) to advise him and make recommendations for a national energy policy. He put Vice President Cheney in charge of the group, which was composed of bureaucrats and various federal agency employees (full and part time). After the NEPDG issued its report to the president, the vice president was sued because it was alleged that energy lobbyists and the heads of large energy corporations (most notoriously, Kenneth Lay of Enron) took an active part in the NEPDG meetings. The plaintiffs were seeking records of the meetings. This is not an FOIA case, but it has all of the elements of what we have referred to as decisional executive privilege, which FOIA Exemption 5 protects. A statute called the Federal Advisory Committee Act imposes open meetings and reporting requirements on committees formed to advise government, but it contains what courts refer to as the de facto membership doctrine. That is, the Act has an exemption that excludes advisory committees from the open meetings and reporting requirements, when the advisory committee is composed of full- and part-time federal employees. In this case, if lobbyists and energy CEOs participated in the meetings, then NEPDG does not qualify for the exemption from open meetings and open records, and the plaintiffs should be able to access the records of the meetings. The narrow issue is whether lobbyists and CEOs participated in the meetings, but the president fought release of any of the information. The district court issued a narrow discovery order to give the plaintiffs an opportunity to try to prove that nongovernment employees took part in the meetings. In a round-about way, the court of appeals upheld the order (more appropriately refused to quash it), and the Supreme Court sent it back to the court of appeals. Although there is no final disposition in the case yet, it is included at the end of this chapter because of the discussion of executive privilege and the fact that this will ultimately become a famous case.

Recall that Exemption 5 has two requirements. First, the material sought has to be inter- or intra-agency communications, and second, it must be privileged (not available to a party suing the agency). The cases above deal with the second requirement or what courts call the deliberative process privilege. There is less case law on what is or is not an "inter/intra agency communication." In a recent case, the Supreme Court had to decide whether communications between a Native American tribe, the Bureau of Indian Affairs, and the Bureau of Reclamation were interagency memos within the meaning of Exemption 5.[38] As the definition of "inter-agency/intra-agency" means within the agency or between agencies and Native American tribes are not federal agencies, you might think the resolution of this is simple. The agencies were in possession of the tribe's communications because the Bureau of Reclamation was in the process of developing a water use plan for the Klamath River Basin and the Bureau of Indian Affairs was involved in water rights litigation in the area (although it was not representing the tribe). An association of water users who depend on Klamath water requested the tribal communications from the agencies under FOIA, and the agencies refused to release under Exemption 5. The issue regarding whether private communications with an agency can be "inter-agency" is complicated by the fact that the Supreme Court has clothed some consulting communications with Exemption 5. Hence, the question here dealt with whether the tribal communications were of the same nature as consulting communications that received the exemption by precedent. The Supreme Court decided that the tribal communications were not the same as consulting communications and should be released under FOIA. The Court reasoned that consulting communications are "as if" they came from the agency or another government entity, whereas the tribal communications reflect the tribe's interest and not that of the agencies or government.

Finally, Exemption 6 is somewhat self-explanatory. It provides for exemptions of "personnel and medical files and similar files the disclosure of which would constitute a clearly unwarranted invasion of personal privacy." Obviously, this exemption was meant to protect against the release of personal information that an agency might possess. The problem is that the language specifies that it is "clearly unwarranted" invasions of privacy that the exemption covers and that presumably it does not protect against incidental invasions of privacy. Because there is no statutory definition of "invasion of privacy," the Court, as it does with special needs warrantless searches and seizures, engages in a balancing test to determine whether the information is exempt or releasable. Although the case that follows is an Exemption 7 case, that exemption contains similar invasion of privacy language to Exemption 6. The balancing test the Court performs is cited as precedent in current invasion of privacy cases.

United States Department of Justice
v. Reporters Committee for Freedom of the Press
489 U.S. 749 (1989)

Justice Stevens delivered the opinion of the Court, in which Chief Justice Rehnquist and Justices White, Marshall, O'Connor, Scalia, and Kennedy joined. Justice Blackmun filed an opinion concurring in the judgment, in which Justice Brennan joined.

The Federal Bureau of Investigation (FBI) has accumulated and maintains criminal identification records, sometimes referred to as "rap sheets," on over 24 million persons. The question presented by this case is whether the disclosure of the contents of such a file to a third party "could reasonably be expected to constitute an unwarranted invasion of personal privacy" within the meaning of the Freedom of Information Act (FOIA), 5 U.S.C. § 552(b) (7) (C).

I

In 1924 Congress appropriated funds to enable the Department of Justice (Department) to establish a program to collect and preserve fingerprints and other criminal identification records. 43 Stat. 217. That statute authorized the Department to exchange such information with "officials of States, cities and other institutions." Ibid. Six years later Congress created the FBI's identification division, and gave it responsibility for "acquiring, collecting, classifying, and preserving criminal identification and other crime records and the exchanging of said criminal identification records with the duly authorized officials of governmental agencies, of States, cities, and penal institutions." Ch. 455, 46 Stat. 554 (codified at 5 U.S.C. § 340 (1934 ed.)); see 28 U.S.C. § 534(a)(4) (providing for exchange of rap-sheet information among "authorized officials of the Federal Government, the States, cities, and penal and other institutions"). Rap sheets compiled pursuant to such authority contain certain descriptive information, such as date of birth and physical characteristics, as well as a history of arrests, charges, convictions, and incarcerations of the subject. Normally a rap sheet is preserved until its subject attains age 80. Because of the volume of rap sheets, they are sometimes incorrect or incomplete and sometimes contain information about other persons with similar names.

The local, state, and federal law enforcement agencies throughout the Nation that exchange rap-sheet data with the FBI do so on a voluntary basis. The principal use of the information is to assist in the detection and prosecution of offenders; it is also used by courts and corrections officials in connection with sentencing and parole decisions. As a matter of executive policy, the Department has generally treated rap sheets as confidential and, with certain exceptions, has restricted their use to governmental purposes. Consistent with the Department's basic policy of treating these records as confidential, Congress in 1957

amended the basic statute to provide that the FBI's exchange of rap-sheet information with any other agency is subject to cancellation "if dissemination is made outside the receiving departments or related agencies." see 28 U.S.C. § 534(b).

As a matter of Department policy, the FBI has made two exceptions to its general practice of prohibiting unofficial access to rap sheets. First, it allows the subject of a rap sheet to obtain a copy, see 28 CFR §§ 16.30–16.34 (1988); and second, it occasionally allows rap sheets to be used in the preparation of press releases and publicity designed to assist in the apprehension of wanted persons or fugitives. See § 20.33(a)(4).

In addition, on three separate occasions Congress has expressly authorized the release of rap sheets for other limited purposes. In 1972 it provided for such release to officials of federally chartered or insured banking institutions and "if authorized by State statute and approved by the Attorney General, to officials of State and local governments for purposes of employment and licensing. . . ." 86 Stat. 1115. In 1975, in an amendment to the Securities Exchange Act of 1934, Congress permitted the Attorney General to release rap sheets to self-regulatory organizations in the securities industry. See 15 U.S.C. § 78q(f)(2). And finally, in 1986 Congress authorized release of criminal-history information to licensees or applicants before the Nuclear Regulatory Commission. See 42 U.S.C. § 2169(a). These three targeted enactments—all adopted after the FOIA was passed in 1966—are consistent with the view that Congress understood and did not disapprove the FBI's general policy of treating rap sheets as nonpublic documents.

Although much rap-sheet information is a matter of public record, the availability and dissemination of the actual rap sheet to the public is limited. Arrests, indictments, convictions, and sentences are public events that are usually documented in court records. In addition, if a person's entire criminal history transpired in a single jurisdiction, all of the contents of his or her rap sheet may be available upon request in that jurisdiction. . . .

The statute known as the FOIA is actually a part of the Administrative Procedure Act (APA).

Section 3 of the APA as enacted in 1946 gave agencies broad discretion concerning the publication of governmental records. In 1966 Congress amended that section to implement a general philosophy of full agency disclosure. . . . If an agency improperly withholds any documents, the district court has jurisdiction to order their production. Unlike the review of other agency action that must be upheld if supported by substantial evidence and not arbitrary or capricious, the FOIA expressly places the burden "on the agency to sustain its action" and directs the district courts to "determine the matter de novo."

Congress exempted nine categories of documents from the FOIA's broad disclosure requirements. Three of those exemptions are arguably relevant to this case. Exemption 3 applies to documents that are specifically exempted from disclosure by another statute. § 552(b)(3).

Exemption 6 protects "personnel and medical files and similar files the disclosure of which would constitute a clearly unwarranted invasion of personal privacy." § 552(b)(6). Exemption 7(C) excludes records or information compiled for law enforcement purposes, "but only to the extent that the production of such [materials] . . . could reasonably be expected to constitute an unwarranted invasion of personal privacy." § 552(b)(7)(C).

Exemption 7(C)'s privacy language is broader than the comparable language in Exemption 6 in two respects. First, whereas Exemption 6 requires that the invasion of privacy be "clearly unwarranted," the adverb "clearly" is omitted from Exemption 7(C). This omission is the product of a 1974 amendment adopted in response to concerns expressed by the President. Second, whereas Exemption 6 refers to disclosures that "would constitute" an invasion of privacy, Exemption 7(C) encompasses any disclosure that "could reasonably be expected to constitute" such an invasion. This difference is also the product of a specific amendment. Thus, the standard for evaluating a threatened invasion of privacy interests resulting from the disclosure of records compiled for law enforcement purposes is somewhat broader than the standard applicable to personnel, medical, and similar files.

III

This case arises out of requests made by a CBS news correspondent and the Reporters Committee for Freedom of the Press (respondents) for information concerning the criminal records of four members of the Medico family. The Pennsylvania Crime Commission had identified the family's company, Medico Industries, as a legitimate business dominated by organized crime figures. Moreover, the company allegedly had obtained a number of defense contracts as a result of an improper arrangement with a corrupt Congressman.

The FOIA requests sought disclosure of any arrests, indictments, acquittals, convictions, and sentences of any of the four Medicos. Although the FBI originally denied the requests, it provided the requested data concerning three of the Medicos after their deaths. In their complaint in the District Court, respondents sought the rap sheet for the fourth, Charles Medico (Medico), insofar as it contained "matters of public record."

The parties filed cross-motions for summary judgment. Respondents urged that any information regarding "a record of bribery, embezzlement or other financial crime" would potentially be a matter of special public interest. In answer to that argument, the Department advised respondents and the District Court that it had no record of any financial crimes concerning Medico, but the Department continued to refuse to confirm or deny whether it had any information concerning nonfinancial crimes. Thus, the issue was narrowed to Medico's nonfinancial-crime history insofar as it is a matter of public record.

The District Court granted the Department's motion for summary judgment. . . . The Court of Appeals reversed. 816 F. 2d 730 (1987). It held that an individual's privacy interest in criminal-history information that is a matter of public record was minimal at best. Noting the absence of any statutory standards by which to judge the public interest in disclosure, the Court of Appeals concluded that it should be bound by the state and local determinations that such information should be made available to the general public. . . .

The Court of Appeals denied rehearing *en banc*, with four judges dissenting. Because of the potential effect of the Court of Appeals' opinion on values of personal privacy, we granted *certiorari.* 485 U.S. 1005 (1988). We now reverse.

IV

Exemption 7(C) requires us to balance the privacy interest in maintaining, as the Government puts it, the "practical obscurity" of the rap sheets against the public interest in their release.

The preliminary question is whether Medico's interest in the nondisclosure of any rap sheet the FBI might have on him is the sort of "personal privacy" interest that Congress intended Exemption 7(C) to protect. As we have pointed out before, "[t]he cases sometimes characterized as protecting 'privacy' have in fact involved at least two different kinds of interests. One is the individual interest in avoiding disclosure of personal matters, and another is the interest in independence in making certain kinds of important decisions." *Whalen v. Roe,* 429 U.S. 589, 598-600 (1977). Here, the former interest, "in avoiding disclosure of personal matters," is implicated. Because events summarized in a rap sheet have been previously disclosed to the public, respondents contend that Medico's privacy interest in avoiding disclosure of a federal compilation of these events approaches zero. We reject respondents' cramped notion of personal privacy. . . .

According to Webster's initial definition, information may be classified as "private" if it is "intended for or restricted to the use of a particular person or group or class of persons: not freely available to the public." Recognition of this attribute of a privacy interest supports the distinction, in terms of personal privacy, between scattered disclosure of the bits of information contained in a rap sheet and revelation of the rap sheet as a whole. The very fact that federal funds have been spent to prepare, index, and maintain these criminal-history files demonstrates that the individual items of information in the summaries would not otherwise be "freely available" either to the officials who have access to the underlying files or to the general public. Indeed, if the summaries were

"freely available," there would be no reason to invoke the FOIA to obtain access to the information they contain. Granted, in many contexts the fact that information is not freely available is no reason to exempt that information from a statute generally requiring its dissemination.

But the issue here is whether the compilation of otherwise hard-to-obtain information alters the privacy interest implicated by disclosure of that information. Plainly there is a vast difference between the public records that might be found after a diligent search of courthouse files, county archives, and local police stations throughout the country and a computerized summary located in a single clearinghouse of information.

This conclusion is supported by the web of federal statutory and regulatory provisions that limits the disclosure of rap-sheet information.

That is, Congress has authorized rap-sheet dissemination to banks, local licensing officials, the securities industry, the nuclear-power industry, and other law enforcement agencies. Further, the FBI has permitted such disclosure to the subject of the rap sheet and, more generally, to assist in the apprehension of wanted persons or fugitives. Finally, the FBI's exchange of rap-sheet information "is subject to cancellation if dissemination is made outside the receiving departments or related agencies." 28 U.S.C. § 534(b). This careful and limited pattern of authorized rap-sheet disclosure fits the dictionary definition of privacy as involving a restriction of information "to the use of a particular person or group or class of persons." Moreover, although perhaps not specific enough to constitute a statutory exemption under FOIA Exemption 3, 5 U.S.C. § 552(b)(3), these statutes and regulations, taken as a whole, evidence a congressional intent to protect the privacy of rap-sheet subjects, and a concomitant recognition of the power of compilations to affect personal privacy that outstrips the combined power of the bits of information contained within. . . .

Also supporting our conclusion that a strong privacy interest inheres in the nondisclosure of compiled computerized information is the Privacy Act of 1974, codified at 5 U.S.C. § 552a. The Privacy Act was passed largely out of concern over "the impact of computer data banks on individual privacy." H.R. Rep. No. 93–1416, p. 7 (1974). The Privacy Act provides generally that "[n]o agency shall disclose any record which is contained in a system of records . . . except pursuant to a written request by, or with the prior written consent of, the individual to whom the record pertains." 5 U.S.C. § 552a(b). Although the Privacy Act contains a variety of exceptions to this rule, including an exemption for information required to be disclosed under the FOIA, see 5 U.S.C. § 552a(b)(2), Congress' basic policy concern regarding the implications of computerized data banks for personal privacy is certainly relevant in our consideration of the privacy interest affected by dissemination of rap sheets from the FBI computer. . . .

V

Exemption 7(C), by its terms, permits an agency to withhold a document only when revelation "could reasonably be expected to constitute an unwarranted invasion of personal privacy." We must next address what factors might warrant an invasion of the interest described in Part IV, supra.

Our previous decisions establish that whether an invasion of privacy is warranted cannot turn on the purposes for which the request for information is made. Except for cases in which the objection to disclosure is based on a claim of privilege and the person requesting disclosure is the party protected by the privilege, the identity of the requesting party has no bearing on the merits of his or her FOIA request. Thus, although the subject of a presentence report can waive a privilege that might defeat a third party's access to that report, *United States Department of Justice v. Julian,* 486 U.S. 1, 13-14 (1988), and although the FBI's policy of granting the subject of a rap sheet access to his own criminal history is consistent with its policy of denying access to all other members of the general public, the rights of the two press respondents in this case are no different from those that might be asserted by any other third party, such as a neighbor or prospective employer. As we have repeatedly

stated, Congress "clearly intended" the FOIA "to give any member of the public as much right to disclosure as one with a special interest [in a particular document]." *NLRB v. Sears, Roebuck & Co.,* 421 U.S. 132, 149 (1975); see *NLRB v. Robbins Tire & Rubber Co.,* 437 U.S. 214, 221 (1978); *FBI v. Abramson,* 456 U.S. 615 (1982). As Professor Davis explained: "The Act's sole concern is with what must be made public or not made public."

Thus whether disclosure of a private document under Exemption 7(C) is warranted must turn on the nature of the requested document and its relationship to "the basic purpose of the Freedom of Information Act 'to open agency action to the light of public scrutiny.'" *Department of Air Force v. Rose,* 425 U.S., at 372, rather than on the particular purpose for which the document is being requested. In our leading case on the FOIA, we declared that the Act was designed to create a broad right of access to "official information." *EPA v. Mink,* 410 U.S. 73, 80 (1973). In his dissent in that case, Justice Douglas characterized the philosophy of the statute by quoting this comment by Henry Steele Commager:

> The generation that made the nation thought secrecy in government one of the instruments of Old World tyranny and committed itself to the principle that a democracy cannot function unless the people are permitted to know what their government is up to. (quoting from *The New York Review of Books,* Oct. 5, 1972, p. 7)

This basic policy of "'full agency disclosure unless information is exempted under clearly delineated statutory language,'" *Department of Air Force v. Rose,* 425 U.S., at 360-361, indeed focuses on the citizens' right to be informed about "what their government is up to." Official information that sheds light on an agency's performance of its statutory duties falls squarely within that statutory purpose. That purpose, however, is not fostered by disclosure of information about private citizens that is accumulated in various governmental files but that reveals little or nothing about an agency's own conduct. In this case—and presumably in the typical case in which one private citizen is seeking information about another—the requester does not intend to discover anything about the conduct of the agency that has possession of the requested records. Indeed, response to this request would not shed any light on the conduct of any government agency or official.

The point is illustrated by our decision in *Rose, supra*. As discussed earlier, we held that the FOIA required the United States Air Force to honor a request for *in camera* submission of disciplinary-hearing summaries maintained in the Academy's Honors and Ethics Code reading files. The summaries obviously contained information that would explain how the disciplinary procedures actually functioned and therefore were an appropriate subject of a FOIA request. All parties, however, agreed that the files should be redacted by deleting information that would identify the particular cadets to whom the summaries related. The deletions were unquestionably appropriate because the names of the particular cadets were irrelevant to the inquiry into the way the Air Force Academy administered its Honor Code; leaving the identifying material in the summaries would therefore have been a "clearly unwarranted" invasion of individual privacy. If, instead of seeking information about the Academy's own conduct, the requests had asked for specific files to obtain information about the persons to whom those files related, the public interest that supported the decision in *Rose* would have been inapplicable. In fact, we explicitly recognized that "the basic purpose of the [FOIA is] to open agency action to the light of public scrutiny."

Respondents argue that there is a twofold public interest in learning about Medico's past arrests or convictions: He allegedly had improper dealings with a corrupt Congressman, and he is an officer of a corporation with defense contracts. But if Medico has, in fact, been arrested or convicted of certain crimes, that information would neither aggravate nor mitigate his allegedly improper relationship with the Congressman; more specifically, it would tell us nothing directly about the character of the Congressman's behavior. Nor would it tell us

anything about the conduct of the Department of Defense (DOD) in awarding one or more contracts to the Medico Company. Arguably a FOIA request to the DOD for records relating to those contracts, or for documents describing the agency's procedures, if any, for determining whether officers of a prospective contractor have criminal records, would constitute an appropriate request for "official information." Conceivably Medico's rap sheet would provide details to include in a news story, but, in itself, this is not the kind of public interest for which Congress enacted the FOIA. In other words, although there is undoubtedly some public interest in anyone's criminal history, especially if the history is in some way related to the subject's dealing with a public official or agency, the FOIA's central purpose is to ensure that the Government's activities be opened to the sharp eye of public scrutiny, not that information about private citizens that happens to be in the warehouse of the Government be so disclosed. Thus, it should come as no surprise that in none of our cases construing the FOIA have we found it appropriate to order a Government agency to honor a FOIA request for information about a particular private citizen. . . .

Finally, we note that Congress has provided that the standard fees for production of documents under the FOIA shall be waived or reduced "if disclosure of the information is in the public interest because it is likely to contribute significantly to public understanding of the operations or activities of the government and is not primarily in the commercial interest of the requester." 5 U.S.C. § 552(a) (4) (A)(iii) (1982 ed., Supp. V). Although such a provision obviously implies that there will be requests that do not meet such a "public interest" standard, we think it relevant to today's inquiry regarding the public interest in release of rap sheets on private citizens that Congress once again expressed the core purpose of the FOIA as "contribute[ing] significantly to public understanding of the operations or activities of the government." . . .

Finally: The privacy interest in maintaining the practical obscurity of rap-sheet information will always be high. When the subject of such a rap sheet is a private citizen and when the information is in the Government's control as a compilation, rather than as a record of "what the Government is up to," the privacy interest protected by Exemption 7(C) is in fact at its apex while the FOIA-based public interest in disclosure is at its nadir.

Such a disparity on the scales of justice holds for a class of cases without regard to individual circumstances; the standard virtues of bright-line rules are thus present, and the difficulties attendant to ad hoc adjudication may be avoided.

Accordingly, we hold as a categorical matter that a third party's request for law enforcement records or information about a private citizen can reasonably be expected to invade that citizen's privacy, and that when the request seeks no "official information" about a Government agency, but merely records that the Government happens to be storing, the invasion of privacy is "unwarranted." The judgment of the Court of Appeals is reversed.

It is so ordered.

Questions

1. What are the two variables that get balanced?
2. The Court says that the reason for the FOIA is so that the citizenry will know what their government is up to. How does this concept enter into the balancing test?

The balancing test for FOIA exemptions relating to invasion of privacy is very similar to the balancing test for special needs warrantless searches and seizures. What gets weighed in the balancing test under FOIA is the individual privacy interest against the public interest in release of private information. In the *Reporter's Committee* case above, the court found a protected privacy interest in the rap sheet that was primarily a matter of public record. Having found a significant privacy interest, the next question was whether the public interest requires invasion of that privacy by release of the rap sheet. What is the public interest in the media's getting hold of Medico's rap sheet? The media says it is in the public interest to know when the "boss" of a crime family has government defense contracts. The Court, however, says that the public interest to be weighed in the balancing test relates to the reason behind the FOIA. The reason behind a requester's request is irrelevant. The purpose of the FOIA is to let citizens learn "what their government is up to." That means the release of information in the public interest is information that would shed light on the agency's performance of its statutory duties. Since release of Medico's rap sheet would not shed light on FBI procedures nor will it help us to assess the defense contracting procedure, release of it would not be in the public interest.

In *Department of Defense v. Federal Labor Relations Authority,* 510 U.S. 487 (1994), a labor union trying to organize federal workers requested the names, work stations, home addresses and other personal information on the civilian employees in the Defense Department. The department released some of the information but withheld the home addresses. The unions filed an unfair labor practice charge against the Department of Defense with the Federal Labor Relations Authority, which ordered the department to produce the addresses. The Court found protected privacy interests in the home addresses and said the public interest would not be served by release of the information. Release of the home information will not help us or the requester assess the performance of the Defense Department and hence is not in the public interest. Furthermore, the Court found that the addresses were protected under the Privacy Act and not releasable under FOIA.

During the late 1980s, American policy toward Haitian nationals who were caught attempting illegal entry into the United States was to return them to Haiti. The Unites States and Haiti had an agreement that we would not grant political asylum and would return them home if Haiti would not persecute them upon return. In an attempt to assess whether Haiti was living up to its end of the agreement, the State Department went to Haiti and interviewed some of the returnees. An American attorney who represented a group of Haitian nationals who sought political asylum in the United States requested the names of the interviewees and other information from the State Department. The agency released nearly all of the information requested, including the findings of the survey, but it blanked out the names of the people it interviewed. In *United States Department of State v. Ray,* 502 U.S. 164 (1991), the Court's decision was consistent with the cases you are familiar with so far. The Court said release of the personal information would not contribute to the public interest of assessing the State Department's performance of its duties.

For more cases in this area of administrative law, see *National Archives and Records Administration v. Favish* (2004), which appears at the end of this chapter; *Bibbles v. Oregon Natural Desert Association,* 519 U.S. 355 (1997); *United States Department of Justice v. Landano,* 508 U.S. 165 (1993); and *Department of the Air Force v. Rose,* 425 U.S. 325 (1976).

We have mentioned elsewhere the concept of unintended or second-order consequences. The FOIA has spawned not only considerable litigation but unintended consequences as well. For example, it can be argued that the foot-dragging in compliance with FOIA requests referred to earlier was not so much evidence of recalcitrance on the part of bureaucrats refusing to comply with the law as it was reflective of a bureaucracy inundated by requests and without the personnel to process them.[39] Estimates are that the federal government receives more than 300,000 FOIA requests each year, that more than 90 percent are granted by the agencies, and that the cost of compliance is upward of $250 million annually.[40] The most common type of request comes from a business attempting to gain an edge on its competition.[41] Furthermore, there is evidence that whereas regulated businesses and parties once turned over information to agencies on request without reservation, those same businesses now resist subpoenas out of fear that the information in agency possession will be turned over to FOIA requesters.[42] Indeed, it appears as though the SEC has found a way around this information problem. SEC staff, rather than asking regulated parties to send information to the agency, are traveling to the regulated businesses to examine information.[43] This way, the information is never in the possession of the agency. Justice Scalia argues that the costs of compliance with the strict deadlines of the FOIA do not outweigh the benefits to society.[44]

This is one of those difficult democratic questions. There appears to be little argument that the American polity is more open now than it was before the FOIA. There also appears to be general agreement that the demands placed on the bureaucracy by the FOIA far exceed early estimates. Compliance is costly.

SUMMARY

Acquisition of Information

1. Generally, there is no violation of the Fifth Amendment's self-incrimination clause whereby an agency requires a regulated business to maintain certain records, the agency inspects those records, and, as a result, the agency imposes sanctions on the regulated business.

2. Agencies do not need probable cause to issue subpoenas for information. Indeed, the courts will allow a "fishing expedition" via the administrative subpoena.

3. When the sufficiency of an agency subpoena is challenged in court, the test is simply whether the topic under inquiry is a topic that the agency is empowered to investigate.

4. Cases involving physical inspections or searches by agencies fall into two broad categories: those that require a warrant and those that do not.

   a. Those that require a warrant are situations where there is a high expectation of privacy in the place searched.

   b. Those that do not require a warrant fall into three categories

      (1) Businesses that are in heavily regulated industries can be searched without a warrant.

      (2) Where there is a reduced expectation of privacy, warrantless searches may be reasonable.

      (3) The special needs doctrine says that warrantless, suspicionless searches and seizures are reasonable depending on the outcome of a balancing test weighing the privacy interests of the individual against the public interest that justifies the special need.

Agency Release of Information Under the Freedom of Information Act

1. The language of the FOIA compels release of information under normal circumstances. There are nine situations in which an agency may withhold information.

2. Although it was not always the case, today, if an agency can withhold information (especially commercial or financial information), it should.

3. Exemption 4 allows the following kind of information to be withheld:

   a. trade secrets

   b. commercial or financial information if (a) it was obtained from a person or business, (b) it is privileged (attorney/client), or (c) it is confidential

4. Commercial or financial information is confidential under the following circumstances:

   a. This information would not normally be released to the public by the individual or business that provided it.

   b. To withhold this information would be consistent with the legislative purposes of the exemption if (a) release would impair the government's ability to obtain such information in the future and (b) release of the information would harm the competitive edge of the provider.

5. Exemption 5 protects privileged information such as attorney/client and executive privilege. To qualify for Exemption 5, the material sought must predate the decision, and it must not have been relied on to make the decision.

6. Exemptions 6 and 7(c) protect citizens from release of information an agency might possess that would constitute a clearly unwarranted invasion of privacy. A balancing test determines whether an invasion of privacy would be "clearly unwarranted." The privacy interest of the individual is weighed against the public interest. The public interest means the citizens' right to know what government is up to. Generally information will fall under the public interest if it helps us assess the agency's performance of its duties.

END-OF-CHAPTER CASES

Dow Chemical Company v. United States
476 U.S. 227 (1986)

Chief Justice Burger delivered the opinion of the Court, in which Justices White, Rehnquist, Stevens, and O'Connor joined, and in Part III of which Justices Brennan, Marshall, Blackmun, and Powell joined. Justice Powell filed an opinion concurring in part and dissenting in part, in which Justices Brennan, Marshall, and Blackmun joined.

We granted certiorari to review the holding of the Court of Appeals (a) that the Environmental Protection Agency's aerial observation of petitioner's plant complex did not exceed EPA's statutory investigatory authority, and (b) that EPA's aerial photography of petitioner's 2,000-acre plant complex without a warrant was not a search under the Fourth Amendment.

I

Petitioner Dow Chemical Co. operates a 2,000-acre facility manufacturing chemicals at Midland, Michigan. The facility consists of numerous covered buildings, with manufacturing equipment and piping conduits located between the various buildings exposed to visual observation from the air. At all times, Dow has maintained elaborate security around the perimeter of the complex barring ground-level public views of these areas. It also investigates any low-level flights by aircraft over the facility. Dow has not undertaken, however, to conceal all manufacturing equipment within the complex from aerial views. Dow maintains that the cost of covering its exposed equipment would be prohibitive.

In early 1978, enforcement officials of EPA, with Dow's consent, made an on-site inspection of two powerplants in this complex. A subsequent EPA request for a second inspection, however, was denied, and EPA did not thereafter seek an administrative search warrant. Instead, EPA employed a commercial aerial photographer, using a standard floor-mounted, precision aerial mapping camera, to take photographs of the facility from altitudes of 12,000, 3,000, and 1,200 feet. At all times the aircraft was lawfully within navigable airspace. EPA did not inform Dow of this aerial photography, but when Dow became aware of it, Dow brought suit in the District Court alleging that EPA's action violated the Fourth Amendment and was beyond EPA's statutory investigative authority. The District Court granted Dow's motion for summary judgment on the ground that EPA had no authority to take aerial photographs and that doing so was a search violating the Fourth Amendment. EPA was permanently enjoined from taking aerial photographs of Dow's premises and from disseminating, releasing, or copying the photographs already taken. The Court of Appeals then held that EPA clearly acted within its statutory powers even absent express authorization for aerial surveillance, concluding that the delegation of general investigative authority to EPA, similar to that of other law enforcement agencies, was sufficient to support the use of aerial photography. Dow claims first that EPA has no authority to use aerial photography to implement its statutory authority for "site inspection" under § 114(a) of the Clean Air Act, 42 U.S.C. § 7414(a); second, Dow claims EPA's use of aerial photography was a "search" of an area that, notwithstanding the large size of the plant, was within an "industrial curtilage" rather than an "open field," and that it had a reasonable expectation of privacy from such photography protected by the Fourth Amendment. . . .

III

Congress has vested in EPA certain investigatory and enforcement authority, without spelling out precisely how this authority was to be exercised in all the myriad circumstances that might arise in monitoring matters relating to clean air and water standards. When Congress invests an agency with enforcement and investigatory authority, it is not necessary to identify explicitly each and every technique that may be used in the course of executing the statutory mission. Aerial observation authority, for example, is not usually expressly extended to police for traffic control, but it could hardly be thought necessary for a legislative body to tell police that aerial observation could be employed for traffic control of a metropolitan area, or to expressly authorize police to send messages to ground highway patrols that a particular over-the-road truck was traveling in excess of 55 miles per hour. Common sense and ordinary human experience teach that traffic violators are apprehended by observation.

Regulatory or enforcement authority generally carries with it all the modes of inquiry and investigation traditionally employed or useful to execute the authority granted. Environmental standards such as clean air and clean water cannot be enforced only in libraries and laboratories, helpful as those institutions may be. . . . We hold that the use of aerial observation and photography is within EPA's statutory authority. . . . We turn now to Dow's contention that taking aerial photographs constituted a search without a warrant, thereby violating Dow's rights under the Fourth Amendment. In making this contention, however, Dow concedes that a simple flyover with naked-eye observation, or the taking of a photograph from a nearby hillside overlooking such a facility, would give rise to no Fourth Amendment problem. We pointed out in *Donovan v. Dewey,* 452 U.S. 594 (1981), that the Government has "greater latitude to conduct warrantless inspections of commercial property" because "the expectation of privacy that the owner of commercial property enjoys in such property differs significantly from the sanctity accorded an individual's home." We emphasized that unlike a homeowner's interest in his dwelling, "[t]he interest of the owner of commercial property is not one in being free from any inspections." And with regard to regulatory inspections, we have held that "[w]hat is observable by the public is observable without a warrant, by the Government inspector as well." *Marshall v. Barlow's, Inc.,* 436 U.S., at 315.

Oliver recognized that in the open field context, "the public and police lawfully may survey lands from the air." 466 U.S., at 179. Here, EPA was not employing some unique sensory device that, for example, could penetrate the walls of buildings and record conversations in Dow's plants, offices, or laboratories, but rather a conventional, albeit precise, commercial camera commonly used in mapmaking. The Government asserts it has not yet enlarged the photographs to any significant degree, but Dow points out that simple magnification permits identification of objects such as wires as small as ½ inch in diameter.

It may well be, as the Government concedes, that surveillance of private property by using highly sophisticated surveillance equipment not generally available to the public, such as satellite technology, might be constitutionally proscribed absent a warrant. But the photographs here are not so revealing of intimate details as to raise constitutional concerns. Although they undoubtedly give EPA more detailed information than naked-eye views, they remain limited to an outline of the facility's buildings and equipment. The mere fact that human vision is enhanced somewhat, at least to the degree here, does not give rise to constitutional problems. An electronic device to penetrate walls or windows so as to hear and record confidential discussions of chemical formulae or other trade secrets would raise very different and far more serious questions; other protections such as trade secret laws are available to protect commercial activities from private surveillance by competitors.

We conclude that the open areas of an industrial plant complex with numerous plant structures spread over an area of 2,000 acres are not analogous to the "curtilage" of a dwelling for purposes of aerial surveillance; such an industrial complex is more comparable to an open field and as such it is open to the view and observation of persons in aircraft lawfully in the public airspace immediately above or sufficiently near the area for the reach of cameras. We hold that the taking of aerial photographs of an industrial plant complex from navigable airspace is not a search prohibited by the Fourth Amendment.

Affirmed.

Ferguson v. City of Charleston
532 U.S. 67 (2001)

Justice Stevens delivered the opinion of the Court, in which Justices O'Connor, Souter, Ginsburg, and Breyer joined. Justice Kennedy filed an opinion concurring in the judgment. Justice Scalia filed a dissenting opinion, in which Chief Justice Rehnquist and Justice Thomas joined as to Part II.

In this case, we must decide whether a state hospital's performance of a diagnostic test to obtain evidence of a patient's criminal conduct for law enforcement purposes is an unreasonable search if the patient has not consented to the procedure. More narrowly, the question is whether the interest in using the threat of criminal sanctions to deter pregnant women from using cocaine can justify a departure from the general rule that an official nonconsensual search is unconstitutional if not authorized by a valid warrant.

I

In the fall of 1988, staff members at the public hospital operated in the city of Charleston by the Medical University of South Carolina (MUSC) became concerned about an apparent increase in the use of cocaine by patients who were receiving prenatal treatment. In response to this perceived increase, as of April 1989,

MUSC began to order drug screens to be performed on urine samples from maternity patients who were suspected of using cocaine. If a patient tested positive, she was then referred by MUSC staff to the county substance abuse commission for counseling and treatment. However, despite the referrals, the incidence of cocaine use among the patients at MUSC did not appear to change.

Some four months later, Nurse Shirley Brown, the case manager for the MUSC obstetrics department, heard a news broadcast reporting that the police in Greenville, South Carolina, were arresting pregnant users of cocaine on the theory that such use harmed the fetus and was therefore child abuse. Nurse Brown discussed the story with MUSC's general counsel, Joseph C. Good, Jr., who then contacted Charleston Solicitor Charles Condon in order to offer MUSC's cooperation in prosecuting mothers whose children tested positive for drugs at birth.

After receiving Good's letter, Solicitor Condon took the first steps in developing the policy at issue in this case. He organized the initial meetings, decided who would participate, and issued the invitations, in which he described his plan to prosecute women who tested positive for cocaine while pregnant. The task force that Condon formed included representatives of MUSC, the police, the County Substance Abuse

Commission and the Department of Social Services. Their deliberations led to MUSC's adoption of a 12-page document entitled "POLICY M-7," dealing with the subject of "Management of Drug Abuse During Pregnancy."

The first three pages of Policy M-7 set forth the procedure to be followed by the hospital staff to "identify/assist pregnant patients suspected of drug abuse." The first section, entitled the "Identification of Drug Abusers," provided that a patient should be tested for cocaine through a urine drug screen if she met one or more of nine criteria [the following are the nine criteria taken from footnote #4 from the opinion of the Court]:

"1. No prenatal care

"2. Late prenatal care after 24 weeks gestation

"3. Incomplete prenatal care

"4. Abruptio placentae

"5. Intrauterine fetal death

"6. Preterm labor 'of no obvious cause'

"7. IUGR [intrauterine growth retardation] 'of no obvious cause'

"8. Previously known drug or alcohol abuse

"9. Unexplained congenital anomalies."

It also stated that a chain of custody should be followed when obtaining and testing urine samples, presumably to make sure that the results could be used in subsequent criminal proceedings. The policy also provided for education and referral to a substance abuse clinic for patients who tested positive. Most important, it added the threat of law enforcement intervention that "provided the necessary 'leverage' to make the policy effective." That threat was, as respondents candidly acknowledge, essential to the program's success in getting women into treatment and keeping them there.

The threat of law enforcement involvement was set forth in two protocols, the first dealing with the identification of drug use during pregnancy, and the second with identification of drug use after labor. Under the latter protocol, the police were to be notified without delay

and the patient promptly arrested. Under the former, after the initial positive drug test, the police were to be notified (and the patient arrested) only if the patient tested positive for cocaine a second time or if she missed an appointment with a substance abuse counselor. In 1990, however, the policy was modified at the behest of the solicitor's office to give the patient who tested positive during labor, like the patient who tested positive during a prenatal care visit, an opportunity to avoid arrest by consenting to substance abuse treatment.

The policy also prescribed in detail the precise offenses with which a woman could be charged, depending on the stage of her pregnancy. If the pregnancy was 27 weeks or less, the patient was to be charged with simple possession. If it was 28 weeks or more, she was to be charged with possession and distribution to a person under the age of 18—in this case, the fetus. If she delivered "while testing positive for illegal drugs," she was also to be charged with unlawful neglect of a child. Under the policy, the police were instructed to interrogate the arrestee in order "to ascertain the identity of the subject who provided illegal drugs to the suspect." Other than the provisions describing the substance abuse treatment to be offered to women who tested positive, the policy made no mention of any change in the prenatal care of such patients, nor did it prescribe any special treatment for the newborns.

II

Petitioners are 10 women who received obstetrical care at MUSC and who were arrested after testing positive for cocaine. Four of them were arrested during the initial implementation of the policy; they were not offered the opportunity to receive drug treatment as an alternative to arrest. The others were arrested after the policy was modified in 1990; they either failed to comply with the terms of the drug treatment program or tested positive for a second time. Respondents include the city of Charleston, law enforcement officials who helped develop and enforce the policy, and representatives of MUSC.

Petitioners' complaint challenged the validity of the policy under various theories, including the claim that warrantless and nonconsensual drug tests conducted for criminal investigatory purposes were unconstitutional searches. Respondents advanced two principal defenses to the constitutional claim: (1) that, as a matter of fact, petitioners had consented to the searches; and (2) that, as a matter of law, the searches were reasonable, even absent consent, because they were justified by special non-law-enforcement purposes. The District Court rejected the second defense because the searches in question "were not done by the medical university for independent purposes. [Instead,] the police came in and there was an agreement reached that the positive screens would be shared with the police." Accordingly, the District Court submitted the factual defense to the jury with instructions that required a verdict in favor of petitioners unless the jury found consent. The jury found for respondents.

Petitioners appealed, arguing that the evidence was not sufficient to support the jury's consent finding. The Court of Appeals for the Fourth Circuit affirmed, but without reaching the question of consent. 186 F.3d 469 (1999). Disagreeing with the District Court, the majority of the appellate panel held that the searches were reasonable as a matter of law under our line of cases recognizing that "special needs" may, in certain exceptional circumstances, justify a search policy designed to serve non-law-enforcement ends.

We granted certiorari, 528 U.S. 1187 (2000), to review the appellate court's holding on the "special needs" issue. Because we do not reach the question of the sufficiency of the evidence with respect to consent, we necessarily assume for purposes of our decision—as did the Court of Appeals—that the searches were conducted without the informed consent of the patients. We conclude that the judgment should be reversed and the case remanded for a decision on the consent issue.

III

Because MUSC is a state hospital, the members of its staff are government actors, subject to the strictures of the Fourth Amendment. *New Jersey v. T. L. O.,* 469 U.S. 325, 335-337 (1985).

Moreover, the urine tests conducted by those staff members were indisputably searches within the meaning of the Fourth Amendment. *Skinner v. Railway Labor Executives' Assn.,* 489 U.S. 602, 617 (1989). Neither the District Court nor the Court of Appeals concluded that any of the nine criteria used to identify the women to be searched provided either probable cause to believe that they were using cocaine, or even the basis for a reasonable suspicion of such use. Rather, the District Court and the Court of Appeals viewed the case as one involving MUSC's right to conduct searches without warrants or probable cause. Furthermore, given the posture in which the case comes to us, we must assume for purposes of our decision that the tests were performed without the informed consent of the patients.

Because the hospital seeks to justify its authority to conduct drug tests and to turn the results over to law enforcement agents without the knowledge or consent of the patients, this case differs from the four previous cases in which we have considered whether comparable drug tests "fit within the closely guarded category of constitutionally permissible suspicionless searches." *Chandler v. Miller,* 520 U.S. 305, 309 (1997). In three of those cases, we sustained drug tests for railway employees involved in train accidents, *Skinner v. Railway Labor Executives' Assn.,* 489 U.S. 602 (1989), for United States Customs Service employees seeking promotion to certain sensitive positions, *Treasury Employees v. Von Raab,* 489 U.S. 656 (1989), and for high school students participating in interscholastic sports, *Vernonia School Dist. 47J v. Acton,* 515 U.S. 646 (1995). In the fourth case, we struck down such testing for candidates for designated state offices as unreasonable. *Chandler v. Miller,* 520 U.S. 305 (1997).

In each of those cases, we employed a balancing test that weighed the intrusion on the individual's interest in privacy against the "special needs" that supported the program. As an initial matter, we note that the invasion of privacy in this case is far more substantial than in those cases. In the previous four cases, there was no misunderstanding about the purpose of the test or the potential use of the test results, and there were protections against the dissemination of the results to third parties. The use of an adverse test result to disqualify one from eligibility for a particular benefit, such as a promotion or an opportunity to participate in an extracurricular activity, involves a less serious intrusion on privacy than the unauthorized dissemination of such results to third parties. The reasonable expectation of privacy enjoyed by the typical patient undergoing diagnostic tests in a hospital is that the results of those tests will not be shared with nonmedical personnel without her consent. . . . In none of our prior cases was there any intrusion upon that kind of expectation. The critical difference between those four drug-testing cases and this one, however, lies in the nature of the "special need" asserted as justification for the warrantless searches. In each of those earlier cases, the "special need" that was advanced as a justification for the absence of a warrant or individualized suspicion was one divorced from the State's general interest in law enforcement. This point was emphasized both in the majority opinions sustaining the programs in the first three cases, as well as in the dissent in the *Chandler* case. In this case, however, the central and indispensable feature of the policy from its inception was the use of law enforcement to coerce the patients into substance abuse treatment. This fact distinguishes this case from circumstances in which physicians or psychologists, in the course of ordinary medical procedures aimed at helping the patient herself, come across information that under rules of law or ethics is subject to reporting requirements, which no one has challenged here. . . .

Respondents argue in essence that their ultimate purpose—namely, protecting the health of both mother and child—is a beneficent one. In *Chandler,* however, we did not simply accept the State's invocation of a "special need." Instead, we carried out a "close review" of the scheme at issue before concluding that the need in question was not "special," as that term has been defined in our cases. 520 U.S. at 322. In this case, a review of the M-7 policy plainly reveals that the purpose actually served by the MUSC searches "is ultimately indistinguishable from the general interest in crime control."

In looking to the programmatic purpose, we consider all the available evidence in order to determine the relevant primary purpose. In this case, as Judge Blake put it in her dissent below, "it . . . is clear from the record that an initial and continuing focus of the policy was on the arrest and prosecution of drug-abusing mothers. . . ." 186 F.3d at 484. Tellingly, the document codifying the policy incorporates the police's operational guidelines. It devotes its attention to the chain of custody, the range of possible criminal charges, and the logistics of police notification and arrests. Nowhere, however, does the document discuss different courses of medical treatment for either mother or infant, aside from treatment for the mother's addiction.

Moreover, throughout the development and application of the policy, the Charleston prosecutors and police were extensively involved in the day-to-day administration of the policy. Police and prosecutors decided who would receive the reports of positive drug screens and what information would be included with those reports. Law enforcement officials also helped determine the procedures to be followed when performing the screens. In the course of the policy's administration, they had access to Nurse Brown's medical files on the women who tested positive, routinely attended the substance abuse team's meetings, and regularly received copies of team documents discussing the women's progress. Police took pains to coordinate the timing and circumstances of the arrests with MUSC staff, and, in particular, Nurse Brown.

While the ultimate goal of the program may well have been to get the women in question into substance abuse treatment and off of drugs, the immediate objective of the searches was to generate evidence for law enforcement purposes in order to reach that goal. The threat of law enforcement may ultimately have been intended as a means to an end, but the direct and primary purpose of MUSC's policy was to ensure the use of those means. In our opinion, this distinction is critical. Because law enforcement involvement always serves some broader social purpose or objective, under respondents' view, virtually any nonconsensual suspicionless search could be immunized under the special needs doctrine by defining the search solely in terms of its ultimate, rather than immediate, purpose. Such an approach is inconsistent with the Fourth Amendment. Given the primary purpose of the Charleston program, which was to use the threat of arrest and prosecution in order to force women into treatment, and given the extensive involvement of law enforcement officials at every stage of the policy, this case simply does not fit within the closely guarded category of "special needs."

The fact that positive test results were turned over to the police does not merely provide a basis for distinguishing our prior cases applying the "special needs" balancing approach to the determination of drug use. It also provides an affirmative reason for enforcing the strictures of the Fourth Amendment. While state hospital employees, like other citizens, may have a duty to provide the police with evidence of criminal conduct that they inadvertently acquire in the course of routine treatment, when they undertake to obtain such evidence from their patients for the specific purpose of incriminating those patients, they have a special obligation to make sure that the patients are fully informed about their constitutional rights, as standards of knowing waiver require. *Miranda v. Arizona,* 384 U.S. 436.

As respondents have repeatedly insisted, their motive was benign rather than punitive. Such a motive, however, cannot justify a departure from Fourth Amendment protections, given the pervasive involvement of law enforcement with the development and application of the MUSC policy. The stark and unique fact that characterizes this case is that Policy M-7 was designed to obtain evidence of criminal conduct by the tested patients that would be turned over to the police and that could be admissible in subsequent criminal prosecutions. While respondents are correct that drug abuse both was and is a serious problem, "the gravity of the threat alone cannot be dispositive of questions concerning what means law enforcement officers may employ to pursue a given purpose."

The Fourth Amendment's general prohibition against nonconsensual, warrantless, and suspicionless searches necessarily applies to such a policy. See, e.g., *Chandler,* 520 U.S. at 308; *Skinner,* 498 U.S. at 619.

Accordingly, the judgment of the Court of Appeals is reversed, and the case is remanded for further proceedings consistent with this opinion.

It is so ordered.

Justice Scalia dissenting, joined by Chief Justice Rehnquist and Justice Thomas as to Part II.

There is always an unappealing aspect to the use of doctors and nurses, ministers of mercy, to obtain incriminating evidence against the supposed objects of their ministration—although here, it is correctly pointed out, the doctors and nurses were ministering not just to the mothers but also to the children whom their cooperation with the police was meant to protect. But whatever may be the correct social judgment concerning the desirability of what occurred here, that is not the issue in the present case. The Constitution does not resolve all difficult social questions, but leaves the vast majority of them to resolution by debate and the democratic process—which would produce a decision by the citizens of Charleston, through their elected representatives, to forbid or permit the police action at issue here. The question before us is a narrower one: whether, whatever the desirability of this police conduct, it violates the Fourth Amendment's prohibition of unreasonable searches and seizures. In my view, it plainly does not.

I

The first step in Fourth Amendment analysis is to identify the search or seizure at issue. What petitioners, the Court, and to a lesser extent the concurrence really object to is not the urine testing, but the hospital's reporting of positive drug-test results to police. But the latter is obviously not a search. At most it may be a "derivative use of the product of a past unlawful search," which, of course, "works no new Fourth Amendment wrong" and "presents a question, not of rights, but of remedies." *United States v. Calandra,* 414 U.S. 338, 354 (1974). There is only one act that could conceivably be regarded as a search of petitioners in the present case: the taking of the urine sample. I suppose the testing of that urine for traces of unlawful drugs could be considered a search of sorts, but the Fourth Amendment protects only against searches of citizens' "persons, houses, papers, and effects"; and it is entirely unrealistic to regard urine as one of the "effects" (i.e., part of the property) of the person who has passed and abandoned it. *California v. Greenwood,* 486 U.S. 35 (1988) (garbage left at curb is not property protected by the Fourth Amendment). Some would argue, I suppose, that testing of the urine is prohibited by some generalized privacy right "emanating" from the "penumbras" of the Constitution (a question that is not before us); but it is not even arguable that the testing of urine that has been lawfully obtained is a Fourth Amendment search. (I may add that, even if it were, the factors legitimizing the taking of the sample, which I discuss below, would likewise legitimize the testing of it.)

It is rudimentary Fourth Amendment law that a search which has been consented to is not unreasonable. There is no contention in the present case that the urine samples were extracted forcibly. The only conceivable bases for saying that they were obtained without consent are the contentions (1) that the consent was coerced by the patients' need for medical treatment, (2) that the consent was uninformed because the patients were not told that the tests would include testing for drugs, and (3) that the consent was uninformed because the patients were not told that the results of the tests would be provided to the police. (When the court below said that it was reserving the factual issue of consent, see 186 F.3d 469, 476 [CA4 1999] it was referring at most to these three— and perhaps just to the last two.)

Under our established Fourth Amendment law, the last two contentions would not suffice, even without reference to the special-needs doctrine. The Court's analogizing of this case to *Miranda v. Arizona,* 384 U.S. 436 (1966), and its claim that "standards of knowing waiver" apply, are flatly contradicted by our jurisprudence, which shows that using lawfully (but deceivingly) obtained material for purposes other than those represented, and giving that material or information derived from it to the police, is not unconstitutional. . . .

Until today, we have never held—or even suggested—that material which a person voluntarily entrusts to someone else cannot be given by that person to the police, and used for whatever evidence it may contain. Without so much as discussing the point, the Court today opens a hole in our Fourth Amendment jurisprudence, the size and shape of which is entirely indeterminate. Today's holding would be remarkable enough if the confidential relationship violated by the police conduct were at least one protected by state law. It would be surprising to learn, for example, that in a State which recognizes a spousal evidentiary privilege the police cannot use evidence obtained from a cooperating husband or wife. But today's holding goes even beyond that, since there does not exist any physician-patient privilege in South Carolina. See, e.g., *Peagler v. Atlantic Coast R. R. Co.,* 101 S.E.2d 821 (1958). Since the Court declines even to discuss the issue, it leaves law enforcement officials entirely in the dark as to when they can use incriminating evidence obtained from "trusted" sources. Presumably the lines will be drawn in the case-by-case development of a whole new branch of Fourth Amendment jurisprudence, taking yet another social judgment (which confidential relationships ought not be invaded by the police) out of democratic control, and confiding it to the uncontrolled judgment of this Court—uncontrolled because there is no common-law precedent to guide it. I would adhere to our established law, which says that information obtained through violation of a relationship of trust is obtained consensually, and is hence not a search.

I think it clear, therefore, that there is no basis for saying that obtaining of the urine sample was unconstitutional. The special-needs doctrine is thus quite irrelevant, since it operates only to validate searches and seizures that are otherwise unlawful. In the ensuing discussion, however, I shall assume (contrary to legal precedent) that the taking of the urine sample was (either because of the patients' necessitous circumstances, or because of failure to disclose that the urine would be tested for drugs, or because of failure to disclose that the results of the test would be given to the police) coerced. Indeed, I shall even assume (contrary to common sense) that the testing of the urine constituted an unconsented search of the patients' effects. On those assumptions, the special-needs doctrine would become relevant; and, properly applied, would validate what was done here.

The conclusion of the Court that the special-needs doctrine is inapplicable rests upon its contention that respondents "undertook to obtain [drug] evidence from their patients" not for any medical purpose, but "for the specific purpose of incriminating those patients." In other words, the purported medical rationale was merely a pretext; there was no special need. See *Skinner v. Railway Labor Executives' Assn.,* 489 U.S. 602, 621 (1989). This contention contradicts the District Court's finding of fact that the goal of the testing policy "was not to arrest patients but to facilitate their treatment and protect both the mother and unborn child." This finding is binding upon us unless clearly erroneous, see Fed. Rule Civ. Proc. 52(a). Not only do I find it supportable; I think any other finding would have to be overturned. . . .

In sum, there can be no basis for the Court's purported ability to "distinguish this case from circumstances in which physicians or psychologists, in the course of ordinary medical procedures aimed at helping the patient herself, come across information that . . . is subject to reporting requirements," unless it is this: That the addition of a law-enforcement-related purpose to a legitimate medical purpose destroys applicability of the "special-needs" doctrine. But that is quite impossible, since the special-needs doctrine was developed, and is ordinarily employed, precisely to enable searches by law enforcement

officials who, of course, ordinarily have a law enforcement objective. Thus, in *Griffin v. Wisconsin,* 483 U.S. 868 (1987), a probation officer received a tip from a detective that petitioner, a felon on parole, possessed a firearm. Accompanied by police, he conducted a warrantless search of petitioner's home. The weapon was found and used as evidence in the probationer's trial for unlawful possession of a firearm. Affirming denial of a motion to suppress, we concluded that the "special need" of assuring compliance with terms of release justified a warrantless search of petitioner's home. . . .

As I indicated at the outset, it is not the function of this Court—at least not in Fourth Amendment cases—to weigh petitioners' privacy interest against the State's interest in meeting the crisis of "crack babies" that developed in the late 1980's. I cannot refrain from observing, however, that the outcome of a wise weighing of those interests is by no means clear. The initial goal of the doctors and nurses who conducted cocaine-testing in this case was to refer pregnant drug addicts to treatment centers, and to prepare for necessary treatment of their possibly affected children. When the doctors and nurses agreed to the program providing test results to the police, they did so because (in addition to the fact that child abuse was required by law to be reported) they wanted to use the sanction of arrest as a strong incentive for their addicted patients to undertake drug-addiction treatment. And the police themselves used it for that benign purpose, as is shown by the fact that only 30 of 253 women testing positive for cocaine were ever arrested, and only 2 of those prosecuted. It would not be unreasonable to conclude that today's judgment, authorizing the assessment of damages against the county solicitor and individual doctors and nurses who participated in the program, proves once again that no good deed goes unpunished.

But as far as the Fourth Amendment is concerned: There was no unconsented search in this case. And if there was, it would have been validated by the special-needs doctrine. For these reasons, I respectfully dissent.

National Archives and Records Administration v. Favish
124 S. Ct. 1570 (2004)

Justice Kennedy delivered the opinion for a unanimous Court.

This case requires us to interpret the Freedom of Information Act (FOIA), 5 U.S.C. § 552. FOIA does not apply if the requested data fall within one or more exemptions. Exemption 7(C) excuses from disclosure "records or information compiled for law enforcement purposes" if their production "could reasonably be expected to constitute an unwarranted invasion of personal privacy." . . .

In *Department of Justice v. Reporters Comm. for Freedom of Press,* 489 U.S. 749, we considered the scope of Exemption 7(C) and held that release of the document at issue would be a prohibited invasion of the personal privacy of the person to whom the document referred. The principal document involved was the criminal record, or rap sheet, of the person who himself objected to the disclosure. Here, the information pertains to an official investigation into the circumstances surrounding an apparent suicide. The initial question is whether the exemption extends to the decedent's family when the family objects to the release of photographs showing the condition of the body at the scene of death. If we find the decedent's family does have a personal privacy interest recognized by the statute, we must then consider whether that privacy claim is outweighed by the public interest in disclosure.

I

Vincent Foster, Jr., deputy counsel to President Clinton, was found dead in Fort Marcy Park, located just outside Washington, D. C. The United States Park Police conducted the initial investigation and took color photographs of the death scene, including 10 pictures of Foster's body. The investigation concluded that Foster committed suicide by shooting himself with a revolver. Subsequent investigations by the Federal Bureau of Investigation, committees of the Senate and the House of Representatives, and independent counsels Robert Fiske and Kenneth Starr reached the same conclusion. Despite the unanimous finding of these five investigations, a citizen interested in the matter, Allan Favish, remained skeptical. Favish is now a respondent in this proceeding. In an earlier proceeding, Favish was the associate counsel for Accuracy in Media (AIM), which applied under FOIA for Foster's death-scene photographs. After the National Park Service, which then maintained custody of the pictures, resisted disclosure, Favish filed suit on behalf of AIM in the District Court for the District of Columbia to compel production. The District Court granted summary judgment against AIM. The Court of Appeals for the District of Columbia unanimously affirmed. *Accuracy in Media, Inc. v. National Park Serv.,* 194 F.3d 120 (1999).

Still convinced that the Government's investigations were "'grossly incomplete and untrustworthy,'" Favish filed the present FOIA request in his own name, seeking, among other things, 11 pictures, 1 showing Foster's eyeglasses and 10 depicting various parts of Foster's body. Like the National Park Service, the Office of Independent Counsel (OIC) refused the request under Exemption 7(C).

Again, Favish sued to compel production, this time in the United States District Court for the Central District of California. . . . On the merits, the court granted partial summary judgment to OIC. With the exception of the picture showing Foster's eyeglasses, the court upheld OIC's claim of exemption. Relying on the so-called Vaughn index provided by the Government—a narrative description of the withheld photos, see *Vaughn v. Rosen,* 84 F.2d 820 (CADC 1973)—the court held, first, that Foster's surviving family members enjoy personal privacy interests that could be infringed by disclosure of the photographs. It then found, with respect to the asserted public interest, that "[Favish] has not sufficiently explained how disclosure of these photographs will advance his investigation into Foster's death." Any purported public interest in disclosure, moreover, "is lessened because of the exhaustive investigation that has already occurred regarding Foster's death." Balancing the competing interests, the court concluded that "the privacy interests of the Foster family members outweigh the public interest in disclosure."

On the first appeal to the Court of Appeals for the Ninth Circuit, the majority reversed and remanded, . . .217 F.3d 1168 (2000). . . .

The Court of Appeals, however, agreed with the District Court that the exemption recognizes the Foster family members' right to personal privacy. . . . Nevertheless, the majority held that the District Court erred in balancing the relevant interests based only on the Vaughn index. . . . It remanded the case to the District Court to examine the photos in camera and, "consistent with [the Court of Appeals'] opinion," "balance the effect of their release on the privacy of the Foster family against the public benefit to be obtained by their release."

On remand, the District Court ordered release of the following five photographs:

"The photograph identified as '3—VF's [Vincent Foster's] body looking down from top of berm' must be released, as the photograph is not so explicit as to overcome the public interest.

"The photograph entitled '5—VF's body—focusing on Rt. side of shoulder arm' is again of such a nature as to be discoverable in that it is not focused in such a manner as to unnecessarily impact the privacy interests of the family.

"The photograph entitled '1—Right hand showing gun & thumb in guard' is discoverable as it may be probative of the public's right to know.

"The photograph entitled '4—VF's body focusing on right side and arm' is discoverable.

"The photograph entitled '5—VF's body—focus on top of head thru heavy foliage' is discoverable."

On the second appeal to the same panel, the majority, affirmed in part. Without providing any explanation, it upheld the release of all the pictures, "except that photo 3—VF's body looking down from top of berm is to be withheld."

We granted OIC's petition for a writ of *certiorari* to resolve a conflict in the Courts of Appeals over the proper interpretation of Exemption 7(C). The only documents at issue in this case are the four photographs the Court of Appeals ordered released in its 2002 unpublished opinion. We reverse.

The OIC terminated its operations on March 23, 2004, and transferred all records—including the photographs that are the subject of Favish's FOIA request—to the National Archives and Records Administration. The National Archives and Records Administration has been substituted as petitioner in the caption of this case. As all the actions relevant to our disposition of the case took place before March 23, 2004, we continue to refer to petitioner as OIC in this opinion.

II

It is common ground among the parties that the death-scene photographs in OIC's possession are "records or information compiled for law enforcement purposes" as that phrase is used in Exemption 7(C). This leads to the question whether disclosure of the four photographs "could reasonably be expected to constitute an unwarranted invasion of personal privacy."

Favish contends the family has no personal privacy interest covered by Exemption 7(C). His argument rests on the proposition that the information is only about the decedent, not his family. FOIA's right to personal privacy, in his view, means only "the right to control information about oneself." . . .

In a sworn declaration filed with the District Court, Foster's sister, Sheila Foster Anthony, stated that the family had been harassed by, and deluged with requests from, "[p]olitical and commercial opportunists" who sought to profit from Foster's suicide. In particular, she was "horrified and devastated by [a] photograph [already] leaked to the press." "Every time I see it," Sheila Foster Anthony wrote, "I have nightmares and heart-pounding insomnia as I visualize how he must have spent his last few minutes and seconds of his life." She opposed the disclosure of the disputed pictures because "I fear that the release of additional photographs certainly would set off another round of intense scrutiny by the media. Undoubtedly, the photographs would be placed on the Internet for world consumption. Once again my family would be the focus of conceivably unsavory and distasteful media coverage." "[R]leasing any photographs," Sheila Foster Anthony continued, "would constitute a painful unwarranted invasion of my privacy, my mother's privacy, my sister's privacy, and the privacy of Lisa Foster Moody (Vince's widow), her three children, and other members of the Foster family."

As we shall explain below, we think it proper to conclude from Congress' use of the term "personal privacy" that it intended to permit family members to assert their own privacy rights against public intrusions long deemed impermissible under the common law and in our cultural traditions. This does not mean that the family is in the same position as the individual who is the subject of the disclosure. We have little difficulty, however, in finding in our case law and traditions the right of family members to direct and control disposition of the body of the deceased and to limit attempts to exploit pictures of the deceased family member's remains for public purposes. . . .

Our ruling that the personal privacy protected by Exemption 7(C) extends to family members who object to the disclosure of graphic details surrounding their relative's death does not end the case. Although this privacy interest is within the terms of the exemption, the statute directs nondisclosure only where the information "could reasonably be expected to constitute an unwarranted invasion" of the family's personal privacy. The term "unwarranted" requires us to balance the family's privacy interest against the public interest in disclosure. See *Reporters Committee*, 489 U.S. 749, at 762.

FOIA is often explained as a means for citizens to know "what the Government is up to."

This phrase should not be dismissed as a convenient formalism. It defines a structural necessity in a real democracy. The statement confirms that, as a general rule, when documents are within FOIA's disclosure provisions, citizens should not be required to explain why they seek the information. A person requesting the information needs no preconceived idea of the uses the data might serve. The information belongs to citizens to do with as they choose. Furthermore, as we have noted, the disclosure does not depend on the identity of the requester. As a general rule, if the information is subject to disclosure, it belongs to all.

When disclosure touches upon certain areas defined in the exemptions, however, the statute recognizes limitations that compete with the general interest in disclosure, and that, in appropriate cases, can overcome it. In the case of Exemption 7(C), the statute requires us to protect, in the proper degree, the personal privacy of citizens against the uncontrolled release of information compiled through the power of the state. The statutory direction that the information not be released if the invasion of personal privacy could reasonably be expected to be unwarranted requires the courts to balance the competing interests in privacy and disclosure. To effect this balance and to give practical meaning to the exemption, the usual rule that the citizen need not offer a reason for requesting the information must be inapplicable.

Where the privacy concerns addressed by Exemption 7(C) are present, the exemption requires the person requesting the information to establish a sufficient reason for the disclosure. First, the citizen must show that the public interest sought to be advanced is a significant one, an interest more specific than having the information for its own sake. Second, the citizen must show the information is likely to advance that interest. Otherwise, the invasion of privacy is unwarranted.

We do not in this single decision attempt to define the reasons that will suffice, or the necessary nexus between the requested information and the asserted public interest that would be advanced by disclosure. On the other hand, there must be some stability with respect to both the specific category of personal privacy interests protected by the statute and the specific category of public interests that could outweigh the privacy claim. Otherwise, courts will be left to balance in an ad hoc manner with little or no real guidance. In the case of photographic images and other data pertaining to an individual who died under mysterious circumstances, the justification most likely to satisfy Exemption 7(C)'s public interest requirement is that the information is necessary to show the investigative agency or other responsible officials acted negligently or otherwise improperly in the performance of their duties. . . .

We hold that, where there is a privacy interest protected by Exemption 7(C) and the public interest being asserted is to show that responsible officials acted negligently or otherwise improperly in the performance of their duties, the requester must establish more than a bare suspicion in order to obtain disclosure. Rather, the requester must produce evidence that would warrant a belief by a reasonable person that the alleged Government impropriety might have occurred. In *United States Dep't of State v. Ray*, 502 U.S. 164 (1991), we held there is a presumption of legitimacy accorded to the Government's official conduct. The presumption perhaps is less a rule of evidence than a general working principle. However the rule is characterized, where the presumption is applicable, clear evidence is usually required to displace it. "In the absence of clear evidence to the contrary, courts presume that [Government agents] have properly discharged their official duties." ("The presumption of regularity supports the official acts of public officers and, in the absence of

clear evidence to the contrary, courts presume that they have properly discharged their official duties"). Given FOIA's prodisclosure purpose, however, the less stringent standard we adopt today is more faithful to the statutory scheme. Only when the FOIA requester has produced evidence sufficient to satisfy this standard will there exist a counterweight on the FOIA scale for the court to balance against the cognizable privacy interests in the requested records. Allegations of government misconduct are "easy to allege and hard to disprove," so courts must insist on a meaningful evidentiary showing. It would be quite extraordinary to say we must ignore the fact that five different inquiries into the Foster matter reached the same conclusion. As we have noted, the balancing exercise in some other case might require us to make a somewhat more precise determination regarding the significance of the public interest and the historical importance of the events in question. We might need to consider the nexus required between the requested documents and the purported public interest served by disclosure. We need not do so here, however. Favish has not produced any evidence that would warrant a belief by a reasonable person that the alleged Government impropriety might have occurred to put the balance into play.

The Court of Appeals erred in its interpretation of Exemption 7(C). . . . The judgment of the Court of Appeals is reversed, and the case is remanded with instructions to grant OIC's motion for summary judgment with respect to the four photographs in dispute.

It is so ordered.

Cheney, Vice President of the United States, v. United States District Court for the District of Columbia
124 S. Ct. 2576 (2004)

Justice Kennedy delivered the opinion of the Court, in which Chief Justice Rehnquist and Justices Stevens, O'Connor, and Breyer joined, and in which Justices Scalia and Thomas joined as to Parts I, II, III, and IV. Justice Stevens filed a

concurring opinion. Justice Thomas filed an opinion concurring in part and dissenting in part, in which Justice Scalia joined. Justice Ginsburg filed a dissenting opinion, in which Justice Souter joined.

The United States District Court for the District of Columbia entered discovery orders directing the Vice President and other senior officials in the Executive Branch to produce information about a task force established to give advice and make policy recommendations to the President. This case requires us to consider the circumstances under which a court of appeals may exercise its power to issue a writ of *mandamus* to modify or dissolve the orders when, by virtue of their overbreadth, enforcement might interfere with the officials in the discharge of their duties and impinge upon the President's constitutional prerogatives.

I

A few days after assuming office, President George W. Bush issued a memorandum establishing the National Energy Policy Development Group (NEPDG or Group). The Group was directed to "develop . . . a national energy policy designed to help the private sector, and government at all levels, promote dependable, affordable, and environmentally sound production and distribution of energy for the future." The President assigned a number of agency heads and assistants—all employees of the Federal Government—to serve as members of the committee. He authorized the Vice President, as chairman of the Group, to invite "other officers of the Federal Government" to participate "as appropriate." Five months later, the NEPDG issued a final report and, according to the Government, terminated all operations.

Following publication of the report, respondents Judicial Watch and the Sierra Club filed these separate actions, which were later consolidated in the District Court. Respondents alleged the NEPDG had failed to comply with the procedural and disclosure requirements of the Federal Advisory Committee Act (FACA or Act), 5 U.S.C. App. § 2, p. 1.

FACA was enacted to monitor the "numerous committees, boards, commissions, councils, and similar groups [that] have been established to advise officers and agencies in the executive branch of the Federal Government," and to prevent the "wasteful expenditure of public funds"

that may result from their proliferation. Subject to specific exemptions, FACA imposes a variety of open-meeting and disclosure requirements on groups that meet the definition of an "advisory committee." As relevant here, an "advisory committee" means "any committee, board, commission, council, conference, panel, task force, or other similar group, or any subcommittee or other subgroup thereof . . . , which is—" (B) "established or utilized by the President, except that [the definition] excludes (i) any committee that is composed wholly of full-time, or permanent part-time, officers or employees of the Federal Government." . . .

Respondents do not dispute the President appointed only Federal Government officials to the NEPDG. They agree that the NEPDG, as established by the President in his memorandum, was "composed wholly of full-time, or permanent part-time, officers or employees of the Federal Government." The complaint alleges, however, that "non-federal employees," including "private lobbyists," "regularly attended and fully participated in non-public meetings." Relying on *Association of American Physicians & Surgeons, Inc. v. Clinton,* 997 F.2d 898 (CADC 1993) respondents contend that the regular participation of the non-Government individuals made them de facto members of the committee. According to the complaint, their "involvement and role are functionally indistinguishable from those of the other [formal] members." As a result, respondents argue, the NEPDG cannot benefit from the Act's exemption under subsection B and is subject to FACA's requirements.

Vice President Cheney, the NEPDG, the Government officials who served on the committee, and the alleged de facto members were named as defendants. The suit seeks declaratory relief and an injunction requiring them to produce all materials allegedly subject to FACA's requirements.

All defendants moved to dismiss. The District Court granted the motion in part and denied it in part. The court acknowledged FACA does not create a private cause of action. On this basis, it dismissed respondents' claims against the non-Government defendants. Because the

NEPDG had been dissolved, it could not be sued as a defendant; and the claims against it were dismissed as well. The District Court held, however, that FACA's substantive requirements could be enforced against the Vice President and other Government participants on the NEPDG under the Mandamus Act, 28 U.S.C. § 1361, and against the agency defendants under the Administrative Procedure Act (APA), 5 U.S.C. § 706. The District Court recognized the disclosure duty must be clear and nondiscretionary for mandamus to issue, and there must be, among other things, "final agency actions" for the APA to apply. According to the District Court, it was premature to decide these questions. It held only that respondents had alleged sufficient facts to keep the Vice President and the other defendants in the case.

The District Court deferred ruling on the Government's contention that to disregard the exemption and apply FACA to the NEPDG would violate principles of separation of powers and interfere with the constitutional prerogatives of the President and the Vice President. Instead, the court allowed respondents to conduct a "tightly-reined" discovery to ascertain the NEPDG's structure and membership, and thus to determine whether the de facto membership doctrine applies. *Judicial Watch, Inc. v. National Energy Policy Dev. Group,* 219 F. Supp.2d 20, 54 (DC 2002). While acknowledging that discovery itself might raise serious constitutional questions, the District Court explained that the Government could assert executive privilege to protect sensitive materials from disclosure. In the District Court's view, these "issues of executive privilege will be much more limited in scope than the broad constitutional challenge raised by the government." The District Court adopted this approach in an attempt to avoid constitutional questions, noting that if, after discovery, respondents have no evidentiary support for the allegations about the regular participation by lobbyists and industry executives on the NEPDG, the Government can prevail on statutory grounds. Furthermore, the District Court explained, even were it appropriate to address constitutional issues, some factual development is necessary to determine the extent of the alleged intrusion into the Executive's constitutional authority. The court denied in part the motion to dismiss and ordered respondents to submit a discovery plan.

In due course the District Court approved respondents' discovery plan, entered a series of orders allowing discovery to proceed (reproducing orders entered on Sept. 9, Oct. 17, and Nov. 1, 2002), and denied the Government's motion for certification under 28 U.S.C. § 1292(b) with respect to the discovery orders. Petitioners sought a writ of mandamus in the Court of Appeals to vacate the discovery orders, to direct the District Court to rule on the basis of the administrative record, and to dismiss the Vice President from the suit. The Vice President also filed a notice of appeal from the same orders.

A divided panel of the Court of Appeals dismissed the petition for a writ of mandamus and the Vice President's attempted interlocutory appeal. *In re Cheney,* 334 F.3d 1096 (CADC 2003). With respect to mandamus, the majority declined to issue the writ on the ground that alternative avenues of relief remained available. Citing *United States v. Nixon,* 418 U.S. 683, the majority held that petitioners, to guard against intrusion into the President's prerogatives, must first assert privilege. Under its reading of *Nixon,* moreover, privilege claims must be made "with particularity.'" In the majority's view, if the District Court sustains the privilege, petitioners will be able to obtain all the relief they seek. If the District Court rejects the claim of executive privilege and creates "an imminent risk of disclosure of allegedly protected presidential communications," "mandamus might well be appropriate to avoid letting 'the cat . . . out of the bag.'" "But so long as the separation of powers conflict that petitioners anticipate remains hypothetical," the panel held, "we have no authority to exercise the extraordinary remedy of mandamus." The majority acknowledged the scope of respondents' requests is overly broad, because it seeks far more than the "limited items" to which respondents would be entitled if "the district court ultimately determines that the NEPDG is subject to FACA." ("The requests to produce also go well beyond FACA's requirements"); ("[Respondents'] discovery also goes well beyond what they need to prove"). It nonetheless agreed with the District Court that petitioners "'shall bear the burden'" of invoking executive privilege and filing objections to the discovery orders with "'detailed precision.'"

For similar reasons, the majority rejected the Vice President's interlocutory appeal. In *United States v. Nixon,* the Court held that the President could appeal an interlocutory subpoena order without having "to place himself in the posture of disobeying an order of a court merely to trigger the procedural mechanism for review." The majority, however, found the case inapplicable because Vice President Cheney, unlike then-President Nixon, had not yet asserted privilege. In the majority's view, the Vice President was not forced to choose between disclosure and suffering contempt for failure to obey a court order. The majority held that to require the Vice President to assert privilege does not create the unnecessary confrontation between two branches of Government described in *Nixon.* . . .

We granted certiorari. We now vacate the judgment of the Court of Appeals and remand the case for further proceedings to reconsider the Government's mandamus petition. . . .

III

We now come to the central issue in the case—whether the Court of Appeals was correct to conclude it "had no authority to exercise the extraordinary remedy of mandamus," on the ground that the Government could protect its rights by asserting executive privilege in the District Court.

The common-law writ of mandamus against a lower court is codified at 28 U.S.C. § 1651(a): "The Supreme Court and all courts established by Act of Congress may issue all writs necessary or appropriate in aid of their respective jurisdictions and agreeable to the usages and principles of law." This is a "drastic and extraordinary" remedy "reserved for really extraordinary causes." *Ex parte Fahey,* 332 U.S. 258, 259-260 (1947).

"The traditional use of the writ in aid of appellate jurisdiction both at common law and in the federal courts has been to confine [the court against which mandamus is sought] to a lawful exercise of its prescribed jurisdiction."

Although courts have not "confined themselves to an arbitrary and technical definition of 'jurisdiction,'" "only exceptional circumstances amounting to a judicial 'usurpation of power,'" or a "clear abuse of discretion, will justify the invocation of this extraordinary remedy."

As the writ is one of "the most potent weapons in the judicial arsenal," three conditions must be satisfied before it may issue. First, "the party seeking issuance of the writ [must] have no other adequate means to attain the relief he desires,"—a condition designed to ensure that the writ will not be used as a substitute for the regular appeals process. Second, the petitioner must satisfy "'the burden of showing that [his] right to issuance of the writ is "clear and indisputable."' Third, even if the first two prerequisites have been met, the issuing court, in the exercise of its discretion, must be satisfied that the writ is appropriate under the circumstances. These hurdles, however demanding, are not insuperable. This Court has issued the writ to restrain a lower court when its actions would threaten the separation of powers by "embarrassing the executive arm of the Government," or result in the "intrusion by the federal judiciary on a delicate area of federal-state relations."

Were the Vice President not a party in the case, the argument that the Court of Appeals should have entertained an action in mandamus, notwithstanding the District Court's denial of the motion for certification, might present different considerations. Here, however, the Vice President and his comembers on the NEPDG are the subjects of the discovery orders. The mandamus petition alleges that the orders threaten "substantial intrusions on the process by which those in closest operational proximity to the President advise the President." These facts and allegations remove this case from the category of ordinary discovery orders where interlocutory appellate review is unavailable, through mandamus or otherwise. It is well established that "a President's communications and activities encompass a vastly wider range of sensitive material than would be true of any 'ordinary individual.'" . . . As *United States v. Nixon* explained, these principles do not mean that the "President is above the law." Rather, they simply acknowledge that the public interest requires that a coequal branch of Government "afford Presidential confidentiality the greatest protection consistent with the fair administration of justice," and give recognition to the paramount necessity of protecting the Executive Branch from vexatious litigation that might distract it from the energetic performance of its constitutional duties.

These separation-of-powers considerations should inform a court of appeals' evaluation of a mandamus petition involving the President or the Vice President. Accepted mandamus standards are broad enough to allow a court of appeals to prevent a lower court from interfering with a coequal branch's ability to discharge its constitutional responsibilities. . . .

IV

The Court of Appeals dismissed these separation-of-powers concerns. Relying on *United States v. Nixon,* it held that even though respondents' discovery requests are overbroad and "go well beyond FACA's requirements," the Vice President and his former colleagues on the NEPDG "shall bear the burden" of invoking privilege with narrow specificity and objecting to the discovery requests with "detailed precision." In its view, this result was required by *Nixon's* rejection of an "absolute, unqualified Presidential privilege of immunity from judicial process under all circumstances." If *Nixon* refused to recognize broad claims of confidentiality where the President had asserted executive privilege, the majority reasoned, *Nixon* must have rejected, a fortiori, petitioners' claim of discovery immunity where the privilege has not even been invoked. According to the majority, because the Executive Branch can invoke executive privilege to maintain the separation of powers, mandamus relief is premature.

This analysis, however, overlooks fundamental differences in the two cases. *Nixon* cannot bear the weight the Court of Appeals puts upon it. First, unlike this case, which concerns respondents' requests for information for use in a civil suit, *Nixon* involves the proper balance between the Executive's interest in the confidentiality of its communications and the "constitutional need for production of relevant evidence in a criminal proceeding." The Court's decision was explicit that it was "not . . . concerned with the balance between the President's generalized interest in confidentiality and the need for relevant evidence in civil litigation. . . . We address only the conflict between the President's assertion of a generalized privilege of confidentiality and the constitutional need for relevant evidence in criminal trials."

. . . The need for information for use in civil cases, while far from negligible, does not share the urgency or significance of the criminal subpoena requests in *Nixon.* As recognized in *Nixon,* the right to production of relevant evidence in civil proceedings does not have the same "constitutional dimensions." . . .

A party's need for information is only one facet of the problem. An important factor weighing in the opposite direction is the burden imposed by the discovery orders. This is not a routine discovery dispute. The discovery requests are directed to the Vice President and other senior Government officials who served on the NEPDG to give advice and make recommendations to the President. The Executive Branch, at its highest level, is seeking the aid of the courts to protect its constitutional prerogatives. As we have already noted, special considerations control when the Executive Branch's interests in maintaining the autonomy of its office and safeguarding the confidentiality of its communications are implicated. This Court has held, on more than one occasion, that "the high respect that is owed to the office of the Chief Executive . . . is a matter that should inform the conduct of the entire proceeding, including the timing and scope of discovery," *Clinton,* 520 U.S. 681, at 707, and that the Executive's "constitutional responsibilities and status [are] factors counseling judicial deference and restraint" in the conduct of litigation against it, *Nixon v. Fitzgerald,* 457 U.S. 731, at 753. Respondents' reliance on cases that do not involve senior members of the Executive Branch, see, e.g., *Kerr v. United States Dist. Court for Northern Dist. of Cal.,* 426 U.S. 394 (1976), is altogether misplaced.

Even when compared against *United States v. Nixon's* criminal subpoenas, which did involve the President, the civil discovery here militates against respondents' position. The observation in *Nixon* that production of confidential information would not disrupt the functioning of the Executive Branch cannot be applied in a mechanistic fashion to civil litigation. . . .

In recognition of these concerns, there is sound precedent in the District of Columbia itself for district courts to explore other avenues, short of forcing the Executive to invoke privilege, when they are asked to enforce against the Executive Branch unnecessarily broad subpoenas. In *United States v. Poindexter,* 727 F. Supp. 1501 (1989), defendant Poindexter, on trial for criminal charges, sought to have the District Court enforce subpoena orders against President Reagan to obtain allegedly exculpatory materials. The Executive considered the subpoenas "unreasonable and oppressive." Rejecting defendant's argument that the Executive must first assert executive privilege to narrow the subpoenas, the District Court agreed with the President that "it is undesirable as a matter of constitutional and public policy to compel a President to make his decision on privilege with respect to a large array of documents." The court decided to narrow, on its own, the scope of the subpoenas to allow the Executive "to consider whether to invoke executive privilege with respect to . . . a smaller number of documents following the narrowing of the subpoenas." This is but one example of the choices available to the District Court and the Court of Appeals in this case.

As we discussed at the outset, under principles of mandamus jurisdiction, the Court of Appeals may exercise its power to issue the writ only upon a finding of "exceptional circumstances amounting to a judicial 'usurpation of power,'" or "a clear abuse of discretion." As this case implicates the separation of powers, the Court of Appeals must also ask, as part of this inquiry, whether the District Court's actions constituted an unwarranted impairment of another branch in the performance of its constitutional duties. This is especially so here because the District Court's analysis of whether mandamus relief is appropriate should itself be constrained by principles similar to those we

have outlined, supra, that limit the Court of Appeals' use of the remedy. The panel majority, however, failed to ask this question. Instead, it labored under the mistaken assumption that the assertion of executive privilege is a necessary precondition to the Government's separation-of-powers objections.

V

In the absence of overriding concerns, . . . we decline petitioners' invitation to direct the Court of Appeals to issue the writ against the District Court. Moreover, this is not a case where, after having considered the issues, the Court of Appeals abused its discretion by failing to issue the writ. Instead, the Court of Appeals, relying on its mistaken reading of *United States v. Nixon,* prematurely terminated its inquiry after the Government refused to assert privilege and did so without even reaching the weighty separation-of-powers objections raised in the case, much less exercised its discretion to determine whether "the writ is appropriate under the circumstances." Because the issuance of the writ is a matter vested in the discretion of the court to which the petition is made, and because this Court is not presented with an original writ of mandamus, we leave to the Court of Appeals to address the parties' arguments with respect to the challenge to APS and the discovery orders. Other matters bearing on whether the writ of mandamus should issue should also be addressed, in the first instance, by the Court of Appeals after considering any additional briefs and arguments as it deems appropriate. We note only that all courts should be mindful of the burdens imposed on the Executive Branch in any future proceedings. Special considerations applicable to the President and the Vice President suggest that the courts should be sensitive to requests by the Government for interlocutory appeals to reexamine, for example, whether the statute embodies the de facto membership doctrine.

The judgment of the Court of Appeals for the District of Columbia is vacated, and the case is remanded for further proceedings consistent with this opinion.

It is so ordered.

Justice Ginsburg, with whom Justice Souter joins, dissenting.

The Government, in seeking a writ of mandamus from the Court of Appeals for the District of Columbia, and on brief to this Court, urged that this case should be resolved without any discovery. In vacating the judgment of the Court of Appeals, however, this Court remands for consideration whether mandamus is appropriate due to the overbreadth of the District Court's discovery orders. But, as the Court of Appeals observed, it appeared that the Government "never asked the district court to narrow discovery." *In re Cheney,* 334 F.3d 1096, 1106 (CADC 2003). Given the Government's decision to resist all discovery, mandamus relief based on the exorbitance of the discovery orders is at least "premature," I would therefore affirm the judgment of the Court of Appeals denying the writ, and allow the District Court, in the first instance, to pursue its expressed intention "tightly [to] rein [in] discovery," should the Government so request.

A

The discovery at issue here was sought in a civil action filed by respondents Judicial Watch, Inc., and Sierra Club. To gain information concerning the membership and operations of an energy-policy task force, the National Energy Policy Development Group (NEPDG), respondents filed suit under the Federal Advisory Committee Act (FACA); respondents named among the defendants the Vice President and senior Executive Branch officials. After granting in part and denying in part the Government's motions to dismiss, the District Court approved respondents' extensive discovery plan, which included detailed and far-ranging interrogatories and sweeping requests for production of documents. In a later order, the District Court directed the Government to "produce non-privileged documents and a privilege log."

The discovery plan drawn by Judicial Watch and Sierra Club was indeed "unbounded in scope." Initial approval of that plan by the District Court, however, was not given in stunning disregard of separation-of-powers concerns. In the order itself, the District Court invited "detailed and precise objections" to any of the discovery requests, and instructed the Government to "identify and explain . . . invocations of privilege with particularity." To avoid duplication, the District Court provided that the Government could identify "documents or information [responsive to the discovery requests] that [it] had already released to [Judicial Watch or the Sierra Club] in different fora." Anticipating further proceedings concerning discovery, the District Court suggested that the Government could "submit [any privileged documents] under seal for the court's consideration," or that "the court [could] appoint the equivalent of a Special Master, maybe a retired judge," to review allegedly privileged documents.

The Government did not file specific objections; nor did it supply particulars to support assertions of privilege. Instead, the Government urged the District Court to rule that Judicial Watch and the Sierra Club could have no discovery at all ("the government position is that . . . no discovery is appropriate. As far as we can tell, petitioners never asked the district court to narrow discovery to those matters [respondents] need to support their allegation that FACA applies to the NEPDG."). In the Government's view, "the resolution of the case had to flow from the administrative record" sans discovery. Without taking up the District Court's suggestion of that court's readiness to rein in discovery, the Government, on behalf of the Vice President, moved, unsuccessfully, for a protective order and for certification of an interlocutory appeal pursuant to 28 U.S.C. § 1292(b). At the District Court's hearing on the Government's motion for a stay pending interlocutory appeal, the Government argued that "the injury is submitting to discovery in the absence of a compelling showing of need by the [respondents]."

Despite the absence from this "flurry of activity," of any Government motion contesting the terms of the discovery plan or proposing a scaled-down substitute plan, this Court states that the Government "did in fact object to the scope of discovery and asked the District Court to narrow it in some way," In support of this statement, the Court points to the Government's objections to the proposed discovery plan, its response to the interrogatories and production requests, and its contention that discovery would be unduly burdensome. . . .

The Government's bottom line was firmly and consistently that "review, limited to the administrative record, should frame the resolution of this case." That administrative record would "consist of the Presidential Memorandum establishing NEPDG, NEPDG's public report, and the Office of the Vice President's response to . . . Judicial Watch's request for permission to attend NEPDG meetings"; it would not include anything respondents could gain through discovery. Indeed, the Government acknowledged before the District Court that its litigation strategy involved opposition to the discovery plan as a whole in lieu of focused objections. (Government stated, "We did not choose to offer written objections to [the discovery plan]. . . .").

Further sounding the Government's leitmotif, in a hearing on the proposed discovery plan, the District Court stated that the Government "didn't file objections" to rein in discovery "because [in the Government's view] no discovery is appropriate." Without endeavoring to correct any misunderstanding on the District Court's part, the Government underscored its resistance to any and all discovery (asserting that respondents are "not entitled to discovery to supplement [the administrative record]"). And in its motion for a protective order, the Government similarly declared its unqualified opposition to discovery. ("[Petitioners] respectfully request that the Court enter a protective order relieving them of any obligation to respond to [respondents'] discovery [requests]." see 334 F.3d at 1106. . . .

Denied § 1292(b) certification by the District Court, the Government sought a writ of mandamus from the Court of Appeals. In its mandamus petition, the Government asked the appellate court to "vacate the discovery orders issued by the district court, direct the court to decide the case on the basis of the administrative record and such supplemental affidavits as it may require, and direct that the Vice President be dismissed as a defendant." In

support of those requests, the Government again argued that the case should be adjudicated without discovery: "The Constitution and principles of comity preclude discovery of the President or Vice President, especially without a demonstration of compelling and focused countervailing interest."

The Court of Appeals acknowledged that the discovery plan presented by respondents and approved by the District Court "goes well beyond what [respondents] need." The appellate court nevertheless denied the mandamus petition, concluding that the Government's separation-of-powers concern "remained hypothetical." Far from ordering immediate "disclosure of communications between senior executive branch officials and those with information relevant to advice that was being formulated for the President," the Court of Appeals observed, the District Court had directed the Government initially to produce only "non-privileged documents and a privilege log." . . .

Throughout this litigation, the Government has declined to move for reduction of the District Court's discovery order to accommodate separation-of-powers concerns. The Court now remands this case so the Court of Appeals can consider whether a mandamus writ should issue ordering the District Court to "explore other avenues, short of forcing the Executive to invoke privilege," and, in particular, to "narrow, on its own, the scope of [discovery]." Nothing in the District Court's orders or the Court of Appeals' opinion, however, suggests that either of those courts would refuse reasonably to accommodate separation-of-powers concerns. When parties seeking a mandamus writ decline to avail themselves of opportunities to obtain relief from the District Court, a writ of mandamus ordering the same relief—i.e., here, reined-in discovery–is surely a doubtful proposition. . . .

Review by mandamus at this stage of the proceedings would be at least comprehensible as a means to test the Government's position that no discovery is appropriate in this litigation. ("Petitioners' separation-of-powers arguments are . . . in the nature of a claim of immunity from discovery."). But in remanding for consideration of discovery-tailoring measures, the Court apparently rejects that no-discovery position. Otherwise, a remand based on the overbreadth of the discovery requests would make no sense. Nothing in the record, however, intimates lower-court refusal to reduce discovery. Indeed, the appeals court has already suggested tailored discovery that would avoid "effectively prejudging the merits of respondents' claim" (respondents "need only documents referring to the involvement of non-federal officials. A few interrogatories or depositions might have determined . . . whether any non-Government employees voted on NEPDG recommendations or drafted portions of the committee's report"). In accord with the Court of Appeals, I am "confident that [were it moved to do so] the district court here [would] protect petitioners' legitimate interests and keep discovery within appropriate limits." I would therefore affirm the judgment of the Court of Appeals.

NOTES

1. Walsh-Healey Act of 1936, 41 U.S.C. 35.

2. The material on types of policies comes from Randall Ripley and Grace Franklin, *Congress, the Bureaucracy, and Public Policy,* 4th ed. (Chicago: Dorsey Press, 1987), 21–28.

3. Ibid., 25.

4. Ernest Gellhorn and Ronald M. Levin, *Administrative Law and Process: In a Nutshell,* 3d ed. (St. Paul, MN: West, 1990), 124.

5. Walter Gellhorn, Clark Byse, and Peter Strauss, *Administrative Law: Cases and Comments,* 7th ed. (Meniola, NY: Foundation Press, 1979), 556.

6. *National Abortion Federation v. Ashcroft,* 2004 U.S. Dist. LEXIS 4530 (March 19, 2004).

7. *Northwestern Memorial Hospital v. Ashcroft* 362 F.3d. 923 (Seventh Cir. 2004).

8. Harold W. Stanley and Richard G. Niemi, *Vital Statistics on American Politics, 2001–2002 Ed.* (Washington, D.C.: Congressional Quarterly Press, 2001), p. 288.

9. *Kyllo v. United States* 533 U.S. 27 (2001).

10. *Marshall v. Barlow's, Incorporated,* 436 U.S. 307, 313 (1978).

11. *National Treasury Employees Union v. Von Raab,* 489 U.S. 656, 665 (1989).

12. *Skinner v. Railway Labor Executives' Association,* 489 U.S. 602 (1989).

13. *Vernonia School District 47J v. Acton,* 515 U.S. 646 (1995).

14. *Bd. of Ed. of Independent School District #92 of Pottowatomie C. v. Earls,* 536 U.S. 822 (2002).

15. *Griffin v. Wisconsin,* 483 U.S. 868 (1987). The *Griffin* case involved a parole revocation but the Court also used the special needs doctrine to justify the suspicionless, warrantless searches in auto check points for drunk drivers.

16. Denise Gellene, "Sears Auto Shops Come Under Fire," *Topeka Capital-Journal,* November 6, 1992, 3A.

17. Lotte E. Feinberg, "Managing the Freedom of Information Act and Federal Information Policy," 46 *Public Administration Review* 615 (1986).

18. 5 U.S.C. 551–59.

19. 5 U.S.C. 552a.

20. 5 U.S.C. 552b.

21. For an excellent analysis on the subject of government and information, see Conrad, "Information Disclosures by Government," ibid., Note #57 (Chapter 2).

22. 44 USCS Sec. 3501. See also Conrad, Ibid., p.527 and Jaime Klima, "The E-Government Act: Promotion of E-Quality or Exaggeration of the Digital Divide?" *Duke Law and Technology Review* 9 (2003).

23. 5 USCS Sec. 552. See also Conrad, Ibid.

24. 44 USCS Sec. 3602.

25. Jim Barnett and Tom Deyzel, "U.S. Balked at Mad Cow Safeguards," *The Oregonian,* January 18, 2004, p. A-1, (Sunday Sunrise Ed.). If you enjoy eating beef, read this article with caution. It discusses the fight over banning "downers" (a cow that cannot walk) from meatpacking plants in America.

26. The material on legal recourse for government release of information comes from Conrad, Ibid., note 22, 532–34.

27. Feinberg, "Managing the Freedom of Information Act," 615.

28. Kristen Uhl, "The Freedom of Informatuion Act Post 9/11: Balancing the Public's Right to Know, Critical Infrastructure Protection and Homeland Security," 53 *American University Law Review* 261 (Oct. 2003).

29. The procedure described is contained in the act, but the condensed description comes from Gellhorn, Byse, and Strauss, *Administrative Law,* 583–84.

30. Ibid., 582.

31. The material on the Attorney General and FOIA comes from Uhl, Ibid. (Note #28).

32. Ibid., 271.

33. Ibid., 272–74.

34. Ibid., 274–82.

35. 18 U.S.C. sec. 1905.

36. Gellhorn and Levin, *Administrative Law and Process,* 156.

37. Daniel Oran, *Oran's Dictionary of the Law* (St. Paul, MN: West, 1983), 133.

38. *Department of Interior and Bureau of Indian Affairs v. Klamath Water Users Protective Association,* 532 U.S. 1 (2001).

39. Gellhorn, Byse, and Strauss, *Administrative Law,* 582–83. See also Robert L. Saloschin, "The FOIA—A Government Perspective," 35 *Public Administration Review* 10 (1975).

40. Arthur E. Bonfield and Michael Asimow, *State and Federal Administrative Law* (St. Paul, MN: West, 1989), 538.

41. Ibid.

42. Gellhorn, Byse, and Strauss, *Administrative Law,* 585.

43. Ibid.

44. Antonin Scalia, "The Freedom of Information Act Has No Clothes," *Regulation,* March/April 1982, 14.

6

INFORMAL AGENCY ACTIVITY

You are already somewhat familiar with the Administrative Procedure Act. In Chapter 3, you learned that the Act imposed standardized decision-making procedures on all federal agencies. In Chapter 4, you became aware of the different standards of court review of agency activity imposed by the Act. Agency decisions resulting from a quasi-judicial hearing require the substantial evidence test, and quasi-legislative decisions are subject to the arbitrary and capricious standard of court review. In the preceding chapter, you became familiar with the Freedom of Information Act (FOIA), which is also part of the Administrative Procedure Act. The next chapter will deal in depth with the Administrative Procedure Act, but because some terms sound similar, you need to know enough about the Administrative Procedure Act to avoid confusion.

Although the Act was intended to standardize and regulate the procedure of agency decision making, it addresses agency decisions in only two contexts. Section 553 regulates quasi-legislative activity or agency rule making through the notice and comment procedure. This procedure is also what has been called rule promulgation. It will also be referred to as a 553 hearing. Sections 554, 556, and 557 regulate quasi-judicial activity. Courts often refer to this type of activity as a 554 hearing. The problem is that agencies engage in a lot of activity and make many decisions that are not the result of either a 553 or a 554 hearing. In fact, much, if not most, of what agencies do falls outside of the activities covered by those sections of the Administrative Procedure Act. Because the 554 hearing is guided by trial-type rules of procedure and a formal record is kept, quasi-judicial agency activity is referred to as *formal rule making*. Quasi-legislative or 553 hearings are called *informal rule making* because they are not guided by trial-type rules, and no formal record is preserved for a court appeal. In administrative law jargon then, there are formal and informal rule-making decisions, and there are simply decisions that get made without any hearing at all. These are unregulated decisions that are not covered by the Administrative Procedure Act, and they fall under what I have termed *informal agency activity*.

The Administrative Procedure Act distinguishes between four types of agency activity based on two dichotomies: rule making versus adjudication and formal versus informal. This four-fold classification produces the grid of agency activity displayed in Figure 6.1. Cells A, B, and to a lesser extent, C are the subject matter of the next chapter, but Cell D is the subject of this chapter. The first thing to note about Cell D is that *informal adjudication* is a misnomer; there is nothing judicial (quasi or otherwise) about what takes place in that cell. The second thing to note about Cell D is that there are no procedures in the Administrative Procedure Act to guide behavior. The activity in this cell is just unregulated decisions and is what we will refer to as informal agency activity. The third thing to note about informal activity is that it constitutes *most* of what agencies do. Professor Edward Rubin has argued that the Administrative Procedure Act was outdated when it was adopted and should be modified to reflect the modern administrative state. He had this to say about informal activity:

> Every time an agency plans its future actions or evaluates its prior ones, allocates its resources, gives advice, makes a promise, issues a threat, negotiates, conducts an investigation, and most of the time it denies an application or makes an exception, it is at least arguably engaged in informal adjudication.[1]

Finally, as you learned in Chapter 4, judicial review of activity in Cell D is the arbitrary and capricious standard of review. Rarely does informal agency activity ever get challenged in court.

	Formal	*Informal*
Rule Making	**Cell A** Formal rule making under Section 554 of the Administrative Procedure Act (a quasi-judicial procedure) Example: When the Food and Drug Administration wanted to increase the peanuts in peanut butter by 2%, the adjudicatory process lasted two decades.	**Cell B** Informal rule making, Section 553 of the Administrative Procedure Act (a quasi-legislative procedure). Example: The Environmental Protection Agency held 553 hearings prior to setting the national ambient air quality standards, and the Department of Transportation held 553 hearings prior to setting standards for tire pressure warning systems.
Adjudication	**Cell C** Formal adjudication, Sections 554, 556, and 557 of the Administrative Procedure Act (a quasi-judicial procedure) Example: Used to adjudicate individual claims or questions of fact: Was game warden Lund's death work-related? (see *State Employees' Retirement System v. Industrial Accident Commission*, Chapter 4)	**Cell D** Informal adjudication is not regulated by the Administrative Procedure Act; it is not an adjudicatory nor a legislative procedure Example: Unregulated decisions such as Secretary of Transportation Volpe's decision to release funds for a six-lane highway through Overton Park (see *Citizens to Preserve Overton Park v. Volpe*, Chapter 4)

Figure 6.1   Four-by-Four Grid of Agency Action Under the Administrative Procedure Act

SOURCE: Adapted from "The Federal Administrative Procedure Act: Codification or Reform?", 56 *Yale Law Journal*, 670, 674-678, 705.

Case in Point:
Let's Count Everybody!
Let's Not and Say We Did

You are probably aware that the U.S. population is counted every 10 years in a decennial census. You may not be aware of how politically charged the process of taking the census is. Over the past few decades, it has become politically charged because the census does not count everybody. People get missed in the count, and this is referred to as the *undercount.* According to the Census Bureau, the undercount from the 1990 census was 1.6 percent.[2] Given a 1990 population of nearly 250 million people,[3] the undercount would represent about 4 million people who were missed. The 2000 census missed 1.2 percent of 281 million people, or about 3.3 million people not counted.[4]

The undercount is a politically charged issue because those who miss being counted are not evenly distributed geographically or socially. This concept is referred to as the *differential undercount.* In the 1990 census, for example, it is estimated that African Americans were undercounted by 4.8 percent, Native Americans by 5.9, and Hispanics by 5.2 percent.[5] By comparison, non-Hispanic whites were undercounted by only .7 of a percent.[6]

This differential undercount is politically charged because both major political parties have an electoral interest in it. While 185 billion federal dollars are distributed annually based on census figures,[7] the constitutional purpose for the decennial census is to set representation in the House of Representatives. The Constitution set the first House at 65 members,[8] but the number in the chamber grew with every census until it was set permanently at 435 in 1910.[9] With the next census, the fighting began because the 1920 census revealed that America had changed from a rural to an urban society. Urban areas would gain representation in the House, and rural areas would lose it.[10]

Today, the fighting has a more partisan ring to it although it still involves geographic considerations. Democrats believe that the differential undercount hurts them because the groups hardest hit have a propensity to vote Democratic. The undercount has a major impact in urbanized areas, almost none in the suburbs, and little effect in rural areas. Again, in terms of voting patterns, this hurts Democrats and helps Republicans. What the census data have shown for several decades is a general population shift from the Northeast and Midwest (the Rust Belt) to the South and the Southwest (the Sun Belt). This trend also benefits Republicans to the detriment of Democrats. In the 1940s, New York, Pennsylvania, Ohio, and Illinois collectively had 127 seats in the House (30 percent of its membership) whereas California, Texas, and Florida had only 52 seats (12 percent of the total). Since the 2000 census, the four Rust Belt states have only 85 seats (20 percent of the membership) whereas the three Sun Belt states have 110 seats (25 percent).[11] That is almost a 111 percent increase for the Sun Belt in 60 years.

Democrats contend that fixing the differential undercount will slow the movement of House seats from the Rust Belt to the Sun Belt. Republicans, concerned about a paper-thin majority in the House, see no virtue in fixing the undercount problem. By way of an extreme example, political scientists generally recognize that the redistricting that occurred after the 1990 census contributed to the Republican victory in the 1994 election. Redistricting is the process of redrawing congressional district lines in the states after the census has told us how many seats each state is supposed to have.

The Republicans picked up 53 seats in the House in the 1994 election, to take control of the House. Of the 53 seats, 18 had once been Rust Belt-Democratic seats, now reassigned to the Republican Sun Belt.[12] Another 13 of the 53 seats were created as a second-order consequence of establishing minority-majority districts in the South subsequent to the 1990 census.[13] A minority-majority district is a congressional district that is drawn in such a way so that a minority group, say African Americans, becomes the majority of voters in that district. This has two consequences. First, it ensures the election of a minority candidate to the House of Representatives. Second, and more important for our discussion, it concentrates African American votes into a single district, which decreases minority voting strength in surrounding districts. The state of Georgia provides a good example. After the 1980 census, Georgia had one congressional district with a majority of black voters and five districts in which black voters accounted for at least 25 percent of the electorate.[14] All six districts were represented by Democrats. By the 1994 election, Georgia had three minority-majority districts, and black Democrats were elected with an average 67 percent of the vote. However, all of the rest of Georgia's congressional districts had few black voters in them. In three districts where white Democrats ran as incumbents, the Democratic percentage of the vote fell from 57 percent in the 1992 election to 46 percent in the 1994 election.[15] In four districts with Republican incumbents, the Democratic percentage of the vote fell from 45 percent in the 1992 election to 35 percent in the 1994 election.[16] Not all of the differential between the 1992 and 1994 elections in Georgia was caused by the "cleansing effect" of creating minority-majority districts; in addition, the Republicans executed a great voter mobilization effort and increased voter turnout in the 1994 election. However, the 1990 census and subsequent reapportionment (moving seats from the Rust Belt to the Sun Belt) and redistricting appears to account for 33 of the 53 seats captured by the Republicans in the 1994 election.

These examples reveal the political aspects of the undercount. Setting aside these political interests, professionals in the Census Bureau were embarrassed at missing so many Americans in their count, and they set about to fix the problem. After the 1980 census (which missed 1.2 percent of the population, or more than 2.5 million people), the bureau engaged in extensive analysis to find a solution to the undercount problem. In preparation for the 1990 census, the bureau proposed several reforms, including expensive and targeted advertising campaigns, a simpler questionnaire, a multilanguage questionnaire, and the use of a statistical adjustment to the actual count of the population. This statistical adjustment triggered the political and legal fighting.

What the census director proposed is a sampling technique called *capture-recapture.* Suppose you wanted to count the number of pumpkins in a pumpkin patch. First, you would choose a specific section of the patch—let's assume, the section is 1/10 the size of the whole patch. At the capture stage, you would take a quick count of the pumpkins in both the whole patch and in your section. Assume the result of this count is 10,000 pumpkins in the patch and 1,000 in your section. At the recapture stage, you would take an exacting count of the pumpkins in the section. If the recapture count of the section revealed a count of 1,100 pumpkins, you could estimate or "adjust" your count by assuming that you missed 100 pumpkins out of every 1,000. Hence, your actual pumpkin patch count would be 11,000 pumpkins.[17]

The Census Bureau refers to this capture-recapture sampling as a *postenumeration survey* (PES), and in the mid-1980s, the director of the census made an informal decision to use PES in the 1990 census. The director's boss is the secretary of commerce, who at that point in history would have been appointed by a Republican president. The secretary of commerce vetoed the director's decision to use PES. That is, the secretary made an informal decision not to statistically adjust the census. States that thought they would have benefited from a statistically adjusted census sued the secretary over the decision.

In *Wisconsin v. New York,* 517 U.S. 1 (1996), the Supreme Court upheld the secretary's decision. Chief Justice Rehnquist pointed out that the Constitution requires a decennial census but delegates to Congress broad power to carry it out. He then went on to say,

> Through the Census Act, Congress has delegated its broad authority over the census to the Secretary, ([the]Secretary shall take a decennial census of the population . . . in such form and content as he may determine . . .). Hence so long as the Secretary's conduct of the census is consistent with the constitutional language and constitutional goal of representation, it is within the limits of the Constitution. In light of the Constitution's broad grant of authority to Congress, the Secretary's decision not to adjust need bear only a reasonable relationship to the accomplishment of an actual enumeration of the population keeping in mind the constitutional purpose of the census.[18]

Again, in preparation for the 2000 census, the Census Bureau pushed for a PES adjustment to the count. By the mid-1990s, a Democrat was in the White House, and obviously, the secretary of commerce was a Democrat as well. The director of the Census Bureau made an informal decision to conduct a PES and to statistically adjust the 2000 census. The secretary approved of the decision and publicly announced that sampling would be used in the coming census. In 1997, the Republican-controlled Congress amended the Census Act to forbid sampling in the census, but President Clinton vetoed it. Next, Congress passed a bill requiring the Census Bureau to issue a report on its intentions for conducting the 2000 census. On receiving the bureau's report, Congress attached a rider to the appropriations bill for the Departments of Commerce, Justice, and State and for the judicial branch. The rider made the secretary's decision to sample a final action by the agency (so that it could be challenged in court right away without having to wait for the statistically adjusted census to be completed) and granted reviewability and standing to any "persons aggrieved" by the sampling. Furthermore, it mandated that any lawsuit challenging the PES would go before a three-judge district court panel and would be reviewed automatically by the Supreme Court, thus skipping the court of appeals step.[19] The secretary was sued before the ink was dry on the legislation, and the district court granted the plaintiffs' request for a permanent injunction forbidding the use of sampling in the census.

In *Department of Commerce v. United States House of Representatives,* 525 U.S. 316 (1999), the Supreme Court affirmed the lower court decision. This time around the Court said that sampling was barred by the Census Act. You will read the Census Case for the 2000 census at the end of this chapter. Should you believe that the census saga is over, you do not fully appreciate the political potential of the census. The census drives three things: (1) apportionment for the House of Representatives, and that part of the saga is indeed at an end; (2) redistricting in the states; and (3) distribution of federal funds. In state redistricting, each state legislature is required to redraw congressional district lines after the census and come as close to one person-one vote as possible. Also, the allotment of $185 billion in federal grant money to the various states is frequently tied to census figures. The Supreme Court said that sampling cannot be used to count the population for apportionment purposes, but it has said nothing about the other purposes. The Census Bureau did indeed use the sampling procedure in the 2000 census with the intention of using the more accurate sampled numbers for redistricting and disbursing federal money. This created two kinds of census data: adjusted (sampled) and unadjusted (the actual count). In early 2001, President George W. Bush's secretary of commerce made an informal decision to release only the unadjusted data for the states to use in redistricting; in the fall of 2001, the secretary made another informal decision to use unadjusted figures for the distribution of federal grants to the states.[20] Two state senators from Oregon made an FOIA request for the adjusted figures, and the Census Bureau denied release, saying the adjusted data were protected under Exemption 5 as a "deliberative process exemption." The two Oregon senators sued for release of the data. The district court ordered the adjusted data released, and the Department of Commerce appealed to the circuit court, which upheld the order to release the adjusted figures. The Department of Commerce, disclaiming their accuracy, released the adjusted data. Without these court decisions, we would not be aware of the undercount for the 2000 census, as the Bush 43 administration did not want it released. As the FOIA suit was working its way through the courts, a host of Democratic officials in state and local government sued the Department of Commerce to force the secretary to use the adjusted figures for the purpose of redistricting. The trial court said that the secretary's decision was a reasonable act of discretion (i.e., it was not arbitrary or capricious). The Court of Appeals upheld the district court decision.[21]

What is important for you to understand is that people within agencies make decisions every day, and most of their decisions are not regulated by the Administrative Procedure Act. The director of the Census Bureau made an informal decision to use sampling for the 1990 census, but the secretary of commerce under President Bush 41 made an informal decision to overrule his census director. The census director made another informal decision to sample for the 2000 census, a decision approved by another informal decision by his boss, President Clinton's secretary of commerce. The secretary of commerce under President Bush 43 made an informal decision not to use the sampled data that had been collected during the 2000 census (actually, two informal decisions—one regarding redistricting and another for federal grants). The same secretary made another informal decision not to release the adjusted data when it was requested under FOIA. Finally, the director of the Census Bureau made an informal decision to disavow the accuracy of the adjusted data.[22] As the case in point illustrates, sometimes these informal decisions can be very important. More often than not, they end up not being reviewed by courts, but you should recognize that when courts review them, the courts will apply the arbitrary and capricious standard of review.

INFORMAL ACTIVITY

Many of the decisions you are familiar with from the cases you have read so far involve informal decisions, in that they were not covered by the Administrative Procedure Act and are examples of unregulated discretion. The following is a list of such decisions:

Collector of Customs' decision to raise the duty on barium oxide	*Hampton v. United States*, 276 U.S. 394 (1928)
The Internal Revenue Service's (IRS) decision to not enforce its policy regarding charitable contributions and private academies	*Allen v. Wright et al.*, 468 U.S. 737 (1984)
The secretary of transportation's decision to run a six-lane highway through a city park	*Citizens to Preserve Overton Park v. Volpe*, 401 U.S. 402 (1971)
The Environmental Protection Agency's (EPA's) decision not to administratively sanction Chicago Steel for years of flagrant violation of environmental reporting laws	*Steel Company, aka Chicago Steel and Pickling Co. v. Citizens for a Better Environment*, 523 U.S. 88 (1998)
All of the informal decisions by the census director and the secretary of commerce regarding sampling and the census	Case in Point, this chapter
The secretary of the interior's decision to allow offroad vehicles in the "wilderness study areas" of Utah	*Norton, Secretary of the Interior v. Southern Utah Wilderness Alliance*, 124 S. Ct. 2373 (2004)
The CIA director's decision to fire an employee because the director disapproved of the employee's sexual orientation	*Webster v. Doe*, 486 U.S. 592 (1988)
The policeman's use of a chokehold (most likely, the chief's policy of allowing the unrestrained and unregulated use of chokeholds also falls into this category)	*City of Los Angeles v. Lyons*, 461 U.S. 55 (1983)
The agency's demand for receipts	*Shapiro v. United States*, 335 U.S. 1 (1948)
Agency decisions to issue subpoenas for information	*Federal Trade Commission v. American Tobacco Company*, 264 U.S. 298 (1924); *Oklahoma Press Publishing Company v. Walling*, 324 U.S. 186 (1946)
The Occupational Safety and Health Administration's (OSHA's) decision to inspect Mr. Barlow's plumbing and heating store	*Marshall v. Barlow's, Incorporated*, 436 U.S. 307 (1978)
All decisions by any agency not to release (or to release) requested information under the FOIA, including the decision by the Defense Logistics Agency to release material that qualified for a FOIA exemption in the *Chrysler* case	

Other obvious agency activity falls into this category. For example, in the processing of applications for nearly any government program, the initial decision on the application is just such an informal decision. Applications for Social Security, food stamps, veterans' benefits, a small business loan, or a federal research grant are examples. Renowned legal scholar Kenneth Culp Davis has argued that 90 percent of what agencies do is informal activity and, furthermore, that rarely are such activities challenged in court.[23]

Gellhorn and Levin have listed nine areas in which considerable informal agency activity takes place:[24]

1. agency settlement, negotiation, and alternative disputes resolution (an agency's decision to settle a potential legal conflict, such as breach of contract, or to enter a consent decree is all at the absolute unregulated discretion of the agency)

2. processing of applications and claims (this has been touched on earlier, but according to Gellhorn and Levin, "In a single year . . . the [Social Security Administration] disburses about two hundred billion dollars and makes over four million determinations in administering the Old-Age, Survivors, Disability and Health Insurance programs")[25]

3. tests and inspections (Chapter 5)

4. suspensions, seizures, and recalls (if an agency considers a product to pose a serious immediate threat to public health or safety—for instance, contaminated food—the summary decision to seize the product or suspend a license is made without a hearing, although one may be required after the fact)

5. agency supervision (nearly constant supervision of banks, for example)

6. agency use of publicity (the decision to leak a story to the media, for example)

7. agency advice (for example, when you call the IRS toll-free number for help in filling out your income tax return—a subject to which we will turn our attention momentarily)

8. contracts and grants (the federal government is certainly the biggest contractor in the United States, and each decision to enter a contract is absolutely at the discretion of an agency; the same is true of grants, although there are general guidelines)

9. agency management (the Bureau of Land Management, Forest Service, and the National Park Service all manage tremendous natural resources and make decisions such as who will get a concession in a national park, who can cut timber and how and where they can cut, and who can graze cattle on public land, practically free).

Although all of these areas have generated some litigation, certainly the area that has generated the most litigation is the area in which a government employee gives advice to a citizen. More particularly, suits are generated when the citizen relies on the governmental advice, but the advice turns out to be wrong and the citizen ends up in trouble or suffering an economic loss.

Estoppel

What happens when a taxpayer calls the toll-free number and gets advice on a deduction from the IRS employee; takes the deduction, which flags an audit; and then finds the IRS wants not only the missing tax money but interest and penalties as well? Does the taxpayer have to pay the interest and penalties? The real-world answer is, "It depends." Factors that go into the resolution are the amount of money involved, how assertive the taxpayer is, how far he or she is willing to fight the IRS through the process, how good the taxpayer's attorney is, and even the mood of the IRS decision maker on the day the taxpayer's case hits his or her desk.[26] The safe and theoretically correct answer, however, is that, yes, the taxpayer is liable for fines and interest accrued as a result of relying on the IRS advice. Why do you suppose this is the case?

In the Spring of 1945, Idaho farmers, the Merrill brothers, applied to the County Agricultural Conservation Committee for federal crop insurance. The Merrills informed the committee that they planned to plant 460 acres of spring wheat, but that 400 of those acres would be reseeded on winter wheat. The committee, acting as the agent for the Federal Crop Insurance Agency within the Department of Agriculture, informed the Merrills that the entire crop would be covered. The committee further recommended to the regional office that the corporation accept the Merrills' application for insurance (although the application itself made no mention of reseeded wheat). The Federal Crop Insurance Corporation accepted the Merrills' application. By July, most of the Merrills' crop was wiped out by drought (a calamity normally covered by the federal insurance program).[27] After the corporation discovered that the destroyed acreage had been reseeded, it refused to cover the loss. The case follows.

Federal Crop Insurance Corporation v. Merrill
332 U.S. 380 (1947)

Justice Frankfurter delivered the opinion of the Court, joined by Chief Justice Vinson and Justices Reed, Murphy, and Burton. Justices Jackson, Black, Douglas, and Rutledge dissented.

The trial court rejected the Corporation's contention, presented by a demurrer to the complaint, that the Wheat Crop Insurance Regulations barred recovery as a matter of law. Evidence was thereupon permitted to go to the jury to the effect that the respondents had no actual knowledge of the Regulations, insofar as they precluded insurance for reseeded wheat, and that they had in fact been misled by petitioner's agent into believing that spring wheat reseeded on winter wheat acreage was insurable by the Corporation. The

jury returned a verdict for the loss on all the 460 acres and the Supreme Court of Idaho affirmed the resulting judgment. 174 P.2d 834. That court in effect adopted the theory of the trial judge, that since the knowledge of the agent of a private insurance company, under the circumstances of this case, would be attributed to, and thereby bind, a private insurance company, the Corporation is equally bound.

The case no doubt presents phases of hardship. We take for granted that, on the basis of what they were told by the Corporation's local agent, the respondents reasonably believed that their entire crop was covered by petitioner's insurance. And so we assume that recovery could be had against a private insurance company. But the Corporation is not a private insurance company. It is too late in the day to urge that the Government is just another private litigant, for purposes of charging it with liability, whenever it takes over a business theretofore conducted by private enterprise or engages in competition with private ventures. Government is not partly public or partly private, depending upon the governmental pedigree of the type of a particular activity or the manner in which the Government conducts it. The Government may carry on its operations through conventional executive agencies or through corporate forms especially created for defined ends. Whatever the form in which the Government functions, anyone entering into an arrangement with the Government takes the risk of having accurately ascertained that he who purports to act for the Government stays within the bounds of his authority. The scope of this authority may be explicitly defined by Congress or be limited by delegated legislation, properly exercised through the rule-making power. And this is so even though, as here, the agent himself may have been unaware of the limitations upon his authority. If the Federal Crop Insurance Act had by explicit language prohibited the insurance of spring wheat which is reseeded on winter wheat acreage, the ignorance of such a restriction, either by the respondents or the Corporation's agent, would be immaterial and recovery could not be had against the Corporation for loss of such reseeded wheat. Congress could hardly define the multitudinous details appropriate for the business of crop insurance when the Government entered it. Inevitably "the terms and conditions" upon which valid governmental insurance can be had must be defined by the agency acting for the Government. And so Congress has legislated in this instance, as in modern regulatory enactments it so often does by conferring the rule-making power upon the agency created for carrying out its policy. . . . Just as everyone is charged with knowledge of the United States Statutes at Large, Congress has provided that the appearance of rules and regulations in the *Federal Register* gives legal notice of their contents.

Accordingly, the Wheat Crop Insurance Regulations were binding on all who sought to come within the Federal Crop Insurance Act, regardless of actual knowledge of what is in the Regulations or of the hardship resulting from innocent ignorance. The oft-quoted observation in *Rock Island, Arkansas & Louisiana R. Co. v. United States,* 254 U.S. 141, that "Men must turn square corners when they deal with the Government," does not reflect a callous outlook. It merely expresses the duty of all courts to observe the conditions defined by Congress for charging the public treasury. The "terms and conditions" defined by the Corporation, under authority of Congress, for creating liability on the part of the Government preclude recovery for the loss of the reseeded wheat no matter with what good reason the respondents thought they had obtained insurance from the Government. Indeed, not only do the Wheat Regulations limit the liability of the Government as if they had been enacted by Congress directly, but they were in fact incorporated by reference in the application, as specifically required by the Regulations. We have thus far assumed, as did the parties here and the courts below, that the controlling regulation in fact precluded insurance coverage for spring wheat reseeded on winter wheat acreage. It explicitly states that the term "wheat crop shall not include . . . winter wheat in the 1945 crop year, and spring wheat which has been reseeded on winter wheat acreage in the 1945 crop year." . . . Wheat Crop Insurance Regulations, 10 F.R. 1591. The circumstances of this case tempt one to read the regulation, since it is for us to read it, with charitable laxity. But not even the temptations of a hard case can elude the clear meaning of the regulation. It precludes recovery for "spring wheat which has been reseeded on winter wheat acreage in the 1945 crop year." Concerning the validity of the regulation, as "not inconsistent with the provisions" of the Federal Crop Insurance Act, no question has been raised.

The judgment is reversed and the cause remanded for further proceedings not inconsistent with this opinion.

Reversed.

Mr. Justice Black, and Mr. Justice Rutledge, dissent.

Justice Jackson, dissenting

I would affirm the decision of the court below. If crop insurance contracts made by agencies of the United States Government are to be judged by the law of the State in which they are written, I find no error in the court below. If, however, we are to hold them subject only to federal law and to declare what that law is, I can see no reason why we should not adopt a rule which recognizes the practicalities of the business.

It was early discovered that fair dealing in the insurance business required that the entire contract between the policyholder and the insurance company be embodied in the writings which passed between the parties, namely the written application, if any, and the policy issued. It may be well enough to make some types of contracts with the Government subject to long and involved regulations published in the Federal Register. To my mind, it is an absurdity to hold that every farmer who insures his crops knows what the Federal Register contains or even knows that there is such a publication. If he were to peruse this voluminous and dull publication as it is issued from time to time in order to make sure whether anything has been promulgated that affects his rights, he would never need crop insurance, for he would never get time to plant any crops. Nor am I convinced that a reading of technically worded regulations would enlighten him much in any event.

In this case, the Government entered a field which required the issuance of large numbers of insurance policies to people engaged in agriculture. It could not expect them to be lawyers, except in rare instances, and one should not be expected to have to employ a lawyer to see whether his own Government is issuing him a policy which in case of loss would turn out to be no policy at all. There was no fraud or concealment, and those who represented the Government in taking on the risk apparently no more suspected the existence of a hidden regulation that would render the contract void than did the policyholder. It is very well to say that those who deal with the Government should turn square corners. But there is no reason why the square corners should constitute a one-way street.

The Government asks us to lift its policies out of the control of the States and to find or fashion a federal rule to govern them. I should respond to that request by laying down a federal rule that would hold these agencies to the same fundamental principles of fair dealing that have been found essential in progressive states to prevent insurance from being an investment in disappointment. Mr. Justice Douglas joins in this opinion.

Question

1. The *Merrill* case is famous because it established a doctrine for dealing with cases like it. The Court was asked to "fashion a federal law," which it did. Can you articulate what the doctrine is?

The *Merrill* case raises questions of *estoppel* (see *estoppel, collateral,* and *equitable estoppel* in your law dictionary). Estoppel is a legal term that means one is stopped from taking some legal action by prior action or activity. In the *Merrill* case, the question is whether the government is estopped from denying the Merrills' insurance claims because the government's agent told them the crop would be covered.

While estopping the government is different and more difficult than estopping a civil party at law, the case of Carolyn Cleveland is instructive on the concept of estoppel. In August of 1993, Carolyn went to work for Policy Management Systems. Her job was to investigate prospective employees and clients of Policy Management's clients. About six months after starting work for Policy Management, she suffered a stroke. Within weeks of the stroke, she applied for social security disability, but after about four months, she felt good enough to return to work. She notified the Social Security Administration of the fact that she was back at work (disability under the Act means that you have a medical disability so severe that you cannot work). Several months later, she received formal notice from the Social Security Administration that her disability claim was denied. A week after she received the notification, her employer fired her because she was not fast and efficient enough in her work. She reapplied for disability, and after several months, she sued Policy Management under the Americans with Disabilities Act (ADA). The ADA forbids employers to discriminate against those with disabilities, and it requires them to make "reasonable accommodations" for disabled employees. A week after she filed suit, the Social Security Administration notified her that she qualified for disability. Discovering that Carolyn was on disability, the defendant moved to dismiss the suit under the concept of estoppel. The argument was that if she is disabled enough to qualify for disability, *a fortiori* she cannot be in the workforce and under the protection of the ADA. Both the district court and the circuit court agreed that a disabled person should be estopped from bringing an ADA suit. The Supreme Court disagreed and reversed saying that there is a legal presumption against pursuing an ADA suit by a plaintiff who qualifies for disability, but the presumption could be overcome by the presentation of evidence. As a matter of law, an ADA suit is not estopped simply because the plaintiff may be on disability. See *Cleveland v. Policy Management Systems,* 526 U.S. 795 (1999).

In the *Merrill* case, the Court gives you guidance about the conditions under which a plaintiff will be unable to estop the government. Using the *Merrill* case as a guide, how would you resolve the following cases?

In 1961, Mr. Montana was 55 years old. He was born in Italy while his parents were temporarily residing there in 1906. His mother was a native-born U.S. citizen, and his father was an Italian citizen. Shortly after his birth, he and his mother entered the United States, and they lived here continuously until 1961, when the Immigration and Naturalization Service (INS) wanted to deport him. His mother apparently wanted to return to America while she was pregnant, but an embassy official erroneously told her she would not be allowed to reenter the country in her condition. One of the questions in the case is whether the United States should be estopped from applying a law that naturalized only the children born outside the country whose fathers were citizens. It appears as though Mr. Montana is not a citizen (and will be deported) only because of the erroneous advice of a government employee.[28]

In 1940, Congress passed the Nationality Act of 1940, which granted U.S. citizenship to noncitizens who served honorably in the U.S. military during World War II. Not only could people like Mr. Hibi become citizens, but they were exempted from certain naturalization requirements (residency and literacy). However, Congress put a deadline on the Act: All who qualified would need to apply before the end of 1947. Mr. Hibi was a citizen of the Philippines when he enlisted in the American army and served honorably until his discharge. However, no one ever told him about the opportunity to become an American citizen, and the United States failed to provide a naturalization officer to the Philippines so that if Mr. Hibi had known about the opportunity, he would have been unable to take advantage of it. He entered the United States on a visa in 1967 to claim his citizenship, arguing that the federal government should be estopped from using the 1947 deadline against him.[29]

An old law called the Rivers and Harbors Act forbids the discharge of any "refuse matter" into navigable waterways in the United States. The Act delegates enforcement power to the Army Corps of Engineers, which enforces the law through a permit system. Historically, permits were issued for dumping into navigable waterways matter that would not impede navigation, but permits were consistently denied for dumping any refuse that would impede navigation. In the early 1970s, there was no Clean Water Act, but environmental groups had raised awareness that our lakes and rivers were dangerously polluted. Environmental lawyers had some success urging government to use the Rivers and Harbors Act to get at companies dumping effluent into rivers. The Pennsylvania Industrial Chemical Corporation, relying on the past behavior of the Army Corps to deny permits only to those who would dump matter that would impede navigation, failed to secure the appropriate permit prior to dumping a chemical into the Monongahela River. The Army Corps brought criminal charges against the chemical company. This case (*United States v. Pennsylvania Industrial Chemical Corporation,* 411 U.S. 655 [1973]) presented a narrow procedural issue of whether the company could present evidence of the Army Corps' past enforcement behavior at trial. Although, technically, this is not an estoppel case, think of the issue this way: Can the government be estopped from bringing criminal charges because its past enforcement behavior misled the company into believing its actions were not criminal? How would you resolve this issue, and why?

Horacio Miranda, a citizen of the Philippines, entered the United States on a visa. While here, he met and married an American citizen. His wife and he both petitioned the INS for an upgrade in his alien status. The INS failed to take any action on either petition for a year and a half. Upon the dissolution of their marriage, the ex-wife withdrew her petition, and then the INS wanted to deport Miranda. Lower courts found that the INS committed *affirmative misconduct* and overruled the deportation. The INS appealed to the Supreme Court.[30]

In *Schweiker v. Hansen,* 450 U.S. 785 (1981), Ms. Hansen asked a Social Security Administration field representative whether she was eligible for her mother's insurance benefits. (She was.) The field representative, however, erroneously told her she was not. Furthermore, the Administration's claims manual instructs field representatives to advise claimants to fill out an application regardless of the advice given, but the representative failed to advise Ms. Hansen to fill out the application. When she found out she was in fact eligible for the benefits, she sued for the year's worth of benefits she had lost. The Social Security Administration's position was that Ms. Hansen was not deserving of the benefits for that year, because the Administration has a rule requiring a written application (just like the crop insurance rule against reseeded wheat). The legal issue is whether the Administration should be estopped from applying the rule to Ms. Hansen because of the erroneous advice given and the failure to inform her by the field agent.

Federal employees who have worked for the government for at least five years are eligible for a federal disability program that is different from the federal disability program administered by the Social Security Administration. The federal employees program terminates if the employee's earning capacity becomes fairly comparable to the current rate of pay for the position held before the disability. The term *fairly comparable,* of course, needs more specificity. Congress said that if earning capacity became 80 percent of the current rate of pay for two years in a row, that would cause the termination of benefits. Congress amended the legislation in 1982 so that the calculation of *fairly comparable* was based on a single year's earnings rather than the two-year computation. Charles Richmond was a welder at a Navy shipyard and applied for the disability based on impaired vision, and his application was approved. He obtained part-time work as a school bus driver. In 1986, he had an opportunity to work some overtime that might push him over the 80 percent limit. He asked an employee relations specialist with the Navy Public Works how much he could earn without going over the 80 percent limit. The specialist erroneously told him about the two-year averaging and provided him with an outdated manual from the federal Office of Personnel Management that had the two-year computation in it. Richmond worked the overtime and eventually was terminated from the disability program for earnings in excess of the 80 percent rule. He is trying to estop the government from applying the one-year income rule to him. This case is the Court's most recent (1990) estoppel case, and it is included at the end of the chapter.

If you resolved any of the cases above and the *Pennsylvania Industrial Chemical Company* case the same way, you are wrong. Indeed, the Social Security Administration was not estopped from applying the written application rule to Ms. Hansen, the INS was not estopped in any of the immigration cases, and you will read about Mr. Richmond's case at the end of this chapter; however, the government was prohibited from pressing criminal charges against the chemical company.

You will see from *Heckler v. Community Health Services* at the end of the chapter that in 1984, the Court articulated a two-pronged test for when a private citizen attempts to estop the government. First, the party claiming estoppel must show that reliance on the government's advice or conduct resulted in a change of position for the worse. Because the Merrills were going to plant the reseeded wheat in any case, they would have been unable to meet this prong of the test. However, all of the other litigants above would have been able to meet this prong of the test. The second prong of the test is that the party claiming estoppel cannot have acted out of ignorance, "and that reliance must have been reasonable in that the party claiming estoppel did not know nor should have known that its adversary's conduct was misleading."[31]

It is the concept in the second prong of the test that is common to all of the cases discussed except the chemical company case. Chief Justice Rehnquist points out that the Court has decided seven estoppel cases, and in five of them, the Court did not estop the government.[32] The two cases in which the government was estopped were unique. The chemical company case, for example, was a criminal case in which the company got into trouble, not out of ignorance, but precisely because it relied on government behavior and therefore had no appropriate warnings of the kind of conduct the government considered illegal.[33]

We have discussed examples of informal agency activity and the exercise of discretion. Let us move to a consideration of how or whether to control such discretion.

Controlling Informal Activity

It is perhaps not a good state of affairs in a democratic country to allow (encourage?) law enforcement officers responding to a minor traffic violation to apply a choke hold that can injure, cripple, or kill a citizen. Neither is it a good indicator of the health of a democracy when an administrative agency threatens the economic well-being of an entire industry by reducing the allowable gasses in the air to the point where the industry cannot comply with the standards. Because the legislative branch cannot be expected to consider every contingency, to foresee every nuance or control for every variable, the administrative state assumes that administrative agencies will exercise discretion. The question then is not whether agencies *should* exercise discretion but, rather, to what degree that discretion should be controlled.

The founding fathers attempted to control the discretion of those in power through a written constitution and the concept of separation of powers. These concepts do not have much application to modern agencies in the administrative state. Legislative delegations of power, which should serve the channeling purposes of the Constitution, are written so loosely and vaguely as to impose almost no constraints at all on agency behavior. There is no separation of powers within agencies (agencies make rules, enforce the rules they make, and adjudicate infractions of those rules). Agencies may, however, be checked by other branches, as in congressional review, the Office of Management and Budget's review, and judicial review. Although a lower-court decision awarded Mr. Lyons money for his injuries, the Supreme Court refused to enjoin the limitless use of choke holds by police. The Court refused to allow the Citizens for a Better Environment to pursue a citizens' suit to enforce the law where Congress had authorized such suits. Executive branch review of agency action is limited to proposed rules, and is likely to be used only when Republicans are in the White House; such review may have constitutional problems. Congressional review only seems to work with veto-proof Republican majorities in Congress and a Democrat in the White House. According to Kenneth Culp Davis, "Judicial review is sometimes available, but much informal action is not even theoretically reviewable and more than ninety-nine percent of what is reviewable is not in fact reviewed."[34]

Davis, who is perhaps the foremost authority on the problem of discretion, argues that much discretion is unnecessary and should be eliminated, and the remaining necessary discretion should be "structured" by rules.[35] For example, prosecutors exercise tremendous discretion in deciding whether to charge, what to charge, and what to recommend regarding bail (whether a defendant is free on bail at the time of trial is related to findings of guilt or innocence). This is probably necessary discretion, but there have been successful attempts to control it. For example, a point system that determines what the prosecutor must recommend in terms of bail reduces the possibility that other factors, such as race, can enter the discretionary decision. Edward Rubin argues that the Administrative Procedure Act should be revised to reflect the realities of the administrative state.[36]

There is no escape from the fact that law enforcement officers must exercise discretion "on the street." That is not to say that we must accept and live with officers' decisions to apply a choke hold to citizens who pose no threat to the officers or other citizens. If the Los Angeles Police Department had adopted an internal procedural rule limiting the application of choke holds to those situations in which officers perceive a threat either to themselves or to other citizens, there would be fewer incidents of "official violence." On the other hand, Davis's solution of limiting discretion through written rules does not always work. There was a written and duly promulgated rule in the *Merrill* case involving the planting of wheat, and apparently the government agent, on whom citizens rely to know the rules, was ignorant of the rule, to the Merrills' detriment. The same can be said in the *Hansen* case on Social Security, the *Montana* and *Hibi* cases involving immigration issues, and the *Richmond* case involving disability payments.

Most of the material in a text such as this deals with challenges to agency activity covered by the Administrative Procedure Act or the enabling legislation. The student should be aware that this constitutes only a small part of agencies' activity. A good deal of agency activity is what we have labeled *informal activity*. This activity affects citizens, but a good deal of it never gets reviewed by courts. This raises serious democratic issues of accountability, but experts are undecided on a solution to the questions it raises.

Summary

1. The two-pronged test from *Heckler v. Community Health Services* consists of the following considerations: (a) The party claiming estoppel must show that reliance on government advice or conduct resulted in a change in their position for the worse. (b) The party claiming estoppel cannot have acted out of ignorance of the law or agency rule.

2. When informal agency decisions or action is reviewed by a court, the proper standard of review is the arbitrary and capricious standard.

END-OF-CHAPTER CASES

Heckler v. Community Health Services
467 U.S. 51 (1984)

Justice Stevens delivered the opinion for a unanimous Court, with Chief Justice Burger and Justice Rehnquist concurring.

Under what is recognized for present purposes as an incorrect interpretation of rather complex federal regulations, during 1975, 1976, and 1977 respondent received and expended $71,480 in federal funds to provide health care services to Medicare beneficiaries to which it was not entitled. The question presented is whether the Government is estopped from recovering those funds because respondent relied on the express authorization of a responsible government agent in making the expenditures.

I

Under the Medicare program, Title XVIII of the Social Security Act, providers of health care services are reimbursed for the reasonable cost of services rendered to Medicare beneficiaries as determined by petitioner, the Secretary of Health and Human Services. Providers receive interim payments at least monthly covering the cost of services they have rendered. Congress recognized, however, that these interim payments would not always correctly reflect the amount of reimbursable costs, and accordingly instructed petitioner to develop mechanisms for making appropriate retroactive adjustments when reimbursement is found to be inadequate or excessive. Pursuant to this statutory mandate, petitioner requires providers to submit annual cost reports which are then audited to determine actual costs. Petitioner may reopen any reimbursement determination within a three-year period and make appropriate adjustments. The Act also permits a provider to elect to receive reimbursement through a "fiscal intermediary." If the intermediary the provider has nominated meets her requirements, petitioner then enters into an agreement with the intermediary to have it perform those administrative responsibilities she assigns it. These duties include receipt, disbursement and accounting for funds used in making Medicare payments, auditing the records of providers in order to ensure payments have been proper, resolving disputes over cost reimbursement, reviewing and reconsidering payments to providers, and recovering over-payments to providers. The fiscal intermediary must also "serve as a center for, and communicate to providers, any information or instructions furnished to it by the Secretary, and serve as a channel of communication from providers to the Secretary."

Respondent Community Health Services of Crawford County, Inc., is a nonprofit corporation. In 1966 it entered into a contract with petitioner's predecessor, the Secretary of Health, Education and Welfare, to provide home health care services to individuals eligible for benefits under Part A of the Medicare program. Under the contract, respondent received reimbursement through a fiscal intermediary, the Travelers Insurance Companies (Travelers).

In 1973 Congress enacted the Comprehensive Employment and Training Act (CETA), now codified as amended at 29 U.S.C. §§ 801–999 authorizing the use of federal funds to provide training and job opportunities for economically disadvantaged persons. In 1975 respondent began participating in the program, which reimbursed it for the salaries and fringe benefits paid to certain of its employees. CETA funds made it possible for respondent to take on additional personnel and to provide additional home health care services.

To prevent what would be in effect double-reimbursement of providers' costs, one of the regulations concerning reasonable costs reimbursable under the Medicare program indicates that grants received by a provider in order to pay specific operating costs must be subtracted from the reasonable costs for which the provider may receive reimbursement. After obtaining a CETA grant, respondent's administrator contacted Travelers to ask whether the salaries of its CETA-funded employees who provided services to patients eligible for Medicare benefits were reimbursable as reasonable costs under Medicare. Travelers' Medicare manager orally advised respondent that the CETA funds were "seed money" within the meaning of the Provider Reimbursement Manual, which is defined as "[g]rants designated for the development of new health care agencies or for expansion of services of established agencies," and therefore, even though the CETA employees' salaries constituted specific operating costs paid by a federal grant, they were reimbursable under the Medicare program. Relying on Travelers' advice, respondent included costs for which it was receiving CETA reimbursement in its cost reports, and received reimbursement for those sums amounting to $7,694, $32,460, and

$31,326 in fiscal 1975, 1976, and 1977, respectively. On several occasions during this period, respondent requested and received from Travelers oral verification of the propriety of this treatment. With these additional funds, respondent expanded its annual number of home health care visits from approximately 4,000 in 1974 to over 81,000 in the next three years. Its annual budget increased during that period from about $53,000 to about $900,000. It is undisputed that correct administrative practice required Travelers to refer respondent's inquiry to the Department of Health and Human Services for a definitive answer. However, Travelers did not do this until August 7, 1977, when a written request for instructions was finally submitted to the Philadelphia office of the Department's Bureau of Health Insurance. Travelers was then formally advised that the CETA funds were not seed money and therefore had to be subtracted from respondent's Medicare reimbursement. On October 7, 1977, Travelers formally notified respondent of this determination. Travelers then reopened respondent's cost reports for the preceding three years and recomputed respondent's reimbursable costs, determining that respondent had been overpaid a total of $71,480.

Estoppel is an equitable doctrine invoked to avoid injustice in particular cases. While a hallmark of the doctrine is its flexible application, certain principles are tolerably clear: "If one person makes a definite misrepresentation of fact to another person having reason to believe that the other will rely upon it and the other in reasonable reliance upon it does an act . . . the first person is not entitled . . . to regain property or its value that the other acquired by the act, if the other in reliance upon the misrepresentation and before discovery of the truth has so changed his position that it would be unjust to deprive him of that which he thus acquired." Restatement (Second) of Torts. Thus, the party claiming the estoppel must have relied on its adversary's conduct "in such a manner as to change his position for the worse." And that reliance must have been reasonable in that the party claiming the estoppel did not know nor should it have known that its adversary's conduct was misleading.

When the Government is unable to enforce the law because the conduct of its agents has given rise to an estoppel, the interest of the citizenry as a whole in obedience to the rule of law is undermined. It is for this reason that it is well-settled that the Government may not be estopped on the same terms as any other litigant. Petitioner urges us to expand this principle into a flat rule that estoppel may not in any circumstances run against the Government. We have left the issue open in the past, and do so again today. Though the arguments the Government advances for the rule are substantial, we are hesitant, when it is unnecessary to decide this case, to say that there are no cases in which the public interest in ensuring that the Government can enforce the law free from estoppel might be outweighed by the countervailing interest of citizens in some minimum standard of decency, honor, and reliability in their dealings with their Government. But however heavy the burden might be when an estoppel is asserted against the Government, the private party surely cannot prevail without at least demonstrating that the traditional elements of an estoppel are present. We are unpersuaded that that has been done in this case with respect to either respondent's change in position or its reliance on Travelers' advice.

III

To analyze the nature of a private party's detrimental change in position, we must identify the manner in which reliance on the Government's misconduct has caused the private citizen to change his position for the worse. In this case the consequences of the Government's misconduct were not entirely adverse. Respondent did receive an immediate benefit as a result of the double reimbursement. Its detriment is the inability to retain money that it should never have received in the first place. Thus, this is not a case in which the respondent has lost any legal right, either vested or contingent, or suffered any adverse change in its status. When a private party is deprived of something to which it was entitled of right, it has surely suffered a detrimental change in its position. Here respondent lost no rights but merely was induced to

something which could be corrected at a later time. . . .

IV

Justice Holmes wrote: "Men must turn square corners when they deal with the Government." This observation has its greatest force when a private party seeks to spend the Government's money. Protection of the public fisc requires that those who seek public funds act with scrupulous regard for the requirements of law; respondent could expect no less than to be held to the most demanding standards in its quest for public funds. This is consistent with the general rule that those who deal with the Government are expected to know the law and may not rely on the conduct of government agents contrary to law.

As a participant in the Medicare program, respondent had a duty to familiarize itself with the legal requirements for cost reimbursement. Since it also had elected to receive reimbursement through Travelers, it also was acquainted with the nature of and limitations on the role of a fiscal intermediary. When the question arose concerning respondent's CETA funds, respondent's own action in consulting Travelers demonstrates the necessity for it to have obtained an interpretation of the applicable regulations; respondent indisputably knew that this was a doubtful question not clearly covered by existing policy statements. The fact that Travelers' advice was erroneous is, in itself, insufficient to raise an estoppel, as is the fact that petitioner had not anticipated this problem and made a clear resolution available to respondent. There is simply no requirement that the Government anticipate every problem that may arise in the administration of a complex program such as Medicare, neither can it be expected to ensure that every bit of informal advice given by its agents in the course of such a program will be sufficiently reliable to justify expenditure of sums of money as substantial as those spent by respondent. Nor was the advice given under circumstances that should have induced respondent's reliance. As a recipient of public funds well-acquainted with the role of a fiscal intermediary, respondent knew Travelers only acted as a conduit; it could not resolve policy questions. The relevant statute, regulations, and reimbursement manual, with which respondent should have been and was acquainted, made that perfectly clear. Yet respondent made no attempt to have the question resolved by petitioner; it was satisfied with the policy judgment of a mere conduit.

The appropriateness of respondent's reliance is further undermined because the advice it received from Travelers was oral. It is not merely the possibility of fraud that undermines our confidence in the reliability of official action that is not confirmed or evidenced by a written instrument. Written advice, like a written judicial opinion, requires its author to reflect about the nature of the advice that is given to the citizen, and subjects that advice to the possibility of review, criticism and reexamination. The necessity for ensuring that governmental agents stay within the lawful scope of their authority, and that those who seek public funds act with scrupulous exactitude, argues strongly for the conclusion that an estoppel cannot be erected on the basis of the oral advice that underlay respondent's cost reports. That is especially true

when a complex program such as Medicare is involved, in which the need for written records is manifest.

In sum, the regulations governing the cost reimbursement provisions of Medicare should and did put respondent on ample notice of the care with which its cost reports must be prepared, and the care which would be taken to review them within the relevant three-year period. Yet respondent prepared those reports on the basis of an oral policy judgment by an official who, it should have known, was not in the business of making policy. That is not the kind of reasonable reliance that would even give rise to an estoppel against a private party. It therefore cannot estop the Government.

Thus, assuming estoppel can ever be appropriately applied against the Government, it cannot be said that the detriment respondent faces is so severe or has been imposed in such an unfair way that petitioner ought to be estopped from enforcing the law in this case. Accordingly, the judgment of the Court of Appeals is reversed and the case is remanded to that court for further proceedings consistent with this opinion.

It is so ordered.

Department of Commerce v. United States House of Representatives
525 U.S. 316 (1999)

Opinion by Justice O'Connor joined by Chief Justice Rehnquist and Justices Scalia, Kennedy, and Thomas. Justices Stevens, Souter, and Ginsburg were in dissent. Justice Breyer concurred in part and dissented in part.

I

Article 1, § 2, cl. 3, of the United States Constitution states that "Representatives . . . shall be apportioned among the several States . . . according to their respective Numbers." It further requires that "the actual Enumeration shall be made within three Years after the first

Meeting of the Congress of the United States, and within every subsequent Term of ten Years, in such Manner as they shall by Law direct." *Ibid.* Finally, § 2 of the Fourteenth Amendment provides that "Representatives shall be apportioned among the several States according to their respective numbers, counting the whole number of persons in each State, excluding Indians not taxed."

Pursuant to this constitutional authority to direct the manner in which the "actual Enumeration" of the population shall be made, Congress enacted the Census Act (hereinafter Census Act or Act), *13 U.S.C. § 1 et seq.,* delegating to the Secretary of Commerce (Secretary) authority to conduct the decennial census. § 4.

The Act provides that the Secretary "shall, in the year 1980 and every 10 years thereafter, take a decennial census of population as of the first day of April of such year." § 141(a). It further requires that "the tabulation of total population by States . . . as required for the apportionment of Representatives in Congress among the several States shall be completed within 9 months after the census date and reported by the Secretary to the President of the United States." § 141(b). Using this information, the President must then "transmit to the Congress a statement showing the whole number of persons in each State . . . and the number of Representatives to which each State would be entitled." 2 U.S.C. § 2a(a). Within 15 days thereafter, the Clerk of the House of Representatives must "send to the executive of each State a certificate of the number of Representatives to which such State is entitled." 2 U.S.C. § 2a(b) (1994 ed., Supp. III).

The instant dispute centers on the problem of "undercount" in the decennial census. For the last few decades, the Bureau has sent census forms to every household, which it asked residents to complete and return. The Bureau followed up on the mailing by sending enumerators to personally visit all households that did not respond by mail. Despite this comprehensive effort to reach every household, the Bureau has always failed to reach—and has thus failed to count—a portion of the population. This shortfall has been labeled the census "undercount."

The Bureau has been measuring the census undercount rate since 1940, and undercount has been the subject of public debate at least since the early 1970's. See M. Anderson, *The American Census: A Social History* 221–222 (1988). It has been measured in one of two ways. Under one method, known as "demographic analysis," the Bureau develops an independent estimate of the population using birth, death, immigration, and emigration records. U.S. Dept. of Commerce, Bureau of the Census, *Report to Congress: The Plan for Census 2000*, p. 2, and n. 1 (Aug. 1997) (hereinafter Census 2000 Report). A second method, first used in 1990, involves a large sample survey, called the "Post-Enumeration Survey," that is conducted in conjunction with the decennial census. The

Bureau compares the information gathered during the survey with the information obtained in the census and uses the comparison to estimate the number of unenumerated people in the census.

Some identifiable groups—including certain minorities, children, and renters—have historically had substantially higher undercount rates than the population as a whole. See Census 2000 Report 3–4. Accordingly, in previous censuses, the Bureau sought to increase the number of persons from whom it obtained information. In 1990, for instance, the Bureau attempted to reach out to traditionally undercounted groups by promoting awareness of the census and its importance, providing access to Spanish language forms, and offering a toll free number for those who had questions about the forms. Indeed, the 1990 census was "better designed and executed than any previous census." Nonetheless, it was less accurate than its predecessor for the first time since the Bureau began measuring the undercount rate in 1940.

In a further effort to address growing concerns about undercount in the census, Congress passed the Decennial Census Improvement Act of 1991, which instructed the Secretary to contract with the National Academy of Sciences (Academy) to study the "means by which the Government could achieve the most accurate population count possible" . . .

In light of these studies and other research, the Bureau formulated a plan for the 2000 census that uses statistical sampling to supplement data obtained through traditional census methods. The Bureau plan provides for two types of sampling that are the subject of the instant challenge. . . .

The Bureau's announcement of its plan to use statistical sampling in the 2000 census led to a flurry of legislative activity. Congress amended the Census Act to provide that, "notwithstanding any other provision of law, no sampling or any other statistical procedure, including any statistical adjustment, may be used in any determination of population for purposes of the apportionment of Representatives in Congress among the several States," H. R. Conf. Rep. No. 105–119, p. 67 (1997), but President Clinton vetoed the bill, see Message to the House of Representatives

Returning Without Approval Emergency Supplemental Appropriations Legislation, 33 Weekly Comp. of Pres. Doc. 846, 847 (1997). Congress then passed, and the President signed, a bill providing for the creation of a "comprehensive and detailed plan outlining [the Bureau's] proposed methodologies for conducting the 2000 Decennial Census and available methods to conduct an actual enumeration of the population," including an explanation of any statistical methodologies that may be used. 1997 Emergency Supplemental Appropriations Act for Recovery From Natural Disasters, and for Overseas Peacekeeping Efforts, Including Those in Bosnia. Pursuant to this directive, the Commerce Department issued the Census 2000 Report. After receiving the Report, Congress passed the 1998 Departments of Commerce, Justice, and State, the Judiciary, and Related Agencies Appropriations Act, § 209, 111 Stat. 2482, which provides that the Census 2000 Report and the Bureau's Census 2000 Operational Plan "shall be deemed to constitute final agency action regarding the use of statistical methods in the 2000 decennial census." The Act also permits any person aggrieved by the plan to use statistical sampling in the decennial census to bring a legal action and requires that any action brought under the Act be heard by a three-judge district court. It further provides for review by appeal directly to this Court. . . .

III

We accordingly arrive at the dispute over the meaning of the relevant provisions of the Census Act. The District Court below examined the plain text and legislative history of the Act and concluded that the proposed use of statistical sampling to determine population for purposes of apportioning congressional seats among the States violates the Act. We agree.

A

An understanding of the historical background of the decennial census and the Act that governs it is essential to a proper interpretation of the Act's present text. From the very first census, the census of 1790, Congress has prohibited the use of statistical sampling in calculating the population for purposes of apportionment. The First Congress enacted legislation requiring census enumerators to swear an oath to make "a just and perfect enumeration" of every person within the division to which they were assigned. Act of Mar. 1, 1790, § 1, 1 Stat. 101. Each enumerator was required to compile a schedule of information for his district, listing by family name the number of persons in each family that fell into each of five specified categories. Congress modified this provision in 1810, adding an express statement that "the said enumeration shall be made by an actual inquiry at every dwelling-house, or of the head of every family within each district, and not otherwise," and expanding the number of specifications in the schedule of information. Act of Mar. 26, 1810, § 1, 2 Stat. 565–566. The requirement that census enumerators visit each home in person appeared in statutes governing the next 14 censuses.

The current Census Act was enacted into positive law in 1954. It contained substantially the same language as did its predecessor statutes, requiring enumerators to "visit personally each dwelling house in his subdivision" in order to obtain "every item of information and all particulars required for any census or survey" conducted in connection with the census. Act of Aug. 31, 1954, § 25(c), 68 Stat. 1012, 1015. Indeed, the first departure from the requirement that the enumerators collect all census information through personal visits to every household in the Nation came in 1957 at the behest of the Secretary. The Secretary asked Congress to amend the Act to permit the Bureau to use statistical sampling in gathering some of the census information. In response, Congress enacted § 195, which provided that, "except for the determination of population for apportionment purposes, the Secretary may, where he deems it appropriate, authorize the use of the statistical method known as 'sampling' in carrying out the provisions of this title." *13 U.S.C. § 195* (1970 ed.). This provision allowed the Secretary to authorize the use of sampling procedures in gathering supplemental, nonapportionment census information regarding population, unemployment, housing, and other matters collected in conjunction with the decennial census—much of which is now collected through what is known as the "long form"—but it did not authorize the use of sampling procedures in connection with apportionment of Representatives. . . .

In 1964, Congress repealed former § 25(c) of the Census Act, see Act of Aug. 31, 1964, 78 Stat. 737, which had required that each enumerator obtain "every item of information" by personal visit to each household. The repeal of this section permitted the Bureau to replace the personal visit of the enumerator with a form delivered and returned via the Postal Service. Pursuant to this new authority, census officials conducted approximately 60 percent of the census through a new "mailout-mailback" system for the first time in 1970. See M. Anderson, *The American Census: A Social History* 210–211 (1988). The Bureau then conducted follow up visits to homes that failed to return census forms. Thus, although the legislation permitted the Bureau to conduct a portion of the census through the mail, there was no suggestion from any quarter that this change altered the prohibition in § 195 on the use of statistical sampling in determining the population for apportionment purposes.

In 1976, the provisions of the Census Act at issue in this case took their present form. Congress revised § 141 of the Census Act, which is now entitled "Population and other census information." It amended subsection (a) to authorize the Secretary to "take a decennial census of population as of the first day of April of such year, which date shall be known as the 'decennial census date,' in such form and content as he may determine, including the use of sampling procedures and special surveys." *13 U.S.C. § 141*(a). Congress also added several subsections to § 141, among them a provision specifying that the term "census of population," as used in § 141, "means a census of population, housing, and matters relating to population and housing." § 141(g). Together, these revisions provided a broad statement that in collecting a range of demographic information during the decennial census, the Bureau would be permitted to use sampling procedures and special surveys.

This broad grant of authority given in § 141(a) is informed, however, by the narrower and more specific § 195, which is revealingly entitled, "Use of Sampling." See *Green v. Bock Laundry Machine Co.*, 490 U.S. 504, 524 (1989). The § 141 authorization to use sampling techniques in the decennial census is not necessarily an authorization to use these techniques in collecting all of the information that is gathered during the decennial census. We look to the remainder of the law to determine what portions of the decennial census the authorization covers. When we do, we discover that, as discussed above, § 195 directly prohibits the use of sampling in the determination of population for purposes of apportionment.

When Congress amended § 195 in 1976, it did not in doing so alter the longstanding prohibition on the use of sampling in matters relating to apportionment. Congress modified the section by changing "apportionment purposes" to "purposes of apportionment of Representative[s] in Congress among the several States" and changing the phrase "may, where he deems it appropriate" to "shall, if he considers it feasible." 90 Stat. 2464. The amended section thus reads: "Except for the determination of population for purposes of apportionment of Representatives in Congress among the several States, the Secretary shall, if he considers it feasible, authorize the use of the statistical method known as 'sampling' in carrying out the provisions of this title." *13 U.S.C. § 195*. As amended, the section now requires the Secretary to use statistical sampling in assembling the myriad demographic data that are collected in connection with the decennial census. But the section maintains its prohibition on the use of statistical sampling in calculating population for purposes of apportionment.

Absent any historical context, the language in the amended § 195 might reasonably be read as either permissive or prohibitive with regard to the use of sampling for apportionment purposes. Indeed, appellees and appellants each cite numerous examples of the "except/shall" sentence structure that support their respective interpretations of the statute. See, e.g., Brief for Appellee Glavin et al. in No. 98–564, p. 36, n. 36 (citing § 2 of the Fourteenth Amendment, which provides that "when the right to vote . . . is denied to any of the male inhabitants of such State . . . *except* for participation in rebellion, or other crime, the basis of representation therein *shall* be reduced in the proportion which the number of such male citizens shall bear to the whole number of male citizens twenty-one years of age in such State"); Brief for Federal Appellant et al. in No. 98–404, p. 29, n. 15 (citing *2 U.S.C. § § 179n*(a)(1) and 384(a) and *5 U.S.C. § 555*(e), which contain the "except/ shall" formulation in contexts where appellants claim "the exception cannot reasonably be construed as prohibiting the excepted activity"). But these dueling examples only serve to illustrate that the interpretation of the "except/shall" structure depends primarily on the broader context in which that structure appears. Here, the context is provided by over 200 years during which federal statutes have prohibited the use of statistical sampling where apportionment is concerned. In light of this background, there is only one plausible reading of the amended § 195: It prohibits the use of sampling in calculating the population for purposes of apportionment.

In fact, the Bureau itself concluded in 1980 that the Census Act, as amended, "clearly" continued the "historical precedent of using the 'actual Enumeration' for purposes of apportionment, while eschewing estimates based on sampling or other statistical procedures, no matter how sophisticated." See *45 Fed. Reg. 69366, 69372 (1980)*. That same year, the Solicitor General argued before this Court that "*13 U.S.C. 195* prohibits the use of statistical 'sampling methods' in determining the state-by-state population totals."

. . . The administration did not adopt the contrary position until 1994, when it first concluded that using statistical sampling to adjust census figures would be consistent with the Census Act. In light of this history, appellants make no claim to deference under *Chevron U.S.A. Inc. v. Natural Resources Defense Council, Inc.,* 467 U.S. 837 (1984), on behalf of the Secretary's interpretation of the Census Act. . . .

B

The conclusion that the Census Act prohibits the use of sampling for apportionment purposes finds support in the debate and discussions

surrounding the 1976 revisions to the Census Act. At no point during the debates over these amendments did a single Member of Congress suggest that the amendments would so fundamentally change the manner in which the Bureau could calculate the population for purposes of apportionment. . . . This is true despite the fact that such a change would profoundly affect Congress by likely shifting the number of seats apportioned to some States and altering district lines in many others. Indeed, it tests the limits of reason to suggest that despite such silence, Members of Congress voting for those amendments intended to enact what would arguably be the single most significant change in the method of conducting the decennial census since its inception. That the 1976 changes to §§ 141 and 195 were not the focus of partisan debate, see *post,* at 5, is almost certainly due to the fact that the Members of Congress voting on the bill read the text of the statute, as do we, to prohibit the use of sampling in determining the population for apportionment purposes. Moreover, it is hard to imagine that, having explicitly prohibited the use of sampling for apportionment purposes in 1957, Congress would have decided to reverse course on such an important issue by enacting [only a subtle change in phraseology.]

IV

For the reasons stated, we conclude that the Census Act prohibits the proposed uses of statistical sampling in calculating the population for purposes of apportionment. Because we so conclude, we find it unnecessary to reach the constitutional question presented. See *Spector Motor Service, Inc. v. McLaughlin,* 323 U.S. 101, 105 (1944) ("If there is one doctrine more deeply rooted than any other in the process of constitutional adjudication, it is that we ought not to pass on questions of constitutionality . . . unless such adjudication is unavoidable"); *Ashwander v. TVA,* 297 U.S. 288, 347 (1936) (Brandeis, J., concurring) ("If a case can be decided on either of two grounds, one involving a constitutional question, the other a question of statutory construction or general law, the Court will decide only the latter"). Accordingly, we affirm the judgment of the District Court for the Eastern District of Virginia in *Clinton v. Glavin, 119 S. Ct. 290.* As this decision also resolves the substantive issues presented by *Department of Commerce v. United States House of Representatives, 1999 U.S. LEXIS 902,* that case no longer presents a substantial federal question. The appeal in that case is therefore dismissed.

It is so ordered.

Justice Stevens dissenting, with whom Justice Souter and Justice Ginsburg join as to Parts I and II, and with whom Justice Breyer joins as to Parts II and III.

The Census Act, *13 U.S.C. § 1 et seq.,* unambiguously authorizes the Secretary of Commerce to use sampling procedures when taking the decennial census. That this authorization is constitutional is equally clear. Moreover, because I am satisfied that at least one of the plaintiffs in each of these cases has standing, I would reverse both District Court judgments.

I

The Census Act, as amended in 1976, contains two provisions that relate to sampling. The first is an unlimited authorization; the second is a limited mandate.

The unlimited authorization is contained in § 141(a). As its text plainly states, that section gives the Secretary of Commerce unqualified authority to use sampling procedures when taking the decennial census, the census used to apportion the House of Representatives. It reads as follows:

"(a) The Secretary shall, in the year 1980 and every 10 years thereafter, take a decennial census of population as of the first day of April of such year, which date shall be known as the 'decennial census date,' in such form and content as he may determine, including the use of sampling procedures and special surveys. *13 U.S.C. § 141*(a)."

The limited mandate is contained in § 195. That section commands the Secretary to use sampling, subject to two limitations: he need

not do so when determining the population for apportionment purposes, and he need not do so unless he considers it feasible. The command reads as follows:

"Except for the determination of population for purposes of apportionment of Representatives in Congress among the several States, the Secretary shall, if he considers it feasible, authorize the use of the statistical method known as 'sampling' in carrying out the provisions of this title." *13 U.S.C. § 195.*

Although § 195 does not command the Secretary to use sampling in the determination of population for apportionment purposes, neither does it prohibit such sampling. Not a word in § 195 qualifies the unlimited grant of authority in § 141(a). Even if its text were ambiguous, § 195 should be construed [consistently with § 141(a).] Moreover, since § 141(a) refers specifically to the decennial census, whereas § 195 refers to the use of sampling in both the mid-decade and the decennial censuses, the former more specific provision would prevail over the latter if there were any conflict between the two. See *Edmond v. United States,* 520 U.S. 651, 657 (1997). In my judgment, however, the text of both provisions is perfectly clear: They authorize sampling in both the decennial and the mid-decade census, but they only command its use when the determination is not for apportionment purposes. . . .

The primary purpose of the 1976 enactment was to provide for a mid-decade census to be used for various purposes other than apportionment. Section 141(a), however, is concerned only with the decennial census. The comment in the Senate Report on the new language in § 141(a) states that this provision was intended "to encourage the use of sampling and surveys in the taking of the decennial census." S. Rep. No. 94–1256, p. 4 (1976). Given that there is only one decennial census, and that it is [the only census that is used for apportionment purposes,] the import of this comment in the Senate Report could not be more clear. See *ibid.* ("It is for the purpose of apportioning Representatives that the United States Constitution establishes a decennial census of population").

Nevertheless, in an unusual *tour de force,* the Court concludes that the amendments made no change in the scope of the Secretary's authority: Both before and after 1976, he could use sampling for any census-related purpose, other than apportionment. The plurality finds an omission in the legislative history of the 1976 enactment more probative of congressional intent than either the plain text of the statute itself or the pertinent comment in the Senate Report. For the plurality, it is incredible that such an important change in the law would not be discussed in the floor debates. It appears, however, that even though other provisions of the legislation were controversial, no one objected to this change. That the use of sampling has since become a partisan issue sheds no light on the views of the legislators who enacted the authorization to use sampling in 1976. Indeed, the bill was reported out of the House Committee by a unanimous vote, both the House and Senate versions easily passed, and the Conference was unanimous in recommending the revised legislation. Surely we must presume that the legislators who voted for the bill were familiar with its text as well as the several references to sampling in the Committee Reports. Given the general agreement on the proposition that "sampling and surveys" should be encouraged because they can both save money and increase the reliability of the population count, it is not at all surprising that no one objected to what was perceived as an obviously desirable change in the law. . . .

The July 1787 debate over future reapportionment of seats in the House of Representatives did not include any dispute about proposed methods of determining the population. Rather, the key questions were whether the rule of reapportionment would be constitutionally fixed and whether subsequent allocations of seats would be based on population or property. See 1 Records of the Federal Convention of 1787, pp. 57–71, 542, 559–562, 566–570, 578–579, 579–580, 586, 594 (M. Farrand ed. 1911); see also Declaration of Jack N. Rakove, App. 387 ("What was at issue . . . were fundamental principles of representation itself . . . not the secondary matter of exactly

how census data was to be compiled"); J. Rakove, *Original Meanings: Politics and Ideas in the Making of the Constitution* 70–74 (1996). The Committee of Style, charged with delivering a polished final version of the Constitution, added the term "actual Enumeration" to the draft reported to the Convention on September 12, 1787—five days before adjournment. 2 Records, *supra,* at 590–591. This stylistic change did not limit Congress' authority to determine the "Manner" of conducting the census.

[The census is intended to serve "the constitutional goal of equal representation." *Franklin v. Massachusetts,* 505 U.S. 788, 804 (1992). That goal is best served by the use of a "Manner" that is most likely to be complete and accurate.] As we repeatedly emphasized in our recent decision in *Wisconsin v. City of New York,* 517 U.S. 1, 3 (1996), our construction of that authorization must respect "the wide discretion bestowed by the Constitution upon Congress." Methodological improvements have been employed to ease the administrative burden of the census and increase the accuracy of the data collected. The "mailout-mailback" procedure now considered a traditional method of enumeration was itself an innovation of the 1970 census. Requiring a face-to-face headcount would yield absurd results: For example, enumerators unable to gain entry to a large and clearly occupied apartment complex would be required to note zero occupants. For this reason, the 1970 census introduced the Postal Vacancy Check—a form of sampling not challenged here—which uses sample households to impute population figures that have been designated vacant but appear to be occupied. Since it is perfectly clear that the use of sampling [will make the census more accurate than an admittedly futile attempt to count every individual by personal inspection, interview, or written interrogatory,] the proposed method is a legitimate means of making the "actual Enumeration" that the Constitution commands . . .

Accordingly, I respectfully dissent in both cases. I would reverse both judgments on the merits.

Office of Personnel Management v. Charles Richmond
496 U.S. 414 (1990)

Justice Kennedy delivered the opinion of the Court, in which Chief Justice Rehnquist and Justices White, Blackmun, O'Connor, and Scalia joined. Justice White filed a concurring opinion, in which Justice Blackmun joined. Justice Stevens filed an opinion concurring in the judgment. Justice Marshall filed a dissenting opinion, in which Justice Brennan joined.

This case presents the question whether erroneous oral and written advice given by a Government employee to a benefit claimant may give rise to estoppel against the Government, and so entitle the claimant to a monetary payment not otherwise permitted by law. We hold that payments of money from the Federal Treasury are limited to those authorized by statute, and we reverse the contrary holding of the Court of Appeals.

I

Respondent was a welder at the Navy Public Works Center in San Diego, California. He left this position in 1981 after petitioner, the Office of Personnel Management (OPM), approved his application for a disability retirement. OPM determined that respondent's impaired eyesight prevented him from performing his job and made him eligible for a disability annuity under 5 U.S.C. § 8337(a). Section 8337(a) provides this benefit for disabled federal employees who have completed five years of service. The statute directs, however, that the entitlement to disability payments will end if the retired employee is "restored to an earning capacity fairly comparable to the current rate of pay of the position occupied at the time of retirement." 5 U.S.C. § 8337(d).

The statutory rules for restoration of earning capacity are central to this case. Prior to 1982, an individual was deemed restored to earning capacity, and so rendered ineligible for a disability annuity, if "in each of 2 succeeding calendar years the income of the annuitant from wages or self-employment . . . equals at least 80 percent of the current rate of pay of the position occupied immediately before retirement."

The provision was amended in 1982 by the Omnibus Budget Reconciliation Act, Pub. L. 97-235, 96 Stat. 792, to change the measuring period for restoration of earning capacity from two years to one:

"Earning capacity is deemed restored if in any calendar year the income of the annuitant from wages or self-employment or both equals at least 80 percent of the current rate of pay of the position occupied immediately before retirement."

After taking disability retirement for his vision impairment, respondent undertook part-time employment as a school bus driver. From 1982 to 1985, respondent earned an average of $12,494 in this job, leaving him under the 80% limit for entitlement to continued annuity payments. In 1986, however, he had an opportunity to earn extra money by working overtime. Respondent asked an Employee Relations Specialist at the Navy Public Works Center's Civilian Personnel Department for information about how much he could earn without exceeding the 80% eligibility limit. Relying upon the terms of the repealed pre-1982 statute, under which respondent could retain the annuity unless his income exceeded the 80% limit in two consecutive years, the specialist gave respondent incorrect advice. The specialist also gave respondent a copy of Attachment 4 to Federal Personnel Manual Letter 831-64, published by petitioner OPM, which also stated the former 2-year eligibility rule. The OPM form was correct when written in 1981; but when given to respondent, the form was out of date and therefore inaccurate. Respondent returned to the Navy in January 1987, and again was advised in error that eligibility would be determined under the old 2-year rule.

After receiving the erroneous information, respondent concluded that he could take on the extra work as a school bus driver in 1986 while still receiving full disability benefits for impaired vision so long as he kept his income for the previous and following years below the statutory level. He earned $19,936 during 1986, exceeding the statutory eligibility limit. OPM discontinued respondent's disability annuity on June 30, 1987. The annuity was restored on January 1, 1988, since respondent did not earn more than allowed by the statute in 1987. Respondent thus lost his disability payments for a 6-month period, for a total amount of $3,993.

Respondent appealed the denial of benefits to the Merit Systems Protection Board (MSPB). He argued that the erroneous advice given him by the Navy personnel should estop OPM and bar its finding him ineligible for benefits under the statute. The MSPB rejected this argument, noting that the officials who misinformed respondent were from the Navy, not OPM. The MSPB observed that, "had [respondent] directed his request for information to the OPM, presumably, he would have learned of the change in the law." The MSPB held that "OPM cannot be estopped from enforcing a statutorily imposed requirement for retirement eligibility. The MSPB denied respondent's petition for review, and respondent appealed to the Court of Appeals for the Federal Circuit.

A divided panel of the Court of Appeals reversed, accepting respondent's contention that the misinformation from Navy personnel estopped the Government, and that the estoppel required payment of disability benefits despite the statutory provision to the contrary. The Court of Appeals acknowledged the longstanding rule that "ordinarily the government may not be estopped because of erroneous or unauthorized statements of government employees when the asserted estoppel would nullify a requirement prescribed by Congress." Nonetheless, the Court of Appeals focused on this Court's statement in an earlier case that "we are hesitant . . . to say that there are no cases" where the Government might be estopped. *Heckler v. Community Health Services of Crawford County, Inc.,* 467 U.S. 51, 60 (1984). The Court of Appeals then discussed other Circuit and District Court opinions that had applied estoppel against the Government. . . .

The Court reasoned that the provision of the out-of-date OPM form was "affirmative misconduct" that should estop the Government from denying respondent benefits in accordance with the statute. The facts of this case, it held, are "sufficiently unusual and extreme that no concern is warranted about exposing the public treasury to estoppel in broad or numerous categories of cases."

We granted certiorari.

II

From our earliest cases, we have recognized that equitable estoppel will not lie against the Government as against private litigants. In *Lee v. Munroe & Thornton,* 11 U.S. 366 (1813), we held that the Government could not be bound by the mistaken representations of an agent unless it were clear that the representations were within the scope of the agent's authority. In *The Floyd Acceptances,* 74 U.S. 666 (1869), we held that the Government could not be compelled to honor bills of exchange issued by the Secretary of War where there was no statutory authority for the issuance of the bills. In *Utah Power & Light Co. v. United States,* 243 U.S. 389, 408–409 (1917), we dismissed the argument that unauthorized representations by agents of the Government estopped the United States to prevent erection of power houses and transmission lines across a public forest in violation of a statute: "Of this it is enough to say that the United States is neither bound nor estopped by the acts of its officers or agents in entering into an arrangement or agreement to do or cause to be done what the law does not sanction or permit."

The principles of these and many other cases were reiterated in *Federal Crop Insurance Corporation v. Merrill,* 332 U.S. 380 (1947), the leading case in our modern line of estoppel decisions. . . . While we recognized the serious hardship caused by the agent's misinformation, we nonetheless rejected the argument that his representations estopped the Government to deny insurance benefits. We recognized that "not even the temptations of a hard case" will provide a basis for ordering recovery contrary to the terms of the regulation, for to do so would disregard "the duty of all courts to observe the conditions defined by Congress for charging the public treasury."

Despite the clarity of these earlier decisions, dicta in our more recent cases have suggested the possibility that there might be some situation in which estoppel against the Government could be appropriate. The genesis of this idea appears to be an observation found at the end of our opinion in *Montana v. Kennedy,* 366 U.S. 308 (1961). In that case, the petitioner brought a declaratory judgment action seeking to establish his American citizenship. After discussing the petitioner's two statutory claims at length, we rejected the final argument that a consular official's erroneous advice to petitioner's mother that she could not return to the United States while pregnant prevented petitioner from having been born in the United States and thus deprived him of United States citizenship. Our discussion was limited to the observation that in light of the fact that no legal obstacle prevented petitioner's mother from returning to the United States, "what may have been only the consular official's well-meant advice—'I am sorry, Mrs., you cannot [return to the United States] in that condition'—falls far short of misconduct such as might prevent the United States from relying on petitioner's foreign birth. In this situation, we need not stop to inquire whether, as some lower courts have held, there may be circumstances in which the United States is estopped to deny citizenship because of the conduct of its officials."

The proposition about which we did not "stop to inquire" in *Kennedy* has since taken on something of a life of its own. Our own opinions have continued to mention the possibility, in the course of rejecting estoppel arguments, that some type of "affirmative misconduct" might give rise to estoppel against the Government. . . .

The Solicitor General proposes to remedy the present confusion in this area of the law with a sweeping rule. As it has in the past, the Government asks us to adopt "a flat rule that estoppel may not in any circumstances run against the Government." *Community Health Services,* supra, at 60. The Government bases its broad rule first upon the doctrine of sovereign immunity. Noting that the "United States, as sovereign,

is immune from suit save as it consents to be sued," *United States v. Mitchell,* 445 U.S. 535, 538 (1980), the Government asserts that the courts are without jurisdiction to entertain a suit to compel the Government to act contrary to a statute, no matter what the context or circumstances. The Government advances as a second basis for this rule the doctrine of separation of powers. The Government contends that to recognize estoppel based on the misrepresentations of Executive Branch officials would give those misrepresentations the force of law, and thereby invade the legislative province reserved to Congress. This rationale, too, supports the Government's contentions that estoppel may never justify an order requiring executive action contrary to a relevant statute, no matter what statute or what facts are involved.

We have recognized before that the "arguments the Government advances for the rule are substantial." And we agree that this case should be decided under a clearer form of analysis than "we will know an estoppel when we see one." *Hansen,* supra, at 792 (Justice Marshall dissenting). But it remains true that we need not embrace a rule that no estoppel will lie against the Government in any case in order to decide this case. We leave for another day whether an estoppel claim could ever succeed against the Government. A narrower ground of decision is sufficient to address the type of suit presented here, a claim for payment of money from the Public Treasury contrary to a statutory appropriation.

III

The Appropriations Clause of the Constitution, Art. I, § 9, cl. 7, provides that: "No Money shall be drawn from the Treasury, but in Consequence of Appropriations made by Law." For the particular type of claim at issue here, a claim for money from the Federal Treasury, the Clause provides an explicit rule of decision. Money may be paid out only through an appropriation made by law; in other words, the payment of money from the Treasury must be authorized by a statute. All parties here agree that the award respondent seeks would be in direct contravention of the federal statute upon which his ultimate claim to the funds must rest, 5 U.S.C. § 8337. The point is made clearer when the appropriation supporting the benefits sought by respondent is examined. In the same subchapter of the United States Code as the eligibility requirements, Congress established the Civil Service Retirement and Disability Fund. 5 U.S.C. § 8348. That section states in pertinent part: "The Fund . . . is appropriated for the payment of . . . benefits as provided by this subchapter. . . ." The benefits respondent claims were not "provided by" the relevant provision of the subchapter; rather, they were specifically denied. It follows that Congress has appropriated no money for the payment of the benefits respondent seeks, and the Constitution prohibits that any money "be drawn from the Treasury" to pay them. . . .

"However, much money may be in the Treasury at any one time, not a dollar of it can be used in payment of any thing not thus previously sanctioned. Any other course would give to the fiscal officers a most dangerous discretion." . . .

We have not had occasion in past cases presenting claims of estoppel against the Government to discuss the Appropriations Clause, for reasons that are apparent. Given the strict rule against estoppel applied as early as 1813 in *Lee v. Munroe & Thornton*, 11 U.S. 366 (1813), claims of estoppel could be dismissed on that ground without more. In our cases following *Montana v. Kennedy* 366 U.S. 308 (1961), reserving the possibility that estoppel might lie on some facts, we have held only that the particular facts presented were insufficient. As discussed above, we decline today to accept the Solicitor General's argument for an across-the-board no-estoppel rule. But this makes it all the more important to state the law and to settle the matter of estoppel as a basis for money claims against the Government.

. . . [T]he [appropriations] Clause has a more fundamental and comprehensive purpose, of direct relevance to the case before us. It is to assure that public funds will be spent according to the letter of the difficult judgments reached by Congress as to the common good, and not according to the individual favor of Government agents or the individual pleas of litigants.

Extended to its logical conclusion, operation of estoppel against the Government in the context of payment of money from the Treasury could in fact render the Appropriations Clause a nullity. If agents of the Executive were able, by their unauthorized oral or written statements to citizens, to obligate the Treasury for the payment of funds, the control over public funds that the Clause reposes in Congress in effect could be transferred to the Executive. If, for example, the President or Executive Branch officials were displeased with a new restriction on benefits imposed by Congress to ease burdens on the fisc (such as the restriction imposed by the statutory change in this case) and sought to evade them, agency officials could advise citizens that the restrictions were inapplicable. Estoppel would give this advice the practical force of law, in violation of the Constitution.

Respondent points to no authority in precedent or history for the type of claim he advances today. Whether there are any extreme circumstances that might support estoppel in a case not involving payment from the Treasury is a matter we need not address. As for monetary claims, it is enough to say that this Court has never upheld [an] assertion of estoppel against the Government by a claimant seeking public funds. In this context there can be no estoppel, for courts cannot estop the Constitution. The judgment of the Court of Appeals is Reversed.

Notes

1. Edward Rubin, "It's Time to Make the Administrative Procedure Act Administrative," 89 *Cornell Law Review* 95, 107–08 (November 2003).

2. Peter Skerry, "Sampling Error: Small Stakes in the Big Census Fight," *The New Republic*, May 31, 1999, p. 18.

3. Harold W. Stanley and Richard Nieme, *Vital Statistics on American Politics*, 5th ed. (Washington, D.C.: Congressional Quarterly Press, 1995), p. 348.

4. Paul Overberg and Douglas Pardue, "Adjusted Census Figures Add 3.3 Million Residents," *USA. Today*, December 6, 2002, p. A2.

5. *Carter v. Department of Commerce,* 186 F.Supp 2d 1147,1149 (D. Oregon, 2001).

6. Ibid.

7. Ibid.

8. Constitution of the United States, Art. I, Sec. 2, Clause 3.

9. Gary Jacobson, *The Politics of Congressional Elections* (New York: Longman, 1997), p. 7.

10. Ibid.

11. Robert T. Gary, "Back to the Drawing Board," 87 *Nation's Business* 48 (Feb. 1999); *CQ's Politics in American 2004: The 108th Congress* (Washington, D.C.: Congressional Quarterly Press, 2003), ix–xii.

12. Morris Fiornia, *Divided Government,* 2nd ed. (Boston: Allyn and Bacon, 1996), p. 137.

13. Ibid. Some have estimated the contribution to Republican gains in the 1994 election from the creation of minority-majority districts to be even higher. See Juan Williams, "Blacked Out in the New Congress," *Washington Post,* November 20, 1994, p. C1.

14. The material on Georgia's congressional districts comes from Rhodes Cook, "Democratic Congressional Base Shredded by November Vote," 52 *Congressional Quarterly* 3518 (December 10, 1994).

15. Ibid.

16. Ibid.

17. The sampling process is described by Chief Justice Rehnquist in his opinion for the Court in *Wisconsin v. New York,* 517 U.S. 1, 15–16 (1996).

18. *Wisconsin v. New York,* 517 U.S. 1, 34–35 (1996).

19. The material on the political posturing prior to the 2000 census comes directly from the Court's opinion in *Department of Commerce v. United States House of Representatives,* 525 U.U. 316, 326–27 (1999).

20. The material on the 2000 census and FOIA comes from the trial court case of *Carter v. DOC* at pp. 1151–52 (note 6). See also *Carter v. DOC,* 307 F.3d. 1084 (9th cir., 2002).

21. *City of Los Angeles et al. v. Department of Commerce,* 307 F.3d. 859 (9th Cir., 2002).

22. Overberg and Pardue, "Adjusted Census Figures."

23. Kenneth Culp Davis, *Administrative Law Treatise,* 2d ed., vol. 1 (San Diego, Calif.: K. C. Davis, 1978), p. 14.

24. Ernest Gellhorn and Ronald Levin, *Administrative Law and Process: In a Nutshell* (St. Paul, Minn.: West, 1990), p. 167.

25. Ibid.

26. In my own case, when I appealed to the regional director's office, the official that I spoke with told me that he believed that I was using the IRS as a case study in my Ph.D. dissertation (I was not), and he absolutely refused to budge, even though I had three district court cases in my favor. When I filed my suit, the IRS offered to settle for half. I took the offer.

27. The facts are contained in the opinion; see *Federal Crop Insurance Corporation v. Merrill,* 332 U.S. 380, 381 (1947).

28. *Montana v. Kennedy,* 366 U.S. 308 (1961).

29. *Immigration and Naturalization Service v. Hibi,* 414 U.S. 5 (1973).

30. *Immigration and Naturalization Service v. Miranda,* 459 U.S. 14 (1982).

31. 467 U.S. 51, 59 (1984).

32. 467 U.S. 51, 68 (1984), Chief Justice Rehnquist concurring.

33. Ibid.

34. Kenneth Culp Davis, *Administrative Law: Cases—Text—Problems,* 6th ed. (St. Paul, Minn.: West, 1977), p. 443.

35. Ibid., p. 444.

36. Rubin, "It's Time to Make," ibid., Note 1.

7

RULE MAKING AND ADJUDICATION

**Case in Point:
"It Depends on What Your
Definition of the Word *Is* Is"**

You may have heard this famous quote by President Clinton when he was being deposed by special prosecutors about possible perjury involving his testimony regarding the nature of his relationship with Monica Lewinsky. In the case in point below, the Court must decide what the word *has* means. Sometimes Congress uses clear language in legislation, and sometimes it does not. Regardless of the clarity of congressional language, agencies will interpret terms used in legislation in their attempts to "faithfully execute the laws" and the courts will be left with reviewing those interpretations.

Probably one of the most important laws passed during the 20th century was the 1964 Civil Rights Act. It forbids discrimination on the basis of race or gender in interstate commerce. The reason Congress felt the need to pass such a law was because, prior to its passage, the federal government had no power to deal with private racial discrimination. The Fourteenth Amendment says in pertinent part, "No state shall . . . deny to any person within its jurisdiction the equal protection of the laws." In *The Civil Rights Cases*, 100 U.S. 3 (1883), the Supreme Court said that the equal protection clause of the Fourteenth Amendment can apply only to official governmental discrimination (i.e., "No *state* shall . . ."), and it cannot form the basis for laws attempting to regulate private or non-governmental discrimination. The Court's 1883 decision is still the law today. Hence, if the federal government wants to legislate against private racial discrimination, it would be forced to find a different way because it cannot rely on the Fourteenth Amendment for legal authority.

The political realignment of 1932 ushered in an era of a more active role for the federal government, and the commerce clause of Art. I, Sec. 8, Cl. 3 of the U.S. Constitution was the vehicle for that more active government. In the middle of the civil rights movement of the 1950s and early 1960s, Congress relied on the commerce clause to ban discrimination other than state-enforced discrimination. It did so in the 1964 Civil Rights Act.

In Chapter 1, the point was made that the Constitution established a limited government. That means that the power of the federal government is limited to those things that can be implied from Art. I, Sec. 8. Because Art. I, Sec. 8, Cl. 3 gives the federal government the power to "regulate commerce . . . among the several states," Congress has the power to ban discrimination in interstate commerce. But that power is limited to interstate commerce. How can we tell when a business or entity is not involved in interstate commerce and thus beyond the reach of the federal government and the 1964 Civil Rights Act?

Congress answered that question in terms of employment discrimination by saying that the Civil Rights Act's ban on discrimination applies "to any employer who *has* 15 or more employees for each working day in each of 20 or more calendar weeks in the current or preceding calendar year." Not only does the Civil Rights Act ban discrimination in interstate commerce, but it also makes it unlawful for an employer to retaliate against any employee who files a claim against the employer before the Equal Employment Opportunity Commission (EEOC).

Darlene Walters[1] was employed by Metropolitan Educational Enterprises, a retail distributor of encyclopedias, dictionaries, and other educational material. After she did not get a promotion to the position of credit manager, Ms. Walters filed a complaint with the EEOC alleging gender discrimination. Metropolitan's reaction was to fire her, so both the EEOC and Walters filed suit in federal district court for a violation of the retaliation clause. The company moved to dismiss the complaint on the grounds that the 1964 Civil Rights Act did not apply to them because they did not *have* 15 or more employees for each working day in each of 20 weeks during 1989 and 1990.

The district court agreed with Metropolitan Educational Enterprises and dismissed the suit, a decision that was upheld by the circuit court. In *Walters v. Metropolitan Educational Enterprises,* 519 U.S. 202 (1997), the Supreme Court reversed. It turns out that there are two ways to count whether an employer *has* 15 or more employees in each working day for 20 weeks. The company had between 15 and 17 employees over the two-year period, but two were part-time and typically did not work on Fridays, so Metropolitan Educational Enterprises only compensated 15 or more employees for nine weeks during either year. This is referred to as the *compensation method* for calculating whether an employer *has* 15 or more employees. You count the number of employees who are compensated "each working day" to see if it adds up to 20 weeks.

The Supreme Court decided to reject the compensation method in favor of the *payroll method* of determining when an employer *has* 15 or more employees. The payroll method simply looks to see whether there was an employer/employee relationship on any given day. In deciding on the payroll method, the Court first turned to the dictionary definition of the word *has*. Also, there are practical problems in calculating whether an employee was compensated on any given day. The Court described those problems as follows:

> In applying it (the compensation method) in the present case required the parties to spend 10 months poring over Metropolitan's payroll registers, time cards, work diaries and other time keeping records to determine, for each working day of the two year period, how many employees were at work, how many were being paid on salary, how many were paid on holiday leave, how many were paid on vacation leave and how many were on paid sick leave. For an employer with 15 employees and a 5 day work-week the number of daily working histories for the two year period is 7,800.[2]

It is worthy of note in a chapter on rule making that the EEOC, which has jurisdiction to enforce the Civil Rights Act, also prefers the payroll method of deciding when an employer *has* 15 or more employees. But when Congress passed the 1964 Civil Rights Act, it failed to give the EEOC any rule-making power. Therefore, the EEOC was forced to litigate its decisions in each case regarding how many employees an employer *had*.

This case involves an area of administrative law referred to as *statutory interpretation.* Here's the process: An agency (EEOC) interprets a term in a statute *(has)*, and the courts have to review the agency's interpretation. You are already familiar with a couple of cases where this was at issue. One of them was *Food and Drug Administration v. Brown & Williamson Corp.*, 529 U.S. 120 (2000), where the Court had to review the FDA's interpretation of whether tobacco is "safe and effective for its intended use." The other case was the case involving the census (*Department of Commerce v. United States House of Representatives*, 525 U.S. 316 [1999])*,* where the Court had to decide whether the term *enumeration* allowed for a sample. As you will soon discover, often when agencies interpret statutory language, they adopt a rule called an interpretive rule.

THE NEED FOR RULE MAKING

In 1899, the Denver Board of Public Works (Board) recommended to the city council that certain streets be paved.[3] The council accepted the recommendation, the mayor ordered the work to be done, and a special assessment district to pay for it was created. After completion of the work, the Board ascertained the total cost of the work and apportioned a special assessment tax on each piece of property according to the extent that each tract benefited from the improvements. The city clerk then published in the newspaper the total cost of the work and each lot's assessment. The notice in the paper further notified affected property owners that they had 30 days to file written complaints with the city council. The city council received complaints, read them into the record, and then voted to accept the Board's apportioned assessments.

The plaintiff property owners sued on the basis of the due process clause of the Fourteenth Amendment, which forbids the state from taking life, liberty, or property without due process of law (*Londoner v. City of Denver,* 210 U.S. 373 [1908]).

The basic elements of due process are (a) a *notice* that government is about to take some action that may affect your life, liberty, or property and (b) an opportunity for those affected to be heard (i.e., *a hearing).* The plaintiffs challenged both the sufficiency of the notice (they thought they should have been notified about the work, not just the assessments) and the sufficiency of the hearing. The Court said that the notice was sufficient, but the procedure was not. The Court noted that the Constitution places few restrictions on a state legislature's power to tax (also true of Congress). That is, a legislature is not required to notify citizens and provide them with an opportunity to speak before it imposes a tax. However, when a legislature delegates the power to lower units of government to decide "whether, in what amount, and upon whom"[4] to levy a tax, lower units of government are required to provide notice and a hearing. At a minimum, that hearing should consist of an opportunity to make arguments and submit proof.[5] Although the Court spoke only of a state legislature's delegation to lower units of government, we can assume that the same logic applies to legislative or congressional delegations to agencies.

Justice Holmes dissented in the *Londoner* case. Seven years later, the Court was presented with the issue again, and this time Justice Holmes wrote the opinion for the majority.

Bi-Metallic Investment Company v. State Board of Equalization
239 U.S. 441 (1915)

Justice Holmes delivered the opinion for a unanimous Court.

This is a suit to enjoin the State Board of Equalization and the Colorado Tax Commission from putting in force and the defendant Pitcher, as assessor of Denver, from obeying, an order of the boards, increasing the valuation of all taxable property in Denver 40 per cent. The order was sustained and the suit directed to be dismissed by the supreme court of the state. The plaintiff is the owner of real estate in Denver, and brings the case here on the ground that it was given no opportunity to be heard, and that therefore its property will be taken without due process of law, contrary to the 14th Amendment of the Constitution of the United States. That is the only question with which we have to deal. For the purposes of decision we assume that the constitutional question is presented in the baldest way—that neither the plaintiff nor the assessor of Denver, who presents a brief on the plaintiff's side, nor any representative of the city and county, was given an opportunity to be heard, other than such as they may have had by reason of the fact that the time of meeting of the boards is fixed by law. On this assumption it is obvious that injustice may be suffered if some property in the county already has been valued at its full worth. But if certain property has been valued at a rate different from that generally prevailing in the county, the owner has had his opportunity to protest and appeal as usual in our system of taxation so that it must be assumed that the property owners in the county all stand alike. The question, then, is whether all individuals have a constitutional right to be heard before a matter can be decided in which all are equally concerned— here, for instance, before a superior board decides that the local taxing officers have adopted a system of undervaluation throughout a county, as notoriously often has been the case. The answer of this court in the *State R. Tax Cases*, 92 U.S. 575, at least, as to any further

notice, was that it was hard to believe that the proposition was seriously made.

Where a rule of conduct applies to more than a few people, it is impracticable that everyone should have a direct voice in its adoption. The Constitution does not require all public acts to be done in town meeting or an assembly of the whole. General statutes within the state power are passed that affect the person or property of individuals, sometimes to the point of ruin, without giving them a chance to be heard. Their rights are protected in the only way that they can be in a complex society, by their power, immediate or remote, over those who make the rule. If the result in this case had been reached, as it might have been by the state's doubling the rate of taxation, no one would suggest that the 14th Amendment was violated unless every person affected had been allowed an opportunity to raise his voice against it before the body entrusted by the state Constitution with the power. In considering this case in this court we must assume that the proper state machinery has been used, and the question is whether, if the state Constitution had declared that Denver had been undervalued as compared with the rest of the state, and had decreed that for the current year the valuation should be 40 per cent higher, the objection now urged could prevail. It appears to us that to put the question is to answer it. There must be a limit to individual argument in such matters if government is to go on. In *Londoner v. Denver*, 210 U.S. 373, a local board had to determine "whether, in what amount, and upon whom" a tax for paving a street should be levied for special benefits. A relatively small number of persons [were] concerned, who were exceptionally affected, in each case upon individual grounds, and it was held that they had a right to a hearing. But that decision is far from reaching a general determination dealing only with the principle upon which all the assessments in a county had been laid.

Judgment affirmed.

The state of the law after 1915 was that where a small number of people each individually and exceptionally are affected, a hearing is required (*Londoner*). Where government action applies to more than a few people and it is impractical to hold a hearing, none is required by due process (*Bi-Metallic*). Just so the student does not assume that these ancient cases have no practical application today, let me provide an example: The state of Kansas adopted an Administrative Procedure Act in 1985, and that Act imposes on all state agencies what we have elsewhere called "notice and comment procedures." It does not, however, impose those procedural requirements on lower units of government. Even into the 21st century, cities and counties and other units of government and their agencies in Kansas looked to *Londoner* and *Bi-Metallic* to determine whether they were required to provide notice and a hearing prior to taking action.[6] This situation is probably true in other states as well. Indeed, some states have yet to pass any sort of administrative procedure act and in those states, the *Londoner/Bi Metallic* doctrine would apply to state level agencies.

Rule Making Under the Administrative Procedure Act

Federal administrative agencies avoid the *Londoner/Bi-Metallic* question by compliance with the Administrative Procedure Act. Section 551 defines a rule as "the whole or a part of an agency statement of general or particular applicability and future effect designed to implement, interpret or prescribe law or policy or describing the organization, procedure or practice requirements of an agency."[7] Section 553 (on pages 535–536 in this book) imposes the constitutional requirements of notice and a hearing on federal agencies. With a few exceptions it requires agencies to publish notice of proposed rule making in the *Federal Register*. It requires that the notice state the time, date, place, and nature of the public hearing on the proposed rule (the nature of the procedure refers to whether the agency will allow oral testimony or whether it will simply accept written input). The procedure requires the agency to cite the legal authority for the rule and provide the gist of the proposed rule. It then requires the agency to consider the input on the proposed rule, to write the rule, to include a "concise general statement of [the rule's] basis and purpose," and to publish the rule in the *Federal Register* again, 30 days after which it becomes a final rule and has the force and effect of law. The process that is described above is what has been referred to so far as rule making, informal rule making, rule promulgation, quasi-legislative procedure or rule, and notice and comment procedure. All of these terms refer to the same thing: a rule adopted through the procedures outlined in § 553 of the Administrative Procedure Act. In cases in which courts have attempted to require more elaborate procedures than those just described, the Supreme Court has reversed those decisions. See the *Vermont Yankee Nuclear Power Company* case at the end of this chapter. Late in the Carter presidency (1977–1981), the secretary of transportation adopted a rule through a § 553 procedure that would require all automobiles manufactured or imported into America to have passive restraint systems (air bags or automatic seat belts) installed by 1984. You will read the history of auto safety regulation in the *State Farm* case at the end of this chapter. Subsequently, President Reagan's secretary of transportation made an informal decision to rescind the passive restraint rule for automobiles and was immediately sued by an auto insurance company that stood to lose millions. The Supreme Court said that once an agency adopts a rule or policy through a § 553 procedure, it can only undo the rule by going through another § 553 process. This is also one of the few cases where the Court voided an agency action because it was arbitrary. The secretary who rescinded the passive restraint rule could not explain why he had done so in light of all the overwhelming evidence that seat belts save lives.

President Clinton fought constantly with a Republican-controlled Congress that wanted to open up more federally owned land for development. Clinton had the Department of Agriculture (Forestry Department) and Department of the Interior hold § 553 hearings in locations across America where national forests are located. More than 2 million people participated in the hearings, which cumulated in the "Roadless Rule."[8] The Roadless Rule made 30 percent of our national forests, some 40 to 60 million acres, *near wilderness* areas. Only Congress can designate land as wilderness, but it delegated to the executive branch the power to designate land as *near wilderness,* which also means no roads. No roads means no development. President Bush 43 and the Republicans in Congress had few options. Congress could not do congressional review because the rule had been implemented by the 60-day time limit. President Bush could attempt to delay implementation of the rule or he could order the Interior and Forestry Departments to hold new rounds of hearings to rescind the rule. It took the Bush Administration three and a half years to propose a counter rule that would allow the states to regulate access to the national forests.

President Clinton's secretary of the interior Bruce Babbitt went through § 553 hearings to change the nation's grazing policy on public lands. Once again, the Clinton Administration turned to the bureaucracy to make public policy rather than submitting legislation to a hostile Congress. From the 1930s when the Taylor Grazing Act was passed to 1995 when the new regulations went into effect, ranchers who lived near public land had an expectation that they would be able to graze cattle on public land and pay little for the privilege. Secretary Babbitt's new regulations were meant to make the rangeland management program "more compatible with ecosystem management" and to change the Bureau of Land Management's practices "into closer conformity with related Forest Service management practices."[9] Specifically, the ranchers who sued the secretary were upset that the new regulations made holders of grazing permits more accountable for the condition of the land. The ranchers also challenged the changed definition of *grazing preference* so that those not engaged in the livestock business could qualify for a permit to use the public's land. Their suit alleged that the regulations exceeded the secretary's authority under the Taylor Act. That made this a jurisdiction case, but the Supreme Court said that the new regulations were consistent with the statute. Justice O'Connor, along with Justice Thomas in a concurring opinion, reminded the ranchers that they had not challenged the regulations as being arbitrary or capricious, and she invited them to file a new round of suits. See the case of *Public Lands Council v. Babbitt,* 529 U.S. 728 (2000).

TYPES OF RULES

In defining a rule, § 553 of the Administrative Procedure Act establishes three different types of rules: (a) interpretive rules, when an agency issues a rule interpreting a statute the agency must apply or work with, as in the definition of *has* 15 or more employees in the Case in Point; (b) procedural rules, which are simply rules stating the agency's procedure for dealing with a situation; and (c) substantive rules, which have the force and effect of law and are the basic way most agencies implement congressional delegations of power. To have the force and effect of law, substantive rules must go through the appropriate § 553 procedure. Procedural and interpretive rules do not need to go through the § 553 or any other procedure, although, once adopted, they must be published in the *Federal*

Register so that those dealing with an agency will be apprised of the agency's interpretation of the law and of its internal procedures.

Interpretive Rules

As mentioned above, when we say an agency adopted an interpretive rule, that means an agency made an informal decision to interpret a term in a statute and published the interpretation in the *Federal Register.* There is no due process notice and hearing prior to the adoption of an interpretive rule. You will not always be able to distinguish between substantive rules and interpretive or procedural rules for they often sound similar. The basic difference is that only substantive rules must go through a § 553 process first. Frequently interpretive rules are challenged in court. In the case below, Congress required states that had not met national air quality standards to adopt a permit system for regulating "new or modified major stationary sources" of air pollution. The Environmental Protection Agency (EPA), charged with implementing the amended Clean Air Act, adopted an interpretation of "new or modified major stationary sources" as a thing referred to as the *bubble concept.* An environmental interest group sued a polluter who was in compliance with the bubble concept. The case boiled down to whether the EPA's interpretation of "new or modified" was reasonable. This is a famous case in the area of statutory interpretation because the Court adopts a doctrine or standard for judicial review of agency statutory interpretation. Make sure you understand the steps a reviewing court should go through.

Chevron, U.S.A., Incorporated v. Natural Resources Defense Council
467 U.S. 837 (1984)

Justice Stevens delivered the opinion for a unanimous court of six. Justices Marshall, O'Connor, and Chief Justice Burger did not participate in the decision.

In the Clean Air Act Amendments of 1977, Pub.L. 95–95, 91 Stat. 685, Congress enacted certain requirements applicable to States that had not achieved the national air quality standards established by the Environmental Protection Agency (EPA) pursuant to earlier legislation. The amended Clean Air Act required these "nonattainment" States to establish a permit program regulating "new or modified major stationary sources" of air pollution. Generally, a permit may not be issued for a new or modified major stationary source unless several stringent conditions are met. The EPA regulation promulgated to implement this permit requirement allows a State to adopt a statewide definition of the term "stationary source." Under this definition, an existing plant that contains several pollution-emitting devices may install or modify one piece of equipment without meeting the permit conditions if the alteration will not increase the total emissions from the plant. The question presented by this case is whether EPA's decision to allow States to treat all of the pollution-emitting devices within the same industrial grouping as though they were encased within a single "bubble" is based on a reasonable construction of the statutory term "stationary source."

I

The EPA regulations containing the plantwide definition of the term *stationary source* were promulgated on October 14, 1981. 46 Fed.Reg.

50766. Respondents filed a timely petition for review in the United States Court of Appeals for the District of Columbia Circuit. The Court of Appeals set aside the regulations. *National Resources Defense Council, Inc. v. Gorsuch*, 685 F.2d 718 (1982).

The court observed that the relevant part of the amended Clean Air Act "does not explicitly define what Congress envisioned as a 'stationary source,' to which the permit program . . . should apply," and further stated that the precise issue was not "squarely addressed in the legislative history." In light of its conclusion that the legislative history bearing on the question was "at best contradictory," it reasoned that "the purposes of the nonattainment program should guide our decision here." Based on two of its precedents concerning the applicability of the bubble concept to certain Clean Air Act programs, the court stated that the bubble concept was "mandatory" in programs designed merely to maintain existing air quality, but held that it was "inappropriate" in programs enacted to improve air quality. Since the purpose of the permit program—its "raison d'etre," in the court's view—was to improve air quality, the court held that the bubble concept was inapplicable in this case under its prior precedents. It therefore set aside the regulations embodying the bubble concept as contrary to law. We granted certiorari to review that judgment, and we now reverse.

II

When a court reviews an agency's construction of the statute which it administers, it is confronted with two questions. First, always, is the question whether Congress has directly spoken to the precise question at issue. If the intent of Congress is clear, that is the end of the matter; for the court, as well as the agency, must give effect to the unambiguously expressed intent of Congress. If, however, the court determines Congress has not directly addressed the precise question at issue, the court does not simply impose its own construction on the statute, as would be necessary in the absence of an administrative interpretation. Rather, if the statute is silent or ambiguous with respect to

the specific issue, the question for the court is whether the agency's answer is based on a permissible construction of the statute.

"The power of an administrative agency to administer a congressionally created . . . program necessarily requires the formulation of policy and the making of rules to fill any gap left, implicitly or explicitly, by Congress." If Congress has explicitly left a gap for the agency to fill, there is an express delegation of authority to the agency to elucidate a specific provision of the statute by regulation. Such legislative regulations are given controlling weight unless they are arbitrary, capricious, or manifestly contrary to the statute. Sometimes the legislative delegation to an agency on a particular question is implicit rather than explicit. In such a case, a court may not substitute its own construction of a statutory provision for a reasonable interpretation made by the administrator of an agency.

We have long recognized that considerable weight should be accorded to an executive department's construction of a statutory scheme it is entrusted to administer, and the principle of deference to administrative interpretations . . . "has been consistently followed by this Court whenever decision as to the meaning or reach of a statute has involved reconciling conflicting policies, and a full understanding of the force of the statutory policy in the given situation has depended upon more than ordinary knowledge respecting the matters subjected to agency regulations. . . ."

In light of these well-settled principles it is clear that the Court of Appeals misconceived the nature of its role in reviewing the regulations at issue. Once it determined, after its own examination of the legislation, that Congress did not actually have an intent regarding the applicability of the bubble concept to the permit program, the question before it was not whether in its view the concept is "inappropriate" in the general context of a program designed to improve air quality, but whether the Administrator's view that it is appropriate in the context of this particular program is a reasonable one. Based on the examination of the legislation and its history which follows, we agree with the Court of Appeals that Congress did not have a specific intention on the applicability of the bubble concept in these cases, and conclude that the EPA's use of that concept here is a reasonable policy choice for the agency to make. The legislative history of the portion of the 1977 Amendments dealing with nonattainment areas does not contain any specific comment on the "bubble concept" or the question whether a plantwide definition of a stationary source is permissible under the permit program. It does, however, plainly disclose that in the permit program Congress sought to accommodate the conflict between the economic interest in permitting capital improvements to continue and the environmental interest in improving air quality. We are not persuaded that parsing of general terms in the text of the statute will reveal an actual intent of Congress. We know full well that this language is not dispositive; the terms are overlapping and the language is not precisely directed to the question of the applicability of a given term in the context of a larger operation. To the extent any congressional "intent" can be discerned from this language, it would appear that the listing of overlapping, illustrative terms was intended to enlarge, rather than to confine, the scope of the agency's power to regulate particular sources in order to effectuate the policies of the Act.

Our review of the EPA's varying interpretations of the word "source"—both before and after the 1977 Amendments—convinces us that the agency primarily responsible for administering this important legislation has consistently interpreted it flexibly—not in a sterile textual vacuum, but in the context of implementing policy decisions in a technical and complex arena. The fact that the agency has from time to time changed its interpretation of the term source does not, as respondents argue, lead us to conclude that no deference should be accorded the agency's interpretation of the statute. An initial agency interpretation is not instantly carved in stone. On the contrary, the agency, to engage in informed rulemaking, must consider varying interpretations and the wisdom of its policy on a continuing basis. Moreover, the fact that the agency has adopted different definitions in different contexts adds force to the argument that the definition itself is

flexible, particularly since Congress has never indicated any disapproval of a flexible reading of the statute.

In this case, the Administrator's interpretation represents a reasonable accommodation of manifestly competing interests and is entitled to deference: the regulatory scheme is technical and complex, the agency considered the matter in a detailed and reasoned fashion, and the decision involves reconciling conflicting policies. Congress intended to accommodate both interests, but did not do so itself on the level of specificity presented by this case. Perhaps that body consciously desired the Administrator to strike the balance at this level, thinking that those with great expertise and charged with responsibility for administering the provision would be in a better position to do so; perhaps it simply did not consider the question at this level; and perhaps Congress was unable to forge a coalition on either side of the question, and those on each side decided to take their chances with the scheme devised by the agency. For judicial purposes, it matters not which of these things occurred.

Judges are not experts in the field, and are not part of either political branch of the Government. Courts must, in some cases, reconcile competing political interests, but not on the basis of the judges' personal policy preferences. In contrast, an agency to which Congress has delegated policymaking responsibilities may, within the limits of that delegation, properly rely upon the incumbent administration's views of wise policy to inform its judgments. While agencies are not directly accountable to the people, the Chief Executive is, and it is entirely appropriate for this political branch of the Government to make such policy choices—resolving the competing interests which Congress itself either inadvertently did not resolve, or intentionally left to be resolved by the agency charged with the administration of the statute in light of everyday realities.

When a challenge to an agency construction of a statutory provision, fairly conceptualized, really centers on the wisdom of the agency's policy, rather than whether it is a reasonable choice within a gap left open by Congress, the challenge must fail. In such a case, federal judges—who have no constituency—have a duty to respect legitimate policy choices made by those who do. The responsibilities for assessing the wisdom of such policy choices and resolving the struggle between competing views of the public interest are not judicial ones: "Our Constitution vests such responsibilities in the political branches."

We hold that the EPA's definition of the term "source" is a permissible construction of the statute which seeks to accommodate progress in reducing air pollution with economic growth. "The Regulations which the Administrator has adopted provide what the agency could allowably view as . . . [an] effective reconciliation of these twofold ends. . . ."

The judgment of the Court of Appeals is reversed.

It is so ordered.

Questions

1. What is the first thing a reviewing court should do when an agency's interpretation of a statute is challenged?
2. If the plain meaning of the statute can be gleaned, what must the reviewing court analyze next?
3. If Congress chooses to obfuscate the issue of clean air by using language such as "new or modified major stationary source," is it constitutionally acceptable for the agency to consider the view of the current occupant of the White House in formulating its interpretation of that language? If so, is it acceptable for that interpretation to change every four to eight years? See *Chamber of Commerce v. Occupational Safety and Health Administration*, 636 F2.d 464 (D.C. Cir. 1980).

Although interpretive and substantive rules may look alike, it is not just the procedure that differentiates them. A substantive rule has the force and effect of law, whereas an interpretive rule does not. If an agency has adopted a rule through the § 553 procedure, then it may legally enforce that rule, perhaps by inspecting a business and imposing a fine for violating the rule. Those adversely affected by the rule, who may wish to challenge the substance of the rule in court, are not likely to succeed. That is because, as you know from Chapter 4, the scope of review for a substantive rule is whether the rule is arbitrary and/or capricious. In very few cases has a court found an agency rule to be arbitrary if it has gone through the proper § 553 procedure.

An agency is not necessarily free, however, to begin to enforce an interpretive rule. In most cases, parties adversely affected by an interpretive rule will have an opportunity to make their case in an adjudicatory hearing before suffering the adverse effects of the rule. That is what it means to say that interpretive rules do not have the force and effect of law.

Haggar Apparel Company cuts the fabric for its slacks in the United States and applies a chemical that, when heated, will permapress the fabric. It then ships the cut fabric, thread, buttons, and zippers to Mexico for assembly and the heating process. The finished slacks are shipped back to the United States to distributors. When the slacks come back into the United States, they are subject to an import tax. Congress has provided importers with a partial tax exemption from the import tax for "articles which 1) are assembled abroad and 2) not advanced in value or improved in condition abroad, except by operations incidental to the assembly process." The Customs Service adopted a rule that interprets the phrase "except by operations incidental to the assembly process." The Customs Service interpretation says that the phrase means "the chemical treatment of components or assembled articles," and it cites permapressing as an example of what it means. Haggar applied for the partial import tax exemption but the customs officials denied the request. Haggar appealed the decision and the interpretation to the Court of International Trade (see the diagram of the federal government in Figure 1.1 on page 13). That court applied an international trade precedent and found in favor of Haggar. In doing so, it did not apply *Chevron* to the agency's interpretation. The circuit court affirmed but the Supreme Court reversed. It sent the case back to the appeals court with orders to apply *Chevron,* and it ordered the lower court to provide judicial deference to the customs interpretation under *Chevron.* See *United States v. Haggar,* 526 U.S. 380 (1999). The point is that Haggar got a chance to argue its case before it was adversely affected by the rule.

Another case involves the Medicare Act, in which Congress authorized the secretary of health and human services to promulgate regulations "establishing the method or methods to be used" to reimburse providers their reasonable costs. In promulgating such rules, the secretary is to consider "principles generally applied by national organizations in computing reimbursement amounts."[10] Health and Human Services promulgated a regulation for reimbursement costs that has the following language: "Standardized definitions, accounting, statistics, and reporting practices that are widely accepted in hospitals and related fields are followed." Subsequent to the adoption of the above § 553 rule, the secretary adopted an informal medical reimbursement guideline called the Medicare Provider Reimbursement Manual (PRM). The manual is an interpretive guideline; it did not go through a § 553 procedure.

A hospital issued bonds to finance capital improvements in 1972 and 1982. In 1985, the hospital refinanced its debt (the bonds) by issuing new bonds. Although the hospital would ultimately save $12 million in interest it would not have to pay, the refinancing resulted in a paper loss of almost $700,000.[11] About half of that loss is reimbursable under Medicare, and it is not the amount that is in dispute. Rather, the conflict is over the timing of the reimbursement.

The hospital argued that the Medicare Act, "principles generally applied by national organizations," the promulgated rule, and standard accounting practices require the application of Generally Accepted Accounting Practices (GAAP). If Health and Human Services applied such practices, the hospital would get the whole $700,000 in one accounting year. The secretary's interpretive PRM, however, required that reimbursements from refinancing bonds be amortized over the life of the old bonds. The $700,000 would be paid out incrementally.

The hospital contended that the PRM substantially modified the § 553 rule, and the agency cannot apply the PRM unless it goes through another § 553 to adopt it. The Supreme Court, in a 5 to 4 decision, said that the PRM did not substantively change the § 553 rule and that it was a reasonable interpretive rule. The point is worth repeating: It is not always easy to differentiate between interpretive and substantive rules. However, interpretive rules have not met the dictates of due process of law (because of a lack of notice and a hearing), so they do not have the force and effect of law, and they do not self-execute. Exceptions will be discussed below.

Court review of interpretive rules is much broader than court review of substantive rules. That is the case because, although courts are required by *Chevron* to show some deference toward agency expertise in interpreting congressional intent, courts are just as capable of determining congressional intent as agencies are. To simply state that interpretive rules do not have the force and effect of law is to oversimplify their effect.

When an agency announces that it plans to proceed a certain way, that is exactly what it plans to do, whether it has gone through a § 553 procedure or not, and this can adversely affect those who deal with the agency. Turn back now to Chapter 5 and reread *Chrysler v. Brown,* 441 U.S. 281 (1979). There, the agency announced a rule that said that even though material requested under the Freedom of Information Act (FOIA) may be exempted from release, the agency was going to release it anyway. By the agency's admission, this rule was an interpretive one, but the agency intended to implement it, to Chrysler's detriment, anyway. Chrysler was forced to spend considerable resources, legal and otherwise, to stop the agency from enforcing a rule that did not have the "force and effect" of law. The interpretive guideline adopted by Health and Human Services cost the Guernsey Memorial Hospital nearly a third of a million dollars.

What if you owned a new business and had secured a contract with a natural gas pipeline company to deliver gas to your plant? Suppose that natural gas is in short supply, so you feel fortunate because of your contract. The federal agency that regulates natural gas, however, has just published an interpretive rule dealing with curtailment of natural gas deliveries due to shortages. The rule says the agency will curtail according to prior use rather than current contract, and all low-volume uses will be completely curtailed before high-volume uses are curtailed at all. Because this is not a substantive rule and does not have the force and effect of law, do you need to worry about keeping your plant in production? Of course, you do. In the actual case challenging the rule, *Pacific Gas and Electric v. Federal Power Commission (FPC),*[12] the Court did not invalidate the rule because no curtailments would actually occur on the basis of the rule alone. Curtailment would follow a quasi-judicial hearing within the agency. So although the rule informed buyers of how the agency intended to proceed, it did not have the force and effect of law, and smaller users could make their case in hearings. Because it is possible for an agency to affect citizens or businesses through interpretive rules without citizen input, there is much discussion involving whether some procedure should be required prior to the adoption of such rules.[13]

Litigation over agency interpretation of statutes is quite common. You are already familiar with *Walters v. Metropolitan Educational Enterprises* and *United States v. Haggar*. What follows is a brief outline of several of the more interesting cases from recent court terms.

In 1983, Betty O'Gilvie died from toxic shock syndrome. Her widower, Kelly, sued the manufacturer of tampons in state court on behalf of himself and their two children. A jury awarded them $1,525,000 in compensatory damages and $10 million in punitive damages. Kelly paid federal income taxes on the punitive damages but immediately filed for a refund. The Internal Revenue Service (IRS) returned the taxable portion for the two children but kept the taxes on Kelly's portion. Kelly sued the IRS, and the IRS countersued the two kids to get their tax money back.

The applicable statute excludes from the calculation of gross income funds that come from "any damages . . . on account of personal injury or sickness." The IRS's interpretation of that phrase is that because punitive damages are awarded to punish and not to compensate, they are not "on account of injury or sickness," and people should pay taxes on them. The counter view is a causal one. But for the injury, there would be no damages—compensatory or punitive—hence "any" and all of the damages are "on account of injury" and should be excluded from the calculation of gross income. Who do you think is right? Has Congress addressed the issue so that congressional intent is clear? If not, is the agency's interpretation a reasonable one? In *O'Gilvie v. United States,* 519 U.S. 79 (1996), the Supreme Court in a 6 to 3 decision sided with the IRS.

Ronald Yeskey was sentenced by a state criminal court to serve 18 to 36 months in a Pennsylvania state prison, but the sentencing judge recommended that Yeskey be sent to a boot camp for first-time offenders. The boot camp program is a straight six-month incarceration and then parole, regardless of the length of the original sentence. When Yeskey was delivered to the Pennsylvania Department of Corrections (PDC), he was given a physical, and it was discovered that he had high blood pressure. Yeskey was denied admission to the boot camp program due to his medical condition and sent to the prison to complete the original sentence. Yeskey sued the PDC under the Americans With Disabilities Act (ADA). The Act prohibits "any public entity from discriminating against any qualified individual on account of that individual's disability." The PDC said that *public entity*" does not include correctional facilities. Who do you think is right? Has Congress addressed the issue in plain language? If the statute says "*any* public entity," and there are no clauses making exceptions, what do you suppose congressional intent must have been? In a unanimous decision, the Supreme Court said the ADA applies to correctional facilities as they are public entities. See *Pennsylvania Department of Corrections v. Yeskey,* 524 U.S. 206 (1998).

Lest you believe that a party who has "won" before the U.S. Supreme Court has actually won their case, you will need to track what happened to Ron Yeskey. The Supreme Court said that the district court that originally dismissed the suit against Yeskey should not have done so, and the Court sent the case back to the district court for a disposition consistent with the Court's opinion (the Supreme Court affirmed the Court of Appeals). Yeskey had been released from prison by the time the Supreme Court spoke. Because he had originally asked for money damages as well as admission to boot camp, the case was not moot, so the case was returned to district court for a determination on the question of money damages. This time around, the PDC moved for summary judgment. Summary judgment is a motion to dismiss a case at the pleading stage and is appropriately granted when there are no material issues of fact between the parties and the judge can decide who wins by simply applying the law. In *Yeskey v. Pennsylvania Department of Corrections,* 76 F. Supp. 2d. 572 (1999), the judge agreed with the PDC and found in their favor (again), saying that Yeskey could not show that boot camp was a "major life activity." Here, the pertinent part of the ADA says that establishing a disability requires a plaintiff to show "a physical or mental impairment that substantially limits one or more of the major life activities." Look again at the original language of the ADA above. It prohibits "discrimination against any *qualified individual.*" An impairment "that substantially limits one or more of the major life activities" is what qualifies an individual under the ADA. The attorney general has interpreted "major life activities" in the following manner: "functions such as caring for one's self, performing manual tasks, walking, seeing, hearing, speaking, breathing, learning and working, all functions that can be grouped together as required for daily living."[14]

Because the exercise required for boot camp is not "walking, seeing, hearing," and so forth, Yeskey was not qualified to be disabled under the ADA, and his suit was dismissed. In case you missed the irony here, Yeskey could not get into the boot camp program because the PDC thought his disability would prevent him from engaging in the rigorous exercise required. Now, he cannot sue the PDC for failure to make reasonable accommodations for him because he *was not disabled.*

Garret's spinal column was severed in a motorcycle accident when he was four years old. He is paralyzed from the neck down, but his mental faculties are good. He gets around by motorized wheelchair and operates a computer by head movements. Garret cannot breathe on his own, without a ventilator, which requires a "responsible person" nearby to help with ventilator-related problems. Garret's parents want him in school in special education classes, but accommodating their request would require the assistance of a licensed practical nurse for Garret while he is in school. The Cedar Rapids Community School District does not think it should have to pay for Garret's nurse.

The Individuals with Disabilities Education Act (IDEA) provides federal grants to the states that agree to provide disabled children with special education and "related services." The Act defines related services as "transportation and such developmental, corrective and other support services . . . as may be required to assist a child with a disability to benefit from special education." The Act goes on to exclude as "related services," "medical services other than for diagnostic or evaluative purposes." The school district says that providing the nurse would be a "medical service" and therefore is not a "related service" under the Act; the district should not have to pay for Garret's nurse. Garret's lawyer said that the nurse is a "related service" that will "assist him in benefiting from special education." Who do you suppose is right? Has Congress addressed the issue in plain language so that congressional intent is clear? If not, is the school board's interpretation reasonable? Even if the board's interpretation is reasonable, the Supreme Court in *Cedar Rapids Community School District v. Garret*, 526 U.S. 66 (1999) cited a precedent that limited the medical services exemption to doctors and sided with Garret in a 7 to 2 decision.

Procedural Rules

Procedural rules, like interpretive rules, are exempted from the requirements of § 553 of the Administrative Procedure Act. It may not always be easy to differentiate a procedural rule from the other types of rules, but generally, they specify an internal agency procedure, and so they are often referred to as *internal procedural agency rules.* It is perhaps not so important to be able to distinguish between an interpretive rule and a procedural rule. What is important is to be aware of two notions: First, neither can be a substantive rule without going through the notice and comment procedure. Second, both interpretive and procedural rules can affect citizens without any citizen input. In the case that follows, the Bureau of Indian Affairs adopted a procedural rule that required the agency to publish eligibility requirements in the *Federal Register.* Although Congress authorized Bureau benefits to be paid to Indians who lived on or near reservations, because of funding insufficient to provide benefits to all such Indians, the Bureau adopted an interpretive rule. The interpretive rule restricted benefits to Indians who lived on a reservation, but the rule was not published in the *Federal Register.* The doctrine from the case is that agencies must adhere to their internal procedural rules.

Morton v. Ruiz
415 U.S. 199 (1974)

Justice Blackmun delivered the opinion for a unanimous Court.

This case presents a narrow but important issue in the administration of the federal general assistance program for needy Indians: Are general assistance benefits available only to those Indians living on reservations in the United States (or in areas regulated by the Bureau of Indian Affairs in Alaska and Oklahoma), and are they thus unavailable to Indians (outside Alaska and Oklahoma) living off, although near, a reservation? The United States District Court for the District of Arizona answered this question favorably to petitioner, the Secretary of the Interior, when, without opinion and on cross-motions for summary judgment, it dismissed the respondents' complaint. The Court of Appeals, one judge dissenting, reversed. 462 F.2d 818 (CA9 1972). We granted certiorari because of the significance of the issue and because of the vigorous assertion that the judgment of the Court of Appeals was inconsistent with long-established policy of the Secretary and of the Bureau.

I

The pertinent facts are agreed upon, although, as to some, the petitioner Secretary denies knowledge but does not dispute them. The respondents, Ramon Ruiz and his wife, Anita, are Papago Indians and United States citizens. In 1940 they left the Papago Reservation in Arizona to seek employment 15 miles away at the Phelps-Dodge copper mines at Ajo. Mr. Ruiz found work there, and they settled in a community at Ajo called the "Indian Village" and populated almost entirely by Papagos. Practically all the land and most of the homes in the Village are owned or rented by Phelps-Dodge. The Ruizes have lived in Ajo continuously since 1940 and have been in their present residence since 1947. A minor daughter lives with them. They speak and understand the Papago language but only limited English. Apart from Mr. Ruiz' employment with Phelps-Dodge, they have not been assimilated into the dominant culture, and they appear to have maintained a close tie with the nearby reservation. . . .

In July 1967, 27 years after the Ruizes moved to Ajo, the mine where he worked was shut down by a strike. It remained closed until the following March. While the strike was in progress, Mr. Ruiz' sole income was a $15 per week striker's benefit paid by the union. He sought welfare assistance from the State of Arizona but this was denied because of the State's apparent policy that striking workers are not eligible for general assistance or emergency relief. . . . On December 11, 1967, Mr. Ruiz applied for general assistance benefits from the Bureau of Indian Affairs (BIA). He was immediately notified by letter that he was ineligible for general assistance because of the provisions (in effect since 1952) in 66 *Indian Affairs Manual* 3.1.4 (1965) that eligibility is limited to Indians living "on reservations" and in jurisdictions under the BIA in Alaska and Oklahoma. An appeal to the Superintendent of the Papago Indian Agency was unsuccessful. A further appeal to the Phoenix Area Director of the BIA led to a hearing, but this, too, proved unsuccessful. The sole ground for the denial of general assistance benefits was that the Ruizes resided outside the boundaries of the Papago Reservation.

II

The Snyder Act, 25 U.S.C. § 13, approved November 2, 1921, provides the underlying congressional authority for most BIA activities including, in particular and importantly, the general assistance program. Prior to the Act, there was no such general authorization. As a result, appropriation requests made by the House Committee on Indian Affairs were frequently stricken on the House floor by point-of-order objections. The Snyder Act was designed to remedy this situation. It is comprehensively worded for the apparent purpose of avoiding these point-of-order motions to strike. Since the passage of the Act, the BIA has presented its budget requests without further interruption of that kind and Congress has enacted appropriation bills annually in response to the requests. . . .

The appropriation legislation at issue here, Department of Interior and Related Agencies Appropriation Act, 1968, Pub.L. 90—28, 81 Stat. 59, 60 (1967), recited: "Bureau of Indian Affairs Education and Welfare Services. For expenses necessary to provide education and welfare services for Indians, either directly or in cooperation with States and other organizations, including payment (in advance or from date of admission) of care, tuition, assistance, and other expenses of Indians in boarding homes, institutions, or schools; grants and other assistance to needy Indians; maintenance of law and order, and payment of rewards for information or evidence concerning violations of law on Indian reservations or lands; and operation of Indian arts and crafts shops; $126,478,000." This wording, except for the amount, is identical to that employed in similar legislation for prior fiscal years and, indeed, for subsequent ones. It is to be that neither the language of the Snyder Act nor that of the Appropriations Act imposes any geographical limitation on the availability of general assistance benefits and does not prescribe eligibility requirements or the details of any program. Instead, the Snyder Act states that the BIA (under the supervision of the Secretary) "shall direct, supervise, and expend . . . for the benefit, care, and assistance of the Indians throughout the United States" for the stated purposes including, as the two purposes first described, "[g]eneral support" and "relief of distress." This is broadly phrased material and obviously is intended to include all BIA activities.

The general assistance program is designed by the BIA to provide direct financial aid to needy Indians where other channels of relief, federal, state, and tribal, are not available. Benefits generally are paid on a scale equivalent to the State's welfare payments. Any Indian, whether living on a reservation or elsewhere, may be eligible for benefits under the various social security programs in which his State participates and no limitation may be placed on social security benefits because of an Indian claimant's residence on a reservation.

III

We are confronted, therefore, with the issues whether the geographical limitation placed on general assistance eligibility by the BIA is consistent with congressional intent and the meaning of the applicable statutes, or, to phrase it somewhat differently, whether the congressional appropriations are properly limited by the BIA's restrictions and, if so, whether the limitation withstands constitutional analysis. On the initial question, the Secretary argues, first, that the Snyder Act is merely an enabling act with no definition of the scope of the general assistance program, that the Appropriation Act did not provide for off-reservation Indian welfare (other than in Oklahoma and Alaska), and that Congress did not intend to expand the program beyond that presented to it by the BIA request. Secondly, he points to the "on reservations" limitation in the *Manual* and suggests that Congress was well acquainted with that limitation, and that, by legislating in the light of the *Manual's* limiting provision, its appropriation amounted to a ratification of the BIA's definitive practice. He notes that, in recent

years, Congress has twice rejected proposals that clearly would have provided off-reservation general assistance for Indians. Thus, it is said, Congress has appropriated no funds for general assistance for off-reservation Indians and, as a practical matter, the Secretary is unable to provide such a program.

Wholly aside from this appropriation subcommittee legislative history, the Secretary suggests that Congress, each year since 1952, appropriated only in accord with the "on reservations" limitation contained in the *BIA Manual*. By legislating annually "in the light of (this) clear provision," the Secretary argues, Congress implicitly ratified the BIA policy. This argument, also, is not convincing. The limitation has not been published in the *Federal Register* or in the *Code of Federal Regulations,* and there is nothing in the legislative history to show that the Manual's provision was brought to the subcommittees' attention, let alone to the entire Congress. To assume that Congress was aware of this provision, contained only in an internally circulated BIA document, would be most strained. But, even assuming that Congress was fully cognizant of the *Manual's* limitation when the 1958 appropriation was made, the language of geographic restriction in the *Manual* must be considered in conjunction with the representations consistently made. There is no reason to assume that Congress did not equate the "on reservations" language with the "on or near" category that continuously was described as the service area. In the light of the Manual's particular inclusion of Oklahoma and Alaska off-reservation Indians, it would seem that this interpretation of the provision would have been the logical one for anyone in Congress, who in fact was aware of it, to accept. . . .

V

Having found that the congressional appropriation was intended to cover welfare services at least to those Indians residing "on or near" the reservation, it does not necessarily follow that the Secretary is without power to create reasonable classifications and eligibility requirements in order to allocate the limited funds available to him for this purpose. Thus, if there were only enough funds appropriated to provide meaningfully for 10,000 needy Indian beneficiaries and the entire class of eligible beneficiaries numbered 20,000, it would be incumbent upon the BIA to develop an eligibility standard to deal with this problem, and the standard, if rational and proper, might leave some of the class otherwise encompassed by the appropriation without benefits. But in such a case the agency must, at a minimum, let the standard be generally known so as to assure that it is being applied consistently and so as to avoid both the reality and the appearance of arbitrary denial of benefits to potential beneficiaries.

The Administrative Procedure Act was adopted to provide, inter alia, that administrative policies affecting individual rights and obligations be promulgated pursuant to certain stated procedures so as to avoid the inherently arbitrary nature of unpublished ad hoc determinations. See generally S.Rep.No.752, 79th Cong., 1st Sess., 12—13 (1945); H.R.Rep.No.1980, 79th Cong., 2d Sess., 21—23 (1946). That Act states in pertinent part: "Each Agency shall separately state and currently publish in the *Federal Register* for the guidance of the public—(D) substantive rules of general applicability adopted as authorized by law, and statements of general policy or interpretations of general applicability formulated and adopted by the agency." 5 U.S.C. § 552(a)(1). The sanction added in 1967 by Pub.L. 90—23, 81 Stat. 54, provides: "Except to the extent that a person has actual and timely notice of the terms thereof, a person may not in any manner be required to resort to, or be adversely affected by, a matter required to be published in the *Federal Register* and not so published."

In the instant case the BIA itself has recognized the necessity of formally publishing its substantive policies and has placed itself under the structure of the APA procedures. The 1968 introduction to the *Manual* reads: "*Code of Federal Regulations:* Directives which relate to the public, including Indians, are published in the *Federal Register* and codified in 25 *Code of Federal Regulations* (25 CFR). These directives inform the public of privileges and benefits

available; eligibility qualifications, requirements, and procedures; and of appeal rights and procedures. They are published in accordance with rules and regulations issued by the Director of the *Federal Register* and the Administrative Procedure Act as amended. . . .

"*Bureau of Indian Affairs Manual:* Policies, procedures, and instructions which do not relate to the public but are required to govern the operations of the Bureau are published in the Bureau of Indian Affairs Manual."

Unlike numerous other programs authorized by the Snyder Act and funded by the annual appropriations, the BIA has chosen not to publish its eligibility requirements for general assistance in the *Federal Register* or in the CFR. This continues to the present time. The only official manifestation of this alleged policy of restricting general assistance to those directly on the reservations is the material in the *Manual* which is, by BIA's own admission, solely an internal-operations brochure intended to cover policies that "do not relate to the public." Indeed, at oral argument the Government conceded that for this to be a "real legislative rule," itself endowed with the force of law, it should be published in the *Federal Register.* Where the rights of individuals are affected, it is incumbent upon agencies to follow their own procedures. This is so even where the internal procedures are possibly more rigorous than otherwise would be required. The BIA, by its *Manual,* has declared that all directives that "inform the public of privileges and benefits available" and of "eligibility requirements" are among those to be published. The requirement that, in order to receive general assistance, an Indian must reside directly "on" a reservation is clearly an important substantive policy that fits within this class of directives. Before the BIA may extinguish the entitlement of these otherwise eligible beneficiaries, it must comply, at a minimum, with its own internal procedures. The Secretary has presented no reason why the requirements of the Administrative Procedure Act could not or should not have been met. The BIA itself has not attempted to defend its rule as a valid exercise of its "legislative power," but rather depends on the argument that Congress itself has not appropriated funds for Indians not directly on the reservations. The conscious choice of the Secretary not to treat this extremely significant eligibility requirement, affecting rights of needy Indians, as a legislative-type rule, renders it ineffective so far as extinguishing rights of those otherwise within the class of beneficiaries contemplated by Congress is concerned. . . .

Before benefits may be denied to these otherwise entitled Indians, the BIA must first promulgate eligibility requirements according to established procedures.

The judgment of the Court of Appeals is affirmed and the case is remanded for further proceedings consistent with this opinion.

It is so ordered.

Affirmed and remanded.

Substantive Rules

Agencies can adopt substantive rules, regulations, or standards by going through either of two procedures. If they go through the § 553 quasi-legislative procedure, the result will have the force and effect of law and will be called a rule, regulation, or a standard. This is what we are calling a *substantive rule*. Agencies can also go through a § 554 quasi-judicial procedure, and the result will have the force and effect of law, but it will be called an order.

Substantive rules can be distinguished from (a) those that do not have the force and effect of law (interpretive and procedural rules) and (b) orders that result from a quasi-judicial hearing but also have the force and effect of law. Refer again to *Chrysler v. Brown*. In that case, Justice Rehnquist defined a substantive rule as opposed to either interpretive or procedural rules. He said that a substantive rule has three properties: (a) It affects individual rights and obligations; (b) its source of authority is a legitimate congressional delegation of power; and (c) it must have been adopted pursuant to the proper procedures as outlined in § 553 of the Administrative Procedure Act.

You may remember that the Office of Federal Contract Compliance Programs had issued a rule indicating its intent to release exemptible material under the FOIA and was about to do just that when Chrysler obtained a temporary restraining order. Ultimately, the case narrowed to the nature and character of the rule. That is because Chrysler's first two lines of attack were not successful. The Court rejected Chrysler's first argument that material qualifying for an FOIA exemption *must* be withheld. The Court also rejected Chrysler's second argument that a criminal law (the Trade Secrets Act) could be used to block release of the information. The question then became whether the Office's rule was a substantive rule "authorized by law." Justice Rehnquist tells us that it is not a substantive rule with the force and effect of law because, although it meets the first criterion (it does affect individual rights and obligations), it does not meet the last two criteria. This is the case because the source of authority for the rule was an executive order, not a congressional delegation of power, and the agency did not observe the § 553 procedure in adopting the rule. Hence, the Office's decision to release exemptible material turned out to be an interpretive rule rather than a substantive one.

Another opinion by Justice Rehnquist distinguished when substantive rules (quasi-legislative) are required as opposed to when agency orders (quasi-judicial) are appropriate. The Interstate Commerce Act authorizes the Interstate Commerce Commission (ICC) to take certain actions "after a hearing."[15] The ICC notified railroads that it was going to look into the question of adopting incentives that would address the boxcar shortage. Later, the ICC required railroads to gather and submit data on boxcar supply and demand. When several railroads complained, the ICC staff met with railroad representatives and left them with the impression that hearings would be held on the question. Further hearings, however, were never held. On the basis of the data provided by the railroads at the agency's request, the ICC promulgated a rule adopting a per diem charge on any boxcar on a railroad's line, if the boxcar did not belong to that railroad. The purpose of the rule was to provide an incentive to quickly return another railroad's boxcar or to make it financially attractive for railroads to purchase more boxcars. After notice in the *Federal Register* that the ICC intended to adopt the per diem rate, several railroad companies objected and requested an oral hearing based on those objections. The ICC modified its proposed rate somewhat but denied all oral hearings.

Railroad companies hurt by the new per diem rate sued, alleging that a quasi-judicial hearing should have been required (*United States v. Florida East Coast Railway Company,* 410 U.S. 224 [1973]). This case presents the issue of when substantive rule making is appropriate as opposed to when a quasi-judicial order is appropriate. Justice Rehnquist first indicated that the Act's simple reference to the term *hearing* does not necessarily connote a quasi-judicial hearing. Indeed, only when the enabling legislation uses the language *hearing on the record* is a quasi-judicial hearing required. Beyond that, the nature of the subject matter suggests which type of hearing is appropriate.

Drawing on the *Londoner/Bi-Metallic* distinction, Justice Rehnquist differentiated between those situations dealing with general applicability requiring legislative-type decision and those involving "a small number of persons, exceptionally affected" and individual grounds that are appropriate for quasi-judicial decision making.

In reality, there are two ways to distinguish legislative-type decision-making situations from those in which quasi-judicial decisions are more appropriate. Justice Rehnquist discussed the general/specific dichotomy, but the Administrative Procedure Act distinguishes between future effect and past effect. A § 553 procedure is appropriate for questions of a more general nature that will apply to future situations. A quasi-judicial (§ 554) procedure is more appropriate in dealing with particularized, individual situations or events that have already occurred.

In the *Florida East Coast Railroad Case,* Justice Rehnquist decided that the issue of per diem fees on railroad cars was one of general application, even though only a few railroads were severely adversely affected by the rate.

The distinctions between future/past and general/specific are the origin of the terms *quasi-legislative* and *judicial*. Legislatures usually pass laws that apply to everybody (general) in the future. Courts look at specific litigants to see whether one of them did something in the past that might incur liability. If the EPA wants to modify the national ambient air quality standards, that would be general and future so the § 553 procedure would be appropriate. If Darlene Walters thinks that Metropolitan Educational Enterprises violated the retaliation clause of the 1964 Civil Rights Act by firing her, that would be about a past event and applicable to an individual, not the general public, so it would be appropriate for a quasi-judicial § 554 hearing at the EEOC.

So that the reader can get a better grasp of federal substantive rule-making activity, what follows is a list of areas involving federal rule making and the agencies that make the rules, most of which appeared on the front page of *The New York Times* over the past few years:

the definition of AIDS (Social Security Administration and Centers for Disease Control)[16]

breast implants (FDA)[17]

the definition of poverty (Census Bureau)[18]

the definition of "Made in the U.S.A." (Federal Trade Commission)[19]

acid rain (EPA)[20]

reduction of the power of air bags (Department of Transportation)[21]

gene therapy experimentation on humans (FDA)[22]

reduction of rain water contamination as water pollution (EPA)[23]

elimination of a farm pesticide (EPA)[24]

requirement that nuclear plants must be prepared to repel attack subsequent to 9/11, specifying tactics (Nuclear Regulatory Commission)[25]

use of human embryos in cell research (National Institutes of Health)[26]

air traffic control and near jet collisions (National Transportation Safety Board)[27]

ergonomic rules to reduce repetitive-stress injuries in the workplace (Occupational Safety and Health Administration)[28]

new entry requirements for foreigners visiting the U.S. (Department of Homeland Security)[29]

approval of a fat-blocking (anti-obesity) drug that blocks the body's ability to store fat as opposed to tricking the brain about hunger (FDA)[30]

regulation of day care centers that receive federal funds (Health and Human Services)[31]

regulation of AIDS-infected health care workers (Centers for Disease Control)[32]

enforcement of existing rules on "single use" medical devices being reused (FDA)[33]

whether doctors who work for health maintenance organizations can unionize (National Labor Relations Board)[34]

subsequent to a scandal in the mutual fund industry, new rules regulating who can sit on their boards and serve as their chairman (Securities and Exchange Commission)[35]

Despite the depth and breadth of the preceding list, bear in mind that although rule making is very important, it constitutes relatively little of what agencies do. Agencies produce procedural and interpretive rules far more often than substantive rules, and from the last chapter, we learned that informal activity constitutes about 90 percent of what agencies do. Although we have not dealt with state agencies except by way of occasional example, the reader should be aware that the real growth in bureaucratic activity in the past 20 years or so has been at the state and local level. California's pollution control agency, for example, promulgated rules to regulate some polluting ingredients in household adhesives, laundry starch, perfumes and colognes, and dusting aids.[36]

Finally, although the § 553 procedure specified in the Administrative Procedure Act is the procedure of choice, Congress has modified the Act to allow for a process called "reg-neg," which stands for *regulation by negotiation* (see description in Appendix A).[37] This is a process by which all interested and potentially affected parties submit proposed regulations and then negotiate the proposals, with the agency acting as a referee. In the early 1990s, environmental interest groups and oil company representatives attempted to negotiate regulations implementing the new Clean Air Act.[38] This process is thought to enhance compliance with agency rules because those who must live by the rules have helped to write them. Actually, that is often the case under normal § 553 procedures as well. In the boxcar case cited earlier, the ICC said it wanted to place a per diem fee on boxcars, but the railroads determined what the rate would be. To help you appreciate the role of expertise in agency rule making, I note here a couple of the questions being hammered out in the Clean Air Act reg-negs: (a) how much volatility gasoline may have (volatility is the rate at which it evaporates) and (b) what statistical formula should be used for calculating minimum levels of oxygenates (an oxygen-carrying molecule in gasoline).[39] No wonder courts defer to agency expertise in court review of agency rule making! If you refer back to Chapter 3 and the discussion of delegation of power, there is mention of a famous case: *Schechter Poultry Corporation v. United States* (the Sick Chicken Case). It is worth noting that the procedure the court declared unconstitutional in that case is almost exactly the reg-neg procedure.

ADJUDICATION

From the earlier discussion, you learned that when the enabling legislation says that the agency shall engage in rule making after a "hearing on the record," that is the language that requires the agency to go through a quasi-judicial hearing. Sometimes, Congress requires this procedure to engage in rule making of a general nature with future applications (as was the case with the *Food and Drug Administration,* where the question was, "Should peanut butter manufacturers be required to increase the peanuts in peanut butter by two percent"). Sometimes, such a hearing is required to decide factual matters (the NLRB is required to conduct a hearing on the record in cases alleging an unfair labor practice). Sometimes, Congress requires this procedure just to make decisions (the Federal Communications Commission (FCC) is required to conduct a hearing on the record to decide whether to grant or renew a license).

When the adjudicative procedure is used for rule making, it is referred to as formal rule making, rule making on the record, or a § 554 procedure (see the Administrative Procedure Act, §§ 554, 556, and 557). Basically, the procedure looks like a trial. The affected parties must receive a formal notice. Pleadings (which assert the facts that may be in dispute) and a discovery process are involved, but they are less formal than in a real trial. Direct and cross-examination of witnesses occurs, but due to the nature of the subject matter, direct examination often involves the submission of a written statement rather than an in-person exchange between a witness and attorney.[40] The purpose of a judicial trial is to discover facts (Did *X* kill *Y*?). In an administrative adjudication, the question may be, "Should the percentage of peanuts in peanut butter be increased by 2 percent?" Agencies are free to adopt procedures, within limits, and some have adopted an *interval hearing* system, in which the government presents its case and the hearing may be recessed for months so the other parties can prepare their case.[41] The proponent of a rule or order has the burden of proof, which is by a "preponderance of the evidence."[42] There are rules of evidence, but, again, because of the nature of the questions involved, the rules of evidence are not as strict as in a court of law. At the close of the adjudication, the parties have an opportunity to submit findings of fact and conclusions of law to the administrative law judge, similar to the submission of jury instructions by attorneys in a trial. The judge then issues a written decision, which must include his or her findings of fact and conclusions of law, along with reasons for accepting certain findings of fact and conclusions of law on "all material issues of fact, law or discretion presented on the record."[43]

Adjudicatory hearings constitute a small amount of agency activity. Although their statistics include the period of time the Reagan Administration was processing numerous disability cases, Gellhorn and Levin document that in 1983, 400,000 new cases were referred to administrative law judges for adjudicatory hearings.[44] Only 275,000 cases were filed in U.S. district courts for the same year.[45]

From Chapter 4, you are aware that when a § 554 hearing is held and the result is challenged in court, the reviewing court will apply the substantial evidence test. The Supreme Court has recently decided only a few cases involving agency § 554 hearings or court review of those hearings.

When a citizen has invented something and seeks to get it patented, the Patent and Trademark Office conducts a § 554 hearing. Mary Zurko invented a method for increasing computer security and applied for a patent. The hearing examiner denied her application saying that what she had discovered was obvious in light of the prior state of the art. On appeal within the agency, the Board of Patent Appeals and Interference upheld the application denial. Appeal of board decisions goes directly to the circuit court of appeals, which applied the "clearly erroneous" standard of review rather than the substantial evidence standard established in the Administrative Procedure Act. Applying the more stringent standard of review, the circuit court reversed the decisions of both the Patent Office and its appeals board. The circuit court of appeals used the "clearly erroneous" standard based on its interpretation of a different section of the Administrative Procedure Act. The Supreme Court reversed the circuit court saying that reviewing courts must use the substantial evidence standard of review for patent cases. See *Dickenson v. Zurko,* 527 U.S. 150 (1999).

When people apply for disability under the Social Security program, their application is generally denied, and the claimant can request a § 554 hearing before an administrative law judge. A dissatisfied claimant can appeal the administrative law judge's decision to the Social Security Appeals Council (SSAC), which has the discretion to review or deny review. The next appeal would be to U.S. district court and then to the circuit court of appeals and perhaps to the Supreme Court.

Juatassa Sims developed a degenerative joint disease as well as carpel tunnel syndrome, and she applied for disability. Upon denial of her application, she requested a hearing before an administrative law judge. While recognizing Juatassa's ailments, the judge denied her disability benefits. Appeal to the SSAC can be made in two ways: (a) fill out a one-page application from the agency or (b) type out your own request for appeal. Juatassa chose the second route, and the SSAC denied her appeal. She sued in district court alleging that: (a) the administrative law judge made selective use of the record in his decision; (b) his questioning of the vocational expert was defective because his questions omitted several of her ailments; and (c) in light of the peculiarities in the medical record, the administrative law judge should have ordered a consultative exam. The district court rejected all three arguments. The circuit court of appeals affirmed the district court on the first issue but said it did not have jurisdiction to rule on the other two issues. The court said that the claimant had not raised those two issues in her letter requesting the appeal to the SSAC, so she had not exhausted those two issues within the agency. This is known as issue exhaustion. At the Supreme Court, the issue narrowed to whether issue exhaustion is required in disability appeals. In a 5 to 4 decision, the Court did not impose issue exhaustion on disability appeals. In *Sims v. Apfel,* 530 U.S. 103 (2000), the Court said that issue exhaustion is normally required in administrative law (as it is in civil and criminal law), but the disability § 554 procedure is so unique that it would make no sense to impose it.

The quasi-judicial procedure in disability hearings is different from all other § 554 hearings because disability hearings are inquisitorial in nature rather than adversarial. That is, the administrative law judge is responsible for investigating the facts both for and against awarding disability benefits. No party is present at the hearing representing the interests of the Social Security Administration. Neither does anyone advocate the interests of the Administration in the SSAC appeal process. The Administration's form to request an appeal of the administrative law judge's decision to the SSAC has only three lines under the area entitled "request for review." Furthermore, the form advises prospective appellants that it should only take 10 minutes to read the instructions, gather necessary facts, and fill out the form. Because an adversarial development of the issues of fact by opposing advocates does not exist in disability hearings, there is no reason to judicially impose issue exhaustion.

In another case, a contractor and employer sued several labor unions for violating the Labor-Management Relations Act for injuries caused by secondary boycotts. The federal district court issued a summary judgment for the unions (this means there was no disagreement between the parties as to material issues of fact, so the judge decided as a matter of law that the unions should win; there was no trial). The contractor then filed an amended complaint, this time alleging, based on the same facts, a violation of the Sherman Antitrust Act. The judge dismissed the amended complaint as reasserting claims that had already been decided. The contractor filed another amended complaint that had a different claim but also reasserted the claims that had been decided. The judge dismissed the already-decided claims and granted another summary judgment to the unions on an antitrust claim; the employer dropped any remaining claims, and the court of appeals affirmed.

While all of this litigation was going on, the unions filed an unfair labor practice claim against the contractor before the NLRB. Employers cannot engage in retaliatory activity against efforts to unionize or collectively bargain. At the § 554 hearing, the NLRB found that the contractor's lawsuits were unmeritorious and retaliatory and imposed sanctions. The NLRB's decision was upheld by the circuit court, but the Supreme Court reversed. The Supreme Court said that the NLRB could not impose sanctions on an employer for filing a losing retaliatory lawsuit if the employer could show that the suit was not objectively baseless (i.e., it was reasonably based but simply unsuccessful). That is because the First Amendment protects a citizen's right to petition government for a redress of grievances, and a lawsuit is one way to petition government. See *B E & K Construction Co. v. NLRB,* 536 U.S. 516 (2002).

AGENCY DISCRETION IN THE USE OF RULE MAKING AND ADJUDICATION

You will want to pay close attention in this section because there is potential for confusion. The subject matter we are about to cover is often called "the choice between rule making and adjudication." So far, we have established that either the enabling legislation, the Administrative Procedure Act, or the nature of the issue determines whether an agency should proceed by a § 553 or a § 554 procedure. Now, you will discover that an agency can proceed any way it wishes and the courts will not interfere. To understand why this is the case, it is necessary to refer to the precedent-setting case from 1947, *Securities and Exchange Commission v. Chenery Corporation,* 332 U.S. 194 (1947), which involved the reorganization of a public utilities holding company. A holding company is a company that does not produce anything but rather just owns stock in other companies, frequently, controlling shares of stock. In this instance, the Securities and Exchange Commission (SEC) had jurisdiction over the reorganization plan. The enabling legislation empowers the SEC to approve the reorganization of public utility holding companies, provided the reorganization is "fair and equitable to the persons affected thereby" (i.e., the stock holders). In this case, corporate officers in the former corporation purchased controlling shares of preferred stock in the reorganized corporation. Today, that would be called a form of *insider trading,* which is illegal, but in 1947, there was no law against it. If the SEC wanted to prohibit that activity, because it would involve a question of general applicability and apply in the future, it should have gone through the due process procedure of § 553 of the Administrative Procedure Act. However, the SEC found itself confronted with this reorganization plan with no controlling law or regulation, and a decision had to be made about whether the plan was "fair and equitable to the persons affected thereby." The SEC held a § 554 hearing and decided that the plan was not "fair and equitable" and forced the officers to surrender the stock at a tremendous financial loss. This action constitutes the civil counterpart to an *ex post facto law* (one that attempts to make an action a crime that was not a crime at the time it was done).[46] It also involves the very essence of due process of law because the corporate officers had no notice that what they did was wrong and the government took their property because of it.

On review, the Supreme Court said that the issue was simply whether there was substantial evidence in the record to sustain the SEC's decision that the plan was not "fair and equitable." The Court said there was substantial evidence to support the decision. The doctrine from the case—and it is still good law today—is that when an agency is faced with a problem (such as whether management can capitalize on corporate reorganization), the choice of whether to deal with the problem by promulgating a general rule or by adjudicating each case is a choice that "lies primarily in the informed discretion of the administrative agency."[47]

In 1969, the NLRB was confronted with the question of whether management should be forced to turn over a list of employees to a union that was trying to unionize the company. That is a question of general application that should apply to all future unionization elections. Furthermore, the National Labor Relations Act (NLRA) requires the NLRB to use the Administrative Procedure Act's § 553 procedure for the adoption of "such rules and regulations as may be necessary to carry out the provisions of this act."[48] Three years before this case, in 1966, the NLRB made its first decision on the unionization issue in an adjudicatory hearing, requiring management to turn over employee lists to the union. In its order, the NLRB did not make its decision apply to the company involved in the adjudication (to avoid ex post facto problems) but issued an order applicable to all future union elections. In the 1969 *Wyman-Gordon* case,[49] relying on its earlier order, the NLRB ordered Wyman-Gordon to produce an employee list and present it to the union. The company refused, the election was held, and the unions lost. The unions appealed to the NLRB, which invalidated the election due to the company's failure to produce the list, ordered new elections, and again ordered the company to produce the list. The company again refused. The NLRB issued a subpoena for the names and addresses of the employees, which the company ignored, so the NLRB went to court to enforce the subpoena. The district court issued an order to enforce the subpoena, but the court of appeals reversed on the basis of the NLRB's failure to promulgate a rule in accordance with the enabling legislation (requiring a § 553 procedure) and the Administrative Procedure Act.

When the case came to the Supreme Court, Justice Fortas wrote an opinion that agreed with everything the court of appeals said, except the resulting decision. Fortas's opinion said that there could not be a rule of general application and future effect with the force and effect of law until the agency had gone through the proper § 553 procedure. Still, Fortas continued, the case was properly before the NLRB on an adjudicating hearing, and the NLRB did have the authority to order the company to produce the list. So the court of appeals, although right, was overruled, and the district court's order to the company to comply with the subpoena was affirmed.

The principle, reaffirmed again in 1974 (the *Bell Aerospace* case at the end of this chapter), seems to be that despite the nature of the subject matter and enabling legislation that would seem to suggest that an agency proceed by rule promulgation, the courts will not interfere with the agency's choice to proceed by adjudication.

The flip side of this principle is called the *Storer* doctrine, and it comes from the next case (see also *Heckler v. Campbell* at the end of this chapter).

United States v. Storer Broadcasting Company
351 U.S. 192 (1956)

Justice Reed delivered the opinion of the Court, joined by Chief Justice Warren and Justices Black, Douglas, Burton, Clark, and Brennan. Justices Frankfurter and Harlan dissented.

The Federal Communications Commission issued, on August 19, 1948, a notice of proposed rule making under the authority of (Communications Act of 1934, as amended, 47 U.S.C. § 301 et seq.) It was proposed, so far as is pertinent to this case, to amend Rules 3.35, 3.240, and 3.636 relating to Multiple Ownership of standard, FM, and television broadcast stations. Those rules provide that licenses for broadcasting stations will not be granted if the applicant, directly or indirectly, has an interest in other stations beyond a limited number. The purpose of the limitations is to avoid overconcentration of broadcasting facilities.

As required, the notice permitted "interested" parties to file statements or briefs. Such parties might also intervene in appeals. Respondent, licensee of a number of radio and television stations, filed a statement objecting to the proposed changes, as did other interested broadcasters. Respondent based its objections largely on the fact that the proposed rules did not allow one person to hold as many FM and television stations as standard stations. Storer argued that such limitations might cause irreparable financial damage to owners of standard stations if an obsolescent standard station could not be augmented by FM and television facilities. In November 1953 the Commission entered an order amending the Rules in question without significant changes from the proposed forms. A review was sought in due course by respondent in the Court of Appeals for the District of Columbia Circuit. Respondent alleged it owned or controlled, within the meaning of the Multiple Ownership Rules, seven standard radio, five FM radio, and five television broadcast stations. It asserted that the Rules complained of were in conflict with the statutory mandates that applicants should be granted licenses if the public interest would be served and that applicants must have a hearing before denial of an application.

Respondent also claimed: . . . "The Rules, in considering the ownership of one (1%) per cent or more of the voting stock of a broadcast licensee corporation as equivalent to ownership, operation or control of the station, are unreasonable and bear no rational relationship to the national Anti-Trust policy." This latter claim was important to respondent because allegedly 20% of its voting stock was in scattered ownership and was traded in by licensed dealers. This stock was thus beyond its control. . . .

On the day the amendments to the Rules were adopted, a pending application of Storer for an additional television station at Miami was dismissed on the basis of the Rules. . . . The Commission asserts that its power to make regulations gives it the authority to limit concentration of stations under a single control. It argues that rules may go beyond the technical aspects of radio, that rules may validly give concreteness to a standard of public interest, and that the right to a hearing does not exist where an applicant admittedly does not meet those standards as there would be no facts to ascertain. The Commission shows that its regulations permit applicants to seek amendments and waivers of or exceptions to its Rules. "This does not mean, of course, that the mere filing of an application for a waiver . . . would necessarily require the holding of a hearing, for if that were the case a rule would no longer be a rule. It means only that it might be an abuse of discretion to fail to hear a request for a waiver which showed, on its face, the existence of circumstances making application of the rule inappropriate."

Respondent defends the position of the Court of Appeals. It urges that an application cannot be rejected under 47 U.S.C. § 309, without a "full hearing" to applicant. We agree that a "full hearing" under § 309 means that every party shall have the right to present his case or defense by oral or documentary evidence, to submit rebuttal evidence, and to conduct such cross-examination as may be required for a full and true disclosure of the facts. Such a hearing is essential for wise and just application of the authority of administrative boards and agencies.

We do not read the hearing requirement, however, as withdrawing from the power of the Commission the rulemaking authority necessary for the orderly conduct of its business. As conceded by Storer, "Section 309(b) does not require the Commission to hold a hearing before denying a license to operate a station in ways contrary to those that the Congress has determined are in the public interest." The challenged Rules contain limitations against licensing not specifically authorized by statute. But

that is not the limit of the Commission's rulemaking authority. 47 U.S.C. § 154(i) and § 303(r) grant general rulemaking power not inconsistent with the Act or law. . . .

This Commission, like other agencies, deals with the public interest. Its authority covers new and rapidly developing fields. Congress sought to create regulation for public protection with careful provision to assure fair opportunity for open competition in the use of broadcasting facilities. Accordingly, we cannot interpret § 309(b) as barring rules that declare a present intent to limit the number of stations consistent with a permissible "concentration of control." It is but a rule that announces the Commission's attitude on public protection against such concentration. The Communications Act must be read as a whole and with appreciation of the responsibilities of the body charged with its fair and efficient operation. The growing complexity of our economy induced the Congress to place regulation of businesses like communication in specialized agencies with broad powers. Courts are slow to interfere with their conclusions when reconcilable with statutory directions. We think the Multiple Ownership Rules, as adopted, are reconcilable with the Communications Act as a whole. An applicant files his application with knowledge of the Commission's attitude toward concentration of control. . . .

Point III of the National Broadcasting Company brief argued the matter under this heading, "The Commission Cannot Escape Its Duty to Evaluate and Decide Each License Application on Its Own Facts." At that time § 309(a) had the hearing provision. It read: "Sec. 309. (a) If upon examination of any application for a station license or for the renewal or modification of a station license the Commission shall determine that public interest, convenience, or necessity would be served by the granting thereof, it shall authorize the issuance, renewal, or modification thereof in accordance with said finding. In the event the Commission upon examination of any such application does not reach such decision with respect thereto, it shall notify the applicant thereof, shall fix and give notice of a time and place for hearing thereon, and shall afford such applicant an opportunity to be heard under such rules and regulations as it may prescribe." 48 Stat. 1085. Change to the present form was merely for more certainty and clarification to avoid the possibility of arbitrary Commission action. . . .

We read the Act and Regulations as providing a "full hearing" for applicants who have reached the existing limit of stations, upon their presentation of applications conforming to Rules 1.361(c) and 1.702, that set out adequate reasons why the Rules should be waived or amended. The Act, considered as a whole, requires no more. We agree with the contention of the Commission that a full hearing, such as is required by § 309(b),

would not be necessary on all such applications. As the Commission has promulgated its Rules after extensive administrative hearings, it is necessary for the accompanying papers to set forth reasons, sufficient if true, to justify a change or waiver of the Rules. We do not think Congress intended the Commission to waste time on applications that do not state a valid basis for a hearing. If any application is aggrieved by a refusal, the way for review is open.

We reverse the judgement of the Court of Appeals and remand the case to that court so that it may consider respondent's other objections to the Multiple Ownership Rules.

Reversed and remanded.

Questions

1. Can you describe the *Storer* Doctrine?
2. Do the results reached in the *Chenery, Wyman-Gordon,* and *Storer* cases seem fair to you? Are they democratic? What do these cases portend for control of agencies by elected (or judicial) branches?

Justice Reed's opinion in the *Storer case* was perhaps not as clear as it might have been. Section 309(A) and (B) of the Federal Communications Act requires the FCC to hold an adjudicatory hearing in each case of a license denial or revocation. The FCC, however, promulgated a rule that limited the number of FM and television stations a company could own to five. Furthermore, the FCC announced its intentions to deny a license to any company that owned five or more stations and also to deny any such company the adjudicatory hearing required under § 309 of the Act. The same principle is applied to disability applicants in *Heckler v. Campbell* at the end of this chapter.

The problem in this area of administrative law lies not so much in the lack of agency hearings but rather in trying to channel discretion by encouraging agencies to go through the proper procedure in making decisions that affect people's lives. Generally, there are statutory requirements that command agencies to go through a specified Administrative Procedure Act procedure to make either a rule or an order. Furthermore, supplemental case law suggests when rule making is appropriate (general and future application) and when an order is more appropriate (specific/past event). There is also somewhat contradictory case law that says (a) that where a statute requires rule promulgation (§ 553) but the agency chooses to proceed on a case-by-case adjudicatory basis, the courts will not interfere (*Chenery, Wyman-Gordon,* and *Bell-Aerospace*) and (b) that where a statute requires a hearing on the record (adjudication), the agency is not precluded (by the courts) from promulgating a rule and denying the adjudicatory hearing to those who do not meet the dictates of the rule (*Storer* and *Campbell;* see also *American Airlines v. Civil Aeronautics Board* [CAB], 359 F.2d 624 [1966]).

SUMMARY

1. The doctrines from the *Londoner* and *Bi-Metallic* cases relate to both due process (next two chapters) and rule making:

   a. Although a state legislature need not provide each citizen a hearing before affecting his or her property or liberty, when the legislature delegates that power, the administrative agency receiving that power is required to hold a hearing. The hearing presumes oral presentation. The hearing is required where agency action affects a small number of people uniquely situated (*Londoner*).

   b. When government action applies to more than a few people (in terms of liberty or property) and it is impractical to hold a hearing, none is required by the due process clause of the Fourteenth Amendment (*Bi-Metallic*).

   c. At the federal level and in most of the states, the *Londoner/Bi-Metallic* jurisprudence has been replaced by legislation requiring agencies to hold hearings (Administrative Procedure Act).

2. There are three different types of rules: interpretive, substantive, and procedural, with their procedural requirements defined in §§ 553, 554, 556, and 557 of the Administrative Procedure Act:

   a. Courts cannot impose procedural requirements above those required in the Administrative Procedure Act (*Vermont Yankee* at the end of this chapter).

   b. When reviewing an agency's interpretation of a statute, a court should look first to whether Congress has clearly addressed the issue. If it has, that is the end of it, and agency interpretation must be consistent with congressional intent. Second, if congressional intent and meaning are obscure, the court must determine whether the agency's interpretation is a reasonable one (*Chevron*).

   c. Where an agency has adopted internal procedural rules, failure to follow those rules will invalidate subsequent agency action (*Ruiz*).

3. Where a statute requires an agency to proceed by § 553 of the Administrative Procedure Act, but an agency chooses instead to deal with an issue on a case-by-case basis via adjudication, the courts will not interfere with the agency's choice (*Chenery*).

4. Where an agency is required by statute to provide a hearing on the record but chooses instead to promulgate a general rule and deny the required hearing to whoever fails to meet the terms of the rule, the courts will not interfere with the agency's choice (*Storer*).

5. The last two doctrines (Nos. 3 and 4) are contemplated in the following quote from *Chenery*: "The choice . . . between proceeding by general rule or by individual, ad hoc litigation is one that lies primarily in the informed discretion of the administrative agency" (332 U.S. 194, 202–3).

END-OF-CHAPTER CASES

Federation of Federal Employees, Local 1309
v. Department of the Interior et al.
526 U.S. 86 (1999)

Justice Breyer delivered the opinion of the Court, in which Justices Stevens, Kennedy, Souter, and Ginsburg joined. Justice O'Connor filed a dissenting opinion, in which Chief Justice Rehnquist joined, and in which Justices Scalia and Thomas joined as to Part I.

I

Congress enacted the Federal Service Labor-Management Relations Statute (Statute or FSLMRS) in 1978. See 5 U.S.C. § 7101 et seq. Declaring that "labor organizations and collective bargaining in the civil service are in the public interest," § 7101(a), the Statute grants federal agency employees the right to organize, provides for collective bargaining, and defines various unfair labor practices. See §§ 7114(a)(1), 7116. It creates the Federal Labor Relations Authority (the Authority) which it makes responsible for implementing the Statute through the exercise of broad adjudicatory, policy-making, and rulemaking powers. §§ 7104, 7105. And it establishes within the Authority a Federal Service Impasses Panel, to which it grants the power to resolve negotiation impasses through compulsory arbitration, § 7119, hence without the strikes that the law forbids to federal employees, § 7116(b)(7).

Of particular relevance here, the Statute requires a federal agency employer to "meet" with the employees' collective-bargaining representative and to "negotiate in good faith for the purposes of arriving at a collective bargaining agreement." § 7114(a)(4). The Courts of Appeals disagree about whether, or the extent to which, this good-faith-bargaining requirement extends to midterm bargaining. Suppose, for example, that the federal agency and the union negotiate a basic 5-year contract. In the

third year a matter arises that the contract does not address. If the union seeks negotiations about the matter, does the Statute require the agency to bargain then and there, or can the agency wait for basic contract renewal negotiations? Does it matter whether the basic contract itself contains a "zipper clause" expressly forbidding such bargaining? Does it matter whether the basic contract itself contains a clause expressly permitting midterm bargaining? Can the parties insist upon bargaining end term (that is, during the negotiations over adopting or renewing a basic labor contract) about whether to include one or the other such clauses in the basic contract itself?

In 1985 the Authority began to answer some of these questions. It considered a union's effort to force midterm negotiations about a matter the basic labor contract did not address, and it held that the Statute did not require the agency to bargain.

The Court of Appeals for the District of Columbia Circuit, however, set aside the Authority's ruling. The court held that in light of the intent and purpose of the Statute, it must be read to require midterm bargaining, inasmuch as it did not create any distinction between bargaining at the end of a labor contract's term and bargaining during that term. *National Treasury Employees Union v. FLRA,* 810 F.2d 295 (1987) (NTEU). On remand the Authority reversed its earlier position. . . .

The Fourth Circuit has taken a different view of the matter. It has held that "union-initiated midterm bargaining is not required by the statute and would undermine the congressional policies underlying the statute." *Social Security Administration v. FLRA,* 956 F.2d 1280, 1281 (1992) *(SSA).* Nor, in its view, may the basic labor contract itself impose a midterm bargaining duty upon the parties. *Department of*

Energy v. FLRA, 106 F.3d 1158, 1163 (1997) (holding unlawful a midterm bargaining clause that the Federal Service Impasses Panel had imposed upon the parties' basic labor contract).

In the present suit, the National Federation of Federal Employees, Local 1309 (Union), representing employees of the United States Geological Survey, a subagency of the Department of the Interior (Agency), proposed including in the basic labor contract a midterm bargaining provision that said, "The Union may request and the Employer will be obliged to negotiate [midterm] on any negotiable matters not covered by the provisions of this [basic] agreement."

The Agency, relying on the Fourth Circuit's view that the Statute prohibits such a provision, refused to accept, or to bargain about, the proposed clause. The Authority, reiterating its own (and the D. C. Circuit's) contrary view, held that the Agency's refusal to bargain amounted to an unfair labor practice. The Statute itself, said the Authority, imposes an obligation to engage in midterm bargaining—an obligation that the proposed clause only reiterates. And even if such an obligation did not exist under the Statute, the Authority added, a proposal to create a contractual obligation to bargain midterm is a fit subject for endterm negotiation. Consequently, the Authority ordered the Agency to bargain over the proposed clause.

The Fourth Circuit set aside the Authority's order. 132 F.3d 157 (1997). The court reiterated its own view that the Statute itself does not impose any midterm bargaining duty. That being so, it concluded, the parties should not be required to bargain endterm about including a clause that would require bargaining midterm. The court reasoned that once bargaining over such a clause began, the employer would have no choice but to accept the clause. Were the employer not to do so (by bargaining to impasse over the proposed clause), the Federal Service Impasses Panel would then inevitably insert the clause over the employer's objection, as the Impasses Panel (like the D. C. Circuit) believes that a midterm bargaining clause would merely reiterate the duty to bargain midterm that the Statute itself imposes.

We granted certiorari to consider the conflicting views of the Circuits.

II

We shall focus primarily upon the basic question that divided the Circuits: Does the Statute itself impose a duty to bargain during the term of an existing labor contract? The Fourth Circuit thought that the Statute did not impose a duty to bargain midterm and that the matter was sufficiently clear to warrant judicial rejection of the contrary view of the agency charged with the Statute's administration. *SSA, supra,* at 1284 (stating that "'Congress has directly spoken to the precise question at issue,'" and quoting *Chevron U.S.A. Inc. v. Natural Resources Defense Council, Inc.,* 467 U.S. 837, 842 [1984]). We do not agree with the Fourth Circuit, for we find the Statute's language sufficiently ambiguous or open on the point as to require judicial deference to reasonable interpretation or elaboration by the agency charged with its execution. See *Chevron, supra,* at 842-845; *Fort Stewart Schools v. FLRA,* 495 U.S. 641, 644-645 (1990).

The D.C. Circuit, the Fourth Circuit, and the Authority all agree that the Statute itself does not expressly address union-initiated midterm bargaining. The Statute's relevant language simply says that federal agency employer and union representative "shall meet and negotiate in good faith for the purposes of arriving at a collective bargaining agreement." 5 U.S.C. § 7114(a)(4). It defines the key term "collective bargaining agreement" as an "agreement entered into as a result of collective bargaining." § 7103(a)(8). And it goes on to define "collective bargaining" as involving the meeting of employer and employee representatives "at reasonable times" to "consult" and to "bargain in a good-faith effort to reach agreement with respect to the conditions of employment," incorporating "any collective bargaining agreement reached" as a result of these negotiations in "a written document." § 7103(a)(12). This language, taken literally, may or may not include a duty to bargain collectively midterm. . . .

First, the Agency makes a variety of linguistic arguments. As an initial matter, it emphasizes the words "arriving at" in the Statute's general statement that the parties must bargain "for the purposes of arriving at a collective bargaining agreement." This statement tends to exclude midterm bargaining, the Agency contends, because parties engage in midterm bargaining, not for the purpose of arriving at, but for the purpose of supplementing, their basic, comprehensive labor contract. In other words, the basic collective-bargaining agreement is the only appropriate destination at which negotiations might "arrive." The Agency adds that "collective bargaining agreement" is a term of art, which only and always refers to basic labor contracts, not to midterm agreements.

Further, while the Agency acknowledges that there is a duty to bargain midterm in the private sector, see *NLRB v. Jacobs Manufacturing Co.,* 196 F.2d 680 (CA2 1952), it argues that this private-sector duty is based upon language in the National Labor Relations Act (NLRA) that is different in significant respects from the language in the Statute here. . . .

In our view, these linguistic arguments, while logical, make too much of too little. One can easily read "arriving at a collective bargaining agreement" as including an agreement reached at the conclusion of midterm bargaining, particularly because the Statute itself does no more than define the relevant term "collective bargaining agreement" in a circular way—as "an agreement entered into as a result of collective bargaining." 5 U.S.C. § 7103(a)(8). Nor have we found any statute, judicial opinion, agency document, or treatise that says whether the words "collective bargaining agreement" are words of art that must necessarily exclude midterm agreements. Finally, the linguistic differences between the NLRA and the FSLMRS tell us little, particularly given the fact that the two labor statutes, like collective bargaining itself, are not otherwise identical in the two sectors. For all these reasons, we find in the relevant statutory language ambiguity, not certainty.

Second, the Agency—like the Fourth Circuit—contends that the Statute's policies demand a reading of the statutory language that would exclude midterm bargaining from its definition of "collective bargaining." The

availability of midterm bargaining, the Agency argues, might lead unions to withhold certain subjects from ordinary endterm negotiations and then to raise them during the term, under more favorable bargaining conditions. A union might conclude, for example, that it is more likely to get what it wants by presenting a proposal during the term (when no other issues are on the table and a compromise is less likely) and then negotiating to impasse, thus leaving the matter for the Federal Service Impasses Panel to resolve. The Agency also points out that public-sector and private-sector bargaining differ in this respect. Private-sector unions enforce their views through strikes, and because they hesitate to strike midterm, they also have no particular incentive to bargain midterm. But public-sector unions enforce their views through compulsory arbitration, not strikes. Hence, the argument goes, public-sector unions have a unique incentive to bargain midterm on a piecemeal basis, thereby threatening to undermine the basic collective-bargaining process. See, e.g., *SSA,* 956 F.2d at 1288-1289.

Other policy concerns, however, argue for a different reading of the Statute. Without midterm bargaining, for example, will it prove possible to find a collective solution to a workplace problem, say a health or safety hazard, that first appeared midterm? The Statute's emphasis upon collective bargaining as "contributing to the effective conduct of public business," 5 U.S.C. § 7101(a)(1)(B), suggests that it would favor joint, not unilateral, solutions to such midterm problems. . . .

Third, the Agency argues that the Statute's history and prior administrative practice support its view that federal agencies have no duty to bargain midterm. The Statute grew out of an Executive Order that previously had governed federal-sector labor relations. See Exec. Order No. 11491, 3 CFR 861 (1966-1970 Comp.). In support, the Agency cites a case in which an Assistant Secretary of Labor, applying that Executive Order, dismissed an unfair labor practice complaint on the ground, among others, that a federal agency need not bargain over midterm union proposals. A single alternative ground, however—in a single, unreviewed decision from before the Statute was enacted—does not demonstrate the kind of historical practice that one might assume would be reflected in the Statute, particularly when at least one treatise suggested at the time that federal labor relations practice was to the contrary. See H. Robinson, *Negotiability in the Federal Sector* 10–11, and n. 9 (1981) (stating that under the Executive Order both unions and agencies had a continuing duty to bargain through the term of a basic labor contract).

The Agency also points to a Senate Report in support of its interpretation of the Statute. That Report speaks of the parties' "mutual duty to bargain" with respect to (1) "changes in established personnel policies proposed by management," and (2) "negotiable proposals initiated by either the agency or [the union] . . . in the context of negotiations leading to a basic collective bargaining agreement." S. Rep. No. 95-969, p. 104 (1978). This Report, however, concerns a bill that contains language similar to the language before us but was not enacted into law. . . .

Fourth, the Agency and the Fourth Circuit contend that the "management rights" provision of the Statute, 5 U.S.C. § 7106, does authorize limited midterm bargaining in respect to certain matters (not here at issue), and that by negative implication it denies permission to bargain midterm in respect to any others. See, e.g., *SSA*, supra, at 1284 ("The inclusion of a specific duty of midterm effects bargaining . . . suggests the inadvisability of reading a more general duty into the statute"). Our examination of that provision, however, finds little support for such a strong negative implication.

Subsection (a) of the management rights provision withdraws from collective bargaining certain subjects that it reserves exclusively for decision by management. It specifies, for example, that federal agency "management officials" will retain their authority to hire, fire, promote, and assign work, and also to determine the agency's "mission, budget, organization, number of employees, and internal security practices." § 7106(a).

Subsection (b), however, permits a certain amount of collective bargaining in respect to the very subjects that subsection (a) withdrew. Subsection (b) states:

"Nothing in this section shall preclude any agency and any labor organization from negotiating—

"(1) at the election of the agency, on the numbers, types, and grades of employees or positions assigned to any organizational subdivision, work project, or tour of duty, or on the technology, methods, and means of performing work;

"(2) procedures which management officials . . . will observe in exercising any authority under this section; or

"(3) appropriate arrangements for employees adversely affected by the exercise of any authority under this section by such management officials." § 7106(b)

The two subsections of the management rights provision, taken together, do not help the Agency. While the provision contemplates that bargaining over the impact and implementation of management changes may take place during the term of the basic labor contract, subsection (b) need not be read to actually impose a duty to bargain midterm. The italicized clause, "nothing in this section shall preclude," indicates only that the delegation of certain rights to management (e.g., promotions) shall not preclude negotiations about certain related matters (e.g., promotion procedures). By its terms, then, subsection (b) does nothing more than create an exception to subsection (a), preserving the duty to bargain with respect to certain matters otherwise committed to the discretion of management. . . .

The upshot of this analysis is that where the Agency and the Fourth Circuit find a clear statutory denial of any midterm bargaining obligation, we find ambiguity created by the Statute's use of general language that might, or might not, encompass various forms of midterm bargaining. That kind of statutory ambiguity is inconsistent both with the Fourth Circuit's absolute reading of the Statute and also with the D.C. Circuit's similarly absolute, but opposite, reading. Compare *SSA*, 956 F.2d at 1284, with *NTEU*, 810 F.2d at 301 (rejecting the Authority's position that there is no duty to bargain midterm on the ground that it is "contrary to the intent of the legislature and the guiding purpose of the statute"). Indeed, the D.C. Circuit's analysis implicitly concedes the need to make at least some midterm bargaining distinctions, when it assumes that the midterm bargaining obligation does not extend to matters that are covered by the basic contract.

The statutory ambiguity is perfectly consistent, however, with the conclusion that Congress delegated to the Authority the power to determine—within appropriate legal bounds, see, e.g., 5 U.S.C. § 706 (Administrative Procedure Act); *Chevron U.S.A. Inc. v. Natural Resources Defense Council, Inc.,* 467 U.S. 837 (1984)—whether, when, where, and what sort of midterm bargaining is required. The Statute's delegation of rulemaking, adjudicatory, and policymaking powers to the Authority supports this conclusion. See 5 U.S.C. § 7105(a)(1) ("Authority shall provide leadership in establishing policies and guidance"); § 7105(a)(2)(E) (Authority "resolves issues relating to the duty to bargain in good faith"); § 7117(c) (Authority resolves disputes about whether the duty to bargain in good faith extends to a particular matter). . . . This conclusion is also supported by precedent recognizing the similarity of the Authority's public-sector and the National Labor Relations Board's private-sector roles. As we have recognized, the Authority's function is "to develop specialized expertise in its field of labor relations and to use that expertise to give content to the principles and goals set forth in the Act," and it "is entitled to considerable deference when it exercises its 'special function of applying the general provisions of the Act to the complexities' of federal labor relations." *Bureau of Alcohol, Tobacco and Firearms v. FLRA,* 464 U.S. 89, 97 (1983) (quoting *NLRB v. Erie Resistor Corp.,* 373 U.S. 221, 236 [1963]).

We conclude that Congress "left" the matters of whether, when, and where midterm bargaining is required "to be resolved by the agency charged with the administration of the statute in light of everyday realities." *Chevron,* supra, at 865–866.

III

The specific question before us is whether an agency must bargain endterm about including in the basic labor contract a clause that would require certain forms of midterm bargaining. As is true of midterm bargaining itself, and for similar reasons, the Statute grants the Authority leeway (within ordinary legal limits) in answering that question as well.

The Authority says that it has determined, as a matter of its own judgment, that the parties must bargain over such a provision. Our reading of its relevant administrative determinations, however, leads us to conclude that its judgment on the matter was occasioned by the D.C. Circuit's holding that the Statute must be read to impose on agencies a duty to bargain midterm. . . . The Authority did indicate below that even if it agreed with the Fourth Circuit's position that the Statute does not impose a duty to bargain midterm, the outcome in this litigation would be no different, as the Authority "has previously upheld the negotiability of proposals despite the absence of a statutory right concerning the matter in question."

This explanation, however, seems more an effort to respond to, and to distinguish, a contrary judicial authority, rather than an independently reasoned effort to develop complex labor policies. Regardless, the Authority's conclusion would seem linked to the D.C. Circuit's basic understanding about the statutory requirements.

In light of our determination that the Statute does not resolve the question of midterm bargaining, nor the related question of bargaining about midterm bargaining, we believe the Authority should have the opportunity to consider these questions aware that the Statute permits, but does not compel, the conclusions it reached.

The decision of the Fourth Circuit is vacated, and the cases are remanded for further proceedings consistent with this opinion.

It is so ordered.

National Credit Union Administration v. First National Bank & Trust Co.
522 U.S. 479 (1998)

Justice Thomas delivered an opinion for the Court. Chief Justice Rehnquist and Justice Kennedy and Ginsburg joined that opinion in full, and Justice Scalia joined except as to footnote 6. Justice O'Connor filed a dissenting opinion, in which Justices Stevens, Souter, and Breyer joined.

Section 109 of the Federal Credit Union Act (FCUA), 12 U.S.C. § 1759, provides that "federal credit union membership shall be limited to groups having a common bond of occupation or association, or to groups within a well-defined neighborhood, community, or rural district." Since 1982, the National Credit Union Administration (NCUA), the agency charged with administering the FCUA, has interpreted § 109 to permit federal credit unions to be composed of multiple unrelated employer groups, each having its own common bond of occupation. In this case, respondents, five banks and the American Bankers Association, have challenged this interpretation on the ground that § 109 unambiguously requires that the same common bond of occupation unite every member of an occupationally defined federal credit union. We granted certiorari to answer two questions. First, do respondents have standing under the Administrative Procedure Act to seek federal court review of the NCUA's interpretation? Second, under the analysis set forth in *Chevron U.S.A. Inc. v. Natural Resources Defense Council, Inc.,* 467 U.S. 837 (1984), is the NCUA's interpretation permissible? We answer the first question in the affirmative and the second question in the negative. We therefore affirm.

I

In 1934, during the Great Depression, Congress enacted the FCUA, which authorizes the chartering of credit unions at the national level and provides that federal credit unions may, as a general matter, offer banking services only to their members. Section 109 of the FCUA, which has remained virtually unaltered since the FCUA's enactment, expressly restricts membership in federal credit unions. In relevant part, it provides: ". . . except that Federal credit union membership shall be limited to groups having a common bond of occupation or association, or to groups within a well-defined neighborhood, community, or rural district." 12 U.S.C. § 1759.

Until 1982, the NCUA and its predecessors consistently interpreted § 109 to require that the same common bond of occupation unite every member of an occupationally defined federal credit union. In 1982, however, the NCUA reversed its longstanding policy in order to permit credit unions to be composed of multiple unrelated employer groups. 47 Fed. Reg. 16775 (1982). It thus interpreted § 109's common bond requirement to apply only to each employer group in a multiple-group credit union, rather than to every member of that credit union. Under the NCUA's new interpretation, all of the employer groups in a multiple-group credit union had to be located "within a well-defined area," ibid., but the NCUA later revised this requirement to provide that each employer group could be located within "an area surrounding the [credit union's] home or a branch office that can be reasonably served by the [credit union] as determined by NCUA." 54 Fed. Reg. 31170 (1989). Since 1982, therefore, the NCUA has permitted federal credit unions to be composed of wholly unrelated employer groups, each having its own distinct common bond.

After the NCUA revised its interpretation of § 109, petitioner AT&T Family Federal Credit Union (ATTF) expanded its operations considerably by adding unrelated employer groups to its membership. As a result, ATTF now has approximately 110,000 members nationwide, only 35% of whom are employees of AT&T and its affiliates. The remaining members are employees of such diverse companies as the Lee Apparel Company, the Coca-Cola Bottling Company, the Ciba-Geigy Corporation, the Duke Power Company, and the American Tobacco Company.

In 1990, after the NCUA approved a series of amendments to ATTF's charter that added several such unrelated employer groups to ATTF's membership, respondents brought this action. Invoking the judicial review provisions of the Administrative Procedure Act (APA), 5 U.S.C. § 702, respondents claimed that the NCUA's approval of the charter amendments was contrary to law because the members of the new groups did not share a common bond of occupation with ATTF's existing members, as respondents alleged § 109 required. ATTF and petitioner Credit Union National Association were permitted to intervene in the case as defendants.

The District Court dismissed the complaint. It held that respondents lacked prudential standing to challenge the NCUA's chartering decision because their interests were not within the "zone of interests" to be protected by § 109, as required by this Court's cases interpreting the APA. *First Nat'l Bank & Trust Co. v. National Credit Union Admin.* 772 F. Supp. 609 (DC 1991). . . .

The Court of Appeals for the District of Columbia Circuit reversed. . . .

On remand, the District Court applied the two-step analysis that we announced in *Chevron U.S.A. Inc. v. Natural Resources Defense Council, Inc.,* 467 U.S. 837 (1984), and held that the NCUA had permissibly interpreted § 109. 863 F. Supp. 9 (DC 1994). It first asked whether, in enacting § 109, Congress had spoken directly to the precise question at issue—whether the same common bond of occupation must unite members of a federal credit union composed of multiple employer groups. It determined that because § 109 could plausibly be understood to permit an occupationally defined federal credit union to consist of several employer "groups," each having its own distinct common bond of occupation, Congress had not unambiguously addressed this question. . . .

The Court of Appeals again reversed. 90 F.3d 525 (CADC 1996). It held that the District Court had incorrectly applied the first step of *Chevron:* Congress had indeed spoken directly to the precise question at issue and had unambiguously indicated that the same common bond of occupation must unite members of a federal credit union composed of multiple employer groups. . . .

II

Based on four of our prior cases finding that competitors of financial institutions have standing to challenge agency action relaxing statutory restrictions on the activities of those institutions, we hold that respondents' interest in limiting the markets that federal credit unions can serve is arguably within the zone of interests to be protected by § 109. Therefore, respondents have prudential standing under the APA to challenge the NCUA's interpretation. . . .

Our prior cases, therefore, have consistently held that for a plaintiff's interests to be arguably within the "zone of interests" to be protected by a statute, there does not have to be an "indication of congressional purpose to benefit the would-be plaintiff." The proper inquiry is simply "whether the interest sought to be protected by the complainant is arguably within the zone of interests to be protected . . . by the statute." *Data Processing,* 397 U.S. at 153. Hence in applying the "zone of interests" test, we do not ask whether, in enacting the statutory provision at issue, Congress specifically intended to benefit the plaintiff. Instead, we first discern the interests "arguably . . . to be protected" by the statutory provision at issue; we then inquire whether the plaintiff's interests affected by the agency action in question are among them.

Section 109 provides that "federal credit union membership shall be limited to groups having a common bond of occupation or association, or to groups within a well-defined neighborhood, community, or rural district." 12 U.S.C. § 1759. By its express terms, § 109 limits membership in every federal credit union to members of definable "groups." Because federal credit unions may, as a general matter, offer banking services only to members, see, e.g., 12 U.S.C. §§ 1757(5)–(6), § 109 also restricts the markets that every federal credit union can serve. Although these markets need not be small, they unquestionably are limited. The link between § 109's regulation of federal credit union membership and its limitation on the markets that federal credit unions can serve is unmistakable. Thus, even if it cannot be said that Congress had the specific purpose of benefiting commercial banks, one of the interests "arguably . . . to be protected" by § 109 is an interest in limiting the markets that federal credit unions can serve. This interest is precisely the interest of respondents affected by the NCUA's interpretation of § 109. As competitors of federal credit unions, respondents certainly have an interest in limiting the markets that federal credit unions can serve, and the NCUA's interpretation has affected that interest by allowing federal credit unions to increase their customer base. . . .

III

Turning to the merits, we must judge the permissibility of the NCUA's current interpretation of § 109 by employing the analysis set forth in *Chevron U.S.A. Inc. v. Natural Resources Defense Council, Inc.*, 467 U.S. 837 (1984). Under that analysis, we first ask whether Congress has "directly spoken to the precise question at issue. If the intent of Congress is clear, that is the end of the matter; for the court, as well as the agency, must give effect to the unambiguously expressed intent of Congress." Id., at 842–843. If we determine that Congress has not directly spoken to the precise question at issue, we then inquire whether the agency's interpretation is reasonable. See id., at 843–844. Because we conclude that Congress has made it clear that the same common bond of occupation must unite each member of an occupationally defined federal credit union, we hold that the NCUA's contrary interpretation is impermissible under the first step of *Chevron*.

As noted, § 109 requires that "federal credit union membership shall be limited to groups having a common bond of occupation or association, or to groups within a well-defined neighborhood, community, or rural district." Respondents contend that because § 109 uses the article "a"—"i.e., one"—in conjunction with the noun "common bond," the "natural reading" of § 109 is that all members in an occupationally defined federal credit union must be united by one common bond. Petitioners reply that because § 109 uses the plural noun "groups," it permits multiple groups, each with its own common bond, to constitute a federal credit union.

Like the Court of Appeals, we do not think that either of these contentions, standing alone, is conclusive. The article "a" could be thought to convey merely that one bond must unite only the members of each group in a multiple-group credit union, and not all of the members in the credit union taken together. Similarly, the plural word "groups" could be thought to refer not merely to multiple groups in a particular credit union, but rather to every single "group" that forms a distinct credit union under the FCUA. See ibid. Nonetheless, as the Court of Appeals correctly recognized, additional considerations compel the conclusion that the same common bond of occupation must unite all of the members of an occupationally defined federal credit union.

First, the NCUA's current interpretation makes the phrase "common bond" surplusage when applied to a federal credit union made up of multiple unrelated employer groups, because each "group" in such a credit union already has its own "common bond." To use the facts of this case, the employees of AT&T and the employees of the American Tobacco Company each already had a "common bond" before being joined together as members of ATTF. The former were bonded because they worked for AT&T, and the latter were bonded because they worked for the American Tobacco Company. If the phrase "common bond" is to be given any meaning when these employees are joined together, a different "common bond"—one extending to each and every employee considered together—must be found to unite them. Such a "common bond" exists when employees of different subsidiaries of the same company are joined together in a federal credit union; it does not exist, however, when employees of unrelated companies are so joined. Put another way, in the multiple employer group context, the NCUA has read the statute as though it merely stated that "federal credit union membership shall be limited to occupational groups," but that is simply not what the statute provides.

Second, the NCUA's interpretation violates the established canon of construction that similar language contained within the same section of a statute must be accorded a consistent meaning. See *Wisconsin Dept. of Revenue v. William Wrigley, Jr., Co.,* 505 U.S. 214, 225 (1992). Section 109 consists of two parallel clauses: Federal credit union membership is limited "to groups having a common bond of occupation or association, or to groups within a well-defined neighborhood, community, or rural district." The NCUA concedes that even though the second limitation permits geographically defined credit unions to have as members more than one "group," all of the groups must come from the same "neighborhood, community, or rural district." The reason that the NCUA has never interpreted, and does not contend that it could interpret, the geographical limitation to allow a credit union to be composed of members from an unlimited number of unrelated geographic units, is that to do so would render the geographical limitation meaningless. Under established principles of statutory interpretation, we must interpret the occupational limitation in the same way. . . .

Finally, by its terms, § 109 requires that membership in federal credit unions "shall be limited." The NCUA's interpretation—under which a common bond of occupation must unite only the members of each unrelated employer group—has the potential to read these words out of the statute entirely. The NCUA has not contested that, under its current interpretation, it would be permissible to grant a charter to a conglomerate credit union whose members would include the employees of every company in the United States. Nor can it: Each company's employees would be a "group," and each such "group" would have its own "common bond of occupation." Section 109, however, cannot be considered a limitation on credit union membership if at the same time it permits such a limitless result.

For the foregoing reasons, we conclude that the NCUA's current interpretation of § 109 is contrary to the unambiguously expressed intent of Congress and is thus impermissible under the first step of *Chevron.*

The judgment of the Court of Appeals is therefore affirmed.

National Labor Relations Board v. Bell Aerospace Company
461 U.S. 267 (1974)

Justice Powell delivered the opinion of the Court, joined by Chief Justice Burger and Justices Douglas, Blackmun, and Rehnquist. Justice White dissented in part and was joined by Justices Brennan, Stewart, and Marshall.

This case presents two questions: first, whether the National Labor Relations Board properly determined that all "managerial employees," except those whose participation in a labor organization would create a conflict of interest with their job responsibilities, are covered by the National Labor Relations Act; and second, whether the Board must proceed by rule-making rather than by adjudication in determining whether certain buyers are "managerial employees." We answer both questions in the negative. . . .

I

Respondent Bell Aerospace Co., Division of Textron, Inc. (company), operates a plant in

Wheatfield, New York, where it is engaged in research and development in the design and fabrication of aerospace products. On July 30, 1970, Amalgamated Local No. 1286 of the United Automobile, Aerospace and Agricultural Implement Workers of America (union) petitioned the National Labor Relations Board (Board) for a representation election to determine whether the union would be certified as the bargaining representative of the 25 buyers in the purchasing and procurement department at the company's plant. The company opposed the petition on the ground that the buyers were "managerial employees" and thus were not covered by the Act.

Absent specific instructions to the contrary, buyers have full discretion, without any dollar limit, to select prospective vendors, draft invitations to bid, evaluate submitted bids, negotiate price and terms, and prepare purchase orders. Buyers execute all purchase orders up to $50,000. They may place or cancel orders of less than $5,000 on their own signature. On commitments in excess of $5,000, buyers must obtain the approval of a superior, with higher levels of approval required as the purchase cost increases. For the Minute Man missile project, which represents 70% of the company's sales, purchase decisions are made by a team of personnel from the engineering, quality assurance, finance, and manufacturing departments. The buyer serves as team chairman and signs the purchase order, but a representative from the pricing and negotiation department participates in working out the terms.

After the representation hearing, the Regional Director transferred the case to the Board. On May 20, 1971, the Board issued its decision holding that the company's buyers constituted an appropriate unit for purposes of collective bargaining and directing an election. 190 N.L.R.B. 431. Relying on its recent decision in *North Arkansas Electric Cooperative, Inc.,* 185 N.L.R.B. 550 (1970), the Board first stated that even though the company's buyers might be "managerial employees," they were nevertheless covered by the Act and entitled to its protections. The Board then rejected the company's alternative contention that representation

should be denied because the buyers' authority to commit the company's credit, select vendors, and negotiate purchase prices would create a potential conflict of interest between the buyers as union members and the company. In essence, the company argued that buyers would be more receptive to bids from union contractors and would also influence "make or buy" decisions in favor of "make," thus creating additional work for sister unions in the plant. The Board thought, however, that any possible conflict was "unsupported conjecture" since the buyers' "discretion and latitude for independent action must take place within the confines of the general directions which the Employer has established" and that "any possible temptation to allow sympathy for sister unions to influence such decisions could effectively be controlled by the Employer." . . .

On June 16, 1971, a representation election was conducted in which 15 of the buyers voted for the union and nine against. On August 12, the Board certified the union as the exclusive bargaining representative for the company's buyers. That same day, however, the Court of Appeals for the Eighth Circuit denied enforcement of another Board order in *NLRB v. North Arkansas Electric Cooperative, Inc.,* 446 F.2d 602, and held that "managerial employees" were not covered by the Act and were therefore not entitled to its protections. . . .

Encouraged by the Eighth Circuit's decision, the company moved the Board for reconsideration of its earlier order. The Board denied the motion, 196 N.L.R.B. 827 (1972), stating that it disagreed with the Eighth Circuit and would adhere to its own decision in *North Arkansas.* In the Board's view, Congress intended to exclude from the Act only those "managerial employees" associated with the "formulation and implementation of labor relations policies." In each case, the "fundamental touchstone" was "whether the duties and responsibilities of any managerial employee or group of managerial employees do or do not include determinations which should be made free of any conflict of interest which could arise if the person involved was a participating member of a labor organization." Turning to the present case, the

Board reiterated its prior finding that the company had not shown that union organization of its buyers would create a conflict of interest in labor relations.

The company stood by its contention that the buyers, as "managerial employees," were not covered by the Act and refused to bargain with the union. An unfair labor practice complaint resulted in a Board finding that the company had violated §§ 8(a)(5) and (1) of the Act, 29 U.S.C. and an order compelling the company to bargain with the union. 197 N.L.R.B. 209 (1972). Subsequently, the company petitioned the United States Court of Appeals for the Second Circuit for review of the order and the Board cross-petitioned for enforcement.

II

We begin with the question whether all "managerial employees," rather than just those in positions susceptible to conflicts of interest in labor relations, are excluded from the protections of the Act. The Board's early decisions, the legislative history of the Taft-Hartley Act of 1947, and subsequent Board and court decisions provide the necessary guidance for our inquiry. In examining these authorities, we draw on several established principles of statutory construction. In addition to the importance of legislative history, a court may accord great weight to the longstanding interpretation placed on a statute by an agency charged with its administration. This is especially so where Congress has re-enacted the statute without pertinent change. In these circumstances, congressional failure to revise or repeal the agency's interpretation is persuasive evidence that the interpretation is the one intended by Congress. We have also recognized that subsequent legislation declaring the intent of an earlier statute is entitled to significant weight. Application of these principles leads us to conclude, as did the Court of Appeals, that Congress intended to exclude from the protections of the Act all employees properly classified as "managerial." . . .

In sum, the Board's early decisions, the purpose and legislative history of the Taft-Hartley

Act of 1947, the Board's subsequent and consistent construction of the Act for more than two decades, and the decisions of the courts of appeals all point unmistakably to the conclusion that "managerial employees" are not covered by the Act. We agree with the Court of Appeals below that the Board "is not now free" to read a new and more restrictive meaning into the Act. . . .

III

The Court of Appeals also held that, although the Board was not precluded from determining that buyers or some types of buyers were not "managerial employees," it could do so only by invoking its rulemaking procedures under § 6 of the Act, 29 U.S.C. § 156. We disagree. At the outset, the precise nature of the present issue must be noted. The question is not whether the Board should have resorted to rulemaking, or in fact improperly promulgated a "rule," when in the context of the prior representation proceeding it held that the Act covers all "managerial employees" except those meeting the new "conflict of interest in labor relations" touchstone. Our conclusion that the Board applied the wrong legal standard makes consideration of that issue unnecessary. Rather, the present question is whether on remand the Board must invoke its rulemaking procedures if it determines, in light of our opinion, that these buyers are not "managerial employees" under the Act. The Court of Appeals thought that rulemaking was required because any Board finding that the company's buyers are not "managerial" would be contrary to its prior decisions and would presumably be in the nature of a general rule designed "to fit all cases at all times." . . .

A similar issue was presented to this Court in its second decision in *SEC v. Chenery Corp.,* 332 U.S. 194 (1947) (*Chenery II*). There, the respondent corporation argued that in an adjudicative proceeding the Commission could not apply a general standard that it had formulated for the first time in that proceeding. Rather, the Commission was required to resort instead to its rulemaking procedures if it desired to promulgate a new standard that would govern future conduct. In rejecting this contention, the Court first noted that the Commission had a statutory duty to decide the issue at hand in light of the proper standards and that this duty remained "regardless of whether those standards previously had been spelled out in a general rule or regulation." The Court continued: . . . "The function of filling in the interstices of the (Securities) Act should be performed, as much as possible, through this quasi-legislative promulgation of rules to be applied in the future. But any rigid requirement to that effect would make the administrative process inflexible and incapable of dealing with many of the specialized problems which arise." . . .

Not every principle essential to the effective administration of a statute can or should be cast immediately into the mold of a general rule. Some principles must await their own development, while others must be adjusted to meet particular, unforeseeable situations. In performing its important functions in these respects, therefore, an administrative agency must be equipped to act either by general rule or by individual order. To insist upon one form of action to the exclusion of the other is to exalt form over necessity. "In other words, problems may arise in a case which the administrative agency could not reasonably foresee, problems which must be solved despite the absence of a relevant general rule. Or the agency may not have had sufficient experience with a particular problem to warrant rigidifying its tentative judgment into a hard and fast rule. Or the problem may be so specialized and varying in nature as to be impossible of capture within the boundaries of a general rule. In those situations, the agency must retain power to deal with the problems on a case-to-case basis if the administrative process is to be effective. There is thus a very definite place for the case-by-case evolution of statutory standards." The Court concluded that "the choice made between proceeding by general rule or by individual, ad hoc litigation is one that lies primarily in the informed discretion of the administrative agency."

And in *NLRB v. Wyman-Gordon Co.,* 394 U.S. 759, 89 S.Ct. 1426, 22 L.Ed.2d 709 (1969), the Court upheld a Board order enforcing an election list requirement first promulgated in an earlier adjudicative proceeding in *Excelsior Underwear Inc.,* 156 N.L.R.B. 1236 (1966). The plurality opinion of Mr. Justice Fortas, joined by the Chief Justice, Mr. Justice Stewart, and Mr. Justice White, recognized that "[a]djudicated cases may and do . . . serve as vehicles for the formulation of agency policies, which are applied and announced therein," and that such cases "generally provide a guide to action that the agency may be expected to take in future cases." *NLRB v. Wyman-Gordon Co.,* supra, at 765–766, 89 S.Ct., at 1429. The concurring opinion of Mr. Justice Black, joined by Mr. Justice Brennan and Mr. Justice Marshall, also noted that the Board had both adjudicative and rule-making powers and that the choice between the two was "within its informed discretion."

The views expressed in *Chenery II* and *Wyman-Gordon* make plain that the Board is not precluded from announcing new principles in an adjudicative proceeding and that the choice between rulemaking and adjudication lies in the first instance within the Board's discretion. Although there may be situations where the Board's reliance on adjudication would amount to an abuse of discretion or a violation of the Act, nothing in the present case would justify such a conclusion. Indeed, there is ample indication that adjudication is especially appropriate in the instant context. The Court of Appeals noted, "[t]here must be tens of thousands of manufacturing, wholesale and retail units which employ buyers, and hundreds of thousands of the latter." Moreover, duties of buyers vary widely depending on the company or industry. It is doubtful whether any generalized standard could be framed which would have more than marginal utility. The Board thus has reason to proceed with caution, developing its standards in a case-by-case manner with attention to the specific character of the buyers' authority and duties in each company. The Board's judgment that adjudication best serves this purpose is entitled to great weight. It is true, of course, that rulemaking would provide the Board with a forum for soliciting the informed views of those affected in industry and labor before embarking on a new course. But surely the Board has discretion to decide that the adjudicative procedures in this case may also produce the relevant information necessary to mature and fair consideration of the issues. Those most immediately affected, the buyers and the company in the particular case, are accorded a full opportunity to be heard before the Board makes its determination.

The judgment of the Court of Appeals is therefore affirmed in part and reversed in part, and the cause remanded to that court with directions to remand to the Board for further proceedings in conformity with this opinion.

Judgment of the Court of Appeals affirmed in part and reversed in part, and cause remanded.

It is so ordered.

Heckler v. Campbell
461 U.S. 458 (1983)

Justice Powell delivered the opinion for seven members of the Court. Justice Brennan concurred, and Justice Marshall concurred in part and dissented in part. The issue is whether the secretary of Health and Human Services may rely on published medical-vocational guidelines to determine a claimant's right to Social Security disability benefits.

I

The Social Security Act defines "disability" in terms of the effect a physical or mental impairment has on a person's ability to function in the work place. It provides disability benefits only to persons who are unable "to engage in any substantial gainful activity by reason of any medically determinable physical or mental impairment." 42 U.S.C. § 423(d)(1)(A). And it specifies that a person must "not only [be] unable to do his previous work but [must be unable], considering his age, education, and work experience, [to] engage in any other kind of substantial gainful work which exists in the national economy, regardless of whether such work exists in the immediate area in which he lives, or whether a specific job vacancy exists for him, or whether he would be hired if he applied for work."

In 1978, the Secretary of Health and Human Services promulgated regulations implementing this definition. See 43 Fed.Reg. 55349 (1978). The regulations recognize that certain impairments are so severe that they prevent a person

from pursuing any gainful work. A claimant who establishes that he suffers from one of these impairments will be considered disabled without further inquiry. If a claimant suffers from a less severe impairment, the Secretary must determine whether the claimant retains the ability to perform either his former work or some less demanding employment. If a claimant can pursue his former occupation, he is not entitled to disability benefits. If he cannot, the Secretary must determine whether the claimant retains the capacity to pursue less demanding work.

The regulations divide this last inquiry into two stages. First, the Secretary must assess each claimant's present job qualifications. The regulations direct the Secretary to consider the factors Congress has identified as relevant: physical ability, age, education, and work experience. Second, she must consider whether jobs exist in the national economy. . . .

Prior to 1978, the Secretary relied on vocational experts to establish the existence of suitable jobs in the national economy. After a claimant's limitations and abilities had been determined at a hearing, a vocational expert ordinarily would testify whether work existed that the claimant could perform. Although this testimony often was based on standardized guides, vocational experts frequently were criticized for their inconsistent treatment of similarly situated claimants. See *Santise v. Schweiker,* 676 F.2d 925 (1982). To improve both the uniformity and efficiency of this determination, the

Secretary promulgated medical-vocational guidelines as part of the 1978 regulations. . . . These guidelines relieve the Secretary of the need to rely on vocational experts by establishing through rulemaking the types and numbers of jobs that exist in the national economy. They consist of a matrix of the four factors identified by Congress—physical ability, age, education, and work experience—and set forth rules that identify whether jobs requiring specific combinations of these factors exist in significant numbers in the national economy. Where a claimant's qualifications correspond to the job requirements identified by a rule, the guidelines direct a conclusion as to whether work exists that the claimant could perform. If such work exists, the claimant is not considered disabled. . . .

II

In 1979, Carmen Campbell applied for disability benefits because a back condition and hypertension prevented her from continuing her work as a hotel maid. After her application was denied, she requested a hearing de novo before an Administrative Law Judge. He determined that her back problem was not severe enough to find her disabled without further inquiry, and accordingly considered whether she retained the ability to perform either her past work or some less strenuous job. He concluded that even though Campbell's back condition prevented her from returning to her work as a maid, she retained the physical capacity to do light work. In accordance with the regulations, he found that Campbell was 52 years old, that her previous employment consisted of unskilled jobs and that she had a limited education. He noted that Campbell, who had been born in Panama, experienced difficulty in speaking and writing English. She was able, however, to understand and read English fairly well. Relying on the medical-vocational guidelines, the Administrative Law Judge found that a significant number of jobs existed that a person of Campbell's qualifications could perform. Accordingly, he concluded that she was not disabled.

This determination was upheld by both the Social Security Appeals Council and the District Court for the Eastern District of New York. The Court of Appeals for the Second Circuit reversed. *Campbell v. Secretary of HHS,* 665 F.2d 48 (CA2 1982). It accepted the Administrative Law Judge's determination that Campbell retained the ability to do light work. And it did not suggest that he had classified Campbell's age, education, or work experience incorrectly. The court noted, however, that it "has consistently required that 'the Secretary identify specific alternative occupations available in the national economy that would be suitable for the claimant' and that 'these jobs be supported by "a job description clarifying the nature of the job, [and] demonstrating that the job does not require" exertion or skills not possessed by the claimant.'" (quoting *Decker v. Harris,* 647 F.2d 291, 298 [CA2 1981]). The court found that the medical-vocational guidelines did not provide the specific evidence that it previously had required. It explained that in the absence of such a showing, "the claimant is deprived of any real chance to present evidence showing that she cannot in fact perform the types of jobs that are administratively noticed by the guidelines." The court concluded that because the Secretary had failed to introduce evidence that specific alternative jobs existed, the determination that Campbell was not disabled was not supported by substantial evidence. We granted certiorari to resolve a conflict among the Courts of Appeals. We now reverse.

[1] The Social Security Act directs the Secretary to "adopt reasonable and proper rules and regulations to regulate and provide for the nature and extent of the proofs and evidence and the method of taking and furnishing the same" in disability cases. As we previously have recognized, Congress has "conferred on the Secretary exceptionally broad authority to prescribe standards for applying certain sections of the [Social Security] Act." *Schweiker v. Gray Panthers,* 453 U.S. 34 (1981). Where, as here, the statute expressly entrusts the Secretary with the responsibility for implementing a provision by regulation, our review is limited to determining

whether the regulations promulgated exceeded the Secretary's statutory authority and whether they are arbitrary and capricious. . . .

[2] We do not think that the Secretary's reliance on medical-vocational guidelines is inconsistent with the Social Security Act. It is true that the statutory scheme contemplates that disability hearings will be individualized determinations based on evidence adduced at a hearing. See 42 U.S.C. § 423(d)(2)(A) (specifying consideration of each individual's condition); 42 U.S.C. § 405(b) (disability determination to be based on evidence adduced at hearing). But this does not bar the Secretary from relying on rulemaking to resolve certain classes of issues. The Court has recognized that even where an agency's enabling statute expressly requires it to hold a hearing, the agency may rely on its rule-making authority to determine issues that do not require case-by-case consideration. *United States v. Storer Broadcasting Co.,* 351 U.S. 192, 205 (1956). A contrary holding would require the agency continually to relitigate issues that may be established fairly and efficiently in a single rulemaking proceeding.

The Secretary's decision to rely on medical-vocational guidelines is consistent with *Texaco* and *Storer.* As noted above, in determining whether a claimant can perform less strenuous work, the Secretary must make two determinations. She must assess each claimant's individual abilities and then determine whether jobs exist that a person having the claimant's qualifications could perform. The first inquiry involves a determination of historic facts, and the regulations properly require the Secretary to make these findings on the basis of evidence adduced at a hearing. We note that the regulations afford claimants ample opportunity both to present evidence relating to their own abilities and to offer evidence that the guidelines do not apply to them. The second inquiry requires the Secretary to determine an issue that is not unique to each claimant—the types and numbers of jobs that exist in the national economy. This type of general factual issue may be resolved as fairly through rulemaking as by introducing the testimony of vocational experts at each disability hearing. See *American Airlines, Inc. v. CAB* [Civil Aeronautics Board], 123 U.S.App.D.C. 310 (1966) (en banc).

IV

The Court of Appeals' decision would require the Secretary to introduce evidence of specific available jobs that respondent could perform. It would limit severely her ability to rely on the medical-vocational guidelines. We think the Secretary reasonably could choose to rely on these guidelines in appropriate cases rather than on the testimony of a vocational expert in each case. Accordingly, the judgment of the Court of Appeals is Reversed.

Vermont Yankee Nuclear Power Corporation v. Natural Resources Defense Council 435 U.S. 519 (1978)

Justice Rehnquist delivered the opinion of the Court of seven Justices. Justices Blackmun and Powell did not participate.

In 1946, Congress enacted the Administrative Procedure Act, which as we have noted elsewhere was not only "a new, basic and comprehensive regulation of procedures in many agencies," but was also a legislative enactment which settled "long-continued and hard-fought contentions, and enacts a formula upon which opposing social and political forces have come to rest." Section 4 of the Act, 5 U.S.C. § 553 dealing with rulemaking, requires in subsection (b) that "notice of proposed rule making shall be published in the Federal Register . . .," describes the contents of that notice, and goes on to require in subsection (c) that after the notice the agency "shall give interested persons an opportunity to participate in the rule making through submission of written data, views, or arguments with or without opportunity for oral presentation. After consideration of the relevant matter presented, the agency shall incorporate in the rules adopted a concise general statement of their basis and purpose." Interpreting this provision of the Act in *United States v. Allegheny-Ludlum Steel Corp.,* 406 U.S. 742 (1972), and *United States v. Florida East Coast R. Co.,* 410 U.S. 224 (1973), we held that generally speaking this section of the Act established the maximum procedural requirements which Congress was willing to have the courts impose upon agencies in conducting rulemaking procedures. Agencies are free to grant additional procedural rights in the exercise of their discretion, but reviewing courts are generally not free to impose them if the agencies have not chosen to grant them. This is not to say necessarily that there are no circumstances which would ever justify a court in overturning agency action because of a failure to employ procedures beyond those required by the statute. But such circumstances, if they exist, are extremely rare.

Even apart from the Administrative Procedure Act this Court has for more than four decades emphasized that the formulation of procedures was basically to be left within the discretion of the agencies to which Congress had confided the responsibility for substantive judgments. The Court explicated this principle, describing it as "an outgrowth of the congressional determination that administrative agencies and administrators will be familiar with the industries which they regulate and will be in a better position than federal courts or Congress itself to design procedural rules adapted to the peculiarities of the industry and the tasks of the agency involved." It is in the light of this background of statutory and decisional law that we granted certiorari to review two judgments of the Court of Appeals for the District of Columbia Circuit because of our concern that they had seriously misread or misapplied this statutory and decisional law cautioning reviewing courts against engrafting their own notions

of proper procedures upon agencies entrusted with substantive functions by Congress. We conclude that the Court of Appeals has done just that in these cases, and we therefore remand them to it for further proceedings. We also find it necessary to examine the Court of Appeals' decision with respect to agency action taken after full adjudicatory hearings. We again conclude that the court improperly intruded into the agency's decisionmaking process, making it necessary for us to reverse and remand with respect to this part of the case also.

I

A

Under the Atomic Energy Act of 1954, 42 U.S.C. § 2011 et seq., the Atomic Energy Commission is given broad regulatory authority over the development of nuclear energy. Under the terms of the Act, a utility seeking to construct and operate a nuclear power plant must obtain a separate permit or license at both the construction and the operation stage of the project. In order to obtain the construction permit, the utility must file a preliminary safety analysis report, an environmental report, and certain information regarding the antitrust implications of the proposed project. This application then undergoes exhaustive review by the Commission's staff and by the Advisory Committee on Reactor Safeguards (ACRS), a group of distinguished experts in the field of atomic energy. Both groups submit to the Commission their own evaluations, which then become part of the record of the utility's application. The Commission staff also undertakes the review required by the National Environmental Policy Act of 1969 (NEPA), 42 U.S.C. § 4321 et seq., and prepares a draft environmental impact statement, which, after being circulated for comment, is revised and becomes a final environmental impact statement.

Thereupon a three-member Atomic Safety and Licensing Board conducts a public adjudicatory hearing, and reaches a decision which can be appealed to the Atomic Safety and Licensing Appeal Board, and currently, in the Commission's discretion, to the Commission itself. The final agency decision may be appealed to the courts of appeals. The same sort of process occurs when the utility applies for a license to operate the plant, except that a hearing need only be held in contested cases and may be limited to the matters in controversy.

These cases arise from two separate decisions of the Court of Appeals for the District of Columbia Circuit. In the first, the court remanded a decision of the Commission to grant a license to petitioner Vermont Yankee Nuclear Power Corp. to operate a nuclear power plant. *Natural Resources Defense Council v. NRC [Nuclear Regulatory Commission]*, 547 F.2d 633 (1976). In the second, the court remanded a decision of that same agency to grant a permit to petitioner Consumers Power Co. to construct two pressurized water nuclear reactors to generate electricity and steam. *Aeschliman v. NRC*, 547 F.2d 622.

B

In December 1967, after the mandatory adjudicatory hearing and necessary review, the Commission granted petitioner Vermont Yankee a permit to build a nuclear power plant in Vernon, Vt. See 4 A.E.C. 36 (1967). Thereafter, Vermont Yankee applied for an operating license. Respondent Natural Resources Defense Council (NRDC) objected to the granting of a license, however, and therefore a hearing on the application commenced on August 10, 1971. Excluded from consideration at the hearings, over NRDC's objection, was the issue of the environmental effects of operations to reprocess fuel or dispose of wastes resulting from the reprocessing operations. This ruling was affirmed by the Appeal Board in June 1972. . . . In November 1972, however, the Commission, making specific reference to the Appeal Board's decision with respect to the Vermont Yankee license, instituted rulemaking proceedings "that would specifically deal with the question of consideration of environmental effects associated with the uranium fuel cycle in the individual cost-benefit analyses for light water cooled nuclear power reactors." The notice of proposed rulemaking offered two

alternatives, both predicated on a report prepared by the Commission's staff entitled Environmental Survey of the Nuclear Fuel Cycle. The first would have required no quantitative evaluation of the environmental hazards of fuel reprocessing or disposal because the Environmental Survey had found them to be slight. The second would have specified numerical values for the environmental impact of this part of the fuel cycle, which values would then be incorporated into a table, along with the other relevant factors, to determine the overall cost-benefit balance for each operating license.

Much of the controversy in this case revolves around the procedures used in the rulemaking hearing which commenced in February 1973. In a supplemental notice of hearing the Commission indicated that while discovery or cross-examination would not be utilized, the Environmental Survey would be available to the public before the hearing along with the extensive background documents cited therein. All participants would be given a reasonable opportunity to present their position and could be represented by counsel if they so desired. Written and, time permitting, oral statements would be received and incorporated into the record. All persons giving oral statements would be subject to questioning by the Commission. At the conclusion of the hearing, a transcript would be made available to the public and the record would remain open for 30 days to allow the filing of supplemental written statements. More than 40 individuals and organizations representing a wide variety of interests submitted written comments. On January 17, 1973, the Licensing Board held a planning session to schedule the appearance of witnesses and to discuss methods for compiling a record. The hearing was held on February 1 and 2, with participation by a number of groups, including the Commission's staff, the United States Environmental Protection Agency, a manufacturer of reactor equipment, a trade association from the nuclear industry, a group of electric utility companies, and a group called Consolidated National Intervenors which represented 79 groups and individuals including respondent NRDC.

After the hearing, the Commission's staff filed a supplemental document for the purpose of clarifying and revising the Environmental Survey. Then the Licensing Board forwarded its report to the Commission without rendering any decision. The Licensing Board identified as the principal procedural question the propriety of declining to use full formal adjudicatory procedures. The major substantive issue was the technical adequacy of the Environmental Survey. In April 1974, the Commission issued a rule which adopted the second of the two proposed alternatives described above. The Commission also approved the procedures used at the hearing, and indicated that the record, including the Environmental Survey, provided an "adequate data base for the regulation adopted." Finally, the Commission ruled that to the extent the rule differed from the Appeal Board decisions in Vermont Yankee "those decisions have no further precedential significance," but that since "the environmental effects of the uranium fuel cycle have been shown to be relatively insignificant, . . . it is unnecessary to apply the amendment to applicant's environmental reports submitted prior to its effective date or to Final Environmental Statements for which Draft Environmental Statements have been circulated for comment prior to the effective date."

But this much is absolutely clear. Absent constitutional constraints or extremely compelling circumstances the "administrative agencies 'should be free to fashion their own rules of procedure and to pursue methods of inquiry capable of permitting them to discharge their multitudinous duties.'" Indeed, our cases could hardly be more explicit in this regard. The Court has, as we noted in FCC v. Schreiber, upheld this principle in a variety of applications, including that case where the District Court, instead of inquiring into the validity of the Federal Communications Commission's exercise of its rulemaking authority, devised procedures to be followed by the agency on the basis of its conception of how the public and private interest involved could best be served.

We have continually repeated this theme through the years, most recently in FPC v. Transcontinental Gas Pipe Line Corp., 423 U.S.

326 (1976), decided just two Terms ago. In that case, in determining the proper scope of judicial review of agency action under the Natural Gas Act, we held that while a court may have occasion to remand an agency decision because of the inadequacy of the record, the agency should normally be allowed to "exercise its administrative discretion in deciding how, in light of internal organization considerations, it may best proceed to develop the needed evidence and how its prior decision should be modified in light of such evidence as develops." We went on to emphasize: "At least in the absence of substantial justification for doing otherwise, a reviewing court may not, after determining that additional evidence is requisite for adequate review, proceed by dictating to the agency the methods, procedures, and time dimension of the needed inquiry and ordering the results to be reported to the court without opportunity for further consideration on the basis of the new evidence by the agency."

Such a procedure clearly runs the risk of "propel[ling] the court into the domain which Congress has set aside exclusively for the administrative agency." SEC v. Chenery Corp., 332 U.S. 194 (1947). Secondly, it is obvious that the court in these cases reviewed the agency's choice of procedures on the basis of the record actually produced at the hearing, and not on the basis of the information available to the agency when it made the decision to structure the proceedings in a certain way. This sort of Monday morning quarterbacking not only encourages but almost compels the agency to conduct all rulemaking proceedings with the full panoply of procedural devices normally associated only with adjudicatory hearings.

Finally, and perhaps most importantly, this sort of review fundamentally misconceives the nature of the standard for judicial review of an agency rule. The court below uncritically assumed that additional procedures will automatically result in a more adequate record because it will give interested parties more of an opportunity to participate in and contribute to the proceedings. But informal rulemaking need not be based solely on the transcript of a hearing held before an agency. Indeed, the agency need not even hold a formal hearing.

See 5 U.S.C. § 553(c). Thus, the adequacy of the "record" in this type of proceeding is not correlated directly to the type of procedural devices employed, but rather turns on whether the agency has followed the statutory mandate of the Administrative Procedure Act or other relevant statutes. If the agency is compelled to support the rule which it ultimately adopts with the type of record produced only after a full adjudicatory hearing, it simply will have no choice but to conduct a full adjudicatory hearing prior to promulgating every rule. In sum, this sort of unwarranted judicial examination of perceived procedural shortcomings of a rulemaking proceeding can do nothing but seriously interfere with that process prescribed by Congress. Thus,

it is clear NEPA cannot serve as the basis for a substantial revision of the carefully constructed procedural specifications of the Administrative Procedure Act.

In short, nothing in the Administrative Procedure Act, NEPA, the circumstances of this case, the nature of the issues being considered, past agency practice, or the statutory mandate under which the Commission operates permitted the court to review and overturn the rulemaking proceeding on the basis of the procedural devices employed (or not employed) by the Commission so long as the Commission employed at least the statutory minima, a matter about which there is no doubt in this case.

Motor Vehicle Manufacturers Association of the United States v. State Farm Mutual Automobile Insurance Company 463 U.S. 29 (1983)

Justice White delivered the opinion, joined by Justices Brennan, Marshall, Blackmun, and Stevens. Justices Burger, Powell, Rehnquist, and O'Connor dissented in part.

Facts: The development of the automobile gave Americans unprecedented freedom to travel, but exacted a high price for enhanced mobility. Since 1929, motor vehicles have been the leading cause of accidental deaths and injuries in the United States. In 1982, 46,300 Americans died in motor vehicle accidents and hundreds of thousands more were maimed and injured. While a consensus exists that the current loss of life on our highways is unacceptably high, improving safety does not admit to easy solution. In 1966, Congress decided that at least part of the answer lies in improving the design and safety features of the vehicle itself. But much of the technology for building safer cars was undeveloped or untested. Before changes in automobile design could be mandated, the effectiveness of these changes had to be studied, their costs examined, and public acceptance considered. This task called for

considerable expertise and Congress responded by enacting the National Traffic and Motor Vehicle Safety Act of 1966 (Act), 15 U.S.C. 1381 et seq. The Act, created for the purpose of "reduc[ing] traffic accidents and deaths and injuries to persons resulting from traffic accidents," directs the Secretary of Transportation or his delegate to issue motor vehicle safety standards that "shall be practicable, shall meet the need for motor vehicle safety, and shall be stated in objective terms." In issuing these standards, the Secretary is directed to consider "relevant available motor vehicle safety data," whether the proposed standard "is reasonable, practicable and appropriate" for the particular type of motor vehicle, and the "extent to which such standards will contribute to carrying out the purposes" of the Act. The Act also authorizes judicial review under the provisions of the Administrative Procedure Act, 5 U.S.C. 706, of all "orders establishing, amending, or revoking a Federal motor vehicle safety standard." Under this authority, we review today whether NHTSA [National Highway Traffic Safety Administration] acted arbitrarily and capriciously in revoking the requirement in Motor Vehicle Safety

Standard 208 that new motor vehicles produced after September 1982 be equipped with passive restraints to protect the safety of the occupants of the vehicle in the event of a collision. Briefly summarized, we hold that the agency failed to present an adequate basis and explanation for rescinding the passive restraint requirement and that the agency must either consider the matter further or adhere to or amend Standard 208 along lines which its analysis supports.

I

The regulation whose rescission is at issue bears a complex and convoluted history. Over the course of approximately 60 rulemaking notices, the requirement has been imposed, amended, rescinded, reimposed, and now rescinded again.

As originally issued by the Department of Transportation in 1967, Standard 208 simply required the installation of seatbelts in all automobiles. 32 Fed. Reg. 2415. It soon became apparent that the level of seatbelt use was too low to reduce traffic injuries to an acceptable level. The Department therefore began consideration of "passive occupant restraint systems"—devices that do not depend for their effectiveness upon any action taken by the occupant except that necessary to operate the vehicle. Two types of automatic crash protection emerged: automatic seatbelts and air bags. The automatic seatbelt is a traditional safety belt, which when fastened to the interior of the door remains attached without impeding entry or exit from the vehicle, and deploys automatically without any action on the part of the passenger. The air bag is an inflatable device concealed in the dashboard and steering column. It automatically inflates when a sensor indicates that deceleration forces from an accident have exceeded a preset minimum, then rapidly deflates to dissipate those forces. The lifesaving potential of these devices was immediately recognized, and in 1977, after substantial on-the-road experience with both devices, it was estimated by NHTSA that passive restraints could prevent approximately

12,000 deaths and over 100,000 serious injuries annually. 42 Fed. Reg. 34298.

In 1969, the Department formally proposed a standard requiring the installation of passive restraints, 34 Fed. Reg. 11148, thereby commencing a lengthy series of proceedings. In 1970, the agency revised Standard 208 to include passive protection requirements, 35 Fed. Reg. 16927, and in 1972, the agency amended the Standard to require full passive protection for all front seat occupants of vehicles manufactured after August 15, 1975. 37 Fed. Reg. 3911. In the interim, vehicles built between August 1973 and August 1975 were to carry either passive restraints or lap and shoulder belts coupled with an "ignition interlock" that would prevent starting the vehicle if the belts were not connected. On review, the agency's decision to require passive restraints was found to be supported by "substantial evidence" and upheld. *Chrysler Corp. v. Department of Transportation,* 472 F.2d 659 (CA6 1972). In preparing for the upcoming model year, most car makers chose the "ignition interlock" option, a decision which was highly unpopular, and led Congress to amend the Act to prohibit a motor vehicle safety standard from requiring or permitting compliance by means of an ignition interlock or a continuous buzzer designed to indicate that safety belts were not in use. The 1974 Amendments also provided that any safety standard that could be satisfied by a system other than seatbelts would have to be submitted to Congress where it could be vetoed by concurrent resolution of both Houses. 15 U.S.C. 1410b(b)(2). The effective date for mandatory passive restraint systems was extended for a year until August 31, 1976. But in June 1976, Secretary of Transportation William T. Coleman, Jr., initiated a new rulemaking on the issue. After hearing testimony and reviewing written comments, Coleman extended the optional alternatives indefinitely and suspended the passive restraint requirements. Although he found passive restraints technologically and economically feasible, the Secretary based his decision on the expectation that there would be widespread public resistance to the new systems. He instead proposed a demonstration project involving up to 500,000 cars installed with passive restraints, in order to smooth the way for public acceptance of mandatory passive restraints at a later date.

Coleman's successor as Secretary of Transportation disagreed. Within months of assuming office, Secretary Brock Adams decided that the demonstration project was unnecessary. He issued a new mandatory passive restraint regulation, known as Modified Standard 208. 42 Fed. Reg. 34289 (1977). The Modified Standard mandated the phasing in of passive restraints beginning with large cars in model year 1982 and extending to all cars by model year 1984. The two principal systems that would satisfy the Standard were air bags and passive belts; the choice of which system to install was left to the manufacturers. In *Pacific Legal Foundation v. Department of Transportation,* 593 F.2d 1338, the Court of Appeals upheld Modified Standard 208 as a rational, nonarbitrary regulation consistent with the agency's mandate under the Act. The Standard also survived scrutiny by Congress, which did not exercise its authority under the legislative veto provision of the 1974 Amendments. Over the next several years, the automobile industry geared up to comply with Modified Standard 208. As late as July 1980, NHTSA reported:

"On the road experience in thousands of vehicles equipped with air bags and automatic safety belts has confirmed agency estimates of the life-saving and injury-preventing benefits of such systems. When all cars are equipped with automatic crash protection systems, each year an estimated 9,000 more lives will be saved, and tens of thousands of serious injuries will be prevented." In February 1981, however, Secretary of Transportation Andrew Lewis reopened the rulemaking due to changed economic circumstances and, in particular, the difficulties of the automobile industry. 46 Fed. Reg. 12033. Two months later, the agency ordered a one-year delay in the application of the Standard to large cars, extending the deadline to September 1982, and at the same time, proposed the possible rescission of the entire Standard. After receiving written comments and

holding public hearings, NHTSA issued a final rule (Notice 25) that rescinded the passive restraint requirement contained in Modified Standard 208.

II

In a statement explaining the rescission, NHTSA maintained that it was no longer able to find, as it had in 1977, that the automatic restraint requirement would produce significant safety benefits. This judgment reflected not a change of opinion on the effectiveness of the technology, but a change in plans by the automobile industry. In 1977, the agency had assumed that air bags would be installed in 60% of all new cars and automatic seatbelts in 40%. By 1981 it became apparent that automobile manufacturers planned to install the automatic seatbelts in approximately 99% of the new cars. For this reason, the lifesaving potential of air bags would not be realized. Moreover, it now appeared that the overwhelming majority of passive belts planned to be installed by manufacturers could be detached easily and left that way permanently. Passive belts, once detached, then required "the same type of affirmative action that is the stumbling block to obtaining high usage levels of manual belts." For this reason, the agency concluded that there was no longer a basis for reliably predicting that the Standard would lead to any significant increased usage of restraints at all.

In view of the possible minimal safety benefits, the automatic restraint requirement no longer was reasonable or practicable in the agency's view. The requirement would require approximately $1 billion to implement and the agency did not believe it would be reasonable to impose such substantial costs on manufacturers and consumers without more adequate assurance that sufficient safety benefits would accrue. In addition, NHTSA concluded that automatic restraints might have an adverse effect on the public's attitude toward safety. Given the high expense and limited benefits of detachable belts, NHTSA feared that many consumers would regard the Standard as an instance of ineffective regulation, adversely affecting the public's view of safety regulation and, in particular, "poisoning . . . popular sentiment toward efforts to improve occupant restraint systems in the future."

The ultimate question before us is whether NHTSA's rescission of the passive restraint requirement of Standard 208 was arbitrary and capricious. We conclude, as did the Court of Appeals, that it was. We also conclude, but for somewhat different reasons, that further consideration of the issue by the agency is therefore required. We deal separately with the rescission as it applies to air bags and as it applies to seatbelts.

A

The first and most obvious reason for finding the rescission arbitrary and capricious is that NHTSA apparently gave no consideration whatever to modifying the Standard to require that air bag technology be utilized. . . .

Given the effectiveness ascribed to air bag technology by the agency, the mandate of the Act to achieve traffic safety would suggest that the logical response to the faults of detachable seatbelts would be to require the installation of air bags. At the very least this alternative way of achieving the objectives of the Act should have been addressed and adequate reasons given for its abandonment. But the agency not only did not require compliance through air bags, it also did not even consider the possibility in its 1981 rulemaking. Not one sentence of its rulemaking statement discusses the air bags-only option. Because, as the Court of Appeals stated, "NHTSA's . . . analysis of air bags was nonexistent," what we said in *Burlington Truck Lines, Inc. v. United States,* 371 U.S., at 167, is apropos here: "There are no findings and no analysis here to justify the choice made, no indication of the basis on which the [agency] exercised its expert discretion. We are not prepared to and the Administrative Procedure Act will not permit us to accept such . . . practice. . . . Expert discretion is the lifeblood of the administrative process, but 'unless we make the requirements for administrative action strict and demanding, expertise, the strength of modern government,

can become a monster which rules with no practical limits on its discretion.' *New York v. United States,* 342 U.S. 882, 884 (dissenting opinion)" [footnote omitted].

B

Although the issue is closer, we also find that the agency was too quick to dismiss the safety benefits of automatic seatbelts. NHTSA's critical finding was that, in light of the industry's plans to install readily detachable passive belts, it could not reliably predict "even a 5 percentage point increase as the minimum level of expected usage increase." The Court of Appeals rejected this finding because there is "not one iota" of evidence that Modified Standard 208 will fail to increase nationwide seatbelt use by at least 13 percentage points, the level of increased usage necessary for the Standard to justify its cost. Given the lack of probative evidence, the court held that "only a well justified refusal to seek more evidence could render rescission non-arbitrary." In these cases, the agency's explanation for rescission of the passive restraint requirement is not sufficient to enable us to conclude that the rescission was the product of reasoned decisionmaking. To reach this conclusion, we do not upset the agency's view of the facts, but we do appreciate the limitations of this record in supporting the agency's decision.

"The Committee intends that safety shall be the overriding consideration in the issuance of standards under this bill. The Committee recognizes . . . that the Secretary will necessarily consider reasonableness of cost, feasibility and adequate leadtime." The agency also failed to articulate a basis for not requiring nondetachable belts under Standard 208. By failing to analyze the continuous seatbelts option in its own right, the agency has failed to offer the rational connection between facts and judgment required to pass muster under the arbitrary-and-capricious standard. The agency also failed to offer any explanation why a continuous passive belt would engender the same adverse public reaction as the ignition interlock, and, as the Court of Appeals concluded, "every indication in the record points the other way."

"An agency's view of what is in the public interest may change, either with or without a change in circumstances. But an agency changing its course must supply a reasoned analysis. . . ." *Greater Boston Television Corp. v. FCC,* 444 F.2d 841, 852 (1970). We do not accept all of the reasoning of the Court of Appeals but we do conclude that the agency has failed to supply the requisite "reasoned analysis" in this case. Accordingly, we vacate the judgment of the Court of Appeals and remand the cases to that court with directions to remand the matter to the NHTSA for further consideration consistent with this opinion.

NOTES

1. The factual material for the case in point comes from the Court's opinion in *Walters v. Metropolitan Educational Enterprises, Inc.,* 519 U.S. 202 (1997).

2. 519 U.S. 202, 210–11 (1997).

3. *Londoner v. City of Denver,* 210 U.S. 373 (1908).

4. Ibid., 385.

5. Ibid., 386.

6. David Ryan, *Kansas Administrative Law With Federal References* (Topeka: Kansas Bar Association, 1985), p. 87.

7. 5 U.S.C. 551 (4).

8. The material on the roadless area controversy comes from: "A Forest Legacy [Editorial]," *The New York Times,* October 18, 1999, p. A22; Douglas Jehl, "Administration Plans Forest Road Ban," *The New York Times,* May 9, 2000, p. A16; Georgia Cappleman, "Clinton Approves Roadless Area Conservation Rule" 11(3) *Florida Environmental Compliance Update* (December, 2000); "Axing of Roadless Rule Hits Taxpayers, Wilderness," *The Tampa Tribune,* July 16, 2004, p. 12.

9. *Public Lands Council v. Babbitt,* 120 S.Ct. 1915, 1822 (2000).

10. The material on Medicare reimbursement comes from *Shalala v. Guernsey Memorial Hospital,* 514 U.S. 87, 91–92 (1995).

11. Ibid., 90.

12. 506 F.2d. 33 (D.C. Cir., 1974).

13. See Michael Asimow, "Public Participation in the Adoption of Interpretive Rules and Policy Statements," 75 *Michigan Law Review* 521 (1977); Michael Asimow, "Nonlegislative Rulemaking and Regulatory Reform," 1985 *Duke Law Journal* 381 (1985); James Hunneycutt, "Another Reason to Reform the Federal Regulatory System: Agencies Treating Nonlegislative Rules as Binding," 41 *Boston College Law Review* 153 (1999).

14. *Yeskey v. Pennsylvania Department of Corrections,* 76 F.Supp. 2d 572, 576 (1999).

15. See *United States v. Florida East Coast Railway Company,* 410 U.S. 224 (1973).

16. Mireya Navarro, "Agency Slowed in Effort to Widen Definition of AIDS," *The New York Times* [national edition], February 10, 1992, pp. A1, A12.

17. Philip J. Hilts, "FDA Seeks Halt in Breast Implants Made of Silicone," *The New York Times* [national edition], January 7, 1992, A1, B6.

18. Louis Uchitelle, "Devising New Math to Define Poverty," *The New York Times,* October 18, 1999, p. A1.

19. Robert D. Hershey Jr., "F.T.C. drops plan to ease Standard of 'made in U.S.A.,'" *The New York Times,* December 2, 1997, p. A1.

20. John H. Cushman, Jr., "U.S. Proposes Regulations to Decrease Acid Rain," *The New York Times* [national edition], October 30, 1991, p. A11.

21. Matthew L. Wald, "Revised Rules for Air Bags Will Reduce Their Power," *The New York Times,* May 5, 2000, p. A14.

22. Sheryl Gay Stalberg, "Youth's Death Shaking Up Field of Gene Experiments on Humans," *The New York Times,* January 27, 2000, p. A1; Phillip J. Hilts, "U.S. Weighs Changes in Rules on Drug Research Conflict," *The New York Times,* August 16, 2000, p. A24.

23. Deborah Hirsch, "Controlling Storm Runoff," *The New York Times,* September 14, 2004, p. A48.

24. Robert Reinhold, "U.S. Moving to End Use of Deadly Farm Pesticide," *The New York Times* [national edition], September 6, 1991, p. A11.

25. Matthew Wald, "Review of Nuclear Plant Security Is Faulted," *The New York Times,* September 15, 2004, p. A18.

26. Nicholas Wade, "New Rules on Use of Human Embryos in Cell Research," *The New York Times,* August 24, 2000, p. A1.

27. John H. Cushman, Jr., "F.A.A. Seeks to Address Rise in Near Jet Collisions," *The New York Times* [national edition], October 18, 1991, p. A11.

28. Robert Pear, "After Long Delay, U.S. Plans to Issue Ergonomic Rules" *The New York Times,* November 22, 1999, p. A12.

29. Rachel Swarns, "U.S. Acts to Notify Foreigners of Tough New Rules for Visits," *The New York Times,* September 11, 2004, p. A16.

30. Sheryl Gay Stolberg, "F.D.A. Approves Fat-Blocking Anti-Obesity Drug," *The New York Times,* April 27, 1999, p. A1.

31. "Child Care Leads to Dispute Over States' Role," *The New York Times* [national edition], July 2, 1991, pp. 1, 8.

32. Laurence K. Altman, "Rules for AIDS-Infected Workers Are Resisted by Medical Groups," *The New York Times* [national edition], August 30, 1991, pp. A1, A13.

33. Gina Kolata, "'Single Use' Medical Devices Are Often Used Several Times," *The New York Times,* October 11, 1999, p. A1.

34. Steven Greenhouse, "Angered by H.M.O.'s Treatment, More Doctors are Joining Unions," *The New York Times,* February 4, 1999, p. A1; Steven Greenhouse, "Interns and Residents Allowed to Unionize," *The New York Times,* November 30, 1999, p. A1.

35. "U.S. Chamber Asks Court to Overturn Rule on Mutual Fund Boards," *The New York Times,* September 3, 2004, p. C9.

36. Mathew Wald, "California Air Agency Limits Personal Goods" *The New York Times* [national edition], January 10, 1992, p. A8.

37. 5 U.S.C. Section 564–570.

38. Mathew Wald, "Environmental Negotiators Flesh Out Bare-Bones Law," *The New York Times* [national edition], June 24, 1991, p. C2.

39. Ibid.

40. Ernest Gellhorn and Ronald Levin, *Administrative Law and Process: In a Nutshell,* 3d ed. (St. Paul, Minn.: West, 1990), 559–60.

41. Ibid., p. 246.

42. 5 U.S.C. 556 (d).

43. 5 U.S.C. 557 (c).

44. Gellhorn and Levin, *Administrative Law and Process,* p. 244.

45. U.S. Bureau of the Census, *Statistical Abstract of the United States 1991,* 111th ed. (Washington, D.C.: U.S. Government Printing Office, 1991), p. 189.

46. Danial Oran, *Oran's Dictionary of the Law* (St. Paul, Minn.: West, 1983), p. 157.

47. 332 U.S. 194, 202–03 (1947).

48. 29 U.S.C. 156.

49. The facts are found at 394 U.S. 759, 761–62 (1969).

PART III

SUBSTANTIVE ISSUES IN ADMINISTRATIVE LAW

8

THE LAW OF PUBLIC EMPLOYMENT

Certain basic principles in the law of public employment apply to anyone who works for government at nearly any level. Those principles could be demonstrated by any line of cases, but because the reader is presently in college and consequently familiar with some of the terminology, we will begin by examining cases in the field of education.

In Chapter 2, which dealt with executive control over agencies through the power of appointment and removal, we learned that only a limited number of policy-making and advisory-level employees serve at the pleasure of the executive. The discussion that follows focuses instead on civil service employees and those who normally do not make policy. Merit, rather than political party considerations, is supposed to guide personnel decisions regarding the employees discussed in the section that follows. Although general principles of the law of public employment will be elucidated, remember, too, that these may be modified from jurisdiction to jurisdiction by labor union contracts and statutes.

Case in Point:
Hale v. Walsh
747 P.2d 1288 (1987)

Dr. Thomas Hale gave up his tenured teaching position at a state university in Louisiana in 1977 to become the untenured chairman of the Department of History at Idaho State University. As part of his teaching load, he was assigned the history seminar that all seniors majoring in history had to take. One student who had transferred to Idaho State University got to the spring semester of his senior year and still had not enrolled in the senior seminar. That spring semester, he was scheduled to student-teach, a role that conflicted with the seminar, and after receiving his degree, he was to begin a teaching position at a local high school. After much negotiation, Dr. Hale agreed to allow this student to complete the senior seminar credits by completion of a research paper. When Dr. Hale received the paper near the end of the semester, he suspected that the paper was plagiarized. After a relatively easy library search, Professor Hale documented the plagiarism and failed the student. As a result of this action, the student would not graduate or get the job.

The student, however, was the son-in-law of a former dean, and the former dean was the best friend of the academic vice president (provost at some universities). The vice president put pressure on Dr. Hale's dean to put pressure on Hale to change the student's grade. Ultimately, the dean's attempts at persuasion failed, so the vice president ordered the dean to threaten Dr. Hale with termination unless the professor changed the grade. Professor Hale refused to compromise academic standards and refused to change the grade. Because of his experience with the Louisiana University system, which is unionized, Professor Hale understood enough of the law of public employment to appreciate that his legal position was precarious and that the university was going to issue him a terminal contract (one more year of teaching at this university); despite the apparent unfairness of the situation, the courts would not hear his case based on the existing situation.

Short of caving in on the academic standard question, Hale could not stop the fact that he was going to lose his job, but he could manipulate the situation so that he could get a court to hear his case. Capitalizing on his previous limited experience with faculty unions in Louisiana, Hale became very active in a union that was trying to become the bargaining agent for the Idaho State faculty (the American Federation of Teachers). Indeed, within a matter of months, he became the chapter president of the union. In that capacity, he made a speech critical of the university president on the steps of the administration building and invited the local media, who gave the event appropriate coverage. Shortly thereafter, Hale received a terminal contract, and a year later, he was out of a job.

Questions

1. It is obvious from the preceding scenario that Hale believed that the union activity and speech would help his legal situation. Do you believe he was right? Why? If so, does that make sense to you?

2. Why was Hale's legal situation hopeless without the union activity and public speech?

Usually, public employees who claim they were unjustly fired must sue under the Fifth Amendment due process clause (if they work for the federal government) or the Fourteenth Amendment due process clause (if they work for state or local government). Both due process clauses prohibit the government from taking an individual's life, liberty, or property without due process of law. Hence, to establish a lawsuit under a due process clause, potential litigants must show that government action is about to take their life or inhibit the exercise of their liberty or the use of their property.

When the government allegedly unjustly fires an employee, is it true that they have taken that employee's property by taking his or her paycheck away? No, not necessarily. The first principle of public employment law is that *the employee must establish either a property interest or a liberty interest to challenge an employment termination in court.* Indeed, one must establish a liberty or property interest to establish a due process suit of any kind.

PROPERTY INTEREST

Almost all employees, whether they work for government or in the private sector, serve a probationary period of employment when they first start a job. Usually, the probationary

357

period of employment is specified, say, six months, and at the end of that period, a supervisor provides some type of formal evaluation of the probationary employee's work (this process is also typically specified in an employee handbook). A decision is made to either retain or terminate the employee as a result of that formal review process.

If the decision is made to retain the employee, then the employee has what the courts refer to as a continuing expectation of employment. That is what establishes a property interest in the law of public employment under the due process clause. Property interests are normally created by state or local law. If the decision is made not to retain the employee, then there is no continuing expectation of employment and therefore no property interest: The employee cannot sue. Employees who lack the requisite property interest simply cannot challenge their employment termination in court (unless they can demonstrate a liberty interest).

In education, a continuing expectation of employment and hence a property interest is established by obtaining tenure. In secondary schools, the probationary employment period is about three years; in universities, it is often five years but can approach eight or even ten years. The normal probationary period for most other public employees is six months to a year.

Board of Regents v. Roth
408 U.S. 564 (1972)

The opinion is by Justice Stewart, joined by Justices Burger, White, Blackmun, and Rehnquist. Justices Brennan, Douglas, and Marshall dissented; Justice Powell took no part in the decision.

Respondent (Roth), hired for a fixed term of one academic year to teach at a state university, was informed without explanation that he would not be rehired for the ensuing year. A statute provided that all state university teachers would be employed initially on probation and that only after four years' continuous service would teachers achieve permanent employment "during efficiency and good behavior," with procedural protection against separation. University rules gave an untenured teacher "dismissed" before the end of the year some opportunity for review of the "dismissal" but provided that no reason need be given for nonretention of an untenured teacher, and no standards were specified for reemployment. Respondent brought this action claiming deprivation of his Fourteenth Amendment rights, alleging infringement of (1) his free speech right because the true reason for his non-retention was his criticism of the university administration, and (2) his procedural due process right because of the university's failure to advise him of the reason for its decision. The District Court granted summary judgment for the respondent on the procedural issue. The Court of Appeals affirmed.

II

"While this Court has not attempted to define with exactness the liberty guaranteed [by the Fourteenth Amendment], the term has received much consideration and some of the included things have been definitely stated. Without doubt, it denotes not merely freedom from bodily restraint but also the right of the individual to contract, to engage in any of the common occupations of life, to acquire useful knowledge, to marry, establish a home and bring up children, to worship God according to the dictates of his own conscience, and generally to enjoy those privileges long recognized as essential to the orderly pursuit of happiness by free men." *Meyer v. Nebraska,* 262 U.S. 390, 399. In a Constitution for a free people, there can be no doubt that the meaning of "liberty" must be broad indeed. See, e.g., *Bolling v. Sharpe,* 347 U.S. 497, 499–500; *Stanley v. Illinois,* 405 U.S. 645.

There might be cases in which a State refused to reemploy a person under such circumstances that interests in liberty would be implicated. But this is not such a case.

The State, in declining to rehire the respondent, did not make any charge against him that might seriously damage his standing and associations in his community. It did not base the nonrenewal of his contract on a charge, for example, that he had been guilty of dishonesty, or immorality. Had it done so, this would be a different case. For "[w]here a person's good name, reputation, honor, or integrity is at stake because of what the government is doing to him, notice and an opportunity to be heard are essential." *Wisconsin v. Constantineau,* 400 U.S. 433, 437. *Wieman v. Updegraff,* 344 U.S. 183, 191; *Joint Anti-Fascist Refugee Committee v. McGrath,* 341 U.S. 123; *United States v. Lovett,* 328 U.S. 303, 316–317; *Peters v. Hobby,* 349 U.S. 331, 352 (Douglas, J., concurring). See *Cafeteria Workers v. McElroy,* 367 U.S. 886, 898. In such a case, due process would accord an opportunity to refute the charge before University officials. In the present case, however, there is no suggestion whatever that the respondent's "good name, reputation, honor, or integrity" is at stake.

Similarly, there is no suggestion that the State, in declining to re-employ the respondent, imposed on him a stigma or other disability that foreclosed his freedom to take advantage of other employment opportunities. The State, for example, did not invoke any regulations to bar the respondent from all other public employment in state universities. Had it done so, this, again, would be a different case. For "[t]o be deprived not only of present government employment but of future opportunity for it certainly is no small injury." *Joint Anti-Fascist Refugee Committee v. McGrath* (Jackson, J., concurring). See *Truax v. Raich,* 239 U.S. 33, 41. The Court has held, for example, that a State, in regulating eligibility for a type of professional employment, cannot foreclose a range of opportunities "in a manner that contravene[s] . . . Due Process," *Schware v. Board of Bar Examiners,* 353 U.S. 232, 238, and, specifically, in a manner that denies the right to a full prior hearing. *Willner v. Committee on*

Character, 373 U.S. 96, 103. See *Cafeteria Workers v. McElroy,* supra, at 898. In the present case, however, this principle does not come into play.

To be sure, the respondent has alleged that the non-renewal of his contract was based on his exercise of his right to freedom of speech. But this allegation is not now before us. The District Court stayed proceedings on this issue, and the respondent has yet to prove that the decision not to rehire him was, in fact, based on his free speech activities.

Hence, on the record before us, all that clearly appears is that the respondent was not rehired for one year at one university. It stretches the concept too far to suggest that a person is deprived of "liberty" when he simply is not rehired in one job but remains as free as before to seek another. *Cafeteria Workers v. McElroy,* supra, at 895–896.

III

The Fourteenth Amendment's procedural protection of property is a safeguard of the security of interests that a person has already acquired in specific benefits. These interests—property interests—may take many forms.

Thus, the Court has held that a person receiving welfare benefits under statutory and administrative standards defining eligibility for them has an interest in continued receipt of those benefits that is safeguarded by procedural due process. *Goldberg v. Kelly,* 397 U.S. 254. See *Flemming v. Nestor,* 363 U.S. 603, 611. Similarly, in the area of public employment, the Court has held that a public college professor dismissed from an office held under tenure provisions, *Slochower v. Board of Education,* 350 U.S. 551, and college professors and staff members dismissed during the terms of their contracts, *Wieman v. Updegraff,* 344 U.S. 183, have interests in continued employment that are safeguarded by due process. Only last year, the Court held that this principle "proscribing summary dismissal from public employment without hearing or inquiry required by due process" also applied to a teacher recently hired without tenure or a formal contract, but nonetheless with a clearly implied promise of continued employment. *Connell v. Higginbotham,* 403 U.S. 207, 208.

Certain attributes of "property" interests protected by procedural due process emerge from these decisions. To have a property interest in a benefit, a person clearly must have more than an abstract need or desire for it. He must have more than a unilateral expectation of it. He must, instead, have a legitimate claim of entitlement to it. It is a purpose of the ancient institution of property to protect those claims upon which people rely in their daily lives, reliance that must not be arbitrarily undermined. It is a purpose of the constitutional right to a hearing to provide an opportunity for a person to vindicate those claims.

Property interests, of course, are not created by the Constitution. Rather, they are created and their dimensions are defined by existing rules or understandings that stem from an independent source such as state law—rules or understandings that secure certain benefits and that support claims of entitlement to those benefits. Thus, the welfare recipients in *Goldberg v. Kelly,* supra, had a claim of entitlement to welfare payments that was grounded in the statute defining eligibility for them. The recipients had not yet shown that they were, in fact, within the statutory terms of eligibility. But we held that they had a right to a hearing at which they might attempt to do so.

Just as the welfare recipients' "property" interest in welfare payments was created and defined by statutory terms, so the respondent's "property" interest in employment at Wisconsin State University–Oshkosh was created and defined by the terms of his appointment. Those terms secured his interest in employment up to June 30, 1969. But the important fact in this case is that they specifically provided that the respondent's employment was to terminate on June 30. They did not provide for contract renewal absent "sufficient cause." Indeed, they made no provision for renewal whatsoever.

Thus, the terms of the respondent's appointment secured absolutely no interest in re-employment for the next year. They supported absolutely no possible claim of entitlement to re-employment. Nor, significantly, was there any state statute or University rule or policy that secured his interest in re-employment or that created any legitimate claim to it. In these circumstances, the respondent surely had an abstract concern in being rehired, but he did not have a property interest sufficient to require the University authorities to give him a hearing when they declined to renew his contract of employment.

IV

Our analysis of the respondent's constitutional rights in this case in no way indicates a view that an opportunity for a hearing or a statement of reasons for nonretention would, or would not, be appropriate or wise in public colleges and universities. For it is a written Constitution that we apply. Our role is confined to interpretation of that Constitution. We must conclude that the summary judgment for the respondent should not have been granted, since the respondent has not shown that he was deprived of liberty or property protected by the Fourteenth Amendment. The judgment of the Court of Appeals, accordingly, is reversed and the case is remanded for further proceedings consistent with this opinion.

It is so ordered.

Questions

1. The Court says that "property interests are not created by the Constitution." What does create a property interest?
2. Roth lost this case. Can you explain why?
3. At this point, you should be able to articulate why Hale's legal position was hopeless prior to his union activity and speech. Can you do that?

We return now to *Hale v. Walsh,* at the beginning of this chapter. The problem for Professor Hale was that because he lacked tenure, he had no expectation of continuing employment and so could not demonstrate to a court a property interest. His suit was a due process action, and because that clause protects against deprivations of property or liberty and he had no property interest, his only hope would be a liberty interest.

LIBERTY INTEREST

An employee can establish a liberty interest if, as a result of the termination, the former employee's reputation is damaged or his or her ability to seek employment is inhibited. Normally, a simple decision not to retain an employee does not sufficiently damage either reputation or employability to establish a liberty interest. If, however, a teacher's contract was not renewed and if the former teacher asked why and was publicly told "because you are incompetent and a terrible teacher," that would establish a liberty interest.

For that reason, one of the canons of personnel management in public administration is that probationary employees who are terminated from employment should *never* be told why. The logic goes like this: Because they are probationary employees, they lack a property interest. To discuss with them the reasons for the termination may provide the grounds to establish a liberty interest. Silence, on the other hand, means that the affected employee will have difficulty getting into court because he or she cannot show a property interest; the silence has ensured the lack of ability to demonstrate a liberty interest. Within the university community, an almost cabalistic silence surrounds the decision to deny a faculty member tenure or, as in Professor Hale's case, not to renew a contract.[1]

A terminated public employee may establish a liberty interest in one more way. Because it is unconstitutional for government to punish an individual as a result of the exercise of a constitutionally protected right (e.g., freedom of speech, freedom of association—i.e., to join a union, to be free from discrimination based on race, gender, age, etc.), it follows that government normally cannot fire an employee for having exercised a constitutional right. Hence, in some cases in which a probationary public employee can demonstrate that the *primary reason* behind a decision to terminate was because the employee exercised a constitutionally protected right, that will establish a liberty interest under the due process clause.

The case presented next, *Pickering v. Board of Education* (1968), is a classic case that discusses the First Amendment protection of public employees. Mr. Pickering was a high school teacher who was fired for writing a letter to the editor in the local paper.

In 1961, the Board of Education for District 205 of Will County submitted two bond issues to the voters; the first was defeated, but the second passed ($5,500,000). Again in 1964, the board submitted two bond issues to the voters, who rejected both. In response to these elections, there were many letters to the editor in the local paper. One of them was sent by Pickering:

> Dear Editor:
>   I enjoyed reading the back issues of your paper which you loaned to me. Perhaps others would enjoy reading them in order to see just how far the two new high schools have deviated from the original promises by the Board of Education. First, let me state that I am referring to the February through November, 1961 issues of your paper, so that it can be checked.

One statement in your paper declared that swimming pools, athletic fields, and auditoriums had been left out of the program. They may have been left out but they got put back in very quickly because Lockport West has both an auditorium and athletic field. In fact, Lockport West has a better athletic field than Lockport Central. It has a track that isn't quite regulation distance even though the board spent a few thousand dollars on it. Whose fault is that? Oh, I forgot, it wasn't supposed to be there in the first place. It must have fallen out of the sky. Such responsibility has been touched on in other letters but it seems one just can't help noticing it. I am not saying the school shouldn't have these facilities, because I think they should, but promises are promises, or are they?

Since there seems to be a problem getting all the facts to the voter on the twice defeated bond issue, many letters have been written to this paper and probably more will follow, I feel I must say something about the letters and their writers. Many of these letters did not give the whole story. Letters by your Board and Administration have stated that teachers' salaries total $1,297,746 for one year. Now that must have been the total payroll, otherwise the teachers would be getting $10,000 a year. I teach at the high school and I know this just isn't the case. However, this shows their "stop at nothing" attitude. To illustrate further, do you know that the superintendent told the teachers, and I quote, "Any teacher that opposes the referendum should be prepared for the consequences." I think this gets at the reason we have problems passing bond issues. Threats take something away; these are insults to voters in a free society. We should try to sell a program on its merits, if it has any.

Remember those letters entitled "District 205 Teachers Speak." I think the voters should know that those letters have been written and agreed to by only five or six teachers, not 98% of the teachers in the high school. In fact, many teachers didn't even know who was writing them. Did you know that those letters had to have the approval of the superintendent before they could be put in the paper? That's the kind of totalitarianism teachers live in at the high school, and your children go to school in.

In last week's paper, the letter written by a few uninformed teachers threatened to close the school cafeteria and fire its personnel. This is ridiculous and insults the intelligence of the voter because properly managed school cafeterias do not cost the school district any money. If the cafeteria is losing money, then the board should not be packing free lunches for athletes on days of athletic contests. Whatever the case, the taxpayer's child should only have to pay about 30 cents for his lunch instead of 35 cents to pay for free lunches for the athletes. In a reply to this letter your Board of Administration will probably state that these lunches are paid for from receipts from the games. But $20,000 in receipts doesn't pay for the $200,000 a year they have been spending on varsity sports while neglecting the wants of teachers. You see we don't need an increase in the transportation tax unless the voters want to keep paying $50,000 or more a year to transport athletes home after practice and to away games, etc. Rest of the $200,000 is made up in coaches' salaries, athletic directors' salaries, baseball pitching machines, sodded football fields, and thousands of dollars for other sports equipment.

These things are all right, provided we have enough money for them. To sod football fields on borrowed money and then not be able to pay teachers' salaries is getting the cart before the horse. If these things aren't enough for you, look at East High. No doors on many of the classrooms, a plant room without any sunlight, no water in a first aid treatment room, are just a few of many things. The taxpayers were really taken to the cleaners. A part of the sidewalk in front of the building has already collapsed. Maybe Mr. Hess would be interested to know that we need blinds on the windows in that building also.

Once again, the board must have forgotten they were going to spend $3,200,000 on the West building and $2,300,000 on the East building.

As I see it, the bond issue is a fight between the Board of Education that is trying to push tax-supported athletics down our throats with education, and a public that has mixed emotions about both of these items because they feel they are already paying enough taxes, and simply don't know whom to trust with any more tax money. I must sign this letter as a citizen, taxpayer and voter, not as a teacher, since that freedom has been taken from the teachers by the administration. Do you really know what goes on behind those stone walls at the high school?

Respectfully,
Marvin L. Pickering

The letter was printed after the elections were over. The school board determined that portions of Pickering's letter were false and that the letter was "detrimental to the efficient operation and administration of the schools." Pickering, who was fired, argued that his letter was protected speech under the First Amendment. After reviewing the board's decision only to determine whether there was substantial supporting evidence in the record, a state trial court sustained the board's decision. The decision was also affirmed by the Illinois Supreme Court, so Pickering appealed to the U.S. Supreme Court.

Pickering v. Board of Education
391 U.S. 563 (1968)

Justice Marshall wrote the opinion for a unanimous Court.

II

To the extent that the Illinois Supreme Court's opinion may be read to suggest that teachers may constitutionally be compelled to relinquish the First Amendment rights they would otherwise enjoy as citizens to comment on matters of public interest in connection with the operation of the public schools in which they work, it proceeds on a premise that has been unequivocally rejected in numerous prior decisions of this Court. E.g., *Wieman v. Updegraff*, 344 U.S. 183 (1952); *Shelton v. Tucker*, 364 U.S. 479 (1960); *Keyishian v. Board of Regents*, 385 U.S. 589 (1967). "[The] theory that public employment which may be denied altogether may be subjected to any conditions, regardless of how unreasonable, has been uniformly rejected." *Keyishian v. Board of Regents*, supra, at 605–606. At the same time it cannot be gainsaid that the State has interests as an employer in regulating the speech of its employees that differ significantly from those it possesses in connection with regulation of the speech of the citizenry in general. The problem in any case is to arrive at a balance between the interests of the teacher, as a citizen, in commenting upon matters of public concern and the interest of the State, as an employer, in promoting the efficiency of the public services it performs through its employees.

III

The Board contends that "the teacher by virtue of his public employment has a duty of loyalty to support his superiors in attaining the generally accepted goals of education and that, if he must speak out publicly, he should do so factually and accurately, commensurate with his education and experience." Appellant, on the other hand, argues that the test applicable to defamatory statements directed against public officials by persons having no occupational relationship with them, namely, that statements to be legally actionable must be made "with knowledge that [they were] false or with reckless disregard of whether [they were] false or not," *New York Times Co. v. Sullivan*, 376 U.S. 254, 280 (1964), should also be applied to public statements made by teachers. Because of the enormous variety of fact situations in which critical statements by teachers and other public employees may be thought by their superiors, against whom the statements are directed, to furnish grounds for dismissal, we do not deem it either appropriate or feasible to attempt to lay down a general standard against which all such statements may be judged. However, in the course of evaluating the conflicting claims of First Amendment protection and the need for orderly school administration in the context of this case, we shall indicate some of the general lines along which an analysis of the controlling interests should run.

An examination of the statements in appellant's letter objected to by the Board reveals that they, like the letter as a whole, consist essentially of criticism of the Board's allocation of school funds between educational and athletic programs, and of both the Board's and the superintendent's methods of informing, or preventing the informing of, the district's taxpayers of the real reasons why additional tax revenues were being sought for the schools. The statements are in no way directed towards any person with whom appellant would normally be in contact in the course of his daily work as a teacher. Thus no question of maintaining either discipline by immediate superiors or harmony among coworkers is presented here. Appellant's employment relationships with the Board and, to a somewhat lesser extent, with the superintendent are not the kind of close working relationships for which it can persuasively be claimed that personal loyalty and confidence are necessary to their proper functioning. Accordingly, to the extent that the Board's position here can be taken to suggest that even comments on matters of public concern that are substantially correct, such as statements (1)–(4) of appellant's letter, may furnish grounds for dismissal if they are sufficiently critical in tone, we unequivocally reject it.

We next consider the statements in appellant's letter which we agree to be false. The Board's original charges included allegations that the publication of the letter damaged the professional reputations of the Board and the superintendent and would foment controversy and conflict among the Board, teachers, administrators, and the residents of the district. However, no evidence to support these allegations was introduced at the hearing. So far as

the record reveals, Pickering's letter was greeted by everyone but its main target, the Board, with massive apathy and total disbelief. The Board must, therefore, have decided, perhaps by analogy with the law of libel, that the statements were per se harmful to the operation of the schools.

However, the only way in which the Board could conclude, absent any evidence of the actual effect of the letter, that the statements contained therein were per se detrimental to the interest of the schools was to equate the Board members' own interests with that of the schools. Certainly an accusation that too much money is being spent on athletics by the administrators of the school system (which is precisely the import of that portion of appellant's letter containing the statements that we have found to be false, see Appendix, infra) cannot reasonably be regarded as per se detrimental to the district's schools. Such an accusation reflects rather a difference of opinion between Pickering and the Board as to the preferable manner of operating the school system, a difference of opinion that clearly concerns an issue of general public interest. In addition, the fact that particular illustrations of the Board's claimed undesirable emphasis on athletic programs are false would not normally have any necessary impact on the actual operation of the schools, beyond its tendency to anger the Board. For example, Pickering's letter was written after the defeat at the polls of the second proposed tax increase. It could, therefore, have had no effect on the ability of the school district to raise necessary revenue, since there was no showing that there was any proposal to increase taxes pending when the letter was written.

More importantly, the question whether a school system requires additional funds is a matter of legitimate public concern on which the judgment of the school administration, including the School Board, cannot, in a society that leaves such questions to popular vote, be taken as conclusive. On such a question free and open debate is vital to informed decision-making by the electorate. Teachers are, as a class, the members of a community most likely to have informed and definite opinions as to how funds allotted to the operation of the schools should be spent. Accordingly, it is essential that they be able to speak out freely on such questions without fear of retaliatory dismissal.

What we do have before us is a case in which a teacher has made erroneous public statements upon issues then currently the subject of public attention, which are critical of his ultimate employer but which are neither shown nor can be presumed to have in any way either impeded the teacher's proper performance of his daily duties in the classroom or to have interfered with the regular operation of the schools generally. In these circumstances we conclude that the interest of the school administration in limiting teachers' opportunities to contribute to public debate is not significantly greater than its interest in limiting a similar contribution by any member of the general public.

In sum, we hold that, in a case such as this, absent proof of false statements knowingly or recklessly made by him, a teacher's exercise of his right to speak on issues of public importance may not furnish the basis for his dismissal from public employment. Since no such showing has been made in this case regarding appellant's letter, his dismissal for writing it cannot be upheld and the judgment of the Illinois Supreme Court must, accordingly, be reversed and the case remanded for further proceedings not inconsistent with this opinion.

It is so ordered.

Questions

1. It is clear that Pickering made some factual representations in his letter that turned out to be wrong. Do false statements receive constitutional protection?
2. It is also clear that Pickering's letter fell on deaf ears and that it was not effective. The Court said, "Pickering's letter was greeted with massive apathy and total disbelief." Do you think a different result would have been reached in this case if Pickering had written prior to the election and the letter was a substantial factor for the defeat of the bond issues? Does the Constitution protect only speech that has no "detrimental" effect?
3. In cases involving a liberty interest, courts will nearly always do a balancing test. Courts will balance the right of the employee (citizen) against the interests of the state (employer). Describe the interests on both sides of the scale.
4. Can you explain now why Professor Hale felt compelled to engage in union activity and give the public speech?

In what other kinds of activities could employees engage that would be constitutionally protected but would upset administrators to the point that they would fire an employee? Professor Aumiller, a homosexual and faculty adviser to the gay rights student organization, gave an interview to the student paper. The university president, fearing a loss of alumni contributions if the alumni sensed that the administration encouraged or tolerated homosexuality, fired Professor Aumiller; the school did not renew his next contract and, of course, refused to say why (*Aumiller v. University of Delaware*, 1973).[2] Professor Duke got fired for teaching Marxism in a Texas state university (*Duke v. North Texas State University*, 1973).[3] Teachers have been fired for criticizing discriminatory conditions in schools (*Givhan v. Western Line Consolidated School District*, 1979;[4] and *Bernasconi v. Tempe Elementary School District*, 1977).[5] Teachers have even been fired for too effectively representing the teacher's union in negotiations with the school board (*Simard v. Board of Education*, 1973).[6] Usually, these cases involve some kind of speech (as in the

Pickering case earlier) or union activity (freedom of association is a constitutionally protected right).

The reader will notice from the discussion in the *Pickering* case that not all speech is protected. The Supreme Court has determined that some forms of expression lie beyond the Constitution's protection. Obscenity is not protected expression. Libel is not protected, nor are "fighting words," or "hate speech." Even though an employee's speech may not fall into one of those categories, it may nevertheless be unprotected speech. If a public employee says something critical about a supervisor or the higher administration, such criticism will be protected only under the following conditions: (a) Ordinarily, it must be a public statement; (b) it must pertain to an issue of public importance; and (c) the expression cannot destroy the working relationship between the employee/employees and administration (for teachers, it cannot disrupt discipline or the orderly educational process). Generally, the speech cannot inhibit the public mission of the employer or the agency.

Absent a property interest then, a probationary public employee can challenge employment termination in a court of law only under the following two conditions: (a) An administrator has publicly discussed the reason for the termination, and that has damaged the former employee's reputation and, consequently, his or her ability to find another job in the field. (b) The administrator has refused to say why employment was terminated, but the employee suspects the primary reason was that he or she may have said something publicly critical of the agency (as in the case of Mr. Pickering).

In the latter types of cases, the plaintiff (terminated employee) must present some evidence to the judge (jury) that some form of constitutionally protected behavior was engaged in and the exercise of that protected behavior was the primary reason for the termination. Once sufficient evidence is presented to that effect, the burden of proof switches to the administration, which can take three courses of action. First, they can try to prove that the exercise of protected behavior was not the primary reason to terminate. Second, and closely related to the first, is the "same decision anyway" defense, which essentially argues that, although the exercise of a protected right may have been part of the decision to terminate, the administration would have reached the decision to terminate on other grounds anyway (say, incompetence or insubordination). Finally, the administration can attempt to argue that the speech is not the kind of speech that is protected under the Constitution (perhaps the speech does not relate to issues of public importance).

So, how did Professor Hale establish a liberty interest sufficient to get his case to court? First, it is important to understand what did not create a liberty interest. Even though the ultimate issue here was the academic integrity of a university, that was not a sufficient enough public issue to clothe it with constitutional protection. Even if Dr. Hale had gone to the press, that would not have turned it into an issue of "public concern." Disputes between the faculty and the administration of a school over academic questions are normally not matters of "public concern" because courts treat such issues as internal squabbling and normally defer to the expertise of the administration. This is true not just for schools but for any public agency.

One can only imagine the conversations that must have taken place between Professor Hale and the dean, but whatever was said, it was not protected speech either. That is because it was not public (although, in some cases, speech between two people has been protected) and ultimately it did not relate to matters of sufficient public interest.

Dr. Hale created a liberty interest by becoming active in union politics and convincing the court that that activity was the primary reason for his nonretention. It was primarily that public speech, clothed in official union activity, that created the liberty interest.

The Court has applied the same jurisprudence to the termination of public contracts. In the case of *Board of County Commissioners v. Umbehr* (at the end of this chapter), a small businessman who had a contract with the county to haul trash successfully sued the commissioners when they cancelled his contract because he had publicly criticized the commission.

At this point, the law of public employment should be fairly clear. If an employee has a continuing expectation of employment (a property interest), the employee can only be fired for cause and there must be a pre-termination hearing. Absent a property interest, a public employee can be fired for no reason at all and has no right to demand an explanation; there will be no pre-termination hearing. Employees without a property interest may be able to get a court to hear their case if they can successfully raise a liberty interest (damage to reputation or infringement of a constitutionally protected right).

On March 30, 1981, a would-be assassin shot and wounded President Reagan. Upon hearing the news, Ardith McPherson, a black deputy constable (sheriff) in Harris County, Texas, engaged another black deputy in a conversation about the direction of the Reagan Administration's policies. At the end of that conversation, she said, "If they go for him again, I hope they get him." This statement was overheard by a third deputy, who told the constable. Constable Rankin called McPherson into his office and questioned her about her speech. She admitted making the statement, and Rankin fired her on the spot. McPherson was a probationary employee. Was she rightly or wrongly fired? You should recognize first that as a probationary employee, she had no right to a pre-termination hearing. The issue should narrow for you to whether her statement was protected. You should recognize that to answer that, courts will apply a balancing test.

First, might McPherson's statement be unprotected? The first variable to examine is whether the speech involved matters of public concern. The Court decided that speech about the policy directions of an administration is sufficiently clothed with public concern to potentially qualify as protected speech. Threats to kill a president are not protected speech, but that is not what McPherson did. The Court did not address the fact that this was private speech between two people; it simply said the speech was potentially protected. Having decided that the speech was potentially protected, the Court next balanced the interests. The potentially protected speech can become unprotected if Rankin can carry the burden of proof that the speech somehow undermined the mission of the Constable's office. By his own admission, the speech did not destroy the working relationship between Rankin and McPherson, nor did it interfere with her working relationship with other employees. Because she was a data entry clerk with no law enforcement function, her speech did not undermine the public safety function of the Constable's office. In *Rankin v. McPherson,* 483 U.S. 378 (1987), the Supreme Court said that the speech was protected and the employer could not carry his burden of proof that the speech damaged internal working relationships or that it harmed the mission of the agency.

On the other hand, see *Rowland v. Mud River School District,* 470 U.S. 1009 (1985), 730 F. 2d 444 (1984). Rowland was a high school guidance counselor. When her secretary repeatedly asked her why she was so happy, Rowland responded that she was in love. As the conversation deepened, Rowland revealed that she was in love with another woman. The secretary told the principal, who fired Rowland. Rowland was a probationary employee. The trial court found as a matter of fact that the administration had no internal reason to fire Rowland other than that she had admitted to a bisexual lifestyle. That is, there was no disruption or inhibition of working relationships or discipline, nor was the educational mission of the school compromised. That court awarded her reinstatement and compensatory damages. The court of appeals reversed with orders to dismiss the suit because the utterance was not a matter of public concern. The Supreme Court denied *certiorari*.

TERMINATION OF PUBLIC EMPLOYEES WHO POSSESS A PROPERTY INTEREST

Apparently, it is fashionable these days for students to refer to tenure as "a job for life." Actually, that is not quite accurate. Once a public employee acquires a property interest, he or she has a continuing expectation of employment. That expectation of employment can be interrupted in two ways. First, public employees with a property interest can be fired for cause. Second, their employment with a public agency can be terminated for financial reasons (referred to as financial exigency).

Termination for Cause

Usually, both public and private employers provide employees with a handbook covering all aspects of employment. This handbook includes the specific period of probationary employment, the process of evaluation at the end of probationary employment, the criteria to be considered in the evaluation process, and the specific reasons for which employees can be terminated once they have passed beyond probationary employment. This employee handbook should also describe the procedure the agency must go through to terminate an employee for cause. What constitutes a for-cause termination varies from agency to agency and from state to state, but criteria often include incompetence, insubordination, malfeasance, immoral conduct, dishonesty, and so on. Even with a property interest, people can be (and many have been) fired for cause.

Remember that the combination of the Fifth and Fourteenth Amendment due process clauses forbids government from taking your life, liberty, or property without due process. This due process notion applies only to government, not to private employers, although labor unions have forced private business to accept some degree of due process through collective bargaining agreements. Also, it is not that government cannot take your liberty or property; it is just that it must go through due process first.

What is due process? It is a procedure that government must follow to avoid the arbitrary, capricious, or mistaken taking of an individual's liberty or property (or, obviously, a life as well). Basically, due process consists of a notice (that government is about to take some action that may affect your liberty or property) and a hearing. Just exactly how intricate that hearing must be is a matter of confusion and the cause of considerable litigation. Due process ranges from a notice from the vice principal (or dean of students) that one is about to be suspended from school for a particular reason and a very simple hearing before that same vice principal or dean on the one hand, to the myriad kinds of protection afforded those accused of capital offenses at the other extreme. So the amount of process due under the law depends on the nature of the liberty or property about to be affected. That is why there is renewed debate about the imposition of capital punishment. Even though the procedure is elaborate, it is obvious that it does not protect against "mistaken" deprivations of life and liberty.

In terms of public employment, no typical due process hearing can be described. Usually, strict rules of evidence do not apply, and attorneys may be present but are not

Table 8.1   Disposition of Termination Cases for Litigants With Tenure

Winner	For Cause	Financial Exigency	Other	Total
Plaintiff/teacher	43% (84)	38% (22)	57% (12)	118
Defendant/board	57% (111)	62% (36)	43% (9)	156
Total	195	58	21	N = 274

SOURCE: Steven Cann, "A Virus in the Ivory Tower," 18 *Educational Considerations* 43-44 (1991).

required. If they are allowed to be present, attorneys often may not have input during the hearing. Generally, reviewing courts look at the procedure first to be satisfied that it is fair.

The reader is already aware from the material in Chapter 4 that courts reviewing quasi-judicial decisions (which due process hearings are) will apply the substantial evidence test on review. To terminate a public employee for cause successfully, administrators must first be certain that the procedure (notice and the hearing) is fair and that sufficient evidence supports the specific charge. If all of that is done, then a reviewing court will simply examine the procedure, and should it find no procedural flaws, the court next will apply the substantial evidence test and most often will sustain the decision.

In a study of 500 teacher termination cases, 274, or 55 percent, involved tenured teachers. Contrary to the popular perception that they have "a job for life," tenured teachers dismissed for cause lost in 57 percent of their appeals to the courts[7] (see Table 8.1). In addition, tenured teachers lost 62 percent of the cases involving either financial exigency or forced retirement. That is only to be expected because the administration or employer is forced by the due process hearing to build a reasonably sound case. Indeed, this research shows that the most frequent reason for a plaintiff/teacher to win a challenged termination-for-cause is that the administration failed to provide adequate procedures. However, once a reviewing court is satisfied with the procedure, the most common disposition of these cases is for the reviewing court to find that there was substantial evidence to support the termination (67 percent of the cases).

Termination for Financial Reasons

Suppose that your state loses millions of dollars in revenue due to a recession. Sales tax receipts fall by several million dollars, and corporate tax revenues drop off by an equal percentage. Suppose, further, that the federal government decides to reduce grants and other federal monies that used to be turned back to the states. In such circumstances, the state legislature has only two courses of action open to it—raise taxes or reduce spending (deficit spending is forbidden in many states). Most states facing exactly these choices in the early 1980s, the late 1980s, and early 1990s, and again from 2001 to 2004 chose to reduce state spending. When governmental units are forced to reduce spending, a common way to go about that is to reduce personnel. Because personnel account for about 70 percent of agency budgets, that is a logical place administrators begin looking to cut costs. There are basically three ways to reduce personnel (the public administration term is RIF, which stands for "reduction in force"). The three methods are referred to as "last hired, first fired"; the attrition method; and program assessment (or evaluation). Two of these options—last hired, first fired and the attrition method—are perhaps the "easier" options for administrators and do not generally involve administrative law or litigation.

The last hired, first fired option means that probationary employees are not offered a contract at the end of the probationary period. The attrition method simply means that as employees die, retire, or transfer, they are not replaced (President Clinton reduced the size of the civilian federal workforce by more than 100,000 employees through the attrition method). Both of these options are easier for administrators than the third option because no due process hearings are required, the actions rarely lead to litigation, and the process is the least disruptive way to accomplish the unpleasant task of reducing the workforce within the agency. However, these two methods are not good options from a planning perspective. To RIF under either of these options could, for example, leave an English Department without faculty to teach, say, creative writing, a business school without someone to teach marketing or finance, a history department without someone to teach early American history; worse yet, a department could be left without a secretary! Indeed, a comptroller general's report concludes that President Clinton's RIF program of attrition had the following consequences: (a) federal agencies are poorly equipped to meet the challenges of the 21st century because employees lack skills in information technology, economics, and management; (b) the reduced influx of young people leaves a void of new knowledge, energy, and ideas and negatively impacts the agency's future leadership; (c) many agencies are left without the manpower to perform their functions.[8]

The third option is to conduct a program assessment, ascertain which programs are not cost-efficient, and eliminate those programs (and their personnel) that are found to be inefficient and/or not necessary to the agency or institution. If the decision is made to RIF an entire program, the likelihood is that employees who possess a property interest will be terminated. That means the institution must provide a due process hearing first.

Usually, reviewing courts will not interfere with administrative decisions relating to financial exigency so long as objective criteria are applied to determine who will be terminated and a due process hearing is available to those who possess a property interest (*Levitt v. Board of Trustees,* 376 F.Supp. 950 [1974]). This assessment of court deference to administrators' RIF decisions is supported by the data in Table 8.1.

CONSEQUENCES OF THE COURT'S JURISPRUDENCE IN PUBLIC EMPLOYMENT LAW

The second-order consequences of the Court's decisions in *Roth* and its progeny have been (a) to create a dual legal subsystem in public employment law, (b) to encourage poor personnel decisions, (c) to encourage disruption (the only way for Professor Hale to get a court to look at his case was to join a union and give a critical speech on the front steps of the administration building), and (d) to cause unnecessary litigation.

The dual legal system in public employment law exists because the Court has created two classes of litigants: those with a property interest, who get administrative law applied to their suits, and those without a property interest, who get constitutional law applied to their cases. Regardless of the reason for the termination, plaintiffs with a property interest have a right to a due process hearing. *A fortiori,* the public employer must make an attempt to provide adequate procedures and supply reasons and evidence at a hearing to support the decision. Because this is a quasi-judicial hearing, the only questions for a reviewing court to answer are (a) whether the procedure is adequate to meet the dictates of due process and (b) whether there is substantial evidence in the record to sustain the decision (classic administrative law, which public employers win nearly 60 percent of the time). Plaintiffs who do not possess a property interest, however, cannot get their case into court without establishing a liberty interest. These frequently involve questions under the First Amendment or the equal protection clause. That being the case, there is no reason to expect a reviewing court to show deference to agency expertise or concentrate on procedural issues (because there is no procedure involved), and there will be no substantial evidence test (because there is no hearing, there is no record). The court will have to determine whether the alleged protected activity was a primary reason in the decision to terminate and whether the activity falls under the Constitution's protection (classic constitutional law, which the plaintiffs win nearly 60 percent of the time).

Poor personnel decisions fall into two categories. In the first, employees with a property interest are retained when they should be let go because employers fear the inevitable lawsuit. Public administrators need to appreciate the fact that the hearing works to protect both the employee and the employer. If the procedure is fair and there is substantial evidence in the record to sustain the decision, it is unlikely that a reviewing court will interfere with the decision. In the second type of bad personnel decisions, employees without a property interest are terminated for reasons that are not related to job performance.

That this jurisprudence encourages disruption should be evident from the case of Professor Hale. The lesson is simple: Public employees without a property interest who fear termination have only one course of action open if they want protection from the courts—turn the issue into a liberty interest by public criticism of their employer.

Finally, there are three situations that would probably not get litigated if probationary public employees were entitled to an internal due process hearing. In the first, cases like Pickering's and Hale's, the mere existence of an internal hearing (116 in my sample of 500 or nearly one fourth) would modify the administration's behavior in a more constitutional direction. Fewer employees in situations such as these would be terminated, hence fewer lawsuits. In the second category of cases, employers present a successful "same decision anyway" defense. That is, at trial, they are able to satisfy the court that there is sufficient evidence to sustain a specific charge (incompetence, insubordination, etc.). A hearing before a board of peers where such evidence is presented would limit employees' propensity to sue. The third category of suits that would be reduced by a pre-termination hearing for employees without a property interest are those that I will call "frivolous," in which the plaintiff can establish neither a property nor a liberty interest; these cases generally are dismissed at an early stage and would probably be screened out of the courts by an internal hearing. These three categories of cases constituted 35 percent of the suits by untenured litigants in my study.[9]

The law of public employment was, until recently, fairly well settled. A property interest meant that a public employee could be terminated only for cause, and there had to be a pre-termination hearing. Absent the property interest, a plaintiff might be able to litigate over the existence of a liberty interest. Most often, such cases involve an analysis of whether a constitutionally protected right was violated.

The law of public employment involves what legal scholars refer to as "bright line rule" jurisprudence as well as a "balancing" jurisprudence. With a "bright line rule," cases are rather cut and dried, and it is often clear who should win. The Court created a bright line rule in *Roth*. If public employees have a property interest, they cannot be terminated without cause, supported at an internal agency due process hearing. Should such a situation be litigated, all the court has to do is determine whether there is a continuing expectation of employment (which is created by state law or federal law in the case of federal employees) and whether an appropriate pre-termination hearing was held. The court would go on to see whether there was substantial evidence in the record from the pre-termination hearing to sustain the decision to terminate. There is little room for subjective judgments by the judge to influence who wins.

On the liberty side of public employment due process, the Court created a balancing test in *Pickering*. With a balancing test, it is nearly impossible to predict who will or should win a case. That is because it is never certain whether or not a majority of five on the Supreme Court will determine that an individual's utterance involves a matter of public concern. Even if certain speech should be classified as involving public concerns by its content, it is uncertain whether or not that speech so adversely affected the work atmosphere as to lose its potential constitutional protection. Whenever the Court creates a balancing test rather than a bright line rule, the Court has reserved for itself the subjective determination of who will win and who will lose. It is easy to manipulate the scales in a balancing test. With a bright line rule, the facts of the case rather than a judge's ideology frequently determine the disposition of the case.

Public employment cases are due process cases, but the Court has always applied a different due process jurisprudence to public employment law than it has to due process cases in other administrative law contexts, which are the subject of the next chapter. There you will become familiar with a case called *Mathews v. Eldridge,* made famous because the Court imposed a balancing test on all administrative law due process cases except those involving public employment. Although the Court had not ruled on the issue, most observers assumed that the *Roth* jurisprudence applied to employee discipline as well as termination. That is, public employees could not be disciplined in a way that threatened their property interest without a pre-deprivation hearing. See *Bush v. Lucas* at the end of Chapter 10, in which hearings were held before a NASA engineer was reassigned and demoted. The case below is a little noticed case in which the Court applied the *Mathews* balancing test to a public employee who was suspended without pay. The employee had a continuing expectation of employment and was suspended following his arrest, but the charges were dropped, so ultimately, the reason for the suspension was a "mistake." As you read the case, bear in mind that the reason for a due process hearing is to avoid government deprivations of property or liberty by mistake. This case has important ramifications for public employment law because it applies the balancing test of *Mathews* to the otherwise bright line rule jurisprudence involving public employees with a property interest.

Gilbert v. Homar
520 U.S. 924 (1997)

Justice Scalia delivered the unanimous opinion of the Court.

This case presents the question whether a State violates the Due Process Clause of the Fourteenth Amendment by failing to provide notice and a hearing before suspending a tenured public employee without pay.

I

Respondent Richard J. Homar was employed as a police officer at East Stroudsburg University (ESU), a branch of Pennsylvania's State System of Higher Education. On August 26, 1992, when respondent was at the home of a family friend, he was arrested by the Pennsylvania

State Police in a drug raid. Later that day, the state police filed a criminal complaint charging respondent with possession of marijuana, possession with intent to deliver, and criminal conspiracy to violate the controlled substance law, which is a felony. The state police notified respondent's supervisor, University Police Chief David Marazas, of the arrest and charges. Chief Marazas in turn informed Gerald Levanowitz, ESU's Director of Human Resources, to whom ESU President James Gilbert had delegated authority to discipline ESU employees. Levanowitz suspended respondent without pay effective immediately. Respondent failed to report to work on the day of his arrest, and learned of his suspension the next day, when he called Chief Marazas to inquire whether he had been suspended. That same day, respondent received a letter from Levanowitz confirming that he had been suspended effective August 26 pending an investigation into the criminal charges filed against him. The letter explained that any action taken by ESU would not necessarily coincide with the disposition of the criminal charges.

Although the criminal charges were dismissed on September 1, respondent's suspension remained in effect while ESU continued with its own investigation. On September 18, Levanowitz and Chief Marazas met with respondent in order to give him an opportunity to tell his side of the story. Respondent was informed at the meeting that the state police had given ESU information that was "very serious in nature," but he was not informed that that included a report of an alleged confession he had made on the day of his arrest; he was consequently unable to respond to damaging statements attributed to him in the police report.

In a letter dated September 23, Levanowitz notified respondent that he was being demoted to the position of groundskeeper effective the next day, and that he would receive backpay from the date the suspension took effect at the rate of pay of a groundskeeper. (Respondent eventually received backpay for the period of his suspension at the rate of pay of a university police officer.) The letter maintained that the demotion was being imposed "as a result of admissions made by yourself to the Pennsylvania

State Police on August 26, 1992 that you maintained associations with individuals whom you knew were dealing in large quantities of marijuana and that you obtained marijuana from one of those individuals for your own use. Your actions constitute a clear and flagrant violation of Sections 200 and 200.2 of the [ESU] Police Department Manual."

Upon receipt of this letter, the president of respondent's union requested a meeting with President Gilbert. The requested meeting took place on September 24, at which point respondent had received and read the police report containing the alleged confession. After providing respondent with an opportunity to respond to the charges, Gilbert sustained the demotion. . . .

II

The protections of the Due Process Clause apply to government deprivation of those perquisites of government employment in which the employee has a constitutionally protected "property" interest. Although we have previously held that public employees who can be discharged only for cause have a constitutionally protected property interest in their tenure and cannot be fired without due process, see *Board of Regents of State Colleges v. Roth,* 408 U.S. 564, 578 (1972); *Perry v. Sindermann,* 408 U.S. 593, 602–603 (1972), we have not had occasion to decide whether the protections of the Due Process Clause extend to discipline of tenured public employees short of termination. Petitioners, however, do not contest this preliminary point, and so without deciding it we will, like the District Court, "assum[e] that the suspension infringed a protected property interest," and turn at once to petitioners' contention that respondent received all the process he was due.

A

In *Cleveland Bd. of Ed. v. Loudermill,* 470 U.S. 532 (1985), we concluded that a public employee dismissible only for cause was entitled to a very limited hearing prior to his termination, to be followed by a more comprehensive post-termination hearing. Stressing that the pretermination hearing "should be an initial check against mistaken decisions—essentially, a determination of whether there are reasonable grounds to believe that the charges against the employee are true and support the proposed action," id., at 545–546, we held that pretermination process need only include oral or written notice of the charges, an explanation of the employer's evidence, and an opportunity for the employee to tell his side of the story, id., at 546. In the course of our assessment of the governmental interest in immediate termination of a tenured employee, we observed that "in those situations where the employer perceives a significant hazard in keeping the employee on the job, it can avoid the problem by suspending with pay." Id., at 544–545.

Relying on this dictum, which it read as "strongly suggesting that suspension without pay must be preceded by notice and an opportunity to be heard in all instances," 89 F.3d at 1015, and determining on its own that such a rule would be "eminently sensible," id., at 1016, the Court of Appeals adopted a categorical prohibition: "[A] governmental employer may not suspend an employee without pay unless that suspension is preceded by some kind of pre-suspension hearing, providing the employee with notice and an opportunity to be heard." Ibid. Respondent (as well as most of his amici) makes no attempt to defend this absolute rule, which spans all types of government employment and all types of unpaid suspensions. This is eminently wise, since under our precedents such an absolute rule is indefensible.

It is by now well established that "'due process,' unlike some legal rules, is not a technical conception with a fixed content unrelated to time, place and circumstances." *Cafeteria & Restaurant Workers v. McElroy,* 367 U.S. 886, 895 (1961). "Due process is flexible and calls for such procedural protections as the particular situation demands." *Morrissey v. Brewer,* 408 U.S. 471, 481 (1972). This Court has recognized, on many occasions, that where a State must act quickly, or where it would be impractical to provide predeprivation process, postdeprivation process satisfies the requirements of the Due Process Clause. See, e.g., *United States v. James Daniel Good Real Property,* 510 U.S.

43, 53 (1993); *Zinermon v. Burch,* 494 U.S. 113, 128 (1990) (collecting cases); *Barry v. Barchi,* 443 U.S. 55, 64–65 (1979); *Dixon v. Love,* 431 U.S. 105, 115 (1977); *North American Cold Storage Co. v. Chicago,* 211 U.S. 306, 314–320 (1908).

Indeed, in *Parratt v. Taylor,* 451 U.S. 527 (1981), overruled in part on other grounds, *Daniels v. Williams,* 474 U.S. 327 (1986), we specifically noted that "we have rejected the proposition that [due process] always requires the State to provide a hearing prior to the initial deprivation of property." 451 U.S. at 540. And in *FDIC v. Mallen,* 486 U.S. 230 (1988), where we unanimously approved the Federal Deposit Insurance Corporation's suspension, without prior hearing, of an indicted private bank employee, we said: "An important government interest, accompanied by a substantial assurance that the deprivation is not baseless or unwarranted, may in limited cases demanding prompt action justify postponing the opportunity to be heard until after the initial deprivation." Id., at 240.

The dictum in *Loudermill* relied upon by the Court of Appeals is of course not inconsistent with these precedents. To say that when the government employer perceives a hazard in leaving the employee on the job it "can avoid the problem by suspending with pay" is not to say that that is the only way of avoiding the problem. Whatever implication the phrase "with pay" might have conveyed is far outweighed by the clarity of our precedents which emphasize the flexibility of due process as contrasted with the sweeping and categorical rule adopted by the Court of Appeals.

B

To determine what process is constitutionally due, we have generally balanced three distinct factors:

"First, the private interest that will be affected by the official action; second, the risk of an erroneous deprivation of such interest through the procedures used, and the probable value, if any, of additional or substitute procedural safeguards; and finally, the Government's interest." *Mathews v. Eldridge,* 424 U.S. 319,

335 (1976). See also, e.g., *Mallen,* supra, at 242; *Logan v. Zimmerman Brush Co.,* 455 U.S. 422, 434 (1982).

Respondent contends that he has a significant private interest in the uninterrupted receipt of his paycheck. But while our opinions have recognized the severity of depriving someone of the means of his livelihood, see, e.g., *Mallen,* supra, at 243; *Loudermill,* 470 U.S. at 543, they have also emphasized that in determining what process is due, account must be taken of "the length" and "finality of the deprivation." *Logan,* supra, at 434. Unlike the employee in *Loudermill,* who faced termination, respondent faced only a temporary suspension without pay. So long as the suspended employee receives a sufficiently prompt postsuspension hearing, the lost income is relatively insubstantial (compared with termination), and fringe benefits such as health and life insurance are often not affected at all.

On the other side of the balance, the State has a significant interest in immediately suspending, when felony charges are filed against them, employees who occupy positions of great public trust and high public visibility, such as police officers. Respondent contends that this interest in maintaining public confidence could have been accommodated by suspending him with pay until he had a hearing. We think, however, that the government does not have to give an employee charged with a felony a paid leave at taxpayer expense. If his services to the government are no longer useful once the felony charge has been filed, the Constitution does not require the government to bear the added expense of hiring a replacement while still paying him. ESU's interest in preserving public confidence in its police force is at least as significant as the State's interest in preserving the integrity of the sport of horse racing, see *Barry v. Barchi,* 443 U.S. at 64, an interest we "deemed sufficiently important . . . to justify a brief period of suspension prior to affording the suspended trainer a hearing," *Mallen,* 486 U.S. at 241.

The last factor in the *Mathews* balancing, and the factor most important to resolution of this case, is the risk of erroneous deprivation and the likely value of any additional procedures. Petitioners argue that any presuspension

hearing would have been worthless because pursuant to an Executive Order of the Governor of Pennsylvania a state employee is automatically to be suspended without pay "as soon as practicable after [being] formally charged with . . . a felony." 4 Pa. Code § 7.173 (1997). According to petitioners, supervisors have no discretion under this rule, and the mandatory suspension without pay lasts until the criminal charges are finally resolved. If petitioners' interpretation of this order is correct, there is no need for any presuspension process since there would be nothing to consider at the hearing except the independently verifiable fact of whether an employee had indeed been formally charged with a felony. See *Codd v. Velger,* 429 U.S. 624, 627–628 (1977). Compare *Loudermill,* supra, at 543. Respondent, however, challenges petitioners' reading of the Code, and contends that in any event an order of the Governor of Pennsylvania is a "mere directive which does not confer a legally enforceable right." We need not resolve this disputed issue of state law because even assuming the Code is only advisory (or has no application at all), the State had no constitutional obligation to provide respondent with a presuspension hearing. We noted in *Loudermill* that the purpose of a pre-termination hearing is to determine "whether there are reasonable grounds to believe the charges against the employee are true and support the proposed action." 470 U.S. at 545–546. By parity of reasoning, the purpose of any pre-suspension hearing would be to assure that there are reasonable grounds to support the suspension without pay. *Mallen,* 486 U.S. at 240. But here that has already been assured by the arrest and the filing of charges.

In *Mallen,* we concluded that an "ex parte finding of probable cause" such as a grand jury indictment provides adequate assurance that the suspension is not unjustified. Id., at 240–241. The same is true when an employee is arrested and then formally charged with a felony. First, as with an indictment, the arrest and formal charges imposed upon respondent "by an independent body demonstrate that the suspension is not arbitrary." Id., at 244. Second, like an indictment, the imposition of felony charges "itself is an objective fact that will in most cases raise serious public concern." Id., at 244–245. It is true, as respondent argues, that there is more reason to believe an employee has committed a felony when he is indicted rather than merely arrested and formally charged; but for present purposes arrest and charge give reason enough. They serve to assure that the state employer's decision to suspend the employee is not "baseless or unwarranted," id., at 240, in that an independent third party has determined that there is probable cause to believe the employee committed a serious crime.

Respondent further contends that since (as we have agreed to assume) Levanowitz had discretion not to suspend despite the arrest and filing of charges, he had to be given an opportunity to persuade Levanowitz of his innocence before the decision was made. We disagree. In *Mallen,* despite the fact that the FDIC had discretion whether to suspend an indicted bank employee, see 64 Stat. 879, as amended, 12 U.S.C. § 1818(g)(1); *Mallen,* supra, at 234–235. We nevertheless did not believe that a pre-suspension hearing was necessary to protect the private interest. Unlike in the case of a termination, where we have recognized that "the only meaningful opportunity to invoke the discretion of the decisionmaker is likely to be before the termination takes effect," *Loudermill,* supra, at 543, in the case of a

suspension there will be ample opportunity to invoke discretion later—and a short delay actually benefits the employee by allowing state officials to obtain more accurate information about the arrest and charges. Respondent "has an interest in seeing that a decision concerning his or her continued suspension is not made with excessive haste." *Mallen,* 486 U.S. at 243. If the State is forced to act too quickly, the decision maker "may give greater weight to the public interest and leave the suspension in place." Ibid.

C

Much of respondent's argument is dedicated to the proposition that he had a due process right to a presuspension hearing because the suspension was open-ended and he "theoretically may not have had the opportunity to be heard for weeks, months, or even years after his initial suspension without pay." But, as respondent himself asserts in his attempt to downplay the governmental interest, "because the employee is entitled, in any event, to a prompt post-suspension opportunity to be heard, the period of the suspension should be short and the amount of pay during the suspension minimal." . . . judgment of the Court of Appeals is reversed, and the case is remanded for further proceedings consistent with this opinion.

It is so ordered.

DISCRIMINATION IN PUBLIC EMPLOYMENT

In 1865, a sufficient number of states in the union ratified the proposed Thirteenth Amendment (outlawing slavery) so that it became the law of the land. The Fourteenth Amendment (1868) and the Fifteenth Amendment (1870) soon followed. Collectively referred to as the Civil War Amendments, they were meant to legally end the system of slavery and apartheid in this country. The Fifteenth Amendment prohibits the states from denying the right to vote on the basis of race. It is primarily the Fourteenth Amendment, forbidding the state from denying citizens equal protection of the laws, on which this discussion will focus. The final section of all three amendments gives Congress the power to pass laws to enforce the amendments. Generally, Congress does this in the form of civil rights acts (or voting rights acts in the case of the Fifteenth Amendment).

During the past 125 years, Congress has passed several civil rights acts, including the Civil Rights Act of 1875, which made it a federal crime for owners of public accommodations (hotels, churches, amusement places, theaters, and common carriers) to discriminate on the basis of race. When the federal government pressed charges against individuals and a railroad for discriminating against blacks, the Supreme Court said that Congress did not have the power to pass such laws regulating private discrimination. The Court reasoned that because the Fourteenth Amendment says "no state shall deny equal protection," the power of Congress to enforce that amendment should be limited to instances of official state discrimination (*Civil Rights Cases,* 109 U.S. 3 [1883]). That precedent, set in 1883, is still valid law today.

Indeed, because of the ruling in the *Civil Rights Cases,* when Congress passed the Civil Rights Act of 1964, it based that act on the commerce clause (banning discrimination in interstate commerce) rather than on the Fourteenth Amendment. Because the federal government's reach is so broad and extensive under the commerce clause (Occupational Safety and Health Administration, minimum wage, pollution control, etc.), that is how the federal government attacks private discrimination today. Recall from the case in point in the preceding chapter that the Court had to define *has.* That was important because an employer or a business does not fall under the jurisdiction of the federal commerce clause unless it *has* 15 or more employees.

Equal Protection of the Law

Generally, administrative law involves government discrimination rather than private discrimination. The aspiring public administrator ought to have some familiarity with equal protection law generally and as it relates to racial discrimination particularly. That is because, as you will discover in Chapter 10, if administrators illegally discriminate against someone, they can and most likely will be sued personally. A court will simply look to see whether the administrator knew or should have known that his or her actions violated someone's rights. The law presumes that mid-level managers and those above them "know or should know" when actions will violate another's constitutional rights.

Although there is no consensus among the nine members of the Supreme Court on the continued use of a three-tiered analysis, the Court presently applies it to equal protection cases. The first and lowest tier is referred to as *the simple rationality test.* It applies only to state regulation of business and assumes that the state's law is constitutional. The party challenging the law has the burden to prove it unconstitutional. Although there is a lack of consensus regarding the precise legislative intent behind the language *equal protection of the laws,* the Supreme Court has come to interpret it as follows: (a) It does not forbid the states from creating categories and treating people differently among the categories, and (b) in the exercise of their police powers, the states are free to create categories so long as the categories are *reasonable and not arbitrary.*[10]

The simple rationality test, then, merely looks to see whether the state had a reason for the category or, as the Court puts it, "a legitimate governmental objective." The City of New York apparently concluded that advertising on the side of vehicles led to increases in accidents, so it passed an ordinance banning advertisement on vehicles but then exempted business advertising on certain business vehicles.[11] The state of Oklahoma passed several measures aimed at putting opticians out of business but then exempted the ready-to-wear glasses industry from the regulations.[12] The City of New Orleans passed an ordinance banning pushcart vendors in the French Quarter but then exempted any vendor who had been in business prior to January 1, 1972.[13]

In these and similar business regulation cases, the Court simply takes the stated reason for the category and then looks to see whether the legislative body could reasonably have believed, at the time the law was passed, that it would accomplish the goal (e.g., reduce traffic accidents in New York City, protect the eyesight of Oklahoma residents, or preserve the aesthetic character of the French Quarter). The reason this standard of review is so lax is that the Supreme Court is extremely sensitive to charges of substituting its economic preferences for those of a legislative body in the area of business regulation. This is exactly what the Supreme Court did between 1932 and 1937, which is what caused Franklin Roosevelt to propose his "court packing plan." This plan caused Chief Justice Hughes to switch his vote, and that created a majority on the Court willing to accept the expanded role of the federal government discussed in Chapter 1.

The middle-tier equal protection analysis is also a reasonableness test, but here, the Court engages in in-depth analysis to see whether the reason for the category, in fact, will accomplish the desired results. The Court will ask not whether there is simply a *legitimate* governmental objective, but rather whether there is an *important* governmental objective and whether the categories created by the policy are rationally related to the achievement of the important governmental objective. The Court applies this middle-tier analysis to social and economic discrimination that does not fit into either of the other two tiers. Gender discrimination cases are common here, as are cases involving discrimination based on age, legitimate birth, and American citizenship.

The Court found that it was unreasonable for the state of Idaho to give a statutory preference to the male where both a male and female were equally qualified to administer an estate. The Court said Idaho's reason (administrative efficiency) was irrational because it was based on outmoded stereotypes.[14] It was also unreasonable for the military to provide a family allowance to any male who got married, whereas a female had to prove that she supplied over half of the family income before she could qualify for the family allowance.[15] The Court found a Florida scheme that provided a property tax break for widows but not for widowers to be a rational classification. The Court agreed with the Florida legislature that women suffer disproportionately when a spouse dies.[16] The Oklahoma legislature, citing statistics that tended to show drunk driving by young males was a leading cause of accidents, passed a law that banned males from purchasing 3.2% beer until the age of 21 but allowed females to purchase such beer at the age of 18. The Supreme Court said that was an irrational and unreasonable classification.[17] Finally, the Court has said that it is reasonable for a state to require state police to retire at age 50 regardless of physical condition[18] and to limit the teaching profession to U.S. citizens[19] (but it is unreasonable to require notary publics to be U.S. citizens).[20]

The third and highest tier of the equal protection analysis is called *strict scrutiny* or the *compelling interest* test. The Court applies this level of analysis to state discrimination involving a suspect class (i.e., race) or a fundamental right (to vote or to travel).

Here, the assumptions are just the opposite of the first tier. Any state classification based on race is assumed to be unconstitutional, and the state has to show a compelling reason to discriminate on such a basis to save its law. Only rarely can a government meet the compelling-interest standard. The federal government was able to demonstrate a compelling interest in its minority business set-aside program, which required that 10 percent of the funds for public works projects go to minority contractors.[21] The Court allowed this discrimination because the program was experimental and closely supervised, it was intended to remedy past discrimination, and Congress has more constitutional power to do this sort of thing than the states do. It is extremely difficult for the states to meet the compelling-interest test.

In 1995, the Supreme Court reversed itself on the issue of minority business set-asides (see *Adarand v. Pena,* 515 U.S. 200 [1995]). Subsequently, the Clinton Administration began the process of reviewing all federal contracts to assure compliance with the *Adarand* decision (i.e., no federal contract can be awarded solely on the basis of race, absent verifiable evidence of past racial discrimination).

Instances involving official state discrimination against blacks are rare these days, but one such case is *Palmore v. Sidoti,*[22] a custody suit in which the divorced father sued for custody of his daughter because his Caucasian ex-wife was cohabiting with a man (who happened to be black). By the time of the trial, the ex-wife and the black man had married, and the Court found both parents to be fit, so the case turned on the welfare of the child. The trial court found that, despite racial gains, children of racially mixed marriages are subjected to social pressures that children of one-race marriages do not face, and the judge awarded custody to the father. The Supreme Court reversed that decision because it was based solely on race (had the former Mrs. Sidoti married a similarly respectable Caucasian, the result would have been different), and the state's reason was not compelling. Speculation about the effects of private racial prejudice on children of interracial marriages is not a compelling reason, the Court said. Also, in 1997, the U.S. Department of Agriculture (USDA) settled with 1,000 black farmers who were part of a class action suit claiming that local farm service agencies in the South had delayed their federal farm loan applications or approved smaller amounts than were due and did so out of racial prejudice.[23] After State Police in New Jersey shot three black men on the turnpike in 1998, a statewide investigation led to a finding of systematic racial profiling, and a U.S. Justice Department consent decree imposed training and federal supervision on the agency. A federal report issued in July 2004, at the end of federal supervision, concluded that the agency had made "remarkable" progress in eliminating racial profiling.[24] These are examples of official purposeful racial discrimination that violate the equal protection clause.

Today, most discrimination against racial minorities is what we call de facto discrimination—that is, discrimination in fact but not mandated by law. Some cases involve discrimination in the workplace (when less than 1 percent of skilled labor jobs are held by blacks and blacks constitute 30 to 50 percent of the labor force [*United Steelworkers v. Weber*] or when less than 1 percent of the contractors in a city are owned by blacks and blacks constitute 50 percent of the population [*Northeastern Florida Chapter of the Associated General Contractors of America v. City of Jacksonville*]). Others involve discrimination in education (all-black and all-white schools within a school district or jurisdiction).

The Court has dealt with this type of racial discrimination by requiring a finding that this discrimination is purposeful before the perpetrator is found to have violated the Constitution.[25] For example, in the city of Topeka, Kansas, 40 years after the famous desegregation decision in 1954 (*Brown v. Board of Education of Topeka*),[26] some schools within the district remained more than 80 percent black or 100 percent white. Because the situation is not mandated by law, it is called de facto segregation, and before it can be found unconstitutional, the plaintiffs have to prove that the segregation exists by design of policymakers. If the racial pattern is the result of forces such as migration and housing patterns, such segregation is not unconstitutional. It was not until the summer of 1999 that the federal court in Topeka finally found, as a matter of fact, that the school district was in compliance with the original *Brown* decision.[27]

Affirmative Action

The most common purposeful discrimination engaged in by state and local governments today is affirmative action. The Court has been badly divided on the question of affirmative action. Its decisions in this area have been unpredictable and make little or no jurisprudential sense. The first Supreme Court case to address the merits of an affirmative action program was *Regents of the University of California v. Bakke,* 438 U.S. 265 (1978). That case involved a special admissions program for admission to medical school at the University of California at Davis. The program was aimed at economically disadvantaged applicants who by virtue of exposure to less sophisticated educational programs could not be expected to perform on the Medical Career Aptitude Test (MCAT) at the same level as those whose socioeconomic level had afforded them private prep schools or public education in the suburbs. Although race was not a written factor in the special admissions process, only blacks had benefited from the affirmative action process. Allan Bakke, a Caucasian who was refused admission twice, had both science and overall grade point averages and MCAT scores in excess of many who were admitted under the special program, and he claimed discrimination on the basis of race. The Court noted that UC Davis proffered laudable reasons for such discrimination (reducing the deficit of minorities in medical school and the medical profession, countering societal discrimination, increasing the number of physicians who will practice in areas currently underserved, and achieving a diverse student body). Of those reasons, the Court found compelling only the diverse student body but declared the affirmative action program unconstitutional anyway because it was not implemented with the least restrictive means. The compelling interest test has two prongs: the state must have a compelling interest, and it must accomplish its program in a way that affects suspect classes or fundamental rights minimally (least restrictive means). The Court said that affirmative action programs may be race conscious so long as race is not the sole criterion. Race may be one among other criteria in affirmative action programs.

In two reapportionment cases in the mid-1990s, the Court moved to a point where it held race-conscious remedies to be valid only in those cases where they were used to eradicate the effects of specifically identifiable past discrimination.[28]

In the summer of 2003, the Court decided two cases involving the University of Michigan's affirmative action program. One case involved the undergraduate school,[29] and the second involved the law school.[30] Although the process was more complex, one facet of the undergraduate affirmative action program awarded 20 admission points to all minority applicants, and this became the focus of the Court's opinion.

The law school's program required a review of every applicant's "hard" and "soft" admissions variables. Hard variables are LSAT score, grade point average, letters of recommendation, and other materials required for an application. Soft variables are things like the enthusiasm of recommenders and the student's own statement on how she/he would contribute to the diversity of the law school. The program called for review of hard and soft variables plus the concept of *critical mass* to make admissions decisions. Critical mass means there must be enough individuals from an underrepresented group so that an admitted individual would not feel like a spokesperson (read token), and there should be enough individuals from an underrepresented group to provide a truly diverse perspective for the other students at the law school. As it had done in *Bakke* 25 years earlier, the Court recognized student body diversity as a compelling enough reason to discriminate on the basis of race. However, the undergraduate program ran afoul of the least restrictive means prong of the test. The law school's affirmative action program, by way of contrast, met both prongs of the test.

To the degree that administrative law deals with discrimination of any kind, it is always public or governmental discrimination. Private discrimination is a matter of constitutional law and statutory law under the 1964 Civil Rights Act and, to a lesser degree, the Thirteenth Amendment. Some of you are probably wondering: What about quotas and anti-affirmative action propositions on ballots? Although this is not a matter of administrative law, it is important enough to take the time to clear confusion.

First, it should be obvious to you from the preceding discussion that no state government or state government agency can have a quota system. It cannot have an affirmative action program in which race is the sole criterion, although race can be a factor. To the degree that a state's medical school or law school has a set-aside program, race cannot be the sole criterion.

Although it has become popular to refer to it as *reverse discrimination,* the more appropriate descriptive term is *affirmative action.* There are affirmative action programs of all kinds. Harvard University (and most Ivy League universities as well) gives bonus points to applicants who attended public schools in states such as Kansas, Iowa, Texas, Oklahoma, Georgia, and so on. The theory for this is simple. Students who are the product of such schools cannot compete on the SAT exam with students who are the product of the Eastern private academies. If Harvard did not do something to level the playing field, it would still be a homogeneous elitist university filled only with the children of the rich who could afford private academies (where the curriculum is geared to producing high SAT scores). It is because a diverse student body is seen as essential to a well-rounded education that affirmative programs of all kinds are appropriate for universities. Indeed, the Supreme Court has said that a diverse student body constitutes a "compelling state interest."

Quotas, however, to the degree that they exist anywhere (they are few and far between) are found almost exclusively in the private sector. Generally, they are created by an agreement between management and a union, and their purpose is to remedy empirically verifiable past discrimination. For example, the United Steel Workers forced an employer to accept a program ensuring that 50 percent of all trainees in an in-plant craft training program were black. This quota was to remain in effect until the number of black skilled craft workers in the plant matched the proportion of blacks in the local workforce.[31] A federal district court found racial discrimination in a union's admission practices and imposed a goal of 29 percent non-White membership in the union by a set date (the 29 percent matched the non-White percentage in the local labor pool).[32] This is how we get quotas. Although the 1964 Civil Rights Act bans discrimination in interstate commerce, the Supreme Court has noted that the Act's purpose was to promote the employment of Blacks who had previously been excluded from participating in the national economy. So private benign discrimination (to make up for past discrimination) is legal under the 1964 Civil Rights Act.[33] Benign racial discrimination by a government is not constitutional under the equal protection clause.

The final area involving what sounds like quotas is the area of preemployment criteria. Requiring applicants for a job with a state correctional agency to be at least five feet, eight inches tall and weigh at least 160 pounds excludes, without reason, 75 percent of the female population. A specific score on a preemployment examination may disproportionately discriminate against a clearly identifiable minority. In the early 1970s, the Court ruled unconstitutional preemployment criteria that (a) have a disproportionate impact on a clearly identifiable minority and (b) are not related to job performance.[34] The Court soon overruled that case and began to employ a purposeful discrimination analysis to preemployment criteria cases. That is, preemployment criteria with a clearly identifiable disproportionate impact on a minority were not unconstitutional unless they could be shown to be part of purposeful discrimination. In 1989, the Court decided another case that made it easier for business to justify such criteria.[35] The civil rights bill negotiated and debated so strongly in 1991 (and often referred to as a "quota bill") was meant to reverse decisions of the Rehnquist Supreme Court in this area.[36]

While the Civil Rights Act of 1991 does not impose or even mention quotas, it restores the Court's original two-pronged test (disproportionate impact and criteria unrelated to job performance), and it forbids the application of purposeful discrimination to these kinds of cases. Some have argued that this Act will cause businesses to "voluntarily" impose "quotas" on themselves to avoid a "disproportionate impact."

Sexual Harassment

As a potential public administrator, you should be especially aware that should you make a decision that happens to violate either a client's or an employee's rights, you personally can be held liable. You can also incur liability for the governmental unit that you work for. Given that, you should be well aware of property and liberty interests under the due process clause. You should know enough not to violate someone's rights under the current jurisprudence applicable to the equal protection clause. Equal protection law, however, is beyond the scope of this text but the law will presume that as a trained public administrator you know enough about it to avoid violating someone's rights. An area of the law that is closely related and mushrooming in terms of litigation is gender discrimination in general and sexual harassment in particular.

Constitutionally, government (usually but not always the legislature), cannot create categories of citizens and treat them differently based on gender without a really good reason. The Supreme Court uses the phrase "important governmental objective." Further, the classification scheme must reasonably be a legitimate means of furthering that important objective. By statute, there are two roads to gender discrimination. Title IX of the Education Act prohibits gender discrimination in education. You should already be aware that Title VII of the 1964 Civil Rights Act prohibits gender discrimination in interstate commerce.

Title IX of the Education Act is really an act of Congress under its Article One Section Eight spending power. It applies to any educational institution that receives federal money (almost all public schools from primary, secondary to college), and it forbids gender discrimination. If such discrimination is reported or otherwise suspected, the educational institution is notified and given an opportunity to correct the situation. If no corrective action is taken, federal funds are cut off.[37] There is nothing in the Act that establishes a plaintiff's right to sue an offending educational institution. The Supreme Court, however, in *Franklin v. Gwinett Co. Public Schools* 503 U.S. 60 (1992), said there was an implied private right to sue. The case involved a teacher/coach who allegedly sexually harassed and abused a female high school student. The Plaintiff alleged "coercive intercourse" and that the other faculty and administrators were aware of the harassment and did nothing. Finally she alleged that the school district dropped all internal investigations once the teacher/coach resigned. The decision was unanimous albeit with concurring opinions.

In 1998, in a five to four decision, the Court decided that a school district was not liable for a high school teacher's sexual harassment of a female student. The teacher and student were caught having an affair but the administration was not aware of the situation. See *Gebser v. Lago Vista Independent School District,* 524 U.S. 274 (1998). A year later the Court decided another Title IX case that received some attention from the media. The case of *Davis v. Monroe County Board of Education,* 526 U.S. 629 (1999) involved an allegation that a fifth-grade male student sexually harassed one of his female classmates, thereby creating a hostile environment. The girl's mother alleged that school authorities were told about the situation and they refused to investigate or to separate the two students. In another five to four decision, this time with Justice O'Connor aligning with Stevens, Souter, Ginsburg and Breyer, she turned the *Gebser* majority into dissenters and decided that the school district was liable. The major variables that seem to incur liability in Title IX cases are whether someone with the authority to resolve a sexual harassment situation is made aware of the problem and whether steps are taken to resolve it. If there is no administrative knowledge, then there is no liability. Administrative knowledge along with insufficient or nonexistent remedies constitutes what courts call *deliberate indifference,* and that will bring damages as well as injunctive relief.

Title VII cases under the 1964 Civil Rights Act are not as clear-cut as the Education Act cases. That is because there are two forms of discrimination involved: discrimination against workers because of their gender and discrimination between males and females in terms of compensation, promotion, assignment, and so on. For example, a study of Texas school superintendents showed that women comprised 75 percent of the teachers, 51 percent of the assistant principals, 47 percent of the principals, and 36 percent of assistant superintendents, but only 8 percent of the superintendents.[38] This is what is known as the "glass ceiling." Second and of more importance to our discussion here, the Equal Employment Opportunity Commission has adopted guidelines on sexual harassment that create two forms of sexual harassment.[39] There is quid pro quo harassment where a person in authority over a worker uses that authority in an attempt to extract sexual favors. There is also a hostile environment where again, usually (but not necessarily), a person in authority makes an employee uncomfortable by sexual innuendo, language, or deeds. More cases involve hostile environment than quid pro quo, but an early case of the latter is *Meritor Savings Bank v. Vinson,* 477 U.S. 57 (1986). The plaintiff was hired by the defendant, who was a bank vice president. She started as a teller trainee and advanced to teller, supervisor, and eventually branch manager over her four-year employment. During that time, she allegedly had sex with the vice president 40 or 50 times out of fear of losing her job. All parties, however, agree that the promotions were based on merit. Her case was dismissed at the trial court because the judge said that she could not recover under Title VII unless she could demonstrate economic or physical injury from the alleged harassment. The Supreme Court reversed and said that the fact of the harassment *is* the injury under Title VII, and a plaintiff need not show economic or psychological injury to sustain the suit.

One of the first hostile work environment cases was *Harris v. Forklift Systems,* 510 U.S. 17 (1993). Here, the plaintiff alleged that the president of the equipment rental company created an abusive work environment that eventually forced her to quit. This is known in legal parlance as a *constructive discharge.* It means in law, if not in fact, or to put it another way, "as if"[40] the employee had been wrongfully terminated. It means that the employer made the work environment so hostile that the employee was left with no choice but to quit. At trial, the plaintiff alleged that the president, in front of other employees, called her a "dumb ass woman," suggested that they go to a hotel to negotiate her raise, asked her to fetch coins out of his front pants pockets, and threw objects on the floor in front of her and asked her to pick them up. The trial judge sided with Forklift Systems, saying that the plaintiff could not show psychological injury from the treatment she had received, which he called a "close call" on the question of creating a hostile work environment. One of the main issues at the Supreme Court was what the plaintiff must show to establish a hostile work environment. Unanimously reversing the trial judge, the Court said that a hostile work environment depends on how frequent and severe the offensive behavior is, whether the offensive behavior is physically threatening or emotionally humiliating, and whether the behavior interferes with the employee's ability to perform the work.

The question before the Court in *Oncale v. Sundowner Offshore Services,* 523 U.S. 75 (1998), was whether a male plaintiff could sue under Title VII for a hostile work environment created by other male employees. The answer is yes; Title VII's prohibition on sex discrimination is not limited to male/female situations.

The concept of vicarious liability, discussed in Chapter 10, is familiar to managers in either the private or the public/nonprofit sector. The concept simply means that sometimes, an employer is liable for the acts of employees. This is the case whether the employer was aware of the employee's behavior or not. The court heard two cases in 1998 that dealt with situations in which an employer could be held liable for the hostile work environment created by management or other employees. One case, *Burlington Industries v. Ellerth,* 524 U.S. 742 (1998), comes from the private sector, and the other case, *Faragher v. City of Boca Raton,* 524 U.S. 775 (1998), originated in the public sector. The 1964 Civil Rights Act applies to both.

In the *Burlington Industries* case, the plaintiff, Ellerth, was allegedly harassed by a supervisor once removed (not her immediate supervisor), who made threats against her continuing employment if she did not "loosen up" and have sex with him. These threats were never carried out, however, and indeed during the period of harassment, the plaintiff was promoted. She was aware that the company had a policy against sexual harassment, but she never lodged a complaint because she knew it would go through the desk of her harasser. She eventually quit (again a potential constructive discharge) and sued. The question was whether Burlington Industries could be held liable for the sexual harassment of a mid-level manager when it had no knowledge of the behavior. To solve this question, the Court turned to the common law of agency or judge-made law about when one person (employee) acts as the agent of another (employer). It also turned to a concept called the *restatement (second)* of agency. A *restatement,* a legal work published by the American Law Institute, is a compilation by judges, lawyers, and legal scholars that describes the law in a given area and suggests the direction it may go.[41] From these sources, the Court indicated that generally an employer is liable for the acts of an employee if the act occurred within the scope of employment. Also, for the most part, when an employee engages in sexual harassment, it is not within the scope of employment.

There are several exceptions regarding when an employee can incur liability against the employer, even acting outside the scope of employment. If supervisors rely on their apparent authority to accomplish the harassment or if they were aided in the harassment by the existence of the agency relationship, the employer may be liable. Ellerth successfully carried her burden of proof to establish potential liability for Burlington. The Court, however, said that an employer could avoid liability by establishing what is now referred to as the *Ellerth/Faragher defense.* First, if an employer can show that it took reasonable measures to correct the situation and, second, that the allegedly harassed employee failed to take reasonable action to avoid the situation, the employer can avoid liability. This is what is known as an *affirmative defense,* which means that defendants who attempt to use it will need to carry the burden of proof (by a preponderance of the evidence). Because Burlington might be able to prove that Ellerth failed to take reasonable action to avoid the situation (by not going through the complaint channels), the case was returned to the lower courts. In this case, the Court downplayed the importance of the distinction between quid pro quo and hostile environment because what started out as a quid pro quo situation turned out in the end to be a hostile environment because the threats were not carried out.

In the *Faragher* case, a female ocean life guard for the city of Boca Raton was allegedly forced to quit her job due to uninvited and offensive touching and lewd remarks from her three supervisors. She sued both the supervisors and the city (i.e., the employer). The city raised the defense against liability by saying it had a sexual harassment policy in place and the plaintiff did not avail herself of it. The problem was that the city failed to distribute its policy to all employees, so that neither the three supervisors nor the victim were aware of it; hence, the city had failed to meet its burden in raising the affirmative defense. When constructive discharge is caused by *tangible employment action* (the employer fires, demotes, reassigns, transfers, etc., the affected employee), the affirmative defense to vicarious liability for sexual harassment is not available to employers. The 2004 case of *Pennsylvania State Police v. Suders* addresses that issue and appears at the end of this chapter.

FUTURE ISSUES IN THE LAW OF PUBLIC EMPLOYMENT

Look for various forms of clashes between public employees and employers over privacy. Expect expanded demands for urine drug tests as a preemployment criterion as well as randomly throughout employment. There could be expanded use of lie detectors and videotaping of employees during their entire shift at work. Finally, employers are increasingly looking to see where their employees go on the World Wide Web. Local governments are increasingly requiring that anyone on the payroll live in the jurisdiction, a concept the Supreme Court has upheld.[42]

SUMMARY

1. Public employees can be categorized as either probationary or permanent employees. Only permanent employees have a property interest in their job.

2. The right to a pretermination hearing is contingent on the ability to demonstrate either a property or a liberty interest.

3. Given a property interest, the right to a predeprivation or predisciplinary hearing depends on the balancing interests from *Mathews v. Eldridge.*

4. Because probationary employees lack a property interest, they must rely on the establishment of a liberty interest.

5. Liberty interests are established in one of two ways: (a) if publicly stated reasons for termination cause damage to one's reputation and/or ability to seek employment in the field, and (b) if the primary reason behind the decision to terminate an employee was the employee's exercise of a constitutionally protected right.

6. The range of constitutionally protected expression is more narrow for public employees than it is for all other citizens (expression that hampers the working relationship between an employee and an administrator is not protected).

7. Employees with a property interest can be terminated for cause (or financial exigency), but a pretermination hearing is required.

8. Government discrimination generally falls under the jurisdiction of the equal protection clause of the Fourteenth Amendment or the Civil Rights Act of 1964. Although the Act was aimed at private discrimination initially, it now applies to government discrimination as well because such discrimination has a significant effect on interstate commerce.

   a. Official (as opposed to private), racial discrimination must be purposeful before it can be illegal. If a plaintiff demonstrates that governmental racial discrimination is purposeful, then the burden of proof switches to the government to demonstrate a compelling interest in the policy. Rarely if ever can states meet the equal protection compelling-interest test.

   b. Other forms of social and economic discrimination must meet the middle tier of equal protection analysis. To have the program or policy survive, government must show: (a) an important governmental objective and (b) that the policy is rationally related to the achievement of that objective.

   c. Affirmative action programs are constitutional so long as race is simply one among many criteria, but race cannot be the sole criterion. Indeed, whether affirmative action, redistricting, child custody, USDA loans to farmers, or racial profiling, race conscious decisions always violate the Constitution. The exception is actions to eradicate the effects of specifically identifiable past invidious discrimination.

9. Sexual harassment falls under the 1964 Civil Rights Act.

   a. There two kinds of sexual harassment, quid pro quo and hostile environment, but the distinction makes no difference in vicarious liability suits.

   b. To sue under quid pro quo, a plaintiff must carry the burden of proof that the harassment happened. The plaintiff need not submit evidence of injury in the form of psychological, physical, emotional, or economic injury. The injury is the sexual abuse.

   c. To succeed in a hostile environment suit, the plaintiff needs to prove the working environment was hostile as opposed to uncivil. To do that, the plaintiff needs to show that the offensive behavior: (a) was either frequent or severe, (b) was either physically threatening or emotionally humiliating; and (c) interfered with the ability to perform the work. If the plaintiff can establish the hostility of the working environment, he or she need not necessarily submit evidence of economic injury. The harassing atmosphere is the injury. Legally, the injury is the change in terms or conditions of employment because of sex, which is what the Civil Rights Act forbids. Often, the concept of a constructive discharge comes into play in these cases.

   d. Vicarious liability for the employer can be established by showing that a supervisor: (a) relied on his or her apparent authority to accomplish the harassment or (b) was aided in the harassment by the existence of the agency relationship to the employer.

(1) An employer can defend against vicarious liability by establishing what is now referred to as the *Ellerth/Faragher* defenses: (a) that the employer took reasonable measures to prevent or discourage employees from engaging in sexual harassment or that it discovered the harassing behavior and took reasonable steps to stop it and (b) that the complaining employee failed to take appropriate steps to alleviate the situation (e.g., failed to file an internal harassment grievance). A strong policy against sexual harassment distributed to all employees along with training and accompanied by a procedural short-circuit, so that a complaining employee will not end up routing the complaint to the harasser, will generally establish the first part of the defense.

(2) The *Ellerth/Faragher* defense is not available to an employer where there was a hostile work environment and tangible employment action (discharge, demotion, reassignment, etc.).

(3) A hostile work environment plaintiff who is also suing for constructive discharge under vicarious liability must show that working conditions were so intolerable that a reasonable person would have felt compelled to resign. If there is no tangible employment action, the *Ellerth/Faragher* defense is available. If there is tangible employment action, the employer is liable (no defense is available).

(4) It is the kiss of death for an employer to have evidence presented that the employer was aware of a harassment situation and did nothing. This is also true where an employer perhaps did not know but *should* have known that a problem might exist. An employer should have known, for example, if there was no harassment policy, it was not distributed to all employees, or it existed but was not taken seriously or not enforced (as in the *Faragher* case).

END-OF-CHAPTER CASES

Bishop v. Wood
426 U.S. 341 (1976)

The facts are contained in the opinion written by Justice Stevens, joined by Justices Burger, Stewart, Powell, and Rehnquist. Justices White, Brennan, Marshall, and Blackmun dissented.

The questions for us to decide are (1) whether petitioner's employment status was a property interest protected by the Due Process Clause of the Fourteenth Amendment, and (2) assuming that the explanation for his discharge was false, whether that false explanation deprived

him of an interest in liberty protected by that Clause.

I

Petitioner was employed by the city of Marion as a probationary policeman on June 9, 1969. After six months he became a permanent employee. He was dismissed on March 31, 1972. He claims that he had either an express or an implied right to continued employment. A city ordinance provides that a permanent employee may be discharged if he fails to perform work up to the standard of his classification, or if he is negligent, inefficient, or unfit to perform his duties. Petitioner first contends that even though the ordinance does not expressly so provide, it should be read to prohibit discharge for any other reason, and therefore to confer tenure on all permanent employees. In addition, he contends that his period of service, together with his "permanent" classification, gave him a sufficient expectancy of continued employment to constitute a protected property interest. A property interest in employment can, of course, be created by ordinance, or by an implied contract. In either case, however, the sufficiency of the claim of entitlement must be decided by reference to state law. The North Carolina Supreme Court has held that an enforceable expectation of continued public employment in that State can exist only if the employer, by statute or contract, has actually granted some form of guarantee. *Still v. Lance,* 279 N.C. 254, 182 S.E. 2d 403 (1971). Whether such a guarantee has been given can be determined only by an examination of the particular statute or ordinance in question. On its face the ordinance on which petitioner relies may fairly be read as conferring such a guarantee. However, such a reading is not the only possible interpretation; the ordinance may also be construed as granting no right to continued employment but merely conditioning an employee's removal on compliance with certain specified procedures.

We do not have any authoritative interpretation of this ordinance by a North Carolina state court. We do, however, have the opinion of the United States District Judge who, of course, sits in North Carolina and practiced law there for many years. Based on his understanding of state law, he concluded that petitioner "held his position at the will and pleasure of the city." This construction of North Carolina law was upheld by the Court of Appeals for the Fourth Circuit, albeit by an equally divided court. In comparable circumstances, this Court has accepted the interpretation of state law in which the District Court and the Court of Appeals have concurred even if an examination of the state-law issue

without such guidance might have justified a different conclusion. In this case, as the District Court construed the ordinance, the City Manager's determination of the adequacy of the grounds for discharge is not subject to judicial review; the employee is merely given certain procedural rights which the District Court found not to have been violated in this case. The District Court's reading of the ordinance is tenable; it derives some support from a decision of the North Carolina Supreme Court, *Still v. Lance,* supra; and it was accepted by the Court of Appeals for the Fourth Circuit. These reasons are sufficient to foreclose our independent examination of the state-law issue.

Under that view of the law, petitioner's discharge did not deprive him of a property interest protected by the Fourteenth Amendment.

II

Petitioner's claim that he has been deprived of liberty has two components. He contends that the reasons given for his discharge are so serious as to constitute a stigma that may severely damage his reputation in the community; in addition, he claims that those reasons were false.

In our appraisal of petitioner's claim we must accept his version of the facts since the District Court granted summary judgment against him. His evidence established that he was a competent police officer; that he was respected by his peers; that he made more arrests than any other officer on the force; that although he had been criticized for engaging in high-speed pursuits, he had promptly heeded such criticism; and that he had a reasonable explanation for his imperfect attendance at police training sessions. We must therefore assume that his discharge was a mistake and based on incorrect information. In *Board of Regents v. Roth,* 408 U.S. 564, we recognized that the nonretention of an untenured college teacher might make him somewhat less attractive to other employers, but nevertheless concluded that it would stretch the concept too far "to suggest that a person is deprived of 'liberty' when he simply is not rehired in one job but remains as free as before to seek another."

Id., at 575. This same conclusion applies to the discharge of a public employee whose position is terminable at the will of the employer when there is no public disclosure of the reasons for the discharge.

In this case the asserted reasons for the City Manager's decision were communicated orally to the petitioner in private and also were stated in writing in answer to interrogatories after this litigation commenced. Since the former communication was not made public, it cannot properly form the basis for a claim that petitioner's interest in his "good name, reputation, honor, or integrity" was thereby impaired. And since the latter communication was made in the course of a judicial proceeding which did not commence until after petitioner had suffered the injury for which he seeks redress, it surely cannot provide retroactive support for his claim. A contrary evaluation of either explanation would penalize forthright and truthful communication between employer and employee in the former instance, and between litigants in the latter. Petitioner argues, however, that the reasons given for his discharge were false. Even so, the reasons stated to him in private had no different impact on his reputation than if they had been true. And the answers to his interrogatories, whether true or false, did not cause the discharge.

The truth or falsity of the City Manager's statement determines whether or not his decision to discharge the petitioner was correct or prudent, but neither enhances nor diminishes petitioner's claim that his constitutionally protected interest in liberty has been impaired. A contrary evaluation of his contention would enable every discharged employee to assert a constitutional claim merely by alleging that his former supervisor made a mistake. The federal court is not the appropriate forum in which to review the multitude of personnel decisions that are made daily by public agencies. We must accept the harsh fact that numerous individual mistakes are inevitable in the day-to-day administration of our affairs. The United States Constitution cannot feasibly be construed to require federal judicial review for every such error.

In the absence of any claim that the public employer was motivated by a desire to curtail or to penalize the exercise of an employee's constitutionally protected rights, we must presume that official action was regular and, if erroneous, can best be corrected in other ways. The Due Process Clause of the Fourteenth Amendment is not a guarantee against incorrect or ill-advised personnel decisions. The judgment is affirmed.

So ordered.

Waters v. Churchill
511 U.S. 661 (1994)

Opinion is by Justice O'Connor joined by the Chief Justice and Justice Ginsburg. Justice Souter filed a concurring opinion as did Justice Scalia, joined by Justices Kennedy and Thomas. Justice Stevens dissented, joined by Justice Blackmun.

In *Connick v. Myers,* 461 U.S. 138 (1983), we set forth a test for determining whether speech by a government employee may, consistently with the First Amendment, serve as a basis for disciplining or discharging that employee. In this case, we decide whether the Connick test should be applied to what the

government employer thought was said, or to what the trier of fact ultimately determines to have been said.

I

This case arises out of a conversation that respondent Cheryl Churchill had on January 16, 1987, with Melanie Perkins-Graham. Both Churchill and Perkins-Graham were nurses working at McDonough District Hospital; Churchill was in the obstetrics department, and Perkins-Graham was considering transferring to that department. The conversation took place at work during a dinner break. Petitioners heard about it, and fired Churchill, allegedly because of it. There is, however, a dispute about what Churchill actually said, and therefore about whether petitioners were constitutionally permitted to fire Churchill for her statements.

The conversation was overheard in part by two other nurses, Mary Lou Ballew and Jean Welty, and by Dr. Thomas Koch, the clinical head of obstetrics. A few days later, Ballew told Cynthia Waters, Churchill's supervisor, about the incident. According to Ballew, Churchill took "the cross trainee into the kitchen for . . . at least 20 minutes to talk about [Waters] and how bad things are in [obstetrics] in general." Ballew said that Churchill's statements led Perkins-Graham to no longer be interested in switching to the department.

Shortly after this, Waters met with Ballew a second time for confirmation of Ballew's initial report. Ballew said that Churchill "was knocking the department" and that "in general [Churchill] was saying what a bad place [obstetrics] is to work." Ballew said she heard Churchill say Waters "was trying to find reasons to fire her." Ballew also said Churchill described a patient complaint for which Waters had supposedly wrongly blamed Churchill.

Waters, together with petitioner Kathleen Davis, the hospital's vice president of nursing, also met with Perkins-Graham, who told them that Churchill "had indeed said unkind and inappropriate negative things about [Waters]." Also, according to Perkins-Graham, Churchill mentioned a negative evaluation that Waters had given Churchill, which arose out of an incident in which Waters had cited Churchill for an insubordinate remark. The evaluation stated that Churchill "promotes an unpleasant atmosphere and hinders constructive communication and cooperation," and "exhibits negative behavior towards [Waters] and [Waters'] leadership through her actions and body language"; the evaluation said Churchill's work was otherwise satisfactory. Churchill allegedly told Perkins-Graham that she and Waters had discussed the evaluation, and that Waters "wanted to wipe the slate clean . . . but [Churchill thought] this wasn't possible." Churchill also allegedly told Perkins-Graham "that just in

general things were not good in OB and hospital administration was responsible." Churchill specifically mentioned Davis, saying Davis "was ruining MDH." Perkins-Graham told Waters that she knew Waters and Davis "could not tolerate that kind of negativism."

Churchill's version of the conversation is different. For several months, Churchill had been concerned about the hospital's "cross-training" policy, under which nurses from one department could work in another when their usual location was overstaffed. Churchill believed this policy threatened patient care because it was designed not to train nurses but to cover staff shortages, and she had complained about this to Davis and Waters. According to Churchill, the conversation with Perkins-Graham primarily concerned the cross-training policy. Churchill denies that she said some of what Ballew and Perkins-Graham allege she said. She does admit she criticized Kathy Davis, saying her staffing policies threatened to "ruin" the hospital because they "seemed to be impeding nursing care." She claims she actually defended Waters and encouraged Perkins-Graham to transfer to obstetrics.

Koch's and Welty's recollections of the conversation match Churchill's. Davis and Waters, however, never talked to Koch or Welty about this, and they did not talk to Churchill until the time they told her she was fired. Moreover, Churchill claims, Ballew was biased against Churchill because of an incident in which Ballew apparently made an error and Churchill had to cover for her.

After she was discharged, Churchill filed an internal grievance. The president of the hospital, petitioner Stephen Hopper, met with Churchill in regard to this and heard her side of the story. He then reviewed Waters' and Davis' written reports of their conversations with Ballew and Perkins-Graham, and had Bernice Magin, the hospital's vice president of human resources, interview Ballew one more time. After considering all this, Hopper rejected Churchill's grievance.

Churchill then sued under 42 U.S.C. § 1983, claiming that the firing violated her First Amendment rights because her speech was protected under *Connick v. Myers*, 461 U.S. 138

(1983). In May 1991, the United States District Court for the Central District of Illinois granted summary judgment to petitioners. The Court held that neither version of the conversation was protected under *Connick*. . . . Therefore, the court held, management could fire Churchill for the conversation with impunity.

The United States Court of Appeals for the Seventh Circuit reversed. 977 F.2d 1114 (1992). The court held that Churchill's speech, viewed in the light most favorable to her, was protected speech under the *Connick* test: It was on a matter of public concern—"the hospital's [alleged] violation of state nursing regulations as well as the quality and level of nursing care it provides its patients," and it was not disruptive.

The court also concluded that the inquiry must turn on what the speech actually was, not on what the employer thought it was.

II

[1] There is no dispute in this case about when speech by a government employee is protected by the First Amendment.

The dispute is over how the factual basis for applying the test—what the speech was, in what tone it was delivered, what the listener's reactions were, is to be determined. Should the court apply the *Connick* test to the speech as the government employer found it to be, or should it ask the jury to determine the facts for itself? The Court of Appeals held that the employer's factual conclusions were irrelevant, and that the jury should engage in its own fact finding. Petitioners argue that the employer's factual conclusions should be dispositive. Respondents take a middle course: They suggest that the court should accept the employer's factual conclusions, but only if those conclusions were arrived at reasonably, something they say did not happen here.

We agree that it is important to ensure not only that the substantive First Amendment standards are sound, but also that they are applied through reliable procedures. This is why we have often held some procedures—a particular allocation of the burden of proof, a particular quantum of proof, a particular type of appellate review, and so on—to be constitutionally required in proceedings that may penalize protected speech. See *Freedman v. Maryland*, 380 U.S. 51 (1965) (government must bear burden of proving that speech is unprotected); *Philadelphia Newspapers, Inc. v. Hepps*, 475 U.S. 767 (1986) (libel plaintiff must bear burden of proving that speech is false); *Masson v. New Yorker Magazine, Inc.*, 501 U.S. 496 (1991) (actual malice must be proved by clear and convincing evidence); *Bose Corp. v. Consumers Union of United States, Inc.*, 466 U.S. 485 (1984) (appellate court must make independent judgment about presence of actual malice).

[2] These cases establish a basic First Amendment principle: Government action based on protected speech may under some circumstances violate the First Amendment even if the government actor honestly believes the speech is unprotected. . . .

Nonetheless, not every procedure that may safeguard protected speech is constitutionally mandated. True, the procedure adopted by the Court of Appeals may lower the chance of protected speech being erroneously punished. A speaker is more protected if she has two opportunities to be vindicated—first by the employer's investigation and then by the jury—than just one. But each procedure involves a different mix of administrative burden, risk of erroneous punishment of protected speech, and risk of erroneous exculpation of unprotected speech. Though the First Amendment creates a strong presumption against punishing protected speech even inadvertently, the balance need not always be struck in that direction. We have never, for instance, required proof beyond a reasonable doubt in civil cases where First Amendment interests are at stake, though such a requirement would protect speech more than the alternative standards would. . . .

We have never set forth a general test to determine when a procedural safeguard is required by the First Amendment—just as we have never set forth a general test to determine what constitutes a compelling state interest, see *Boos v. Barry*, 485 U.S. 312 (1988), or what categories of speech are so lacking in value that they fall outside the protection of the First Amendment, *New York v. Ferber,* 458 U.S. 747 (1982), or many other matters—and we do not purport to do so now. But though we agree with Justice Scalia that the lack of such a test is inconvenient, this does not relieve us of our responsibility to decide the case that is before us today. Both Justice Scalia and we agree that some procedural requirements are mandated by the First Amendment and some are not. None of us have discovered a general principle to determine where the line is to be drawn. We must therefore reconcile ourselves to answering the question on a case-by-case basis, at least until some workable general rule emerges.

[3] Accordingly, all we say today is that the propriety of a proposed procedure must turn on the particular context in which the question arises—on the cost of the procedure and the relative magnitude and constitutional significance of the risks it would decrease and increase. And to evaluate these factors here we have to return to the issue we dealt with in *Connick* and in the cases that came before it: What is it about the government's role as employer that gives it a freer hand in regulating the speech of its employees than it has in regulating the speech of the public at large?

B

[4] We have never explicitly answered this question, though we have always assumed that its premise is correct—that the government as employer indeed has far broader powers than does the government as sovereign. See, *Pickering,* supra, at 568 (1973); *Connick,* 461 U.S., at 147. This assumption is amply borne out by considering the practical realities of government employment, and the many situations in which, we believe, most observers would agree that the government must be able to restrict its employees' speech.

To begin with, even many of the most fundamental maxims of our First Amendment jurisprudence cannot reasonably be applied to speech by government employees. The First Amendment demands a tolerance of "verbal tumult, discord, and even offensive utterance,"

as "necessary side effects of . . . the process of open debate," *Cohen v. California,* 403 U.S. 15 (1971). But we have never expressed doubt that a government employer may bar its employees from using Mr. Cohen's offensive utterance to members of the public, or to the people with whom they work. "Under the First Amendment there is no such thing as a false idea," *Gertz,* supra, at 339, the "fitting remedy for evil counsels is good ones," *Whitney v. California,* 274 U.S. 357 (1927) (Brandeis, J., concurring). But when an employee counsels her coworkers to do their job in a way with which the public employer disagrees, her managers may tell her to stop, rather than relying on counter-speech. The First Amendment reflects the "profound national commitment to the principle that debate on public issues should be uninhibited, robust, and wide-open." *New York Times Co. v. Sullivan,* 376 U.S. 254 (1964). But though a private person is perfectly free to uninhibitedly and robustly criticize a state governor's legislative program, we have never suggested that the Constitution bars the governor from firing a high-ranking deputy for doing the same thing. Cf. *Branti v. Finkel,* 445 U.S. 507 (1980). Even something as close to the core of the First Amendment as participation in political campaigns may be prohibited to government employees. *Broadrick v. Oklahoma,* 413 U.S. 601 (1973); *Public Workers v. Mitchell,* 330 U.S. 75 (1947).

[5] Government employee speech must be treated differently with regard to procedural requirements as well. For example, speech restrictions must generally precisely define the speech they target. *Baggett v. Bullitt,* 377 U.S. 360, 367–368 (1964); *Hustler Magazine, Inc. v. Falwell,* 485 U.S. 46, 55 (1988). Yet surely a public employer may, consistently with the First Amendment, prohibit its employees from being "rude to customers," a standard almost certainly too vague when applied to the public at large. Cf. *Arnett v. Kennedy,* 416 U.S. 134, 158–162 (1974) (plurality opinion) (upholding a regulation that allowed discharges for speech which hindered the "efficiency of the service"); id., at 164 (Powell, J., concurring in part and concurring in result in part) (agreeing on this point).

Likewise, we have consistently given greater deference to government predictions of harm used to justify restriction of employee speech than to predictions of harm used to justify restrictions on the speech of the public at large. Few of the examples we have discussed involve tangible, present interference with the agency's operation. The danger in them is mostly speculative. One could make a respectable argument that political activity by government employees is generally not harmful, see *Public Workers v. Mitchell,* supra, 330 U.S. at 99, 67 S.Ct., at 569, or that high officials should allow more public dissent by their subordinates, see *Connick,* supra, 461 U.S., at 168–169 (Brennan, J., dissenting); Whistleblower Protection Act of 1989, 103 Stat. 16, or that even in a government workplace the free market of ideas is superior to a command economy. But we have given substantial weight to government employers' reasonable predictions of disruption, even when the speech involved is on a matter of public concern, and even though when the government is acting as sovereign our review of legislative predictions of harm is considerably less deferential. Compare, e.g., *Connick,* supra, at 151-152; *Letter Carriers,* supra, 413 U.S., at 566–567 with *Sable Communications of Cal., Inc. v. FCC,* 492 U.S. 115, 129 (1989); *Texas v. Johnson,* 491 U.S. 397, 409 (1989). Similarly, we have refrained from intervening in government employer decisions that are based on speech that is of entirely private concern. Doubtless some such speech is sometimes nondisruptive; doubtless it is sometimes of value to the speakers and the listeners. But we have declined to question government employers' decisions on such matters. *Connick,* supra, 461 U.S., at 146–149.

[6] This does not, of course, show that the First Amendment should play no role in government employment decisions. Government employees are often in the best position to know what ails the agencies for which they work; public debate may gain much from their informed opinions, *Pickering v. Board of Ed. of Township High School Dist.,* 391 U.S., at 572. And a government employee, like any citizen, may have a strong, legitimate interest in speaking out on public matters. In many such situations the government may have to make a substantial showing that the speech is, in fact, likely to be disruptive before it may be punished. See, e.g., *Rankin v. McPherson,* 483 U.S. 378, 388 (1987); *Connick,* 461 U.S., at 152; *Pickering,* supra, 391 U.S., at 569–571. Moreover, the government may certainly choose to give additional protections to its employees beyond what is mandated by the First Amendment, out of respect for the values underlying the First Amendment, values central to our social order as well as our legal system. See, e.g., Whistleblower Protection Act of 1989, supra.

[7] But the above examples do show that constitutional review of government employment decisions must rest on different principles than review of speech restraints imposed by the government as sovereign. The restrictions discussed above are allowed not just because the speech interferes with the government's operation. Speech by private people can do the same, but this does not allow the government to suppress it.

Rather, the extra power the government has in this area comes from the nature of the government's mission as employer. Government agencies are charged by law with doing particular tasks. Agencies hire employees to help do those tasks as effectively and efficiently as possible. When someone who is paid a salary so that she will contribute to an agency's effective operation begins to do or say things that detract from the agency's effective operation, the government employer must have some power to restrain her. The reason the governor may, in the example given above, fire the deputy is not that this dismissal would somehow be narrowly tailored to a compelling government interest. It is that the governor and the governor's staff have a job to do, and the governor justifiably feels that a quieter subordinate would allow them to do this job more effectively.

[8] The key to First Amendment analysis of government employment decisions, then, is this: The government's interest in achieving its goals as effectively and efficiently as possible is elevated from a relatively subordinate interest when it acts as sovereign to a significant one

when it acts as employer. The government cannot restrict the speech of the public at large just in the name of efficiency. But where the government is employing someone for the very purpose of effectively achieving its goals, such restrictions may well be appropriate.

C

1

The problem with the Court of Appeals' approach—under which the facts to which the *Connick* test is applied are determined by the judicial fact finder—is that it would force the government employer to come to its factual conclusions through procedures that substantially mirror the evidentiary rules used in court. The government manager would have to ask not what conclusions she, as an experienced professional, can draw from the circumstances, but rather what conclusions a jury would later draw. If she relies on hearsay, or on what she knows about the accused employee's character, she must be aware that this evidence might not be usable in court. If she knows one party is, in her personal experience, more credible than another, she must realize that the jury will not share that personal experience. If she thinks the alleged offense is so egregious that it is proper to discipline the accused employee even though the evidence is ambiguous, she must consider that a jury might decide the other way.

[9] But employers, public and private, often do rely on hearsay, on past similar conduct, on their personal knowledge of people's credibility, and on other factors that the judicial process ignores. Such reliance may sometimes be the most effective way for the employer to avoid future recurrences of improper and disruptive conduct. What works best in a judicial proceeding may not be appropriate in the employment context. If one employee accuses another of misconduct, it is reasonable for a government manager to credit the allegation more if it is consistent with what the manager knows of the character of the accused. Likewise, a manager may legitimately want to discipline an employee based on complaints by patrons that

the employee has been rude, even though these complaints are hearsay.

[10] On the other hand, we do not believe that the court must apply the *Connick* test only to the facts as the employer thought them to be, without considering the reasonableness of the employer's conclusions. Even in situations where courts have recognized the special expertise and special needs of certain decision-makers, the deference to their conclusions has never been complete. Cf. *New Jersey v. T.L.O.,* 469 U.S. 325, 342–343 (1985); *United States v. Leon,* 468 U.S. 897, 914 (1984); *Universal Camera Corp. v. NLRB,* 340 U.S. 474, 490–491 (1951). It is necessary that the decisionmaker reach its conclusion about what was said in good faith, rather than as a pretext; but it does not follow that good faith is sufficient. Justice Scalia is right in saying that we have often held various laws to require only an inquiry into the decisionmaker's intent, see post, at 1895, but, as discussed supra in Part II-A, this has not been our view of the First Amendment.

We think employer decision making will not be unduly burdened by having courts look to the facts as the employer reasonably found them to be. It may be unreasonable, for example, for the employer to come to a conclusion based on no evidence at all. Likewise, it may be unreasonable for an employer to act based on extremely weak evidence when strong evidence is clearly available—if, for instance, an employee is accused of writing an improper letter to the editor, and instead of just reading the letter, the employer decides what it said based on unreliable hearsay.

[11] If an employment action is based on what an employee supposedly said, and a reasonable supervisor would recognize that there is a substantial likelihood that what was actually said was protected, the manager must tread with a certain amount of care. This need not be the care with which trials, with their rules of evidence and procedure, are conducted. It should, however, be the care that a reasonable manager would use before making an employment decision—discharge, suspension, reprimand, or whatever else—of the sort involved in the particular case. Justice Scalia correctly points out

that such care is normally not constitutionally required unless the employee has a protected property interest in her job, post, at 1894; see also *Board of Regents of State Colleges v. Roth,* 408 U.S. 564, 576–578 (1972); but we believe that the possibility of inadvertently punishing someone for exercising her First Amendment rights makes such care necessary. . . .

Of course, there will often be situations in which reasonable employers would disagree about who is to be believed, or how much investigation needs to be done, or how much evidence is needed to come to a particular conclusion. In those situations, many different courses of action will necessarily be reasonable. Only procedures outside the range of what a reasonable manager would use may be condemned as unreasonable.

III

[13] Applying the foregoing to this case, it is clear that if petitioners really did believe Perkins-Graham's and Ballew's story, and fired Churchill because of it, they must win. Their belief, based on the investigation they conducted, would have been entirely reasonable. After getting the initial report from Ballew, who overheard the conversation, Waters and Davis approached and interviewed Perkins-Graham, and then interviewed Ballew again for confirmation. In response to Churchill's grievance, Hopper met directly with Churchill to hear her side of the story, and instructed Magin to interview Ballew one more time. Management can spend only so much of their time on any one employment decision. By the end of the termination process, Hopper, who made the final decision, had the word of two trusted employees, the endorsement of those employees' reliability by three hospital managers, and the benefit of a face-to-face meeting with the employee he fired. With that in hand, a reasonable manager could have concluded that no further time needed to be taken. As respondents themselves point out, "if the belief an employer forms supporting its adverse personnel action is 'reasonable,' an employer has no need to investigate further."

[14] And under the *Connick* test, Churchill's speech as reported by Perkins-Graham and Ballew was unprotected. Even if Churchill's criticism of cross-training reported by Perkins-Graham and Ballew was speech on a matter of public concern—something we need not decide—the potential disruptiveness of the speech as reported was enough to outweigh whatever First Amendment value it might have had. According to Ballew, Churchill's speech may have substantially dampened Perkins-Graham's interest in working in obstetrics. Discouraging people from coming to work for a department certainly qualifies as disruption. Moreover, Perkins-Graham perceived Churchill's statements about Waters to be "unkind and inappropriate," and told management that she knew they could not continue to "tolerate that kind of negativism" from Churchill. This is strong evidence that Churchill's complaining, if not dealt with, threatened to undermine management's authority in Perkins-Graham's eyes. And finally, Churchill's statement, as reported by Perkins-Graham, that it "wasn't possible" to "wipe the slate clean" between her and Waters could certainly make management doubt Churchill's future effectiveness. As a matter of law, this potential disruptiveness was enough to outweigh whatever First Amendment value the speech might have had.

[15] This is so even if, as Churchill suggests, Davis and Waters were "[d]eliberately [i]ndifferent," to the possibility that much of the rest of the conversation was solely about cross-training. So long as Davis and Waters discharged Churchill only for the part of the speech that was either not on a matter of public concern, or on a matter of public concern but disruptive, it is irrelevant whether the rest of the speech was, unbeknownst to them, both on a matter of public concern and nondisruptive. The *Connick* test is to be applied to the speech for which Churchill was fired. Cf. *Connick,* supra, 461 U.S., at 149, 103 S.Ct., at 1691 (evaluating the disruptiveness of part of plaintiff's speech because that part was "upon a matter of public concern and contributed to [plaintiff's] discharge" (emphasis added)); *Mt. Healthy,* supra, 429 U.S., at 286–287. An employee who makes an unprotected statement is not immunized from discipline by the fact that this statement is surrounded by protected statements.

Nonetheless, we agree with the Court of Appeals that the District Court erred in granting summary judgment in petitioners' favor. Though Davis and Waters would have been justified in firing Churchill for the statements outlined above, there remains the question whether Churchill was actually fired because of those statements, or because of something else. See *Mt. Healthy*, supra, at 286–287.

Rather, we vacate the judgment of the Court of Appeals and remand the case for further proceedings consistent with this opinion.

So ordered.

Justice Stevens, with whom Justice Blackmun joins, dissenting.

This is a free country. Every American has the right to express an opinion on issues of public significance. In the private sector, of course, the exercise of that right may entail unpleasant consequences. Absent some contractual or statutory provision limiting its prerogatives, a private-sector employer may discipline or fire employees for speaking their minds. The First Amendment, however, demands that the Government respect its employees' freedom to express their opinions on issues of public importance. As long as that expression is not unduly disruptive, it simply may not provide the basis for discipline or termination. The critical issues in a case of this kind are (1) whether the speech is protected, and (2) whether it was the basis for the sanction imposed on the employee.

Applying these standards to the case before us is quite straightforward. Everyone agrees that respondent Cheryl Churchill was fired because of what she said in a conversation with co-workers during a dinner break. Given the posture in which this case comes to us, we must assume that Churchill's statements were fully protected by the First Amendment. Nevertheless, the plurality concludes that a dismissal for speech is valid as a matter of law as long as the public employer reasonably believed that the employee's speech was unprotected. This conclusion is erroneous because it provides less protection for a fundamental constitutional right than the law ordinarily provides for less exalted rights, including contractual and statutory rights applicable in the private sector.

If, for example, a hospital employee had a contract providing that she could retain her job for a year if she followed the employer's rules and did competent work, that employee could not be fired because her supervisor reasonably but mistakenly believed she had been late to work or given a patient the wrong medicine. Ordinarily, when someone acts to another person's detriment based upon a factual judgment, the actor assumes the risk that an impartial adjudicator may come to a different conclusion. Our legal system generally delegates the determination of facts upon which important rights depend to neutral factfinders, notwithstanding the attendant risks of error and overdeterrence.

Federal constitutional rights merit at least the normal degree of protection. Doubts concerning the ability of juries to find the truth, an ability for which we usually have high regard, should be resolved in favor of, not against, the protection of First Amendment rights. See, e.g., *New York Times Co. v. Sullivan*, 376 U.S. 254, 279–280 (1964). Unfortunately, the plurality underestimates the importance of freedom of speech for the more than 18 million civilian employees of this country's Federal, State, and local Governments, and subordinates that freedom to an abstract interest in bureaucratic efficiency. The need for governmental efficiency that so concerns the plurality is amply protected by the substantive limits on public employees' rights of expression. See generally *Connick v. Myers*, 461 U.S. 138 (1983); *Pickering v. Board of Ed. of Township High School Dist.*, 391 U.S. 563 (1968). Efficiency does not demand an additional layer of deference to employers' "reasonable" factual errors. Today's ruling will surely deter speech that would be fully protected under *Pickering* and *Connick*.

The plurality correctly points out that we have never decided whether the governing version of the facts in public employment free speech cases is "what the government employer thought was said, or . . . what the trier of fact ultimately determines to have been said." Ante, at 1882. To me it is clear that the latter must be controlling. The First Amendment assures public employees that they may express their views on issues of public concern without fear of discipline or termination as long as they do so in an appropriate manner and at an appropriate time and place. A violation occurs when a public employee is fired for uttering speech on a matter of public concern that is not unduly disruptive of the operations of the relevant agency. The violation does not vanish merely because the firing was based upon a reasonable mistake about what the employee said. A First Amendment claimant need not allege bad faith; the controlling question is not the regularity of the agency's investigative procedures, or the purity of its motives, but whether the employee's freedom of speech has been "abridged."

The risk that a jury may ultimately view the facts differently from even a conscientious employer, is not, as the plurality would have it, a needless fetter on public employers' ability to discharge their duties. It is the normal means by which our legal system protects legal rights and encourages those in authority to act with care. Here, for example, attention to "conclusions a jury would later draw," ante, at 1888, about the content of Churchill's speech might have caused petitioners to talk to Churchill about what she said before deciding to fire her. There is nothing unfair or onerous about putting the risk of error on an employer in these circumstances.

Government agencies are often the site of sharp differences over a wide range of important public issues. In offices where the First Amendment commands respect for candid deliberation and individual opinion, such disagreements are both inevitable and desirable. When those who work together disagree, reports of speech are often skewed, and supervisors are apt to misconstrue even accurate reports. The plurality, observing that managers "can spend only so much of their time on any one employment decision," ante, at 1890, adopts a rule that invites discipline, rather than further discussion, when such disputes arise. That rule is unwise, for deliberation within the government, like deliberation about it, is an essential part of our "profound national commitment" to the freedom of speech. Cf. New York Times, 376 U.S., at 270. A proper regard for that principle requires that, before firing a public employee for her speech, management get its facts straight.

I would affirm the judgment of the Court of Appeals.

Cleveland Board of Education v. Loudermill
470 U.S. 532 (1985)

Justice White delivered the opinion of the Court, joined by Chief Justice Burger and Justices Blackmun, Powell, Stevens, and O'Connor. Justice Marshall concurred, Justice Brennan concurred in part and dissented in part, and Justice Rehnquist dissented.

In these cases we consider what pretermination process must be accorded a public employee who can be discharged only for cause.

I

In 1979 the Cleveland Board of Education, petitioner in No. 83–1362, hired respondent James Loudermill as a security guard. On his job application, Loudermill stated that he had never been convicted of a felony. Eleven months later, as part of a routine examination of his employment records, the Board discovered that in fact Loudermill had been convicted of grand larceny in 1968. By letter dated November 3, 1980, the Board's Business Manager informed Loudermill that he had been dismissed because of his dishonesty in filling out the employment application. Loudermill was not afforded an opportunity to respond to the charge of dishonesty or to challenge his dismissal. On November 13, the Board adopted a resolution officially approving the discharge. Under Ohio law, Loudermill was a "classified civil servant." Such employees can be terminated only for cause, and may obtain administrative review if discharged. Pursuant to this provision, Loudermill filed an appeal with the Cleveland Civil Service Commission on November 12. The Commission appointed a referee, who held a hearing on January 29, 1981. Loudermill argued that he had thought that his 1968 larceny conviction was for a misdemeanor rather than a felony. The referee recommended reinstatement. On July 20, 1981, the full Commission heard argument and orally announced that it would uphold the dismissal. Proposed findings of fact and conclusions of law followed on August 10, and Loudermill's attorneys were advised of the result by mail on August 21.

Although the Commission's decision was subject to judicial review in the state courts, Loudermill instead brought the present suit in the Federal District Court for the Northern District of Ohio. The complaint alleged that § 124.34 was unconstitutional on its face because it did not provide the employee an opportunity to respond to the charges against him prior to removal. As a result, discharged employees were deprived of liberty and property without due process. The complaint also alleged that the provision was unconstitutional as applied because discharged employees were not given sufficiently prompt postremoval hearings. . . .

The Due Process Clause provides that certain substantive rights—life, liberty, and property—cannot be deprived except pursuant to constitutionally adequate procedures. The categories of substance and procedure are distinct. Were the rule otherwise, the Clause would be reduced to a mere tautology. "Property" cannot be defined by the procedures provided for its deprivation any more than can life or liberty. The right to due process "is conferred, not by legislative grace, but by constitutional guarantee. While the legislature may elect not to confer a property interest in [public] employment, it may not constitutionally authorize the deprivation of such an interest, once conferred, without appropriate procedural safeguards."

In short, once it is determined that the Due Process Clause applies, "the question remains what process is due." *Morrissey v. Brewer,* 408 U.S. 471, 481 (1972). The answer to that question is not to be found in the Ohio statute.

III

An essential principle of due process is that a deprivation of life, liberty, or property "be preceded by notice and opportunity for hearing appropriate to the nature of the case." *Mullane v. Central Hanover Bank & Trust Co.,* 339 U.S. 306 (1950). We have described "the root requirement" of the Due Process Clause as being "that an individual be given an opportunity for a hearing before he is deprived of any significant property interest." *Boddie v. Connecticut,* 401 U.S. 371 (1971). This principle requires "some kind of a hearing" prior to the discharge of an employee who has a constitutionally protected property interest in his employment. . . .

The need for some form of pretermination hearing, recognized in these cases, is evident from a balancing of the competing interests at stake. These are the private interests in retaining employment, the governmental interest in the expeditious removal of unsatisfactory employees and the avoidance of administrative burdens, and the risk of an erroneous termination. See *Mathews v. Eldridge,* 424 U.S. 319, 335 (1976).

First, the significance of the private interest in retaining employment cannot be gainsaid. We have frequently recognized the severity of depriving a person of the means of livelihood. While a fired worker may find employment elsewhere, doing so will take some time and is likely to be burdened by the questionable circumstances under which he left his previous job.

Second, some opportunity for the employee to present his side of the case is recurringly of obvious value in reaching an accurate decision. Dismissals for cause will often involve factual disputes. Even where the facts are clear, the appropriateness or necessity of the discharge may not be; in such cases, the only meaningful opportunity to invoke the discretion of the decisionmaker is likely to be before the termination takes effect. See *Goss v. Lopez,* 419 U.S., at 583–584. . . .

The cases before us illustrate these considerations. Both respondents had plausible arguments to make that might have prevented their discharge. The fact that the Commission saw fit to reinstate Donnelly suggests that an error might have been avoided had he been provided an opportunity to make his case to the Board. As for Loudermill, given the Commission's ruling we cannot say that the discharge was mistaken. Nonetheless, in light of the referee's recommendation, neither can we say that a fully informed decisionmaker might not have exercised its discretion and decided not to dismiss him, notwithstanding its authority to do so. In any event, the termination involved arguable issues, and the right to a hearing does not depend on a demonstration of certain success.

Loudermill's dismissal turned not on the objective fact that he was an ex-felon or the inaccuracy of his statement to the contrary, but on the subjective question whether he had lied on his application form. His explanation for the false statement is plausible in light of the fact that he received only a suspended 6-month sentence and a fine on the grand larceny conviction.

The governmental interest in immediate termination does not outweigh these interests. As we shall explain, affording the employee an opportunity to respond prior to termination would impose neither a significant administrative burden nor intolerable delays. Furthermore, the employer shares the employee's interest in avoiding disruption and erroneous decisions; and until the matter is settled, the employer would continue to receive the benefit of the employee's labors. It is preferable to keep a qualified employee on than to train a new one. A governmental employer also has an interest in keeping citizens usefully employed rather than taking the possibly erroneous and counterproductive step of forcing its employees onto the welfare rolls. Finally, in those situations where the employer perceives a significant hazard in keeping the employee on the job, it can avoid the problem by suspending with pay. . . .

IV

The foregoing considerations indicate that the pretermination "hearing," though necessary,

need not be elaborate. We have pointed out that "[t]he formality and procedural requisites for the hearing can vary, depending upon the importance of the interests involved and the nature of the subsequent proceedings." In general, "something less" than a full evidentiary hearing is sufficient prior to adverse administrative action. *Mathews v. Eldridge,* 424 U.S., at 343. Under state law, respondents were later entitled to a full administrative hearing and judicial review. The only question is what steps were required before the termination took effect.

In only one case, *Goldberg v. Kelly,* 397 U.S. 254 (1970), has the Court required a full adversarial evidentiary hearing prior to adverse governmental action. However, as the *Goldberg* Court itself pointed out, that case presented significantly different considerations than are present in the context of public employment. Here, the pretermination hearing need not definitively resolve the propriety of the discharge. It should be an initial check against mistaken decisions—essentially, a determination of whether there are reasonable grounds to believe that the charges against the employee are true and support the proposed action. See *Bell v. Burson,* 402 U.S., at 540. . . .

The essential requirements of due process, and all that respondents seek or the Court of Appeals required, are notice and an opportunity to respond. The opportunity to present reasons, either in person or in writing, why proposed action should not be taken is a fundamental due process requirement. See Friendly, "Some Kind of Hearing," 123 U.Pa.L.Rev. 1267, 1281 (1975). The tenured public employee is entitled to oral or written notice of the charges against him, an explanation of the employer's evidence, and an opportunity to present his side of the story. To require more than this prior to termination would intrude to an unwarranted extent on the government's interest in quickly removing an unsatisfactory employee.

VI

We conclude that all the process that is due is provided by a pretermination opportunity to respond, coupled with post-administrative procedures as provided by the Ohio statute. Because respondents allege in their complaints that they had no chance to respond, the District Court erred in dismissing for failure to state a claim. The judgment of the Court of Appeals is affirmed, and the case is remanded for further proceedings consistent with this opinion.

Board of County Commissioners, Wabaunsee County v. Umbehr
518 U.S. 669 (1996)

Justice O'Connor delivered the opinion of the Court, joined by Chief Justice Rehnquist (except for a small part of the opinion which he disagreed with) and Justices Stevens, Kennedy, Souter, Ginsburg, and Breyer. Justice Scalia's dissent was joined by Justice Thomas.

This case requires us to decide whether, and to what extent, the First Amendment protects independent contractors from the termination of at-will government contracts in retaliation for their exercise of the freedom of speech.

I

Under state law, Wabaunsee County, Kansas (County) is obliged to provide for the disposal of solid waste generated within its borders. In 1981, and, after renegotiation, in 1985, the County contracted with respondent Umbehr for him to be the exclusive hauler of trash for cities in the county at a rate specified in the contract. Each city was free to reject or, on 90 days' notice, to opt out of, the contract. By its terms, the contract between Umbehr and the County was automatically renewed annually unless either party terminated it by giving notice at least 60 days before the end of the year or a renegotiation was instituted on 90 days' notice. Pursuant to the contract, Umbehr hauled trash for six of the County's seven cities from 1985 to 1991 on an exclusive and uninterrupted basis.

During the term of his contract, Umbehr was an outspoken critic of petitioner, the Board of County Commissioners of Wabaunsee County (Board), the three-member governing body of the County. Umbehr spoke at the Board's meetings, and wrote critical letters and editorials in local newspapers regarding the County's landfill user rates, the cost of obtaining official documents from the County, alleged violations by the Board of the Kansas Open Meetings Act, the County's alleged mismanagement of taxpayers' money, and other topics. His allegations of violation of the Kansas Open Meetings Act were vindicated in a consent decree signed by the Board's members. Umbehr also ran unsuccessfully for election to the Board.

The Board's members allegedly took Umbehr's criticism badly, threatening the official county newspaper with censorship for publishing his writings. In 1990, they voted, 2-to-1, to terminate (or prevent the automatic renewal of) Umbehr's contract with the County. That attempt at termination failed because of a technical defect, but in 1991, the Board succeeded in terminating Umbehr's contract, again by a 2-to-1 vote. Umbehr subsequently negotiated new contracts with five of the six cities that he had previously served.

In 1992, Umbehr brought this suit against the two majority Board members in their individual and official capacities under 42 U.S.C. § 1983, alleging that they had terminated his government contract in retaliation for his criticism of the County and the Board. The Board members moved for summary judgment. The District Court . . . held that . . . as an independent contractor, Umbehr was not entitled to the First Amendment protection afforded to public employees. *Umbehr v. McClure,* 840 F.Supp. 837, 839 (D.Kan.1993).

The United States Court of Appeals for the Tenth Circuit reversed holding that "an independent contractor is protected under the First

Amendment from retaliatory governmental action, just as an employee would be."

We agree with the Tenth Circuit that independent contractors are protected, and that the *Pickering* balancing test, adjusted to weigh the government's interests as contractor rather than as employer, determines the extent of their protection. We therefore affirm.

II

This Court has not previously considered whether and to what extent the First Amendment restricts the freedom of federal, state, or local governments to terminate their relationships with independent contractors because of the contractors' speech. We have, however, considered the same issue in the context of government employees' rights on several occasions. The similarities between government employees and government contractors with respect to this issue are obvious. The government needs to be free to terminate both employees and contractors for poor performance, to improve the efficiency, efficacy and responsiveness of service to the public, and to prevent the appearance of corruption. And, absent contractual, statutory or constitutional restriction, the government is entitled to terminate them for no reason at all. But either type of relationship provides a valuable financial benefit, the threat of the loss of which in retaliation for speech may chill speech on matters of public concern by those who, because of their dealings with the government, "are often in the best position to know what ails the agencies for which they work," *Waters v. Churchill,* 114 S.Ct. 1878. Because of these similarities, we turn initially to our government employment precedents for guidance.

Those precedents have long since rejected Justice Holmes' famous dictum, that a policeman "may have a constitutional right to talk politics, but he has no constitutional right to be a policeman," *McAuliffe v. Mayor of New Bedford,* 29 N.E. 517 (1892). Recognizing that "constitutional violations may arise from the deterrent, or 'chilling,' effect of governmental [efforts] that fall short of a direct prohibition against the exercise of First Amendment rights,"

Laird v. Tatum, 408 U.S. 1 (1972), our modern "unconstitutional conditions" doctrine holds that the government "may not deny a benefit to a person on a basis that infringes his constitutionally protected . . . freedom of speech" even if he has no entitlement to that benefit, *Perry v. Sindermann,* 408 U.S. 593 (1972). We have held that government workers are constitutionally protected from dismissal for refusing to take an oath regarding their political affiliation, *Wieman v. Updegraff,* 344 U.S. 183 (1952); *Keyishian v. Board of Regents of Univ. of State of N.Y.,* 385 U.S. 589 (1967), for publicly or privately criticizing their employer's policies, see *Perry,* supra; for expressing hostility to prominent political figures, see *Rankin v. McPherson,* 483 U.S. 378 (1987), or, except where political affiliation may reasonably be considered an appropriate job qualification, for supporting or affiliating with a particular political party, see, *Branti v. Finkel,* 445 U.S. 507 (1980). See also *United States v. Treasury Employees,* 115 S.Ct. 1310 (1995) (government employees are protected from undue burdens on their expressive activities created by a prohibition against accepting honoraria); *Abood v. Detroit Bd. of Ed.,* 431 U.S. 209 (1977) (government employment cannot be conditioned on making or not making financial contributions to particular political causes).

While protecting First Amendment freedoms, we have, however, acknowledged that the First Amendment does not create property or tenure rights, and does not guarantee absolute freedom of speech. The First Amendment's guarantee of freedom of speech protects government employees from termination because of their speech on matters of public concern. See *Connick v. Myers,* 461 U.S. 138 (1983) (speech on merely private employment matters is unprotected). To prevail, an employee must prove that the conduct at issue was constitutionally protected, and that it was a substantial or motivating factor in the termination. If the employee discharges that burden, the government can escape liability by showing that it would have taken the same action even in the absence of the protected conduct. See *Mt. Healthy,* supra. And even termination because of protected speech may be justified when legitimate countervailing government interests are sufficiently strong. Government employees' First Amendment rights depend on the "balance between the interests of the [employee], as a citizen, in commenting upon matters of public concern and the interest of the State, as an employer, in promoting the efficiency of the public services it performs through its employees." *Pickering*, 391 U.S., at 568. In striking that balance, we have concluded that "[t]he government's interest in achieving its goals as effectively and efficiently as possible is elevated from a relatively subordinate interest when it acts as sovereign to a significant one when it acts as employer." *Waters*, 114 S.Ct., at 1888 (plurality opinion). We have, therefore, "consistently given greater deference to government predictions of harm used to justify restriction of employee speech than to predictions of harm used to justify restrictions on the speech of the public at large." Id., at 114 S.Ct., at 1887; . . .

Both parties observe that independent contractors in general, and Umbehr in particular, work at a greater remove from government officials than do most government employees. In the Board's view, the key feature of an independent contractor's contract is that it does not give the government the right to supervise and control the details of how work is done. The Board argues that the lack of day-to-day control accentuates the government's need to have the work done by someone it trusts, and to resort to the sanction of termination for unsatisfactory performance. Umbehr, on the other hand, argues that the government interests in maintaining harmonious working environments and relationships recognized in our government employee cases are attenuated where the contractor does not work at the government's workplace and does not interact daily with government officers and employees. He also points out that to the extent that he is publicly perceived as an independent contractor, any government concern that his political statements will be confused with the government's political positions is mitigated. The Board and the dissent retort that the cost of fending off litigation, and the potential for government contracting practices to ossify into prophylactic rules to avoid potential litigation and liability, outweigh the interests of independent contractors, who are typically less financially dependent on their government contracts than are government employees.

Each of these arguments for and against the imposition of liability has some force. But all of them can be accommodated by applying our existing framework for government employee cases to independent contractors. *Mt. Healthy* assures the government's ability to terminate contracts so long as it does not do so in retaliation for protected First Amendment activity. *Pickering* requires a fact-sensitive and deferential weighing of the government's legitimate interests. The dangers of burdensome litigation and the de facto imposition of rigid contracting rules necessitate attentive application of the *Mt. Healthy* requirement of proof of causation and substantial deference, as mandated by *Pickering*, *Connick*, and *Waters*, to the government's reasonable view of its legitimate interests, but not a per se denial of liability. Nor can the Board's and the dissent's generalization that independent contractors may be less dependent on the government than government employees, justify denial of all First Amendment protection to contractors. The tests that we have established in our government employment cases must be judicially administered with sensitivity to governmental needs, but First Amendment rights must not be neglected. . . .

We therefore see no reason to believe that proper application of the *Pickering* balancing test cannot accommodate the differences between employees and independent contractors.

In sum, neither the Board nor Umbehr have persuaded us that there is a "difference of constitutional magnitude," 414 U.S., at 83, between independent contractors and employees in this context. Independent government contractors are similar in most relevant respects to government employees, although both the speaker's and the government's interests are typically—though not always—somewhat less strong in the independent contractor case. We therefore conclude that the same form of balancing analysis should apply to each. . . .

III

Finally, we emphasize the limited nature of our decision today. Because Umbehr's suit concerns the termination of a pre-existing commercial relationship with the government, we need not address the possibility of suits by bidders or applicants for new government contracts who cannot rely on such a relationship.

Subject to these limitations and caveats, however, we recognize the right of independent government contractors not to be terminated for exercising their First Amendment rights. The judgment of the Court of Appeals is, therefore, affirmed, and the case is remanded for proceedings consistent with this opinion.

It is so ordered.

Pennsylvania State Police v. Nancy Drew Suders
542 U.S. 129 (2004)

The facts are contained in the opinion written by Justice Ginsburg, joined by Justices Rehnquist, Stevens, O'Connor, Scalia, and Breyer. Justice Thomas dissented.

Plaintiff-respondent Nancy Drew Suders alleged sexually harassing conduct by her supervisors, officers of the Pennsylvania State Police (PSP), of such severity she was forced to resign. The question presented concerns the proof burdens parties bear when a sexual harassment/constructive discharge claim of that character is asserted under Title VII of the Civil Rights Act of 1964.

To establish hostile work environment, plaintiffs like Suders must show harassing behavior "sufficiently severe or pervasive to alter the conditions of [their] employment." *Meritor Savings Bank v. Vinson,* 477 U.S. 57, 67 (1986); see *Harris v. Forklift Systems, Inc.,* 510 U.S. 17, 22 (1993) ("[T]he very fact that the discriminatory conduct was so severe or pervasive that it created a work environment abusive to employees because of their . . . gender . . . offends Title VII's broad rule of workplace equality."). Beyond that, we hold, to establish "constructive discharge," the plaintiff must make a further showing: She must show that the abusive working environment became so intolerable that her resignation qualified as a fitting response. An employer may defend against such a claim by showing both (1) that it had installed a readily accessible and effective policy for reporting and

resolving complaints of sexual harassment, and (2) that the plaintiff unreasonably failed to avail herself of that employer-provided preventive or remedial apparatus. This affirmative defense will not be available to the employer, however, if the plaintiff quits in reasonable response to an employer-sanctioned adverse action officially changing her employment status or situation, for example, a humiliating demotion, extreme cut in pay, or transfer to a position in which she would face unbearable working conditions. In so ruling today, we follow the path marked by our 1998 decisions in *Burlington Industries, Inc. v. Ellerth,* 524 U.S. 742, and *Faragher v. Boca Raton,* 524 U.S. 775.

I

Because this case was decided against Suders in the District Court on the PSP's motion for summary judgment, we recite the facts, as summarized by the Court of Appeals, in the light most favorable to Suders. In March 1998, the PSP hired Suders as a police communications operator for the McConnellsburg barracks. Suders' supervisors were Sergeant Eric D. Easton, Station Commander at the McConnellsburg barracks, Patrol Corporal William D. Baker, and Corporal Eric B. Prendergast. Those three supervisors subjected Suders to a continuous barrage of sexual harassment that ceased only when she resigned from the force.

Easton "would bring up [the subject of] people having sex with animals" each time

Suders entered his office. He told Prendergast, in front of Suders, that young girls should be given instruction in how to gratify men with oral sex. Easton also would sit down near Suders, wearing spandex shorts, and spread his legs apart. Apparently imitating a move popularized by television wrestling, Baker repeatedly made an obscene gesture in Suders' presence by grabbing his genitals and shouting out a vulgar comment inviting oral sex. Baker made this gesture as many as five-to-ten times per night throughout Suders' employment at the barracks. Suders once told Baker she "'d[id]n't think [he] should be doing this'"; Baker responded by jumping on a chair and again performing the gesture, with the accompanying vulgarity. Further, Baker would "rub his rear end in front of her and remark 'I have a nice ass, don't I?'" Prendergast told Suders "'the village idiot could do her job'"; wearing black gloves, he would pound on furniture to intimidate her.

In June 1998, Prendergast accused Suders of taking a missing accident file home with her. After that incident, Suders approached the PSP's Equal Employment Opportunity Officer, Virginia Smith-Elliott, and told her she "might need some help." Smith-Elliott gave Suders her telephone number, but neither woman followed up on the conversation. On August 18, 1998, Suders contacted Smith-Elliott again, this time stating that she was being harassed and was afraid. Smith-Elliott told Suders to file a complaint, but did not tell her how to obtain the necessary form. Smith-Elliott's response and the manner in which it was conveyed appeared to Suders insensitive and unhelpful. Two days later, Suders' supervisors arrested her for theft, and Suders resigned from the force. The theft arrest occurred in the following circumstances. Suders had several times taken a computer-skills exam to satisfy a PSP job requirement. Each time, Suders' supervisors told her that she had failed. Suders one day came upon her exams in a set of drawers in the women's locker room. She concluded that her supervisors had never forwarded the tests for grading and that their reports of her failures were false. Regarding the tests as her property, Suders removed them from the locker room. Upon finding that the

exams had been removed, Suders' supervisors devised a plan to arrest her for theft. The officers dusted the drawer in which the exams had been stored with a theft-detection powder that turns hands blue when touched. As anticipated by Easton, Baker, and Prendergast, Suders attempted to return the tests to the drawer, whereupon her hands turned telltale blue. The supervisors then apprehended and handcuffed her, photographed her blue hands, and commenced to question her. Suders had previously prepared a written resignation, which she tendered soon after the supervisors detained her. Nevertheless, the supervisors initially refused to release her. Instead, they brought her to an interrogation room, gave her warnings under *Miranda v. Arizona,* 384 U.S. 436 (1966), and continued to question her. Suders reiterated that she wanted to resign, and Easton then let her leave. The PSP never brought theft charges against her.

In September 2000, Suders sued the PSP in Federal District Court, alleging, inter alia, that she had been subjected to sexual harassment and constructively discharged, in violation of Title VII of the Civil Rights Act of 1964. At the close of discovery, the District Court granted the PSP's motion for summary judgment. Suders' testimony, the District Court recognized, sufficed to permit a trier of fact to conclude that the supervisors had created a hostile work environment. The court nevertheless held that the PSP was not vicariously liable for the supervisors' conduct. . . . Suders' hostile work environment claim was untenable as a matter of law, the District Court stated, because she "unreasonably failed to avail herself of the PSP's internal procedures for reporting any harassment." Resigning just two days after she first mentioned anything about harassment to Equal Employment Opportunity Officer Smith-Elliott, the court noted, Suders had "never given [the PSP] the opportunity to respond to [her] complaints." The District Court did not address Suders' constructive discharge claim. . . .

The Court of Appeals for the Third Circuit reversed and remanded the case for disposition on the merits. The Third Circuit agreed with the District Court that Suders had presented evidence sufficient for a trier of fact to conclude that the supervisors had engaged in a "pattern of sexual harassment that was pervasive and regular." . . . The Court of Appeals then made the ruling challenged here: It held that "a constructive discharge, when proved, constitutes a tangible employment action." Under *Ellerth* and *Faragher,* the court observed, such an action renders an employer strictly liable and precludes employer recourse to the affirmative defense announced in those decisions. The Third Circuit recognized that the Courts of Appeals for the Second and Sixth Circuits had ruled otherwise. A constructive discharge resulting from a supervisor-created hostile work environment, both Circuits had held, does not qualify as a tangible employment action, and therefore does not stop an employer from invoking the *Ellerth/Faragher* affirmative defense. . . . The Third Circuit, however, reasoned that a constructive discharge "'constitutes a significant change in employment status' by ending the employer-employee relationship" and "also inflicts the same type of 'direct economic harm'" as the tangible employment actions *Ellerth* and *Faragher* offered by way of example (discharge, demotion, undesirable reassignment). Satisfied that Suders had "raised genuine issues of material fact as to her claim of constructive discharge," and that the PSP was "precluded from asserting the affirmative defense to liability advanced in support of its motion for summary judgment," the Court of Appeals remanded Suders' Title VII claim for trial.

This Court granted certiorari to resolve the disagreement among the Circuits on the question whether a constructive discharge brought about by supervisor harassment ranks as a tangible employment action and therefore precludes assertion of the affirmative defense articulated in *Ellerth* and *Faragher.* . . . We conclude that an employer does not have recourse to the *Ellerth/Faragher* affirmative defense when a supervisor's official act precipitates the constructive discharge; absent such a "tangible employment action," however, the defense is available to the employer whose supervisors are charged with harassment. We therefore vacate the Third Circuit's judgment and remand the case for further proceedings.

II

A

Under the constructive discharge doctrine, an employee's reasonable decision to resign because of unendurable working conditions is assimilated to a formal discharge for remedial purposes. . . . The inquiry is objective: Did working conditions become so intolerable that a reasonable person in the employee's position would have felt compelled to resign?

The constructive discharge concept originated in the labor-law field in the 1930's; the National Labor Relations Board (NLRB) developed the doctrine to address situations in which employers coerced employees to resign, often by creating intolerable working conditions, in retaliation for employees' engagement in collective activities. . . . Although this Court has not had occasion earlier to hold that a claim for constructive discharge lies under Title VII, we have recognized constructive discharge in the labor-law context, . . . We agree with the lower courts and the EEOC that Title VII encompasses employer liability for a constructive discharge.

B

This case concerns an employer's liability for one subset of Title VII constructive discharge claims: constructive discharge resulting from sexual harassment, or "hostile work environment," attributable to a supervisor. Our starting point is the framework *Ellerth* and *Faragher* established to govern employer liability for sexual harassment by supervisors. As earlier noted, . . . those decisions delineate two categories of hostile work environment claims: (1) harassment that "culminates in a tangible employment action," for which employers are strictly liable, . . . (2) harassment that takes place in the absence of a tangible employment action, to which employers may assert an affirmative defense . . . With the background set out above in mind, we turn to the key issues here at stake: Into which *Ellerth/Faragher* category do hostile-environment constructive discharge claims fall—and what proof burdens do the parties bear in such cases.

The Law of Public Employment • 393

In *Ellerth* and *Faragher,* the plaintiffs-employees sought to hold their employers vicariously liable for sexual harassment by their supervisors, even though the plaintiffs "suffer[ed] no adverse, tangible job consequences." Setting out a framework for employer liability in those decisions, this Court noted that Title VII's definition of "employer" includes the employer's "agent[s]." We viewed that definition as a direction to "interpret Title VII based on agency principles." . . . We then identified "a class of cases where, beyond question, more than the mere existence of the employment relation aids in commission of the harassment: when a supervisor takes a tangible employment action against the subordinate." A tangible employment action, the Court explained, "constitutes a significant change in employment status, such as hiring, firing, failing to promote, reassignment with significantly different responsibilities, or a decision causing a significant change in benefits." Unlike injuries that could equally be inflicted by a co-worker, we stated, tangible employment actions "fall within the special province of the supervisor," who "has been empowered by the company as . . . [an] agent to make economic decisions affecting other employees under his or her control." The tangible employment action, the Court elaborated, is, in essential character, "an official act of the enterprise, a company act." It is "the means by which the supervisor brings the official power of the enterprise to bear on subordinates." Often, the supervisor will "use [the company's] internal processes" and thereby "obtain the imprimatur of the enterprise." Ordinarily, the tangible employment decision "is documented in official company records, and may be subject to review by higher level supervisors." In sum, we stated, "when a supervisor takes a tangible employment action against a subordinate[,] . . . it would be implausible to interpret agency principles to allow an employer to escape liability." When a supervisor's harassment of a subordinate does not culminate in a tangible employment action, the Court next explained, it is "less obvious" that the agency relation is the driving force. We acknowledged that a supervisor's "power and

authority invests his or her harassing conduct with a particular threatening character, and in this sense, a supervisor always is aided by the agency relation." But we also recognized that "there are acts of harassment a supervisor might commit which might be the same acts a coemployee would commit, and there may be some circumstances where the supervisor's status [would] mak[e] little difference."

An "aided-by-the-agency-relation" standard, the Court suggested, was insufficiently developed to press into service as the standard governing cases in which no tangible employment action is in the picture. . . . Accordingly, we held that when no tangible employment action is taken, the employer may defeat vicarious liability for supervisor harassment by establishing, as an affirmative defense, both that "the employer exercised reasonable care to prevent and correct promptly any sexually harassing behavior," and that "the plaintiff employee unreasonably failed to take advantage of any preventive or corrective opportunities provided by the employer or to avoid harm otherwise."

Ellerth and *Faragher* also clarified the parties' respective proof burdens in hostile environment cases. Title VII, the Court noted, "borrows from tort law the avoidable consequences doctrine," under which victims have "a duty 'to use such means as are reasonable under the circumstances to avoid or minimize the damages' that result from violations of the statute." The *Ellerth/Faragher* affirmative defense accommodates that doctrine by requiring plaintiffs reasonably to stave off avoidable harm. But both decisions place the burden squarely on the defendant to prove that the plaintiff unreasonably failed to avoid or reduce harm. . . .

Suders' claim is of the same genre as the hostile work environment claims the Court analyzed in *Ellerth* and *Faragher*. Essentially, Suders presents a "worse case" harassment scenario, harassment ratcheted up to the breaking point. Like the harassment considered in our path-marking decisions, harassment so intolerable as to cause a resignation may be effected through co-worker conduct, unofficial supervisory conduct, or official company acts. Unlike an actual termination, which is always effected through an official act of the company, a constructive discharge need not be. A constructive discharge involves both an employee's decision to leave and precipitating conduct: The former involves no official action; the latter, like a harassment claim without any constructive discharge assertion, may or may not involve official action. . . .

We note, finally, two recent Court of Appeals decisions that indicate how the "official act" (or "tangible employment action") criterion should play out when constructive discharge is alleged. Both decisions advance the untangled approach we approve in this opinion. In *Reed v. MBNA Marketing Systems, Inc.,* 333 F.3d 27 (CA1 2003), the plaintiff claimed a constructive discharge based on her supervisor's repeated sexual comments and an incident in which he sexually assaulted her. The First Circuit held that the alleged wrongdoing did not preclude the employer from asserting the *Ellerth/Faragher* affirmative defense. As the court explained in *Reed,* the supervisor's behavior involved no official actions. Unlike, "e.g., an extremely dangerous job assignment to retaliate for spurned advances," the supervisor's conduct in *Reed* "was exceedingly unofficial and involved no direct exercise of company authority"; indeed, it was "exactly the kind of wholly unauthorized conduct for which the affirmative defense was designed." In contrast, in *Robinson v. Sappington,* 351 F.3d 317 (CA7 2003), after the plaintiff complained that she was sexually harassed by the judge for whom she worked, the presiding judge decided to transfer her to another judge, but told her that "her first six months [in the new post]

probably would be 'hell,'" and that it was in her "'best interest to resign.'" The Seventh Circuit held that the employer was precluded from asserting the affirmative defense to the plaintiff's constructive discharge claim. The *Robinson* plaintiff's decision to resign, the court explained, "resulted, at least in part, from [the presiding judge's] official actio[n] in transferring" her to a judge who resisted placing her on his staff. The courts in *Reed* and *Robinson* properly recognized that *Ellerth* and *Faragher,* which divided the universe of supervisor-harassment claims according to the presence or absence of an official act, mark the path constructive discharge claims based on harassing conduct must follow. . . .

. . . Following *Ellerth* and *Faragher,* the plaintiff who alleges no tangible employment action has the duty to mitigate harm, but the defendant bears the burden to allege and prove that the plaintiff failed in that regard. The plaintiff might elect to allege facts relevant to mitigation in her pleading or to present those facts in her case in chief, but she would do so in anticipation of the employer's affirmative defense, not as a legal requirement.

We agree with the Third Circuit that the case, in its current posture, presents genuine issues of material fact concerning Suders' hostile work environment and constructive discharge claims.[11] We hold, however, that the Court of Appeals erred in declaring the affirmative defense described in *Ellerth* and *Faragher* never available in constructive discharge cases. Accordingly, we vacate the Third Circuit's judgment and remand the case for further proceedings consistent with this opinion.

---

[11] Although most of the discriminatory behavior Suders alleged involved unofficial conduct, the events surrounding her computer-skills exams were less obviously unofficial.

NOTES

1. Because it takes, say, five years to get tenure, employment consists of 5 one-year contracts until the tenure decision.

2. 434 F.Supp. 1273 (D. Del., 1977).

3. 469 F.2d 829 (5th Cir., 1972).

4. 439 U.S. 410 (1979).

5. 548 F.2d 857 (9th Cir., 1977).

6. 473 F.2d 988 (2d Cir., 1973).

7. Steven Cann, "A Virus in the Ivory Tower," 18 *Educational Considerations* 43 (1991).

8. Robert Pear, "Financial Problems in Government Are Rife, Nation's Top Auditor Says," *New York Times,* January 18, 2001, p. A12.

9. Cann, "A Virus," p. 44.

10. For an early interpretation that the Court has continued to sustain, see *Lindsley v. Natural Carbonic Gas Company,* 220 U.S. 61, 78 (1911).

11. *Railway Express Agency v. New York,* 336 U.S. 106 (1949).

12. *Williamson v. Lee Optical Company,* 348 U.S. 483 (1955).

13. *New Orleans v. Dukes,* 427 U.S. 297 (1976).

14. *Reed v. Reed,* 404 U.S. 71 (1971).

15. *Frantinero v. Richardson,* 411 U.S. 677 (1973).

16. *Kahn v. Shevin,* 416 U.S. 351 (1974).

17. *Craig v. Borne,* 429 U.S. 190 (1976).

18. *Massachusetts Board of Retirement v. Murgia,* 427 U.S. 307 (1976).

19. *Ambach v. Norwick,* 441 U.S. 68 (1979).

20. *Bernal v. Fainter,* 467 U.S. 216 (1984).

21. *Fullilove v. Klutznick,* 448 U.S. 448 (1980).

22. 466 U.S. 429 (1984).

23. Kevin Sack, "To Vestige of Black Farmers, Bias Settlement Is Too Late," *The New York Times,* June 1, 1999, p. A1.

24. David Kocieniewski and Robert Hanley, "Racial Profiling Was the Routine, New Jersey Finds," *The New York Times,* November 28, 2000, p. A1; Jessica Bruder, "Progress for State Police," *The New York Times,* July 25, 2004, p. 6.

25. *Washington v. Davis,* 426 U.S. 229 (1976).

26. 347 U.S. 483 (1954).

27. *Brown v. Board of Education* has been in litigation almost constantly since 1954. The Supreme Court, in a 1955 implementation decision, said desegregation had to be implemented "with all deliberate speed" (*Brown II,* 349 U.S. 294 [1955]). There was a *Brown III* in the 1970s (892 F.2d 851 [1979]), and *Brown IV* in the 1980s (892 F.2d 851 [10th Cir., 1989]). In *Brown IV,* the district court found no purposeful discrimination, but the circuit court did. The Supreme Court sent the case back to the circuit court, *Brown v. Board of Education,* 503 U.S. 978 (1992), in light of its recent decision in *Board of Education of Oklahoma City Public Schools v. Dowell,* 498 U.S. 237 (1991). On October 28, 1992, the Tenth Circuit Court of Appeals, after reconsidering *Brown IV,* once again found the requisite purposeful discrimination. The Topeka School Board decided not to litigate further and adopted a magnet school plan for the primary schools. It was not until the summer of 1999 that the Topeka school district was finally found to be in compliance with the 1954 *Brown* decision. The case is still titled *Brown v. Board of Education,* because Linda Brown, the lead child-plaintiff in the original case, had two children who were plaintiffs. See Steven Cann, "Politics in Brown and White: Resegregation in America," 88(2) *Judicature* 74, 76–77 (2004).

28. *Shaw v. Reno,* 509 U.S. 630 (1993); *Miller v. Johnson,* 515 U.S. 900 (1995).

29. *Gratz v. Bollinger,* 539 U.S. 244 (2003).

30. *Grutter v. Bollinger,* 539 U.S. 306 (2003).

31. *United Steelworkers of America v. Weber,* 443 U.S. 193 (1979).

32. *Local 28 Sheet Metal Workers Union v. Equal Employment Opportunity Commission,* 478 U.S. 421 (1986).

33. *United Steelworkers of America v. Weber,* 443 U.S. 193 (1979).

34. *Griggs v. Duke Power Company,* 401 U.S. 424 (1971).

35. *Wards Cove Packing v. Atonio,* 490 U.S. 642 (1989).

36. Adam Clymer, "White House and Senate Republicans Reach Agreement on Civil Rights Bill," *The New York Times* [national edition], October 25, 1991, p. A10; Adam Clymer, "Senate Approves Rights Bill, Ending Bitter Job-Bias Rift," *The New York Times* [national edition], October 31, 1991, p. A10; Adam Clymer, "Civil Rights Bill Is Passed by House," *The New York Times* [national edition], November 18, 1991, p. A10.

37. Robert D. Lee Jr. and Paul S. Greenlaw, "Employer Liability for Employee Sexual Harassment: A Judicial Policy-Making Study," 60 *Public Administration Review* 124 (March/April 2000).

38. Kenneth Meier and Vicky Wilkins, "Gender Differences in Agency Head Salaries: The Case of Public Education," 62(4) *Public Administration Review* 405, 407 (July–August 2002).

39. Ibid., p. 125.

40. Ibid., p. 126.

41. Ibid., p. 128.

42. *Hicks v. Miranda,* 422 U.S. 332 (1975); *McCarthy v. Philadelphia Civil Service Commission,* 424 U.S. 645 (1976).

9

DUE PROCESS OF LAW
IN OTHER CONTEXTS

Case in Point:
Mathews v. Eldridge
424 U.S. 319 (1976)

There was a somewhat notorious ward boss in the Tammany Hall machine whose name was George Washington Plunkett. In response to reporters' questions about enriching himself through Tammany Hall graft and corruption, Mr. Plunkett would simply reply, "I seen my opportunities and I took 'em."

In the case of *Mathews v. Eldridge,* the Supreme Court "seen its opportunity" and took it. The four Nixon appointees (Burger, Blackmun, Powell, and Rehnquist) coalesced with Justices White and Stewart to restrict what had become known as the due process revolution.

The due process revolution started with a landmark case called *Goldberg v. Kelly.*[1] In that case, New York welfare officials sent a termination of benefits notice to a recipient of Aid to Families With Dependent Children (AFDC). The procedure required the notice and allowed for an internal paper review; if the beneficiary lost at that stage, benefits would cease, but there could be a posttermination adjudicatory hearing. The issue in *Goldberg* was whether the due process clause of the Fourteenth Amendment requires a pretermination hearing under these circumstances (i.e., prior to termination of benefits). The Court answered in the affirmative.

Despite the specific language of the due process clause, there are several circumstances in which government can take property without holding a due process hearing first. Those situations include the summary seizure of mislabeled vitamins,[2] the seizure of food inventory suspected of being spoiled,[3] the freezing of rents during and after World War II,[4] the destruction of an imported ornamental tree,[5] the disqualification of a contractor doing business with the federal government,[6] and firing a cook for a concession in a defense contractor's plant.[7] Most of these summary takings of property are justified as threats to the public health or safety or are emergency situations, and the Court has said that a postdeprivation hearing or a "just compensation" lawsuit satisfies the due process clause.

After the *Goldberg* decision in 1970, however, the Court decided a series of cases, all of which required a predeprivation hearing and constituted the due process revolution. Those cases involved the revocation of parole,[8] probation,[9] and good time credit for inmates;[10] the suspension of a driver's license;[11] and a suspension from high school.[12] The Court also required a due process hearing before the state of Wisconsin could publicly post the names of people deemed unfit to consume alcohol[13] and before a state could evict people from a public housing project.[14] Hearings were required before the state could play a role in the repossession of property[15] or the garnishment of wages,[16] and the Court said it violated the due process clause for a state to prohibit a student from establishing residency to reduce tuition while attending college (this created the unconstitutional, unrebuttable presumption that once a noncitizen, always a noncitizen).[17]

Against this background of expanding due process protections for citizens adversely affected by government action, *Mathews v. Eldridge* was decided.

George Eldridge dropped out of school in the fifth grade and went to work as a laborer for a railroad until he got drafted into the military.[18] While in the military, he was involved in an accident in a military jeep. After his military discharge, Eldridge went back to work for the railroad in the early 1950s. By then, he had been diagnosed with spinal arthritis, but lacking enough education to find less strenuous work and facing the financial pressure of providing for his family, Eldridge saw no choice but to keep working hard. Eventually, he quit the railroad and took a job as a deliveryman for Royal Crown Cola. He worked for that company for about eight years; then, one day when he got down from his truck, he was unable to move his legs. He was hospitalized for over a month and eventually developed diabetes as well. Eldridge applied for disability benefits in 1967, and his application was denied, a decision that was upheld in an internal paper reconsideration process. Eldridge asked for and received a hearing before an administrative law judge, whose decision reversed the denial of benefits, and in June 1968, Eldridge was placed on disability benefits. About a year later, he received a notice from the disability office asking him to submit evidence that he was still disabled. This he did. In early 1970, he was notified that he was no longer disabled, and his benefits would cease in February. By this time, Eldridge owed a mortgage on a house; he had six children, and his wife had cancer. He immediately started the reconsideration and appeals process, but he knew from his first experience with the agency that it would take at least a year to get to the administrative law judge. From his perspective, he had proved that he was totally disabled; he knew that he could not work and nothing had changed. He thought he should have a right to make his case to someone before the government shut off his income, so while continuing the appeals process, he went to see a lawyer. Eldridge's lawyer filed suit in federal district court, arguing that disability beneficiaries have a constitutional right to a due process hearing prior to the termination of benefits.

In June 1970, the trial judge ordered the Social Security Administration (SSA) to continue benefits to Eldridge until the case was decided. From February to June 1970, the Eldridge family survived on his $136-a-month disability check from the Veterans Administration (VA). Mrs. Eldridge died of cancer in June of that year. As the lawsuit moved through the court, the appeals process continued at the SSA. In March 1971, Eldridge finally got his second hearing before an administrative law judge, albeit a different judge from the 1968 hearing, who also declared Eldridge to be totally disabled, ordered the benefits to continue, and ordered back pay. As a result of this decision, the district court judge declared Eldridge's case to be moot and dismissed the suit.

In May 1972, Eldridge received another letter from the SSA asking him to submit proof of his continuing disability. Once again, he filled out the papers, included the names of treating physicians, and sent along a rather calm letter, given the circumstances. In his letter, Eldridge reminded the SSA that he had documented his total disability twice in the past four years and that nothing had changed since then. He also clarified that the ailment he suffered from was arthritis of the spine, rather than the "strained back" the SSA had claimed, and he admonished the agency to check its own records on that score.

Nevertheless, in June 1972, the SSA informed Eldridge that his benefits were to be terminated because he was no longer disabled. This time, rather than going through the internal review process, he just went to court. The issue was the same as it had been in the first suit: whether the Constitution required an oral hearing before disability benefits could be terminated.

In April 1973, the district court judge entered a decision in Eldridge's favor based on the Supreme Court's decision in *Goldberg* and its progeny.[19] The SSA appealed to the Fourth Circuit Court of Appeals, which in April 1974 upheld the district court decision in favor of Eldridge.[20] The SSA appealed to the U.S. Supreme Court, which handed down a decision in the spring of 1976.

Justice Powell's decision applied a balancing test that involved three considerations: First, there is a need to analyze the private interest involved. In this case, the private interest was Eldridge's property interest in continued disability benefits. According to Powell, although this indeed involved a property interest under the due process clause, it was not the same kind of property interest that was involved in *Goldberg*. *Goldberg* involved benefits that a recipient had to show poverty to receive. Almost by definition, the termination of those benefits would leave one destitute. Because disability benefits do not depend on income or need, it does not necessarily follow that the termination of disability benefits would leave one without a means of support.

The second consideration was what Justice Powell termed "the risk of an erroneous decision." Here, the Court reasoned that the risk of error was high in AFDC termination cases but was very low in disability termination cases. That is because of the nature of the evidence. Evidence that an AFDC beneficiary is no longer eligible might be based on hearsay and very subjective, whereas evidence of a disability is scientific and not likely to produce erroneous decisions.

The third consideration is the balance between all of the preceding and the government's (people's?) interest. Here, administrative efficiency and the cost to the taxpayers of requiring a pretermination hearing should be considered, given the benefits of such a hearing.

Weighing all of these factors in Eldridge's case, the Court concluded that (a) the property interest of disability claimants, as a class, were not as acute as the property interests of AFDC beneficiaries; (b) the risk of making an erroneous decision in disability termination cases was minimal and would not be reduced by adding more procedural requirements; and (c) the government's interests were substantial enough that a posttermination hearing in disability cases would satisfy the due process requirements.

With the announcement of the Court's decision in Eldridge's case, he initiated the internal appeals process again to see if he could get his benefits restored. His case was reconsidered within the agency a year and a half after he made the appeal, and that decision, again, upheld his termination.[21] In March 1978, two years after the Court's decision, George received his third hearing before an administrative law judge. The judge again declared Eldridge to be totally disabled and ordered restoration of benefits with back pay.[22] During his fight with the SSA over his disability, the bank had foreclosed on Eldridge's home loan. He and his six children moved into a trailer, but their furniture was repossessed, so they all had to sleep in one bed.[23]

Questions

1. Does the evidence from Eldridge's case support the Court's conclusion that an erroneous decision in disability cases is unlikely? What do you make of the Court's test, given that administrative law judges overturn 50 percent of SSA determinations that claimants are not disabled? What does that say about the "nature of evidence and unlikelihood of error"?
2. In your opinion, is this case an example of judicial activism or a case of judicial self-restraint? Why?
3. At the time, Solicitor General Robert Bork told the Court in his brief that if Eldridge won and the government had to continue to pay benefits to those terminated until after they had a hearing, it would cost taxpayers an additional $25 million a year. Assuming that Bork's figures are correct and given the suffering of George Eldridge (and hundreds like him), is it cost-efficient to provide the predetermination hearing? Why or why not?

DUE PROCESS AND YOUR POTENTIAL FUTURE

If you are reading this book, you are probably in a political science, public administration, or prelaw class of some kind. Given that the average liberal arts college graduate changes careers (not just jobs) four times, even if you are not thinking about public service right now, you may end up at some point working for the government. You will discover in the next chapter that as a government employee, you may be sued as a consequence of decisions you make. One of the constitutional tests involving whether a government employee has incurred liability is whether the employee knew or should have known that his or her actions would violate the constitutional rights of another. This test presumes that the employee knows and understands the Constitution and constitutional rights.

The constitutional right most frequently involved in such suits is the due process clause. That is why this book spends two chapters on it. It would be nice to be able to assure you that after mastery of a few principles, you will understand due process, but the concept is too slippery for that. Actually, it is not that the concept itself is so difficult but that changes of personnel on the Supreme Court have led to inconsistent decisions and confusing opinions.

Due process analysis is fairly straightforward. It consists of answering the following questions:

1. Is there state action?

2. Is there a liberty or a property interest involved?

3. If the answer to the first two questions is yes, then how much process is due?

STATE ACTION

We have discussed elsewhere that the prohibitions of the Fourteenth Amendment (against violating due process, equal protection, or the privileges and immunities of citizenship) only protect a citizen against the actions of government. Neither the Fourteenth Amendment nor any civil rights legislation passed to enforce it will apply to the actions of a private individual or entity.

Therefore, in any due process litigation, the first question to ask is who took the action that caused the injury that led to the suit. If a government acted, then the court can proceed with further due process analysis. If the injury was caused by a private entity, then the due process suit is over.

Normally, you would think it is easy to tell whether an actor is the government or a private entity. However, government has become more involved in what used to be private spheres of activity, and governments are more frequently relying on private entities to implement government policy. Increasingly, as government turns to privatization and outsourcing, the issue of whether action is private or government has been obfuscated.

Two early cases during the civil rights movement began the process of creating a doctrine that clothes private individuals with a sufficient connection to government that private activity can fall under the jurisdiction of the Fourteenth Amendment. This concept is referred to as *state action.* In one of those early cases, the Supreme Court said that a state court could not enforce a private contract to discriminate on the basis of race.[24] In the second case, the Court found that a privately owned coffee shop that refused to serve blacks was a state actor. The coffee shop was located in a government-owned parking garage, and there were intricate landlord-tenant issues.[25]

If your local power company cut off your electricity without notifying you or giving you an opportunity to discuss it, would that be a due process violation? The power company would not exist if it were not for its government-sanctioned monopoly, so is the power company a private or a government actor? Do you have a property or a liberty interest in the electric current that runs into your house? The answer is no; the power company is a private entity, so you have no due process rights in dealing with it.[26] However, you should begin to realize how complicated theses issues can become. If in your state, you do have a right to notice from the utility company before it terminates service, it is because the bureaucracy that regulates the company has imposed that requirement.

The Court decided that in spite of a long history of government regulation, a Moose Lodge lounge and dining room that refused to serve a black guest was not a state actor, hence there could be no equal protection suit.[27] However, the black plaintiff could have pursued a 1964 Civil Rights Act suit against the Moose Lodge. All he would have had to show was that the organization had a substantial effect on interstate commerce, and he would have won the suit. The Court has also said that neither the U.S. Olympic Committee[28] nor the National Collegiate Athletic Association (NCAA)[29] is a state actor.

You have probably heard about a "patients' bill of rights," and your doctor may be part of a health maintenance organization (HMO). An interesting case in this area is *Grijalva v. Shalala,* 152 F. 3d. 1115 (1998); the Circuit Court decision in the first round is found at the end of this chapter. People who have reached retirement age and qualify for social security also have medical coverage in the form of Medicare. There are two ways to access medical care coverage under Medicare. First is the fee-for-service route. Here, the patient goes to a private health care provider, and the government reimburses either the patient or the health care provider for reasonable costs. More recently, the government has added an

HMO option. Under this plan, no up-front cash or service is at risk. The government pays the HMO a contracted fee per enrollee, and the HMO can decide which medical services it will cover. The HMOs are guided by statute and heavily regulated in their partnership with the Department of Health and Human Services (HHS). In 1993, several retirees who were enrolled in the HMO plan sued the secretary because their HMO refused to cover certain services without notice or predeprivation hearing. In *Grijalva*, one of the main issues is whether the HMO is a private or a state actor.

Because of the actions of HMOs, the movement for a patients' bill of rights has gained momentum. The various legislative proposals for such a bill of rights would impose some sort of due process on the HMOs, whether the courts will or not. Both Democrats and Republicans agree on the need for a patients' bill of rights, but at the beginning of the 21st century, they are still fighting over whether to allow patients to sue an HMO, so there is no legislation. The *graveman* of the complaint in the *Grijalva* case is that the patients allege that they were not provided with a notice and opportunity to present evidence before the HMO made adverse decisions. They want a due process predeprivation hearing, but they have a constitutional right to one only if the HMO is a state actor and there exists a liberty and property interest.

On the same day in 1982, the Supreme Court decided two state action cases. In *Blum v. Yaretsky,*[30] the Court said that a utilization review committee was not a state actor in a 7 to 2 decision. A utilization review committee is composed of private physicians who make recommendations to the state about the proper level of nursing home care for the Medicaid program (Medicaid is government health care for the poor). When a utilization review committee decided that Yaretsky needed a lesser level of nursing home care, he sued under the due process clause, and he lost.

More significant, in *Lugar v. Edmondson Oil Co.,*[31] the Court created a test to determine when private action becomes state action. In a 5 to 4 decision, the Court decided that a private creditor was a state actor when it secured a prejudgment attachment of a debtor's property. That is, the creditor took the debtor's property without due process of law, and because the creditor was a state actor, the debtor won the case. The Court created a two-pronged test to tell when the actions of private people are clothed with state action. The first prong of the test is *whether the claimed constitutional deprivation resulted from the exercise of a right or privilege having its source in state authority.* The second prong of the test is *whether the party charged with the deprivation can in all fairness be described as a state actor.* There are three variables the Court uses in analyzing the second prong of the test:

1. the extent to which the private actor relied on government assistance or benefits

2. whether the actor is performing a traditional government function

3. whether the injury caused is aggravated in a unique way by the incidence of government authority

In 1988, the Court applied the test to decide whether a doctor who contracted with a state prison to perform medical services was a state actor when he refused to perform surgery on an inmate.[32] The Court, in a unanimous decision, said that he was a state actor. In 1991, in a 6 to 3 decision, the Court found that a private attorney in a civil law suit was a state actor. In *Edmonson v. Leesville Concrete Co.,*[33] the attorney for a defendant in a simple negligence case exercised two of his three preemptory challenges to exclude blacks from sitting on a jury where the plaintiff was black. Because the attorney was a state actor, his actions violated both the due process and equal protection clauses of the Constitution.

Of more relevance to the *Grijalva* case is *American Manufacturer's Mutual Insurance Company v. Sullivan,* 526 U.S. 40 (1999). In an 8 to 1 decision, but with a lot of concurring opinions, the Court determined that a utilization review organization is not a state actor. This case, which appears later in this chapter, involves the workers' compensation program in Pennsylvania. Normally, under workers' compensation programs, once an employee is found to have a work-related injury, there is no argument about liability or fault. Either the employer pays into a state fund that pays the medical bills, or in some states, employers are required to carry private insurance. Pennsylvania has the latter, but it revised the law to allow for utilization review organizations. When an employer's insurance company receives a bill from a workers' compensation case, it can have the organization review the bills and medical history of the injured worker to assess the "reasonableness" and "necessity" of continuing the treatment of the employee. This review takes place before the insurance company has to pay any medical bills. If an injured worker has had treatment and the utilization review organization decides it was unreasonable or unnecessary, you know who gets stuck with the bill. Also, any further medical treatment will not be paid for by the employer's insurer. The injured worker is provided no notice or hearing before the utilization review organization's decision. The issue, similar to the one in *Grijalva* and the HMO, was whether the organization was a private actor, immune from the due process requirements, or whether it is clothed with state action; the Court said it was a private actor. Furthermore, the Court went on to say that injured workers have no property interests in workers' compensation treatment. The utilization review organization is simply a group of private health care providers, but its relationship to the state's workers' compensation program is not as involved and partnership-like as the HMO's relationship to the implementation of the Medicare program.

In *Grijalva,* the district court found the HMO to be a state actor and ordered the secretary of health and human services to write new regulations increasing due process protection. The circuit court of appeals agreed, but the Supreme Court kicked the case back down to the appellate court for consideration, in an action not inconsistent with its decision in *American Manufacturers Mutual Insurance.* The circuit court kicked it back down to the original district court.

Let me stress again that as state, local, and federal governments expand privatization and contracting out of government services, more and more decisions that affect people's lives will be made by private entities looking out for the bottom line. In more and more lawsuits, the question will be whether the action of a private party is really private or whether the action is clothed with government action.

The public situation is even worse than this suggests. Increasingly, the public administration literature documents and discusses *quasi-governments* and *hybrid organizations.* These entities range from official government agencies that have governing bodies from the private sector (the Federal Reserve Board or the Legal Services Corporation) to private entities that perform government functions (HMO review boards or the Federal Home Loan Mortgage Corporation, Freddie Mac). Ronald Moe has categorized these hundreds of entities as follows:

1. quasi-official agencies

2. government-sponsored enterprises

3. federally funded research and development corporations

4. agency-related nonprofit organizations

5. venture capital funds

6. congressionally chartered nonprofit organizations

7. instrumentalities of indeterminate character[34]

Pause for a moment and contemplate category No. 7. These entities defy categorization or description. Moe notes that a quasi-government entity ignited the American Revolution. The British East India Company was a private corporation authorized by the British government to exploit the British colonies for private gain and profit. The company collected taxes, which led to the Boston Tea Party, which led to . . . [35] Moe's point is that in current American government, these quasi-governments are mostly unaccountable to political bodies that must stand for election. What is of more concern is that Moe's article is limited to a discussion of the federal government. It did not consider all of the similar activity at the state and local level. More to the point for this text, the more the U.S. Supreme Court refuses to clothe these entities with state action, the more our democracy is threatened.

LIBERTY OR PROPERTY INTEREST

You are already familiar with the notion of liberty and property interests from the previous chapter. Liberty and property interests are derived from the language of the two due process clauses in the Fifth and Fourteenth Amendments: "No person shall be . . . deprived of life, liberty or property without due process of law." For administrative law, we know that agencies cannot inhibit your liberty or the use of your property without a notice and some kind of hearing. The Constitution does not tell us, however, which liberties or properties are to receive due process protection. As a practical matter, that means that on any given day in any given due process suit, a coalition of five justices of the Supreme Court gets to decide which liberties are in and which are out. Ditto for property. It might be nice if I could tell you that the Court had created a test to determine which interests get protection, but no such test exists. You will be reading some of the classic administrative law due process cases in the following pages, and you will get a feel for the kinds of liberty and property interests that are and are not protected. As you read the cases, bear in mind that protected interests are created by transitory majorities on the Court. Each new appointee can change the contour or direction of due process jurisprudence.

The due process revolution was created by the Warren Court during the late 1950s and into the next decade. It ended with four Nixon appointees, who ultimately produced a majority in *Mathews v. Eldridge* and created the balancing test that would soon end the due process revolution. Today, four Reagan/Bush appointees (Scalia, O'Connor, Kennedy, and Thomas) plus the Chief Justice are even more conservative and hostile toward due process claims than were the Nixon appointees who stopped the revolution. The Court today is unwilling to recognize new liberties that might receive protection, and the same can be said for property interests. The conservative justices seem unable to create a coalition that can overrule precedent, so whatever was protected prior to the *Eldridge* case is still protected, but few if any new liberty or property interests have received protection since the 1976 decision in *Mathews v. Eldridge*. The case of *Gilbert v. Homar,* which you read in the last chapter, is typical of the current Court's treatment of due process claims. While recognizing that the plaintiff had a property interest in that he was not a probationary employee, the Court refused to extend due process protection to him when he was wrongly suspended without pay. Indeed, Justice Scalia's majority opinion is unwilling to concede that the due process protections apply at all to employee discipline less severe than termination, a matter most of us thought was well settled the other way long ago.

Two recent cases might appear to cast some doubt on the conservative justices' hostility to due process claims. In 2000, the Court declared that a Washington statute violated due process. The Washington law expanded the rights of people other than parents to obtain court-ordered visitation with children. Grandparents initiated court action to get more visitation with their grandchildren than the mother wanted to allow. The Court said the Washington law violated the mother's liberty interest in making decisions concerning the care, custody, and control of her children.[36]

Lawrence v. Texas[37] generated a fair amount of publicity at the time it was decided. In 1986, the Supreme Court decided that Georgia's sodomy law did not violate the Constitution. In the *Lawrence* case in 2003, the Court said that a Texas sodomy law violated due process as it invaded the two men's liberty interest of privacy. As indicated above, the conservative bloc of the Court does not have the votes to eliminate liberty interests that existed prior to 1976. Liberty interests in privacy and privacy within the family context have been recognized for quite some time.

A case that flows directly from the events of 9/11 was decided in the summer of 2004, *Hamdi v. Rumsfeld.*[38] Hamdi was an American citizen who had never lived in the United States, but rather in Saudi Arabia. He was caught in Afghanistan during the American invasion subsequent to 9/11. Afghan forces said he was armed and turned him over to the American military. Hamdi said he was in Afghanistan doing missionary work. He was transferred to military prisons in America and held as an enemy combatant, and he was denied legal representation and the opportunity to challenge his status as an enemy combatant. His father filed a habeas corpus petition, and the trial judge ordered the government to produce evidence of Hamdi's enemy status for an in-chambers inspection. The government refused and appealed. The Supreme Court said Hamdi had a right to challenge his enemy status and sent the case back to district court for a due process hearing on the issue. The government chose not to present its case and released Hamdi back to Saudi Arabia.

The two cases that follow both deal with the same liberty interest, a right to the continued use of an individual's good name. The disposition of the cases illustrates the disparate treatment of liberty interests during and after the due process revolution.

Wisconsin v. Constantineau
400 U.S. 433 (1971)

Justice Douglas delivered the opinion of the Court, joined by Justices Brennan, Stewart, White, and Marshall. Chief Justice Burger dissented, joined by Justices Blackmun and Black.

Appellee is an adult resident of Hartford, Wis. She brought suit in a federal district court in Wisconsin to have a Wisconsin statute declared unconstitutional. A three-judge court was convened. That court, by a divided vote, held the Act unconstitutional, 302 F.Supp. 861, and we noted probable jurisdiction. . . .

The Act, Wis.Stat. § 176.26 (1967), provides that designated persons may in writing forbid the sale or gift of intoxicating liquors to one who "by excessive drinking" produces described conditions or exhibits specified traits, such as exposing himself or family "to want" or becoming "dangerous to the peace" of the community. The chief of police of Hartford, without notice or hearing to appellee, caused to be posted a notice in all retail liquor outlets in Hartford that sales or gifts of liquors to appellee were forbidden for one year. Thereupon this suit was brought against the chief of police claiming damages and asking for injunctive relief. The State of Wisconsin intervened as a defendant on the injunctive phase of the case and that was the only issue tried and decided, the three-judge court holding the Act unconstitutional on its face and enjoining its enforcement. The court said: "In 'posting' an individual, the particular city official or spouse is doing more than denying him the ability to purchase alcoholic beverages within the city limits. In essence, he is giving notice to the public that he has found the particular individual's behavior to fall within one of the categories enumerated in the statutes. It would be naive not to recognize that such 'posting' or characterization of an individual will expose him to public embarrassment and ridicule, and it is our opinion that procedural due process requires that before one acting pursuant to State statute can make such a quasi-judicial determination, the individual involved must be given notice of the intent to post and an opportunity to present his side of the matter."

We have no doubt as to the power of a State to deal with the evils described in the Act. The police power of the States over intoxicating liquors was extremely broad even prior to the Twenty-First Amendment. The only issue present here is whether the label or characterization given a person by "posting," though a mark of serious illness to some, is to others such a stigma or badge of disgrace that procedural due process requires notice and an opportunity to be heard. We agree with the District Court that the private interest is such that those requirements of procedural due process must be met.

It is significant that most of the provisions of the Bill of Rights are procedural, for it is procedure that marks much of the difference between rule by law and rule by fiat.

We reviewed in *Cafeteria and Restaurant Workers Union, Local 473, A.F.L.-C.I.O. v.*

McElroy, 367 U.S. 886, the nature of the various "private interest(s)" that have fallen on one side or the other of the line. See also *Sniadach v. Family Finance Corp.,* 395 U.S. 337. Generalizations are hazardous as some state and federal administrative procedures are summary by reason of necessity or history. Yet certainly where the State attaches "a badge of infamy" to the citizen, due process comes into play. *Wieman v. Updegraff,* 344 U.S. 183. "[T]he right to be heard before being condemned to suffer grievous loss of any kind, even though it may not involve the stigma and hardships of a criminal conviction, is a principle basic to our society." *Joint Anti-Fascist Refugee Committee v. McGrath,* 341 U.S. 123.

Where a person's good name, reputation, honor, or integrity is at stake because of what the government is doing to him, notice and an opportunity to be heard are essential. "Posting" under the Wisconsin Act may to some be merely the mark of illness, to others it is a stigma, an official branding of a person. The label is a degrading one. Under the Wisconsin Act, a resident of Hartford is given no process at all. This appellee was not afforded a chance to defend herself. She may have been the victim of an official's caprice. Only when the whole proceedings leading to the pinning of an unsavory label on a person are aired can oppressive results be prevented.

It is suggested that the three-judge court should have stayed its hand while the aggrieved person repaired to the state courts to obtain a construction of the Act or relief from it. The fact that Wisconsin does not raise the point does not, of course, mean that it lacks merit. Yet the suggestion is not in keeping with the precedents.

Congress could, of course, have routed all federal constitutional questions through the state court systems, saving to this Court the final say when it came to review of the state court judgments. But our First Congress resolved differently and created the federal court system and in time granted the federal courts various heads of jurisdiction, which today involve most federal constitutional rights. Once that jurisdiction was granted, the federal courts resolved those questions even when they were enmeshed with state law questions.

In the present case the Wisconsin Act does not contain any provision whatsoever for notice and hearing. There is no ambiguity in the state statute. There are no provisions which could fairly be taken to mean that notice and hearing might be given under some circumstances or under some construction but not under others. The Act on its face gives the chief of police the power to do what he did to the appellee. Hence the naked question, uncomplicated by an unresolved state law, is whether that Act on its face is unconstitutional. As we said in *Zwickler v. Koota,*

389 U.S. 241, abstention should not be ordered merely to await an attempt to vindicate the claim in a state court. Where there is no ambiguity in the state statute, the federal court should not abstain but should proceed to decide the federal constitutional claim. We would negate the history of the enlargement of the jurisdiction of the federal district courts, if we held the federal court should stay its hand and not decide the question before the state courts decided it.

Affirmed.

Paul v. Davis
424 U.S. 693 (1976)

Justice Rehnquist delivered the opinion of the Court, joined by Chief Justice Burger and Justices Stewart, Blackmun, Powell, and Stevens. Justices Brennan, Marshall, and White dissented.

We granted certiorari, in this case to consider whether respondent's charge that petitioners' defamation of him, standing alone and apart from any other governmental action with respect to him, stated a claim for relief under 42 U.S.C. § 1983 and the Fourteenth Amendment. For the reasons hereinafter stated, we conclude that it does not.

Petitioner Paul is the Chief of Police of the Louisville, Ky., Division of Police, while petitioner McDaniel occupies the same position in the Jefferson County, Ky., Division of Police. In late 1972 they agreed to combine their efforts for the purpose of alerting local area merchants to possible shoplifters who might be operating during the Christmas season. In early December petitioners distributed to approximately 800 merchants in the Louisville metropolitan area a "flyer," which began as follows: "TO: BUSINESS MEN IN THE METROPOLITAN AREA. The Chiefs of the Jefferson County and City of Louisville Police Departments, in an effort to keep their officers advised on shoplifting activity, have approved the attached alphabetically arranged flyer of subjects known to be active in this criminal field. This flyer is being distributed

to you, the business man, so that you may inform your security personnel to watch for these subjects. These persons have been arrested during 1971 and 1972 or have been active in various criminal fields in high density shopping areas. Only the photograph and name of the subject is shown on this flyer, if additional information is desired, please forward a request in writing."

The flyer consisted of five pages of "mug shot" photos, arranged alphabetically. Each page was headed:

"NOVEMBER 1972
CITY OF LOUISVILLE
JEFFERSON COUNTY
POLICE DEPARTMENTS
ACTIVE SHOPLIFTERS"

In approximately the center of page 2 there appeared photos and the name of the respondent, Edward Charles Davis III.

Respondent appeared on the flyer because on June 14, 1971, he had been arrested in Louisville on a charge of shoplifting. He had been arraigned on this charge in September 1971, and, upon his plea of not guilty, the charge had been "filed away with leave (to reinstate)," a disposition which left the charge outstanding. Thus, at the time petitioners caused the flyer to be prepared and circulated respondent had been charged with shoplifting but his guilt or innocence of that offense had never been resolved. Shortly after circulation of the flyer the charge against respondent was finally dismissed by a judge of the Louisville Police Court.

At the time the flyer was circulated respondent was employed as a photographer by the *Louisville Courier-Journal* and *Times*. The flyer, and respondent's inclusion therein, soon came to the attention of respondent's supervisor, the executive director of photography for the two newspapers. This individual called respondent in to hear his version of the events leading to his appearing in the flyer. Following this discussion, the supervisor informed respondent that although he would not be fired, he "had best not find himself in a similar situation" in the future.

Respondent thereupon brought this § 1983 action in the District Court for the Western District of Kentucky, seeking redress for the alleged violation of rights guaranteed to him by the Constitution of the United States. Claiming jurisdiction under 28 U.S.C. § 1343(3), respondent sought damages as well as declaratory and injunctive relief. Petitioners moved to dismiss this complaint. The District Court granted this motion, ruling that "[t]he facts alleged in this case do not establish that plaintiff has been deprived of any right secured to him by the Constitution of the United States."

Respondent appealed to the Court of Appeals for the Sixth Circuit which recognized that, under our decisions, for respondent to establish a claim cognizable under § 1983 he had to show that petitioners had deprived him of a right secured by the Constitution of the United States, and that any such deprivation was achieved under color of law. *Adickes v. Kress & Co.,* 398 U.S. 144 (1970). The Court of Appeals concluded that respondent had set forth a § 1983 claim "in that he has alleged facts that constitute a denial of due process of law." 505 F.2d 1180 (1974). In its view our decision in *Wisconsin v. Constantineau,* 400 U.S. 433 (1971), mandated reversal of the District Court. . . .

I

Respondent's due process claim is grounded upon his assertion that the flyer, and in particular the phrase "Active Shoplifters" appearing at the head of the page upon which his name and photograph appear, impermissibly deprived him of some "liberty" protected by the Fourteenth Amendment. His complaint asserted that the "active shoplifter" designation would inhibit him from entering business establishments for fear of being suspected of shoplifting and possibly apprehended, and would seriously impair his future employment opportunities. Accepting that such consequences may flow from the flyer in question, respondent's complaint would appear to state a classical claim for defamation actionable in the courts of virtually every State. Imputing criminal behavior to an individual is generally considered defamatory per se, and actionable without proof of special damages.

Respondent brought his action, however, not in the state courts of Kentucky, but in a United States District Court for that State. He asserted not a claim for defamation under the laws of Kentucky, but a claim that he had been deprived of rights secured to him by the Fourteenth Amendment of the United States Constitution. Concededly if the same allegations had been made about respondent by a private individual, he would have nothing more than a claim for defamation under state law. But, he contends, since petitioners are respectively an official of city and of county government, his action is thereby transmuted into one for deprivation by the State of rights secured under the Fourteenth Amendment.

II

The result reached by the Court of Appeals, which respondent seeks to sustain here, must be bottomed on one of two premises. The first is that the Due Process Clause of the Fourteenth Amendment and § 1983 make actionable many wrongs inflicted by government employees which had heretofore been thought to give rise only to state-law tort claims. The second premise is that the infliction by state officials of a "stigma" to one's reputation is somehow different in kind from the infliction by the same official of harm or injury to other interests protected by state law, so that an injury to reputation is actionable under § 1983 and the

Fourteenth Amendment even if other such harms are not. We examine each of these premises in turn.

The second premise upon which the result reached by the Court of Appeals could be rested, that the infliction by state officials of a "stigma" to one's reputation is somehow different in kind from infliction by a state official of harm to other interests protected by state law, is equally untenable. The words "liberty" and "property" as used in the Fourteenth Amendment do not in terms single out reputation as a candidate for special protection over and above other interests that may be protected by state law. While we have in a number of our prior cases pointed out the frequently drastic effect of the "stigma" which may result from defamation by the government in a variety of contexts, this line of cases does not establish the proposition that reputation alone, apart from some more tangible interests such as employment, is either "liberty" or "property" by itself sufficient to invoke the procedural protection of the Due Process Clause. As we have said, the Court of Appeals, in reaching a contrary conclusion, relied primarily upon *Wisconsin v. Constantineau*, 400 U.S. 433 (1971). We think the correct import of that decision, however, must be derived from an examination of the precedents upon which it relied, as well as consideration of the other decisions by this Court, before and after *Constantineau*, which bear upon the relationship between governmental defamation and the guarantees of the Constitution. While not uniform in their treatment of the subject, we think that the weight of our decisions establishes no constitutional doctrine converting every defamation by a public official into a deprivation of liberty within the meaning of the Due Process Clause of the Fifth or Fourteenth Amendment. . . .

III

It is apparent from our decisions that there exists a variety of interests which are difficult of definition but are nevertheless comprehended within the meaning of either "liberty" or "property" as meant in the Due Process Clause. These interests attain this constitutional status by virtue of the fact that they have been initially recognized and protected by state law, and we have repeatedly ruled that the procedural guarantees of the Fourteenth Amendment apply whenever the State seeks to remove or significantly alter that protected status. In *Bell v. Burson*, 402 U.S. 535 (1971), for example, the State by issuing drivers' licenses recognized in its citizens a right to operate a vehicle on the highways of the State. The Court held that the State could not withdraw this right without giving petitioner due process. In *Morrissey v. Brewer*, 408 U.S. 471 (1972), the State afforded parolees the right to remain at liberty as long as the conditions of their parole were not violated. Before the State could alter the status of a parolee because of alleged violations of these conditions, we held that the Fourteenth Amendment's guarantee of due process of law required certain procedural safeguards. Kentucky law does not extend to respondent any legal guarantee of present enjoyment of reputation which has been altered as a result of petitioners' actions. Rather his interest in reputation is simply one of a number which the State may protect against injury by virtue of its tort law, providing a forum for vindication of those interests by means of damages actions. And any harm or injury to that interest, even where as here inflicted by an officer of the State, does not result in a deprivation of any "liberty" or "property" recognized by state or federal law, nor has it worked any change of respondent's status as theretofore recognized under the State's laws. For these reasons we hold that the interest in reputation asserted in this case is neither "liberty" nor "property" guaranteed against state deprivation without due process of law.

Respondent in this case cannot assert denial of any right vouchsafed to him by the State and thereby protected under the Fourteenth Amendment. That being the case, petitioners' defamatory publications, however seriously they may have harmed respondent's reputation, did not deprive him of any "liberty" or "property" interests protected by the Due Process Clause. The judgment of the Court of Appeals holding otherwise is Reversed.

Questions

1. What was the interest in *Constantineau?*
2. What was interest in *Paul v. Davis?*
3. Can you explain why one's interest in a good name and reputation in a liquor store posting *(Constantineau)* deserves more protection than when one's good name and reputation have been slandered by being falsely branded as a shoplifter *(Paul)?*

Megan's Law refers to certain sex offender laws in all the states that require the states to notify the public of the whereabouts of convicted sex offenders who have been released into society. These laws are named after a child who was sexually assaulted and murdered by a neighbor who had a record of sex offenses against minors; Megan's parents were not aware of the situation. In Connecticut, Megan's Law requires the Department of Public Safety to maintain a Website with addresses and photos of released sex offenders. When citizens access the Website and enter a zip code, names, addresses, and photos of sex offenders resident in that zip code will appear. The Website has a disclaimer that says the state does not know whether any of the offenders in the registry are currently dangerous. If you assume that the purpose of the law is to warn the public, then it is safe to assume a presumption of dangerousness about the people on the list. If they are not dangerous, why maintain the registry? A listed sex offender who claims to offer proof that he is not "a dangerous sex offender" sued the state for violating his due process of law under the liberty interest of damage to his reputation. He argues that Connecticut has implied that he is dangerous when in fact he is not, and this was done without a hearing that allowed him to challenge his altered status. Indeed, his suit was a class action brought on behalf of himself and all other similarly situated individuals. The federal district judge certified the class and decided in favor of the plaintiff. The judge halted the public disclosure provisions of the law. The court of appeals affirmed, but in a 2003 case, the Supreme Court reversed. See *Connecticut Department of Public Safety v. John Doe.*[39]

In my opinion, the trend in due process cases in administrative law is toward those involving situations where the provision of government services has been contracted out to a private entity. That means there will be an increasing number of state action cases. The case below is a state action case, but it also involves the property interest of the plaintiffs. It is a somewhat important case because it establishes an atmosphere regarding how the Court views the legal interests of private actors who contract to provide government services. Only a few private provider due process cases are moving through the federal judicial system, and the one below is the most on-point.

You read about *Blum v. Yaretsky* in the state action section of this chapter. As you will recall, the role of the review committee was simply to make a recommendation to the government agency that would ultimately make a decision about the level of nursing home care required. In the case below, the private utilization review organization makes the actual decision about whether the medical treatment received by an employee is "reasonable" or "necessary." This is the case that the Court cited when it dispatched the HMO case back to the lower courts.

American Manufacturers Mutual Insurance Company v. Sullivan
526 U.S. 40 (1999)

Chief Justice Rehnquist delivered the opinion of the Court, Parts I and II of which were joined by Justices O'Connor, Scalia, Kennedy, Souter, Thomas, and Breyer and Part III of which was joined by Justices O'Connor, Kennedy, Thomas, and Ginsburg. Justice Ginsburg filed an opinion concurring in part and concurring in the judgment. Justice Breyer filed an opinion concurring in part and concurring in the judgment, in which Justice Souter joined. Justice Stevens filed an opinion concurring in part and dissenting in part.

Pennsylvania provides in its workers' compensation regime that an employer or insurer may withhold payment for disputed medical treatment pending an independent review to determine whether the treatment is reasonable and necessary. We hold that the insurers are not "state actors" under the Fourteenth Amendment, and that the Pennsylvania regime does not deprive disabled employees of property within the meaning of that Amendment.

I

Before the enactment of workers' compensation laws, employees who suffered a work-related injury or occupational disease could recover compensation from their employers only by resort to traditional tort remedies available at common law. In the early 20th century, States began to replace the common-law system, which often saddled employees with the difficulty and expense of establishing negligence or proving damages, with a compulsory insurance system requiring employers to compensate employees for work-related injuries without regard to fault.

Following this model, Pennsylvania's Workers' Compensation Act, first enacted in 1915, creates a system of no-fault liability for work-related injuries and makes employers' liability under this system "exclusive . . . of any

and all other liability." All employers subject to the Act must either (1) obtain workers' compensation insurance from a private insurer, (2) obtain such insurance through the State Workers' Insurance Fund (SWIF), or (3) seek permission from the State to self-insure. Once an employer becomes liable for an employee's work-related injury—because liability either is not contested or is no longer at issue—the employer or its insurer must pay for all "reasonable" and "necessary" medical treatment, and must do so within 30 days of receiving a bill.

To assure that insurers pay only for medical care that meets these criteria, and in an attempt to control costs, Pennsylvania amended its workers' compensation system in 1993. Most important for our purposes, the 1993 amendments created a "utilization review" procedure under which the reasonableness and necessity of an employee's past, ongoing, or prospective medical treatment could be reviewed before a medical bill must be paid. Under this system, if an insurer "disputes the reasonableness or necessity of the treatment provided," it may request utilization review (within the same 30-day period) by filing a one-page form with the Workers' Compensation Bureau of the Pennsylvania Department of Labor and Industry (Bureau). The form identifies (among other things) the employee, the medical provider, the date of the employee's injury, and the medical treatment to be reviewed. The Bureau makes no attempt, as the Court of Appeals stated, to "address the legitimacy or lack thereof of the request," but merely determines whether the form is "properly completed—i.e., that all information required by the form is provided." Upon the proper filing of a request, an insurer may withhold payment to health care providers for the particular services being challenged.

The Bureau then notifies the parties that utilization review has been requested and forwards the request to a randomly selected "utilization review organization" (URO). URO's are private organizations consisting of health care providers who are "licensed in the same profession and have the same or similar specialty as that of the provider of the treatment under review," The purpose of utilization review, and the sole authority conferred upon a URO, is to determine "whether the treatment under review is reasonable or necessary for the medical condition of the employee" in light of "generally accepted treatment protocols." Reviewers must examine the treating provider's medical records and must give the provider an opportunity to discuss the treatment under review. Any doubt as to the reasonableness and necessity of a given procedure must be resolved in favor of the employee.

URO's are instructed to complete their review and render a determination within 30 days of a completed request. If the URO finds in favor of the insurer, the employee may appeal the determination to a workers' compensation judge for a de novo review, but the insurer need not pay for the disputed services unless the URO's determination is overturned by the judge, or later by the courts. If the URO finds in favor of the employee, the insurer must pay the disputed bill immediately, with 10 percent annual interest, as well as the cost of the utilization review.

Respondents are 10 individual employees and 2 organizations representing employees who received medical benefits under the Act. They claimed to have had payment of particular benefits withheld pursuant to the utilization review procedure set forth in the Act. They sued under 42 U.S.C. § 1983, acting individually and on behalf of a class of similarly situated employees. Named as defendants were various Pennsylvania officials who administer the Act, the director of the SWIF, the School District of Philadelphia (which self-insures), and a number of private insurance companies who provide workers' compensation coverage in Pennsylvania. Respondents alleged that in withholding workers' compensation benefits without predeprivation notice and an opportunity to be heard, the state and private defendants, acting "under color of state law," deprived them of property in violation of due process. They sought declaratory and injunctive relief, as well as damages.

The District Court dismissed the private insurers from the lawsuit on the ground that they are not "state actors," *Sullivan v. Barnett,* 913 F. Supp. 895, 905 (ED Pa. 1996), and later dismissed the state officials who remained as defendants, as well as the school district, on the ground that the Act does not violate due process.

The Court of Appeals for the Third Circuit disagreed on both issues. . . .

We granted certiorari to resolve a conflict on the status of private insurers providing workers' compensation coverage under state laws, and to review the Court of Appeals' holding that due process prohibits insurers from withholding payment for disputed medical treatment pending review.

II

To state a claim for relief in an action brought under § 1983, respondents must establish that they were deprived of a right secured by the Constitution or laws of the United States, and that the alleged deprivation was committed under color of state law. Like the state-action requirement of the Fourteenth Amendment, the under-color-of-state-law element of § 1983 excludes from its reach "'merely private conduct, no matter how discriminatory or wrongful,'" *Blum v. Yaretsky,* 457 U.S. 991, 1002 (1982) (quoting *Shelley v. Kreamer,* 334 U.S. 1, 13 (1948)). . . .

(S)tate action requires both an alleged constitutional deprivation "caused by the exercise of some right or privilege created by the State or by a rule of conduct imposed by the State or by a person for whom the State is responsible," and that "the party charged with the deprivation must be a person who may fairly be said to be a state actor." *Lugar v. Edmondson Oil Co.,* 457 U.S. 922, 937 (1982); see *Flagg Bros., Inc. v. Brooks,* 436 U.S. 149, 156 (1978). In this case, while it may fairly be said that private insurers act "with knowledge of and pursuant to" the state statute, ibid., thus satisfying the first requirement, respondents still must satisfy the second, whether the allegedly unconstitutional conduct is fairly attributable to the State. . . .

Here, respondents named as defendants both public officials and a class of private insurers and self-insured employers. Also named is the director of the SWIF and the School District of Philadelphia, a municipal corporation. The complaint alleged that the state and private defendants, acting under color of state law and pursuant to the Act, deprived them of property in violation of due process by withholding payment for medical treatment without prior notice and an opportunity to be heard. All agree that the public officials responsible for administering the workers' compensation system and the director of SWIF are state actors. Thus, the issue we address, in accordance with our cases, is whether a private insurer's decision to withhold payment for disputed medical treatment may be fairly attributable to the State so as to subject insurers to the constraints of the Fourteenth Amendment. Our answer to that question is "no."

In cases involving extensive state regulation of private activity, we have consistently held that "the mere fact that a business is subject to state regulation does not by itself convert its action into that of the State for purposes of the Fourteenth Amendment." *Jackson v. Metropolitan Edison Co.,* 419 U.S. 345, 350 (1974); see *Blum,* 457 U.S. at 1004. Faithful application of the state-action requirement in these cases ensures that the prerogative of regulating private business remains with the States and the representative branches, not the courts. Thus, the private insurers in this case will not be held to constitutional standards unless "there is a sufficiently close nexus between the State and the challenged action of the regulated entity so that the latter may be fairly treated as that of the State itself." Ibid. Whether such a "close nexus" exists, our cases state, depends on whether the State "has exercised coercive power or has provided such significant encouragement, either overt or covert, that the choice must in law be deemed to be that of the State." Ibid.; see *Flagg Bros.,* supra., 166; *Jackson,* supra, at 357; *Moose Lodge No. 107 v. Irvis,* 407 U.S. 163, 173 (1972); *Adickes v. S. H. Kress & Co.,* 398 U.S. 144, 170 (1970). Action taken by private entities with the mere approval or acquiescence of the State is not state action. *Blum,* supra, at

1004–1005; *Flagg Bros.,* supra, at 154–165; *Jackson,* supra, at 357.

Here, respondents do not assert that the decision to invoke utilization review should be attributed to the State because the State compels or is directly involved in that decision. Obviously the State is not so involved.

It authorizes, but does not require, insurers to withhold payments for disputed medical treatment. The decision to withhold payment, like the decision to transfer Medicaid patients to a lower level of care in *Blum,* is made by concededly private parties, and "turns on . . . judgments made by private parties" without "standards . . . established by the State." *Blum,* 457 U.S. at 1008.

Respondents do assert, however, that the decision to withhold payment to providers may be fairly attributable to the State because the State has "authorized" and "encouraged" it. Respondents' primary argument in this regard is that, in amending the Act to provide for utilization review and to grant insurers an option they previously did not have, the State purposely "encouraged" insurers to withhold payments for disputed medical treatment. This argument reads too much into the State's reform, and in any event cannot be squared with our cases. . . .

The State's decision to allow insurers to withhold payments pending review can just as easily be seen as state inaction, or more accurately, a legislative decision not to intervene in a dispute between an insurer and an employee over whether a particular treatment is reasonable and necessary. See *Flagg Bros.,* 436 U.S. at 164–165. Before the 1993 amendments, Pennsylvania restricted the ability of an insurer (after liability had been established, of course) to defer workers' compensation medical benefits, including payment for unreasonable and unnecessary treatment, beyond 30 days of receipt of the bill. The 1993 amendments, in effect, restored to insurers the narrow option, historically exercised by employers and insurers before the adoption of Pennsylvania's workers' compensation law, to defer payment of a bill until it is substantiated. The most that can be said of the statutory scheme, therefore, is that whereas it previously prohibited insurers from withholding payment for disputed medical services, it no longer does so. Such permission of a private choice cannot support a finding of state action. As we have said before, our cases will not tolerate "the imposition of Fourteenth Amendment restraints on private action by the simple device of characterizing the State's inaction as 'authorization' or 'encouragement.'"

Nor does the State's role in creating, supervising, and setting standards for the URO process differ in any meaningful sense from the creation and administration of any forum for resolving disputes. While the decision of a URO, like that of any judicial official, may properly be considered state action, a private party's mere use of the State's dispute resolution machinery, without the "overt, significant assistance of state officials," *Tulsa,* supra, at 486, cannot.

The State, in the course of administering a many-faceted remedial system, has shifted one facet from favoring the employees to favoring the employer. This sort of decision occurs regularly in legislative review of such systems. But it cannot be said that such a change "encourages" or "authorizes" the insurer's actions as those terms are used in our state-action jurisprudence. . . .

Respondents next contend that state action is present because the State has delegated to insurers "powers traditionally exclusively reserved to the State." *Jackson,* 419 U.S. at 352. Their argument here is twofold. Relying on *West v. Atkins,* 487 U.S. 42 (1988), respondents first argue that workers' compensation benefits are state-mandated "public benefits" and that the State has delegated the provision of these "public benefits" to private insurers. They also contend that the State has delegated to insurers the traditionally exclusive government function of determining whether and under what circumstances an injured worker's medical benefits may be suspended. The Court of Appeals apparently agreed on both points, stating that insurers "providing public benefits which honor State entitlements . . . become an arm of the State, fulfilling a uniquely governmental obligation," 139 F.3d at 168, and that "the right to invoke the supersedeas, or to stop payments, is a power that traditionally was held in the hands of the State," ibid. We think neither argument has merit. *West* is readily distinguishable: there

the State was constitutionally obligated to provide medical treatment to injured inmates, and the delegation of that traditionally exclusive public function to a private physician gave rise to a finding of state action. See 487 U.S. at 54–56. Here, on the other hand, nothing in Pennsylvania's constitution or statutory scheme obligates the State to provide either medical treatment or workers' compensation benefits to injured workers. See *Blum,* supra, at 1011. Instead, the State's workers' compensation law imposes that obligation on employers. This case is therefore not unlike *Jackson,* supra, where we noted that "while the Pennsylvania statute imposes an obligation to furnish service on regulated utilities, it imposes no such obligation on the State." 419 U.S. at 352; see also *San Francisco Arts & Athletics, Inc. v. United States Olympic Comm.,* 483 U.S. 522, 544 (1987) ("The fact 'that a private entity performs a function which serves the public does not make its acts [governmental] action'") (quoting *Rendell-Baker v. Kohn,* 457 U.S. 830, 842 (1982)). . . .

But before Pennsylvania ever adopted its workers' compensation law, an insurer under contract with an employer to pay for its workers' reasonable and necessary medical expenses could withhold payment, for any reason or no reason, without any authorization or involvement of the State. The insurer, of course, might become liable to the employer (or its workers) if the refusal to pay breached the contract or constituted "bad faith," but the obligation to pay would only arise after the employer had initiated a claim and reduced it to a judgment. That Pennsylvania first recognized an insurer's traditionally private prerogative to withhold payment, then restricted it, and now (in one limited respect) has restored it, cannot constitute the delegation of a traditionally exclusive public function. Like New York in *Flagg Bros.,* Pennsylvania "has done nothing more than authorize (and indeed limit—without participation by any public official—what [private insurers] would tend to do, even in the absence of such authorization," i.e., withhold payment for disputed medical treatment pending a determination that the treatment is, in fact, reasonable and necessary. 436 U.S. at 162, . . .

Burton was one of our early cases dealing with "state action" under the Fourteenth Amendment, and later cases have refined the vague "joint participation" test embodied in that case. *Blum* and *Jackson,* in particular, have established that "privately owned enterprises providing services that the State would not necessarily provide, even though they are extensively regulated, do not fall within the ambit of *Burton.*" *Blum,* 457 U.S. at 1011; see *Jackson,* supra, at 357–358. Here, workers' compensation insurers are at least as extensively regulated as the private nursing facilities in *Blum* and the private utility in *Jackson.* Like those cases, though, the state statutory and regulatory scheme leaves the challenged decisions to the judgment of insurers. . . .

We conclude that an insurer's decision to withhold payment and seek utilization review of the reasonableness and necessity of particular medical treatment is not fairly attributable to the State. Respondents have therefore failed to satisfy an essential element of their § 1983 claim.

III

Though our resolution of the state-action issue would be sufficient by itself to reverse the judgment of the Court of Appeals, we believe the court fundamentally misapprehended the nature of respondents' property interest at stake in this case, with ramifications not only for the state officials who are concededly state actors, but also for the private insurers who (under our holding in Part II) are not. If the Court of Appeals' ruling is left undisturbed, SWIF, which insures both public and private employers, will be required to pay for all medical treatment (reasonable and necessary or not) within 30 days, while private insurers will be able to defer payment for disputed treatment pending utilization review. Although we denied the petitions for certiorari filed by the school district and the various state officials we granted both questions presented in the petition filed by the private insurance companies. The second question therein states:

"Whether the Due Process Clause requires workers' compensation insurers to pay disputed medical bills prior to a determination that the medical treatment was reasonable and necessary."

This question has been briefed and argued, it is an important one, and it is squarely presented for review. We thus proceed to address it.

The first inquiry in every due process challenge is whether the plaintiff has been deprived of a protected interest in "property" or "liberty." See U.S. Const., Amdt. 14 ("nor shall any State deprive any person of life, liberty, or property without due process of law"); *Mathews v. Eldridge,* 424 U.S. 319, 332 (1976). Only after finding the deprivation of a protected interest do we look to see if the State's procedures comport with due process. Id. at 332.

Here, respondents contend that Pennsylvania's workers' compensation law confers upon them a protected property interest in workers' compensation medical benefits. Under state law, respondents assert, once an employer's liability is established for a particular work-related injury, the employer is obligated to pay for certain benefits, including partial wage replacement, compensation for permanent injury or disability, and medical care. It follows from this, the argument goes, that medical benefits are a state-created entitlement, and thus an insurer cannot withhold payment of medical benefits without affording an injured worker due process.

In *Goldberg v. Kelly,* 397 U.S. 254 (1970), we held that an individual receiving federal welfare assistance has a statutorily created property interest in the continued receipt of those benefits. Likewise, in *Mathews,* supra, we recognized that the same was true for an individual receiving Social Security disability benefits. In both cases, an individual's entitlement to benefits had been established, and the question presented was whether predeprivation notice and a hearing were required before the individual's interest in continued payment of benefits could be terminated. See *Goldberg,* supra, at 261–263; *Mathews,* supra, at 332.

Respondents' property interest in this case, however, is fundamentally different. Under Pennsylvania law, an employee is not entitled to payment for all medical treatment once the employer's initial liability is established, as respondents' argument assumes. Instead, the law expressly limits an employee's entitlement to "reasonable" and "necessary" medical treatment, and requires that disputes over the reasonableness and necessity of particular treatment must be resolved before an employer's obligation to pay—and an employee's entitlement to benefits—arise. ("The employer shall provide payment . . . for reasonable surgical and medical services"); ("All payments to providers for treatment . . . shall be made within thirty (30) days of receipt of such bills and records unless the employer or insurer disputes the reasonableness or necessity of the treatment"). Thus, for an employee's property interest in the payment of medical benefits to attach under state law, the employee must clear two hurdles: First, he must prove that an employer is liable for a work-related injury, and second, he must establish that the particular medical treatment at issue is reasonable and necessary. Only then does the employee's interest parallel that of the beneficiary of welfare assistance in *Goldberg* and the recipient of disability benefits in *Mathews*.

Respondents obviously have not cleared both of these hurdles. While they indeed have established their initial eligibility for medical treatment, they have yet to make good on their claim that the particular medical treatment they received was reasonable and necessary. Consequently, they do not have a property interest—under the logic of their own argument—in having their providers paid for treatment that has yet to be found reasonable and necessary. To state the argument is to refute it, for what respondents ask in this case is that insurers be required to pay for patently unreasonable, unnecessary, and even fraudulent medical care without any right, under state law, to seek reimbursement from providers. Unsurprisingly, the Due Process Clause does not require such a result.

Having concluded that respondents' due process claim falters for lack of a property interest in the payment of benefits, we need go no further.

The judgment of the Court of Appeals is Reversed.

How Much Process Is Due?

Having established that a government entity or agent took action (that there is state action) that affected the property or liberty interest of another, the final question is what kind of procedure should be required. The short answer is that it depends on the nature of the affected interest.

Suppose the administration of your university accused you of taking part in a demonstration that resulted in the destruction of property and wanted to expel you. Is there a liberty or property interest? What is it? What kind of procedures would the university have to provide? Suppose the university was going to suspend you for academic reasons. Would the situation be any different?

To a degree, the *Goldberg* and *Eldridge* cases you are already somewhat familiar with represent the extremes in the notion of how elaborate a hearing must be (and at what point it is required). The *Goldberg* case, which follows, requires what have been labeled the "ten Goldberg requirements" at a predeprivation hearing. This case was the start of the due process revolution. Following it is *Mathews v. Eldridge*, which ended the due process revolution just six years later.

Goldberg v. Kelly
397 U.S. 254 (1970)

Justice Brennan delivered the opinion of the Court, joined by Justices Douglas, Harlan, White, Marshall, and Blackmun. Chief Justice Burger and Justice Black dissented. Justice Stewart dissented in the companion case, 397 U.S. 282, 285.

The question for decision is whether a State that terminates public assistance payments to a particular recipient without affording him the opportunity for an evidentiary hearing prior to termination denies the recipient procedural due process in violation of the Due Process Clause of the Fourteenth Amendment.

This action was brought in the District Court for the Southern District of New York by residents of New York City receiving financial aid under the federally assisted program of Aid to Families with Dependent Children (AFDC) or under New York State's general Home Relief program. Their complaint alleged that the New York State and New York City officials administering these programs terminated, or were about to terminate, such aid without prior notice and hearing, thereby denying them due process of law. At the time the suits were filed there was no requirement of prior notice or hearing of any kind before termination of financial aid. However, the State and city adopted procedures for notice and hearing after the suits were brought, and the plaintiffs, appellees here, then challenged the constitutional adequacy of those procedures.

The State Commissioner of Social Services amended the State Department of Social Services' Official Regulations to require that local social services officials proposing to discontinue or suspend a recipient's financial aid do so according to a procedure that conforms to either subdivision (a) or subdivision (b) of § 351.26 of the regulations as amended. The City of New York elected to promulgate a local procedure according to subdivision (b). That subdivision, so far as here pertinent, provides

that the local procedure must include the giving of notice to the recipient of the reasons for a proposed discontinuance or suspension at least seven days prior to its effective date, with notice also that upon request the recipient may have the proposal reviewed by a local welfare official holding a position superior to that of the supervisor who approved the proposed discontinuance or suspension, and, further, that the recipient may submit, for purposes of the review, a written statement to demonstrate why his grant should not be discontinued or suspended. The decision by the reviewing official whether to discontinue or suspend aid must be made expeditiously, with written notice of the decision to the recipient.

The section further expressly provides that "[a]ssistance shall not be discontinued or suspended prior to the date such notice of decision is sent to the recipient and his representative, if any, or prior to the proposed effective date of discontinuance or suspension, whichever occurs later." This case presents no issue of the validity or construction of the federal regulations. It is only subdivision (b) of § 351.26 of the New York State regulations and implementing procedure 68–18 of New York City that pose the constitutional question before us. Even assuming that the constitutional question might be avoided in the context of AFDC by construction of the Social Security Act or of the present federal regulations thereunder, or by waiting for the new regulations to become effective, the question must be faced and decided in the context of New York's Home Relief program, to which the procedures also apply.

Pursuant to subdivision (b), the New York City Department of Social Services promulgated Procedure No. 68–18. A caseworker who has doubts about the recipient's continued eligibility must first discuss them with the recipient. If the caseworker concludes that the recipient is no longer eligible, he recommends termination of aid to a unit supervisor. If the latter concurs, he sends the recipient a letter stating the reasons for proposing to terminate aid and notifying him that within seven days he may request that a higher official review the record, and may support the request with a written statement prepared personally or with the aid of an attorney or other person. If the reviewing official affirms the determination of ineligibility, aid is stopped immediately and the recipient is informed by letter of the reasons for the action. Appellees' challenge to this procedure emphasizes the absence of any provisions for the personal appearance of the recipient before the reviewing official, for oral presentation of evidence, and for confrontation and cross-examination of adverse witnesses. However, the letter does inform the recipient that he may request a post-termination "fair hearing." This is a proceeding before an independent state hearing officer at which the recipient may appear personally, offer oral evidence, confront and cross-examine the witnesses against him, and have a record made of the hearing. If the recipient prevails at the "fair hearing" he is paid all funds erroneously withheld. A recipient whose aid is not restored by a "fair hearing" decision may have judicial review. The recipient is so notified.

I

The constitutional issue to be decided, therefore, is the narrow one whether the Due Process Clause requires that the recipient be afforded an evidentiary hearing before the termination of benefits. Under all the circumstances, we hold that due process requires an adequate hearing before termination of welfare benefits, and the fact that there is a later constitutionally fair proceeding does not alter the result. Although state officials were party defendants in the action, only the Commissioner of Social Services of the City of New York appealed. We noted probable jurisdiction, to decide important issues that have been the subject of disagreement in principle between the three-judge court in the present case and that convened in *Wheeler v. Montgomery,* 397 U.S. 280. We affirm.

"Consideration of what procedures due process may require under any given set of circumstances must begin with a determination of the precise nature of the government function involved as well as of the private interest that has been affected by governmental action." See also *Hannah v. Larche,* 363 U.S. 420, 1307 (1960). It is true, of course, that some governmental benefits may be administratively terminated without affording the recipient a pre-termination evidentiary hearing. But we agree with the District Court that when welfare is discontinued, only a pre-termination evidentiary hearing provides the recipient with procedural due process. Cf. *Sniadach v. Family Finance Corp.,* 395 U.S. 337 (1969). For qualified recipients, welfare provides the means to obtain essential food, clothing, housing, and medical care. Thus the crucial factor in this context—a factor not present in the case of the blacklisted government contractor, the discharged government employee, the taxpayer denied a tax exemption, or virtually anyone else whose governmental entitlements are ended—is that termination of aid pending resolution of a controversy over eligibility may deprive an eligible recipient of the very means by which to live while he waits. Since he lacks independent resources, his situation becomes immediately desperate. His need to concentrate upon finding the means for daily subsistence, in turn, adversely affects his ability to seek redress from the welfare bureaucracy. Moreover, important governmental interests are promoted by affording recipients a pre-termination evidentiary hearing. From its founding the Nation's basic commitment has been to foster the dignity and well-being of all persons within its borders. We have come to recognize that forces not within the control of the poor contribute to their poverty. This perception, against the background of our traditions, has significantly influenced the development of the contemporary public assistance system. Welfare, by meeting the basic demands of subsistence, can help bring within the reach of the poor the same opportunities that are available to others to participate meaningfully in the life of the community. At the same time, welfare guards against the societal malaise that may flow from a widespread sense of unjustified frustration and insecurity. Public assistance, then, is not mere charity, but a means to "promote the general Welfare, and secure the Blessings of Liberty to ourselves and our Posterity." The same governmental interests that counsel the provision of welfare, counsel as well its uninterrupted provision to those eligible to receive it; pre-termination evidentiary hearings are indispensable to that end.

II

We also agree with the District Court, however, that the pre-termination hearing need not take the form of a judicial or quasi-judicial trial. We bear in mind that the statutory "fair hearing" will provide the recipient with a full administrative review. Accordingly, the pre-termination hearing has one function only: to produce an initial determination of the validity of the welfare department's grounds for discontinuance of payments in order to protect a recipient against an erroneous termination of his benefits. Thus, a complete record and a comprehensive opinion, which would serve primarily to facilitate judicial review and to guide future decisions, need not be provided at the pre-termination stage. We recognize, too, that both welfare authorities and recipients have an interest in relatively speedy resolution of questions of eligibility, that they are used to dealing with one another informally, and that some welfare departments have very burdensome caseloads. These considerations justify the limitation of the pre-termination hearing to minimum procedural safeguards, adapted to the particular characteristics of welfare recipients, and to the limited nature of the controversies to be resolved. We wish to add that we, no less than the dissenters, recognize the importance of not imposing upon the States or the Federal Government in this developing field of law any procedural requirements beyond those demanded by rudimentary due process.

"The fundamental requisite of due process of law is the opportunity to be heard." The hearing must be "at a meaningful time and in a meaningful manner." In the present context these principles require that a recipient have timely and adequate notice detailing the reasons for a proposed termination, and an effective opportunity to defend by confronting any adverse witnesses and by presenting his own arguments and evidence orally. These rights are important in cases such as those before us, where recipients have challenged proposed terminations as resting on incorrect or misleading factual premises or on misapplication of rules or policies to the facts of particular cases.

The city's procedures presently do not permit recipients to appear personally with or without counsel before the official who finally determines continued eligibility. Thus a recipient is not permitted to present evidence to that official orally, or to confront or cross-examine adverse witnesses. These omissions are fatal to the constitutional adequacy of the procedures.

The opportunity to be heard must be tailored to the capacities and circumstances of those who are to be heard. It is not enough that a welfare recipient may present his position to the decision maker in writing or second-hand through his caseworker. Therefore a recipient must be allowed to state his position orally. Informal procedures will suffice; in this context due process does not require a particular order of proof or mode of offering evidence.

In almost every setting where important decisions turn on questions of fact, due process requires an opportunity to confront and cross-examine adverse witnesses. What we said in *Greene v. McElroy,* 360 U.S. 474 (1959) is particularly pertinent here: "Certain principles have remained relatively immutable in our jurisprudence. One of these is that where governmental action seriously injures an individual, and the reasonableness of the action depends on fact findings, the evidence used to prove the Government's case must be disclosed to the individual so that he has an opportunity to show that it is untrue. While this is important in the case of documentary evidence, it is even more important where the evidence consists of the testimony of individuals whose memory might be faulty or who, in fact, might be perjurers or persons motivated by malice, vindictiveness, intolerance, prejudice, or jealousy. We have formalized these protections in the requirements of confrontation and cross-examination. They have ancient roots. They find expression in the Sixth Amendment. "The right to be heard would be, in many cases, of little avail if it did not comprehend the right to be heard by counsel." *Powell v. Alabama*, 287 U.S. 45 (1932). We do not say that counsel must be provided at the pre-termination hearing, but only that the recipient must be allowed to retain an attorney if he so desires. Counsel can help delineate the issues, present the factual contentions in an orderly manner, conduct cross-examination, and generally safeguard the interests of the recipient. We do not anticipate that this assistance will unduly prolong or otherwise encumber the hearing. Evidently HEW has reached the same conclusion.

Finally, the decision maker's conclusion as to a recipient's eligibility must rest solely on the legal rules and evidence adduced at the hearing. To demonstrate compliance with this elementary requirement, the decision maker should state the reasons for his determination and indicate the evidence he relied on, *Wichita R. & Light Co. v. PUC*, 260 U.S. 48 (1922) though his statement need not amount to a full opinion or even formal findings of fact and conclusions of law. And, of course, an impartial decision maker is essential. We agree with the District Court that prior involvement in some aspects of a case will not necessarily bar a welfare official from acting as a decision maker. He should not, however, have participated in making the determination under review.

Affirmed.

Questions

1. What is the affected interest?
2. Can you list the 10 requirements of the hearing?

Mathews v. Eldridge
424 U.S. 319 (1976)

Justice Powell delivered the opinion of the Court, joined by Chief Justice Burger and Justices White, Stewart, Blackmun, and Rehnquist. Justices Brennan and Marshall dissented. Justice Stevens did not participate.

The issue in this case is whether the Due Process Clause of the Fifth Amendment requires that prior to the termination of Social Security disability benefit payments the recipient be afforded an opportunity for an evidentiary hearing.

Cash benefits are provided to workers during periods in which they are completely disabled under the disability insurance benefits

program created by the 1956 amendments to Title II of the Social Security Act. 42 U.S.C. § 423. Respondent Eldridge was first awarded benefits in June 1968. In March 1972, he received a questionnaire from the state agency charged with monitoring his medical condition. Eldridge completed the questionnaire, indicating that his condition had not improved and identifying the medical sources, including physicians, from whom he had received treatment recently. The state agency then obtained reports from his physician and a psychiatric consultant. After considering these reports and other information in his file the agency informed Eldridge by letter that it had made a tentative determination that his disability had ceased in May 1972. The letter included a statement of reasons for the proposed termination of benefits, and advised Eldridge that he might request reasonable time in which to obtain and submit additional information pertaining to his condition. In his written response, Eldridge disputed one characterization of his medical condition and indicated that the agency already had enough evidence to establish his disability. The state agency then made its final determination that he had ceased to be disabled in May 1972. This determination was accepted by the Social Security Administration (SSA), which notified Eldridge in July that his benefits would terminate after that month. The notification also advised him of his right to seek reconsideration by the state agency of this initial determination within six months.

Instead of requesting reconsideration Eldridge commenced this action challenging the constitutional validity of the administrative procedures established by the Secretary of Health, Education, and Welfare for assessing whether there exists a continuing disability. He sought an immediate reinstatement of benefits pending a hearing on the issue of his disability. 361 F.Supp. 520 (W.D.Va. 1973). The Secretary moved to dismiss on the grounds that Eldridge's benefits had been terminated in accordance with valid administrative regulations and procedures and that he had failed to exhaust available remedies. In support of his contention that due process requires a pretermination hearing, Eldridge relied exclusively upon this Court's decision in *Goldberg v. Kelly*, 397 U.S. 254 (1970), which established a right to an "evidentiary hearing" prior to termination of welfare benefits. The Secretary contended that *Goldberg* was not controlling since eligibility for disability benefits, unlike eligibility for welfare benefits, is not based on financial need and since issues of credibility and veracity do not play a significant role in the disability entitlement decision, which turns primarily on medical evidence.

The District Court concluded that the administrative procedures pursuant to which the Secretary had terminated Eldridge's benefits abridged his right to procedural due process.

The court viewed the interest of the disability recipient in uninterrupted benefits as indistinguishable from that of the welfare recipient in *Goldberg*. It further noted that decisions subsequent to *Goldberg* demonstrated that the due process requirement of pretermination hearings is not limited to situations involving the deprivation of vital necessities. See *Fuentes v. Shevin*, 407 U.S. 67, 88–89 (1972); *Bell v. Burson*, 402 U.S. 535 (1971). Reasoning that disability determinations may involve subjective judgments based on conflicting medical and nonmedical evidence, the District Court held that prior to termination of benefits Eldridge had to be afforded an evidentiary hearing of the type required for welfare beneficiaries under Title IV of the Social Security Act. 361 F.Supp., at 528. Relying entirely upon the District Court's opinion, the Court of Appeals for the Fourth Circuit affirmed the injunction barring termination of Eldridge's benefits prior to an evidentiary hearing. 493 F.2d 1230 (1974). We reverse. . . .

III

A

Procedural due process imposes constraints on governmental decisions which deprive individuals of "liberty" or "property" interests within the meaning of the Due Process Clause of the Fifth or Fourteenth Amendment. The Secretary does not contend that procedural due process is inapplicable to terminations of Social Security disability benefits. He recognizes, as has been implicit in our prior decisions, that the interest of an individual in continued receipt of these benefits is a statutorily created "property" interest protected by the Fifth Amendment. Rather, the Secretary contends that the existing administrative procedures, detailed below, provide all the process that is constitutionally due before a recipient can be deprived of that interest.

This Court consistently has held that some form of hearing is required before an individual is finally deprived of a property interest. *Wolff v. McDonnell*, 418 U.S. 539 (1974). See, e.g., *Phillips v. Commissioner of Internal Revenue*, 283 U.S. 589 (1931). See also *Dent v. West*

Virginia, 129 U.S. 114 (1889). The "right to be heard before being condemned to suffer grievous loss of any kind, even though it may not involve the stigma and hardships of a criminal conviction, is a principle basic to our society." *Joint Anti-Fascist Comm. v. McGrath,* 341 U.S. 123 (1951) (Frankfurter, J., concurring). The fundamental requirement of due process is the opportunity to be heard "at a meaningful time and in a meaningful manner." Eldridge agrees that the review procedures available to a claimant before the initial determination of ineligibility becomes final would be adequate if disability benefits were not terminated until after the evidentiary hearing stage of the administrative process. The dispute centers upon what process is due prior to the initial termination of benefits, pending review.

These decisions underscore the truism that "[d]ue process," unlike some legal rules, is not a technical conception with a fixed content unrelated to time, place and circumstances. "[D]ue process is flexible and calls for such procedural protections as the particular situation demands." Accordingly, resolution of the issue whether the administrative procedures provided here are constitutionally sufficient requires analysis of the governmental and private interests that are affected. More precisely, our prior decisions indicate that identification of the specific dictates of due process generally requires consideration of three distinct factors: First, the private interest that will be affected by the official action; second, the risk of an erroneous deprivation of such interest through the procedures used, and the probable value, if any, of additional or substitute procedural safeguards; and finally, the Government's interest, including the function involved and the fiscal and administrative burdens that the additional or substitute procedural requirement would entail. . . .

C

Despite the elaborate character of the administrative procedures provided by the Secretary, the courts below held them to be constitutionally inadequate, concluding that due process requires an evidentiary hearing prior to termination. In light of the private and governmental interests at stake here and the nature of the existing procedures, we think this was error.

Since a recipient whose benefits are terminated is awarded full retroactive relief if he ultimately prevails, his sole interest is in the uninterrupted receipt of this source of income pending final administrative decision on his claim. His potential injury is thus similar in nature to that of the welfare recipient in *Goldberg,* the nonprobationary federal employee in *Arnett,* see 416 U.S., at 146, and the wage earner in *Sniadach.*

Only in *Goldberg* has the Court held that due process requires an evidentiary hearing prior to a temporary deprivation. It was emphasized there that welfare assistance is given to persons on the very margin of subsistence: "The crucial factor in this context, a factor not present in the case of virtually anyone else whose governmental entitlements are ended, is that termination of aid pending resolution of a controversy over eligibility may deprive an eligible recipient of the very means by which to live while he waits." Eligibility for disability benefits, in contrast, is not based upon financial need. Indeed, it is wholly unrelated to the worker's income or support from many other sources, such as earnings of other family members, workmen's compensation awards, tort claims awards, savings, private insurance, public or private pensions, veterans' benefits, food stamps, public assistance, or the "many other important programs, both public and private, which contain provisions for disability payments affecting a substantial portion of the work force. . . ."

In view of the torpidity of this administrative review process, and the typically modest resources of the family unit of the physically disabled worker, the hardship imposed upon the erroneously terminated disability recipient may be significant. Still, the disabled worker's need is likely to be less than that of a welfare recipient. In addition to the possibility of access to private resources, other forms of government assistance will become available where the termination of disability benefits places a worker or his family below the subsistence level. In view of these potential sources of temporary income, there is less reason here than in *Goldberg* to depart from the ordinary principle, established by our decisions, that something less than an evidentiary hearing is sufficient prior to adverse administrative action.

D

An additional factor to be considered here is the fairness and reliability of the existing pretermination procedures, and the probable value, if any, of additional procedural safeguards. Central to the evaluation of any administrative process is the nature of the relevant inquiry. See Friendly, Some Kind of Hearing, 123 *U.Pa.L.Rev.* 1267, 1281 (1975). In order to remain eligible for benefits the disabled worker must demonstrate by means of "medically acceptable clinical and laboratory diagnostic techniques," that he is unable "to engage in any substantial gainful activity by reason of any medically determinable physical or mental impairment." In short, a medical assessment of the worker's physical or mental condition is required. This is a more sharply focused and easily documented decision than the typical determination of welfare entitlement. In the latter case, a wide variety of information may be deemed relevant, and issues of witness credibility and veracity often are critical to the decisionmaking process. *Goldberg* noted that in such circumstances "written submissions are a wholly unsatisfactory basis for decision."

By contrast, the decision whether to discontinue disability benefits will turn, in most cases, upon "routine, standard, and unbiased medical reports by physician specialists," concerning a subject whom they have personally examined.

In striking the appropriate due process balance the final factor to be assessed is the public interest. This includes the administrative burden and other societal costs that would be associated with requiring, as a matter of constitutional right, an evidentiary hearing upon demand in all cases prior to the termination of disability benefits. The most visible burden would be the incremental cost resulting from the increased number of hearings and the expense of providing benefits to ineligible recipients pending decision. No one can predict the extent of the increase, but the fact that full benefits would continue until after such hearings would assure the exhaustion in most cases of this attractive option. Nor would the theoretical right of the Secretary to recover undeserved benefits result, as a practical matter, in any substantial offset to the added outlay of public funds. The parties submit widely varying estimates of the probable additional financial cost. We only need say that experience with the constitutionalizing of government procedures suggests that the ultimate additional cost in terms of money and administrative burden would not be insubstantial.

Financial cost alone is not a controlling weight in determining whether due process requires a particular procedural safeguard prior to some administrative decision. But the Government's interest, and hence that of the public, in conserving scarce fiscal and administrative resources is a factor that must be weighed. At some point the benefit of an additional safeguard to the individual affected by the administrative action and to society in terms of increased assurance that the action is just, may be outweighed by the cost. Significantly, the cost of protecting those whom the preliminary administrative process has identified as likely to be found undeserving may in the end come out of the pockets of the deserving since resources available for any particular program of social welfare are not unlimited.

But more is implicated in cases of this type than ad hoc weighing of fiscal and administrative burdens against the interests of a particular category of claimants. The ultimate balance involves a determination as to when, under our constitutional system, judicial-type procedures must be imposed upon administrative action to assure fairness. We reiterate the wise admonishment of Mr. Justice Frankfurter that differences in the origin and function of administrative agencies "preclude wholesale transplantation of the rules of procedure, trial and review which have evolved from the history and experience of courts." *FCC v. Pottsville Broadcasting Co.*, 309 U.S. 134, 143 (1940). The judicial model of an evidentiary hearing is neither a required, nor even the most effective, method of decisionmaking in all circumstances. The essence of due process is the requirement that "a person in jeopardy of serious loss (be given) notice of the case against him and opportunity to meet it." All that is necessary is that the procedures be tailored, in light of the decision to be made, to "the capacities and circumstances of those who are to be heard," to insure that they are given a meaningful opportunity to present their case. This is especially so where, as here, the prescribed procedures not only provide the claimant with an effective process for asserting his claim prior to any administrative action, but also assure a right to an evidentiary hearing, as well as to subsequent judicial review, before the denial of his claim becomes final.

We conclude that an evidentiary hearing is not required prior to the termination of disability benefits and that the present administrative procedures fully comport with due process.

The judgment of the Court of Appeals is Reversed.

Justice Brennan, dissenting. Justice Marshall concurred with Justice Brennan's dissent.

For the reasons stated in my dissenting opinion in *Richardson v. Wright*, 405 U.S. 208, 212 (1972), I agree with the District Court and the Court of Appeals that, prior to termination of benefits, Eldridge must be afforded an evidentiary hearing of the type required for welfare beneficiaries under Title IV of the Social Security Act, 42 U.S.C. § 601 et seq. See *Goldberg v. Kelly*, 397 U.S. 254 (1970). I would add that the Court's consideration that a discontinuance of disability benefits may cause the recipient to suffer only a limited deprivation is no argument. It is speculative. Moreover, the very legislative determination to provide disability benefits, without any prerequisite determination of need in fact, presumes a need by the recipient which is not this Court's function to denigrate. Indeed, in the present case, it is indicated that because disability benefits were terminated there was a foreclosure upon the Eldridge home and the family's furniture was repossessed, forcing Eldridge, his wife, and their children to sleep in one bed. Finally, it is also no argument that a worker, who has been placed in the untenable position of having been denied disability benefits, may still seek other forms of public assistance.

Questions

1. Why, do you suppose, did the Court's statement of the facts not mention that Eldridge had already been through the termination process twice before?
2. Can you articulate what has become known as due process test from *Mathews v. Eldridge*? For a modern application of the test, see *Walters v. National Association of Radiation Survivors* at the end of the chapter.

The case you are about to read next, *Goss v. Lopez*, requires a due process hearing prior to a 10-day suspension from high school (the Court said "preferably prior to"). This case was decided just one year before the decisions in *Paul v. Davis* and *Eldridge*.

Goss v. Lopez
419 U.S. 565 (1975)

Justice White delivered the opinion of the Court, joined by Justices Brennan, Stewart, Marshall, and Stevens. Justice Powell filed a dissent joined by Chief Justice Burger and Justices Blackmun and Rehnquist.

This appeal by various administrators of the Columbus, Ohio, Public School System (CPSS) challenges the judgment of a three-judge federal court, declaring that appellees—various high school students in the CPSS—were denied due process of law contrary to the command of the Fourteenth Amendment in that they were temporarily suspended from their high schools without a hearing either prior to suspension or within a reasonable time thereafter, and enjoining the administrators to remove all references to such suspensions from the students' records.

I

Ohio law, Rev.Code Ann. § 3313.64 (1972), provides for free education to all children between the ages of six and 21. Section 3313.66 of the Code empowers the principal of an Ohio public school to suspend a pupil for misconduct for up to 10 days or to expel him. In either case, he must notify the student's parents within 24 hours and state the reasons for his action. A pupil who is expelled, or his parents, may appeal the decision to the Board of Education and in connection therewith shall be permitted to be heard at the board meeting. The Board may reinstate the pupil following the hearing. No similar procedure is provided in § 3313.66 or any other provision of state law for a suspended student. Aside from a regulation tracking the statute, at the time of the imposition of the suspensions in this case the CPSS itself had not issued any written procedure applicable to suspensions. Nor, so far as the record reflects, had any of the individual high schools involved in this case. Each, however, had formally or informally described the conduct for which suspension could be imposed. The nine named appellees, each of whom alleged that he or she had been suspended from public high school in Columbus for up to 10 days without a hearing pursuant to § 3313.66, filed an action under 42 U.S.C. § 1983 against the Columbus Board of Education and various administrators of the CPSS. The complaint sought a declaration that § 3313.66 was unconstitutional in that it permitted public school administrators to deprive plaintiffs of their rights to an education without a hearing of any kind, in violation of the procedural due process component of the Fourteenth Amendment. It also sought to enjoin the public school officials from issuing future suspensions pursuant to § 3313.66 and to require them to remove references to the past suspensions from the records of the students in question.

The proof below established that the suspensions arose out of a period of widespread student unrest in the CPSS during February and March 1971. Six of the named plaintiffs, Rudolph Sutton, Tyrone Washington, Susan Cooper, Deborah Fox, Clarence Byars, and Bruce Harris, were students at the Marion-Franklin High School and were each suspended for 10 days on account of disruptive or disobedient conduct committed in the presence of the school administrator who ordered the suspension. One of these, Tyrone Washington, was among a group of students demonstrating in the school auditorium while a class was being conducted there. He was ordered by the school principal to leave, refused to do so, and was suspended. Rudolph Sutton, in the presence of the principal, physically attacked a police officer who was attempting to remove Tyrone Washington from the auditorium. He was immediately suspended. The other four Marion-Franklin students were suspended for similar conduct. None was given a hearing to determine the operative facts underlying the suspension, but each, together with his or her parents, was offered the opportunity to attend a conference, subsequent to the effective date of the suspension, to discuss the student's future. Two named plaintiffs, Dwight Lopez and Betty Crome, were students at the Central High School and McGuffey Junior High School, respectively. The former was suspended in connection with a disturbance in the lunchroom which involved some physical damage to school property. Lopez testified that at least 75 other students were suspended from his school on the same day. He also testified below that he was not a party to the destructive conduct but was instead an innocent bystander. Because no one from the school testified with regard to this incident, there is no evidence in the record indicating the official basis for concluding otherwise. Lopez never had a hearing. Betty Crome was present at a demonstration at a high school other than the one she was attending. There she was arrested together with others, taken to the police station, and released without being formally charged. Before she went to school on the following day, she was notified that she had been suspended for a 10-day period. Because no one from the school testified with respect to this incident, the record does not disclose how the McGuffey Junior High School principal went about making the decision to suspend Crome, nor does it disclose on what information the decision was based. It is clear from the record that no hearing was ever held.

There was no testimony with respect to the suspension of the ninth named plaintiff, Carl Smith. The school files were also silent as to his suspension, although as to some, but not all, of the other named plaintiffs the files contained either direct references to their suspensions or copies of letters sent to their parents advising them of the suspension.

On the basis of this evidence, the three-judge court declared that plaintiffs were denied due process of law because they were "suspended without hearing prior to suspension or within a reasonable time thereafter," and that Ohio Rev.Code Ann. § 3313.66 (1972) and regulations issued pursuant thereto were unconstitutional in permitting such suspensions. It was ordered that all references to plaintiffs' suspensions be removed from school files.

II

At the outset, appellants contend that because there is no constitutional right to an education at public expense, the Due Process Clause does not protect against expulsions from the public school system. This position misconceives the nature of the issue and is refuted by prior decisions. The Fourteenth Amendment forbids the State to deprive any person of life, liberty, or property without due process of law. Protected interests in property are normally "not created by the Constitution. Rather, they are created and their dimensions are defined" by an independent source such as state statutes or rules entitling the citizen to certain benefits. *Board of Regents v. Roth,* 408 U.S. 564 (1972).

Here, on the basis of state law, appellees plainly had legitimate claims of entitlement to a public education. Ohio Rev.Code Ann. §§ 3313.48 and 3313.64 (1972 and Supp.1973) direct local authorities to provide a free education to all residents between five and 21 years of age, and a compulsory-attendance law requires attendance for a school year of not less than 32 weeks. It is true that § 3313.66 of the Code permits school principals to suspend students for up to 10 days; but suspensions may not be imposed without any grounds whatsoever. All of the schools had their own rules specifying the grounds for expulsion or suspension. Having chosen to extend the right to an education to people of appellees' class generally, Ohio may not withdraw that right on grounds of misconduct absent fundamentally fair procedures to determine whether the misconduct has occurred.

Among other things, the State is constrained to recognize a student's legitimate entitlement to a public education as a property interest which is protected by the Due Process Clause and which may not be taken away for misconduct without adherence to the minimum procedures required by that Clause.

The Due Process Clause also forbids arbitrary deprivations of liberty. "Where a person's good name, reputation, honor, or integrity is at stake because of what the government is doing to him," the minimal requirements of the Clause must be satisfied. *Wisconsin v. Constantineau,* 400 U.S. 433 (1971); *Board of Regents v. Roth, supra,* 408 U.S. at 573. School authorities here suspended appellees from school for periods of up to 10 days based on charges of misconduct. If sustained and recorded, those charges could seriously damage the students' standing with their fellow pupils and their teachers as well as interfere with later opportunities for higher education and employment. It is apparent that the claimed right of the State to determine unilaterally and without process whether that misconduct has occurred immediately collides with the requirements of the Constitution.

III

"Once it is determined that due process applies, the question remains what process is due." We turn to that question, fully realizing as our cases regularly do that the interpretation and application of the Due Process Clause are intensely practical matters and that "[t]he very nature of due process negates any concept of inflexible procedures universally applicable to every imaginable situation."

Students facing temporary suspension have interests qualifying for protection of the Due Process Clause, and due process requires, in connection with a suspension of 10 days or less, that the student be given oral or written notice of the charges against him and, if he denies them, an explanation of the evidence the authorities have and an opportunity to present his side of the story. The Clause requires at least these rudimentary precautions against unfair or mistaken findings of misconduct and arbitrary exclusion from school. There need be no delay between the time notice is given and the time of the hearing. In the great majority of cases the disciplinarian may informally discuss the alleged misconduct with the student minutes after it has occurred. We hold only that, in being given an opportunity to explain his version of the facts at this discussion, the student first be told what he is accused of doing and what the basis of the accusation is.

Since the hearing may occur almost immediately following the misconduct, it follows that as a general rule notice and hearing should precede removal of the student from school. We agree with the District Court, however, that there are recurring situations in which prior notice and hearing cannot be insisted upon. Students whose presence poses a continuing danger to persons or property or an ongoing threat of disrupting the academic process may be immediately removed from school. In such cases, the necessary notice and rudimentary hearing should follow as soon as practicable, as the District Court indicated.

Affirmed.

Questions

1. What is the interest involved?
2. What procedure is required?
3. Must the procedure be administered predeprivation?

The Court says in *Goss* that suspended students must be notified of the charges, provided an explanation of the evidence the school officials have, and given an opportunity to explain their side of the facts. In this case, Dwight Lopez said he was a bystander in a disturbance in the school cafeteria, that he took no part in activities that led to destruction of property, and that he was suspended along with 75 other students. Betty Crome, a junior high student, was present at a demonstration at a high school, where she was rounded up with students, taken to the police station, and then released without being charged. In both cases, the students would be going before the very vice principal who wanted to suspend them prior to the Court ordering a hearing first. How much protection against a "wrongful suspension" do you think the process provides?

The next case involves the issue of academic suspensions. Compare the result in *Horowitz* to the decision in *Goss*.

Board of Curators of the University
of Missouri v. Horowitz
435 U.S. 78 (1978)

Justice Rehnquist delivered the opinion of the Court.

Respondent, a student at the University of Missouri-Kansas City Medical School, was dismissed by petitioner officials of the school during her final year of study for failure to meet academic standards. Respondent sued petitioners under 42 U.S.C. § 1983 in the United States District Court for the Western District of Missouri alleging, among other constitutional violations, that petitioners had not accorded her procedural due process prior to her dismissal. The District Court, after conducting a full trial, concluded that respondent had been afforded all of the rights guaranteed her by the Fourteenth Amendment to the United States Constitution and dismissed her complaint. The Court of Appeals for the Eighth Circuit reversed, 538 F.2d 1317 (1976), and a petition for rehearing en banc was denied by a divided court. We granted certiorari, to consider what procedures must be accorded to a student at a state educational institution whose dismissal may constitute a deprivation of "liberty" or "property" within the meaning of the Fourteenth Amendment. We reverse the judgment of the Court of Appeals.

I

Respondent was admitted with advanced standing to the Medical School in the fall of 1971. During the final years of a student's education at the school, the student is required to pursue in "rotational units" academic and clinical studies pertaining to various medical disciplines such as obstetrics-gynecology, pediatrics, and surgery. Each student's academic performance at the school is evaluated on a periodic basis by the Council on Evaluation, a body composed of both faculty and students, which can recommend various actions including probation and dismissal. The recommendations of the Council are reviewed by the Coordinating Committee, a body composed solely of faculty members, and must ultimately be approved by the Dean. Students are not typically allowed to appear before either the Council or the Coordinating Committee on the occasion of their review of the student's academic performance.

In the spring of respondent's first year of study, several faculty members expressed dissatisfaction with her clinical performance during a pediatrics rotation. The faculty members noted that respondent's "performance was below that of her peers in all clinical patient-oriented settings," that she was erratic in her attendance at clinical sessions, and that she lacked a critical concern for personal hygiene. Upon the recommendation of the Council on Evaluation, respondent was advanced to her second and final year on a probationary basis.

Faculty dissatisfaction with respondent's clinical performance continued during the following year. For example, respondent's docent, or faculty adviser, rated her clinical skills as "unsatisfactory." In the middle of the year, the Council again reviewed respondent's academic progress and concluded that respondent should not be considered for graduation in June of that year; furthermore, the Council recommended that, absent "radical improvement," respondent be dropped from the school.

Respondent was permitted to take a set of oral and practical examinations as an "appeal" of the decision not to permit her to graduate. Pursuant to this "appeal," respondent spent a substantial portion of time with seven practicing physicians in the area who enjoyed a good reputation among their peers. The physicians were asked to recommend whether respondent should be allowed to graduate on schedule and, if not, whether she should be dropped immediately or allowed to remain on probation. Only two of the doctors recommended that respondent be graduated on schedule. Of the other five, two recommended that she be immediately dropped from the school. The remaining three recommended that she not be allowed to graduate in June and be continued on probation pending further reports on her clinical progress. Upon receipt of these recommendations, the Council on Evaluation reaffirmed its prior position.

The Council met again in mid-May to consider whether respondent should be allowed to remain in school beyond June of that year. Noting that the report on respondent's recent surgery rotation rated her performance as "low-satisfactory," the Council unanimously recommended that "barring receipt of any reports that Miss Horowitz has improved radically, [she] not be allowed to re-enroll in the . . . School of Medicine." The Council delayed making its recommendation official until receiving reports on other rotations; when a report on respondent's emergency rotation also turned out to be negative, the Council unanimously reaffirmed its recommendation that respondent be dropped from the school. The Coordinating Committee and the Dean approved the recommendation and notified respondent, who appealed the decision in writing to the University's Provost for Health Sciences. The Provost sustained the school's actions after reviewing the record compiled during the earlier proceedings.

II

A

To be entitled to the procedural protections of the Fourteenth Amendment, respondent must in a case such as this demonstrate that her dismissal from the school deprived her of either a "liberty" or a "property" interest. Respondent has never alleged that she was deprived of a property interest. Because property interests are creatures of state law, respondent would have been required to show at trial that her seat at the Medical School was a "property" interest recognized by Missouri state law. Instead, respondent argued that her dismissal deprived her of "liberty" by substantially impairing her opportunities to continue her medical

education or to return to employment in a medically related field.

The Court of Appeals agreed, citing this Court's opinion in *Board of Regents v. Roth,* 408 U.S. 564 (1972). . . .

B

We need not decide, however, whether respondent's dismissal deprived her of a liberty interest in pursuing a medical career. Nor need we decide whether respondent's dismissal infringed any other interest constitutionally protected against deprivation without procedural due process. Assuming the existence of a liberty or property interest, respondent has been awarded at least as much due process as the Fourteenth Amendment requires. The school fully informed respondent of the faculty's dissatisfaction with her clinical progress and the danger that this posed to timely graduation and continued enrollment. The ultimate decision to dismiss respondent was careful and deliberate. These procedures were sufficient under the Due Process Clause of the Fourteenth Amendment. We agree with the District Court that respondent "was afforded full procedural due process by the [school]. In fact, the Court is of the opinion, and so finds, that the school went beyond [constitutionally required] procedural due process by affording [respondent] the opportunity to be examined by seven independent physicians in order to be absolutely certain that their grading of the [respondent] in her medical skills was correct." . . .

Since the issue first arose 50 years ago, state and lower federal courts have recognized that there are distinct differences between decisions to suspend or dismiss a student for disciplinary purposes and similar actions taken for academic reasons which may call for hearings in connection with the former but not the latter. These prior decisions of state and federal courts, over a period of 60 years, unanimously holding that formal hearings before decisionmaking bodies need not be held in the case of academic dismissals, cannot be rejected lightly . . . Academic evaluations of a student, in contrast to disciplinary determinations, bear little resemblance to the judicial and administrative fact-finding proceedings to which we have traditionally attached a full-hearing requirement. In *Goss,* the school's decision to suspend the students rested on factual conclusions that the individual students had participated in demonstrations that had disrupted classes, attacked a police officer, or caused physical damage to school property. The requirement of a hearing, where the student could present his side of the factual issue, could under such circumstances "provide a meaningful hedge against erroneous action." The decision to dismiss respondent, by comparison, rested on the academic judgment of school officials that she did not have the necessary clinical ability to perform adequately as a medical doctor and was making insufficient progress toward that goal. Such a judgment is by its nature more subjective and evaluative than the typical factual questions presented in the average disciplinary decision. Like the decision of an individual professor as to the proper grade for a student in his course, the determination whether to dismiss a student for academic reasons requires an expert evaluation of cumulative information and is not readily adapted to the procedural tools of judicial or administrative decisionmaking.

The judgment of the Court of Appeals is therefore Reversed.

Questions

1. How much process is due in academic suspensions?
2. Do you think it makes a difference that this involved a graduate program?
3. What role does court deference to expertise play in this case?

In 1985, the Court revisited the issues in *Horowitz* in the case of *Regents of the University of Michigan v. Ewing,* 474 U.S. 124 (1985). Ewing had been accepted into a special accelerated six-year program that led to the award of both a bachelor's and a medical degree. Before enrollees could complete the last two years of the program, they had to pass a two-day written test administered by the National Board of Medical Examiners (NBME) (the NBME exam). Ewing received the lowest score on the exam that any student in the program had ever received. He was not allowed to retake the exam and was expelled from the program. Ewing had opportunities to make his case before the Committee that expelled him so this is not a procedural due process case. The essence of his complaint was that other students had been given opportunities to retake the NBME, and because he was not afforded such an opportunity, the decision to expel him was arbitrary under the due process clause. The Court did find that Ewing had a property interest in continuing enrollment in the program, but he had been accorded all the procedural due process necessary, and the Committee's decision not to let him retake the Boards was based on the totality of his record and was not arbitrary.

If a hearing (of some kind) is necessary prior to termination of AFDC benefits, disciplinary suspensions from both high school and college, state cooperation in garnishment and repossession of personal property, the suspension of a driver's license, and the posting of a name to inhibit the individual's ability to purchase alcohol, what kind of a hearing do you suppose is required before a public school administrator can administer corporal punishment to a student?

Ingraham v. Wright
430 U.S. 651 (1977)

Justice Powell delivered the opinion of the Court, joined by Chief Justice Burger and Justices Stewart, Blackmun, and Rehnquist. Justices White, Brennan, Marshall, and Stevens dissented.

This case presents questions concerning the use of corporal punishment in public schools: First, whether the paddling of students as a means of maintaining school discipline constitutes cruel and unusual punishment in violation of the Eighth Amendment; and, second, to the extent that paddling is constitutionally permissible, whether the Due Process Clause of the Fourteenth Amendment requires prior notice and an opportunity to be heard.

I

Petitioners James Ingraham and Roosevelt Andrews filed the complaint in this case on January 7, 1971, in the United States District Court for the Southern District of Florida. At the time both were enrolled in the Charles R. Drew Junior High School in Dade County, Fla., Ingraham in the eighth grade and Andrews in the ninth. The complaint contained three counts, each alleging a separate cause of action for deprivation of constitutional rights, under 42 U.S.C. §§ 1981–1988. Counts one and two were individual actions for damages by Ingraham and Andrews based on paddling incidents that allegedly occurred in October 1970 at Drew Junior High School. Count three was a class action for declaratory and injunctive relief filed on behalf of all students in the Dade County schools. Named as defendants in all counts were respondents Willie J. Wright (principal at Drew Junior High School), Lemmie Deliford (an assistant principal), Solomon Barnes (an assistant to the principal), and Edward L. Whigham (superintendent of the Dade County School System).

Petitioners' evidence may be summarized briefly. In the 1970–1971 school year many of the 237 schools in Dade County used corporal punishment as a means of maintaining discipline pursuant to Florida legislation and a local School Board regulation. The statute then in effect authorized limited corporal punishment by negative inference, proscribing punishment which was "degrading or unduly severe" or which was inflicted without prior consultation with the principal or the teacher in charge of the school. Fla.Stat.Ann. § 232.27 (1961). The regulation, Dade County School Board Policy 5144, contained explicit directions and limitations. The authorized punishment consisted of paddling the recalcitrant student on the buttocks with a flat wooden paddle measuring less than two feet long, three to four inches wide, and about one-half inch thick. The normal punishment was limited to one to five "licks" or blows with the paddle and resulted in no apparent physical injury to the student. School authorities viewed corporal punishment as a less drastic means of discipline than suspension or expulsion. Contrary to the procedural requirements of the statute and regulation, teachers often paddled students on their own authority without first consulting the principal. . . .

Petitioners focused on Drew Junior High School, the school in which both Ingraham and Andrews were enrolled in the fall of 1970. In an apparent reference to Drew, the District Court found that "[t]he instances of punishment which could be characterized as severe, accepting the students' testimony as credible, took place in one junior high school." The evidence, consisting mainly of the testimony of 16 students, suggests that the regime at Drew was exceptionally harsh. The testimony of Ingraham and Andrews, in support of their individual claims for damages, is illustrative. Because he was slow to respond to his teacher's instructions, Ingraham was subjected to more than 20 licks with a paddle while being held over a table in the principal's office. The paddling was so severe that he suffered a hematoma requiring medical attention and keeping him out of school for several days. Andrews was paddled several times for minor infractions. On two occasions he was struck on his arms, once depriving him of the full use of his arm for a week. . . .

The Eighth Amendment provides: "Excessive bail shall not be required, nor excessive fines imposed, nor cruel and unusual punishments inflicted." Bail, fines, and punishment traditionally have been associated with the criminal process, and by subjecting the three to parallel limitations the text of the Amendment suggests an intention to limit the power of those entrusted with the criminal-law function of government. An examination of the history of the Amendment and the decisions of this Court construing the proscription against cruel and unusual punishment confirms that it was designed to protect those convicted of crimes. We adhere to this longstanding limitation and hold that the Eighth Amendment does not apply to the paddling of children as a means of maintaining discipline in public schools. . . .

IV

The Fourteenth Amendment prohibits any state deprivation of life, liberty, or property without due process of law. Application of this prohibition requires the familiar two-stage analysis: We must first ask whether the asserted individual interests are encompassed within the Fourteenth Amendment's protection of "life, liberty or property"; if protected interests are implicated, we then must decide what procedures constitute "due process of law." Following that analysis here, we find that corporal punishment in public schools implicates a constitutionally protected liberty interest, but we hold that the traditional common-law remedies are fully adequate to afford due process.

While the contours of this historic liberty interest in the context of our federal system of government have not been defined precisely, they always have been thought to encompass freedom from bodily restraint and punishment. It is fundamental that the state cannot hold and physically punish an individual except in accordance with due process of law. . . .

This constitutionally protected liberty interest is at stake in this case. There is, of course a de minimis level of imposition with which the Constitution is not concerned. But at least where school authorities, acting under color of state law, deliberately decide to punish a child

for misconduct by restraining the child and inflicting appreciable physical pain, we hold that Fourteenth Amendment liberty interests are implicated. . . .

B

"[T]he question remains what process is due." Were it not for the common-law privilege permitting teachers to inflict reasonable corporal punishment on children in their care, and the availability of the traditional remedies for abuse, the case for requiring advance procedural safeguards would be strong indeed. But here we deal with a punishment-paddling within that tradition, and the question is whether the common-law remedies are adequate to afford due process. . . .

"[D]ue process," unlike some legal rules, is not a technical conception with a fixed content unrelated to time, place and circumstances. . . . Representing a profound attitude of fairness. . . ."due process" is compounded of history, reason, the past course of decisions, and stout confidence in the strength of the democratic faith which we profess . . . Whether in this case the common-law remedies for excessive corporal punishment constitute due process of law must turn on an analysis of the competing interests at stake, viewed against the background of "history, reason, (and) the past course of decisions." The analysis requires consideration of three distinct factors: "First, the private interest that will be affected; second, the risk of an erroneous deprivation of such interest and the probable value, if any, of additional or substitute procedural safeguards; and, finally, the (state) interest, including the function involved and the fiscal and administrative burdens that the additional or substitute procedural requirement would entail."

1

Because it is rooted in history, the child's liberty interest in avoiding corporal punishment while in the care of public school authorities is subject to historical limitations. Under the common law, an invasion of personal security gave rise to a right to recover damages in a subsequent judicial proceeding. But the right of recovery was qualified by the concept of justification. Thus, there could be no recovery against a teacher who gave only "moderate correction" to a child. To the extent that the force used was reasonable in light of its purpose, it was not wrongful, but rather "justifiable or lawful." The concept that reasonable corporal punishment in school is justifiable continues to be recognized in the laws of most States . . .

2

Florida has continued to recognize, and indeed has strengthened by statute, the common-law right of a child not to be subjected to excessive corporal punishment in school. Under Florida law the teacher and principal of the school decide in the first instance whether corporal punishment is reasonably necessary under the circumstances in order to discipline a child who has misbehaved. But they must exercise prudence and restraint. For Florida has preserved the traditional judicial proceedings for determining whether the punishment was justified. If the punishment inflicted is later found to have been excessive, not reasonably believed at the time to be necessary for the child's discipline or training, the school authorities inflicting it may be held liable in damages to the child and, if malice is shown, they may be subject to criminal penalties . . .

Although students have testified in this case to specific instances of abuse, there is every reason to believe that such mistreatment is an aberration. The uncontradicted evidence suggests that corporal punishment in the Dade County schools was, "[w]ith the exception of a few cases, . . . unremarkable in physical severity." Moreover, because paddlings are usually inflicted in response to conduct directly observed by teachers in their presence, the risk that a child will be paddled without cause is typically insignificant. In the ordinary case, a disciplinary paddling neither threatens seriously to violate any substantive rights nor condemns the child "to suffer grievous loss of any kind."

3

But even if the need for advance procedural safeguards were clear, the question would remain whether the incremental benefit could justify the cost. Acceptance of petitioners' claims would work a transformation in the law governing corporal punishment in Florida and most other States. Given the impracticability of formulating a rule of procedural due process that varies with the severity of the particular imposition, the prior hearing petitioners seek would have to precede any paddling, however moderate or trivial. . . .

Such a universal constitutional requirement would significantly burden the use of corporal punishment as a disciplinary measure. . . .

Elimination or curtailment of corporal punishment would be welcomed by many as a societal advance. But when such a policy choice may result from this Court's determination of an asserted right to due process, rather than from the normal processes of community debate and legislative action, the societal costs cannot be dismissed as insubstantial.

V

Petitioners cannot prevail on either of the theories before us in this case. The Eighth Amendment's prohibition against cruel and unusual punishment is inapplicable to school paddlings, and the Fourteenth Amendment's requirement of procedural due process is satisfied by Florida's preservation of common-law constraints and remedies. We therefore agree with the Court of Appeals that petitioners' evidence affords no basis for injunctive relief, and that petitioners cannot recover damages on the basis of any Eighth Amendment or procedural due process violation.

Affirmed.

Question

1. Aside from the awkwardness of a due process hearing prior to the administration of corporal punishment, the Court provides another legal reason why due process might not be necessary. Can you explain the reason?

In a 1988 case, a bank president was indicted for making false statements to the Federal Deposit Insurance Corporation (FDIC). Shortly after the indictment, the FDIC terminated him from his job and barred his employment with any FDIC-insured bank. The applicable statute gave the FDIC the power to summarily terminate in such circumstances, and it provided for a posttermination hearing to be held within 90 days of the termination. Furthermore, the FDIC could decide whether to allow oral testimony at the hearing. The plaintiff challenged both the timing of the hearing and the sufficiency of the hearing process as violations of due process. See *FDIC v. Mallen* (1988).[40]

In 1998, a Los Angeles police officer had Mr. David's car towed because it was parked in a no parking zone. David claimed that he could not see the no parking sign because the city had not trimmed the trees around the sign. He paid the $134.50 to retrieve his car and requested a hearing for a refund. About a month later, the city gave him his hearing and denied his refund. His case went to the Supreme Court on the sufficiency of the timing of the hearing. See *City of Los Angeles v. David* (2003).[41] In both cases, the Court applied the *Eldridge* test and decided against the plaintiffs.

LICENSING

One area of administrative law that has been touched on only tangentially is licensing. When the federal government requires a license, that frequently touches on a property interest, and therefore, the quasi-judicial procedure of § 554 of the Administrative Procedure Act is required. The states issue licenses not only to drivers but also to workers in a whole host of occupations, including physicians, lawyers, plumbers, electricians, and barbers. Professor Walter Gellhorn had this to say about occupational licensing in the states:

> Possibly the founding fathers knew of restrictions in some of the new American states on the practices of law and medicine. They would, however, have been aghast to learn that in many parts of this country today aspiring bee keepers, embalmers, lightning rod salesmen, septic tank cleaners, taxidermists, and tree surgeons must obtain official approval before seeking the public's patronage. After examining the roster of those who must receive official permission to function, a cynic might conclude that virtually the only people who remain unlicensed in at least one of the United States are clergymen and university professors, presumably because they are nowhere taken seriously.[42]

The reader should have passing familiarity with the subject of licensing because the decisions and procedures of licensing boards can have serious property implications. The Kansas Board of Medical Examiners revoked a physician's license because the doctor claimed publicly to have had contact with extraterrestrial beings. In some cases, those who sit on licensing boards have used their power to enrich themselves at the expense of those lacking access to the board.[43] In Georgia, the liquor license procedure called for the board to consider patronage as well as statutory requirements, which led a federal court to declare a license denial based on the patronage criterion to be a violation of due process.[44]

To this point, you have been exposed to the seminal cases in administrative law of due process. As a result, you know:

- A fairly elaborate pretermination hearing was required prior to termination of AFDC benefits (but AFDC no longer exists)
- A posttermination hearing before an administrative law judge is sufficient due process in a disability termination case; Congress, however, has amended the process to allow a face-to-face hearing in which the claimant can present his or her case at the reconsideration stage
- Notice and an opportunity to refute are required before a state may post the name of an individual forbidden to purchase alcohol, but none is required to post the name of a cleared "shoplifter"
- Notice and an opportunity to refute are required before suspension from a public school for disciplinary reasons, but no due process is necessary for suspension from school for academic reasons or for the imposition of corporal punishment.

Can you detect a pattern in these decisions?

It is difficult to summarize due process because the Court has not been consistent in recognizing property or liberty interest and in determining what procedures are due at what point. We can identify some common notions about due process in administrative law. First, so long as minimal due process protections exist, courts are likely to show deference to administrative agencies. Second, so long as the potential loss is not a severe deprivation of liberty or property, minimal acceptable due process appears to consist of notice, some kind of opportunity to explain and/or refute, and an impartial decision maker. Administrative agencies get into trouble in terms of due process and judicial review when they fail to provide any hearing at all or when the procedure is not fair. The *Eldridge* case aside, the purpose of due process in public administration is to avoid the likelihood of error in taking citizens' property or in limiting the exercise of their liberties. Generally, where minimal due process procedures are in place, that risk of error is reduced enough to satisfy reviewing courts.

We have mentioned the due process ramifications of privatization and outsourcing before in this chapter. There are two sides of this issue, but only one side has been discussed so far. Not only are individual citizens likely to be adversely affected by the decisions of private entities like reviewing committees or HMOs, but the private companies can also be adversely affected by government treatment of them. Courts will have to consider the due process rights of both the customers and the providers. *Shalala v. Illinois Council on Long Term Care, Inc.,* 529 U.S. 1 (2000), involved a legal attack by an association of health care providers on the secretary of health and human services' authority to sanction providers in the Medicare program. The Court said that Congress and HHS have created elaborate internal procedures; the Medicare statute disallows a federal court challenge in the manner the plaintiffs used. None of the association's members had been sanctioned, and they did not go through the internal procedures.

SUMMARY

1. Due process litigation requires government or state action.

2. Liberty and property interests are created by state law or authority (not by the U.S. Constitution).

3. *Goldberg* is the only case in which the Court has required full due process protection in a predeprivation administrative context. Presumably, that is because the deprivation means certain destitution for the parent and children.

4. For cases in which the deprivation is not as severe as in *Goldberg*, minimal due process will usually suffice.

5. Minimal due process appears to be (a) notice, (b) appraisal of evidence against, (c) some form of opportunity to refute and explain, and (d) generally, a neutral decision maker.

6. Whether a pre- or a postdeprivation hearing will suffice is sometimes determined by applying the three-pronged balancing test from *Mathews v. Eldridge:* (a) What is the private interest? (b) What is the risk of an erroneous decision? What would the value be in requiring additional procedures? (c) What is the government's interest?

END-OF-CHAPTER CASES

Grijalva v. Shalala
152 F.3d 1115 (1998)

Circuit Judges Herbert Y. C. Choy, Mary M. Schroeder, and Charles Wiggins. Opinion by Judge Wiggins.

Medicare beneficiaries enrolled in health maintenance organizations ("HMOs") in Arizona sued the Secretary of Health and Human Services ("Secretary"). Their suit alleged a failure to enforce due process requirements and a failure to monitor HMO denials of medical services to enrolled Medicare beneficiaries. The district court granted Plaintiffs summary judgment, holding that HMO denials of medical services to Medicare beneficiaries constitute state action and that the regulations issued by the Secretary fail to provide due process. The district court issued an injunction mandating certain procedural protections for Medicare beneficiaries enrolled in HMOs. The Secretary appeals. We affirm.

I. Background

Congress passed the Medicare Act, Title XVIII of the Social Security Act, 42 U.S.C. §§ 1395 et seq., in 1965 to provide a federal health insurance program for the elderly and the disabled. Today, a Medicare beneficiary can receive Medicare services in two different ways. The first is to receive Medicare on a fee-for-service basis. Under this option, the beneficiary goes to a health care provider for the necessary

covered services; either the provider or the beneficiary will be reimbursed by the government for the cost of the services. The second, newer option is to enroll in an HMO or other eligible organization. See 42 U.S.C. § 1395 mm(b).

In 1982, Congress authorized the Secretary to enter into "risk-sharing" contracts with HMOs. See § 1395mm. Under these contracts, HMOs provide to enrolled Medicare beneficiaries all the Medicare services provided in the statute in exchange for a monthly flat payment from the Secretary.

The Medicare statute establishes in § 1395mm(c) procedural protections for those beneficiaries that enroll in HMOs. Among these, the HMO must "provide meaningful procedures for hearing and resolving grievances between the organization . . . and members enrolled . . ." § 1395mm (c)(5)(A). HMO members must also have certain appeal rights:

A member enrolled with an eligible organization under this section who is dissatisfied by reason of his failure to receive any health service to which he believes he is entitled and at no greater charge than he believes he is required to pay is entitled, if the amount in controversy is $100 or more, to a hearing before the Secretary to the same extent as is provided in [42 U.S.C. § 405(b)], and in any such hearing the Secretary shall make the eligible organization a party. If the amount in controversy is $1,000 or more, the individual or eligible organization shall, upon notifying the other party, be entitled to judicial review of the Secretary's final decision as provided in [42 U.S.C. § 405(g)]. . . . § 1395mm(c)(5)(B).

The Secretary created additional appeal protections in subsequent regulations. See 42 C.F.R. §§ 417.600–417.638. Under § 417.604, each HMO must establish appeal procedures and ensure that beneficiaries receive written information about the appeal and grievance procedures. If the HMO makes an "organization determination" (defined in § 417.606) adverse to the enrollee, "it must notify the enrollee of the determination within 60 days of receiving the enrollee's request for payment for services." An example of an adverse organization determination is an HMO's decision that certain medical services are not covered by Medicare. The notice to the beneficiary must "state the specific reasons for the determination" and inform the enrollee of his or her "right to a reconsideration." § 417.608(b). Failure to provide timely notice is an adverse determination and may be appealed by the enrollee. See § 417.608(c).

If the enrollee is dissatisfied with an adverse determination, a request for reconsideration may be filed within 60 days from the date of the notice. Within 60 days of the request, the HMO may make a decision fully favorable to the enrollee. If it decides to make a decision that partially or completely affirms the adverse determination, it must explain its decision in writing and forward the case to the Health Care Financing Administration ("HCFA"). See § 417.620(b). If the enrollee is dissatisfied with the result of the reconsideration, and the amount remaining in controversy is $100 or more, the enrollee has a right to a hearing before an administrative law judge ("ALJ"). See § 417.630. The enrollee can appeal that hearing decision to the Appeals Council and then to the district court.

The Secretary possesses a number of sanctions to ensure HMO compliance with the Medicare statute and the Secretary's regulations. First, the Secretary "may not enter into a contract . . . with

an [HMO] unless it meets the requirements of [§ 1395mm(c)] and [§ 1395mm(e)]." 42 U.S.C. § 1395mm(c)(1). The specified sections require the HMO, inter alia, to provide all Medicare services to eligible enrollees, to have particular open enrollment periods, to provide enrollees annually with information on their rights, including appeal rights, to provide covered services "with reasonable promptness," to provide the aforementioned procedural protections, and not to exceed certain limits on rates charged to beneficiaries and the Secretary.

Second, the Secretary may terminate any contract with an HMO if she determines that the HMO has not met the terms of the contract or has not satisfied the statutory or regulatory requirements. If the Secretary determines that an HMO has failed to provide necessary covered services to an enrollee and that failure has adversely affected the individual, the Secretary may seek civil money penalties, suspend enrollment, or suspend payment to the HMO.

In 1993, five Medicare beneficiaries enrolled in an Arizona HMO sued the Secretary. Among other claims, Plaintiffs alleged that the Secretary "has failed and refused to take effective action to implement beneficiaries' notice and appeal rights when they are denied health care services by their HMOs," and "has failed and refused to provide Medicare beneficiaries enrolled in HMOs with a procedure of obtaining review of HMO denial decisions contemporaneously with the denial decisions." In a decision not on appeal, the district court certified a nationwide plaintiff class.

In October 1996, the district court granted partial summary judgment to Plaintiffs on the claims described above. See Grijalva v. Shalala, 946 F. Supp. 747 (D. Ariz. 1996). The court held that the "organization determinations" made by HMOs constitute state action, triggering constitutional due process requirements. The court also held that the regulations promulgated by the Secretary regarding adverse determinations by HMOs fail to provide sufficient due process to enrollees under Mathews v. Eldridge, 424 U.S. 319 (1976). In particular, the district court found that the notices issued by HMOs failed to provide adequate notice: they were often illegible, failed to specify the reason for the denial, and failed to inform the beneficiary that he or she had the right to present additional evidence to the HMO. Therefore, "subsequent due process, available in the administrative review phase of the appeal, comes too late in many cases. . . ." Id. at 759. The district court also found that the language of § 1395mm(c)(1) ("The Secretary may not enter into a contract . . . with an eligible organization unless it meets the requirements of this subsection") was mandatory, requiring the Secretary to enforce her regulations by refusing to renew a contract with an HMO if the denial notices of that HMO fail to provide due process.

The district court found that the Secretary violated § 1395mm(c)(1) by entering into a contract with any HMO that failed to provide timely notice for any and all denials of service. The court held that the notice must be legible (at least 12-point type), state clearly the reason for the denial, inform the enrollee of all appeal rights, explain hearing rights and procedures, and provide "instruction on how to obtain supporting evidence, including medical records and supporting affidavits from the attending physician." Id. at 760-61. The district court also held that any hearing must be "informal, in-person communication with the decision-maker," available upon request for all service denials, and timely. Id. at 761. The district court also required expedited hearings for "acute care service denials." Id. . . .

The actions of private parties are not subject to the requirements of constitutional due process unless they can fairly be considered government action. See *Shelley v. Kraemer,* 334 U.S. 1, 13 (1948). We use the same standards to attribute the actions of private actors to the federal government under the Fifth Amendment as we do to attribute private actions to state governments under the Fourteenth Amendment. See *Kitchens v. Bowen,* 825 F.2d 1337, 1340 (9th Cir. 1987). The actions of private entities constitute state action under particular circumstances. In order to show that a private action is in fact state action, the plaintiff must show that "'there is a sufficiently close nexus between the

State and the challenged action of the regulated entity so that the action of the latter may be fairly treated as that of the State itself.'" *Blum v. Yaretsky,* 457 U.S. 991, 1004 (1982) (quoting *Jackson v. Metropolitan Edison Co.,* 419 U.S. 345, 351 (1974)). The government's regulation of the private actor is insufficient alone to show federal action. See *Blum,* 457 U.S. at 1004; *Jackson,* 419 U.S. at 350. Government action exists if there is a symbiotic relationship with a high degree of interdependence between the private and public parties such that they are "joint participants in the challenged activity." See *Burton v. Wilmington Parking Auth.,* 365 U.S. 715, 725 (1961). Government action exists if the challenged private action occurs under government compulsion. See *Adickes v. S. H. Kress & Co.,* 398 U.S. 144, 170-71 (1970). The government must do more, however, than merely acquiesce in the challenged action. See *Flagg Bros., Inc. v. Brooks,* 436 U.S. 149, 164 (1978) (holding that government inaction is insufficient for state action). A detailed inquiry into the facts of the particular case may be necessary to determine whether there is state or federal action. See *Jackson,* 419 U.S. at 351.

In this case, the question is whether the challenged action—HMO denials of services to Medicare beneficiaries with inadequate notice—may fairly be treated as that of the federal government. We agree with the district court's cogent analysis and conclusion that, in the circumstances of the Secretary's regulation of and delegation of Medicare coverage decisions to HMOs, HMO denials of services to Medicare beneficiaries with inadequate notice constitute federal action.

We find that HMOs and the federal government are essentially engaged as joint participants to provide Medicare services such that the actions of HMOs in denying medical services to Medicare beneficiaries and in failing to provide adequate notice may fairly be attributed to the federal government. The Secretary extensively regulates the provision of Medicare services by HMOs. HMOs are required, by the Medicare statute and their contracts with the Secretary, to comply with all federal laws and regulations. The Secretary is required to ensure, inter alia, that HMOs provide adequate notice and meaningful appeal procedures to beneficiaries. The Secretary pays HMOs for each enrolled Medicare beneficiary (regardless of the services provided). The federal government has created the legal framework—the standards and enforcement mechanisms—within which HMOs make adverse determinations, issue notices, and guarantee appeal rights. Medicare beneficiaries enrolled in HMOs may appeal an HMO's adverse determination to the Secretary, who has the power to overturn the HMO's decision. Each of these factors alone might not be sufficient to establish federal action. Together they show federal action. See *Catanzano v. Dowling,* 60 F.3d 113, 117–120 (2d Cir. 1995) (similar analysis in Medicaid context); *J.K. v. Dillenberg,* 836 F. Supp. 694, 697–99 (D. Ariz. 1993) (same). . . .

Unlike the nursing home doctors and administrators in *Blum,* the HMOs in this case are not making decisions to which the government merely responds. HMOs are following congressional and regulatory orders and are making decisions as a governmental proxy—they are deciding that Medicare does not cover certain medical services. In *Blum,* by contrast, the nursing homes decided that certain medical services were no longer medically necessary. While such an inquiry may occur in HMO service denials, the decisions in the case at hand are more accurately described as coverage decisions—interpretations of the Medicare statute—rather than merely medical judgments (particularly when no reason for the denial is given other than that the service does not meet "Medicare guidelines . . . based upon [the HMO's] understanding and interpretation of Medicare . . . coverage policies and guidelines," to quote a typical notice provided by Plaintiffs). . . .

B. Due Process and *Mathews v. Eldridge*

The parties agree that the balancing test used by the Supreme Court in *Mathews v. Eldridge,* 424 U.S. 319 (1976), applies to determine the necessary procedural protections to ensure that due process is provided to Medicare beneficiaries enrolled in HMOs. . . .

1. Private Interest at Stake

The district court held that the private interest at stake from an HMO's initial denial of Medicare coverage is the potential that medical care will be precluded altogether. The court held that this interest is a substantial private interest in additional protections such as timely and effective notice of service denials. We agree. . . .

The district court was correct in holding that Plaintiffs' interest in Medicare benefits is greater than the interest of the plaintiff in *Eldridge.* As the district court noted, "unlike *Eldridge,* the deprivation suffered from an HMO denial to provide care cannot so easily be remedied by retroactive recoupment of benefits." 946 F. Supp. at 757. An HMO's denial of coverage is an initial refusal to provide any medical services. The mere fact that the enrollee may be able to go elsewhere and pay for the services herself is of little comfort to an elderly, poor patient—particularly one who is ill and whose skilled nursing care has been terminated without a specific reason or description of how to appeal. . . .

2. Risk of Erroneous Deprivation

The district court also held that factor two weighed in favor of greater procedural protections for Medicare beneficiaries enrolled in HMOs. The court reviewed Plaintiffs' analysis of notice failures and conducted its own review of the notices provided to Plaintiffs. The court held that the notices failed to provide adequate explanation for the denials. See 946 F. Supp. at 757–58. We agree. This failure creates a high risk of erroneous deprivation of medical care to Medicare beneficiaries. The appeal rights and other procedural protections available to Medicare beneficiaries are meaningless if the beneficiaries are unaware of the reason for service denial and therefore cannot argue against the denial. "Due process requires notice that gives an agency's reason for its action in sufficient detail that the affected party can prepare a responsive defense." *Barnes v. Healy,* 980 F.2d 572, 579 (9th Cir. 1992). Therefore, inadequate notice creates the risk of erroneous deprivation by undermining the appeal process.

The Secretary attacks the district court's analysis of this factor by arguing that the court simply identified an "arguable problem" faced by enrollees—inadequate notice—rather than address whether that problem actually results in deprivations. The Secretary argues that the district court "simply assumed that the perceived failures of notice resulted in fewer appeals, and that more appeals would diminish erroneous deprivations." The Secretary fails to recognize the real problem: Inadequate notice renders the existence of an appeal process meaningless. Moreover, the question established by *Eldridge* is not whether the inadequate notices actually resulted in erroneous deprivations, but whether the inadequate notices created an unjustifiably high risk of erroneous deprivation. Because due process has at its foundation the notion of adequate notice, the risk of erroneous deprivation caused by ineffective notices points towards the need for added procedural protections for Medicare beneficiaries enrolled in HMOs.

3. The Government's Interest

The Secretary argues that the district court paid only cursory attention to this factor, dismissing the government's concerns. The Secretary argues that the procedures sought by plaintiffs would impose a large burden on HMOs, which would accordingly affect the benefits received by enrollees.

The district court did not engage in as detailed an analysis of this third factor as of the other two. A shorter analysis, however, does not mean the analysis is cursory or dismissive. The Secretary has failed to show that the added procedural protections sought by Plaintiffs would result in significant additional costs to the government. Unlike the plaintiff in *Eldridge*, Plaintiffs do not seek a hearing prior to every denial, which would greatly increase costs.

Adequate notices do not impose a burden on HMOs that outweighs the beneficiaries' need for them. "[A] weighing of the *[Mathews v. Eldridge]* factors suggests that the administrative burden of providing an explanation for denying a [certain benefit] is minimal in light of the added potential for spotting erroneously withheld [benefits]." *Barnes v. Healy,* 980 F.2d 572, 579 (9th Cir. 1992).

The Secretary fails to advance any convincing argument that an additional burden on the government outweighs the effects of the other factors such that additional procedural safeguards are not necessary.

Taken together, the *Eldridge* factors point to a need for additional procedural protections for Medicare beneficiaries enrolled in HMOs, in particular for adequate notice of service denials, including the specific reason for the denial and an explanation of appeal rights, and expedited review for critical care denials. We therefore affirm the district court's holdings on *Eldridge.* . . .

IV. Conclusion

For the foregoing reasons, we AFFIRM the district court's summary judgment and injunction in favor of Plaintiffs.

Affirmed.

[Note: The U.S. Supreme Court sent this case back to the Circuit Court in light of its decision in *American Manufacturers Mutual Insurance Co. v. Sullivan* in May of 1999 (526 U.S. 1096). The Circuit Court sent it back down to the District Court in light of the same case in September of 1999 (185 F.3d 1075). There is no evidence of recent activity as of the writing of this edition.]

Walters v. National Association of Radiation Survivors
473 U.S. 305 (1985)

Justice Rehnquist delivered the opinion of the Court, joined by Justices White, Powell, and Scalia. Justices O'Connor and Blackmun concurred. Justices Brennan, Marshall, and Stevens dissented.

Title 38 U.S.C. § 3404(c) limits to $10 the fee that may be paid an attorney or agent who represents a veteran seeking benefits for service-connected death or disability. The United States District Court for the Northern District of

California held that this limit violates the Due Process Clause of the Fifth Amendment, and the First Amendment, because it denies veterans or their survivors the opportunity to retain counsel of their choice in pursuing their claims. We noted probable jurisdiction of the Government's appeal, and we now reverse.

I

Congress has by statute established an administrative system for granting service-connected death or disability benefits to veterans. See 38 U.S.C. § 301 et seq. The amount of the benefit award is not based upon need, but upon service connection—that is, whether the disability is causally related to an injury sustained in the service—and the degree of incapacity caused by the disability. A detailed system has been established by statute and Veterans' Administration (VA) regulation for determining a veteran's entitlement, with final authority resting with an administrative body known as the Board of Veterans' Appeals (BVA). Judicial review of VA decisions is precluded by statute. 38 U.S.C. § 211(a); *Johnson v. Robison,* 415 U.S. 361 (1974). The controversy in this case centers on the opportunity for a benefit applicant or recipient to obtain legal counsel to aid in the presentation of his claim to the VA. Section 3404(c) of Title 38 provides: "The Administrator shall determine and pay fees to agents or attorneys recognized under this section in allowed claims for monetary benefits under laws administered by the Veterans' Administration. Such fees. . . . (2) shall not exceed $10 with respect to any one claim ." Section 3405 provides criminal penalties for any person who charges fees in excess of the limitation of § 3404. . . .

Congress began providing veterans pensions in early 1789, and after every conflict in which the nation has been involved Congress has, in the words of Abraham Lincoln, "provided for him who has borne the battle, and his widow and his orphan." The VA was created by Congress in 1930, and since that time has been responsible for administering the congressional program for veterans' benefits. In 1978, the year

covered by the report of the Legal Services Corporation to Congress that was introduced into evidence in the District Court, approximately 800,000 claims for service-connected disability or death and pensions were decided by the 58 regional offices of the VA. Slightly more than half of these were claims for service-connected disability or death, and the remainder were pension claims. Of the 800,000 total claims in 1978, more than 400,000 were allowed, and some 379,000 were denied. Sixty-six thousand of these denials were contested at the regional level; about a quarter of these contests were dropped, 15% prevailed on reconsideration at the local level, and the remaining 36,000 were appealed to the BVA. At that level some 4,500, or 12%, prevailed, and another 13% won a remand for further proceedings. Although these figures are from 1978, the statistics in evidence indicate that the figures remain fairly constant from year to year.

As might be expected in a system which processes such a large number of claims each year, the process prescribed by Congress for obtaining disability benefits does not contemplate the adversary mode of dispute resolution utilized by courts in this country. A claimant is "entitled to a hearing at any time on any issue involved in a claim." Proceedings in front of the rating board "are ex parte in nature," no Government official appears in opposition. The principal issues are the extent of the claimant's disability and whether it is service connected. The board is required by regulation "to assist a claimant in developing the facts pertinent to his claim," and to consider any evidence offered by the claimant. In deciding the claim the board generally will request the applicant's Armed Service and medical records, and will order a medical examination by a VA hospital. Moreover, the board is directed by regulation to resolve all reasonable doubts in favor of the claimant. . . .

After reviewing the evidence the board renders a decision either denying the claim or assigning a disability "rating" pursuant to detailed regulations developed for assessing various disabilities. Money benefits are calculated based on the rating. The claimant is notified of the board's decision and its reasons, and the claimant may then initiate an appeal by filing a "notice of disagreement" with the local agency. If the local agency adheres to its original decision it must then provide the claimant with a "statement of the case"—a written description of the facts and applicable law upon which the board based its determination—so that the claimant may adequately present his appeal to the BVA. Hearings in front of the BVA are subject to the same rules as local agency hearings—they are ex parte, there is no formal questioning or cross-examination, and no formal rules of evidence apply. The BVA's decision is not subject to judicial review. . . .

In reaching its conclusions the court relied heavily on the problems presented by what it described as "complex cases"—a class of cases also focused on in the depositions. Though never expressly defined by the District Court, these cases apparently include those in which a disability is slow developing and therefore difficult to find service connected, such as the claims associated with exposure to radiation or harmful chemicals, as well as other cases identified by the deponents as involving difficult matters of medical judgment. Nowhere in the opinion of the District Court is there any estimate of what percentage of the annual VA caseload of 800,000 these cases comprise, nor is there any more precise description of the class. There is no question but what the 3 named plaintiffs and the plaintiff veteran's widow asserted such claims, and in addition there are declarations in the record from 12 other claimants who were asserting such claims. The evidence contained in the record, however, suggests that the sum total of such claims is extremely small; in 1982, for example, roughly 2% of the BVA caseload consisted of "agent orange" or "radiation" claims, and what evidence there is suggests that the percentage of such claims in the regional offices was even less—perhaps as little as 3 in 1,000.

With respect to the service representatives, the court again found the representation unsatisfactory. Although admitting that this was not due to any "lack of dedication," the court found that a heavy caseload and the lack of legal training combined to prevent service representatives from adequately researching a claim. Facts are not developed, and "it is standard practice for service organization representatives to submit merely a one to two page handwritten brief."

Based on the inability of the VA and service organizations to provide the full range of services that a retained attorney might, the court concluded that appellees had demonstrated a "high risk of erroneous deprivation" from the process as administered. Ibid. The court then found that the Government had "failed to demonstrate that it would suffer any harm if the statutory fee limitation were lifted." The only Government interest suggested was the "paternalistic" assertion that the fee limitation is necessary to ensure that claimants do not turn substantial portions of their benefits over to unscrupulous lawyers. The court suggested that there were "less drastic means" to confront this problem. . . .

In the face of this congressional commitment to the fee limitation for more than a century, the District Court had only this to say with respect to the governmental interest: "The government has neither argued nor shown that lifting the fee limit would harm the government in any way, except as the paternalistic protector of claimants' supposed best interests. To the extent the paternalistic role is valid, there are less drastic means available to ensure that attorneys' fees do not deplete veterans' death or disability benefits." 589 F.Supp., at 1323.

It is not for the District Court or any other federal court to invalidate a federal statute by so cavalierly dismissing a long-asserted congressional purpose. If "paternalism" is an insignificant Government interest, then Congress first went astray in 1792, when by its Act of March 23 of that year it prohibited the "sale, transfer or mortgage of the pension [of a] soldier before the same shall become due." Acts of Congress long on the books, such as the Fair Labor Standards Act, might similarly be described as "paternalistic"; indeed, this Court once opined that "[s]tatutes of the nature of that under review, limiting the hours in which grown and intelligent men may labor to earn their living, are mere meddlesome interferences with the rights of the individual." *Lochner v. New York,* 198 U.S. 45, 61 (1905). That day is fortunately long gone, and with it the condemnation of rational paternalism as a legitimate legislative goal.

There can be little doubt that invalidation of the fee limitation would seriously frustrate the oft-repeated congressional purpose for enacting it. Attorneys would be freely employable by claimants to veterans' benefits, and the claimant would as a result end up paying part of the award, or its equivalent, to an attorney.

The flexibility of our approach in due process cases is intended in part to allow room for other forms of dispute resolution; with respect to the individual interests at stake here, legislatures are to be allowed considerable leeway to formulate such processes without being forced to conform to a rigid constitutional code of procedural necessities. It would take an extraordinarily strong showing of probability of error under the present system—and the probability that the presence of attorneys would sharply diminish that possibility—to warrant a holding that the fee limitation denies claimants due process of law. We have no hesitation in deciding that no such showing was made out on the record before the District Court.

Thus none of our cases dealing with constitutionally required representation by counsel requires the conclusion reached by the District Court. Especially in light of the Government interests at stake, the evidence adduced before the District Court as to success rates in claims handled with or without lawyers shows no such great disparity as to warrant the inference that the congressional fee limitation under consideration here violates the Due Process Clause of the Fifth Amendment. What evidence we have been pointed to in the record regarding complex cases falls far short of the kind which would warrant upsetting Congress' judgment that this is the manner in which it wishes claims for veterans' benefits adjudicated. The District Court abused its discretion in holding otherwise.

In 1992, the Supreme Court declared that the state of Louisiana violated the due process clause when it continued to hold a person in civil commitment when the state admitted the person was no longer insane. Foucha was found not guilty by reason of insanity. He was sent to a state hospital for the criminally insane where he was treated, and the hospital certified him for release. Before he could obtain his release, he had to go to court and prove that he was no longer a danger to society even though everyone in the court room agreed he was not mentally ill. The Court said this procedure violated the due process clause. In *Foucha v. Louisiana,* 504 U.S. 71 (1992), there was a five-to-four decision with White, Blackmun, Stevens, O'Connor, and Souter in the majority. Kennedy, Rehnquist, Scalia, and Thomas dissented. The case below is another civil commitment case, this time for "sexual predators." (Foucha had been charged with burglary and illegally discharging a firearm). As you will see, Justice O'Connor switched her vote in this case.

Kansas v. Hendricks
521 U.S. 346 (1997)

Justice Thomas delivered the opinion of the Court, in which Chief Justice Rehnquist and Justices O'Connor, Scalia, and Kennedy joined. Justice Kennedy filed a concurring opinion. Justice Breyer filed a dissenting opinion, in which

Justices Stevens and Souter joined, and in which Justice Ginsburg joined as to Parts II and III.

In 1994, Kansas enacted the Sexually Violent Predator Act, which establishes procedures for the civil commitment of persons who, due to a "mental abnormality" or a "personality disorder," are likely to engage in "predatory acts of sexual violence." Kan. Stat. Ann. § 59–29a01 et seq. (1994). The State invoked the Act for the first time to commit Leroy Hendricks, an inmate who had a long history of sexually molesting children, and who was scheduled for release from prison shortly after the Act became law. Hendricks challenged his commitment on, inter alia, "substantive" due process, double jeopardy, and ex post facto grounds. The Kansas Supreme Court invalidated the Act, holding that its pre-commitment condition of a "mental abnormality" did not satisfy what the court perceived to be the "substantive" due process requirement that involuntary civil commitment must be predicated on a finding of "mental illness." The State of Kansas petitioned for certiorari. Hendricks subsequently filed a cross-petition in which he reasserted his federal double jeopardy and ex post facto claims. We granted certiorari on both the petition and the cross-petition and now reverse the judgment below. . . .

(T)he Legislature found it necessary to establish "a civil commitment procedure for the long-term care and treatment of the sexually violent predator." The Act defined a "sexually violent predator" as:

"any person who has been convicted of or charged with a sexually violent offense and who suffers from a mental abnormality or personality disorder which makes the person likely to engage in the predatory acts of sexual violence." § 59–29 a02(a).

A "mental abnormality" was defined, in turn, as a "congenital or acquired condition affecting the emotional or volitional capacity which predisposes the person to commit sexually violent offenses in a degree constituting such person a menace to the health and safety of others." § 59–29a02(b).

As originally structured, the Act's civil commitment procedures pertained to: (1) a presently confined person who, like Hendricks, "has been convicted of a sexually violent offense" and is scheduled for release; (2) a person who has been "charged with a sexually violent offense" but has been found incompetent to stand trial; (3) a person who has been found "not guilty by reason of insanity of a sexually violent offense"; and (4) a person found "not guilty" of a sexually violent offense because of a mental disease or defect. § 59–29a03(a), § 22–3221 (1995).

The initial version of the Act, as applied to a currently confined person such as Hendricks, was designed to initiate a specific series of procedures. The custodial agency was required to notify the local prosecutor 60 days before the anticipated release of a person who might have met the Act's criteria. The prosecutor was then obligated, within 45 days, to decide whether to file a petition in state court seeking the person's involuntary commitment. If such a petition were filed, the court was to determine whether "probable cause" existed to support a finding that the person was a "sexually violent predator" and thus eligible for civil commitment. Upon such a determination, transfer of the individual to a secure facility for professional evaluation would occur. After that evaluation, a trial would be held to determine beyond a reasonable doubt whether the individual was a sexually violent predator. If that determination were made, the person would then be transferred to the custody of the Secretary of Social and Rehabilitation Services (Secretary) for "control, care and treatment until such time as the person's mental abnormality or personality disorder has so changed that the person is safe to be at large." . . .

In 1984, Hendricks was convicted of taking "indecent liberties" with two 13-year-old boys. After serving nearly 10 years of his sentence, he was slated for release to a halfway house. Shortly before his scheduled release, however, the State filed a petition in state court seeking Hendricks' civil confinement as a sexually violent predator. On August 19, 1994, Hendricks appeared before the court with counsel and moved to dismiss the petition on the grounds that the Act violated various federal constitutional provisions. Although the court reserved ruling on the Act's constitutionality, it concluded that there was probable cause to support a finding that Hendricks was a sexually violent predator, and therefore ordered that he be evaluated at the Larned State Security Hospital.

Hendricks subsequently requested a jury trial to determine whether he qualified as a sexually violent predator. During that trial, Hendricks' own testimony revealed a chilling history of repeated child sexual molestation and abuse, beginning in 1955 when he exposed his genitals to two young girls. At that time, he pleaded guilty to indecent exposure. Then, in 1957, he was convicted of lewdness involving a young girl and received a brief jail sentence. In 1960, he molested two young boys while he worked for a carnival. After serving two years in prison for that offense, he was paroled, only to be rearrested for molesting a 7-year-old girl. Attempts were made to treat him for his sexual deviance, and in 1965 he was considered "safe to be at large," and was discharged from a state psychiatric hospital.

Shortly thereafter, however, Hendricks sexually assaulted another young boy and girl—he performed oral sex on the 8-year-old girl and fondled the 11-year-old boy. He was again imprisoned in 1967, but refused to participate in a sex offender treatment program, and thus remained incarcerated until his parole in 1972. Diagnosed as a pedophile, Hendricks entered into, but then abandoned, a treatment program. He testified that despite having received professional help for his pedophilia, he continued to harbor sexual desires for children. Indeed, soon after his 1972 parole, Hendricks began to abuse his own stepdaughter and stepson. He forced the children to engage in sexual activity with him over a period of approximately four years. Then, as noted above, Hendricks was convicted of "taking indecent liberties" with two adolescent boys after he attempted to fondle them. As a result of that conviction, he was once again imprisoned, and was serving that sentence when he reached his conditional release date in September 1994.

Hendricks admitted that he had repeatedly abused children whenever he was not confined. He explained that when he "gets stressed out," he "can't control the urge" to molest children. Although Hendricks recognized that his behavior harms children, and he hoped he would not sexually molest children again, he stated that the only sure way he could keep from sexually abusing children in the future was "to die." Hendricks readily agreed with the state physician's diagnosis that he suffers from pedophilia and that he is not cured of the condition; indeed, he told the physician that "treatment is bull—." The jury unanimously found beyond a reasonable doubt that Hendricks was a sexually violent predator. The trial court subsequently determined, as a matter of state law, that pedophilia qualifies as a "mental abnormality" as defined by the Act, and thus ordered Hendricks committed to the Secretary's custody. . . .

II

Kansas argues that the Act's definition of "mental abnormality" satisfies "substantive" due process requirements. We agree. Although freedom from physical restraint "has always been at the core of the liberty protected by the Due Process Clause from arbitrary governmental action," *Foucha v. Louisiana,* 504 U.S. 71, 80 (1992), that liberty interest is not absolute. The Court has recognized that an individual's constitutionally protected interest in avoiding physical restraint may be overridden even in the civil context:

> "The liberty secured by the Constitution of the United States to every person within its jurisdiction does not import an absolute right in each person to be, at all times and in all circumstances, wholly free from restraint. There are manifold restraints to which every person is necessarily subject for the common good. On any other basis organized society could not exist with safety to its members." *Jacobson v. Massachusetts,* 197 U.S. 11, 26 (1905).

Accordingly, States have in certain narrow circumstances provided for the forcible civil detainment of people who are unable to control their behavior and who thereby pose a danger to the public health and safety. . . .

The challenged Act unambiguously requires a finding of dangerousness either to one's self or to others as a prerequisite to involuntary confinement. Commitment proceedings can be initiated only when a person "has been convicted of or charged with a sexually violent offense," and "suffers from a mental abnormality or personality disorder which makes the person likely to engage in the predatory acts of sexual violence." Kan. Stat. Ann. § 59–29a02(a) (1994). The statute thus requires proof of more than a mere predisposition to violence; rather, it requires evidence of past sexually violent behavior and a present mental condition that creates a likelihood of such conduct in the future if the person is not incapacitated. As we have recognized, "previous instances of violent behavior are an important indicator of future violent tendencies." *Heller v. Doe,* 509 U.S. 312, 323 (1993) . . .

Hendricks nonetheless argues that our earlier cases dictate a finding of "mental illness" as a prerequisite for civil commitment, citing *Foucha* and *Addington.* He then asserts that a "mental abnormality" is not equivalent to a "mental illness" because it is a term coined by the Kansas Legislature, rather than by the psychiatric community. Contrary to Hendricks' assertion, the term "mental illness" is devoid of any talismanic significance. Not only do "psychiatrists disagree widely and frequently on what constitutes mental illness," *Ake v. Oklahoma,* 470 U.S. 68, 81 (1985), but the Court itself has used a variety of expressions to describe the mental condition of those properly subject to civil confinement. See, e.g., *Addington,* 441 U.S. at 425–426 (using the terms "emotionally disturbed" and "mentally ill"); *Jackson,* 406 U.S. at 732, 737 (using the terms "incompetency" and "insanity"); cf. *Foucha,* 504 U.S. at 88 (O'CONNOR, J., concurring in part and concurring in judgment) (acknowledging State's authority to commit a person when there is "some medical justification for doing so"). . . .

To the extent that the civil commitment statutes we have considered set forth criteria relating to an individual's inability to control his dangerousness, the Kansas Act sets forth comparable criteria and Hendricks' condition doubtless satisfies those criteria. The mental health professionals who evaluated Hendricks diagnosed him as suffering from pedophilia, a condition the psychiatric profession itself classifies as a serious mental disorder. See, 1 American Psychiatric Association, *Treatments of Psychiatric Disorders,* 617–633 (1989); Abel & Rouleau, Male Sex Offenders, in *Handbook of Outpatient Treatment of Adults* 271 (M. Thase, B. Edelstein, & M. Hersen, eds. 1990). Hendricks even conceded that, when he becomes "stressed out," he cannot "control the urge" to molest children. This admitted lack of volitional control, coupled with a prediction of future dangerousness, adequately distinguishes Hendricks from other dangerous persons who are perhaps more properly dealt with exclusively through criminal proceedings. Hendricks' diagnosis as a pedophile, which qualifies as a "mental abnormality" under the Act, thus plainly suffices for due process purposes.

B

We granted Hendricks' cross-petition to determine whether the Act violates the Constitution's double jeopardy prohibition or its ban on ex post facto lawmaking. The thrust of Hendricks' argument is that the Act establishes criminal proceedings; hence confinement under it necessarily constitutes punishment. He contends that where, as here, newly enacted "punishment" is predicated upon past conduct for which he has already been convicted and forced to serve a prison sentence, the Constitution's Double Jeopardy and Ex Post Facto Clauses are violated. We are unpersuaded by Hendricks' argument that Kansas has established criminal proceedings.

The categorization of a particular proceeding as civil or criminal "is first of all a question of statutory construction." *Allen,* 478 U.S. at 368. We must initially ascertain whether the legislature meant the statute to establish "civil" proceedings. If so, we ordinarily defer to the legislature's stated intent. Here, Kansas' objective to create a civil proceeding is evidenced by its placement of the Sexually Violent Predator Act within the Kansas probate code, instead of the criminal code, as well as its description of the Act as creating a "civil commitment procedure." Kan. Stat. Ann., Article 29 (1994)

("Care and Treatment for Mentally Ill Persons"), § 59–29a01. Nothing on the face of the statute suggests that the legislature sought to create anything other than a civil commitment scheme designed to protect the public from harm.

Although we recognize that a "civil label is not always dispositive," *Allen,* supra, at 369, we will reject the legislature's manifest intent only where a party challenging the statute provides "the clearest proof" that "the statutory scheme [is] so punitive either in purpose or effect as to negate [the State's] intention" to deem it "civil." *United States v. Ward,* 448 U.S. 242, 248–249 (1980). In those limited circumstances, we will consider the statute to have established criminal proceedings for constitutional purposes. Hendricks, however, has failed to satisfy this heavy burden. . . .

Finally, Hendricks argues that the Act is necessarily punitive because it fails to offer any legitimate "treatment." Without such treatment, Hendricks asserts, confinement under the Act amounts to little more than disguised punishment. Hendricks' argument assumes that treatment for his condition is available, but that the State has failed (or refused) to provide it. The Kansas Supreme Court, however, apparently rejected this assumption, explaining:

> "It is clear that the overriding concern of the legislature is to continue the segregation of sexually violent offenders from the public. Treatment with the goal of reintegrating them into society is incidental, at best. The record reflects that treatment for sexually violent predators is all but nonexistent.
>
> The legislature concedes that sexually violent predators are not amenable to treatment under [the existing Kansas involuntary commitment statute]. If there is nothing to treat under [that statute], then there is no mental illness. In that light, the provisions of the Act for treatment appear somewhat disingenuous." 259 Kan. at 258, 912 P.2d at 136.

It is possible to read this passage as a determination that Hendricks' condition was untreatable under the existing Kansas civil commitment statute, and thus the Act's sole purpose was incapacitation. Absent a treatable mental illness, the Kansas court concluded, Hendricks could not be detained against his will.

Accepting the Kansas court's apparent determination that treatment is not possible for this category of individuals does not obligate us to adopt its legal conclusions. We have already observed that, under the appropriate circumstances and when accompanied by proper procedures, incapacitation may be a legitimate end of the civil law. See *Allen,* supra, at 373; *Salerno,* 481 U.S. at 748–749. Accordingly, the Kansas court's determination that the Act's "overriding concern" was the continued "segregation of sexually violent offenders" is consistent with our conclusion that the Act establishes civil proceedings, 259 Kan. at 258, 912 P.2d at 136, especially when that concern is coupled with the State's ancillary goal of providing treatment to those offenders, if such is possible. While we have upheld state civil commitment statutes that aim both to incapacitate and to treat, see *Allen,* supra, we have never held that the Constitution prevents a State from civilly detaining those for whom no treatment is available, but who nevertheless pose a danger to others. . . .

Where the State has "disavowed any punitive intent"; limited confinement to a small segment of particularly dangerous individuals; provided strict procedural safeguards; directed that confined persons be segregated from the general prison population and afforded the same status as others who have been civilly committed; recommended treatment if such is possible; and permitted immediate release upon a showing that the individual is no longer dangerous or mentally impaired, we cannot say that it acted with punitive intent. We therefore hold that the Act does not establish criminal proceedings and that involuntary confinement pursuant to the Act is not punitive.

Our conclusion that the Act is nonpunitive thus removes an essential prerequisite for both Hendricks' double jeopardy and ex post facto claims. . . .

III

We hold that the Kansas Sexually Violent Predator Act comports with due process requirements and neither runs afoul of double jeopardy principles nor constitutes an exercise in impermissible ex post facto lawmaking.

Accordingly, the judgment of the Kansas Supreme Court is reversed.

It is so ordered.

The Supreme Court has been struggling with the question of when a jury award of punitive damages violates due process. Remember that punitive damages are the civil counterpart to criminal law. They are meant to punish and to deter future similar behavior. Hence, there should be notice of potential risk, and there should be a relationship between the injury, the compensatory damages, and the award of punitive damages.

In 1991, the Court said that an award of $1,040,000 did not violate due process where an insurance company willfully and fraudulently led city employees to believe they were covered when they were not. When one of them went to the hospital, employees discovered they were not covered by the city's insurer because the agent had skipped town with the premiums, and the insurance company had hidden this fact from the city. The jury award did not separate compensatory and punitive damages, so we really do not know how large the punitive award was, but the hospitalized employee's out-of-pocket damages were around $5,000. See *Pacific Mutual Life Insurance Co. v. Haslip*, 499 U.S. 1 (1991).

The Court also refused to nullify a punitive damage award of $10 million on top of $19,000 in compensatory damages for corporate slander. See *TXO Production Corp. v. Alliance Resources Corp.*, 509 U.S. 443 (1993). In all of these cases, the Court warned that one of these days, a jury would go too far.

BMW of North America, Inc., v. Gore
517 U.S. 559 (1996)

Justice Stevens delivered the opinion of the Court, in which Justices O'Connor, Kennedy, Souter, and Breyer joined. Justice Breyer filed a concurring opinion, in which Justices O'Connor and Souter joined. Justice Scalia filed a dissenting opinion, in which Justice Thomas joined. Justice Ginsburg filed a dissenting opinion, in which Chief Justice Rehnquist joined.

In January 1990, Dr. Ira Gore, Jr. (respondent), purchased a black BMW sports sedan for $40,750.88 from an authorized BMW dealer in Birmingham, Alabama. After driving the car for approximately nine months, and without noticing any flaws in its appearance, Dr. Gore took the car to "Slick Finish," an independent detailer, to make it look "'snazzier than it normally would appear.'" 646 So. 2d 619, 621 (Ala. 1994). Mr. Slick, the proprietor, detected

evidence that the car had been repainted. Convinced that he had been cheated, Dr. Gore brought suit against petitioner BMW of North America (BMW), the American distributor of BMW automobiles. Dr. Gore alleged, inter alia, that the failure to disclose that the car had been repainted constituted suppression of a material fact. The complaint prayed for $500,000 in compensatory and punitive damages, and costs.

At trial, BMW acknowledged that it had adopted a nationwide policy in 1983 concerning cars that were damaged in the course of manufacture or transportation. If the cost of repairing the damage exceeded 3 percent of the car's suggested retail price, the car was placed in company service for a period of time and then sold as used. If the repair cost did not exceed 3 percent of the suggested retail price, however, the car was sold as new without advising the dealer that any repairs had been made. Because the $601.37 cost of repainting Dr. Gore's car was only about 1.5 percent of its suggested retail price, BMW did not disclose the damage or repair to the Birmingham dealer.

Dr. Gore asserted that his repainted car was worth less than a car that had not been refinished. To prove his actual damages of $4,000, he relied on the testimony of a former BMW dealer, who estimated that the value of a repainted BMW was approximately 10 percent less than the value of a new car that had not been damaged and repaired. To support his claim for punitive damages, Dr. Gore introduced evidence that since 1983 BMW had sold 983 refinished cars as new, including 14 in Alabama, without disclosing that the cars had been repainted before sale at a cost of more than $300 per vehicle. Using the actual damage estimate of $4,000 per vehicle, Dr. Gore argued that a punitive award of $4 million would provide an appropriate penalty for selling approximately 1,000 cars for more than they were worth.

In defense of its disclosure policy, BMW argued that it was under no obligation to disclose repairs of minor damage to new cars and that Dr. Gore's car was as good as a car with the original factory finish. It disputed Dr. Gore's assertion that the value of the car was impaired by the repainting and argued that this good-faith belief made a punitive award inappropriate. BMW also maintained that transactions in jurisdictions other than Alabama had no relevance to Dr. Gore's claim.

The jury returned a verdict finding BMW liable for compensatory damages of $4,000. In addition, the jury assessed $4 million in punitive damages, based on a determination that the nondisclosure policy constituted "gross, oppressive or malicious" fraud. . . .

The trial judge denied BMW's post-trial motion, holding, inter alia, that the award was not excessive. On appeal, the Alabama Supreme Court also rejected BMW's claim that the award exceeded the constitutionally permissible amount. 646 So. 2d 619 (1994). The court's excessiveness inquiry applied the factors articulated in *Green Oil Co. v. Hornsby,* 539 So. 2d 218, 223–224 (Ala. 1989), and approved in

Pacific Mut. Life Ins. Co. v. Haslip, 499 U.S. 1, 21-22 (1991). 646 So. 2d at 624-625. Based on its analysis, the court concluded that BMW's conduct was "reprehensible"; the nondisclosure was profitable for the company; the judgment "would not have a substantial impact upon [BMW's] financial position"; the litigation had been expensive; no criminal sanctions had been imposed on BMW for the same conduct; the award of no punitive damages in *Yates* reflected "the inherent uncertainty of the trial process"; and the punitive award bore a "reasonable relationship" to "the harm that was likely to occur from [BMW's] conduct as well as . . . the harm that actually occurred." 646 So. 2d at 625–627.

The Alabama Supreme Court did, however, rule in BMW's favor on one critical point: The court found that the jury improperly computed the amount of punitive damages by multiplying Dr. Gore's compensatory damages by the number of similar sales in other jurisdictions. Id., at 627. Having found the verdict tainted, the court held that "a constitutionally reasonable punitive damages award in this case is $2,000,000," id., at 629, . . .

Because we believed that a review of this case would help to illuminate "the character of the standard that will identify unconstitutionally excessive awards" of punitive damages, see *Honda Motor Co. v. Oberg,* 512 U.S. 415, 420 (1994), we granted certiorari, 513 U.S. 1125 (1995).

II

Punitive damages may properly be imposed to further a State's legitimate interests in punishing unlawful conduct and deterring its repetition. *Gertz v. Robert Welch, Inc.,* 418 U.S. 323, 350 (1974); *Newport v. Fact Concerts, Inc.,* 453 U.S. 247, 266–267 (1981); *Haslip,* 499 U.S. at 22. In our federal system, States necessarily have considerable flexibility in determining the level of punitive damages that they will allow in different classes of cases and in any particular case. Most States that authorize exemplary damages afford the jury similar latitude, requiring only that the damages awarded be reasonably necessary to vindicate the State's legitimate interests in punishment and deterrence. [See *TXO*, 509 U.S. at 456; *Haslip*, 499 U.S. at 21, 22.] Only when an award can fairly be categorized as "grossly excessive" in relation to these interests does it enter the zone of arbitrariness that violates the Due Process Clause of the Fourteenth Amendment. Cf. *TXO*, 509 U.S. at 456. For that reason, the federal excessiveness inquiry appropriately begins with an identification of the state interests that a punitive award is designed to serve. We therefore focus our attention first on the scope of Alabama's legitimate interests in punishing BMW and deterring it from future misconduct.

No one doubts that a State may protect its citizens by prohibiting deceptive trade practices and by requiring automobile distributors to disclose presale repairs that affect the value of a new car.

But the States need not, and in fact do not, provide such protection in a uniform manner. Some States rely on the judicial process to formulate and enforce an appropriate disclosure requirement by applying principles of contract and tort law. Other States have enacted various forms of legislation that define the disclosure obligations of automobile manufacturers, distributors, and dealers. The result is a patchwork of rules representing the diverse policy judgments of lawmakers in 50 States. . . .

We think it follows from these principles of state sovereignty and comity that a State may not impose economic sanctions on violators of its laws with the intent of changing the tortfeasors' lawful conduct in other States. Before this Court Dr. Gore argued that the large punitive damages award was necessary to induce BMW to change the nationwide policy that it adopted in 1983. But by attempting to alter BMW's nationwide policy, Alabama would be infringing on the policy choices of other States. To avoid such encroachment, the economic penalties that a State such as Alabama inflicts on those who transgress its laws, whether the penalties take the form of legislatively authorized fines or judicially imposed punitive damages, must be supported by the State's interest in protecting its own consumers and its own

economy. Alabama may insist that BMW adhere to a particular disclosure policy in that State. Alabama does not have the power, however, to punish BMW for conduct that was lawful where it occurred and that had no impact on Alabama or its residents.

Nor may Alabama impose sanctions on BMW in order to deter conduct that is lawful in other jurisdictions.

In this case, we accept the Alabama Supreme Court's interpretation of the jury verdict as reflecting a computation of the amount of punitive damages "based in large part on conduct that happened in other jurisdictions." 646 So. 2d at 627. As the Alabama Supreme Court noted, neither the jury nor the trial court was presented with evidence that any of BMW's out-of-state conduct was unlawful. "The only testimony touching the issue showed that approximately 60% of the vehicles that were refinished were sold in states where failure to disclose the repair was not an unfair trade practice." Id., at 627. The Alabama Supreme Court therefore properly eschewed reliance on BMW's out-of-state conduct, id., at 628, and based its remitted award solely on conduct that occurred within Alabama. The award must be analyzed in the light of the same conduct, with consideration given only to the interests of Alabama consumers, rather than those of the entire Nation. When the scope of the interest in punishment and deterrence that an Alabama court may appropriately consider is properly limited, it is apparent—for reasons that we shall now address—that this award is grossly excessive.

III

Elementary notions of fairness enshrined in our constitutional jurisprudence dictate that a person receive fair notice not only of the conduct that will subject him to punishment, but also of the severity of the penalty that a State may impose. Three guideposts, each of which indicates that BMW did not receive adequate notice of the magnitude of the sanction that Alabama might impose for adhering to the nondisclosure policy adopted in 1983, lead us to the conclusion that the $2 million award against BMW is grossly excessive: the degree of reprehensibility of the nondisclosure; the disparity between the harm or potential harm suffered by Dr. Gore and his punitive damages award; and the difference between this remedy and the civil penalties authorized or imposed in comparable cases. We discuss these considerations in turn.

Perhaps the most important indicium of the reasonableness of a punitive damages award is the degree of reprehensibility of the defendant's conduct. As the Court stated nearly 150 years ago, exemplary damages imposed on a defendant should reflect "the enormity of his offense." . . . This principle reflects the accepted view that some wrongs are more blameworthy than others. Thus, we have said that "nonviolent crimes are less serious than crimes marked by violence or the threat of violence." *Solem v. Helm,* 463 U.S. 277, 292–293 (1983). Similarly, "trickery and deceit," *TXO,* 509 U.S. at 462, are more reprehensible than negligence. In *TXO,* both the West Virginia Supreme Court and the Justices of this Court placed special emphasis on the principle that punitive damages may not be "grossly out of proportion to the severity of the offense." Indeed, for JUSTICE KENNEDY, the defendant's intentional malice was the decisive element in a "close and difficult" case. Id., at 468.

In this case, none of the aggravating factors associated with particularly reprehensible conduct is present. The harm BMW inflicted on Dr. Gore was purely economic in nature. The presale refinishing of the car had no effect on its performance or safety features, or even its appearance for at least nine months after his purchase. BMW's conduct evinced no indifference to or reckless disregard for the health and safety of others. To be sure, infliction of economic injury, especially when done intentionally through affirmative acts of misconduct, or when the target is financially vulnerable, can warrant a substantial penalty. But this observation does not convert all acts that cause economic harm into torts that are sufficiently reprehensible to justify a significant sanction in addition to compensatory damages.

Dr. Gore contends that BMW's conduct was particularly reprehensible because nondisclosure of the repairs to his car formed part of a nationwide pattern of tortious conduct. Certainly, evidence that a defendant has repeatedly engaged in prohibited conduct while knowing or suspecting that it was unlawful would provide relevant support for an argument that strong medicine is required to cure the defendant's disrespect for the law. Our holdings that a recidivist may be punished more severely than a first offender recognize that repeated misconduct is more reprehensible than an individual instance of malfeasance. See *Gryger v. Burke,* 334 U.S. 728, 732 (1948). . . .

We recognize, of course, that only state courts may authoritatively construe state statutes. As far as we are aware, at the time this action was commenced no state court had explicitly addressed whether its State's disclosure statute provides a safe harbor for nondisclosure of presumptively minor repairs or should be construed instead as supplementing common-law duties. A review of the text of the statutes, however, persuades us that in the absence of a state-court determination to the contrary, a corporate executive could reasonably interpret the disclosure requirements as establishing safe harbors. In California, for example, the disclosure statute defines "material" damage to a motor vehicle as damage requiring repairs costing in excess of 3 percent of the suggested retail price or $500, whichever is greater. Cal. Veh. Code Ann. § 9990 (West Supp. 1996). The Illinois statute states that in cases in which disclosure is not required, "nondisclosure does not constitute a misrepresentation or omission of fact." Ill. Comp. Stat., ch. 815, § 710/5 (1994). Perhaps the statutes may also be interpreted in another way. We simply emphasize that the record contains no evidence that BMW's decision to follow a disclosure policy that coincided with the strictest extant state statute was sufficiently reprehensible to justify a $2 million award of punitive damages.

. . . We do not think it can be disputed that there may exist minor imperfections in the finish of a new car that can be repaired (or indeed, left unrepaired) without materially affecting the car's value. There is no evidence that BMW acted in bad faith when it sought to establish the appropriate line between presumptively minor damage and damage requiring disclosure to purchasers. For this purpose, BMW could reasonably rely on state disclosure statutes for guidance. In this regard, it is also significant that there is no evidence that BMW persisted in a course of conduct after it had been adjudged unlawful on even one occasion, let alone repeated occasions.

Finally, the record in this case discloses no deliberate false statements, acts of affirmative misconduct, or concealment of evidence of improper motive, such as were present in *Haslip* and *TXO*. *Haslip*, 499 U.S. at 5; *TXO*, 509 U.S. at 453. We accept, of course, the jury's finding that BMW suppressed a material fact which Alabama law obligated it to communicate to prospective purchasers of repainted cars in that State. But the omission of a material fact may be less reprehensible than a deliberate false statement, particularly when there is a good-faith basis for believing that no duty to disclose exists.

That conduct is sufficiently reprehensible to give rise to tort liability, and even a modest award of exemplary damages does not establish the high degree of culpability that warrants a substantial punitive damages award.

Because this case exhibits none of the circumstances ordinarily associated with egregiously improper conduct, we are persuaded that BMW's conduct was not sufficiently reprehensible to warrant imposition of a $2 million exemplary damages award.

Ratio

The second and perhaps most commonly cited indicium of an unreasonable or excessive punitive damages award is its ratio to the actual harm inflicted on the plaintiff. See *TXO*, 509 U.S. at 459; *Haslip*, 499 U.S. at 23. The principle that exemplary damages must bear a "reasonable relationship" to compensatory damages has a long pedigree. Scholars have identified a number of early English statutes authorizing the award of multiple damages for

particular wrongs. Some 65 different enactments during the period between 1275 and 1753 provided for double, treble, or quadruple damages. Our decisions in both *Haslip* and *TXO* endorsed the proposition that a comparison between the compensatory award and the punitive award is significant. . . .

In *Haslip* we concluded that even though a punitive damages award of "more than 4 times the amount of compensatory damages" might be "close to the line," it did not "cross the line into the area of constitutional impropriety." 499 U.S. at 23–24. *TXO*, following dicta in *Haslip*, refined this analysis by confirming that the proper inquiry is "'whether there is a reasonable relationship between the punitive damages award and the harm likely to result from the defendant's conduct as well as the harm that actually has occurred.'" *TXO*, 509 U.S. at 460, quoting *Haslip*, 499 U.S. at 21. Thus, in upholding the $10 million award in *TXO*, we relied on the difference between that figure and the harm to the victim that would have ensued if the tortious plan had succeeded. That difference suggested that the relevant ratio was not more than 10 to 1. . . .

The $2 million in punitive damages awarded to Dr. Gore by the Alabama Supreme Court is 500 times the amount of his actual harm as determined by the jury. Moreover, there is no suggestion that Dr. Gore or any other BMW purchaser was threatened with any additional potential harm by BMW's nondisclosure policy. The disparity in this case is thus dramatically greater than those considered in *Haslip* and *TXO*.

Of course, we have consistently rejected the notion that the constitutional line is marked by a simple mathematical formula, even one that compares actual and potential damages to the punitive award. *TXO*, 509 U.S. at 458. Indeed, low awards of compensatory damages may properly support a higher ratio than high compensatory awards, if, for example, a particularly egregious act has resulted in only a small amount of economic damages. A higher ratio may also be justified in cases in which the injury is hard to detect or the monetary value of noneconomic harm might have been difficult to determine. It is appropriate, therefore, to reiterate our rejection of a categorical approach. Once again, "we return to what we said . . . in *Haslip*: 'We need not, and indeed we cannot, draw a mathematical bright line between the constitutionally acceptable and the constitutionally unacceptable that would fit every case. We can say, however, that [a] general concer[n] of reasonableness . . . properly enter[s] into the constitutional calculus.'" Id., at 458 (quoting *Haslip*, 499 U.S. at 18). In most cases, the ratio will be within a constitutionally acceptable range, and remittitur will not be justified on this basis. When the ratio is a breathtaking 500 to 1, however, the award must surely "raise a suspicious judicial eyebrow." *TXO*, 509 U.S. at 481 (O'CONNOR, J., dissenting).

Sanctions for Comparable Misconduct

Comparing the punitive damages award and the civil or criminal penalties that could be imposed for comparable misconduct provides a third indicium of excessiveness. As JUSTICE O'CONNOR has correctly observed, a reviewing court engaged in determining whether an award of punitive damages is excessive should "accord 'substantial deference' to legislative judgments concerning appropriate sanctions for the conduct at issue." *Browning-Ferris Industries of Vt., Inc. v. Kelco Disposal, Inc.*, 492 U.S. at 301 (opinion concurring in part and dissenting in part). In *Haslip*, 499 U.S. at 23, the Court noted that although the exemplary award was "much in excess of the fine that could be imposed," imprisonment was also authorized in the criminal context. In this case the $2 million economic sanction imposed on BMW is substantially greater than the statutory fines available in Alabama and elsewhere for similar malfeasance.

The maximum civil penalty authorized by the Alabama Legislature for a violation of its Deceptive Trade Practices Act is $2,000; other States authorize more severe sanctions, with the maxima ranging from $5,000 to $10,000. . . .

The sanction imposed in this case cannot be justified on the ground that it was necessary to deter future misconduct without considering whether less drastic remedies could be expected to achieve that goal. The fact that a multimillion dollar penalty prompted a change in policy sheds no light on the question whether a lesser deterrent would have adequately protected the interests of Alabama consumers. In the absence of a history of noncompliance with known statutory requirements, there is no basis for assuming that a more modest sanction would not have been sufficient to motivate full compliance with the disclosure requirement imposed by the Alabama Supreme Court in this case.

We assume, as the juries in this case and in the *Yates* case found, that the undisclosed damage to the new BMW's affected their actual value. Notwithstanding the evidence adduced by BMW in an effort to prove that the repainted cars conformed to the same quality standards as its other cars, we also assume that it knew, or should have known, that as time passed the repainted cars would lose their attractive appearance more rapidly than other BMW's. Moreover, we of course accept the Alabama courts' view that the state interest in protecting its citizens from deceptive trade practices justifies a sanction in addition to the recovery of compensatory damages. We cannot, however, accept the conclusion of the Alabama Supreme Court that BMW's conduct was sufficiently egregious to justify a punitive sanction that is tantamount to a severe criminal penalty. . . .

As in *Haslip*, we are not prepared to draw a bright line marking the limits of a constitutionally acceptable punitive damages award. Unlike that case, however, we are fully convinced that the grossly excessive award imposed in this case transcends the constitutional limit. Whether the appropriate remedy requires a new trial or merely an indepenent determination by the Alabama Supreme Court of the award necessary to vindicate the economic interests of Alabama consumers is a matter that should be addressed by the state court in the first instance.

The judgment is reversed, and the case is remanded for further proceedings not inconsistent with this opinion.

It is so ordered.

NOTES

1. 397 U.S. 254 (1970).

2. *Ewing v. Mytinger and Casselberry, Incorporated,* 339 U.S. 594 (1950).

3. *North American Cold Storage Company v. Chicago,* 211 U.S. 306 (1908).

4. *Yakus v. United States,* 321 U.S. 414 (1944).

5. *Miller v. Schoene,* 276 U.S. 272 (1928).

6. *Gonzalez v. Freeman,* 334 F. 2d. 570 (D.C. Cir. 1964).

7. *Cafeteria and Restaurant Workers Union v. McElroy,* 367 U.S. 886 (1961).

8. *Morrissey v. Brewer,* 408 U.S. 471 (1972).

9. *Gagnon v. Scarpelli,* 411 U.S. 778 (1973).

10. *Wolff v. McDonnell,* 418 U.S. 539 (1974).

11. *Bell v. Burson,* 402 U.S. 535 (1971).

12. *Goss v. Lopez,* 419 U.S. 565 (1975).

13. *Wisconsin v. Constantineau,* 400 U.S. 208 (1971).

14. *Caulker v. Durham,* 433 F.2d 998 (4th Cir., 1970), Cert. denied 401 U.S. 1003 (1971).

15. *Fuentes v. Shevin,* 407 U.S. 67 (1972).

16. *Sniadach v. Family Finance Corporation,* 395 U.S. 337 (1969).

17. *Vlandis v. Kline,* 412 U.S. 441 (1973).

18. Because the Court's treatment of the facts in this case was, to be generous, antiseptic, additional factual information in this scenario comes from Phillip J. Cooper, *Public Law and Public Administration,* 2d ed. (Englewood Cliffs, NJ: Prentice Hall, 1988), 403–52.

19. *Eldridge v. Weinberger,* 651 F.Supp. 520 (1973).

20. 493 F.2d. 1230 (4th Cir., 1974).

21. Cooper, *Public Law and Public Administration,* p. 447.

22. Ibid.

23. Ibid., p. 404.

24. *Shelley v. Kraemer,* 334 U.S. 1 (1948).

25. *Burton v. Wilmington Parking Authority,* 365 U.S. 716 (1961).

26. *Jackson v. Metropolitan Edison Company,* 419 U.S. 345 (1974).

27. *Moose Lodge #107 v. Irvis,* 407 U.S. 163 (1972).

28. *San Francisco Arts and Athletic Inc. v. U.S. Olympic Committee,* 483 U.S. 522 (1987).

29. *National Collegiate Athletic Association v. Tarkanian,* 488 U.S. 179 (1988).

30. 457 U.S. 991 (1982).

31. 457 U.S. 922 (1982).

32. *West v. Atkins,* 487 U.S. 42 (1988).

33. 500 U.S. 614 (1991).

34. Ronald Moe, "The Emerging Federal Quasi-Government: Issues of Management and Accountability," 61(3) *Public Administration Review* 290 (May/June 2001).

35. Ibid., p. 307.

36. *Troxel v. Granville,* 530 U.S. 57 (2000).

37. 539 U.S. 558 (2003).

38. 124 S.Ct. 2633 (2004).

39. 538 U.S. 1 (2003). See also *Smith v. Doe,* 538 U.S. 84 (2003), where the Court decided that the application of Megan's Law to sex offenders who had been convicted and released before Megan's Law was enacted is not a violation of the prohibition of ex post facto laws.

40. 486 U.S. 230 (1988).

41. 538 U.S. 715 (2003).

42. Walter Gellhorn, "The Abuse of Occupational Licensing," 44 *University of Chicago Law Review* 6 (1976).

43. See, for example, *Gibson v. Berryhill,* 411 U.S. 564 (1973).

44. *Hornsby v. Allen,* 326 F.2d. 605 (5th Cir., 1964).

10

SUING THE GOVERNMENT

Case in Point:
Dalehite v. United States
346 U.S. 15 (1953)

At the end of World War II, a good deal of Europe lay in ruins. To help preserve the peace and the stability of European governments, the United States embarked on a policy of helping Europe to feed itself. It was not possible for America to send enough food, so part of the policy adopted was to send fertilizer to help Europe grow plentiful crops as soon as possible. The fertilizer chosen was fertilizer grade ammonium nitrate (FGAN). At the time, ammonium nitrate was a component found in explosives. The government reopened munitions plants that had been closed after the war and produced the ammonium nitrate. The nitrate was sent to private companies (DuPont and Hercules Powder Company), who contracted with the government to produce FGAN. An army ordinance officer was assigned to each plant that produced FGAN to oversee its production.

The government of France purchased 2,800 tons of FGAN and stored it in a warehouse for three weeks in Texas City, Texas, while waiting for ships to transport the fertilizer to France. On June 15, 1947, 1,850 tons of FGAN were loaded into a hold on a French ship, the *Grandcamp,* which also held substantial amounts of other explosives. Another 1,000 tons were loaded into the *High Flyer,* which also held 2,000 tons of sulfur. On June 16, at 8:15 a.m., smoke led to the discovery of a fire in the *Grandcamp* hold where the FGAN was stored. All hatches were closed, and steam was introduced into the hold, but it did not retard the fire. The captain ordered the ship to be vacated, and less than an hour after the smoke was first detected, the FGAN in the hold exploded, causing the FGAN in the other holds to explode, which then caused the other explosives aboard the *Grandcamp* to explode. The force of the explosion threw fire to the dock area of the city and to the *High Flyer,* which was at the next pier. Efforts to contain the blaze aboard the *High Flyer* were unsuccessful, as was an attempt to tow it out to sea. At 1 a.m. on June 17, the sulfur and FGAN aboard the *High Flyer* exploded with a vengeance that leveled what was left of the burning dock area of the city. The explosions and fire claimed the lives of 560 people, injured 3,000,[1] and caused property damage in the neighborhood of $200 million.[2]

The survivors of Henry G. Dalehite were among 300 parties who sued the government for negligence. The plaintiffs claimed in this case[3]—and the trial judge found as a matter of fact—that the controlling negligence law was that of the place where the negligent act (or omission) occurred. The FGAN involved in the Texas City incident was manufactured in Iowa and Nebraska, so their negligence laws were controlling. The Erie Doctrine[4] requires that in a federal court action where there is no federal law to apply (Congress does not pass tort or negligence laws because they are the sole province of the states), the federal courts must apply appropriate state law. The negligence laws of both Nebraska and Iowa hold that a manufacturer is liable for defects in its product that could have been avoided by the exercise of reasonable care (sometimes called due care). The plaintiffs also claimed, and the trial judge found, that the government failed to exercise reasonable care by (a) discontinuing the testing of FGAN when tests at that point indicated "suspected but unverified dangers," (b) packaging the FGAN in paper bags at temperatures that were too high, (c) ignoring a history of unexplained fires and explosions involving ammonium nitrate, and (d) failing to warn (by labeling the sacks of FGAN as "fertilizer" instead of warning of the explosive nature of the product).

This last finding, failure to warn, is important because the cause of the fire was either spontaneous combustion or a smoldering cigarette left by a longshoreman. If it was the latter, then the failure to warn becomes almost dispositive of the case. The *Dalehite* plaintiffs were awarded $75,000 by the trial judge.[5]

The plaintiffs in this case sued the federal government under an act of Congress called the Federal Tort Claims Act (FTCA),[6] which was passed in 1946 and waived sovereign immunity for the federal government. Sovereign immunity is the notion that a sovereign (the people in the United States) cannot be sued without the sovereign's consent. The FTCA is the vehicle through which the federal government consented to allow itself to be held liable for its torts (negligence).

Prior to the passage of the FTCA, when citizens were injured as a result of government's (or a government employee's) negligence, they simply could not sue the government to recover damages. The only process available was to have their representative submit a private bill in Congress. In the 70th Congress (1927–29), 2,268 private bills claiming damages from government wrongs were introduced.[7] These bills sought more than $100 million collectively, and Congress passed 336 of them, for a total expenditure of $2,830,000. Over the next eight Congresses (up to 1945), 2,118 such private bills were introduced per session. Only 408 (19 percent) passed, calling for $1.5 million per Congress (the figures are averages).

Because the government has the power to decide whether it can be sued, it can also decide under what conditions it will allow itself to be sued. Hence, the FTCA has certain exceptions or situations under which the government will not be liable. The exception involved in this case, the *discretionary function exception,* is found in Section 2680 of the Act and reads as follows:

> The provisions of this chapter . . . shall not apply to . . . (a) any claim based upon an act or omission of an employee of the government, exercising due care, in the execution of a statute or regulation, whether or not the statute or regulation be valid [this part of the exception is meant to bar citizens from using tort suits to challenge the legality of acts of Congress or regulations] or based upon the exercise or performance or the failure to exercise or perform a discretionary function or duty on the part of a federal agency or an employee of the government, whether or not the discretion involved be abused.

The second part is the *discretionary function exception,* and its purpose is to make acts of discretion immune from negligence suits so that those in government will not hesitate to make a decision out of fear of a lawsuit.

When the government lost in the *Dalehite* case at the trial court, it appealed to the circuit court, which overturned the trial judge. On review by the Supreme Court, the question narrowed to an interpretation of the discretionary exception clause. (That is, whether the decisions to stop testing FGAN, to bag it at high temperatures, to put it in paper bags rather than something more stable, and to label it as fertilizer were acts of discretion within the meaning of the exception.) In a 4 to 3 decision (two justices did not participate), the Court said the exception was meant to make immune acts of discretion in the exercise of government functions. Whether there is negligence or not, the Act meant to protect, for example, flood control, irrigation, and activities of the Federal Trade Commission, the Securities and Exchange Commission, and other regulatory agencies. Indeed, the Court said the only government negligence that was not exempted under the Act was the "common law torts of employees of agencies," such as negligence in driving an automobile. Therefore, all of the above-mentioned decisions claimed by the plaintiff to constitute negligence, whether they were negligent or not, are exempted under Section 2680 of the Act. The Dalehite plaintiffs (and all the rest of them as well) lost their suit, and Justice Jackson wrote a strong dissent:

> Many acts of government officials deal only with the housekeeping side of federal activities. The Government, as landowner, as manufacturer, as shipper, as warehouseman, as shipowner and operator, is carrying on activities indistinguishable from those performed by private persons. In this area, there is no good reason to stretch the legislative text to immunize the Government or its officers from responsibility for their acts, if done without appropriate care for the safety of others. Many official decisions even in this area may involve a nice balancing of various considerations, but this is the same kind of balancing which citizens do at their peril and we think it is not within the exception of the statute.
>
> The Government's negligence here was not in policy decisions of a regulatory or governmental nature, but involved actions akin to those of a private manufacturer, contractor, or shipper. Reading the discretionary exception as we do, in a way both workable and faithful to legislative intent, we would hold that the Government was liable under these circumstances. Surely a statute so long debated was meant to embrace more than traffic accidents. If not, the ancient and discredited doctrine that "The King can do no wrong" has not been uprooted; it has merely been amended to read, "The King can do only little wrongs." (346 U.S. 15, 60)

Questions

1. What was the legal situation of the affected citizens of Texas City after the Court's ruling? Did they have a remedy at all, or were they simply out of luck (and money)?[8]
2. Does this decision seem to you to be democratically acceptable? Why or why not?

Sovereign Immunity

As a good deal of American law does, the concept of sovereign immunity dates from medieval England. It means, as Justice Jackson said in dissent in the *Dalehite* case, that the king (or sovereign) can do no wrong and therefore cannot be sued. Lest you believe that sovereign immunity is a concept with no practical consequences in the 21st century, the case of *Lane v. Pena,* 518 U.S. 187 (1996), should be instructive.

Mr. Lane entered the United States Merchant Marine Academy in 1991 after passing a Defense Department physical examination. During his freshman year, however, he was diagnosed with diabetes by a private physician. Lane informed the academy's medical staff, and a hearing was held to determine whether his condition would prevent service in the Merchant Marine or in the Navy. The hearing found that insulin-dependent diabetes was a disqualifying condition, and Lane was involuntarily separated from the academy. He challenged his involuntary separation at a § 554 hearing within the Department of Transportation [DOT], which runs the Merchant Marine Academy. His challenge was on the basis of the Rehabilitation Act of 1973. The Act forbids any activity receiving federal funds or any program run by a federal executive branch agency (DOT) from discriminating against any individual solely on the basis of a disability. After Lane lost at the agency hearing, he sued in federal district court alleging a violation of the Rehabilitation Act. As remedies for discriminating against him on the basis of his disability, Lane sought reinstatement into the Academy plus money damages. Regarding sovereign immunity and money damages, § 505 of the Rehabilitation Act says, "The remedies, . . . set forth in Title VI of the Civil Rights Act of 1964 shall be available to any person aggrieved by any act . . . [of] any recipient of federal assistance or federal provider of such assistance." As money damages are available as a remedy under the 1964 Civil Rights Act, Lane must have assumed they were available to him under the Rehabilitation Act.

However, the Supreme Court has said that it is not enough for Congress to simply waive sovereign immunity. If Congress intends to waive sovereign immunity, that intention must be clear and "unequivocally expressed in statutory text"; there can be no such thing as an implied waiver. The Court was willing to accept that Congress had unequivocally waived sovereign immunity for programs receiving federal assistance. But the language of § 505, quoted above, fails to mention executive branch programs; hence, Congress had not clearly and unequivocally waived sovereign immunity for suits like Lane's. Lane was reinstated, but no money damages were allowed due to a lack of a waiver of sovereign immunity.

Hence, sovereign immunity is alive and well. Indeed, a few state legislatures still have not waived their respective sovereign immunities. The point that you should understand is that citizens cannot sue government unless government consents to be sued. Indeed, it is not enough for a governmental unit to consent to be sued. As you just read in *Lane v. Pena,* sovereign immunity is not waived until five justices of the Supreme Court have decided that the government has "clearly and unequivocally" consented to be sued. In *West v. Gibson,* 527 U.S. 212 (1999) at the end of this chapter, the issue is whether a 1991 amendment to the 1964 Civil Rights Act authorizing compensatory damages "clearly and unequivocally" provides the Equal Employment Opportunity Commission (EEOC) with the power to award compensatory damages against another federal agency.

The Supreme Court refused to recognize a waiver of federal sovereign immunity in *The Department of the Army v. Blue Fox, Inc.,* 525 U.S 225 (1999). Section 702 of the Administrative Procedure Act (in Appendix A) appears to waive the sovereign immunity of federal agencies in legal actions for remedies "other than for money damages." The Miller Act requires prime federal contractors to post a bond to protect the interests of sub-contractors. In this case, the Department of the Army required no Miller bond on a project, and the prime contractor failed to pay a subcontractor (Blue Fox). Blue Fox obtained a court judgment against the prime contractor but still feared it would never see the money, as the contractor had already been paid. Blue Fox sued the Army in district court seeking an equitable lien against funds still held by the Army for the project and an order directing payment. Despite the fact that this is an action by an aggrieved party against a federal agency for a remedy other than money damages, the Supreme Court said the action was outside Section 702's waiver of immunity. Blue Fox could not sue the Army because of sovereign immunity.

The sovereign immunity of the states relative to the Eleventh Amendment is a hot legal topic recently. The Eleventh Amendment was adopted in 1795 as a reaction against a Supreme Court decision in the 1793 case of *Chisholm v. Georgia*.[9] Chisholm was a citizen of South Carolina who sued the state of Georgia in federal court. As Article III of the Constitution clearly specified that federal court jurisdiction extended to suits between "a state and citizens of another state," the *Chisholm* suit was allowed to proceed. Two years later, the Eleventh Amendment was adopted, withdrawing federal court jurisdiction from suits where a state is sued by a citizen of another state (or of a foreign state). The notion that a sovereign cannot be sued unless it consents is the Eleventh Amendment's underpinning.

The commerce clause of the Constitution (Article I, section 8, clause 3), grants to Congress the power to regulate commerce between the states, between states and foreign countries, and with the Indian tribes. Pursuant to that authority, Congress passed the Indian Gaming Regulatory Act in an attempt to bring order to the process of gambling on Indian reservations (which are federal enclaves located within states). The law requires the states to negotiate with Indian tribes that wish to establish gambling on their reservations, and it admonishes the states to conduct those negotiations "in good faith." Indeed, the law authorized the tribes to sue the states in federal court, should a tribe suspect that a state is not negotiating in good faith. The Seminole tribe sued the state of Florida in federal court for failure to negotiate in good faith, but the Supreme Court said the part of the Gaming Act that authorized unconsenting states to be sued was unconstitutional.[10] Indeed, in making that decision, the Court overruled a 1989 case that established the power of Congress to abrogate a state's Eleventh Amendment sovereign immunity pursuant to an exercise of power under the commerce clause.[11]

The Fair Labor Standards Act, a piece of New Deal legislation, is our nation's current minimum wage law. When Congress debates whether to raise the minimum wage, what it is really doing is debating an amendment to the Act. The Act imposes not only a federal minimum wage but also a 40-hour work week and a requirement that any employee who works more than the 40-hour limit will be paid time and a half. The Act applies to all governments and private employers (who *have* 15 or more employees . . .), and it creates a private right of action (so a citizen can sue the offending employer). When probation officers sued their employer (the State of Maine) in the state courts of Maine for violations of the overtime provision, the Supreme Court said no.[12] The Court said that the sovereign immunity created by the Eleventh Amendment means that Congress is without the power to authorize citizen suits against a state government in either state or federal court. The upshot of this and similar recent cases is that the states are free to ignore the Fair Labor Standards Act, and affected employees have no remedy available unless the secretary of labor wants to sue the state on behalf of the workers.

The Court has not been consistent in its Eleventh Amendment jurisprudence. The Americans With Disabilities Act (ADA) was passed by Congress, not under the commerce clause, but under the enforcement provisions of the Fourteenth Amendment (which forbids the states from denying to their citizens due process of law or the equal protection of the laws). The enforcement provision grants to Congress the authority to see that the dictates of the Fourteenth Amendment are enforced. The ADA forbids any entity (including the states) from discriminating against people on account of their disabilities. It further authorizes any citizen who has been discriminated against because of a disability to sue in the federal courts. In a 2001 case, two disabled employees of the state of Alabama sued the state in federal court for damages caused by an alleged violation of the ADA.[13]

Two criteria must be met before Congress can constitutionally abrogate the states' Eleventh Amendment sovereign immunity: (a) Congress must "unequivocally" indicate its intent to do so in the statutory language, and (b) it can only be done pursuant to a proper constitutional grant of authority. Congress met the first criterion in passing the ADA. The question in the *Alabama* case was whether Congress met the second criterion. We already know from the *Seminole* and the *Maine* cases that Congress lacks the power to authorize suits against the states under its commerce clause power. The Court had previously held, however, that Congress does possess the power to abrogate Eleventh Amendment immunity under the enforcement provisions of the Fourteenth Amendment. The problem for the Alabama employee-plaintiffs was that the Court has severely limited congressional Fourteenth Amendment enforcement powers relative to the Eleventh Amendment. Before Congress can authorize Fourteenth Amendment enforcement citizen-suits against the states, there must be a record of a pattern of discrimination by the states (for example, racial discrimination), and the remedy authorized by Congress must be proportional to the documented discrimination. The Alabama plaintiffs lost this case because the Court found that Congress had failed to document a history of state discrimination against the disabled. This was a 5 to 4 decision, with Chief Justice Rehnquist and Justices O'Connor, Scalia, Kennedy, and Thomas in the majority.

Compare, however, the 2004 case of *Tennessee v. Lane.*[14] Whereas the *Alabama* case involved one plaintiff who suffered from cancer and another who was afflicted with asthma and sleep apnea, the *Tennessee* case involved paraplegics. The facts of the *Lane* litigation are compelling and worth repeating. Lane, who was confined to a wheelchair, was apparently charged with some criminal violations. When he showed up for his first court appearance, he must have been chagrined to discover that the hearing was scheduled for a second-floor courtroom, and the courthouse had no elevator. Lane crawled up the two flights of stairs for his hearing and presumably had to slide back down. On his return for a second appearance, once again in a second-floor courtroom, Lane refused to crawl up the stairs a second time, and he refused to allow deputies to carry him. As a consequence of his refusal, Lane was arrested and jailed for failure to appear.

The *Tennessee* case involved a paraplegic court reporter who lost jobs because she was unable to access courtrooms. In the 2004 case, Justice O'Connor switched sides to create another 5 to 4 decision, this time with a majority composed of Justices Stevens, O'Connor, Souter, Ginsburg, and Breyer. Applying the same two-pronged test it applied in the *Alabama* case, this Court found that there was sufficient congressional documentation of state discrimination against the disabled and that the remedy was appropriate. Whereas the *Alabama* case involved Title One of the ADA (which generally forbids discrimination against the disabled and requires employers to make reasonable accommodations for their disabled employees), the Tennessee case involved Title Two (which forbids excluding the disabled from "programs and activities of a public entity").

In 1996, Congress passed the Telecommunications Act to make the telephone and Internet industries more competitive. It requires that incumbent local exchange carriers (in this case, Verizon) provide interconnection with existing networks to new competitors who wish to enter the incumbent's local market (in this case, MCI Worldcom). The Act requires that agreements between incumbent carriers and new competitors must be approved by the respective state's public utilities commission (PUC) and that the PUC's actions can be reviewed in the federal courts. Verizon and Worldcom entered into the required agreement, which was approved by the Maryland PUC. Several months later, a dispute erupted between the two companies, and Verizon refused to abide by part of the contract. Worldcom petitioned the Maryland PUC for relief, and the PUC sided with Worldcom and ordered Verizon to pay Worldcom. Instead, Verizon sued the Maryland PUC and its individual commissioners in federal court. This suit was not barred by the Eleventh Amendment because of a 1908 doctrine called the *ex parte Young* doctrine that provides federal court jurisdiction in a suit against a state seeking to enjoin state action that allegedly violates federal law, even where the state itself is immune under the Eleventh Amendment. The case is *Verizon v. Public Service Commission of Maryland,* and it is a 2002 case.[15]

The Constitution grants to Congress the power to regulate bankruptcies, and using that power, Congress has stipulated that student loans typically cannot be discharged in a bankruptcy proceeding, except where the failure to discharge them would constitute an "undue hardship" on the debtor. To discharge a student loan in bankruptcy, the debtor is required to go through a separate lawsuit to prove the undue hardship. In a 2004 case, a debtor initiated the separate lawsuit to discharge her student loans, but she had to sue a state agency that had acquired her student loan indebtedness.[16] The state agency claimed Eleventh Amendment immunity from the suit. Certiorari was granted in this case to determine whether Congress possessed the power under its Article I, Section 8 bankruptcy authority to abrogate a state's Eleventh Amendment immunity, but according to the dissent, the Court ducked the issue and decided on narrower grounds. The Court found that in admiralty law, when a state possesses property, the federal courts have jurisdiction over the property (called *in rem* jurisdiction) in a lawsuit over the property. Such suits are not barred by the Eleventh Amendment. The Court reasoned that holding a student loan in a bankruptcy proceeding was like holding property in an admiralty case, so the bankruptcy suit against the state was not barred by sovereign immunity.

Finally, regarding the state of sovereign immunity, the Eleventh Amendment, and administrative law, there was a 2002 case involving the Federal Maritime Commission, which appears at the end of this chapter. A cruise ship company requested a docking berth in the Charleston, South Carolina, harbor from the South Carolina State Ports Authority, which denied the request because the ship would be used exclusively for gambling, which is contrary to South Carolina's public policy. The cruise ship company filed a complaint with the Federal Maritime Commission complaining that the ports authority's decision violated the Shipping Act of 1984. The company wanted the commission to order the ports authority to pay reparations, stop violating the Shipping Act, and provide a berth in the Charleston harbor. While this might sound like the *Verizon* case above, you will need to read the case to see how the Court resolved it.

Sovereign immunity is alive and well both at the federal and at the state level. However, as local units of government are not sovereigns, they are not clothed with immunity from suit. As we move through the chapter, you will find that sometimes, some government employees cannot be sued either. That is called a *qualified immunity.*

Waiving Sovereign Immunity: The Federal Tort Claims Act

Whether state or federal, a tort claims act is necessary if citizens are going to be able to sue government for its acts of negligence. Any time a lawsuit is filed, it contains identifiable components. A suit is started by the filing of a complaint, which states the name and address of the plaintiff (to help establish jurisdiction), alleges that the defendant (also identified by name and address) did certain acts that resulted in injury to the plaintiff, and asks the court for certain relief—known in American jurisprudence as a *remedy.* American remedies fall into two categories: common-law remedies and equitable remedies. Common-law remedies involve money damages, and equitable remedies are allowed only where a common-law remedy is not adequate to take care of the plaintiff's situation. There are several equitable remedies, but perhaps the most common are injunctions and declaratory judgments. An injunction is a court order stopping certain action, and a declaratory judgment is one by which a court declares a law or agency activity to be unconstitutional or otherwise unlawful. Of the cases that began each chapter, only two have involved common-law remedies: the *Dalehite* case and *Hale v. Walsh* in Chapter 8, in which Professor Hale asked the Court for both types of remedies (compensatory damages for lost wages and retraining expenses incurred, and reinstatement to his position as professor of history—an equity remedy).

So long as a government refuses to waive its sovereign immunity, theoretically, neither type of action—common-law or equity—can be maintained against the government. The federal legislation permitting suits in equity against the government is found in Section 702 of the Administrative Procedure Act, although the language permitting equity actions was not added until 1976. There is some inconsistent case law involving declaratory judgments and injunctions instituted against the government prior to that amendment.

At least one type of suit at common law was permitted with the passage of the FTCA in 1946: torts. A tort is a "legal wrong done to another person."[17] To prevail in a tort suit, the plaintiff needs to establish the existence of a legal duty and the breach of that duty, which is the proximate cause of harm to the plaintiff's person or property. There are two categories of torts: intentional and unintentional. You are probably familiar with at least the names of intentional torts: invasion of privacy, defamation of character (libel and slander), assault, battery, false imprisonment, malicious prosecution, and so on. Negligence is the unintentional tort. Because most intentional torts are exempt under the FTCA, our discussion will focus on negligence.

Just as criminal law presumes that all adults know and understand the law and are possessed of free will to choose right from wrong, so negligence law imposes a legal duty on all adults to take reasonable care (due care) that their actions (or failures to act) do not cause harm to others. Because the latter is a legal duty, negligence suits often narrow to whether the defendant took reasonable care. Such was the essence of the *Dalehite* case at the trial court, and the trial judge found as a matter of fact that the government had breached its duty to exercise reasonable care.

How would one know whether another had failed to take reasonable care? Domino's Pizza advertised nationally that customers would get their pizza free if it was not delivered within a half hour. The survivors of a Domino's delivery boy sued the company when the boy was killed in an auto accident caused by his speeding to meet the deadline. Has the company breached its duty to take reasonable care through its scheme to capture a larger share of the pizza delivery market? Yes, because the average reasonable person would have foreseen that the scheme, and the way it was implemented (the free pizza came out of the delivery person's pocket, not company profits), could lead to injury. Hence, the test for whether the duty to exercise reasonable care has been breached is whether the average reasonable person would have foreseen that the actions taken by the defendant could cause harm. Foreseeability does not have to be specific. (That is, the average reasonable person would not have had to foresee a delivery boy's speeding and getting killed or two ships blowing up and leveling a city along with its citizens.) One only needs to foresee that some general harm might result from the defendant's actions, and that is a question of fact often submitted to a jury (except that juries are forbidden under the FTCA).

Aside from the question of how much money in damages should be awarded, a successful negligence action requires that the plaintiff prove that the failure to exercise reasonable care was the proximate cause of the injuries to the plaintiff. Although first-year law students spend considerable time trying to master proximate cause, it is introduced here only so you can appreciate a tort claims lawsuit. Kimble's survivors sued a company when its roof fell in and killed Kimble. The negligence alleged was that the roof was in disrepair, and the defendant had failed to repair it; hence the failure to exercise reasonable care was the proximate cause of Kimble's death. In defense, the company admitted that the roof was in need of repair but claimed it fell in because of a violent storm; hence, the proximate cause of Kimble's death was an act of God and not the company's negligence.[18] These questions are often resolved by applying the "but-for" test. But for the negligence of the defendant, would the plaintiff have been injured? This, too, is a question of fact to be determined by the trier of fact (judge or jury). In the *Kimble* case, if the plaintiff's attorney could establish that no other roofs fell in during the storm, that would probably satisfy the but-for test.

The Discretionary Function Exception

In a typical negligence action, then, the plaintiff must prove (a) there was a failure to exercise reasonable care, (b) the failure was the proximate cause of the injury, and (c) the failure to exercise reasonable care resulted in a specific dollar amount of injury. In an FTCA case, the plaintiff has another hurdle to clear, for the government can say: "Yes, we were negligent and our negligence was the proximate cause of injury, but the negligence arose out of an act of discretion; therefore, we are not liable." Indeed, in the *Dalehite* case, nearly all of these elements were in dispute. The government attorneys claimed that the acts complained of (stopping the test, bagging at high temperatures and in paper, and labeling) did not amount to a failure to exercise reasonable care because there was a rational scientific explanation for each. The cause of the fire was in dispute, and the amount of damages was also disputed, as was whether the alleged acts of negligence were covered by the discretionary exception.

Over the years, the Court's interpretation of the discretionary function has not changed much from the Court's view of it in 1953. Theoretically, it is not simply "the common law torts of employees" that fall within the exception. Today, the courts distinguish between acts of discretion with policy implications and acts of discretion simply implementing policy (or planning versus operational acts of discretion). The former are covered by the discretionary exception, but the latter, presumably are not. Actually, the planning/operational dichotomy was recognized in *Dalehite,* with the trial judge finding the acts complained of to be operational but the Supreme Court finding them to be planning in nature.[19]

The discretionary function exception is controversial because the whole reason for a tort claims act is to soften the blow of sovereign immunity and to make government accountable to its citizens when government action causes injury or death. The exception, however, takes a potentially huge chunk of governmental activity and reimmunizes it. William Weaver and Thomas Longoria[20] recite a bone-chilling list of government actions that left innocent citizens dead or maimed, including turning southern Utah citizens into nuclear fallout guinea pigs[21] and releasing a biological agent on an unsuspecting San Francisco citizenry.[22]

The Supreme Court has considered the discretionary function exception in only four cases. You are already familiar with one of them, the *Dalehite* case in 1953. In 1984, the Court heard *United States v. Varig Airlines,*[23] which case involved a Boeing 707 aircraft that was sold to a Brazilian air carrier. On a 1973 flight from Rio de Janeiro to Paris, a fire that broke out in one of the lavatories and filled the cabin with toxic smoke. All but 11 of the 135 passengers and crew died. The lawsuits were filed on behalf of the Brazilian company, which wanted to be reimbursed for the lost aircraft, and the survivors of the dead. The plaintiffs allege that whatever caused the fire was exacerbated by the fact that fire-resistant material was not used in the lavatory as required by federal regulations. The essence of the complaint was that a government agency (predecessor to the Federal Aviation Administration [FAA], but we will use FAA here) negligently certified an aircraft to be airworthy when in fact, it was not. The FAA has an elaborate procedure for certifying the airworthiness of aircraft. The procedure involves agency review of manufacturing documents and physical inspections of the planes. The problem was that the FAA employed fewer than 400 engineers and consequently lacked the manpower to review all the documents and conduct all the inspections. Hence, the FAA hired the manufacturer's engineers to act as its agents in the certification process and adopted a system of spot checks; in fact, each plane is not really inspected by the FAA. That is how an aircraft that was not in compliance with regulations got into the air. The Supreme Court said the decisions to use the manufacturer's employees and to adopt a system of spot checks were acts of discretion with policy implications, which were meant to be protected from lawsuit by the discretionary function exception.

Four years after the *Varig Airlines* case, the Court said that a suit against the National Institutes of Health (NIH) and the Food and Drug Administration (FDA) was not necessarily barred by the discretionary exception. Kevan Berkovitz, a two-year-old infant, contracted polio by ingesting an oral polio vaccine. The lawsuit alleged that the Division of Biological Standards, a bureau under the NIH, wrongfully licensed a manufacturer to make the vaccine and the FDA wrongfully approved release to the public of the lot containing Kevan's dose. The government argued that the lawsuit should be blocked by the discretionary function exception. The plaintiffs allege that the Division of Biological Standards licensed the production of the vaccine without first receiving required data from the manufacturer. While Kevan's claim against the FDA was more complex, his claim against the Biological Standards Division was not barred by the discretionary function exception. The doctrine from the case is that agencies are not free to utilize discretion to ignore statutory commands or regulatory standards. Both the congressional act that commands them and the subsequent agency regulations require that before a license for a vaccine can be issued, the Biological Standards Division must receive test data from the manufacturer relating to the product's compliance with regulatory standards. As Kevan has alleged that the Division issued the license without receiving the required data, the agency cannot have the lawsuit barred by claiming that it exercised its discretion to license the product without receiving and reviewing the data.

The Court's most recent statement on the discretionary function exception came in a 1991 case in which a federal banking agency took over a healthy financial institution and mismanaged it so badly that it became insolvent. The case is reproduced below.

United States v. Gaubert
499 U.S. 315 (1991)

Justice White delivered the opinion for a unanimous Court. Justice Scalia filed a concurring opinion.

When the events in this case occurred, the Home Owners' Loan Act of 1933, provided for the chartering and regulation of federal savings and loan associations (FSLA's). Section 1464(a) authorized the Federal Home Loan Bank Board (FHLBB) "under such rules and regulations as it may prescribe, to provide for the organization, incorporation, examination, operation, and regulation" of FSLA's, and to issue charters, "giving primary consideration to the best practices of thrift institutions in the United States." In this case the FHLBB and the Federal Home Loan Bank—Dallas (FHLB-D) undertook to advise about and oversee certain aspects of the operation of a thrift institution. Their conduct in this respect was challenged by a suit against the United States under the Federal Tort Claims Act (FTCA), asserting that the FHLBB and FHLB-D had been negligent in carrying out their supervisory activities. The question before us is whether certain actions taken by the FHLBB and FHLB-D are within the "discretionary function" exception to the liability of the United States under the FTCA. The Court of Appeals for the Fifth Circuit answered this question in the negative. We have the contrary view and reverse.

I

This FTCA suit arises from the supervision by federal regulators of the activities of Independent American Savings Association (IASA), a Texas-chartered and federally insured savings and loan. Respondent Thomas M. Gaubert was IASA's chairman of the board and largest shareholder. In 1984, officials at the FHLBB sought to have IASA merge with Investex Savings, a failing Texas thrift. Because the FHLBB and FHLB-D were concerned about Gaubert's other financial dealings, they requested that he sign a "neutralization agreement" which effectively removed him from IASA's management. They also asked him to post a $25 million interest in real property as security for his personal guarantee that IASA's net worth would exceed regulatory minimums. Gaubert agreed to both conditions. Federal officials then provided regulatory and financial advice to enable IASA to consummate the merger with Investex. Throughout this period, the regulators instituted no formal action against IASA. Instead, they relied on the likelihood that IASA and Gaubert would follow their suggestions and advice.

In the spring of 1986, the regulators threatened to close IASA unless its management and board of directors were replaced; all of the directors agreed to resign. The new officers and directors, including the chief executive officer who was a former FHLB-D employee, were recommended by FHLB-D. After the new management took over, FHLB-D officials became more involved in IASA's day-to-day business. They recommended the hiring of a certain consultant to advise IASA on operational and financial matters; they advised IASA concerning whether, when, and how its subsidiaries should be placed into bankruptcy; they mediated salary disputes; they reviewed the draft of a complaint to be used in litigation; they urged IASA to convert from state to federal charter; and they actively intervened when the Texas Savings and Loan Department attempted to install a supervisory agent at IASA. In each instance, FHLB-D's advice was followed.

Although IASA was thought to be financially sound while Gaubert managed the thrift, the new directors soon announced that IASA had a substantial negative net worth. On May 20, 1987, Gaubert filed an administrative tort claim with the FHLBB, FHLB-D, and FSLIC, seeking $75 million in damages for the lost value of his shares and $25 million for the property he had forfeited under his personal guarantee. That same day, the FSLIC assumed the receivership of IASA. After Gaubert's administrative claim was denied six months later, he filed the instant FTCA suit in the United States District Court for the Northern District of Texas. His amended complaint sought $100 million in damages for the alleged negligence of federal officials in selecting the new officers and directors and in participating in the day-to-day management of IASA. The District Court granted the motion to dismiss filed by the United States, finding that all of the challenged actions of the regulators fell within the discretionary function exception to the FTCA.

The Court of Appeals for the Fifth Circuit affirmed in part and reversed in part. 885 F. 2d 1284 (1989). Relying on this Court's decision in *Indian Towing Co. v. United States,* 350 U.S. 61 (1955), the court distinguished between "policy decisions," which fall within the exception, and "operational actions," which do not. . . . [T]he Court of Appeals affirmed the District Court's dismissal of the claims which concerned the merger, neutralization agreement, personal guarantee, and replacement of IASA management, but reversed the dismissal of the claims which concerned the regulators' activities after they assumed a supervisory role in IASA's day-to-day affairs. We granted certiorari and now reverse.

II

The liability of the United States under the FTCA is subject to the various exceptions contained in § 2680, including the "discretionary function" exception at issue here. That exception provides that the Government is not liable for "any claim based upon an act or omission of an employee of the Government, exercising due care, in the execution of a statute or regulation, whether or not such statute or regulation be valid, or based upon the exercise or performance or the failure to exercise or perform a discretionary function or duty on the part of a federal agency or an employee of the Government, whether or not the discretion involved be abused."

The exception covers only acts that are discretionary in nature, acts that "involve an element of judgment or choice," and "it is the nature of the conduct, rather than the status of the actor" that governs whether the exception applies. The requirement of judgment or choice is not satisfied if a "federal statute, regulation, or policy specifically prescribes a course of action for an employee to follow," because "the employee has no rightful option but to adhere to the directive."

Furthermore, even "assuming the challenged conduct involves an element of judgment," it remains to be decided "whether that judgment is of the kind that the discretionary function exception was designed to shield." Because the purpose of the exception is to "prevent judicial 'second-guessing' of legislative and administrative decisions grounded in social, economic, and political policy through the medium of an action in tort," when properly construed, the exception "protects only governmental actions and decisions based on considerations of public policy."

Where Congress has delegated the authority to an independent agency or to the Executive Branch to implement the general provisions of a regulatory statute and to issue regulations to that end, there is no doubt that planning-level decisions establishing programs are protected by the discretionary function exception, as is the promulgation of regulations by which the agencies are to carry out the programs. In addition, the actions of Government agents involving the necessary element of choice and grounded in the social, economic, or political goals of the statute and regulations are protected.

Thus, in *Dalehite,* the exception barred recovery for claims arising from a massive fertilizer explosion. The fertilizer had been manufactured, packaged, and prepared for export pursuant to detailed regulations as part of a comprehensive federal program aimed at increasing the food supply in occupied areas after World War II. Not only was the cabinet-level decision to institute the fertilizer program discretionary, but so were the decisions concerning the specific requirements for manufacturing the fertilizer.

Nearly 30 years later, in *Varig Airlines,* the Federal Aviation Administration's actions in formulating and implementing a "spot-check" plan for airplane inspection were protected by the discretionary function exception because of the agency's authority to establish safety standards for airplanes. Actions taken in furtherance of the program were likewise protected, even if those particular actions were negligent. Most recently, in *Berkovitz,* we examined a comprehensive regulatory scheme governing the licensing of laboratories to produce polio vaccine and the release to the public of particular drugs. We found that some of the claims fell outside the exception, because the agency employees had failed to follow the specific directions contained in the applicable regulations, i.e., in those instances, there was no room for choice or judgment. We then remanded the case for an analysis of the remaining claims in light of the applicable regulations.

Under the applicable precedents, therefore, if a regulation mandates particular conduct, and the employee obeys the direction, the Government will be protected because the action will be deemed in furtherance of the policies which led to the promulgation of the regulation. If the employee violates the mandatory regulation, there will be no shelter from liability because there is no room for choice and the action will be contrary to policy. On the other hand, if a regulation allows the employee discretion, the very existence of the regulation creates a strong presumption that a discretionary act authorized by the regulation involves consideration of the same policies which led to the promulgation of the regulations.

Not all agencies issue comprehensive regulations, however. Some establish policy on a case-by-case basis, whether through adjudicatory proceedings or through administration of agency programs. Others promulgate regulations on some topics, but not on others. In addition, an agency may rely on internal guidelines rather than on published regulations. In any event, it will most often be true that the general aims and policies of the controlling statute will be evident from its text.

When established governmental policy, as expressed or implied by statute, regulation, or agency guidelines, allows a Government agent to exercise discretion, it must be presumed that the agent's acts are grounded in policy when exercising that discretion. For a complaint to survive a motion to dismiss, it must allege facts which would support a finding that the challenged actions are not the kind of conduct that can be said to be grounded in the policy of the regulatory regime. The focus of the inquiry is not on the agent's subjective intent in exercising the discretion conferred by statute or regulation, but on the nature of the actions taken and on whether they are susceptible to policy analysis.

III

In light of our cases and their interpretation of § 2680(a), it is clear that the Court of Appeals erred in holding that the exception does not reach decisions made at the operational or management level of the bank involved in this case. A discretionary act is one that involves choice or judgment; there is nothing in that description that refers exclusively to policymaking or planning functions. Day-to-day management of banking affairs, like the management of other businesses, regularly requires judgment as to which of a range of permissible courses is the wisest. Discretionary conduct is not confined to the policy or planning level. "It is the nature of the conduct, rather than the status of the actor, that governs whether the discretionary function exception applies in a given case." . . .

The Court's first use of the term "operational" in connection with the discretionary function exception occurred in *Dalehite,* where the Court noted that "the decisions held culpable were all responsibly made at a planning rather than operational level and involved considerations more or less important to the practicability of the Government's fertilizer program." Gaubert relies upon this statement as support for his argument that the Court of Appeals applied the appropriate analysis to the allegations of the amended complaint, but the distinction in *Dalehite* was merely description of the level at which the challenged conduct occurred. There was no suggestion that decisions made at an operational level could not also be based on policy.

Neither is the decision below supported by *Indian Towing.* There the Coast Guard had negligently failed to maintain a lighthouse by allowing the light to go out.

The United States was held liable, not because the negligence occurred at the operational level but because making sure the light was operational "did not involve any permissible exercise of policy judgment." Indeed, the Government did not even claim the benefit of the exception but unsuccessfully urged that maintaining the light was a governmental function for which it could not be liable. The Court of Appeals misinterpreted *Berkovitz's* reference to *Indian Towing* as perpetuating a nonexistent dichotomy between discretionary functions and operational activities.

Consequently, once the court determined that some of the actions challenged by Gaubert occurred at an operational level, it concluded, incorrectly, that those actions must necessarily have been outside the scope of the discretionary function exception.

IV

We now inquire whether the Court of Appeals was correct in holding that some of the acts alleged in Gaubert's amended complaint were not discretionary acts within the meaning of § 2680(a). The decision we review was entered on a motion to dismiss. We therefore "accept all of the factual allegations in [Gaubert's] complaint as true" and ask whether the allegations state a claim sufficient to survive a motion to dismiss.

These claims asserted that the regulators had achieved "a constant federal presence" at IASA. In describing this presence, the amended complaint alleged that the regulators "consulted as to day-to-day affairs and operations of IASA," "participated in management decisions" at IASA board meetings, "became involved in giving advice, making recommendations, urging, or directing action or procedures at IASA"; and "advised their hand-picked directors and officers on a variety of subjects." Specifically, the complaint enumerated seven instances or kinds of objectionable official involvement.

First, the regulators "arranged for the hiring for IASA of . . . consultants on operational and financial matters and asset management." Second, the officials "urged or directed that IASA convert from a state-chartered savings and loan to federally-chartered savings and loan in part so that it could become the exclusive government entity with power to control IASA." Third, the regulators "gave advice and made recommendations concerning whether, when, and how to place IASA subsidiaries into bankruptcy." Fourth, the officials "mediated salary disputes between IASA and its senior officers." Fifth, the regulators "reviewed a draft complaint in litigation" that IASA's board contemplated filing and were "so actively involved in giving advice, making recommendations, and directing matters related to IASA's litigation policy that they were able successfully to stall the Board of Directors' ultimate decision to file the complaint until the Bank Board in Washington had reviewed, advised on, and commented on the draft." Sixth, the regulators "actively intervened with the Texas Savings and Loan Department (IASA's principal regulator) when the State attempted to install a supervisory agent at IASA." Finally, the FHLB-D president wrote the IASA board of directors "affirming that his agency had placed that Board of Directors into office, and describing their mutual goal to protect the FSLIC insurance fund." According to Gaubert, the losses he suffered were caused by the regulators' "assumption of the duty to participate in, and to make, the day-to-day decisions at IASA and [the] negligent discharge of that assumed duty."

Moreover, he alleged that "the involvement of the FHLB-Dallas in the affairs of IASA went beyond its normal regulatory activity, and the agency actually substituted its decisions for those of the directors and officers of the association."

We first inquire whether the challenged actions were discretionary, or whether they were instead controlled by mandatory statutes or regulations. Although the FHLBB, which oversaw the other agencies at issue, had promulgated extensive regulations which were then in effect, neither party has identified formal regulations governing the conduct in question. As already noted, 12 U.S.C. § 1464(a) authorizes the FHLBB to examine and regulate FSLA's, "giving primary consideration to the best practices of thrift institutions in the United States." Both the District Court and the Court of Appeals recognized that the agencies possessed broad statutory authority to supervise financial institutions. The relevant statutory provisions were not mandatory, but left to the judgment of the agency the decision of when to institute proceedings against a financial institution and which mechanism to use. For example, the FSLIC had authority to terminate an institution's insured status, issue cease-and-desist orders, and suspend or remove an institution's officers, if "in the opinion of the corporation" such action was warranted because the institution or its officers were engaging in an "unsafe or unsound practice" in connection with the business of the institution. The FHLBB had parallel authority to issue cease-and-desist orders and suspend or remove an institution's officers. Although the statute enumerated specific grounds warranting an appointment by the FHLBB of a conservator or receiver, the determination of whether any of these grounds existed depended upon "the opinion of the Board." The agencies here were not bound to act in a particular way; the exercise of their authority involved a great "element of judgment or choice."

We are unconvinced by Gaubert's assertion that because the agencies did not institute formal proceedings against IASA, they had no discretion to take informal actions as they did. Although the statutes provided only for formal proceedings, there is nothing in the language or structure of the statutes that prevented the regulators from invoking less formal means of supervision of financial institutions. Not only was there no statutory or regulatory mandate which compelled the regulators to act in a particular way, but there was no prohibition against the use of supervisory mechanisms not specifically set forth in statute or regulation.

Gaubert also argues that the challenged actions fall outside the discretionary function exception because they involved the mere application of technical skills and business expertise. But this is just another way of saying that the considerations involving the day-to-day management of a business concern such as IASA are so precisely formulated that decisions at the operational level never involve the exercise of discretion within the meaning of § 2680(a), a notion that we have already rejected in disapproving the rationale of the Court of Appeals' decision. It may be that certain decisions resting on mathematical calculations, for example, involve no choice or judgment in carrying out the calculations, but the regulatory acts alleged here are not of that genre. Rather, it is plain to us that each of the challenged actions involved the exercise of choice and judgment.

We are also convinced that each of the regulatory actions in question involved the kind of policy judgment that the discretionary function exception was designed to shield. The FHLBB Resolution quoted above, coupled with the relevant statutory provisions, established governmental policy which is presumed to have been furthered when the regulators exercised their discretion to choose from various courses of action in supervising IASA. Although Gaubert contends that day-to-day decisions concerning IASA's affairs did not implicate social, economic, or political policies, even the Court of Appeals recognized that these day-to-day "operational" decisions were undertaken for policy reasons of primary concern to the regulatory agencies: . . .

In the end, Gaubert's Amended Complaint alleges nothing more than negligence on the part of the regulators. Indeed, the two substantive counts seek relief for "negligent selection of directors and officers" and "negligent involvement in day-to-day operations." Gaubert asserts that the discretionary function exception protects only those acts of negligence which occur in the course of establishing broad policies, rather than individual acts of negligence which occur in the course of day-to-day activities. But we have already disposed of that submission. If the routine or frequent nature of a decision were sufficient to remove an otherwise discretionary act from the scope of the exception, then countless policy based decisions by regulators exercising day-to day supervisory authority would be actionable. This is not the rule of our cases.

V

Because from the face of the amended complaint, it is apparent that all of the challenged actions of the federal regulators involved the exercise of discretion in furtherance of public policy goals, the Court of Appeals erred in failing to find the claims barred by the discretionary function exception of the FTCA. We therefore reverse the decision of the Court of Appeals for the Fifth Circuit and remand for proceedings consistent with this opinion.

It is so ordered.

Questions

1. Do you think the policy/operational distinction still exists?
2. Can you summarize the main variables that lead to government immunity under the discretionary function exception?

INTENTIONAL TORTS

The other exclusion in the FTCA is intentional torts. Assault (putting one in fear or apprehension) and battery (an unauthorized touching) are two intentional torts with which you are probably familiar. Defamation of character (slander and libel) is another. As originally passed, the FTCA maintained sovereign immunity for the government in the event that one of its employees committed an intentional tort. As this chapter moves to the notion of official immunity, you will be introduced to the case of *Barr v. Matteo,* in which federal employees who had been libeled by their boss sued him individually for the tort of libel. In a case similar to *Dalehite*, the jury found that the employer had libeled the employees, but the Supreme Court said the boss was clothed with (a different kind of) immunity.

In the early 1970s, many events caused policymakers to question the wisdom of continuing the intentional tort exception.[24] There were, for example, the wholesale arrests of thousands who demonstrated in Washington, D.C., on May Day in 1971. (They were held in a football stadium.) There was a Supreme Court decision in a case called *Bivens v. Six Unknown Named Agents of the Federal Bureau of Narcotics* (which you will read shortly), which was handed down in June 1971. There were the shootings at Kent State University and Jackson State University in May 1970. But it was the accumulation of several events in and around St. Louis in 1973 that caused Congress to amend the intentional tort exception to the FTCA in March 1974.

A former federal program called Drug Abuse Law Enforcement (DALE) was a special effort by state and local law enforcement agents and Bureau of Narcotics and Dangerous Drugs officers to get at drug trafficking in the United States. One of the regional DALE offices was in St. Louis. DALE officers frequently worked undercover and were described by several citizens who had contact with them as "shabbily dressed and with long hair."[25]

Herbert and Evelyn Giglotto, who lived in Collinsville, Illinois, were awakened at 9:30 p.m. on April 23, 1973, by the sound of someone breaking down their front door. According to Boger, Gitenstein, and Verkuil, who studied the case, Mr. Giglotto was met in the hallway outside the bedroom by five shabbily dressed men who grabbed him and dragged him back to the bedroom, threw him on the bed, tied his hands behind his back, put a gun to his head, and told him that if he moved they would kill him. The men shouted abuse at Mr. Giglotto, then grabbed his wife (who was wearing only a negligee), threw her on the bed, and gave her the same treatment her husband had received. The men identified themselves as federal agents, and, eventually, 15 or so of them had entered and left the bedroom. After about 15 minutes, one of the agents came into the bedroom with Giglotto's checkbook and other documents and announced, "Well, we have the wrong people." The couple were untied and allowed to sit on the bed but not allowed to get dressed. The agents left without explanation, "leaving behind a smashed television, a broken camera, scattered books, scratched furniture and a shattered antique vase,"[26] not to mention the lack of a front door. DALE agents would later arrest a man who lived next door to the Giglottos.

A half hour later, across town, shabbily dressed men broke into the home of the Askews, who were accosted at the dinner table. Mr. Askew would eventually testify that from the appearance of the men and the weapons they brandished (sawed-off shotguns), he first thought that his son had been in a fight with a motorcycle gang member, and now the gang had come to his house to kill the boy.[27] After Mrs. Askew, who had fainted, was revived, the DALE agents were able to convince the Askews that they were federal agents. The Askews were not treated with the abuse, verbal or physical, that the Giglottos had received, but the house was searched while they were held at gunpoint. Eventually, one of the agents said it must have been a "bad tip," and they left. Different and more pleasant agents appeared at both houses the next day with assurances that the property damage would be paid for, but no apology was forthcoming, and there was no offer to pay for the trauma that DALE agents had caused the two families.

The actions of the DALE agents constitute the torts of assault, battery, and false imprisonment, but because of the intentional tort exclusion in the FTCA, the Giglottos and Askews were without a legal remedy.

It turned out that several of the agents involved in the April 23 raids had been involved in two similar incidents over the preceding year. A special assistant attorney general said that he had suspended the four agents. One of the suspended agents, however, was caught by the press at another raid shortly after the suspension. It turned out the four agents had simply been reassigned to planning and coordinating the raids.

The incidents received nationwide coverage in the press. The administrative reaction was to create a new agency, the Drug Enforcement Agency (DEA); severely restrict the use of "no-knock" entries; stress the importance of obtaining a warrant (it appears there was no warrant in either case); and, finally, to see to it that federal agents wear identifying clothing in raids and searches. The Giglottos and the Askews went to Washington, D.C., to testify, and as a result of the publicity surrounding this incident, Congress amended the FTCA to remove sovereign immunity for intentional torts such as assault, battery, and false imprisonment, when committed by a federal law enforcement officer.

OFFICIAL OR QUALIFIED IMMUNITY

One of the things the FTCA does is to absolve the individual federal employee of liability and spread the financial burden to the taxpayers. In the case you are about to read next,

Federal Bureau of Narcotics Agents entered (they broke in) a man's apartment, searched him and the apartment, and arrested him for alleged narcotics violations—all without a warrant. Except to the extent that it may involve a battery or false imprisonment (which at the time—1971—were intentional torts exempted under the FTCA), this is not an action for a tort. The man, Mr. Bivens, was suing the narcotics agents individually (not the agency or the federal government) for violating his Fourth Amendment rights. If Congress has never authorized such suits, can they be maintained?

Bivens v. Six Unknown Named Agents of the Federal Bureau of Narcotics
403 U.S. 388 (1971)

Justice Brennan delivered the opinion of the Court, joined by Justices Douglas, Stewart, White, and Marshall. Justice Harlan concurred, and Chief Justice Burger and Justices Black and Blackmun filed dissents.

The Fourth Amendment provides that: "The right of the people to be secure in their persons, houses, papers, and effects, against unreasonable searches and seizures, shall not be violated. . . ." In *Bell v. Hood,* 327 U.S. 678 (1946), we reserved the question whether violation of that command by a federal agent acting under color of his authority gives rise to a cause of action for damages consequent upon his unconstitutional conduct. Today we hold that it does.

This case has its origin in an arrest and search carried out on the morning of November 26, 1965. Petitioner's complaint alleged that on that day respondents, agents of the Federal Bureau of Narcotics acting under claim of federal authority, entered his apartment and arrested him for alleged narcotics violations. The agents manacled petitioner in front of his wife and children, and threatened to arrest the entire family. They searched the apartment from stem to stern. Thereafter, petitioner was taken to the federal courthouse in Brooklyn, where he was interrogated, booked, and subjected to a visual strip search.

On July 7, 1967, petitioner brought suit in Federal District Court. In addition to the allegations above, his complaint asserted that the arrest and search were effected without a warrant, and

that unreasonable force was employed in making the arrest; fairly read, it alleges as well that the arrest was made without probable cause. Petitioner claimed to have suffered great humiliation, embarrassment, and mental suffering as a result of the agents' unlawful conduct, and sought $15,000 damages from each of them. The District Court, on respondents' motion, dismissed the complaint on the ground, inter alia, that it failed to state a cause of action. 276 F.Supp. 12 1967. The Court of Appeals, one judge concurring specially, affirmed on that basis. 409 F.2d 718 (CA2 1969). We granted certiorari. We reverse. . . .

I

Respondents do not argue that petitioner should be entirely without remedy for an unconstitutional invasion of his rights by federal agents. In respondents' view, however, the rights that petitioner asserts—primarily rights of privacy—are creations of state and not of federal law. Accordingly, they argue, petitioner may obtain money damages to redress invasion of these rights only by an action in tort, under state law, in the state courts. In this scheme the Fourth Amendment would serve merely to limit the extent to which the agents could defend the state law tort suit by asserting that their actions were a valid exercise of federal power: if the agents were shown to have violated the Fourth Amendment, such a defense would be lost to them and they would stand before the state law merely as private individuals. Candidly admitting that it is the policy of the Department of Justice to remove all such suits from the state to the federal courts for decision, respondents nevertheless urge that we uphold dismissal of petitioner's complaint in federal court, and remit him to filing an action in the state courts in order that the case may properly be removed to the federal court for decision on the basis of state law. We think that respondents' thesis rests upon an unduly restrictive view of the Fourth Amendment's protection against unreasonable searches and seizures by federal agents, a view that has consistently been rejected by this Court. Respondents seek to treat the relationship between a citizen and a federal agent unconstitutionally exercising his authority as no different from the relationship between two private citizens. In so doing, they ignore the fact that power, once granted, does not disappear like a magic gift when it is wrongfully used. An agent acting—albeit unconstitutionally—in the name of the United States possesses a far greater capacity for harm than an individual trespasser exercising no authority other than his own.

Accordingly, as our cases make clear, the Fourth Amendment operates as a limitation upon the exercise of federal power regardless of whether the State in whose jurisdiction that power is exercised would prohibit or penalize the identical act if engaged in by a private citizen. It guarantees to citizens of the United States the absolute right to be free from unreasonable searches and seizures carried out by virtue of federal authority. And "where federally protected rights have been invaded, it has been the rule from the beginning that courts will be alert to adjust their remedies so as to grant the necessary relief." . . .

Second. The interests protected by state laws regulating trespass and the invasion of privacy, and those protected by the Fourth Amendment's guarantee against unreasonable searches and seizures, may be inconsistent or even hostile. Thus, we may bar the door against an unwelcome private intruder, or call the police if he persists in seeking entrance. The availability of such alternative means for the protection of privacy may lead the State to restrict imposition of liability for any consequent trespass. A private

citizen, asserting no authority other than his own, will not normally be liable in trespass if he demands, and is granted, admission to another's house. But one who demands admission under a claim of federal authority stands in a far different position. The mere invocation of federal power by a federal law enforcement official will normally render futile any attempt to resist an unlawful entry or arrest by resort to the local police; and a claim of authority to enter is likely to unlock the door as well. . . .

Third. That damages may be obtained for injuries consequent upon a violation of the Fourth Amendment by federal officials should hardly seem a surprising proposition. Historically, damages have been regarded as the ordinary remedy for an invasion of personal interests in liberty. . . .

Of course, the Fourth Amendment does not in so many words provide for its enforcement by an award of money damages for the consequences of its violation. But "it is well settled that where legal rights have been invaded, and a federal statute provides for a general right to sue for such invasion, federal courts may use any available remedy to make good the wrong done." The question is merely whether petitioner, if he can demonstrate an injury consequent upon the violation by federal agents of his Fourth Amendment rights, is entitled to redress his injury through a particular remedial mechanism normally available in the federal courts. "The very essence of civil liberty certainly consists in the right of every individual to claim the protection of the laws, whenever he receives an injury." *Marbury v. Madison*, 1 Cranch 137, 163, 2 L.Ed. 60 (1803). Having concluded that petitioner's complaint states a cause of action under the Fourth Amendment, we hold that petitioner is entitled to recover money damages for any injuries he has suffered as a result of the agents' violation of the Amendment.

II

In addition to holding that petitioner's complaint had failed to state facts making out a cause of action, the District Court ruled that in any event respondents were immune from liability by virtue of their official position. 276 F.Supp., at 15. This question was not passed upon by the Court of Appeals, and accordingly we do not consider it here. The judgment of the Court of Appeals is reversed and the case is remanded for further proceedings consistent with this opinion.

So ordered.

Judgment reversed and case remanded.

Questions

1. What is the holding in *Bivens?*
2. Do you think this is a good or a bad decision? Why?

Some have attributed to *Bivens* the notion of qualified immunity, but as you can tell from reading the case, the Court passed on the question of immunity. Some government officials have absolute immunity. That means they cannot be sued at all in their official capacity. Judges, prosecutors, and presidents are examples.[28] Most government officials possess what is called a qualified immunity for *Bivens*-type suits. This means that sometimes they can be sued, and sometimes they are immune from suit.

In the 1950s, the acting director of the Office of Rent Stabilization (Barr) issued a press release that a jury later found to have slandered former employees (Matteo and Madigan). This was not a *Bivens*-type action but, rather, a tort suit. It was not an FTCA suit, however, because the plaintiffs were not suing the government but, instead, were suing Barr personally for an intentional tort. One of the defenses Barr raised was that even if his actions did amount to slander, because he was acting in an official capacity, he should enjoy immunity. The Supreme Court agreed, saying, "The fact that the action here taken was within the outer perimeter of petitioner's line of duty is enough to render the privilege applicable."[29]

The "privilege" the Court spoke of is official immunity (as opposed to governmental immunity), and in saying that official immunity extended all the way to the "outer perimeters of official duty," the Court effectively created an absolute immunity for governmental officials.

The *Bivens* case signaled the end of absolute official immunity. Indeed, on remand to the circuit court, the *Bivens* defendants were found to have acted beyond the outer perimeters of their line of duty. The case you are about to read, although it is not the most recent case on federal official immunity, is famous for its official immunity jurisprudence.

Butz v. Economou
438 U.S. 478 (1978)

Justice White delivered the opinion of the Court, joined by Justices Brennan, Marshall, Blackmun, and Powell. Justice Rehnquist filed an opinion concurring in part and dissenting in part, joined by Chief Justice Burger and Justices Stewart and Stevens.

This case concerns the personal immunity of federal officials in the Executive Branch from claims for damages arising from their violations of citizens' constitutional rights. Respondent filed suit against a number of officials in the Department of Agriculture claiming that they had instituted an investigation and an administrative proceeding against him in retaliation for his criticism of that agency. The District Court dismissed the action on the ground that the individual defendants, as federal officials, were entitled to absolute immunity for all discretionary acts within the scope of their authority. The Court of Appeals reversed, holding that the defendants were entitled only to the qualified immunity available to their counterparts in state government. *Economou v. U.S. Dept. of Agriculture*, 535 F.2d 688 (1976). Because of the importance of immunity doctrine to both the vindication of constitutional guarantees and the effective functioning of government, we granted certiorari. . . .

I

Respondent controls Arthur N. Economou and Co., Inc., which was at one time registered with the Department of Agriculture as a commodity futures commission merchant. Most of respondent's factual allegations in this lawsuit focus on an earlier administrative proceeding in which the Department of Agriculture sought to revoke or suspend the company's registration. On February 19, 1970, following an audit, the Department of Agriculture issued an administrative complaint alleging that respondent, while a registered merchant, had willfully failed to maintain the minimum financial requirements prescribed by the Department. After another audit, an amended complaint was issued on June 22, 1970. A hearing was held before the Chief Hearing Examiner of the Department, who filed a recommendation sustaining the administrative complaint. The Judicial Officer of the Department, to whom the Secretary had delegated his decisional authority in enforcement proceedings, affirmed the Chief Hearing Examiner's decision. On respondent's petition for review, the Court of Appeals for the Second Circuit vacated the order of the Judicial Officer. It reasoned that "the essential finding of willfulness . . . was made in a proceeding instituted without the customary warning letter, which the Judicial Officer conceded might well have resulted in prompt correction of the claimed insufficiencies." *Economou v. U.S. Department of Agriculture*, 494 F.2d 519 (1974).

While the administrative complaint was pending before the Judicial Officer, respondent filed this lawsuit in Federal District Court. Respondent sought initially to enjoin the progress of the administrative proceeding, but he was unsuccessful in that regard. On March 31, 1975, respondent filed a second amended complaint seeking damages. Named as defendants were the individuals who had served as Secretary and Assistant Secretary of Agriculture during the relevant events; the Judicial Officer and Chief Hearing Examiner; several officials in the Commodity Exchange Authority; the Agriculture Department attorney who had prosecuted the enforcement proceeding; and several of the auditors who had investigated respondent or were witnesses against respondent. . . .

The complaint stated that prior to the issuance of the administrative complaints respondent had been "sharply critical of the staff and operations of Defendants and carried on a vociferous campaign for the reform of Defendant Commodity Exchange Authority to obtain more effective regulation of commodity trading." The complaint also stated that, some time prior to the issuance of the February 19 complaint, respondent and his company had ceased to engage in activities regulated by the defendants. The complaint charged that each of the administrative complaints had been issued without the notice or warning required by law; that the defendants had furnished the complaints "to interested persons and others without furnishing respondent's answers as well"; and that following the issuance of the amended complaint, the defendants had issued a "deceptive" press release that "falsely indicated to the public that [respondent's] financial resources had deteriorated, when Defendants knew that their statement was untrue and so acknowledge[d] previously that said assertion was untrue." . . .

The complaint then presented 10 "causes of action," some of which purported to state claims for damages under the United States Constitution. For example, the first "cause of action" alleged that respondent had been denied due process of law because the defendants had instituted unauthorized proceedings against him without proper notice and with the knowledge that respondent was no longer subject to their regulatory jurisdiction. The third "cause of action" stated that by means of such actions "the Defendants discouraged and chilled the campaign of criticism [plaintiff] directed against them, and thereby deprived the [plaintiff] of [his] rights to free expression guaranteed by the First Amendment of the United States Constitution." . . .

The defendants moved to dismiss the complaint on the ground that "as to the individual defendants it is barred by the doctrine of official immunity." . . .

II

The single submission by the United States on behalf of petitioners is that all of the federal officials sued in this case are absolutely immune from any liability for damages even if in the course of enforcing the relevant statutes they infringed respondent's constitutional rights and even if the violation was knowing and deliberate. Although the position is earnestly and ably presented by the United States, we are quite sure that it is unsound and consequently reject it.

Bivens established that compensable injury to a constitutionally protected interest could be vindicated by a suit for damages invoking the general federal-question jurisdiction of the federal courts, but we reserved the question whether the agents involved were "immune from liability by virtue of their official position," and remanded the case for that determination. On remand the Court of Appeals for the Second Circuit, as has every other Court of Appeals that has faced the question, held that the agents were not absolutely immune and that the public interest would be sufficiently protected by according the agents and their superiors a qualified immunity. . . .

"[I]n varying scope, a qualified immunity is available to officers of the executive branch of government, the variation being dependent upon the scope of discretion and responsibilities of the office and all the circumstances as they reasonably appeared at the time of the action on which liability is sought to be based. It is the existence of reasonable grounds for the belief formed at the time and in light of all the circumstances, coupled with good-faith belief,

that affords a basis for qualified immunity of executive officers for acts performed in the course of official conduct." . . .

We agree with the perception of these courts that, in the absence of congressional direction to the contrary, there is no basis for according to federal officials a higher degree of immunity from liability when sued for a constitutional infringement as authorized by *Bivens* than is accorded state officials when sued for the identical violation under § 1983. The constitutional injuries made actionable by § 1983 are of no greater magnitude than those for which federal officials may be responsible. The pressures and uncertainties facing decisionmakers in state government are little if at all different from those affecting federal officials. We see no sense in holding a state governor liable but immunizing the head of a federal department; in holding the administrator of a federal hospital immune where the superintendent of a state hospital would be liable; in protecting the warden of a federal prison where the warden of a state prison would be vulnerable; or in distinguishing between state and federal police participating in the same investigation. Surely, federal officials should enjoy no greater zone of protection when they violate federal constitutional rules than do state officers. . . .

This is not to say that considerations of public policy fail to support a limited immunity for federal executive officials. We consider here, as we did in *Scheuer*, the need to protect officials who are required to exercise their discretion and the related public interest in encouraging the vigorous exercise of official authority. Yet *Scheuer* and other cases have recognized that it is not unfair to hold liable the official who knows or should know he is acting outside the law, and that insisting on an awareness of clearly established constitutional limits will not unduly interfere with the exercise of official judgment. We therefore hold that, in a suit for damages arising from unconstitutional action, federal executive officials exercising discretion are entitled only to the qualified immunity specified in *Scheuer*, subject to those exceptional situations where it is demonstrated that absolute immunity is essential for the conduct of the public business.

We think that the Court of Appeals placed undue emphasis on the fact that the officials sued here are—from an administrative perspective—employees of the Executive Branch. Judges have absolute immunity not because of their particular location within the Government but because of the special nature of their responsibilities. . . . We think that adjudication within a federal administrative agency shares enough of the characteristics of the judicial process that those who participate in such adjudication should also be immune from suits for damages. . . .

We therefore hold that persons subject to these restraints and performing adjudicatory functions within a federal agency are entitled to absolute immunity from damages liability for their judicial acts. Those who complain of error in such proceedings must seek agency or judicial review.

We also believe that agency officials performing certain functions analogous to those of a prosecutor should be able to claim absolute immunity with respect to such acts. The decision to initiate administrative proceedings against an individual or corporation is very much like the prosecutor's decision to initiate or move forward with a criminal prosecution. An agency official, like a prosecutor, may have broad discretion in deciding whether a proceeding should be brought and what sanctions should be sought.

We turn finally to the role of an agency attorney in conducting a trial and presenting evidence on the record to the trier of fact. We can see no substantial difference between the function of the agency attorney in presenting evidence in an agency hearing and the function of the prosecutor who brings evidence before a court. . . .

We therefore hold that an agency attorney who arranges for the presentation of evidence on the record in the course of an adjudication is absolutely immune from suits based on the introduction of such evidence. . . .

VI

There remains the task of applying the foregoing principles to the claims against the particular petitioner-defendants involved in this case. Rather than attempt this here in the first instance, we vacate the judgment of the Court of Appeals and remand the case to that court with instructions to remand the case to the District Court for further proceedings consistent with this opinion.

So ordered.

Question

1. The Court here clearly establishes a qualified official immunity for federal officials. Can you describe when such officials will be liable and when they enjoy immunity?

In 1994, The Supreme Court ruled that a *Bivens* action would not be available when suing a federal agency; it only applies to individual employees.[30] A similar issue was decided by the Court in 2001 where the issue was whether an injured plaintiff can use a *Bivens* action to sue a private corporation that was running a federal halfway house under federal contract. The case is *Correctional Services Corporation v. Malesko*, and it appears at the end of this chapter.

IMMUNITY IN THE STATES

Because sovereign immunity was the jurisprudential status quo in the United States and both the state and the federal governments are sovereign entities, it follows that state governments are clothed with sovereign immunity. They cannot be sued without their consent. Today, there are still 10 states that have refused to relinquish sovereign immunity.[31] The rest have passed tort claims acts, most of which are similar to the FTCA in that there are numerous exceptions.

What about county and city government? Because they are creatures of the state legislature, they are not sovereign and hence do not enjoy sovereign immunity. Local governments did, however, have an immunity created by the courts. Local governments could not be sued so long as they were engaged in a governmental function or activity but could be sued if engaged in a proprietary function, one that could be performed by a private business. The state of North Dakota, for example, runs a bank and a mill and elevator and, at one time, brewed beer. These are proprietary functions. The distinction between proprietary and governmental functions no longer exists, as you will discover as you read the *Owen* case below.

Part of the Civil Rights Act of 1871 is 42 U.S.C.1983 imposes civil liability on "any person" who, acting under color of law, deprives another of their federally protected rights. Lawsuits filed under 42 U.S.C. 1983 are referred to as 1983 suits or § 1983 suits. For a long time, the term *person* in the Act was not read to include cities, counties, or local units of government. Cities had an absolute immunity from suit under § 1983. All of that changed in *Monell v. New York City Department of Social Services,* 436 U.S. 658 (1978). Female employees of the agency sued under § 1983 when they were forced to take leave from work due to pregnancy before there was any medical justification to do so. The Court decided that cities and their agencies are *persons* within the Act. There would no longer be absolute immunity for local government under § 1983. The question of whether local government should enjoy a qualified immunity was left for the case below.

Owen v. City of Independence
445 U.S. 622 (1980)

Justice Brennan delivered the opinion of the Court, joined by Justices White, Marshall, Blackmun, and Stevens. Justice Powell filed a dissent joined by Justices Stewart and Rehnquist and Chief Justice Burger.

Monell v. New York City Dept. of Social Services, 436 U.S. 658 (1978), overruled *Monroe v. Pape,* 365 U.S. 167 (1961), insofar as *Monroe* held that local governments were not among the "persons" to whom 42 U.S.C. § 1983 applies and were therefore wholly immune from suit under the statute. *Monell* reserved decision, however, on the question whether local governments, although not entitled to an absolute immunity, should be afforded some form of official immunity in

§ 1983 suits. In this action brought by petitioner in the District Court for the Western District of Missouri, the Court of Appeals for the Eighth Circuit held that respondent city of Independence, Mo., "is entitled to qualified immunity from liability" based on the good faith of its officials: "We extend the limited immunity the district court applied to the individual defendants to cover the City as well, because its officials acted in good faith and without malice." 589 F.2d 335 (1978). We granted certiorari. We reverse. . . .

I

The events giving rise to this suit are detailed in the District Court's findings of fact, 421 F.Supp. 1110 (1976). On February 20, 1967, Robert L.

Broucek, then City Manager of respondent city of Independence, Mo., appointed petitioner George D. Owen to an indefinite term as Chief of Police. In 1972, Owen and a new City Manager, Lyle W. Alberg, engaged in a dispute over petitioner's administration of the Police Department's property room. In March of that year, a handgun, which the records of the Department's property room stated had been destroyed, turned up in Kansas City in the possession of a felon. This discovery prompted Alberg to initiate an investigation of the management of the property room. Although the probe was initially directed by petitioner, Alberg soon transferred responsibility for the investigation to the city's Department of Law, instructing the City Counselor to supervise its conduct and to inform him directly of its findings. . . . While Alberg was away on the weekend of April 15 and 16, two developments occurred. Petitioner, having consulted with counsel, sent Alberg a letter demanding written notice of the charges against him and a public hearing with a reasonable opportunity to respond to those charges. At approximately the same time, City Councilman Paul L. Roberts asked for a copy of the investigative report on the Police Department property room. Although petitioner's appeal received no immediate response, the Acting City Manager complied with Roberts' request and supplied him with the audit report and witness statements. . . . On the evening of April 17, 1972, the City Council held its regularly scheduled meeting. After completion of the planned agenda, Councilman Roberts read a statement he had prepared on the investigation. Among other allegations, Roberts charged that petitioner had misappropriated Police Department property for his own use, that narcotics and money had "mysteriously disappeared" from his office, that traffic tickets had been manipulated, that high ranking police officials had made "inappropriate" requests affecting the police court, and that "things have occurred causing the unusual release of felons." At the close of his statement, Roberts moved that the investigative reports be released to the news media and turned over to the prosecutor for presentation to the grand jury, and that the City Manager "take all direct and appropriate action" against those persons "involved in illegal, wrongful, or gross inefficient activities brought out in the investigative reports." After some discussion, the City Council passed Roberts' motion with no dissents and one abstention. . . .

City Manager Alberg discharged petitioner the very next day. Petitioner was not given any reason for his dismissal; he received only a written notice stating that his employment as Chief of Police was "[t]erminated under the provisions of Section 3.3(1) of the City Charter." Petitioner's earlier demand for a specification of charges and a public hearing was ignored, and a subsequent request by his attorney for an appeal of the discharge decision was denied by the city on the grounds that "there is no appellate procedure or forum provided by the Charter or ordinances of the City of Independence, Missouri, relating to the dismissal of Mr. Owen." . . . The local press gave prominent coverage both to the City Council's action and petitioner's dismissal, linking the discharge to the investigation. As instructed by the City Council, Alberg referred the investigative reports and witness statements to the Prosecuting Attorney of Jackson County, Mo., for consideration by a grand jury. The results of the audit and investigation were never released to the public, however. The grand jury subsequently returned a "no true bill," and no further action was taken by either the City Council or City Manager Alberg.

II

Petitioner named the city of Independence, City Manager Alberg, and the present members of the City Council in their official capacities as defendants in this suit. Alleging that he was discharged without notice of reasons and without a hearing in violation of his constitutional rights to procedural and substantive due process, petitioner sought declaratory and injunctive relief, including a hearing on his discharge, backpay from the date of discharge, and attorney's fees. The District Court, after a bench trial, entered judgment for respondents. 421 F.Supp. 1110 (1976).

The Court of Appeals initially reversed the District Court. . . . Respondents petitioned for review of the Court of Appeals' decision. Certiorari was granted, and the case was remanded for further consideration in light of our supervening decision in *Monell v. New York City Dept. of Social Services,* 436 U.S. 658 (1978). The Court of Appeals on the remand reaffirmed its original determination that the city had violated petitioner's rights under the Fourteenth Amendment, but held that all respondents, including the city, were entitled to qualified immunity from liability. 589 F.2d 335 (1978).

Monell held that "a local government may not be sued under § 1983 for an injury inflicted solely by its employees or agents. Instead, it is when execution of a government's policy or custom, whether made by its lawmakers or by those whose edicts or acts may fairly be said to represent official policy, inflicts the injury that the government as an entity is responsible under § 1983." The Court of Appeals held in the instant case that the municipality's official policy was responsible for the deprivation of petitioner's constitutional rights: "[T]he stigma attached to [petitioner] in connection with his discharge was caused by the official conduct of the City's lawmakers, or by those whose acts may fairly be said to represent official policy. Such conduct amounted to official policy causing the infringement of [petitioner's] constitutional rights, in violation of section 1983." . . . We turn now to the reasons for our disagreement with this holding. . . .

III

Because the question of the scope of a municipality's immunity from liability under § 1983 is essentially one of statutory construction, see *Wood v. Strickland,* 420 U.S. 308 (1975); the starting point in our analysis must be the language of the statute itself. By its terms, § 1983 "creates a species of tort liability that on its face admits of no immunities." Its language is absolute and unqualified; no mention is made of any privileges, immunities, or defenses that may be asserted. Rather, the Act imposes

liability upon "every person" who, under color of state law or custom, "subjects, or causes to be subjected, any citizen of the United States . . . to the deprivation of any rights, privileges, or immunities secured by the Constitution and laws." And *Monell* held that these words were intended to encompass municipal corporations as well as natural "persons." . . . But there is no tradition of immunity for municipal corporations, and neither history nor policy supports a construction of § 1983 that would justify the qualified immunity accorded the city of Independence by the Court of Appeals. We hold, therefore, that the municipality may not assert the good faith of its officers or agents as a defense to liability under § 1983. . . .

To be sure, there were two doctrines that afforded municipal corporations some measure of protection from tort liability. The first sought to distinguish between a municipality's "governmental" and "proprietary" functions; as to the former, the city was held immune, whereas in its exercise of the latter, the city was held to the same standards of liability as any private corporation. The second doctrine immunized a municipality for its "discretionary" or "legislative" activities, but not for those which were "ministerial" in nature. A brief examination of the application and the rationale underlying each of these doctrines demonstrates that Congress could not have intended them to limit a municipality's liability under § 1983.

In sum, we can discern no "tradition so well grounded in history and reason" that would warrant the conclusion that in enacting § 1 of the Civil Rights Act, the 42d Congress *sub silentio* extended to municipalities a qualified immunity based on the good faith of their officers. Absent any clearer indication that Congress intended so to limit the reach of a statute expressly designed to provide a "broad remedy for violations of federally protected civil rights," *Monell v. New York City Dept. of Social Services,* 436 U.S., at 685, we are unwilling to suppose that injuries occasioned by a municipality's unconstitutional conduct were not also meant to be fully redressable through its sweep.

. . . Moreover, § 1983 was intended not only to provide compensation to the victims of past abuses, but to serve as a deterrent against future constitutional deprivations, as well. See *Robertson v. Wegmann,* 436 U.S. 584 (1978); *Carey v. Piphus,* 435 U.S. 247 (1978). The knowledge that a municipality will be liable for all of its injurious conduct, whether committed in good faith or not, should create an incentive for officials who may harbor doubts about the lawfulness of their intended actions to err on the side of protecting citizens' constitutional rights. Furthermore, the threat that damages might be levied against the city may encourage those in a policymaking position to institute internal rules and programs designed to minimize the likelihood of unintentional infringements on constitutional rights. Such procedures are particularly beneficial in preventing those "systemic" injuries that result not so much from the conduct of any single individual, but from the interactive behavior of several government officials, each of whom may be acting in good faith. . . .

In *Scheuer v. Rhodes,* supra, 416 U.S., at 240, the Chief Justice identified the two "mutually dependent rationales" on which the doctrine of official immunity rested: "(1) the injustice, particularly in the absence of bad faith, of subjecting to liability an officer who is required, by the legal obligations of his position, to exercise discretion; (2) the danger that the threat of such liability would deter his willingness to execute his office with the decisiveness and the judgment required by the public good." . . .

The first consideration is simply not implicated when the damages award comes not from the official's pocket, but from the public treasury. . . .

It has been argued, however, that revenue raised by taxation for public use should not be diverted to the benefit of a single or discrete group of taxpayers, particularly where the municipality has at all times acted in good faith. On the contrary, the accepted view is that stated in *Thayer v. Boston*—"that the city, in its corporate capacity, should be liable to make good the damage sustained by an [unlucky] individual, in consequence of the acts thus done." 36 Mass., at 515. After all, it is the

public at large which enjoys the benefits of the government's activities, and it is the public at large which is ultimately responsible for its administration. Thus, even where some constitutional development could not have been foreseen by municipal officials, it is fairer to allocate any resulting financial loss to the inevitable costs of government borne by all the taxpayers, than to allow its impact to be felt solely by those whose rights, albeit newly recognized, have been violated. . . .

The second rationale mentioned in *Scheuer* also loses its force when it is the municipality, in contrast to the official, whose liability is at issue. At the heart of this justification for a qualified immunity for the individual official is the concern that the threat of personal monetary liability will introduce an unwarranted and unconscionable consideration into the decisionmaking process, thus paralyzing the governing official's decisiveness and distorting his judgment on matters of public policy. The inhibiting effect is significantly reduced, if not eliminated, however, when the threat of personal liability is removed.

IV

In sum, our decision holding that municipalities have no immunity from damages liability flowing from their constitutional violations harmonizes well with developments in the common law and our own pronouncements on official immunities under § 1983. Doctrines of tort law have changed significantly over the past century, and our notions of governmental responsibility should properly reflect that evolution. No longer is individual "blameworthiness" the acid test of liability; the principle of equitable loss-spreading has joined fault as a factor in distributing the costs of official misconduct.

We believe that today's decision, together with prior precedents in this area, properly allocates these costs among the three principals in the scenario of the § 1983 cause of action: the victim of the constitutional deprivation; the officer whose conduct caused the injury; and the public, as represented by the municipal entity. The innocent individual who is harmed by an abuse of governmental authority is assured that he will be compensated for his injury. The offending official, so long as he conducts himself in good faith, may go about his business secure in the knowledge that a qualified immunity will protect him from personal liability for damages that are more appropriately chargeable to the populace as a whole. And the public will be forced to bear only the costs of injury inflicted by the "execution of a government's policy or custom, whether made by its lawmakers or by those whose edicts or acts may fairly be said to represent official policy."

Reversed.

Question

1. Do local units of government have qualified immunity?

Owen, the plaintiff in the preceding case, was suing the city under 42 U.S.C., § 1983. The law creates a constitutional suit against state officials, just as the decision in *Bivens* created one for federal officials and the *Monell* case creates the same kind of suit against a local government. Such suits are referred to as "1983 suits," and they constitute a mushrooming proportion of cases filed in federal courts.[32] Court interpretation of § 1983 created a qualified official immunity for state officials, just as the immunity articulated in *Butz* created a qualified immunity for federal officials. However, the decision in *Owen* does not allow for a qualified immunity for local governments. It is important that you understand the state of 1983 jurisprudence after *Owen*. Local governments can be sued. They have no immunity. However to successfully sue a local government, a plaintiff must show that the action that caused the injury was the official policy of the city. The case of *Pembaur v. Cincinnati* at the end of this chapter addresses that issue.

Another lawsuit involving issues of immunity was filed by Walter McMillian, who sat on Alabama's death row for six years. His case is somewhat famous because *60 Minutes* did a piece on him that eventually led to his release, and a best-selling book has been written about his experience.[33] On a Saturday morning in November 1986, while Ronda Morrison was being brutally murdered in the back of a dry cleaning store, Walter McMillian was attending an outdoor barbecue with about 100 other black friends and neighbors in Monroeville, Alabama. Several months later, Walter was arrested, convicted after a trial that lasted less than three days, and sentenced to be executed in Alabama's electric chair. The State has since admitted that coerced false testimony was used against him at trial and exculpatory evidence was withheld from Walter's attorney and the jury. Walter eventually sued the sheriff who coerced the false testimony and the county under § 1983. In the courts, this suit boiled down to a question of policy. The Supreme Court, in a 5 to 4 decision, held that the county had no policy-making role in county law enforcement. Hence, whatever may or may not have happened in McMillian's criminal trial was not the result of policy by Monroe County. It could not be sued under § 1983. Just as the city manager's actions incurred § 1983 liability for the city in the *Owen* case, the issue now turned to whether the sheriff by his policy actions incurred liability for Monroe County. The answer was no because the court determined that while the sheriff was a policymaker, he worked for the state, not the county. Walter lost this round of suits. He could still sue the sheriff as an individual under § 1983, but he would face the hurdle of *judgment proof,* a concept familiar to law students. Try to answer the question, "Why cannot Walter sue Alabama"? See *McMillian v. Monroe County, Alabama*, 520 U.S. 781 (1997).

In another case, B. J. Moore, who was the sheriff of Bryan County, Oklahoma, hired Burns, a relative, as a reserve officer for the department. Burns and a deputy sheriff stopped the Browns' truck and ordered the occupants to exit. When they did not comply fast enough to suit Burns, he grabbed the passenger and threw her out of the truck. Mrs. Brown's knees hit the pavement, damaging them so severely that they needed to be replaced surgically. The Browns sued Bryan County for the cost of the knee replacement surgery under § 1983. The suit alleged that the sheriff's hiring policy should incur 1983 liability for the county. Had the sheriff done a normal law enforcement background check on Burns, he would have discovered a violent history, including a string of misdemeanor convictions for assault. The Supreme Court said that the county would be liable if a policymaker acted on behalf of the county with deliberate indifference toward a citizen. Plus, the deliberate indifference must cause the injury. The Court concluded that one bad hiring decision did not constitute deliberate indifference sufficient to incur § 1983 liability for Bryan County. See *Board of Commissioners of Bryan County v. Brown*, 520 U.S. 397 (1997).

The two cases that follow show the evolution of doctrine in state official immunity cases. The *Wood* case articulates the present constitutional test to determine when a state official has crossed the line from immunity to liability.

Scheuer v. Rhodes
416 U.S. 232 (1974)

Chief Justice Burger delivered the opinion for a unanimous court. Justice Douglas did not participate.

We granted certiorari in these cases to resolve whether the District Court correctly dismissed civil damage actions, brought under 42 U.S.C. § 1983, on the ground that these actions were, as a matter of law, against the State of Ohio, and hence barred by the Eleventh Amendment to the Constitution and, alternatively, that the actions were against state officials who were immune from liability for the acts alleged in the complaints. These cases arise out of the same period of alleged civil disorder on the campus of Kent State University in Ohio during May 1970 which was before us, in another context, in *Gilligan v. Morgan*, 413 U.S. 1 (1973). . . . In these cases the personal representatives of the estates of three students who died in that episode seek damages against the Governor,

the Adjutant General, and his assistant, various named and unnamed officers and enlisted members of the Ohio National Guard, and the president of Kent State University. The complaints in both cases allege a cause of action under the Civil Rights Act of 1871, now 42 U.S.C. § 1983. Petitioner Scheuer also alleges a cause of action under Ohio law on the theory of pendent jurisdiction. Petitioners Krause and Miller make a similar claim, asserting jurisdiction on the basis of diversity of citizenship. . . .

The District Court dismissed the complaints for lack of jurisdiction over the subject matter on the theory that these actions, although in form against the named individuals, were, in substance and effect, against the State of Ohio and thus barred by the Eleventh Amendment. The Court of Appeals affirmed the action of the District Court, agreeing that the suit was in legal effect one against the State of Ohio and, alternatively, that the common-law doctrine of executive immunity barred action against the state officials who are respondents here. 471 F.2d 430 (1972). We are confronted with the narrow threshold question whether the District Court properly dismissed the complaints. We hold that dismissal was inappropriate at this stage of the litigation and accordingly reverse the judgments and remand for further proceedings. We intimate no view on the merits of the allegations since there is no evidence before us at this stage.

I

The complaints in these cases are not identical but their thrust is essentially the same. In essence, the defendants are alleged to have "intentionally, recklessly, willfully and wantonly" caused an unnecessary deployment of the Ohio National Guard on the Kent State campus and, in the same manner, ordered the Guard members to perform allegedly illegal actions which resulted in the death of plaintiffs' decedents. Both complaints allege that the action was taken "under color of state law" and that it deprived the decedents of their lives and rights without due process of law. Fairly read, the complaints allege that each of the named defendants, in undertaking such actions, acted either outside the scope of his respective office or, if within the scope, acted in an arbitrary manner, grossly abusing the lawful powers of office. The complaints were dismissed by the District Court for lack of jurisdiction without the filing of an answer to any of the complaints. The only pertinent documentation before the court in addition to the complaints [was] two proclamations issued by the respondent Governor. The first proclamation ordered the Guard to duty to protect against violence arising from wildcat strikes in the trucking industry; the other recited an account of the conditions prevailing at Kent State University at that time. In dismissing these complaints for want of subject matter jurisdiction at that early stage, the District Court held, as we noted earlier, that the defendants were being sued in their official and representative capacities and that the actions were therefore in effect against the State

of Ohio. The primary question presented is whether the District Court acted prematurely and hence erroneously in dismissing the complaints on the stated ground, thus precluding any opportunity for the plaintiffs by subsequent proof to establish a claim. . . .

Whatever the plaintiffs may or may not be able to establish as to the merits of their allegations, their claims, as stated in the complaints, given the favorable reading required by the Federal Rules of Civil Procedure, are not barred by the Eleventh Amendment. Consequently, the District Court erred in dismissing the complaints for lack of jurisdiction. . . .

III

The Court of Appeals relied upon the existence of an absolute "executive immunity" as an alternative ground for sustaining the dismissal of the complaints by the District Court. If the immunity of a member of the executive branch is absolute and comprehensive as to all acts allegedly performed within the scope of official duty, the Court of Appeals was correct; if, on the other hand, the immunity is not absolute but rather one that is qualified or limited, an executive officer may or may not be subject to liability depending on all the circumstances that may be revealed by evidence. The concept of the immunity of government officers from personal liability springs from the same root considerations that generated the doctrine of sovereign immunity. While the latter doctrine— that the "King can do no wrong"—did not protect all government officers from personal liability, the common law soon recognized the necessity of permitting officials to perform their official functions free from the threat of suits for personal liability. This official immunity apparently rested, in its genesis, on two mutually dependent rationales: (1) the injustice, particularly in the absence of bad faith, of subjecting to liability an officer who is required, by the legal obligations of his position, to exercise discretion; (2) the danger that the threat of such liability would deter his willingness to execute his office with the decisiveness and the judgment required by the public good. . . .

Under the criteria developed by precedents of this Court, § 1983 would be drained of meaning were we to hold that the acts of a governor or other high executive officer have "the quality of a supreme and unchangeable edict, overriding all conflicting rights of property and unreviewable through the judicial power of the federal government." *Sterling v. Constantin,* 287 U.S., at 397. In *Sterling,* Mr. Chief Justice Hughes put it in these terms: "If this extreme position could be deemed to be well taken, it is manifest that the fiat of a state Governor, and not the Constitution of the United States, would be the supreme law of the land; that the restrictions of the Federal Constitution upon the exercise of state power would be but impotent phrases, the futility of which the State may at any time disclose by the simple process of transferring powers of legislation to the Governor to be exercised by him, beyond control, upon his assertion of necessity. Under our system of government, such a conclusion is obviously untenable. There is no such avenue of escape from the paramount authority of the Federal Constitution. When there is a substantial showing that the exertion of state power has overridden private rights secured by that Constitution, the subject is necessarily one for judicial inquiry in an appropriate proceeding directed against the individuals charged with the transgression." . . .

V

The documents properly before the District Court at this early pleading stage specifically placed in issue whether the Governor and his subordinate officers were acting within the scope of their duties under the Constitution and laws of Ohio; whether they acted within the range of discretion permitted the holders of such office under Ohio law and whether they acted in good faith both in proclaiming an emergency and as to the actions taken to cope with the emergency so declared. Similarly, the complaints place directly in issue whether the lesser officers and enlisted personnel of the Guard acted in good-faith obedience to the orders of their superiors. Further proceedings, either by way of summary judgment or by trial on the merits, are required. The complaining parties are entitled to be heard more fully than is possible on a motion to dismiss a complaint.

We intimate no evaluation whatever as to the merits of the petitioners' claims or as to whether it will be possible to support them by proof. We hold only that, on the allegations of their respective complaints, they were entitled to have them judicially resolved.

The judgments of the Court of Appeals are reversed and the cases are remanded for further proceedings consistent with this opinion.

It is so ordered.

Wood v. Strickland
420 U.S. 308 (1975)

Justice White delivered the opinion of the Court, joined by Justices Brennan, Stewart, Marshall, and Stevens. Justice Powell filed an opinion concurring in part and dissenting in part, which was joined by Chief Justice Burger and Justices Blackmun and Rehnquist.

Respondents Peggy Strickland and Virginia Crain brought this lawsuit against petitioners, who were members of the school board at the

time in question, two school administrators, and the Special School District of Mena, Ark., purporting to assert a cause of action under 42 U.S.C. § 1983, and claiming that their federal constitutional rights to due process were infringed under color of state law by their expulsion from the Mena Public High School on the grounds of their violation of a school regulation prohibiting the use or possession of intoxicating beverages at school or school activities. The complaint as amended prayed for compensatory and punitive damages against all petitioners, injunctive relief allowing respondents to resume attendance, preventing petitioners from imposing any sanctions as a result of the expulsion, and restraining enforcement of the challenged regulations, declaratory relief as to the constitutional invalidity of the regulation, and expunction of any record of their expulsion. After the declaration of a mistrial arising from the jury's failure to reach a verdict, the District Court directed verdicts in favor of petitioners on the ground that petitioners were immune from damages suits absent proof of malice in the sense of ill will toward respondents. 348 F.Supp. 244 (WD Ark. 1972). The Court of Appeals, finding that the facts showed a violation of respondents' rights to "substantive due process," reversed and remanded for appropriate injunctive relief and a new trial on the question of damages. 485 F.2d 186 (CA8 1973). A petition for rehearing en banc was denied, with three judges dissenting. Certiorari was granted to consider whether this application of due process by the Court of Appeals was warranted and whether that court's expression of a standard governing immunity for school board members from liability for compensatory damages under 42 U.S.C. § 1983 was the correct one. . . .

I

The violation of the school regulation prohibiting the use or possession of intoxicating beverages at school or school activities with which respondents were charged concerned their "spiking" of the punch served at a meeting of an extracurricular school organization attended by parents and students. At the time in question, respondents were 16 years old and were in the 10th grade. The relevant facts begin with their discovery that the punch had not been prepared for the meeting as previously planned. The girls then agreed to "spike" it. Since the county in which the school is located is "dry," respondents and a third girl drove across the state border into Oklahoma and purchased two 12-ounce bottles of "Right Time," a malt liquor. They then bought six 10-ounce bottles of a soft drink, and, after having mixed the contents of

the eight bottles in an empty milk carton, returned to school. Prior to the meeting, the girls experienced second thoughts about the wisdom of their prank, but by then they were caught up in the force of events and the intervention of other girls prevented them from disposing of the illicit punch. The punch was served at the meeting, without apparent effect. . . .

Ten days later, the teacher in charge of the extracurricular group and meeting, Mrs. Curtis Powell, having heard something about the "spiking," questioned the girls about it. Although first denying any knowledge, the girls admitted their involvement after the teacher said that she would handle the punishment herself. The next day, however, she told the girls that the incident was becoming increasingly the subject of talk in the school and that the principal, P. T. Waller, would probably hear about it. She told them that her job was in jeopardy but that she would not force them to admit to Waller what they had done. If they did not go to him then, however, she would not be able to help them if the incident became "distorted." The three girls then went to Waller and admitted their role in the affair. He suspended them from school for a maximum two-week period, subject to the decision of the school board. Waller also told them that the board would meet that night, that the girls could tell their parents about the meeting, but that the parents should not contact any members of the board.

Neither the girls nor their parents attended the school board meeting that night. Both Mrs. Powell and Waller, after making their reports concerning the incident, recommended leniency. At this point, a telephone call was received by S. L. Inlow, then the superintendent of schools, from Mrs. Powell's husband, also a teacher at the high school, who reported that he had heard that the third girl involved had been in a fight that evening at a basketball game. Inlow informed the meeting of the news, although he did not mention the name of the girl involved. Mrs. Powell and Waller then withdrew their recommendations of leniency, and the board voted to expel the girls from school for the remainder of the semester, a period of approximately three months.

The board subsequently agreed to hold another meeting on the matter, and one was held approximately two weeks after the first meeting. The girls, their parents, and their counsel attended this session. The board began with a reading of a written statement of facts as it had found them. The girls admitted mixing the malt liquor into the punch with the intent of "spiking" it, but asked the board to forgo its rule punishing such violations by such substantial suspensions. Neither Mrs. Powell nor Waller was present at this meeting. The board voted not to change its policy and, as before, to expel the girls for the remainder of the semester. . . .

Petitioners as members of the school board assert here, as they did below, an absolute immunity from liability under § 1983 and at the very least seek to reinstate the judgment of the District Court. If they are correct and the District Court's dismissal should be sustained, we need go no further in this case. Moreover, the immunity question involves the construction of a federal statute, and our practice is to deal with possibly dispositive statutory issues before reaching questions turning on the construction of the Constitution. We essentially sustain the position of the Court of Appeals with respect to the immunity issue. . . .

The nature of the immunity from awards of damages under § 1983 available to school administrators and school board members is not a question which the lower federal courts have answered with a single voice. There is general agreement on the existence of a "good faith" immunity, but the courts have either emphasized different factors as elements of good faith or have not given specific content to the good-faith standard. . . .

Therefore, in the specific context of school discipline, we hold that a school board member is not immune from liability for damages under § 1983 if he knew or reasonably should have known that the action he took within his sphere of official responsibility would violate the constitutional rights of the student affected, or if he took the action with the malicious intention to cause a deprivation of constitutional rights or other injury to the student. That is not to say that school board members are "charged with predicting the future course of constitutional law." A compensatory award will be appropriate only if the school board member has acted with such an impermissible motivation or with such disregard of the student's clearly established constitutional rights that his action cannot reasonably be characterized as being in good faith. . . .

IV

Respondents' complaint alleged that their procedural due process rights were violated by the action taken by petitioners. The District Court did not discuss this claim in its final opinion, but the Court of Appeals viewed it as presenting a substantial question. It concluded that the girls were denied procedural due process at the first school board meeting, but also intimated that the second meeting may have cured the initial procedural deficiencies. Having found a substantive due process violation, however, the court did not reach a conclusion on this procedural issue.

Respondents have argued here that there was a procedural due process violation which also supports the result reached by the Court of Appeals. But because the District Court did not discuss it, and the Court of Appeals did not decide it, it would be preferable to have the Court of Appeals consider the issue in the first instance.

The judgment of the Court of Appeals is vacated and the case remanded for further proceedings consistent with this opinion.

So ordered.

Although they do not relate so much to administrative law, the student should be aware that there are many other forms of immunity from suit. Members of Congress and state legislators are immune from both suit and criminal prosecution under constitutional speech and debate clauses. City Council members and County Commissioners have an absolute immunity for their legislative decisions. Where a city administrator filed a 1983 suit against the mayor and the vice president of the city council for vindictively eliminating her agency (and hence her job), the Court said they were immune because it was legislative activity.[34] Prosecutors normally enjoy an absolute immunity from suit. However, a prosecutor swore as to the veracity of facts in an affidavit supporting an arrest warrant, but the facts turned out to be wrong. After the charges were dropped and he was released from jail, the individual who was arrested sued the prosecutor under § 1983. The Court said that the prosecutor was acting in the capacity of a witness rather than as an advocate for the jurisdiction so she was not immune from suit in this instance.[35] States can make charities immune from their torts, and the Supreme Court recently created a different kind of immunity for HMOs in certain kinds of suits.[36]

KINDS OF LAWSUITS PROMINENT IN LITIGATION WITH GOVERNMENT

We have covered many different kinds of lawsuits, and you need to keep them straight. They can be confusing. Remember from Chapter 4 that under the Administrative Procedure Act, it is theoretically possible to force an agency to act when it refuses to do so. However, the Supreme Court has never allowed that to happen. It is also possible under the Act to challenge actions taken by agencies, but to do so: (a) the challenged activity must be reviewable, (b) the court must have jurisdiction, (c) the case must be ripe and cannot be moot, (d) the plaintiff must have standing, (e) the plaintiff must have exhausted all avenues of appeal within the agency, and (f) there must not be a primary jurisdiction problem. If all of those conditions are met, one may sue a federal agency.

Federal Tort Claims Act

Under an FTCA suit, a plaintiff needs to show that there was a breach of a legal duty to exercise reasonable care (foreseeability), that the injury was caused by the breach of the duty to exercise reasonable care (proximate cause), and that the suit is not barred by the discretionary exception. The policy-making/policy implementation dichotomy appears not to exist since the 1991 *Gaubert* decision. Apparently, if government action involves an act of discretion in the furtherance of government policy, that agency action will be immune from lawsuit.[37] The individual employee is absolved of liability in an FTCA suit. You will want to check your own state's tort claims act for different exceptions. If your state does not have a tort claims act, it is one of those few states that have not waived sovereign immunity, and the state cannot be sued.

Constitutional Torts

This is a *Bivens* suit. The plaintiff sues an individual federal employee, alleging that the employee violated the plaintiff's constitutionally protected rights. Federal employees enjoy a qualified immunity. The qualified immunity is established where the defendant/employee acted in good faith. To establish a lack of good faith, a plaintiff can show that the employee either knew or should have known that his or her actions would violate the plaintiff's constitutionally protected rights. A plaintiff might also try to prove that the employee acted maliciously to deprive the plaintiff of a protected right. If this suit is successful, the individual employee must pay the damages, not the government or an agency.

Section 1983

Success in Section 1983 lawsuits depends on who or what is being sued. To sue an individual state or local government employee, a plaintiff must show that the employee showed the same lack of good faith discussed above under *Bivens.* It is the employee who will pay, not the government.

To sue a county, city, or other lower unit of government (the states are protected by sovereign immunity), the plaintiff either can sue the unit of government directly or can sue an individual employee on the theory of vicarious liability. There is no qualified immunity. Whether the employee acted in good faith does not matter. The plaintiff must show that the employee was a policymaker for the governmental unit and made the final policy that deprived the plaintiff of federally protected rights. For example, there is no question that the sheriff of Monroe County took actions that violated several of Walter McMillian's constitutionally protected rights. Nor is there a question that the sheriff is a law enforcement policymaker. The problem for McMillian's suit was that the sheriff was not a final policymaker. Only the attorney general of Alabama has the power to make final law enforcement policy. If a plaintiff is suing the governmental unit directly rather than an individual acting on its behalf, the plaintiff needs to show that the injury resulted from the final, official policy of the unit of government.

It is possible to sue a private individual acting on behalf of the state. We have previously discussed the popular trend toward privatization. Where a state privatized several of its prisons and guards violated a prisoner's rights, the prisoner filed a § 1983 suit. There is no question about state action; the "private" guards are state actors for § 1983 purposes. The question in *Richardson v. McKnight,* 521 U.S. 399 (1997), was whether the private guards should have the same qualified immunity that a state prison guard would have (whether they knew or should have known). The answer is no. Private employees when acting as state actors do not possess a qualified immunity. But compare the *Malesko* case at the end of this chapter, where the Court said that a *Bivens* suit was not available in a suit against a private corporation operating under a federal contract. That is, even though it is a "state actor," because it is an entity and not an individual, it cannot be sued under *Bivens.*

There is a criminal counterpart to § 1983. Whereas 42 U.S.C. 1983 provides for civil damages for a violation of an individual's federally protected rights, 42 U.S.C. 242 provides for criminal penalties for the same thing. A state judge was sentenced to 25 years in prison for sexually assaulting a woman in his chambers, when the woman had legal matters pending before his court. See *United States v. Lanier,* 520 U.S. 259 (1997).

Both *Bivens* and § 1983 lawsuits are unique because the individual is legally liable and financially responsible for a court judgment, not the related government. Almost more important than the salary an employee will receive are considerations about what benefits the employer offers. If you interview for employment with a government, you should inquire into employer-provided liability insurance to protect you against § 1983 judgments.

Additional Related Kinds of Lawsuits

Americans with Disabilities Act. The ADA applies to both private and government employers. However, the Eleventh Amendment may prevent suits against the states, but not lower units of government. It forbids discrimination against individuals with disabilities and requires employers to make "reasonable accommodations" for their disabled employees. In an interesting recent case, an employee suffered a stroke. After rehabilitation, she returned to work but got fired after three months. The company said she was slow, and her work was unsatisfactory. She applied for and obtained federal disability. To receive disability benefits, applicants must prove that they are unable to perform their previous work and that there is no job in the national economy they can do. Under the ADA, employers are required to make reasonable accommodations to allow the disabled employees to "perform the essential functions of their job." The plaintiff sued the employer for failing to make reasonable accommodations for her. The company's position was that if she has already demonstrated that she cannot perform her job (by qualifying for disability), *a fortiori* the company need not try to reasonably accommodate her.

The precise legal issue was whether a plaintiff on disability is estopped from pursuing an ADA suit. The Court said that disability plaintiffs are not automatically estopped from suing under the ADA. The presumptions of the statutes are contradictory, however, and the plaintiff would need to explain how she could be qualified for disability, on the one hand (she cannot work), and demand that an employer reasonably accommodate her so she can perform the essential functions of the job, on the other hand. See *Cleveland v. Policy Management Systems, Inc.,* 526 U.S. 795 (1999).

The 1964 Civil Rights Act. The Civil Rights Act does a host of things, but of most relevance here, it forbids discrimination in interstate commerce on the basis of race, color, religion, national origin, and in the case of employment, gender. It applies to all levels of government as well as private industry (provided a business *has* 15 or more employees. . .). Plaintiffs need to show specific discrimination toward them or prove that the discrimination has a disproportionate impact on a clearly identifiable protected group (race, color, religion, etc.). The Act allows benign discrimination and does not require a showing of purposeful discrimination (as the equal protection clause does for racial discrimination). The EEOC has been delegated enforcement authority. A plaintiff files a complaint with the EEOC, which investigates the complaint and holds a hearing. The EEOC can find the complaint is not legitimate, it can find discrimination under the Act and award remedies, or it can give permission to sue in federal court. There is no immunity from Civil Rights Act suits, qualified or otherwise. By a 1991 amendment, either the EEOC or the courts can award compensatory damages for intentional violations of the law (see *West v. Gibson* at the end of this chapter). The 1991 amendment also allows for the award of punitive damages where a plaintiff can show that the intentional discrimination was done with malice or "reckless indifference."[38]

Equal protection suits. These apply only to government or private parties when they are acting for the government (state action). The equal protection clause of the Fourteenth Amendment is not meant to prohibit government from treating groups or people differently. That is the essence of what governments do when adopting public policy: Some will benefit, and some will not. What the equal protection clause does is prohibit government from treating people differently without a reason for doing so. A three-tier level of analysis is applied to equal protection doctrine, with each tier requiring a more substantial reason for the challenged desperate treatment. The first tier is called simple rationality. It applies to government regulation of business and only requires that government have a believable reason for disparate treatment. The second tier is called heightened scrutiny and applies to any form of social or economic discrimination that is not a first or third tier.

Typically, in public administration, the middle tier cases will involve either gender or age discrimination. At this level, to be allowed to continue disparate treatment, government must (a) proffer an important governmental interest and (b) demonstrate that the disparate treatment will accomplish the important interest. The third tier is called the compelling interest test, and it applies where government has discriminated on the basis of race (called suspect classes) or on the basis of a fundamental right (to vote, to travel, or to retain family privacy). Here, for the government's disparate treatment to survive, the government must proffer a compelling reason to treat people differently, and they must implement the disparate treatment in a manner that is the least restrictive on the liberties of individuals. Governments almost never survive court application of the compelling interest test.

Race discrimination. Official governmental action that treats people differently based on racial considerations is almost nonexistent today. Only the University of Michigan's Law School was able to survive the compelling interest test, and then by a close 5 to 4 decision of the Supreme Court (see Chapter 8). More subtle forms of racial discrimination are gaining attention. The issue of resegregation of America's schools has gained a lot of attention with the 50th anniversary of the *Brown v. Bd. of Education* case.

Gender discrimination. A claim of gender discrimination could be litigated under the 1964 Civil Rights Act, primarily but not exclusively against a private employer or against the government under the equal protection clause. Official government policy that discriminates on the basis of sex is not as prevalent as it was a few decades ago. However, Congress has passed an immigration law that covers the citizenship of children born out of wedlock in a foreign country when one parent is a citizen and the other is not. The law provides that if the mother is a citizen, the child is a citizen at birth, but if the father is the citizen, then the father needs to go through certain steps before the child can be a citizen. Tuan Ahn Nguyen was born in Vietnam to an American father and a Vietnamese mother in 1969. Tuan moved to America at the age of six and lived with his father. He became a permanent resident of the United States, but the father never went through the hoops required by law to make Tuan a citizen (some of those hoops need to be accomplished before the child turns 18). In 1992, Tuan pleaded guilty to some criminal charges in Texas, and three years later, the Immigration and Naturalization Services instituted proceedings to deport him back to Vietnam. The question before the Supreme Court narrowed to whether Congress's disparate treatment of the sexes was constitutional (while the equal protection clause only applies to state governments, the courts apply middle-tier analysis under the Fifth Amendment's due process clause to federal gender discrimination). The Court decided, 5 to 4, that the government had important interests that justified the discrimination (assurances that both a biological and family relationship existed between the child and the father) and that the law would accomplish those objectives. Tuan was deported back to Vietnam.[39]

Age discrimination. People who believe they have been discriminated against because of their age have two legal options. If it is government that has discriminated, they can sue under the equal protection clause of the Fourteenth Amendment. Such a suit gets middle-tier analysis, and the court will ask whether there is an important governmental objective and whether the discrimination is rationally related to the achievement of that objective. If the answer to both questions is yes, then it is not unconstitutional for the government to discriminate on the basis of age.

Also, Congress passed the Age Discrimination in Employment Act (ADEA), not under its commerce power, but under its power to enforce the Fourteenth Amendment. The Act forbids discrimination in employment against anyone older than 40, and it provides for a private right of action. Several governmental employees sued their states, alleging that particular policies relating to evaluation for merit pay and salary scales created a disparate impact on older employees. The states moved to dismiss based on the Eleventh Amendment's sovereign immunity (see the discussion early in this chapter on the Eleventh Amendment). The Supreme Court unanimously found that congressional enforcement powers under the Fourteenth Amendment were powerful enough to abrogate the Eleventh Amendment's sovereign immunity (where the commerce clause was not). Next, splitting 5 to 4, the Court said that Congress lacked the power to stipulate that discrimination against individuals older than 40 was illegal. That is because the Supreme Court has established that the Constitution allows age discrimination so long as it is rational (see the two-pronged test described in the previous paragraph). If Congress wants to ban discrimination against people older than 40, it will have to pass a constitutional amendment to do so (or alternatively wait until sufficient personnel changes on the Court do away with the two-pronged test). See *Kimel v. Florida Board of Regents*, 528 U.S. 62 (2000).

SUMMARY

1. *Sovereign immunity.* Both state and federal governments in America are clothed with sovereign immunity. They can be sued only with their consent and only under the conditions they set:

   a. Section 702 of the Administrative Procedure Act sanctions suits in equity against the federal government.

   b. A tort claims act is the vehicle through which most state and federal governments agree to be held liable in money damages for their torts (mostly for the unintentional tort of negligence).

To pursue a successful negligence suit against the federal government, plaintiffs must show that (a) there was a failure to exercise reasonable care (foreseeability measured by the average reasonable person), (b) the failure to exercise reasonable care was the proximate cause of injuries, (c) a dollar amount can be attached to the injuries, and (d) the negligent action was not the result of the exercise of discretion in furtherance of public policy.

The tort claims act absolves the individual employee of legal liability (so long as the negligence occurred in the scope of employment) and spreads the cost to the taxpayers.

2. *Federal official or qualified immunity* is a term used to connote that individual employees of the federal government can be sued for their acts that violate the constitutional rights of another but that they have a qualified immunity in that sometimes they are immune from such suits: (a) when there is a lack of malice (i.e., they acted in good faith) and (b) when they did not know and could not have known that their actions would violate the constitutional rights of another (e.g., *Butz v. Economou*). This qualified immunity comes from the *Butz* case. This kind of lawsuit makes the individual employee liable for money damages; it is not the government or the agency that gets sued. Such lawsuits were not created by statute; they

were created by the Supreme Court in the *Bivens* case and are referred to as *Bivens* suits. In two situations, a plaintiff who otherwise could sue under *Bivens* cannot maintain a successful *Bivens* action:

a. Where the defendant demonstrates special factors counseling hesitation in the absence of affirmative action by Congress (see *Bush v. Lucas*[40]).

b. Where the defendant shows that Congress has provided an equally effective remedy at law (see *Carlson v. Green*[41]).

3. *Qualified immunity at the state and local level.* State employees are exposed to liability for violating another person's rights by § 1983 of the Civil Rights Act of 1871. Like federal employees, they have a qualified immunity: (a) when there is absence of malice and (b) when they did not know and could not have known that their actions would violate the constitutional rights of another.

4. *Immunity for city and county governments.* City and county governments can also be sued under § 1983 (*Owen v. City of Independence*). However, such suits can be successful only if the violation of citizens' rights was the result of a local policy. To hold a local unit of government liable under § 1983, plaintiffs need to show that their constitutional rights were violated and the violation resulted from a local government official policy or the actions of a local official who can be said to represent official policy (for example, the city administrator for the city of Independence, Missouri, but not the sheriff of Monroe County, Alabama). There is no qualified immunity for local governments under § 1983.

END-OF-CHAPTER CASES

Federal Maritime Commission v. South Carolina State Ports Authority
535 U.S. 743 (2002)

Justice Thomas delivered the opinion of the Court, joined by Justices Rehnquist, O'Connor, Scalia, and Kennedy. Justice Stevens filed a dissenting opinion. Justice Breyer filed a dissenting opinion, in which Justices Stevens, Souter, and Ginsburg joined.

This case presents the question whether state sovereign immunity precludes petitioner Federal Maritime Commission (FMC or Commission) from adjudicating a private party's complaint that a state-run port has violated the Shipping Act of 1984, 46 U.S.C. § 1701. We hold that state sovereign immunity bars such an adjudicative proceeding.

I

On five occasions, South Carolina Maritime Services, Inc. (Maritime Services), asked respondent South Carolina State Ports Authority (SCSPA) for permission to berth a cruise ship, the M/V Tropic Sea, at the SCSPA's port facilities in Charleston, South Carolina. Maritime Services intended to offer cruises on the M/V Tropic Sea originating from the Port of Charleston. Some of these cruises would stop in the Bahamas while others would merely travel in international waters before returning to Charleston with no intervening ports of call. On all of these trips, passengers would be permitted to participate in gambling activities while on board.

The SCSPA repeatedly denied Maritime Services' requests, contending that it had an established policy of denying berths in the Port of Charleston to vessels whose primary purpose was gambling. As a result, Maritime Services filed a complaint with the FMC, contending that the SCSPA's refusal to provide berthing space to the M/V Tropic Sea violated the Shipping Act. Maritime Services alleged in its complaint that the SCSPA had implemented its antigambling policy in a discriminatory fashion by providing berthing space in Charleston to two Carnival Cruise Lines vessels even though Carnival offered gambling activities on these ships. Maritime Services therefore complained that the SCSPA had unduly and unreasonably preferred Carnival over Maritime Services . . . and unreasonably refused to deal or negotiate with Maritime Services in violation of [the Shipping Act]. It further alleged that the SCSPA's unlawful actions had inflicted upon Maritime Services a "loss of profits, loss of earnings, loss of sales, and loss of business opportunities."

To remedy its injuries, Maritime Services prayed that the FMC: (1) seek a temporary restraining order and preliminary injunction in the United States District Court for the District of South Carolina "enjoining [the SCSPA] from utilizing its discriminatory practice to refuse to provide berthing space and passenger services to Maritime Services;" (2) direct the SCSPA to pay reparations to Maritime Services as well as interest and reasonable attorneys' fees; (3) issue an order commanding, among other things, the SCSPA to cease and desist from violating the Shipping Act; and (4) award Maritime Services "such other and further relief as is just and proper."

Consistent with the FMC's Rules of Practice and Procedure, Maritime Services' complaint was referred to an administrative law judge (ALJ). The SCSPA then filed . . . a motion to dismiss, asserting . . . that the SCSPA, as an arm of the State of South Carolina, was "entitled to Eleventh Amendment immunity" from Maritime Services' suit. . . .

The ALJ agreed, concluding that recent decisions of this Court "interpreting the 11th Amendment and State sovereign immunity

from private suits . . . required that [Maritime Services'] complaint be dismissed." . . . The ALJ noted, however, that his decision did not deprive the FMC of its "authority to look into [Maritime Services'] allegations of Shipping Act violations and enforce the Shipping Act." For example, the FMC could institute its own formal investigatory proceeding or refer Maritime Services' allegations to its Bureau of Enforcement.

While Maritime Services did not appeal the ALJ's dismissal of its complaint, the FMC on its own motion decided to review the ALJ's ruling to consider whether state sovereign immunity from private suits extends to proceedings before the Commission. It concluded that "the doctrine of state sovereign immunity . . . is meant to cover proceedings before judicial tribunals, whether Federal or state, not executive branch administrative agencies like the Commission." As a result, the FMC held that sovereign immunity did not bar the Commission from adjudicating private complaints against state-run ports and reversed the ALJ's decision dismissing Maritime Services' complaint.

The SCSPA filed a petition for review, and the United States Court of Appeals for the Fourth Circuit reversed. Observing that "any proceeding where a federal officer adjudicates disputes between private parties and unconsenting states would not have passed muster at the time of the Constitution's passage nor after the ratification of the Eleventh Amendment," the Court of Appeals reasoned that "such an adjudication is equally as invalid today, whether the forum be a state court, a federal court, or a federal administrative agency." Reviewing the "precise nature" of the procedures employed by the FMC for resolving private complaints, the Court of Appeals concluded that the proceeding "walks, talks, and squawks very much like a lawsuit" and that "its placement within the Executive Branch cannot blind us to the fact that the proceeding is truly an adjudication." The Court of Appeals therefore held that because the SCSPA is an arm of the State of South Carolina, sovereign immunity precluded the FMC from adjudicating Maritime Services' complaint, and remanded the case with instructions that it be dismissed. 234 F.3rd 165 179 (CA4 2001).

We granted the FMC's petition for certiorari, 534 U.S. 971 (2001), and now affirm.

II

Dual sovereignty is a defining feature of our Nation's constitutional blueprint. States, upon ratification of the Constitution, did not consent to become mere appendages of the Federal Government. Rather, they entered the Union "with their sovereignty intact." *Blatchford v. Native Village of Noatak,* 501 U.S. 775, 779 (1991). An integral component of that "residuary and inviolable sovereignty," retained by the States is their immunity from private suits. . . .

States, in ratifying the Constitution, did surrender a portion of their inherent immunity by consenting to suits brought by sister States or by the Federal Government. See *Alden v. Maine,* 527 U.S. 706, 755 (1999). Nevertheless, the Convention did not disturb States' immunity from private suits, thus firmly enshrining this principle in our constitutional framework. "The leading advocates of the Constitution assured the people in no uncertain terms that the Constitution would not strip the States of sovereign immunity."

The States' sovereign immunity, however, fell into peril in the early days of our Nation's history when this Court held in *Chisholm v. Georgia,* 2 U.S. 419 (1793), that Article III authorized citizens of one State to sue another State in federal court. In order to overturn *Chisholm,* Congress quickly passed the Eleventh Amendment and the States ratified it speedily. The Amendment clarified that "the judicial Power of the United States shall not be construed to extend to any suit in law or equity, commenced or prosecuted against one of the United States by Citizens of another State, or by Citizens or Subjects of any Foreign State."

Instead of explicitly memorializing the full breadth of the sovereign immunity retained by the States when the Constitution was ratified, Congress chose in the text of the Eleventh Amendment only to "address the specific provisions of the Constitution that had raised concerns during the ratification debates and formed the basis of the *Chisholm* decision." As a result, the Eleventh Amendment does not define the scope of the States' sovereign immunity; it is but one particular exemplification of that immunity. *Cf. Blatchford,* supra, at 779 ("We have understood the Eleventh Amendment to stand not so much for what it says, but for the presupposition of our constitutional structure which it confirms").

III

We now consider whether the sovereign immunity enjoyed by States as part of our constitutional framework applies to adjudications conducted by the FMC. Petitioner FMC and respondent United States initially maintain that the Court of Appeals erred because sovereign immunity only shields States from exercises of "judicial power" and FMC adjudications are not judicial proceedings. As support for their position, they point to the text of the Eleventh Amendment and contend that "the Amendment's reference to 'judicial Power' and 'to any suit in law or equity' clearly mark it as an immunity from judicial process."

For purposes of this case, we will assume, arguendo, that in adjudicating complaints filed by private parties under the Shipping Act, the FMC does not exercise the judicial power of the United States. Such an assumption, however, does not end our inquiry as this Court has repeatedly held that the sovereign immunity enjoyed by the States extends beyond the literal text of the Eleventh Amendment. See, e.g., *Alden,* supra (holding that sovereign immunity shields States from private suits in state courts pursuant to federal causes of action); *Blatchford,* supra (applying state sovereign immunity to suits by Indian tribes); *Principality of Monaco v. Mississippi,* 292 U.S. 313 (1934) (applying state sovereign immunity to suits by foreign nations); *Ex parte New York,* 256 U.S. 490 (1921) (applying state sovereign immunity to admiralty proceedings); *Smith v. Reeves,* 178 U.S. 436 (1900) (applying state sovereign immunity to suits by federal corporations); *Hans v. Louisiana,* 134 U.S. 1 (1890) (applying state sovereign immunity to suits by a State's own citizens under federal-question jurisdiction). Adhering to that well-reasoned precedent, we must determine whether the sovereign immunity embedded in our constitutional structure and retained by the States when they joined the Union extends to FMC adjudicative proceedings.

A

"Look[ing] first to evidence of the original understanding of the Constitution," as well as early congressional practice, we find a relatively barren historical record, from which the parties draw radically different conclusions. . . .

Because formalized administrative adjudications were all but unheard of in the late 18th century and early 19th century, the dearth of specific evidence indicating whether the Framers believed that the States' sovereign immunity would apply in such proceedings is unsurprising.

This Court, however, has applied a presumption—first explicitly stated in *Hans v. Louisiana,* supra—that the Constitution was not intended to "raise up" any proceedings against the States that were "anomalous and unheard of when the Constitution was adopted." We therefore attribute great significance to the fact that States were not subject to private suits in administrative adjudications at the time of the founding or for many years thereafter. For instance, while the United States asserts that "state entities have long been subject to similar administrative enforcement proceedings," the earliest example it provides did not occur until 1918 (citing *California Canneries Co. v. Southern Pacific Co.,* 51 I.C.C. 500 (1918)).

B

To decide whether the *Hans* presumption applies here, however, we must examine FMC adjudications to determine whether they are the type of proceedings from which the Framers would have thought the States possessed immunity when they agreed to enter the Union.

In another case asking whether an immunity present in the judicial context also applied to administrative adjudications, this Court considered whether administrative law judges share the same absolute immunity from suit as do Article III judges. See *Butz v. Economou,* 438 U.S. 478 (1978). . . .

Beyond the similarities between the role of an ALJ and that of a trial judge, this Court also noted the numerous common features shared by administrative adjudications and judicial proceedings: . . .

This Court therefore concluded in Butz that administrative law judges were "entitled to absolute immunity from damages liability for their judicial acts."

Turning to FMC adjudications specifically, neither the Commission nor the United States disputes the Court of Appeals' characterization below that such a proceeding "walks, talks, and squawks very much like a lawsuit." Nor do they deny that the similarities identified in *Butz* between administrative adjudications and trial court proceedings are present here.

A review of the FMC's Rules of Practice and Procedure confirms that FMC administrative proceedings bear a remarkably strong resemblance to civil litigation in federal courts. . . .

Given both this interest in protecting States' dignity and the strong similarities between FMC proceedings and civil litigation, we hold that state sovereign immunity bars the FMC from adjudicating complaints filed by a private party against a nonconsenting State. Simply put, if the Framers thought it an impermissible affront to a State's dignity to be required to answer the complaints of private parties in federal courts, we cannot imagine that they would have found it acceptable to compel a State to do exactly the same thing before the administrative tribunal of an agency, such as the FMC. . . . The affront to a State's dignity does not lessen when an adjudication takes place in an administrative tribunal as opposed to an Article III court. In both instances, a State is required to defend itself in an adversarial proceeding against a private party before an impartial federal officer. Moreover, it would be quite strange to prohibit Congress from exercising its Article I powers to abrogate state sovereign immunity in Article III judicial proceedings, but permit the use of those same Article I powers to create court-like administrative tribunals where sovereign immunity does not apply.

D

... The United States suggests two reasons why we should distinguish FMC administrative adjudications from judicial proceedings for purposes of state sovereign immunity. Both of these arguments are unavailing.

1

The United States first contends that sovereign immunity should not apply to FMC adjudications because the Commission's orders are not self-executing. Whereas a court may enforce a judgment through the exercise of its contempt power, the FMC cannot enforce its own orders. Rather, the Commission's orders can only be enforced by a federal district court.

The United States presents a valid distinction between the authority possessed by the FMC and that of a court. For purposes of this case, however, it is a distinction without a meaningful difference. To the extent that the United States highlights this fact in order to suggest that a party alleged to have violated the Shipping Act is not coerced to participate in FMC proceedings, it is mistaken. The relevant statutory scheme makes it quite clear that, absent sovereign immunity, States would effectively be required to defend themselves against private parties in front of the FMC. ...

2

The United States next suggests that sovereign immunity should not apply to FMC proceedings because they do not present the same threat to the financial integrity of States as do private judicial suits. The Government highlights the fact that, in contrast to a nonreparation order, for which the Attorney General may seek enforcement at the request of the Commission, a reparation order may be enforced in a United States district court only in an action brought by the private party to whom the award was made. The United States then points out that a State's sovereign immunity would extend to such a suit brought by a private party.

This argument, however, reflects a fundamental misunderstanding of the purposes of sovereign immunity. While state sovereign immunity serves the important function of shielding state treasuries and thus preserving "the States' ability to govern in accordance with the will of their citizens," the doctrine's central purpose is to "accord the States the respect owed them as" joint sovereigns. It is for this reason, for instance, that sovereign immunity applies regardless of whether a private plaintiff's suit is for monetary damages or some other type of relief. ...

IV

Two final arguments raised by the FMC and the United States remain to be addressed. Each is answered in part by reference to our decision in Seminole Tribe.

A

The FMC maintains that sovereign immunity should not bar the Commission from adjudicating Maritime Services' complaint because "the constitutional necessity of uniformity in the regulation of maritime commerce limits the States' sovereignty with respect to the Federal Government's authority to regulate that commerce." This Court, however, has already held that the States' sovereign immunity extends to cases concerning maritime commerce. See, e.g., Ex parte New York, 256 U.S. 490 (1921). Moreover, Seminole Tribe precludes us from creating a new "maritime commerce" exception to state sovereign immunity. ...

B

Finally, the United States maintains that even if sovereign immunity were to bar the FMC from adjudicating a private party's complaint against a state-run port for purposes of issuing a reparation order, the FMC should not be precluded from considering a private party's request for other forms of relief, such as a cease-and-desist order. As we have previously noted, however, the primary function of sovereign immunity is not to protect State treasuries, but to afford the States the dignity and respect due sovereign entities. As a result, we explained in Seminole Tribe that "the relief sought by a plaintiff suing a State is irrelevant to the question whether the suit is barred by the Eleventh Amendment." We see no reason why a different principle should apply in the realm of administrative adjudications.

While some might complain that our system of dual sovereignty is not a model of administrative convenience, that is not its purpose. Rather, "the 'constitutionally mandated balance of power' between the States and the Federal Government was adopted by the Framers to ensure the protection of 'our fundamental liberties.'" . . . By guarding against encroachments by the Federal Government on fundamental aspects of state sovereignty, such as sovereign immunity, we strive to maintain the balance of power embodied in our Constitution and thus to "reduce the risk of tyranny and abuse from either front." *Gregory v. Ashcroft,* 501 U.S., at 458. Although the Framers likely did not envision the intrusion on state sovereignty at issue in today's case, we are nonetheless confident that it is contrary to their constitutional design, and therefore affirm the judgment of the Court of Appeals.

It is so ordered.

Justice Breyer, with whom Justice Stevens, Justice Souter, and Justice Ginsburg join, dissenting.

The Court holds that a private person cannot bring a complaint against a State to a federal administrative agency where the agency (1) will use an internal adjudicative process to decide if the complaint is well founded, and (2) if so, proceed to court to enforce the law. Where does the Constitution contain the principle of law that the Court enunciates? I cannot find the answer to this question in any text, in any tradition, or in any relevant purpose. In saying this, I do not simply reiterate the dissenting views set forth in many of the Court's recent sovereign immunity decisions. . . . For even were I to believe that those decisions properly stated the law—which I do not—I still could not accept the Court's conclusion here.

I

At the outset one must understand the constitutional nature of the legal proceeding before us.

The legal body conducting the proceeding, the Federal Maritime Commission, is an "independent" federal agency. Constitutionally speaking, an "independent" agency belongs neither to the Legislative Branch nor to the Judicial Branch of Government. Although Members of this Court have referred to agencies as a "fourth branch" of Government, the agencies, even "independent" agencies, are more appropriately considered to be part of the Executive Branch. . . .

The Court long ago laid to rest any constitutional doubts about whether the Constitution permitted Congress to delegate rulemaking and adjudicative powers to agencies. . . . That, in part, is because the Court established certain safeguards surrounding the exercise of these powers. And the Court denied that those activities as safeguarded, however much they might resemble the activities of a legislature or court, fell within the scope of Article I or Article III of the Constitution. . . . Consequently, in exercising those powers, the agency is engaging in an Article II, Executive Branch activity. And the powers it is exercising are powers that the Executive Branch of Government must possess if it is to enforce modern law through administration.

This constitutional understanding explains why both commentators and courts have often attached the prefix "quasi" to descriptions of an agency's rulemaking or adjudicative functions. . . . The terms "quasi legislative" and "quasi adjudicative" indicate that the agency uses legislative like or court like procedures but that it is not, constitutionally speaking, either a legislature or a court. See *Whitman v. American Trucking Assns., Inc.,* 531 U.S. 457, 472–473 (2001).

The case before us presents a fairly typical example of a federal administrative agency's use of agency adjudication. Congress has enacted a statute, the Shipping Act of 1984 (Act or Shipping Act), 46 U.S.C. § 1701 (1994), which, among other things, forbids marine terminal operators to discriminate against terminal users. The Act grants the Federal Maritime Commission the authority to administer the Act. The law grants the Commission the authority to enforce the Act in a variety of ways, for example, by making rules and regulations, by issuing or revoking licenses, and by conducting investigations and issuing reports. It also permits a private person to file a complaint, which the Commission is to consider. Interestingly enough, it does not say that the Commission must determine the merits of the complaint through agency adjudication,—though, for present purposes, I do not see that this statutory lacuna matters. . . .

The Court's decision threatens to deny the Executive and Legislative Branches of Government the structural flexibility that the Constitution permits and which modern government demands. The Court derives from the abstract notion of state "dignity" a structural principle that limits the powers of both Congress and the President. Its reasoning rests almost exclusively upon the use of a formal analogy, which, as I have said, jumps ordinary separation-of-powers bounds. It places "great significance" upon the 18th century absence of 20th century administrative proceedings. And its conclusion draws little support from considerations of constitutional purpose or related consequence. In its readiness to rest a structural limitation on so little evidence and in its willingness to interpret that limitation so broadly, the majority ignores a historical lesson, reflected in a constitutional understanding that the Court adopted long ago: An overly restrictive judicial interpretation of the Constitution's structural constraints (unlike its protections of certain basic liberties) will undermine the Constitution's own efforts to achieve its far more basic structural aim, the creation of a representative form of government capable of translating the people's will into effective public action.

This understanding, underlying constitutional interpretation since the New Deal, reflects the Constitution's demands for structural flexibility sufficient to adapt substantive laws and institutions to rapidly changing social, economic, and technological conditions. It reflects the comparative inability of the Judiciary to understand either those conditions or the need for new laws and new administrative forms they may create. It reflects the Framers' own aspiration to write a document that would "constitute" a democratic, liberty-protecting form of government that would endure through centuries of change. This understanding led the New Deal Court to reject overly restrictive formalistic interpretations of the Constitution's structural provisions, thereby permitting Congress to enact social and economic legislation that circumstances had led the public to demand. And it led that Court to find in the Constitution authorization for new forms of administration, including independent administrative agencies, with the legal authority flexibly to implement, i.e., to "execute," through adjudication, through rule-making, and in other ways, the legislation that Congress subsequently enacted.

Where I believe the Court has departed from this basic understanding I have consistently dissented. . . . These decisions set loose an interpretive principle that restricts far too severely the authority of the Federal Government to regulate innumerable relationships between State and citizen. Just as this principle has no logical starting place, I fear that neither does it have any logical stopping point.

Today's decision reaffirms the need for continued dissent—unless the consequences of the Court's approach prove anodyne, as I hope, rather than randomly destructive, as I fear.

Correctional Services Corporation v. John E. Malesko
534 U.S. 61 (2001)

Chief Justice Rehnquist delivered the opinion of the Court joined by Justices O'Connor, Scalia, Kennedy, and Thomas. Justice Scalia filed a concurring opinion, in which Justice Thomas joined. Justice Stevens filed a dissenting opinion, in which Justices Souter, Ginsburg, and Breyer joined.

We decide here whether the implied damages action first recognized in *Bivens v. Six Unknown Fed. Narcotics Agents,* 403 U.S. 388 (1971), should be extended to allow recovery against a private corporation operating a halfway house under contract with the Bureau of Prisons. We decline to so extend *Bivens*.

Petitioner Correctional Services Corporation (CSC), under contract with the federal Bureau of Prisons (BOP), operates Community Corrections Centers and other facilities that house federal prisoners and detainees. Since the late 1980's, CSC has operated Le Marquis Community Correctional Center (Le Marquis), a halfway house located in New York City. Respondent John E. Malesko is a former federal inmate who, having been convicted of federal securities fraud in December 1992, was sentenced to a term of 18 months' imprisonment under the supervision of the BOP. During his imprisonment, respondent was diagnosed with a heart condition and treated with prescription medication. Respondent's condition limited his ability to engage in physical activity, such as climbing stairs.

In February 1993, the BOP transferred respondent to Le Marquis where he was to serve the remainder of his sentence. Respondent was assigned to living quarters on the fifth floor. On or about March 1, 1994, petitioner instituted a policy at Le Marquis requiring inmates residing below the sixth floor to use the staircase rather than the elevator to travel from the first-floor lobby to their rooms. There is no dispute that respondent was exempted from this policy on account of his heart condition. Respondent alleges that on March 28, 1994, however, Jorge Urena, an employee of petitioner, forbade him to use the elevator to reach his fifth-floor bedroom. Respondent protested that he was specially permitted elevator access, but Urena was adamant. Respondent then climbed the stairs, suffered a heart attack, and fell, injuring his left ear.

Three years after this incident occurred, respondent filed a pro se action against CSC and unnamed CSC employees in the United States District Court for the Southern District of New York. Two years later, now acting with counsel, respondent filed an amended complaint which named Urena as 1 of the 10 John Doe defendants. The amended complaint alleged that CSC, Urena, and unnamed defendants were "negligent in failing to obtain requisite medication for [respondent's] condition and were further negligent by refusing [respondent] the use of the elevator." It further alleged that respondent injured his left ear and aggravated a pre-existing condition "as a result of the negligence of the Defendants." Respondent demanded judgment in the sum of $1 million in compensatory damages, $3 million in anticipated future damages, and punitive damages "for such sum as the Court and/or jury may determine."

The District Court treated the amended complaint as raising claims under *Bivens v. Six Unknown Fed. Narcotics Agents,* supra, and dismissed respondent's cause of action in its entirety. Relying on our decision in *FDIC v. Meyer,* 510 U.S. 471, (1994), the District Court reasoned that "a *Bivens* action may only be maintained against an individual," and thus was not available against petitioner, a corporate entity. With respect to Urena and the unnamed individual defendants, the complaint was dismissed on statute of limitations grounds.

The Court of Appeals for the Second Circuit affirmed in part, reversed in part, and remanded. 229 F.3d 374 (2000). That court affirmed dismissal of respondent's claims against individual defendants as barred by the statute of limitations. . . . and the parties agree that the question whether a Bivens action might lie against a private individual is not presented here. . . . But the court reasoned that private entities like petitioner should be held liable under Bivens to "accomplish the . . . important Bivens goal of providing a remedy for constitutional violations."

We granted certiorari and now reverse.

In *Bivens v. Six Unknown Fed. Narcotics Agents,* we recognized for the first time an implied private action for damages against federal officers alleged to have violated a citizen's constitutional rights. Respondent now asks that we extend this limited holding to confer a right of action for damages against private entities acting under color of federal law. He contends that the Court must recognize a federal remedy at law wherever there has been an alleged constitutional deprivation, no matter that the victim of the alleged deprivation might have alternative remedies elsewhere, and that the proposed remedy would not significantly deter the principal wrongdoer, an individual private employee. We have heretofore refused to imply new substantive liabilities under such circumstances, and we decline to do so here.

Our authority to imply a new constitutional tort, not expressly authorized by statute, is anchored in our general jurisdiction to decide all cases "arising under the Constitution, laws, or treaties of the United States." We first exercised this authority in *Bivens,* where we held that a victim of a Fourth Amendment violation by federal officers may bring suit for money damages against the officers in federal court. *Bivens* acknowledged that Congress had never provided for a private right of action against federal officers, and that "the Fourth Amendment does not in so many words provide for its enforcement by award of money damages for the consequences of its violation." Nonetheless, relying largely on earlier decisions implying private damages actions into federal statutes, . . . and finding "no special factors counseling hesitation in the absence of affirmative action by Congress," we found an implied damages remedy available under the Fourth Amendment.

In the decade following *Bivens,* we recognized an implied damages remedy under the Due Process Clause of the Fifth Amendment, *Davis v. Passman,* 442 U.S. 228 (1979), and the Cruel and Unusual Punishment Clause of the Eighth Amendment, *Carlson v. Green,* 446 U.S. 14 (1980). In both *Davis* and *Carlson,* we applied the core holding of *Bivens,* recognizing in limited circumstances a claim for money damages against federal officers who abuse their constitutional authority. In *Davis,* we inferred a new right of action chiefly because the plaintiff lacked any other remedy for the alleged constitutional deprivation. In *Carlson,* we inferred a right of action against individual prison officials where the plaintiff's only alternative was a Federal Tort Claims Act (FTCA) claim against the United States. We reasoned that the threat of suit against the United States was insufficient to deter the unconstitutional

acts of individuals. ("Because the *Bivens* remedy is recoverable against individuals, it is a more effective deterrent than the FTCA remedy"). We also found it "crystal clear" that Congress intended the FTCA and *Bivens* to serve as "parallel" and "complementary" sources of liability.

Since *Carlson* we have consistently refused to extend *Bivens* liability to any new context or new category of defendants. In *Bush v. Lucas,* supra, we declined to create a *Bivens* remedy against individual Government officials for a First Amendment violation arising in the context of federal employment. Although the plaintiff had no opportunity to fully remedy the constitutional violation, we held that administrative review mechanisms crafted by Congress provided meaningful redress and thereby foreclosed the need to fashion a new, judicially crafted cause of action. We further recognized Congress' institutional competence in crafting appropriate relief for aggrieved federal employees as a "special factor counseling hesitation in the creation of a new remedy." . . . We have reached a similar result in the military context, *Chappell v. Wallace,* 462 U.S. 296 (1983), even where the defendants were alleged to have been civilian personnel, *United States v. Stanley,* 483 U.S. 669 (1987). . . .

From this discussion, it is clear that the claim urged by respondent is fundamentally different from anything recognized in *Bivens* or subsequent cases. In 30 years of *Bivens* jurisprudence we have extended its holding only twice, to provide an otherwise nonexistent cause of action against individual officers alleged to have acted unconstitutionally, or to provide a cause of action for a plaintiff who lacked any alternative remedy for harms caused by an individual officer's unconstitutional conduct. Where such circumstances are not present, we have consistently rejected invitations to extend *Bivens,* often for reasons that foreclose its extension here.

The purpose of *Bivens* is to deter individual federal officers from committing constitutional violations. *Meyer* made clear that the threat of litigation and liability will adequately deter federal officers for *Bivens* purposes no matter that they may enjoy qualified immunity, are indemnified by the employing agency or entity, or are acting pursuant to an entity's policy. *Meyer* also made clear that the threat of suit against an individual's employer was not the kind of deterrence contemplated by *Bivens*. This case is, in every meaningful sense, the same. For if a corporate defendant is available for suit, claimants will focus their collection efforts on it, and not the individual directly responsible for the alleged injury. . . . On the logic of *Meyer*, inferring a constitutional tort remedy against a private entity like CSC is therefore foreclosed. . . .

. . . [R]espondent's situation [is] altogether different from *Bivens,* in which we found alternative state tort remedies to be "inconsistent or even hostile" to a remedy inferred from the Fourth Amendment. When a federal officer appears at the door and requests entry, one cannot always be expected to resist. ("[A] claim of authority to enter is likely to unlock the door"). Yet lack of resistance alone might foreclose a cause of action in trespass or privacy. Therefore, we reasoned in *Bivens* that other than an implied constitutional tort remedy, "there remained . . . but the alternative of resistance, which may amount to a crime." Such logic does not apply to respondent, whose claim of negligence or deliberate indifference requires no resistance to official action, and whose lack of alternative tort remedies was due solely to strategic choice.

Inmates in respondent's position also have full access to remedial mechanisms established by the BOP, including suits in federal court for injunctive relief and grievances filed through the BOP's Administrative Remedy Program (ARP). This program provides yet another means through which allegedly unconstitutional actions and policies can be brought to the attention of the BOP and prevented from recurring. And unlike the *Bivens* remedy, which we have never considered a proper vehicle for altering an entity's policy, injunctive relief has long been recognized as the proper means for preventing entities from acting unconstitutionally.

In sum, respondent is not a plaintiff in search of a remedy as in *Bivens* and *Davis*. Nor does he seek a cause of action against an individual officer, otherwise lacking, as in *Carlson*.

Respondent instead seeks a marked extension of *Bivens*, to contexts that would not advance *Bivens'* core purpose of deterring individual officers from engaging in unconstitutional wrongdoing. The caution toward extending *Bivens* remedies into any new context, a caution consistently and repeatedly recognized for three decades, forecloses such an extension here.

The judgment of the Court of Appeals is reversed.

It is so ordered.

Justice Stevens, with whom Justice Souter, Justice Ginsburg, and Justice Breyer join, dissenting.

In *Bivens v. Six Unknown Fed. Narcotics Agents,* the Court affirmatively answered the question that it had reserved in *Bell v. Hood,* 327 U.S. 678 (1946): whether a violation of the Fourth Amendment "by a federal agent acting under color of his authority gives rise to a cause of action for damages consequent upon his unconstitutional conduct." Nearly a decade later, in *Carlson v. Green,* we held that a violation of the Eighth Amendment by federal prison officials gave rise to a *Bivens* remedy despite the fact that the plaintiffs also had a remedy against the United States under the Federal Tort Claims Act (FTCA). We stated: "*Bivens* established that the victims of a constitutional violation by a federal agent have a right to recover damages against the official in federal court despite the absence of any statute conferring such a right."

In subsequent cases, we have decided that a *Bivens* remedy is not available for every conceivable constitutional violation. We have never, however, qualified our holding that Eighth Amendment violations are actionable under *Bivens*. Nor have we ever suggested that a category of federal agents can commit Eighth Amendment violations with impunity.

The parties before us have assumed that respondent's complaint has alleged a violation of the Eighth Amendment. The violation was committed by a federal agent—a private corporation employed by the Bureau of Prisons to perform functions that would otherwise be performed by individual employees of the Federal Government. Thus, the question presented by this case is whether the Court should create an exception to the straightforward application of *Bivens* and *Carlson*, not whether it should extend our cases beyond their "core premise," This point is evident from the fact that prior to our recent decision in *FDIC v. Meyer*, the Courts of Appeals had consistently and correctly held that corporate agents performing federal functions, like human agents doing so, were proper defendants in *Bivens* actions.

Meyer, which concluded that federal agencies are not suable under *Bivens*, does not lead to the outcome reached by the Court today. In that case, we did not discuss private corporate agents, nor suggest that such agents should be viewed differently from human ones. Rather, in *Meyer*, we drew a distinction between "federal agents" and "an agency of the Federal Government." Indeed, our repeated references to the Federal Deposit Insurance Corporation's (FDIC) status as a "federal agency" emphasized the FDIC's affinity to the federal sovereign. We expressed concern that damages sought directly from federal agencies, such as the FDIC, would "create a potentially enormous financial burden for the Federal Government." And it must be kept in mind that *Meyer* involved the FDIC's waiver of sovereign immunity, which, had the Court in *Meyer* recognized a cause of action, would have permitted the very sort of lawsuit that *Bivens* presumed impossible: "a direct action against the Government." . . .

Because *Meyer* does not dispose of this case, the Court claims that the rationales underlying *Bivens*—namely, lack of alternative remedies and deterrence—are not present in cases in which suit is brought against a private corporation serving as a federal agent. However, common sense, buttressed by all of the reasons that supported the holding in *Bivens*, leads to the conclusion that corporate agents should not be treated more favorably than human agents. . . .

It is apparent from the Court's critical discussion of the thoughtful opinions of Justice Harlan and his contemporaries, and from its erroneous statement of the question presented by this case as whether *Bivens* "should be extended" to allow recovery against a private corporation employed as a federal agent, that the driving force behind the Court's decision is a disagreement with the holding in *Bivens* itself. There are at least two reasons why it is improper for the Court to allow its decision in this case to be influenced by that predisposition. First, as is clear from the legislative materials cited in *Carlson*, Congress has effectively ratified the *Bivens* remedy; surely Congress has never sought to abolish it. Second, a rule that has been such a well-recognized part of our law for over 30 years should be accorded full respect by the Members of this Court, whether or not they would have endorsed that rule when it was first announced. For our primary duty is to apply and enforce settled law, not to revise that law to accord with our own notions of sound policy.

I respectfully dissent.

Pembaur v. Cincinnati
475 U.S. 469 (1986)

Justice Brennan delivered the opinion of the Court with respect to Parts I, II-A, and II-C, in which Justices White, Marshall, Blackmun, Stevens, and O'Connor (except for Part II-C) joined, and an opinion with respect to Part II-B, in which Justices White, Marshall, and Blackmun joined. Justice White filed a concurring opinion, and Justices Stevens and

O'Connor filed opinions concurring in part and concurring in the judgment. Justice Powell filed a dissenting opinion, in which Chief Justice Burger and Justice Rehnquist joined.

In *Monell v. New York City Dept. of Social Services*, 436 U.S. 658 (1978), the Court concluded that municipal liability under 42 U.S.C.

§ 1983 is limited to deprivations of federally protected rights caused by action taken "pursuant to official municipal policy of some nature. . . ." The question presented is whether, and in what circumstances, a decision by municipal policymakers on a single occasion may satisfy this requirement.

I

Bertold Pembaur is a licensed Ohio physician and the sole proprietor of the Rockdale Medical Center, located in the city of Cincinnati in Hamilton County. Most of Pembaur's patients are welfare recipients who rely on government assistance to pay for medical care. During the spring of 1977, Simon Leis, the Hamilton County Prosecutor, began investigating charges that Pembaur fraudulently had accepted payments from state welfare agencies for services not actually provided to patients. A grand jury was convened, and the case was assigned to Assistant Prosecutor William Whalen. In April, the grand jury charged Pembaur in a six-count indictment.

During the investigation, the grand jury issued subpoenas for the appearance of two of Pembaur's employees. When these employees failed to appear as directed, the Prosecutor obtained capiases for their arrest and detention from the Court of Common Pleas of Hamilton County. . . . On May 19, 1977, two Hamilton County Deputy Sheriffs attempted to serve the capiases at Pembaur's clinic. Although the reception area is open to the public, the rest of the clinic may be entered only through a door next to the receptionist's window. Upon arriving, the Deputy Sheriffs identified themselves to the receptionist and sought to pass through this door, which was apparently open. The receptionist blocked their way and asked them to wait for the doctor. When Pembaur appeared a moment later, he and the receptionist closed the door, which automatically locked from the inside, and wedged a piece of wood between it and the wall. Returning to the receptionist's window, the Deputy Sheriffs identified themselves to Pembaur, showed him the capiases and explained why they were there. Pembaur refused to let them enter, claiming that the

police had no legal authority to be there and requesting that they leave. He told them that he had called the Cincinnati police, the local media, and his lawyer. The Deputy Sheriffs decided not to take further action until the Cincinnati police arrived.

Shortly thereafter, several Cincinnati police officers appeared. The Deputy Sheriffs explained the situation to them and asked that they speak to Pembaur. The Cincinnati police told Pembaur that the papers were lawful and that he should allow the Deputy Sheriffs to enter. When Pembaur refused, the Cincinnati police called for a superior officer. When he too failed to persuade Pembaur to open the door, the Deputy Sheriffs decided to call their supervisor for further instructions. Their supervisor told them to call Assistant Prosecutor Whalen and to follow his instructions. The Deputy Sheriffs then telephoned Whalen and informed him of the situation. Whalen conferred with County Prosecutor Leis, who told Whalen to instruct the Deputy Sheriffs to "go in and get [the witnesses]." Whalen in turn passed these instructions along to the Deputy Sheriffs.

After a final attempt to persuade Pembaur voluntarily to allow them to enter, the Deputy Sheriffs tried unsuccessfully to force the door. City police officers, who had been advised of the County Prosecutor's instructions to "go in and get" the witnesses, obtained an axe and chopped down the door. The Deputy Sheriffs then entered and searched the clinic. Two individuals who fit descriptions of the witnesses sought were detained, but turned out not to be the right persons.

After this incident, the Prosecutor obtained an additional indictment against Pembaur for obstructing police in the performance of an authorized act. Although acquitted of all other charges, Pembaur was convicted for this offense. The Ohio Court of Appeals reversed, reasoning that Pembaur was privileged under state law to exclude the deputies because the search of his office violated the Fourth Amendment. The Ohio Supreme Court reversed and reinstated the conviction. *State v. Pembaur,* 459 N.E.2d 217 (1984). The Supreme Court held that the state-law privilege applied only to bad-faith conduct by law enforcement officials, and that, under the circumstances of this case, Pembaur was obliged to acquiesce to the search and seek redress later in a civil action for damages.

On April 20, 1981, Pembaur filed the present action in the United States District Court for the Southern District of Ohio against the city of Cincinnati, the County of Hamilton, the Cincinnati Police Chief, the Hamilton County Sheriff, the members of the Hamilton Board of County Commissioners (in their official capacities only), Assistant Prosecutor Whalen, and nine city and county police officers. Pembaur sought damages under 42 U.S.C. § 1983, alleging that the county and city police had violated his rights under the Fourth and Fourteenth Amendments. His theory was that, absent exigent circumstances, the Fourth Amendment prohibits police from searching an individual's home or business without a search warrant even to execute an arrest warrant for a third person. We agreed with that proposition in *Steagald v. United States,* 451 U.S. 204 (1981), decided the day after Pembaur filed this lawsuit. Pembaur sought $10 million in actual and $10 million in punitive damages, plus costs and attorney's fees. . . .

II

A

Our analysis must begin with the proposition that "Congress did not intend municipalities to be held liable unless action pursuant to official municipal policy of some nature caused a constitutional tort." *Monell v. New York City Dept. of Social Services,* 436 U.S., at 691. As we read its opinion, the Court of Appeals held that a single decision to take particular action, although made by municipal policymakers, cannot establish the kind of "official policy" required by *Monell* as a predicate to municipal liability under § 1983. The Court of Appeals reached this conclusion without referring to *Monell*—indeed, without any explanation at all. However, examination of the opinion in *Monell* clearly demonstrates that the Court of Appeals misinterpreted its holding. . . . The conclusion that tortious conduct, to be the basis

for municipal liability under § 1983, must be pursuant to a municipality's "official policy" is contained in this discussion. The "official policy" requirement was intended to distinguish acts of the municipality from acts of employees of the municipality, and thereby make clear that municipal liability is limited to action for which the municipality is actually responsible. *Monell* reasoned that recovery from a municipality is limited to acts that are, properly speaking, acts "of the municipality"—that is, acts which the municipality has officially sanctioned or ordered.

B

Having said this much, we hasten to emphasize that not every decision by municipal officers automatically subjects the municipality to § 1983 liability. Municipal liability attaches only where the decisionmaker possesses final authority to establish municipal policy with respect to the action ordered. The fact that a particular official—even a policymaking official—has discretion in the exercise of particular functions does not, without more, give rise to municipal liability based on an exercise of that discretion. See, e.g., *Oklahoma City v. Tuttle,* 471 U.S., at 822–824. The official must also be responsible for establishing final government policy respecting such activity before the municipality can be held liable. Authority to make municipal policy may be granted directly by a legislative enactment or may be delegated by an official who possesses such authority, and of course, whether an official had final policymaking authority is a question of state law.

C

Applying this standard to the case before us, we have little difficulty concluding that the Court of Appeals erred in dismissing petitioner's claim against the county. The Deputy Sheriffs who attempted to serve the capiases at petitioner's clinic found themselves in a difficult situation. Unsure of the proper course of action to follow, they sought instructions from their supervisors. The instructions they received were to follow the orders of the County Prosecutor. The Prosecutor made a considered decision based on his understanding of the law and commanded the officers forcibly to enter petitioner's clinic. That decision directly caused the violation of petitioner's Fourth Amendment rights.

Respondent argues that the County Prosecutor lacked authority to establish municipal policy respecting law enforcement practices because only the County Sheriff may establish policy respecting such practices. Respondent suggests that the County Prosecutor was merely rendering "legal advice" when he ordered the Deputy Sheriffs to "go in and get" the witnesses. Consequently, the argument concludes, the action of the individual Deputy Sheriffs in following this advice and forcibly entering petitioner's clinic was not pursuant to a properly established municipal policy.

We might be inclined to agree with respondent if we thought that the Prosecutor had only rendered "legal advice." However, the Court of Appeals concluded, based upon its examination of Ohio law, that both the County Sheriff and the County Prosecutor could establish county policy under appropriate circumstances, a conclusion that we do not question here. Ohio Rev.Code Ann. § 309.09(A) (1979) provides that county officers may "require . . . instructions from [the County Prosecutor] in matters connected with their official duties." Pursuant to standard office procedure, the Sheriff's Office referred this matter to the Prosecutor and then followed his instructions. The Sheriff testified that his Department followed this practice under appropriate circumstances and that it was "the proper thing to do" in this case. We decline to accept respondent's invitation to overlook this delegation of authority by disingenuously labeling the Prosecutor's clear command mere "legal advice." In ordering the Deputy Sheriffs to enter petitioner's clinic the County Prosecutor was acting as the final decisionmaker for the county, and the county may therefore be held liable under § 1983.

The decision of the Court of Appeals is reversed, and the case is remanded for further proceedings consistent with this opinion.

It is so ordered.

DeShaney v. Winnebago County Department of Social Services
489 U.S. 189 (1989)

Chief Justice Rehnquist delivered the opinion of the Court, joined by Justices White, Stevens, O'Connor, Scalia, and Kennedy. Justices Brennan, Marshall, and Blackmun dissented.

Petitioner is a boy who was beaten and permanently injured by his father, with whom he lived. Respondents are social workers and other local officials who received complaints that petitioner was being abused by his father and had reason to believe that this was the case, but nonetheless did not act to remove petitioner from his father's custody. Petitioner sued respondents claiming that their failure to act deprived him of his liberty in violation of the Due Process Clause of the Fourteenth Amendment to the United States Constitution. We hold that it did not.

I

The facts of this case are undeniably tragic. Petitioner Joshua DeShaney was born in 1979. In 1980, a Wyoming court granted his parents a divorce and awarded custody of Joshua to his father, Randy DeShaney. The father shortly thereafter moved to Neenah, a city located in Winnebago County, Wisconsin, taking the infant Joshua with him. There he entered into a second marriage, which also ended in divorce.

The Winnebago County authorities first learned that Joshua DeShaney might be a victim of child abuse in January 1982, when his father's second wife complained to the police, at the time of their divorce, that he had previously "hit the boy causing marks and [was] a prime case for child abuse." The Winnebago County Department of Social Services (DSS) interviewed the father, but he denied the accusations, and DSS did not pursue them further. In January 1983, Joshua was admitted to a local hospital with multiple bruises and abrasions. The examining physician suspected child abuse and notified DSS, which immediately obtained an order from a Wisconsin juvenile court placing Joshua in the temporary custody of the hospital. Three days later, the county convened an ad hoc "Child Protection Team"—consisting of a pediatrician, a psychologist, a police detective, the county's lawyer, several DSS caseworkers, and various hospital personnel—to consider Joshua's situation. At this meeting, the Team decided that there was insufficient evidence of child abuse to retain Joshua in the custody of the court. The Team did, however, decide to recommend several measures to protect Joshua, including enrolling him in a preschool program, providing his father with certain counselling services, and encouraging his father's girlfriend to move out of the home. Randy DeShaney entered into a voluntary agreement with DSS in which he promised to cooperate with them in accomplishing these goals.

Based on the recommendation of the Child Protection Team, the juvenile court dismissed the child protection case and returned Joshua to the custody of his father. A month later, emergency room personnel called the DSS caseworker handling Joshua's case to report that he had once again been treated for suspicious injuries. The caseworker concluded that there was no basis for action. For the next six months, the caseworker made monthly visits to the DeShaney home, during which she observed a number of suspicious injuries on Joshua's head; she also noticed that he had not been enrolled in school, and that the girlfriend had not moved out. The caseworker dutifully recorded these

incidents in her files, along with her continuing suspicions that someone in the DeShaney household was physically abusing Joshua, but she did nothing more. In November 1983, the emergency room notified DSS that Joshua had been treated once again for injuries that they believed to be caused by child abuse. On the caseworker's next two visits to the DeShaney home, she was told that Joshua was too ill to see her. Still DSS took no action.

In March 1984, Randy DeShaney beat 4-year-old Joshua so severely that he fell into a life-threatening coma. Emergency brain surgery revealed a series of hemorrhages caused by traumatic injuries to the head inflicted over a long period of time. Joshua did not die, but he suffered brain damage so severe that he is expected to spend the rest of his life confined to an institution for the profoundly retarded. Randy DeShaney was subsequently tried and convicted of child abuse.

Joshua and his mother brought this action under 42 U.S.C. § 1983 in the United States District Court for the Eastern District of Wisconsin against respondents Winnebago County, DSS, and various individual employees of DSS. The complaint alleged that respondents had deprived Joshua of his liberty without due process of law, in violation of his rights under the Fourteenth Amendment, by failing to intervene to protect him against a risk of violence at his father's hands of which they knew or should have known. The District Court granted summary judgment for respondents.

The Court of Appeals for the Seventh Circuit affirmed, 812 F.2d 298 (1987), holding that petitioners had not made out an actionable § 1983 claim for two alternative reasons. First, the court held that the Due Process Clause of the Fourteenth Amendment does not require a state or local governmental entity to protect its citizens from "private violence, or other mishaps not attributable to the conduct of its employees." In so holding, the court specifically rejected the position endorsed by a divided panel of the Third Circuit in *Estate of Bailey by Oare v. County of York*, 768 F.2d 503 (CA3 1985), and by dicta in *Jensen v. Conrad*, 747 F.2d 185 (CA4 1984), that once the State learns that a particular child is in danger of abuse from third parties and actually undertakes to protect him from that danger, a "special relationship" arises between it and the child which imposes an affirmative constitutional duty to provide adequate protection.

Second, the court held, in reliance on our decision in *Martinez v. California,* 444 U.S. 277 (1980), that the causal connection between respondents' conduct and Joshua's injuries was too attenuated to establish a deprivation of constitutional rights actionable under § 1983. The court therefore found it unnecessary to reach the question whether respondents' conduct evinced the "state of mind" necessary to make out a due process claim after *Daniels v. Williams,* 474 U.S. 327 (1986), and *Davidson v. Cannon,* 474 U.S. 344 (1986). Because of the inconsistent approaches taken by the lower courts in determining when, if ever, the failure of a state or local governmental entity or its agents to provide an individual with adequate protective services constitutes a violation of the individual's due process rights, and the importance of the issue to the administration of state and local governments, we granted certiorari. We now affirm.

II

The Due Process Clause of the Fourteenth Amendment provides that "[n]o State shall . . . deprive any person of life, liberty, or property, without due process of law." Petitioners contend that the State deprived Joshua of his liberty interest in "free[dom] from . . . unjustified intrusions on personal security," *Ingraham v. Wright,* 430 U.S. 651 (1977), by failing to provide him with adequate protection against his father's violence. The claim is one invoking the substantive rather than the procedural component of the Due Process Clause; petitioners do not claim that the State denied Joshua protection without according him appropriate procedural safeguards, but that it was categorically obligated to protect him in these circumstances.

But nothing in the language of the Due Process Clause itself requires the State to protect the life, liberty, and property of its citizens against invasion by private actors. The Clause is phrased as a limitation on the State's power to act, not as a guarantee of certain minimal levels of safety and security. It forbids the State itself to deprive individuals of life, liberty, or property without "due process of law," but its language cannot fairly be extended to impose an affirmative obligation on the State to ensure that those interests do not come to harm through other means.

Consistent with these principles, our cases have recognized that the Due Process Clauses generally confer no affirmative right to governmental aid, even where such aid may be necessary to secure life, liberty, or property interests of which the government itself may not deprive the individual. See, e.g., *Harris v. McRae,* 448 U.S. 297 (1980) (no obligation to fund abortions or other medical services) (discussing Due Process Clause of Fifth Amendment); *Lindsey v. Normet,* 405 U.S. 56 (1972) (no obligation to provide adequate housing) (discussing Due Process Clause of Fourteenth Amendment); see also *Youngberg v. Romeo,* supra, 457 U.S., at 317 ("As a general matter, a State is under no constitutional duty to provide substantive services for those within its border"). As we said in *Harris v. McRae:* "Although the liberty protected by the Due Process Clause affords protection against unwarranted government interference . . . , it does not confer an entitlement to such [governmental aid] as may be necessary to realize all the advantages of that freedom." If the Due Process Clause does not require the State to provide its citizens with particular protective services, it follows that the State cannot be held liable under the Clause for injuries that could have been averted had it chosen to provide them. As a general matter, then, we conclude that a State's failure to protect an individual against private violence simply does not constitute a violation of the Due Process Clause.

The *Estelle-Youngberg* analysis simply has no applicability in the present case. Petitioners concede that the harms Joshua suffered did not occur while he was in the State's custody, but while he was in the custody of his natural father, who was in no sense a state actor. While the State may have been aware of the dangers that Joshua faced in the free world, it played no part in their creation, nor did it do anything to render him any more vulnerable to them. That the State once took temporary custody of Joshua does not alter the analysis, for when it returned him to his father's custody, it placed him in no worse position than that in which he would have been had it not acted at all; the State does not become the permanent guarantor of an individual's safety by having once offered him shelter.

Under these circumstances, the State had no constitutional duty to protect Joshua.

Judges and lawyers, like other humans, are moved by natural sympathy in a case like this to find a way for Joshua and his mother to receive adequate compensation for the grievous harm inflicted upon them. But before yielding to that impulse, it is well to remember once again that the harm was inflicted not by the State of Wisconsin, but by Joshua's father. The most that

can be said of the state functionaries in this case is that they stood by and did nothing when suspicious circumstances dictated a more active role for them. In defense of them it must also be said that had they moved too soon to take custody of the son away from the father, they would likely have been met with charges of improperly intruding into the parent-child relationship, charges based on the same Due Process Clause that forms the basis for the present charge of failure to provide adequate protection.

The people of Wisconsin may well prefer a system of liability which would place upon the State and its officials the responsibility for failure to act in situations such as the present one. They may create such a system, if they do not have it already, by changing the tort law of the State in accordance with the regular lawmaking process. But they should not have it thrust upon them by this Court's expansion of the Due Process Clause of the Fourteenth Amendment.

Affirmed.

West v. Gibson
527 U.S. 212 (1999)

Justice Breyer delivered the opinion of the Court, in which Justices Stevens, O'Connor, Souter, and Ginsburg joined. Justice Kennedy filed a dissenting opinion, in which Chief Justice Rehnquist and Justices Scalia and Thomas joined.

The question in this case is whether the Equal Employment Opportunity Commission (EEOC) possesses the legal authority to require federal agencies to pay compensatory damages when they discriminate in employment in violation of Title VII of the Civil Rights Act of 1964, 42 U.S.C. § 2000e. We conclude that the EEOC does have that authority.

I

Title VII of the Civil Rights Act of 1964 forbids employment discrimination. In 1972 Congress

extended Title VII so that it applies not only to employment in the private sector, but to employment in the Federal Government as well. See Equal Employment Opportunity Act of 1972, 42 U.S.C. § 2000e-16. This 1972 Title VII extension, found in § 717 of Title VII, has three relevant subsections.

The first subsection, § 717(a), sets forth the basic Federal Government employment antidiscrimination standard. It says that

"all personnel actions affecting employees or applicants for employment [of specified Government agencies and departments] . . . shall be made free from any discrimination based on race, color, religion, sex, or national origin." 42 U.S.C. § 2000e-16(a).

The second subsection, § 717(b), provides the EEOC with the power to enforce the standard. It says (among other things) that "the Equal Employment Opportunity Commission shall have authority to enforce the provisions of subsection (a) . . . through appropriate remedies, including reinstatement or hiring of employees with or without back pay, as will effectuate the policies of this section. . . ." 42 U.S.C. § 2000e- 16(b).

The third subsection, § 717(c), concerns a court's authority to enforce the standard. It says that, after an agency or the EEOC takes final action on a complaint (or fails to take action within a certain time),

"an employee or applicant . . . [who is still] aggrieved . . . may file a civil action as provided in section [706, dealing with discrimination by private employers] . . . in which civil action the head of the department, agency, or unit, as appropriate, shall be the defendant." 42 U.S.C. § 2000e- 16(c).

In 1991 Congress again amended Title VII. The amendment relevant here permits victims of intentional employment discrimination (whether within the private sector or the Federal Government) to recover compensatory damages. See Civil Rights Act of 1991, 42 U.S.C. § 1981a(a)(1). The relevant portion of that amendment, which we shall call the Compensatory Damages Amendment (CDA), says:

"In an action brought by a complaining party under section 706 [dealing with discrimination by private employers] or 717 [dealing with discrimination by the Federal Government] against a respondent who engaged in unlawful intentional discrimination . . . the complaining party may recover compensatory . . . damages . . ." 42 U.S.C. § 1981a(a)(1).

The CDA also sets forth certain conditions and exceptions. It imposes, for example, a cap on compensatory damages (of up to $ 300,000 for large employers, § 1981a (b)(3)(D)). And it adds: "If a complaining party seeks compensatory . . . damages under this section . . . any party may demand a trial by jury. . . ."

§ 1981a(c). Once the CDA became law, the EEOC began to grant compensatory damages awards in Federal Government employment discrimination cases. . . .

B

Respondent, Michael Gibson, filed a complaint with the Department of Veterans Affairs charging that the Department had discriminated against him by denying him a promotion on the basis of his gender. The Department found against Gibson. The EEOC, however, subsequently found in Gibson's favor and awarded the promotion plus backpay. Three months later Gibson filed a complaint in Federal District Court, asking the court to order the Department to comply immediately with the EEOC's order and also to pay compensatory damages. Complaint. The Department then voluntarily complied with the EEOC's order, but it continued to oppose Gibson's claim for compensatory damages.

Eventually, the District Court dismissed Gibson's compensatory damages claim. On appeal, the Department supported the District Court's dismissal with the argument that Gibson had failed to exhaust his administrative remedies in respect to his compensatory damages claim; hence, he could not bring that claim in court. *Gibson v. Brown,* 137 F.3d 992, 994 (CA7 1998).

The Seventh Circuit, however, reversed the District Court's dismissal. It rejected the Department's argument because, in its view, the EEOC lacked the legal power to award compensatory damages; consequently there was no administrative remedy to exhaust. Id. at 995–998.

Because the circuits have disagreed about whether the EEOC has the power to award compensatory damages, . . . we granted certiorari in order to decide that question.

II

The language, purposes, and history of the 1972 Title VII extension and the 1991 CDA convince us that Congress has authorized the EEOC to award compensatory damages in Federal Government employment discrimination cases. Read literally, the language of the statutes is consistent with a grant of that authority. The relevant portion of the Title VII extension, namely, § 717(b), says that the EEOC "shall have authority" to enforce § 717(a) "through appropriate remedies, including reinstatement or hiring of employees with or without back pay." 42 U.S.C. § 2000e-16(b). After enactment of the 1991 CDA, an award of compensatory damages is a "remedy" that is "appropriate."

We recognize that subsection 717(b) explicitly mentions certain equitable remedies, namely, reinstatement, hiring, and back pay, and it does not explicitly refer to compensatory damages. But the preceding word "including" makes clear that the authorization is not limited to the specified remedies there mentioned; and the 1972 Title VII extension's choice of examples is not surprising, for in 1972 (and until 1991) Title VII itself authorized only equitable remedies. See Civil Rights Act of 1964, 42 U.S.C. § 2000e–5(g) (private sector discrimination); Equal Employment Opportunity Act of 1972, 42 U.S.C. 2000e–16 (federal sector discrimination) . . . .

The meaning of the word "appropriate" permits its scope to expand to include Title VII remedies that were not appropriate before 1991, but in light of legal change are appropriate now. The word "including" makes clear that "appropriate remedies" are not limited to the examples that follow that word. See *Phelps Dodge Corp. v. NLRB,* 313 U.S. 177, 189 (1941). And in context the word "appropriate" most naturally refers to forms of relief that Title VII itself authorizes—at least where that relief is of a kind that agencies typically can provide. Thus, Congress' decision in the 1991 CDA to permit a "complaining party" to "recover compensatory damages" in "an action brought under section . . . 717," by adding compensatory damages to Title VII's arsenal of remedies, could make that form of relief "appropriate" under § 717(b) as well.

An examination of the purposes of the 1972 Title VII extension shows that this permissible reading of the language is also the correct reading. Section 717's general purpose is to remedy discrimination in federal employment. It does so in part by creating a dispute resolution system that requires a complaining party to pursue administrative relief prior to court action, thereby encouraging quicker, less formal, and less expensive resolution of disputes within the Federal Government and outside of court. See 42 U.S.C. § 2000e-16(c) (court action permitted only where complainant disagrees with final agency disposition or, if complainant pursued discretionary appeal to EEOC, with EEOC disposition; or if either agency or EEOC disposition is delayed); . . .

The history of the CDA reinforces this point. The CDA's sponsors and supporters spoke frequently of the need to create a new remedy in order, for example, to "help make victims whole." H. R. Rep. No. 102-40, pt. 1, pp. 64-65 (1991). But the CDA's sponsors and supporters said nothing about limiting the EEOC's ability to use the new Title VII remedy or suggesting that it would be desirable to distinguish the new Title VII remedy from old Title VII remedies in that respect. This total silence is not surprising. What reason could there be for Congress, anxious to have the EEOC consider as a preliminary matter every other possible remedy, not to want the EEOC similarly to consider compensatory damages as well?

Respondent makes three important arguments in favor of a more limited interpretation of the statutes—an interpretation that would deprive the EEOC of the power to award compensatory damages. First, respondent points out that the CDA says nothing about the EEOC, or EEOC proceedings, but rather states only that a complaining party may recover compensatory damages "in an action brought under section . . . 717." 42 U.S.C. § 1981a(a)(1). And the word "action" often refers to judicial cases, not to administrative "proceedings." See *New York Gaslight Club, Inc. v. Carey,* 447 U.S. 54, 60–62 (1980) (distinguishing civil "actions" from administrative "proceedings").

Had Congress thought it important so to limit the scope of the CDA, however, it could easily have cross-referenced § 717(c), the civil action subsection itself, rather than cross-referencing the whole of § 717, which includes authorization for the EEOC to enforce the section through "appropriate remedies." Regardless, the question, as we see it, is whether, by using the word "action," Congress intended to deny that compensatory damages is "appropriate" administrative relief within the terms of § 717(b). In light of the previous discussion, we do not believe the simple use of the word "action" in the context of a cross-reference to the whole of § 717 indicates an intent to deprive the EEOC of that authority.

Second, in an effort to explain why Congress might have wanted to impose a special EEOC-related limitation in respect to compensatory damages, respondent points to the language in the CDA that says: "If a complaining party seeks compensatory . . . damages under this section . . . any party may demand a trial by jury." 42 U.S.C. § 1981a(c). Respondent notes that an EEOC compensatory damages award would not involve a jury. And an agency cannot proceed to court under § 717(c) because that subsection makes a court action available only to an aggrieved complaining party, not to the agency. § 2000e-16(c). Thus, respondent concludes that the CDA must implicitly forbid any such EEOC award, for that award would take place without the jury trial that § 1981a(c) guarantees.

This argument, however, draws too much from too little. One easily can read the jury trial provision in § 1981a(c) as simply guaranteeing either party a jury trial in respect to compensatory damages if a complaining party proceeds to court under § 717(c). . . .

Finally, respondent argues that insofar as the law permits the EEOC to award compensatory damages, it waives the Government's sovereign immunity, and we must construe any such waiver narrowly. See *Lane v. Pena,* 518 U.S. 187, 192 (1996); *Lehman v. Nakshian,* 453 U.S. 156, 160–161 (1981). There is no dispute, however, that the CDA waives sovereign immunity in respect to an award of compensatory damages. Whether, in light of that waiver, the CDA permits the EEOC to consider the same matter at an earlier phase of the employment discrimination claim is a distinct question concerning how the waived damages remedy is to be administered. Because the relationship of this kind of administrative question to the goals and

purposes of the doctrine of sovereign immunity may be unclear, ordinary sovereign immunity presumptions may not apply. In the Government's view here, for example, the EEOC's preliminary consideration, by lowering the costs of resolving disputes, does not threaten, but helps to protect, the public fisc. Regardless, if we must apply a specially strict standard in such a case, which question we need not decide, that standard is met here. We believe that the statutory language, taken together with statutory purposes, history, and the absence of any convincing reason for denying the EEOC the relevant power, produce evidence of a waiver that satisfies the stricter standard.

For these reasons, we conclude that the EEOC possesses the legal authority to enforce § 717 through an award of compensatory damages.

III

Respondent asks us to affirm on alternative grounds the Seventh Circuit's judgment permitting his case to proceed in the District Court. The Seventh Circuit considered whether Gibson had "asked the EEOC for compensatory damages." 137 F.3d at 994. It added that if "he did, then the government's failure-to-exhaust argument obviously is a non-starter." Ibid. But the Court of Appeals concluded that Gibson did not "put the EEOC on notice that he was seeking compensatory damages." Ibid. Respondent claims that he can proceed in District Court because he did satisfy the law's exhaustion requirements, even if the EEOC has the legal power to award compensatory damages and even if he did not give notice to the EEOC that he sought compensatory damages. He argues that is so because (1) the requirement of notice for exhaustion purposes is unusually weak in respect to compensatory damages, (2) he did request a "monetary cash award," and (3) special circumstances estop the Government from asserting a "no exhaustion" claim in this case.

These matters fall outside the scope of the question presented in the Government's petition for certiorari. We remand the case so that the Court of Appeals can determine whether these questions have been properly raised and, if so, decide them.

The decision of the Court of Appeals is vacated, and the case is remanded for further proceedings consistent with this opinion.

It is so ordered.

Justice Kennedy, with whom the Chief Justice, Justice Scalia, and Justice Thomas join, dissenting.

The rules governing this case are clear and well established, or at least had been before the majority's unsettling opinion today. Relief may not be awarded against the United States unless it has waived its sovereign immunity. See *Department of Army v. Blue Fox, Inc.,* 142 L. Ed. 2d 718 (1999). The waiver must be expressed in unequivocal statutory text and cannot be implied. *Lane v. Pena,* 518 U.S. 187, 192 (1996). Even when the United States has waived its immunity, the waiver must be "strictly construed, in terms of its scope, in favor of the sovereign," *Blue Fox,* 1999 U.S. LEXIS 746, *Lane,* supra, at 192, for "'this Court has long decided that limitations and conditions upon which the Government consents to be sued must be strictly observed and exceptions thereto are not to be implied,'" *Lehman v. Nakshian,* 453 U.S. 156, 161 (1981), quoting *Soriano v. United States,* 352 U.S. 270, 276 (1957). Not only do these rules reserve authority over the public fisc to the branch of Government with which the Constitution has placed it, they also form an important part of the background of settled legal principles upon which Congress relied in enacting various statutes authorizing suits against the United States, such as the Tucker Act, 28 U.S.C. § 1491; § 10(a) of the Administrative Procedure Act, 5 U.S.C. § 702; and the Federal Tort Claims Act, 28 U.S.C. § 2671. The rules governing waivers of sovereign immunity make clear that the Equal Employment Opportunity Commission (EEOC) may not award or authorize compensatory damages against the United States unless it is permitted to do so by a statutory provision which waives the United States' immunity to the awards in clear and unambiguous terms.

Section 717(b) of Title VII of the Civil Rights Act of 1964, 42 U.S.C. § 2000e–16(b), which authorizes the EEOC to enforce federal compliance with Title VII "through appropriate remedies, including reinstatement or hiring of employees with or without back pay," effects a waiver of the United States' sovereign immunity for some purposes. Unlike other similar statutes, however, the provision does not mention awards of compensatory damages. A waiver of immunity to other types of relief does not provide the unequivocal statement required to establish a waiver of immunity to damages awards. . . .

Nor does the statutory grant of authority to the EEOC to enforce Title VII through appropriate remedies include, in unequivocal terms or even by necessary implication, the power to award or authorize compensatory damages. Even if the phrase "appropriate remedies" had been intended, as the majority maintains, to incorporate relief authorized for violations of Title VII under other statutory provisions, it is not obvious that the phrase's meaning would have been intended also to "expand" to include remedies that were not available at the time § 717 was adopted. . . .

Unlike § 717(b), 42 U.S.C. § 1981a does authorize awards of compensatory damages against the United States. Although it is clear the statute authorizes courts to award damages, however, § 1981a does not so much as mention the EEOC, much less empower it to award or authorize money damages. It is settled law that a waiver of sovereign immunity in one forum does not effect a waiver in other forums. See, e.g., *McElrath v. United States,* 102 U.S. 426, 440 (1880). . . .

The majority's attempt to read 42 U.S.C. § 1981a(a)(1) to authorize administrative awards of compensatory damages is not persuasive. Section 1981a(a)(1) provides:

"In an action brought by a complaining party under section 706 or 717 of the Civil Rights Act of 1964 . . . the complaining party may recover compensatory and punitive damages as allowed in subsection (b) of this section, in addition to any relief authorized by section 706(g) of the Civil Rights Act of 1964. . . ."

The provision authorizes an award of compensatory damages in an "action" brought under § 717; the word "action" is often used to distinguish judicial cases from administrative "proceedings." See *New York Gaslight Club, Inc. v. Carey,* 447 U.S. 54, 60–62 (1980). . . .

While falling short of embracing the argument as its own, the majority flirts with the contention that allowing agencies rather than juries to award compensatory damages lowers the costs of resolving employment disputes and protects the public fisc. It is not clear to me that juries would be less protective of the fisc than would one group of Government employees who deem themselves empowered by agency interpretation to award Government funds to fellow employees. When a Government employee seeks damages from the Government itself, there may be advantages in insisting upon the expertise of a trial court with experience in awarding damages in all types of cases, with the additional safeguards of trial in a forum of high visibility, trial by jury if either party chooses to ask for it, and appellate review. These factors are disregarded by the majority, which seems instead to suggest that the nature

and convenience of administrative proceedings will by necessity provide a financial advantage to the Government.

In all events, speculation does not suffice to overcome the rule that waivers of sovereign immunity must be clear and express. An unequivocal waiver of the United States' sovereign immunity to administrative awards of compensatory damages cannot be found in the relevant statutory provisions. To the extent the majority relies on textual analysis, it establishes at most (if at all) that the statutes might be read to authorize such awards, not that the statutes must be so read. To the extent the majority relies on legislative history and other extratextual sources, it contradicts our precedents and sets us on a new course, for before today it was well settled that "[a] statute's legislative history cannot supply a waiver that does not appear clearly in any statutory text." *Lane,* 518 U.S. at 192; *Nordic Village,* 503 U.S. at 37 ("The 'unequivocal expression' of elimination of sovereign immunity that we insist upon is an expression in statutory text. If clarity does not exist there, it cannot be supplied by a committee report"). With respect, I dissent.

Notes

1. *Dalehite v. United States,* 346 U.S. 15, 47–48 (1953).

2. Ibid., 16.

3. There was an agreement among all the plaintiffs and defendants that the trial judge's findings of fact and interpretation of law as to the federal government's liability in the *Dalehite* litigation would be accepted in all the remaining suits, 346 U.S. 15, 16.

4. *Erie Railroad Company v. Tompkins,* 304 U.S. 64 (1938).

5. 346 U.S. 15, 55.

6. 28 U.S.C. 1346 and 2671–80.

7. The material on private bills comes from footnote 9 in *Dalehite v. United States,* 346 U.S. 15, 25.

8. The only available remedy for the Texas City plaintiffs was to return to the activity the FTCA was intended to stop—the private bill. By 1957, when

Congress passed the last private bill from this incident, it passed 1,394 awards for a total of almost $17 million. See Donald Barry and Howard Whitcomb, *The Legal Foundations of Public Administration,* 2d ed. (St. Paul, Minn.: West, 1987), p. 268.

9. *Chisholm v. Georgia,* 2 Dall. 419 (1793).

10. *Seminole Tribe of Florida v. Florida,* 517 U.S. 44 (1996).

11. *Pennsylvania v. Union Gas Co.,* 491 U.S. 1 (1989).

12. *Alden v. Maine,* 527 U.S. 706 (1999).

13. *Board of Trustees of the University of Alabama v. Garrett,* 531 U.S. 536 (2001).

14. *Tennessee v. Lane,* 124 S.Ct. 1978 (2004).

15. 535 U.S. 635 (2002).

16. *Tennessee Student Assistance Corporation v. Hood,* 541 U.S. 440 (2004).

17. Daniel Oran, *Oran's Dictionary of the Law* (St. Paul, Minn.: West, 1983), p. 424.

18. *Kimble v. Machintosh Hemphill Company,* 59 A. 2d 68 (1948).

19. 346 U.S. 15, 35–36.

20. William G. Weaver and Thomas Longoria, "Bureaucracy that Kills: Federal Sovereign Immunity and the Discretionary Function Exemption," 96(2) *American Political Science Review* 335 (June 2002).

21. *Allen v. United States,* 588 F.Supp. 247, 336 (D. Ut. 1984).

22. *Nevin v. United States,* 696 F.2d. 1229 (9th Cir. 1983).

23. 346 U.S. 15 (1983).

24. The material on the Giglotto and Askew raids comes from Jack Boger, Mark Gitenstein, and Paul Verkuil, "The Federal Tort Claims Act Intentional Torts Amendment: An Interpretative Analysis," 54 *North Carolina Law Review* 498 (1976).

25. Ibid., pp. 501, 502.

26. Ibid., p. 501.

27. Ibid.

28. But see *Forrester v. White,* 108 S.Ct. 538 (1988), where a judge was held not to be immune in the execution of administrative duties as opposed to judicial duties.

29. *Barr v. Matteo,* 360 U.S. 564, 575 (1959).

30. *Federal Deposit Insurance Corporation v. Meyer,* 510 U.S. 471 (1994).

31. Arthur Bonfield and Michael Asimow, *State and Federal Administrative Law* (St. Paul, Minn.: West, 1989), p. 640.

32. Sande Buhai, "Symposium: Social Justice in the 21st Century: In the meantime: State Protection of Disability and Civil Rights," 37 *Loyola of Los Angeles Law Review* 1065, 1072 (Spring 2004).

33. Pete Earley, *Circumstantial Evidence: Death, Life, and Justice in a Southern Town* (New York: Bantam Books, 1995).

34. *Bogan v. Scott-Harris,* 523 U.S. 44 (1998).

35. *Kalina v. Fletcher,* 522 U.S. 118 (1997).

36. *Pegram v. Herdrich,* 530 U.S. 211 (2000).

37. See *United States v. Gaubert,* 499 U.S. 315 (1991), at p. 326, where the Court says, "the Court of Appeals misinterpreted *Berkovitz's* reference to *Indian Towing* as perpetuating a *nonexistent dichotomy* [emphasis mine] between discretionary functions and operational activities."

38. *Kolstad v. American Dental Association,* 527 U.S. 526 (1999).

39. See *Nguyen and Boulais v. Immigration and Naturalization Service,* 533 U.S. 53 (2001).

40. 426 U.S. 367 (1983).

41. 446 U.S. 14 (1980).

11

SUMMARY AND CONCLUSIONS

The field a farmer plowed typified the work setting of an agricultural society.
The factory assembly line was the distinctive setting for the industrial society.
Bureaucracy is the predominant work setting for the postindustrial era.[1]

This book began with the proposition that we live in an era characterized by the administrative state. That is, the fourth branch of government, bureaucracy, makes policy decisions based on expertise rather than on electoral accountability. Bureaucracy enforces its own policies and adjudicates infractions of those policies. Through the cases you have read, it may strike you that the policy choices often made by agencies do not simply involve the "filling in of details" but, rather, can be significant and far-reaching policy choices. Evidence was presented in Chapters 2 and 3 that we cannot always count on the current occupant of the White House or on Congress to exert significant control over the fourth branch. If all that I have previously said is true, then you and I as citizens do not exercise control over many policies, either directly or indirectly through our elected representatives.

Think about some of the policy decisions that have been made by agencies. The Department of Transportation adopted a policy that by a certain date, all vehicles manufactured in the United States would have passive restraints, either automatic seatbelts or airbags. That policy cost industry and consumers billions of dollars by the time compliance rippled through the economy. Similarly, the Department of Energy promulgated standards (i.e., adopted a policy) requiring that every major appliance manufactured in the United States operate at a certain level of efficiency.[2] In the case commonly known as the Benzene Case,[3] discussed in Chapter 3, Congress delegated to the secretary of labor nothing less than the power to make the choice between workers' safety and industry profits. In a case discussed in Chapter 7, *Pacific Gas and Electric v. Federal Power Commission,* 506 F.2d 33 (D.C. Cir. 1974), the Federal Power Commission adopted a rule regarding the allocation of natural gas in the event of a shortage that would have voided otherwise valid contracts between buyers and sellers of natural gas. In yet another case, briefly discussed in Chapter 10, the Atomic Energy Commission (AEC; now the Nuclear Regulatory Commission) adopted policies to conduct above-ground nuclear testing and not to warn or educate those citizens who live downwind of the test sight about nuclear fallout. The commission's failure to warn has allegedly led to above-normal incidences of cancer among residents of southern Utah. Although this issue is not discussed in the current edition of this book, President Reagan's Secretary of Health and Human Services Margaret Heckler ordered a massive purge of the disability rolls.[4] In the 1980 election, candidate Reagan tried to sell voters on the idea that one of the fixes for a sagging economy and massive federal deficits would be to go after welfare cheats, and he pointed his finger at the disability program. After his election, Heckler took action. Para- and quadriplegics and the mentally retarded were informed by their government to stop faking disabilities and to get to work like the rest of us. When ordered by more than one U.S. circuit court of appeals to cease and desist, Heckler adopted a policy of nonacquiescence. Following this strategy, an agency will implement a court decision involving the specific litigant but refuse to apply the court's decision to all others dealing with the agency. In this case, the appellate courts told the secretary she could not terminate anyone from disability unless there was evidence of medical improvement so that they would no longer be medically disabled. The secretary's nonacquiescence policy meant she applied the medical improvement standard to the immediate litigant but continued to apply a different standard to the thousands of disability recipients whose cases she was reviewing. The Supreme Count winked at the nonacquiescence policy.[5]

Case in Point:
Ergonomics Regulation

In January of 2001, the Occupational Safety and Health Administration (OSHA) issued its final version of ergonomics rules. Ergonomics, an applied science concerned with designing and arranging things so that people can use them without injury, responds to injuries called repetitive stress syndrome or repetitive stress injury (RSI), which is caused by repetitive activity. Your doctor knows it as musculoskeletal disorder. The National Academy of Sciences estimates that 1.8 million RSIs each year cost the economy $54 billion in workers compensation, lost work time, and reduced productivity.[6]

For years, organized labor and women's groups lobbied OSHA to produce a rule on RSI, and business interest groups fought it tooth and nail. The agency finally did produce a rule during the final days of the Clinton presidency. The rule would force employers to evaluate their workspace for its potential to create RSI, to train and inform employees about RSI, and to eliminate the causes of RSI in their businesses.[7] The rule "was expected to be the most expensive safety and health standard in OSHA's 30-year history and was expected to have a greater impact on more employers in more sectors of employment than any other OSHA regulatory activity."[8]

In Chapter 3's discussion of the congressional review process, you learned that Congress passed a resolution forbidding OSHA from promulgating regulations in the field of ergonomics, which President Bush 43 signed into law on March 20, 2001. You may not, however, be aware that on April 5, 2002, OSHA announced its new ergonomics policy. The new regulation of RSI would consist of "voluntary" industry-specific guidelines, targeted enforcement, workplace outreach, and advanced research. When Congress passed the Occupational Safety and Health Act, it inserted a clause that is known today as the general duty clause. This clause says that employers have a legal duty not to create "recognized hazards" in the workplace. OSHA developed voluntary guidelines of some industries (starting with the nursing home industry regarding the physical lifting of patients) and encouraged the remaining industries to develop their own voluntary guidelines.

Arguing that excessive lifting is a recognized hazard, OSHA has used the general duty clause to justify 1,300 inspections and to issue 12 citations for excessive lifting (67% of them in nursing homes).[9]

This book has argued that to be consistent with basic notions of democracy, agencies that make public policy need to be controlled by elected officials so that political consumers can say yes or no to the public situation. Let me summarize the public situation with regard to OSHA and ergonomics: After the Supreme Court declared the congressional veto to be unconstitutional and similarly dealt a blow to the Office of Management and Budget's (OMB's) control of agency rules (*Chadha* and the *Steelworkers* cases, respectively), Congress restored them both. Today, the White House, through the OMB and the Office of Information and Regulatory Affairs (OIRA), reviews both existing and proposed rules, with the power to derail proposals that the current occupant of the White House may disapprove of and to compel the modification of existing rules. Provided that Congress acts before the Administrative Procedure Act's 60-day clock turns a proposed rule into a real one with the force and effect of law, Congress can stop the proposed rule from becoming a reality. An agency (OSHA) proposed a rule (regarding ergonomics) that would have far-ranging conse-quences. The occupant of the White House at the time favored the rule, so there was mini-mal interference from OMB. A majority of both houses of Congress did not favor the rule but had to wait a few weeks for a new occupant of the White House, because the old occu-pant would have vetoed a congressional review resolution against the rule. With a new occu-pant in the White House, Congress expressed the people's will—we forbid the adoption of any rules in the area of RSI—and the new president signed the resolution into law. Undeterred by this flurry of activity against it, OSHA adopted a new RSI policy (this time without going through 553 public hearings). The policy requires businesses to adhere to the agency's voluntary guidelines, and the agency is armed with the will and the power to con-duct inspections and issue citations for violations of those guidelines. All the while, President Bush 43 presumably opposes what the agency is doing, along with his directors of OMB and OIRA, his chief of staff, and his secretary of labor. Presuming that the director of OSHA has joined the senior executive service, all of the above-named executive and White House offi-cials have the power to order the director of OSHA to stop and fire him or her if the offend-ing activity does not stop. It may be worth paraphrasing Congressman Tom DeLay (from Chapter 3), the Majority leader of the House of Representatives, who summarized the public situation by pointing out that despite conservative-probusiness majorities in both houses of Congress and in the White House (I would add the Supreme Court as well), bureaucracies can still tell people how to live their lives.

Question

1. As a political consumer, who do you think you should reward or punish with your next vote on this public situation?

SUMMARIZING CONTROL OF BUREAUCRACY

Political Control

To comport with democratic theory, if policy-making power is given away by the body that constitutionally possesses it, there should be some way for elected officials to control the exercise of that power. Chapter 3's discussion of congressional control of bureaucracy indicated that control could come at either the front end or the back end of the regulatory process. That is, Congress can control delegations of power before bureaucracy gets hold of policy-making authority, or it can exercise control by checking agency policies after they are proposed. It may well be that Congress has given away too much power, and now with conservative majorities, it is having some trouble taking a good deal of it back. However, delegation of power is a complicated issue; there are practical and political reasons for it, and philosophical reasons against it. Indeed, although conservative Republican majorities in Congress are uneasy with the broad discretion given to the OSHA or the Environmental Protection Agency (EPA), they do not balk at delegating lots of power and discretion to the new Department of Homeland Security. Delegation of power is probably here to stay (it has actually been "here" from the start of government under this Constitution). Some have argued that when Congress delegates its power, it should do so more narrowly and carefully. If you reread the Chief Justice's concurring opinion in the Benzene case (Chapter 3), you may appreciate why it is easier to admonish Congress to make better delegations than it is to accomplish that goal.

In any case, we should not hold our breath for front-end control. Perhaps, back-end control is the best our political system can offer. Congress has accomplished that by adopting the congressional review procedure. Because of the *Chadha* decision, that procedure is as good as it can get. Once a proposed agency rule is published in the *Federal Register* the second time, it turns into a substantive rule in 60 days. That is when it has the force and effect of law and becomes public policy. Public policy can only be modified by going through the legislative process described in Article I of the Constitution, bicameralism and presentment. That is why the congressional review process has a 60-day window, in which both houses of Congress can adopt an expedited resolution, and the president can sign it. The practical effect is that the procedure worked well in 2001, when both houses of Congress and the presidency were controlled by the same political party. The procedure will not be as smooth when the same political party does not control both institutions. Indeed, Congress has done more than just adopt the congressional review procedure. It also adopted what has become known as the Data Quality Act, which is supposed to ensure the integrity of information and data used by agencies. The Act also allows citizens to access that information or data and challenge it. Congress attempted to pass guidance legislation that would have required agencies to conduct cost-benefit analysis and regulatory impact analysis on all proposed rules, but the law did not pass for political reasons. Congress appeared content to delegate the power to control agencies to the White House. With conservative Republican ranks increased by the 2004 election, perhaps the 109th Congress will take up the task again.

President George W. Bush has been able to achieve the administrative presidency. His appointees in the OMB and OIRA have power and control over existing agency rules and proposed rules. The OIRA has mandated cost-benefit analysis and regulatory impact analysis on all proposed rules. It has also exercised control over agency information and data (a delegation from the Data Quality Act). The problem is that all of these devices to control agency policy are tied to paperwork or "major bills" or those affecting small business; in addition, the agencies get to decide what has paperwork implications, what has a major impact, and so on. That is why guidance legislation controlling agencies would be more effective.

Finally, it is not constitutionally clear that the White House can modify congressional policy by having OIRA manipulate its implementation. The Founding Fathers specified that the president shall *faithfully* [emphasis mine] execute the laws of Congress. If a former (Democratic) Congress mandated clean air and water and workplace safety, there is no legal certainty that the current occupant of the White House can revise those mandates at his or her pleasure. The Supreme Court has addressed this issue in a case that you read in Chapter 7 (the *Chevron* case), but it did so in dicta. The Court will eventually need to address what *faithfully* means in Article Two.

> An agency to which Congress had delegated policymaking responsibilities may, within the limits of that delegation, properly rely upon the incumbent administration's view of wise policy to inform its judgements. While agencies are not directly accountable to the people, the Chief Executive is, and it is entirely appropriate for this political branch of government to make such policy choices.[10]

Finally, effective executive control of agencies waxes and wanes with the partisanship of whoever occupies the presidency. Midway through the first decade of the 21st century, there is more accountability in our political system then there has been for a very long time. As the 2006 election approaches, political consumers will have no difficulty identifying who to reward or who to blame for the public situation (OSHA and ergonomics excepted).

Judicial Control

The corollary proposition to the existence of the administrative state and varying control over the so-called fourth branch by elected branches of government was that by default, the task of controlling the fourth branch fell to the courts. What kind of job have the courts done? Although the cases presented in this text are diverse and in some instances not consistent, some broad trends can be identified, especially with regard to democracy. Through a number of decisions, the Court has restricted a citizen's ability to challenge agency actions in the courts.

First, the Court has narrowed standing to challenge agency action. The full-blown adoption of the three-pronged test for standing from *Lujan* means more individuals "adversely affected by agency action" will be unable to get a court to review that agency action. For example, in *Allen v. Wright et al.* (Chapter 4), the Court refused to recognize the possibility of a connection between an Internal Revenue Service grant of tax-exempt status to discriminatory private schools and the Wrights' inability to send their children to desegregated public schools. In *City of Los Angeles v. Lyons* (Chapter 4), the Court refused to find an appropriate legal connection between the victim of police brutality and the victim's legal ability to challenge a police department policy that led to the act of brutality. From the Case in Point in Chapter 4, you saw that although Congress specifically authorized private citizen suits to enforce environmental laws, the Citizens for a Better Environment could not sue a flagrant violator of the law.

Second, consistent with court deference to agency expertise, the Court has refused to narrow estoppel against the government. The consequence of this is that the average citizen dare not rely on the advice or information provided by the agency with the expertise. The two-pronged test for estoppel against the government adopted in *Heckler v. Community Health Services* (Chapter 6) in 1984 does little to move beyond the Court's 1920 pronouncement that "men must turn square corners when they deal with the government."[11]

Third, as the trend toward privatization of government services mushrooms, Court decisions in the area of state action put citizens at risk. Conservative majorities on the Rehnquist

Court have consistently failed to find state action where government has contracted out the delivery of services. If government provides the service, citizen/consumers are protected to an extent by the Constitution and an array of public laws and policies. Where those services are transferred to private parties, the citizen consumer is significantly less protected unless courts find that the private actor is clothed with government action.[12]

Fourth, also related to privatization, the Court has refused to extend the possibility of a *Bivens* suit to a private company that was unquestionably a state actor. See *Correctional Services Corp. v. Malesko* in Chapter 10. Citizens cannot sue a federal agency under *Bivens,* either; they can sue only an individual employee. If the employee happens not to have liability insurance, the citizen might as well not bother with the suit.

Fifth, the Court has broadened the discretionary function exemption under the Federal Tort Claims Act (FTCA). There is no longer (if there ever was) a policy/implementation dichotomy. Agency actions are insulated from citizen suit in any situation where an actor in the agency exercised discretion in the implementation of policy. We are back to where we were during the Texas City incident after World War II. Government is only liable for the simple negligence of its employees in traffic accidents or if an employee took action that was contrary to a statutory command.

Sixth, the Court's Eleventh Amendment decisions broadening sovereign immunity insulate a whole host of governmental actions from redressing via a suit against the government. The states are free to refuse to negotiate in good faith as required by statute (*Seminole Tribe* case); to refuse to abide by federal minimum wage and hour provisions (*Alden v. Maine*); and to discriminate illegally against shipping companies in awarding port berths without worrying about the Shipping Act of 1984, which prohibits such discrimination (*FMC v. South Carolina).* It is unclear at this time whether the states need to worry about the Americans With Disabilities Act or not.

A final line of cases in which the Court has inhibited a citizen's ability to challenge agency activity in the courts is in the area of due process. The Court has not developed a new test; it has simply restricted the situations in which a liberty or property interest either exists or requires a due process hearing.

Bearing in mind that the purpose of the due process requirement is to guard against arbitrary or mistaken deprivations of liberty or property by government, the following cases are representative of the Court's due process jurisprudence over the past 30 years: *Paul v. Davis,* 424 U.S. 623 (1976) (no liberty interest in the erroneous posting of plaintiff's picture as a shoplifter); *Bishop v. Wood,* 426 U.S. 341 (1976) (federal courts do not function to rectify the erroneous discharge of a local public employee); *Ingraham v. Wright,* 438 U.S. 651 (1977) (no due process requirement for the administration of corporal punishment in the public schools); *Board of Curators of the University of Missouri v. Horowitz,* 435 U.S. 78 (1978) (no due process required for the academic suspension of a college student); *Waters v. Churchill,* 511 U.S. 661 (1994) (what an employer reasonably *thought* was said, as opposed to what was *really* said, will provide the legal basis for an employee termination under the due process clause); *Connick v. Myers,* 461 U.S. 138 (1983) (although it is perfectly acceptable for management to assess the performance of employees, there was no due process violation where an employee was fired for attempting to assess the administrative ability of management); *National Treasury Employees Union v. Von Raab,* 489 U.S. 656 (1989) (no sufficient liberty interest in the compelled collection of urine samples from certain public employees); *Pacific Mutual Life Insurance v. Haslip,* 499 U.S. 1 (1991) (no due process violation in the apparently arbitrary jury award of punitive damages); *Collins v. City of Harker Heights,* 503 U.S. 115 (1992) (no liberty interest where city's failure to properly train and warn its employees led to employee's death); *Gilbert v. Homar,* 520 U.S. 924 (1997) (no due process violation where employee with a property interest was wrongfully suspended without pay and no predeprivation hearing was held); and *Kansas v. Hendricks,* 521 U.S. 346 (1997) (no due process violation to civilly commit a prisoner after he has served his criminal sentence).

A series of cases that are unrelated to citizen access to the courts nevertheless allow agencies to cut a wide swath in terms of how they deal with clients or the public. The cases referred to here involve situations in which Congress has mandated that the agencies proceed according to a specific procedure, the agency has employed a different procedure, and the courts have refused to make the agency comply with the required procedure. In *National Labor Relations Board v. Bell Aerospace Company,* 461 U.S. 267 (1974) (Chapter 7), both Congress and the nature of the subject matter dictated that the agency use rule promulgation in decision making, but the agency used a quasi-judicial adjudication instead. The Supreme Court, deferring to agency expertise, condoned the agency's choice of a case-by-case procedure. In the case of *Heckler v. Campbell,* 461 U.S. 458 (1983) (Chapter 7), the Court reaffirmed the *Storer* doctrine that when an agency is required by Congress to proceed by adjudication, the agency is not precluded from promulgating a rule and denying the adjudicatory hearing to those who do not meet the rule's requirements.

OTHER POSSIBLE MEASURES OF ACCOUNTABILITY

Is it reasonable to expect the judicial branch of government to make decisions that enhance citizen control of bureaucracy? It is the role of the federal courts to interpret the Constitution, and as was discussed in Chapter 1, the Constitution is not a particularly democratic document, at least not as democracy has been defined in this book. If we wait for the courts to deliver us from the administrative state, we would wait for a very long time.

The fourth branch of government is a fact of life, and policy making by insulated bureaucrats is here to stay for the foreseeable future. The task is to at least begin the discussion about how to make the fourth branch more accountable. As Robert Reich, professor of economics and secretary of labor during President Clinton's first term, points out, volumes have been written about making judicial review compatible with democracy, but very little has been written about making the administrative state compatible with democracy.[13]

According to a concept called functional representation, those who make the policy should in fact be representative of the polity. By way of a counterexample, we pay our senators and representatives in Congress about $150,000 a year. Almost everyone elected to that body is so rich that they must accept a cut in pay to take the job. More than 15 percent of the members of the House and a quarter of U.S. senators are millionaires, whereas the percentage for the general population is one twentieth of one percent.[14] So we do not have functional representation in this country. The theory behind functional representation is that there will be a closer fit between the constituency's demands and public policy when the legislative body reflects the socioeconomic and demographic makeup of the citizenry. The former Soviet Union had functional representation. The National People's Congress in China is based on functional representation. There are hints of the concept in Hong Kong and in India's Parliament. Despite evidence of the same glass ceiling in American public service that there is in the private economy, the American bureaucracy is very close to being functionally representative.[15] One out of every six people in the civilian workforce works for government.[16] "[T]he average bureaucrat is middle-aged and middle class and in that sense pretty 'ordinary.' The federal bureaucrat . . . is on the average forty-two years old, has worked for the government for thirteen years, has a year or two of college and makes $40,000 a year."[17]

The term *bureaucrat* has a bad connotation that is not deserved. It turns out that the media and politicians have been denigrating public servants, while the empirical evidence indicates that the myths about bureaucrats are not true.[18] Members of Congress, for example, sleep with bureaucrats by day in cozy triangles, working hand in hand on constituency service and bringing home the pork. But when politicians return to the home district, they make speeches about the faceless bureaucrats in Washington, D.C. It has become too easy in our political system for elected representatives to delegate to the bureaucracy the power to choose between industry profits or worker safety and then make a public speech attacking the bureaucrat who made the choice. Empirical evidence indicates that when American citizens come into contact with bureaucrats, the experience is positive, helpful, and satisfying.[19] Indeed, in a study of juror evaluation of jury duty for the Kansas Supreme Court, only 9 respondents out of 1,747 (.005%) said that courthouse employees were not courteous and helpful.[20] Perhaps, one possibility is simply not to worry about insulated policy making by bureaucrats because the bureaucracy is you and I, whereas our elected officials are nothing like us.

Another possibility involves leadership by agency heads. The idea is for agency heads to encourage citizen debate prior to agency action. Secretary Reich calls it *civic discovery*,[21] but 30 years ago, a famous political scientist, E. E. Schattschneider, referred to the same concept as the *socialization of conflict*.[22] Schattschneider argued that conflict could be either expanded (socialization of conflict) or constricted (privatization of conflict). His thesis was that socialization or broadening of conflict is more compatible with democracy than is the privatization of conflict. The socialization of conflict is compatible with democracy because socialization of conflict leads to citizen input on policy making through political parties via elections. The privatization of conflict, on the other hand, leads to pluralism and policy making by interest groups, bureaucrats, cozy triangles, and, I would add, the administrative state.

Secretary Reich argues for a variant of Schattschneider's thesis. Rather than agencies' making policy by cost-benefit analysis or in collusion with interest groups with vested interests (see the reg-neg process referred to in Chapter 7), Reich argues that the agency should open the question to citizen debate. Reich recounts how it worked in Tacoma, Washington.[23]

The EPA had to make the same kind of choice in Tacoma that the secretary of labor made in the Benzene case, discussed in Chapter 3—that is, a choice between human life or economic well-being. A mainstay of Tacoma's economy, the American Smelting and Refining Company (ASARCO) employed 570 workers with a payroll of $23 million and local annual purchases of $12 million. ASARCO produced inorganic arsenic as a by-product of its smelting process, which it released into the air. Inorganic arsenic is a documented cause of lung cancer, and the EPA was charged by Congress to provide an "ample margin of safety to protect the public health." Rather than make a unilateral decision within the agency, the director of EPA, William Ruckelshaus, opened the question for public debate in a series of town meetings. The price of copper on the world market eventually forced the plant to close, but not before the citizens of Tacoma encouraged the city policymakers to diversify the Tacoma economy.

The § 553 notice and comment procedure in the Administrative Procedure Act is an attempt to broaden participation in the administrative process. Theoretically, any citizen could show up at any agency hearing and provide input into the agency decision-making process. The real world problem is that citizens would have to read the weekly *Federal Register* to find out where and when the hearing was scheduled. As a consequence, the record on public comment on proposed agency rules is not good.[24] In practice, § 553 procedures are privatized decision-making affairs between the agencies and those groups with a vested interest in the outcome of the proposed rule.[25] One facet of President Clinton's reinvention of government was to broaden participation in agency rule making. At the beginning of the 21st century, most agencies with significant rule-making authority have a Web page with options for participation.[26] Called E-Government, this simplifies a citizen's ability to know what government is up to. In those instances where there is interactive cyber communication with agencies, there is very good potential for democracy.

Chapter 7 described the neg-reg procedure in which the agency negotiates a proposed rule with affected parties. This more closely resembles a mediation than a legislative hearing. These negotiations can fit either the privatization mode, or they can socialize the conflict. When the agency manipulates situation so that only a chosen few clients participate, you have privatized business as usual. However, when the agency opens up the participation to all groups that have an interest to discuss, you get socialization of conflict. You also get increased compliance with the rule, fewer infractions of the rule, and fewer lawsuits over the rule. The concept is called *stakeholder involvement*, which means that those who must live by a rule (or a law) live better with it if they have had a hand in crafting the rule. It is simple democracy at a mini-level, and some successful reg-neg outcomes have spurred some agencies to go in search of citizen input.[27]

In our federal system, the states have played a role as experimental laboratories from the beginning. Several states have been taking steps to enhance the accountability of their agencies. More than two thirds of the states use sunset laws,[28] allotting an agency a specific life span, which can be renewed only after some type of action by the state legislature. Although the legislative veto (Chapter 3) has been declared unconstitutional for the federal government and in eight states, it is still used in more than a third of the remaining states.[29] More than half of the states have adopted some form of zero or reduced-based budgeting,[30] in which agency budgets are not determined by last year's appropriation plus inflation; rather, agencies must justify an increase. The states have taken the lead in broadening representation on boards and commissions[31] (lay representation on licensing boards, ombudsmen office, etc.). One should not assume, however, that simply because a legislature or a chief executive has imposed a reform on the bureaucracy, the reform will have the desired effect—or any effect at all for that matter.[32] Studies show that Government Performance and Results Act and reinvention of government have had little effect on agency behavior.[33] You may not be receptive to the idea of creating another bureaucracy to deal with the existing bureaucracy, but that is exactly what an ombudsman's office does. In 1969, Hawaii became the first state to create an ombudsman agency. Nebraska, Iowa, Alaska, Arizona, Detroit, Seattle, and Boise, Idaho, have followed suit.[34] Three decades worth of data show that the ombudsman's office disposed of more than 74,000 complaints against state agencies; the office also handles requests for information and questions. In 39 percent of those complaints, the ombudsman either vindicated the agency on a preliminary inquiry, required the complainant to pursue internal procedures with the agency, or explained to the citizen why the agency acted and the citizen dropped the complaint. After a thorough investigation, 36 percent of the complaints were found to have no basis, and the agency was vindicated. In the remaining quarter of complaints, the office sustained the complaint, and in 86 percent of those, the ombudsman persuaded the agency to rectify the complaint.

The point was made before in this book that the average liberal arts graduate changes careers four times in a working life. If you are taking a course in administrative law, chances are that you may find yourself in a decision-making position within a government agency or a nonprofit agency someday. The temptation will be great to privatize the conflict and make a decision based on the expertise of those within the agency who advise you or on the expertise of those groups with a vested interest in the decision. To be a democratic decision maker is neither easy nor efficient. Secretary Ruckelshaus, in the Tacoma example earlier, received criticism from all sides—industry, environmentalists, and organized labor. He was also criticized by the media for not unilaterally making a decision. *The New York Times* said it was "inexcusable . . . for him to impose such an impossible choice on Tacomans."[35] Whose choice should it be?

NOTES

1. Everett Carl Ladd, *The American Polity*, 5th ed. (New York: Norton, 1985), p. 25.

2. Leif Carter, *Administrative Law and Politics: Cases and Comments* (Boston: Little, Brown, 1983), p. 30.

3. *Industrial Union Department AFL-CIO v. American Petroleum Institute*, 448 U.S. 607 (1980).

4. The material on purging the disability rolls and nonacquiescence policy comes from Susan Gluck Mezey, *No Longer Disabled: The Federal Courts and the Politics of Social Security Disability* (New York: The Greenwood Press, 1988), 75–82.

5. *Heckler v. Lopez*, 464 U.S. 879 (1983).

6. Editoral, "Bush and RSI," *Pittsburgh Post-Gazzette,* June 16, 2004, p. A14.

7. The information on OSHA and new ergonomic rules comes from Charles H. Morgan, "OSHA Ergonomic Guidelines," 26(20) *National Law Journal* 17 (January12, 2004).

8. Ibid.

9. Ibid.

10. *Chevron U.S.A., Inc. v. Natural Resources Defense Council*, 467 U.S. 837,865 (1984).

11. *Rock Island, Arkansas and Louisiana Railroad Company v. United States*, 254 U.S. 141, 143 (1920).

12. Robert S. Gilmour and Laura S. Jensen, "Reinventing Government Accountability: Public Functions, Privatization, and the Meaning of 'State Action'," 58 *Public Administration Review* 247 (May/June 1998).

13. Robert B. Reich, "Policy Making in a Democracy," in *Current Issues in Public Administration,* ed. Frederick S. Lane, 5th ed. (New York: St. Martin's, 1994), p. 115.

14. Susan Welch, John Gruhl, John Comer, Susan M. Rigdon, and Jan Vermeer, *Understanding American Government,* 5th ed. (Belmont, Calif.: West/Wadsworth, 1999), 271–72.

15. Charles T. Goodsell, *The Case For Bureaucracy: A Public Administration Polemic,* 4th ed. (Washington, D.C.: Congressional Quarterly Press, 2004), p. 85.

16. Goodsell, *The Case for Bureaucracy*, 4th ed., p. 83.

17. Goodsell, *The Case for Bureaucracy*, 4th ed., p. 104. See also Chapter 5 on the demographics, personality, and ideology of government employees.

18. Charles T. Goodsell, *The Case for Bureaucracy,* 3rd ed. (Chatham, N.J.: Chatham House), 49–77.

19. Ibid., pp. 30–31.

20. Steven Cann and Michael Kaye, "Juror Satisfaction With the Kansas Court System," *Report to the Chief Justice of The Kansas Supreme Court,* 1998, 12.

21. Reich, "Policy Making in a Democracy," p. 129.

22. E. E. Schattschneider, *The Semisovereign People* (Hinsdale, Ill.: Dryden, 1975), 7–19.

23. All of the material on the EPA, ASARCO, and Tacoma comes from Reich, "Policy Making in a Democracy," 131–33.

24. Cornelius M. Kerwin, *Rulemaking: How Government Agencies Write Law and Make Policy,* 3rd ed. (Washington, D.C.: C.Q. Press, 2003), 179–84.

25. Ibid.

26. Ibid., p.195.

27. Phillip J. Harder, "In Search of Goldilocks: Democracy, Participation, and Government," 10 *Pennsylvania State Environmental Law Review* 113 (Summer 2002).

28. William T. Gormley, Jr., "Accountability Battles in State Administration" in *Current Issues in Public Administration,* ed. Frederick S. Lane, 5th ed. (New York: St. Martin's, 1994), 141–42.

29. Gormley, "Accountability Battles," p. 142.

30. Gormley, "Accountability Battles," p. 143.

31. Gormley, "Accountability Battles," 143–44.

32. David B. Spence, "Agency Discretion and the Dynamics of Procedural Reform," 59 *Public Administration Review* 425 (September/October 1999). Also, see generally, Paul Light, *Tides of Reform* (New Haven, Conn.: Yale University Press, 1997).

33. James Thompson, "Reinventing as Reform: Assessing the National Performance Review," 60 *Public Administration Review* 508 (November/December 2000).

34. The information on the ombudsman comes from Larry B. Hill, "The Ombudsman Revisited: Thirty Years of Hawaiian Experience," 62(1) *Public Administration Review* 24 (January/February 2002).

35. Reich, "Policy Making in a Democracy," p.132.

APPENDIX A

Administrative Procedure Act

Material from Parts II and II of Title 5 relating to administrative law judges has been omitted. If you were to actually use the United States Code Annotated, you would see that Subchapter III is really entitled "The Administrative Conference of the United States" (which has been omitted). There are two Subchapter IVs, one on negotiated rule making and the other on alternative disputes resolution. For simplicity, we have presented the index for you as outlined above.

UNITED STATES CODE ANNOTATED

TITLE 5. GOVERNMENT ORGANIZATION AND EMPLOYEES
CHAPTER—ADMINISTRATIVE PROCEDURE

**§ 552. Public Information; Agency Rules,
Opinions, Orders, Records, and Proceedings**

(a) Each agency shall make available to the public information as follows:

(1) Each agency shall separately state and currently publish in the *Federal Register* for the guidance of the public—

(A) descriptions of its central and field organization and the established places at which, the employees (and in the case of a uniformed service, the members) from whom, and the methods whereby, the public may obtain information, make submittals or requests, or obtain decisions;

(B) statements of the general course and method by which its functions are channeled and determined, including the nature and requirements of all formal and informal procedures available;

(C) rules of procedure, descriptions of forms available or the places at which forms may be obtained, and instructions as to the scope and contents of all papers, reports, or examinations;

(D) substantive rules of general applicability adopted as authorized by law, and statements of general policy or interpretations of general applicability formulated and adopted by the agency; and

(E) each amendment, revision, or repeal of the foregoing.

Except to the extent that a person has actual and timely notice of the terms thereof, a person may not in any manner be required to resort to, or be adversely affected by, a matter required to be published in the *Federal Register* and not so published. For the purpose of this paragraph, matter reasonably available to the class of persons affected thereby is deemed published in the *Federal Register* when incorporated by reference therein with the approval of the Director of the *Federal Register.*

(2) Each agency, in accordance with published rules, shall make available for public inspection and copying—

(A) final opinions, including concurring and dissenting opinions, as well as orders, made in the adjudication of cases;

(B) those statements of policy and interpretations which have been adopted by the agency and are not published in the *Federal Register;* and

(C) administrative staff manuals and instructions to staff that affect a member of the public; unless the materials are promptly published and copies offered for sale. To the extent required to prevent a clearly unwarranted invasion of personal privacy, an agency may delete identifying details when it makes available or publishes an opinion, statement of policy, interpretation, or staff manual or instruction. However, in each case the justification for the deletion shall be explained fully in writing. Each agency shall also maintain and make available for public inspection and copying current indexes providing identifying information for the public as to any matter issued, adopted, or promulgated after July 4, 1967, and required by this paragraph to be made available or published. Each agency shall promptly publish, quarterly or more frequently, and distribute (by sale or otherwise) copies of each index or supplements thereto unless it determines by order published in the *Federal Register* that the publication would be unnecessary and impracticable, in which case the agency shall nonetheless provide copies of such index on request at a cost not to exceed the direct cost of duplication. A final order, opinion, statement of policy, interpretation, or staff manual or instruction that affects a member of the public may be relied on, used, or cited as precedent by an agency against a party other than an agency only if—

(i) it has been indexed and either made available or published as provided by this paragraph; or

(ii) the party has actual and timely notice of the terms thereof.

(3) Except with respect to the records made available under paragraphs (1) and (2) of this subsection, each agency, upon any request for records which (A) reasonably describes such records and (B) is made in accordance with published rules stating the time, place, fees (if any), and procedures to be followed, shall make the records promptly available to any person.

(4)(A)(i) In order to carry out the provisions of this section, each agency shall promulgate regulations, pursuant to notice and receipt of public comment, specifying the schedule of fees applicable to the processing of requests under this section and establishing procedures and guidelines for determining when such fees should be waived or reduced. Such schedule shall conform to the guidelines which shall be promulgated, pursuant to notice and receipt of public comment, by the Director of the Office of Management and Budget and which shall provide for a uniform schedule of fees for all agencies.

(ii) Such agency regulations shall provide that—

(I) fees shall be limited to reasonable standard charges for document search, duplication, and review, when records are requested for commercial use;

(II) fees shall be limited to reasonable standard charges for document duplication when records are not sought for commercial use and the request is made by an educational or noncommercial scientific institution, whose purpose is scholarly or scientific research; or a representative of the news media; and

(III) for any request not described in (I) or (II), fees shall be limited to reasonable standard charges for document search and duplication.

(iii) Documents shall be furnished without any charge or at a charge reduced below the fees established under clause (ii) if disclosure of the information is in the public interest because it is likely to contribute significantly to public understanding of the operations or activities of the government and is not primarily in the commercial interest of the requester.

(iv) Fee schedules shall provide for the recovery of only the direct costs of search, duplication, or review. Review costs shall include only the direct costs incurred during the initial examination of a document for the purposes of determining whether the documents must be disclosed under this section and for the purposes of withholding any portions exempt from disclosure under this section. Review costs may not include any costs incurred in resolving issues of law or policy that may be raised in the course of processing a request under this section. No fee may be charged by any agency under this section—

    (I) if the costs of routine collection and processing of the fee are likely to equal or exceed the amount of the fee; or

    (II) for any request described in clause (ii)(II) or (III) of this subparagraph for the first two hours of search time or for the first one hundred pages of duplication.

(v) No agency may require advance payment of any fee unless the requester has previously failed to pay fees in a timely fashion, or the agency has determined that the fee will exceed $250.

(vi) Nothing in this subparagraph shall supersede fees chargeable under a statute specifically providing for setting the level of fees for particular types of records.

(vii) In any action by a requester regarding the waiver of fees under this section, the court shall determine the matter de novo: Provided, that the court's review of the matter shall be limited to the record before the agency.

(B) On complaint, the district court of the United States in the district in which the complainant resides, or has his principal place of business, or in which the agency records are situated, or in the District of Columbia, has jurisdiction to enjoin the agency from withholding agency records and to order the production of any agency records improperly withheld from the complainant. In such a case the court shall determine the matter de novo, and may examine the contents of such agency records in camera to determine whether such records or any part thereof shall be withheld under any of the exemptions set forth in subsection (b) of this section, and the burden is on the agency to sustain its action.

(C) Notwithstanding any other provision of law, the defendant shall serve an answer or otherwise plead to any complaint made under this subsection within thirty days after service upon the defendant of the pleading in which such complaint is made, unless the court otherwise directs for good cause shown.

(D) Repealed. Pub.L. 98–620, Title IV, § 402(2), Nov. 8, 1984, § 98 Stat. 3357

(E) The court may assess against the United States reasonable attorney fees and other litigation costs reasonably incurred in any case under this section in which the complainant has substantially prevailed.

(F) Whenever the court orders the production of any agency records improperly withheld from the complainant and assesses against the United States reasonable attorney fees and other litigation costs, and the court additionally issues a written finding that the circumstances surrounding the withholding raise questions whether agency personnel acted arbitrarily or capriciously with respect to the withholding, the Special Counsel shall promptly initiate a proceeding to determine whether disciplinary action is warranted against the officer or employee who was primarily responsible for the withholding. The Special Counsel, after investigation and consideration of the evidence submitted, shall submit his findings and recommendations to the administrative authority of the agency concerned and shall send copies of the findings and recommendations to the officer or employee or his representative. The administrative authority shall take the corrective action that the Special Counsel recommends.

(G) In the event of noncompliance with the order of the court, the district court may punish for contempt the responsible employee, and in the case of a uniformed service, the responsible member.

(5) Each agency having more than one member shall maintain and make available for public inspection a record of the final votes of each member in every agency proceeding.

(6) (A) Each agency, upon any request for records made under paragraph (1), (2), or (3) of this subsection, shall

(i) determine within ten days (excepting Saturdays, Sundays, and legal public holidays) after the receipt of any such request whether to comply with such request and shall immediately notify the person making such request of such determination and the reasons therefor, and of the right of such person to appeal to the head of the agency any adverse determination; and

(ii) make a determination with respect to any appeal within twenty days (excepting Saturdays, Sundays, and legal public holidays) after the receipt of such appeal. If on appeal the denial of the request for records is in whole or in part upheld, the agency shall notify the person making such request of the provisions for judicial review of that determination under paragraph (4) of this subsection.

(B) In unusual circumstances as specified in this subparagraph, the time limits prescribed in either clause (i) or clause (ii) of subparagraph (A) may be extended by written notice to the person making such request setting forth the reasons for such extension and the date on which a determination is expected to be dispatched. No such notice shall specify a date that would result in an extension for more than ten working days. As used in this subparagraph, "unusual circumstances" means, but only to the extent reasonably necessary to the proper processing of the particular request—

(i) the need to search for and collect the requested records from field facilities or other establishments that are separate from the office processing the request;

(ii) the need to search for, collect, and appropriately examine a voluminous amount of separate and distinct records which are demanded in a single request; or

(iii) the need for consultation, which shall be conducted with all practicable speed, with another agency having a substantial interest in the determination of the request or among two or more components of the agency having substantial subject-matter interest therein.

(C) Any person making a request to any agency for records under paragraph (1), (2), or (3) of this subsection shall be deemed to have exhausted his administrative remedies with respect to such request if the agency fails to comply with the applicable time limit provisions of this paragraph. If the Government can show exceptional circumstances exist and that the agency is exercising due diligence in responding to the request, the court may retain jurisdiction and allow the agency additional time to complete its review of the records. Upon any determination by an agency to comply with a request for records, the records shall be made promptly available to such person making such request. Any notification of denial of any request for records under this subsection shall set forth the names and titles or positions of each person responsible for the denial of such request.

(b) This section does not apply to matters that are—

(1) (A) specifically authorized under criteria established by an executive order to be kept secret in the interest of national defense or foreign policy and (B) are in fact properly classified pursuant to such executive order;

(2) related solely to the internal personnel rules and practices of an agency;

(3) specifically exempted from disclosure by statute (other than section 552b of this title), provided that such statute (A) requires that the matters be withheld from the public in such a manner as to leave no discretion on the issue, or (B) establishes particular criteria for withholding or refers to particular types of matters to be withheld;

(4) trade secrets and commercial or financial information obtained from a person and privileged or confidential;

(5) inter-agency or intra-agency memorandums or letters which would not be available by law to a party other than an agency in litigation with the agency;

(6) personnel and medical files and similar files the disclosure of which would constitute a clearly unwarranted invasion of personal privacy;

(7) records or information compiled for law enforcement purposes, but only to the extent that the production of such law enforcement records or information (A) could reasonably be expected to interfere with enforcement proceedings, (B) would deprive a person of a right to a fair trial or an impartial adjudication, (C) could reasonably be expected to constitute an unwarranted invasion of personal privacy, (D) could reasonably be expected to disclose the identity of a confidential source, including a State, local, or foreign agency or authority or any private institution which furnished information on a confidential basis, and, in the case of a record or information compiled by criminal law enforcement authority in the course of a criminal investigation or by an agency conducting a lawful national security intelligence investigation, information furnished by a confidential source, (E) would disclose techniques and procedures for law enforcement investigations or prosecutions, or would disclose guidelines for

law enforcement investigations or prosecutions if such disclosure could reasonably be expected to risk circumvention of the law, or (F) could reasonably be expected to endanger the life or physical safety of any individual;

(8) contained in or related to examination, operating, or condition reports prepared by, on behalf of, or for the use of an agency responsible for the regulation or supervision of financial institutions; or

(9) geological and geophysical information and data, including maps, concerning wells. Any reasonable segregable portion of a record shall be provided to any person requesting such record after deletion of the portions which are exempt under this subsection.

(c)(1) Whenever a request is made which involves access to records described in subsection (b)(7)(A) and—

(A) the investigation or proceeding involves a possible violation of criminal law; and

(B) there is reason to believe that (i) the subject of the investigation or proceeding is not aware of its pendency, and (ii) disclosure of the existence of the records could reasonably be expected to interfere with enforcement proceedings, the agency may, during only such time as that circumstance continues, treat the records as not subject to the requirements of this section.

(2) Whenever informant records maintained by a criminal law enforcement agency under an informant's name or personal identifier are requested by a third party according to the informant's name or personal identifier, the agency may treat the records as not subject to the requirements of this section unless the informant's status as an informant has been officially confirmed.

(3) Whenever a request is made which involves access to records maintained by the Federal Bureau of Investigation pertaining to foreign intelligence or counterintelligence, or international terrorism, and the existence of the records is classified information as provided in subsection (b)(1), the Bureau may, as long as the existence of the records remains classified information, treat the records as not subject to the requirements of this section.

(d) This section does not authorize withholding of information or limit the availability of records to the public, except as specifically stated in this section. This section is not authority to withhold information from Congress.

(e) On or before March 1 of each calendar year, each agency shall submit a report covering the preceding calendar year to the Speaker of the House of Representatives and President of the Senate for referral to the appropriate committees of the Congress. The report shall include—

(1) the number of determinations made by such agency not to comply with requests for records made to such agency under subsection (a) and the reasons for each such determination;

(2) the number of appeals made by persons under subsection (a)(6), the result of such appeals, and the reason for the action upon each appeal that results in a denial of information;

(3) the names and titles or positions of each person responsible for the denial of records requested under this section, and the number of instances of participation for each;

(4) the results of each proceeding conducted pursuant to subsection (a)(4)(F), including a report of the disciplinary action taken against the officer or employee who was primarily responsible for improperly withholding records or an explanation of why disciplinary action was not taken;

(5) a copy of every rule made by such agency regarding this section;

(6) a copy of the fee schedule and the total amount of fees collected by the agency for making records available under this section; and

(7) such other information as indicates efforts to administer fully this section.

The Attorney General shall submit an annual report on or before March 1 of each calendar year which shall include for the prior calendar year a listing of the number of cases arising under this section, the exemption involved in each case, the disposition of such case, and the cost, fees, and penalties assessed under subsections (a)(4)(E), (F), and (G). Such report shall also include a description of the efforts undertaken by the Department of Justice to encourage agency compliance with this section.

(f) For purposes of this section, the term "agency" as defined in section 551(1) of this title includes any executive department, military department, Government corporation, Government controlled corporation, or other establishment in the executive branch of the Government (including the Executive Office of the President), or any independent regulatory agency.

§ 553. Rule Making

(a) This section applies, according to the provisions thereof, except to the extent that there is involved—

(1) a military or foreign affairs function of the United States; or

(2) a matter relating to agency management or personnel or to public property, loans, grants, benefits, or contracts.

(b) General notice of proposed rule making shall be published in the *Federal Register,* unless persons subject thereto are named and either personally served or otherwise have actual notice thereof in accordance with law. The notice shall include—

(1) a statement of the time, place, and nature of public rule-making proceedings;

(2) reference to the legal authority under which the rule is proposed; and

(3) either the terms or substance of the proposed rule or a description of the subjects and issues involved.

Except when notice or hearing is required by statute, this subsection does not apply—

(A) to interpretative rules, general statements of policy, or rules of agency organization, procedure, or practice; or

(B) when the agency for good cause finds (and incorporates the finding and a brief statement of reasons therefor in the rules issued) that notice and public procedure thereon are impracticable, unnecessary, or contrary to the public interest.

(c) After notice required by this section, the agency shall give interested persons an opportunity to participate in the rule making through submission of written data, views, or arguments with or without opportunity for oral presentation. After consideration of the relevant matter presented, the agency shall incorporate in the rules adopted a concise general statement of their basis and purpose. When rules are required by statute to be made on the record after opportunity for an agency hearing, sections 556 and 557 of this title apply instead of this subsection.

(d) The required publication or service of a substantive rule shall be made not less than 30 days before its effective date, except—

  (1) a substantive rule which grants or recognizes an exemption or relieves a restriction;

  (2) interpretative rules and statements of policy; or

  (3) as otherwise provided by the agency for good cause found and published with the rule.

(e) Each agency shall give an interested person the right to petition for the issuance, amendment, or repeal of a rule.

§ 554. Adjudication

(a) This section applies, according to the provisions thereof, in every case of adjudication required by statute to be determined on the record after opportunity for an agency hearing, except to the extent that there is involved—

  (1) a matter subject to a subsequent trial of the law and the facts de novo in a court;

  (2) the selection or tenure of an employee, except an administrative law judge appointed under section 3105 of this title;

  (3) proceedings in which decisions rest solely on inspections, tests, or elections;

  (4) the conduct of military or foreign affairs functions;

  (5) cases in which an agency is acting as an agent for a court; or

  (6) the certification of worker representatives.

(b) Persons entitled to notice of an agency hearing shall be timely informed of—

  (1) the time, place, and nature of the hearing;

  (2) the legal authority and jurisdiction under which the hearing is to be held; and

  (3) the matters of fact and law asserted.

When private persons are the moving parties, other parties to the proceeding shall give prompt notice of issues controverted in fact or law; and in other instances agencies may by rule require responsive pleading. In fixing the time and place for hearings, due regard shall be had for the convenience and necessity of the parties or their representatives.

(c)   The agency shall give all interested parties opportunity for—

　　(1)   the submission and consideration of facts, arguments, offers of settlement, or proposals of adjustment when time, the nature of the proceeding, and the public interest permit; and

　　(2)   to the extent that the parties are unable so to determine a controversy by consent, hearing and decision on notice and in accordance with sections 556 and 557 of this title.

(d)   The employee who presides at the reception of evidence pursuant to section 556 of this title shall make the recommended decision or initial decision required by section 557 of this title, unless he becomes unavailable to the agency. Except to the extent required for the disposition of ex parte matters as authorized by law, such an employee may not—

　　(1)   consult a person or party on a fact in issue, unless on notice and opportunity for all parties to participate; or

　　(2)   be responsible to or subject to the supervision or direction of an employee or agent engaged in the performance of investigative or prosecuting functions for an agency.

An employee or agent engaged in the performance of investigative or prosecuting functions for an agency in a case may not, in that or a factually related case, participate or advise in the decision, recommended decision, or agency review pursuant to section 557 of this title, except as witness or counsel in public proceedings. This subsection does not apply—

　　(A)   in determining applications for initial licenses;

　　(B)   to proceedings involving the validity or application of rates, facilities, or practices of public utilities or carriers; or

　　(C)   to the agency or a member or members of the body comprising the agency.

(e)   The agency, with like effect as in the case of other orders, and in its sound discretion, may issue a declaratory order to terminate a controversy or remove uncertainty.

§ 555. Ancillary Matters

(a)   This section applies, according to the provisions thereof, except as otherwise provided by this subchapter.

(b)   A person compelled to appear in person before an agency or representative thereof is entitled to be accompanied, represented, and advised by counsel or, if permitted by the agency, by other qualified representative. A party is entitled to appear in person or by or with counsel or other duly qualified representative in an agency proceeding. So far as the orderly conduct of public business permits, an interested person may appear before an agency or its responsible employees for the presentation, adjustment, or determination of an issue, request, or controversy in a proceeding, whether interlocutory, summary, or otherwise, or in connection with an agency function. With due regard for the convenience and necessity of the parties or their representatives and within a reasonable time, each agency shall proceed to conclude a matter presented to it. This subsection does not grant or deny a person who is not a lawyer the right to appear for or represent others before an agency or in an agency proceeding.

(c) Process, requirement of a report, inspection, or other investigative act or demand may not be issued, made, or enforced except as authorized by law. A person compelled to submit data or evidence is entitled to retain or, on payment of lawfully prescribed costs, procure a copy or transcript thereof, except that in a nonpublic investigatory proceeding the witness may for good cause be limited to inspection of the official transcript of his testimony.

(d) Agency subpoenas authorized by law shall be issued to a party on request and, when required by rules of procedure, on a statement or showing of general relevance and reasonable scope of the evidence sought. On contest, the court shall sustain the subpoena or similar process or demand to the extent that it is found to be in accordance with law. In a proceeding for enforcement, the court shall issue an order requiring the appearance of the witness or the production of the evidence or data within a reasonable time under penalty of punishment for contempt in case of contumacious failure to comply.

(e) Prompt notice shall be given of the denial in whole or in part of a written application, petition, or other request of an interested person made in connection with any agency proceeding. Except in affirming a prior denial or when the denial is self-explanatory, the notice shall be accompanied by a brief statement of the grounds for denial.

§ 556. Hearings; Presiding Employees; Powers and Duties; Burden of Proof; Evidence; Record as Basis of Decision

(a) This section applies, according to the provisions thereof, to hearings required by section 553 or 554 of this title to be conducted in accordance with this section.

(b) There shall preside at the taking of evidence—

 (1) the agency;

 (2) one or more members of the body which comprises the agency; or

 (3) one or more administrative law judges appointed under section 3105 of this title.

This subchapter does not supersede the conduct of specified classes of proceedings, in whole or in part, by or before boards or other employees specially provided for by or designated under statute. The functions of presiding employees and of employees participating in decisions in accordance with section 557 of this title shall be conducted in an impartial manner. A presiding or participating employee may at any time disqualify himself. On the filing in good faith of a timely and sufficient affidavit of personal bias or other disqualification of a presiding or participating employee, the agency shall determine the matter as a part of the record and decision in the case.

(c)   Subject to published rules of the agency and within its powers, employees presiding at hearings may—

   (1)   administer oaths and affirmations;

   (2)   issue subpoenas authorized by law;

   (3)   rule on offers of proof and receive relevant evidence;

   (4)   take depositions or have depositions taken when the ends of justice would be served;

   (5)   regulate the course of the hearing;

   (6)   hold conferences for the settlement or simplification of the issues by consent of the parties or by the use of alternative means of dispute resolution as provided in subchapter IV of this chapter;

   (7)   inform the parties as to the availability of one or more alternative means of dispute resolution, and encourage use of such methods;

   (8)   require the attendance at any conference held pursuant to paragraph (6) of at least one representative of each party who has authority to negotiate concerning resolution of issues in controversy;

   (9)   dispose of procedural requests or similar matters;

   (10)   make or recommend decisions in accordance with section 557 of this title; and

   (11)   take other action authorized by agency rule consistent with this subchapter.

(d)   Except as otherwise provided by statute, the proponent of a rule or order has the burden of proof. Any oral or documentary evidence may be received, but the agency as a matter of policy shall provide for the exclusion of irrelevant, immaterial, or unduly repetitious evidence. A sanction may not be imposed or rule or order issued except on consideration of the whole record or those parts thereof cited by a party and supported by and in accordance with the reliable, probative, and substantial evidence. The agency may, to the extent consistent with the interests of justice and the policy of the underlying statutes administered by the agency, consider a violation of section 557(d) of this title sufficient grounds for a decision adverse to a party who has knowingly committed such violation or knowingly caused such violation to occur. A party is entitled to present his case or defense by oral or documentary evidence, to submit rebuttal evidence, and to conduct such cross-examination as may be required for a full and true disclosure of the facts. In rule making or determining claims for money or benefits or applications for initial licenses an agency may, when a party will not be prejudiced thereby, adopt procedures for the submission of all or part of the evidence in written form.

(e)   The transcript of testimony and exhibits, together with all papers and requests filed in the proceeding, constitutes the exclusive record for decision in accordance with section 557 of this title and, on payment of lawfully prescribed costs, shall be made available to the parties. When an agency decision rests on official notice of a material fact not appearing in the evidence in the record, a party is entitled, on timely request, to an opportunity to show the contrary.

§ 557. Initial Decisions; Conclusiveness; Review by Agency; Submissions by Parties; Contents of Decisions; Record

(a) This section applies, according to the provisions thereof, when a hearing is required to be conducted in accordance with section 556 of this title.

(b) When the agency did not preside at the reception of the evidence, the presiding employee or, in cases not subject to section 554(d) of this title, an employee qualified to preside at hearings pursuant to section 556 of this title, shall initially decide the case unless the agency requires, either in specific cases or by general rule, the entire record to be certified to it for decision. When the presiding employee makes an initial decision, that decision then becomes the decision of the agency without further proceedings unless there is an appeal to, or review on motion of, the agency within time provided by rule. On appeal from or review of the initial decision, the agency has all the powers which it would have in making the initial decision except as it may limit the issues on notice or by rule. When the agency makes the decision without having presided at the reception of the evidence, the presiding employee or an employee qualified to preside at hearings pursuant to section 556 of this title shall first recommend a decision, except that in rule making or determining applications for initial licenses—

  (1) instead thereof the agency may issue a tentative decision or one of its responsible employees may recommend a decision; or

  (2) this procedure may be omitted in a case in which the agency finds on the record that due and timely execution of its functions imperatively and unavoidably so requires.

(c) Before a recommended, initial, or tentative decision, or a decision on agency review of the decision of subordinate employees, the parties are entitled to a reasonable opportunity to submit for the consideration of the employees participating in the decisions—

  (1) proposed findings and conclusions; or

  (2) exceptions to the decisions or recommended decisions of subordinate employees or to tentative agency decisions; and

  (3) supporting reasons for the exceptions or proposed findings or conclusions.

The record shall show the ruling on each finding, conclusion, or exception presented. All decisions, including initial, recommended, and tentative decisions, are a part of the record and shall include a statement of—

  (A) findings and conclusions, and the reasons or basis therefor, on all the material issues of fact, law, or discretion presented on the record; and

  (B) the appropriate rule, order, sanction, relief, or denial thereof.

(d)(1)　In any agency proceeding which is subject to subsection (a) of this section, except to the extent required for the disposition of ex parte matters as authorized by law—

(A)　no interested person outside the agency shall make or knowingly cause to be made to any member of the body comprising the agency, administrative law judge, or other employee who is or may reasonably be expected to be involved in the decisional process of the proceeding, an ex parte communication relevant to the merits of the proceeding;

(B)　no member of the body comprising the agency, administrative law judge, or other employee who is or may reasonably be expected to be involved in the decisional process of the proceeding, shall make or knowingly cause to be made to any interested person outside the agency an ex parte communication relevant to the merits of the proceeding;

(C)　a member of the body comprising the agency, administrative law judge, or other employee who is or may reasonably be expected to be involved in the decisional process of such proceeding who receives, or who makes or knowingly causes to be made, a communication prohibited by this subsection shall place on the public record of the proceeding:

(i)　all such written communications;

(ii)　memoranda stating the substance of all such oral communications; and

(iii)　all written responses, and memoranda stating the substance of all oral responses, to the materials described in clauses (i) and (ii) of this subparagraph;

(D)　upon receipt of a communication knowingly made or knowingly caused to be made by a party in violation of this subsection, the agency, administrative law judge, or other employee presiding at the hearing may, to the extent consistent with the interests of justice and the policy of the underlying statutes, require the party to show cause why his claim or interest in the proceeding should not be dismissed, denied, disregarded, or otherwise adversely affected on account of such violation; and

(E)　the prohibitions of this subsection shall apply beginning at such time as the agency may designate, but in no case shall they begin to apply later than the time at which a proceeding is noticed for hearing unless the person responsible for the communication has knowledge that it will be noticed, in which case the prohibitions shall apply beginning at the time of his acquisition of such knowledge.

(2)　This subsection does not constitute authority to withhold information from Congress.

§ 558. Imposition of Sanctions; Determination of Applications for Licenses; Suspension, Revocation and Expiration of Licenses

(a)　This section applies, according to the provisions thereof, to the exercise of a power or authority.

(b) A sanction may not be imposed or a substantive rule or order issued except within jurisdiction delegated to the agency and as authorized by law.

(c) When application is made for a license required by law, the agency, with due regard for the rights and privileges of all the interested parties or adversely affected persons and within a reasonable time, shall set and complete proceedings required to be conducted in accordance with sections 556 and 557 of this title or other proceedings required by law and shall make its decision. Except in cases of willfulness or those in which public health, interest, or safety requires otherwise, the withdrawal, suspension, revocation, or annulment of a license is lawful only if, before the institution of agency proceedings therefor, the licensee has been given—

    (1) notice by the agency in writing of the facts or conduct which may warrant the action; and

    (2) opportunity to demonstrate or achieve compliance with all lawful requirements.

When the licensee has made timely and sufficient application for a renewal or a new license in accordance with agency rules, a license with reference to an activity of a continuing nature does not expire until the application has been finally determined by the agency.

§ 559. Effect on Other Laws; Effect of Subsequent Statute

This subchapter, chapter 7, and sections 1305, 3105, 3344, 4301(2)(E), 5372, and 7521 of this title, and the provisions of section 5335(a)(B) of this title that relate to administrative law judges, do not limit or repeal additional requirements imposed by statute or otherwise recognized by law. Except as otherwise required by law, requirements or privileges relating to evidence or procedure apply equally to agencies and persons. Each agency is granted the authority necessary to comply with the requirements of this subchapter through the issuance of rules or otherwise. Subsequent statute may not be held to supersede or modify this subchapter, chapter 7, sections 1305, 3105, 3344, 4301(2)(E), 5372, or 7521 of this title, or the provisions of section 5335(a)(B) of this title that relate to administrative law judges, except to the extent that it does so expressly.

TITLE 5. GOVERNMENT ORGANIZATION AND EMPLOYEES

PART I—THE AGENCIES GENERALLY

CHAPTER 5—ADMINISTRATIVE PROCEDURE

SUBCHAPTER III—NEGOTIATED RULE-MAKING PROCEDURE

§ 564. Publication of Notice; Application for Membership on Committees

(a) Publication of notice.—If, after considering the report of a convener or conducting its own assessment, an agency decides to establish a negotiated rule-making committee, the agency shall publish in the *Federal Register* and, as appropriate, in trade or other specialized publications, a notice which shall include—

    (1) an announcement that the agency intends to establish a negotiated rule-making committee to negotiate and develop a proposed rule;

(2)   a description of the subject and scope of the rule to be developed, and the issues to be considered;

(3)   a list of the interests which are likely to be significantly affected by the rule;

(4)   a list of the persons proposed to represent such interests and the person or persons proposed to represent the agency;

(5)   a proposed agenda and schedule for completing the work of the committee, including a target date for publication by the agency of a proposed rule for notice and comment;

(6)   a description of administrative support for the committee to be provided by the agency, including technical assistance;

(7)   a solicitation for comments on the proposal to establish the committee, and the proposed membership of the negotiated rule-making committee; and

(8)   an explanation of how a person may apply or nominate another person for membership on the committee, as provided under subsection (b).

(b)   Applications for membership or committee.—Persons who will be significantly affected by a proposed rule and who believe that their interests will not be adequately represented by any person specified in a notice under subsection (a)(4) may apply for, or nominate another person for, membership on the negotiated rule-making committee to represent such interests with respect to the proposed rule. Each application or nomination shall include—

(1)   the name of the applicant or nominee and a description of the interests such person shall represent;

(2)   evidence that the applicant or nominee is authorized to represent parties related to the interests the person proposes to represent;

(3)   a written commitment that the applicant or nominee shall actively participate in good faith in the development of the rule under consideration; and

(4)   the reasons that the persons specified in the notice under subsection (a)(4) do not adequately represent the interests of the person submitting the application or nomination.

(c)   Period for submission of comments and applications.—The agency shall provide for a period of at least 30 calendar days for the submission of comments and applications under this section.

§ 565. Establishment of Committee

(a)   Establishment.—

(1)   Determination to establish committee.—If after considering comments and applications submitted under section 564, the agency determines that a negotiated rule-making committee can adequately represent the interests that will be significantly affected by a proposed rule and that it is feasible and appropriate in the particular rule-making, the agency may establish a negotiated rule-making committee. In establishing and administering such a committee, the agency

shall comply with the Federal Advisory Committee Act with respect to such committee, except as otherwise provided in this subchapter.

(2) Determination not to establish committee.—If after considering such comments and applications, the agency decides not to establish a negotiated rule-making committee, the agency shall promptly publish notice of such decision and the reasons therefor in the *Federal Register* and, as appropriate, in trade or other specialized publications, a copy of which shall be sent to any person who applied for, or nominated another person for, membership on the negotiated rule-making committee to represent such interests with respect to the proposed rule.

(b) Membership.—The agency shall limit membership on a negotiated rule-making committee to 25 members, unless the agency head determines that a greater number of members is necessary for the functioning of the committee or to achieve balanced membership. Each committee shall include at least one person representing the agency.

(c) Administrative Support.—The agency shall provide appropriate administrative support to the negotiated rule-making committee, including technical assistance.

§ 566. Conduct of Committee Activity

(a) Duties of Committee.—Each negotiated rule-making committee established under this subchapter shall consider the matter proposed by the agency for consideration and shall attempt to reach a consensus concerning a proposed rule with respect to such matter and any other matter the committee determines is relevant to the proposed rule.

(b) Representatives of Agency on Committee.—The person or persons representing the agency on a negotiated rule-making committee shall participate in the deliberations and activities of the committee with the same rights and responsibilities as other members of the committee, and shall be authorized to fully represent the agency in the discussions and negotiations of the committee.

(c) Selecting Facilitator.—Notwithstanding section 10(e) of the Federal Advisory Committee Act, an agency may nominate either a person from the Federal Government or a person from outside the Federal Government to serve as a facilitator for the negotiations of the committee, subject to the approval of the committee by consensus. If the committee does not approve the nominee of the agency for facilitator, the agency shall submit a substitute nomination. If a committee does not approve any nominee of the agency for facilitator, the committee shall select by consensus a person to serve as facilitator. A person designated to represent the agency in substantive issues may not serve as facilitator or otherwise chair the committee.

(d) Duties of Facilitator.—A facilitator approved or selected by a negotiated rule-making committee shall—

(1) chair the meetings of the committee in an impartial manner;

(2) impartially assist the members of the committee in conducting discussions and negotiations; and

(3) manage the keeping of minutes and records as required under section 10(b) and (c) of the Federal Advisory Committee Act, except that any personal notes and materials of the facilitator or of the members of a committee shall not be subject to section 552 of this title.

(e) Committee Procedures.—A negotiated rule-making committee established under this subchapter may adopt procedures for the operation of the committee. No provision of section 553 of this title shall apply to the procedures of a negotiated rule-making committee.

(f) Report of Committee.—If a committee reaches a consensus on a proposed rule, at the conclusion of negotiations the committee shall transmit to the agency that established the committee a report containing the proposed rule. If the committee does not reach a consensus on a proposed rule, the committee may transmit to the agency a report specifying any areas in which the committee reached a consensus. The committee may include in a report any other information, recommendations, or materials that the committee considers appropriate. Any committee member may include as an addendum to the report additional information, recommendations, or materials.

(g) Records of Committee.—In addition to the report required by subsection (f), a committee shall submit to the agency the records required under section 10(b) and (c) of the Federal Advisory Committee Act.

§ 567. Termination of Committee

A negotiated rule-making committee shall terminate upon promulgation of the final rule under consideration, unless the committee's charter contains an earlier termination date or the agency, after consulting the committee, or the committee itself specifies an earlier termination date.

§ 568. Services, Facilities, and Payment of Committee Member Expenses

(a) Services of Conveners and Facilitators.—

(1) In general.—An agency may employ or enter into contracts for the services of an individual or organization to serve as a convener or facilitator for a negotiated rule-making committee under this subchapter, or may use the services of a Government employee to act as a convener or a facilitator for such a committee.

(2) Determination of conflicting interests.—An agency shall determine whether a person under consideration to serve as convener or facilitator of a committee under paragraph (1) has any financial or other interest that would preclude such person from serving in an impartial and independent manner.

(b) Services and Facilities of Other Entities.—For purposes of this subchapter, an agency may use the services and facilities of other Federal agencies and public and private agencies and instrumentalities with the consent of such agencies and instrumentalities, and with or without reimbursement to such agencies and instrumentalities, and may accept voluntary and uncompensated services without regard to the provisions of section 1342 of title 31. The Federal Mediation and Conciliation Service may provide services and facilities, with or without reimbursement, to assist agencies under this subchapter, including furnishing conveners, facilitators, and training in negotiated rule making.

(c) Expenses of Committee Members.—Members of a negotiated rule-making committee shall be responsible for their own expenses of participation in such committee, except that an agency may, in accordance with section 7(d) of the Federal Advisory Committee Act, pay for a member's reasonable travel and per diem expenses, expenses to obtain technical assistance, and a reasonable rate of compensation, if—

(1) such member certifies a lack of adequate financial resources to participate in the committee; and

(2) the agency determines that such member's participation in the committee is necessary to assure an adequate representation of the member's interest.

(d) Status of Member as Federal Employee.—A member's receipt of funds under this section or section 569 shall not conclusively determine for purposes of sections 202 through 209 of title 18 whether that member is an employee of the United States Government.

§ 569. Role of the Administrative Conference of the United States and Other Entities

(a) Consultation by Agencies.—An agency may consult with the Administrative Conference of the United States or other public or private individuals or organizations for information and assistance in forming a negotiated rule-making committee and conducting negotiations on a proposed rule.

(b) Roster of Potential Conveners and Facilitators.—The Administrative Conference of the United States, in consultation with the Federal Mediation and Conciliation Service, shall maintain a roster of individuals who have acted as or are interested in serving as conveners or facilitators in negotiated rule-making proceedings. The roster shall include individuals from government agencies and private groups, and shall be made available upon request. Agencies may also use rosters maintained by other public or private individuals or organizations.

(c) Procedures to Obtain Conveners and Facilitators.—

(1) Procedures.—The Administrative Conference of the United States shall develop procedures which permit agencies to obtain the services of conveners and facilitators on an expedited basis.

(2) Payment for services.—Payment for the services of conveners or facilitators shall be made by the agency using the services, unless the Chairman of the Administrative Conference agrees to pay for such services under subsection (f).

(d)   Compilation of Data on Negotiated Rule-making; Report to Congress.—

    (1)   Compilation of data.—The Administrative Conference of the United States shall compile and maintain data related to negotiated rule-making and shall act as a clearinghouse to assist agencies and parties participating in negotiated rule-making proceedings.

    (2)   Submission of information by agencies.—Each agency engaged in negotiated rule-making shall provide to the Administrative Conference of the United States a copy of any reports submitted to the agency by negotiated rule-making committees under section 566 and such additional information as necessary to enable the Administrative Conference of the United States to comply with this subsection.

    (3)   Reports to congress.—The Administrative Conference of the United States shall review and analyze the reports and information received under this subsection and shall transmit a biennial report to the Committee on Governmental Affairs of the Senate and the appropriate committees of the House of Representatives that—

        (A)   provides recommendations for effective use by agencies of negotiated rule making; and

        (B)   describes the nature and amounts of expenditures made by the Administrative Conference of the United States to accomplish the purposes of this subchapter.

(e)   Training in Negotiated Rule Making.—The Administrative Conference of the United States is authorized to provide training in negotiated rule-making techniques and procedures for personnel of the Federal Government either on a reimbursable or non-reimbursable basis. Such training may be extended to private individuals on a reimbursable basis.

(f)   Payment of Expenses of Agencies.—The Chairman of the Administrative Conference of the United States is authorized to pay, upon request of an agency, all or part of the expenses of establishing a negotiated rule-making committee and conducting a negotiated rule making. Such expenses may include, but are not limited to—

    (1)   the costs of conveners and facilitators;

    (2)   the expenses of committee members determined by the agency to be eligible for assistance under section 568(c); and

    (3)   training costs.

Determinations with respect to payments under this section shall be at the discretion of such Chairman in furthering the use by Federal agencies of negotiated rule making.

(g)   Use of Funds of the Conference.—The Administrative Conference of the United States may apply funds received under section 595(c)(12) of this title to carry out the purposes of this subchapter.

§ 570. Judicial Review

Any agency action relating to establishing, assisting, or terminating a negotiated rule-making committee under this subchapter shall not be subject to judicial review. Nothing in this section shall bar judicial review of a rule if such judicial review is otherwise provided by law. A rule which is the product of negotiated rule making and is subject to judicial review shall not be accorded any greater deference by a court than a rule which is the product of other rule-making procedures.

TITLE 5.

GOVERNMENT ORGANIZATION AND EMPLOYEES

PART I—THE AGENCIES GENERALLY

CHAPTER 7—JUDICIAL REVIEW

§ 701. Application; Definitions

(a)   This chapter applies, according to the provisions thereof, except to the extent that—

(1)   statutes preclude judicial review; or

(2)   agency action is committed to agency discretion by law.

(b)   For the purpose of this chapter—

(1)   "agency" means each authority of the Government of the United States, whether or not it is within or subject to review by another agency, but does not include—

(A)   the Congress;

(B)   the courts of the United States;

(C)   the governments of the territories or possessions of the United States;

(D)   the government of the District of Columbia;

(E)   agencies composed of representatives of the parties or of representatives of organizations of the parties to the disputes determined by them;

(F)   court martial and military commissions;

(G)   military authority exercised in the field in time of war or in occupied territory; or

(H)   functions conferred by sections 1738, 1739, 1743, and 1744 of title 12; chapter 2 of title 41; or sections 1622, 1884, 1891–1902, and former section 1641(b)(2), of title 50, appendix; and

(2)   "person," "rule," "order," "license," "sanction," "relief," and "agency action" have the meanings given them by section 551 of this title.

§ 702. Right of Review

A person suffering legal wrong because of agency action, or adversely affected or aggrieved by agency action within the meaning of a relevant statute, is entitled to judicial review thereof. An action in a court of the United States seeking relief other than money damages and stating a claim that an agency or an officer or employee thereof acted or failed to act in an official capacity or under color of legal authority shall not be dismissed nor relief therein be denied on the ground that it is against the United States or that the United States is an indispensable party. The United States may be named as a defendant in any such action, and a judgment or decree may be entered against the United States: Provided, that any mandatory or injunctive decree shall specify the Federal officer or officers (by name or by title), and their successors in office, personally responsible for compliance. Nothing herein (1) affects other limitations on judicial review or the power or duty of the court to dismiss any action or deny relief on any other appropriate legal or equitable ground; or (2) confers authority to grant relief if any other statute that grants consent to suit expressly or impliedly forbids the relief which is sought.

§ 703. Form and Venue of Proceeding

The form of proceeding for judicial review is the special statutory review proceeding relevant to the subject matter in a court specified by statute or, in the absence or inadequacy thereof, any applicable form of legal action, including actions for declaratory judgments or writs of prohibitory or mandatory injunction or habeas corpus, in a court of competent jurisdiction. If no special statutory review proceeding is applicable, the action for judicial review may be brought against the United States, the agency by its official title, or the appropriate officer. Except to the extent that prior, adequate, and exclusive opportunity for judicial review is provided by law, agency action is subject to judicial review in civil or criminal proceedings for judicial enforcement.

§ 704. Actions Reviewable

Agency action made reviewable by statute and final agency action for which there is no other adequate remedy in a court are subject to judicial review. A preliminary, procedural, or intermediate agency action or ruling not directly reviewable is subject to review on the review of the final agency action. Except as otherwise expressly required by statute, agency action otherwise final is final for the purposes of this section whether or not there has been presented or determined an application for a declaratory order, for any form of reconsideration, or, unless the agency otherwise requires by rule and provides that the action meanwhile is inoperative, for an appeal to superior agency.

§ 705. Relief Pending Review

When an agency finds that justice so requires, it may postpone the effective date of action taken by it, pending judicial review. On such conditions as may be required and to the extent necessary to prevent irreparable injury, the reviewing court, including the court to which a case may be taken on appeal from or on application for certiorari or other writ to a reviewing court, may issue all necessary and appropriate process to postpone the effective date of an agency action or to preserve status or rights pending conclusion of the review proceedings.

§ 706. Scope of Review

To the extent necessary to decision and when presented, the reviewing court shall decide all relevant questions of law, interpret constitutional and statutory provisions, and determine the meaning or applicability of the terms of an agency action. The reviewing court shall—

(1)   compel agency action unlawfully withheld or unreasonably delayed; and

(2)   hold unlawful and set aside agency action, findings, and conclusions found to be—

(A)   arbitrary, capricious, an abuse of discretion, or otherwise not in accordance with law;

(B)   contrary to constitutional right, power, privilege, or immunity;

(C)   in excess of statutory jurisdiction, authority, or limitations, or short of statutory right;

(D)   without observance of procedure required by law;

(E)   unsupported by substantial evidence in a case subject to sections 556 and 557 of this title or otherwise reviewed on the record of an agency hearing provided by statute; or

(F)   unwarranted by the facts to the extent that the facts are subject to trial de novo by the reviewing court.

In making the foregoing determinations, the court shall review the whole record or those parts of it cited by a party, and due account shall be taken of the rule of prejudicial error.

APPENDIX B

The United States Constitution

We the People of the United States, in Order to form a more perfect Union, establish Justice, insure domestic Tranquility, provide for the common defence, promote the general Welfare, and secure the Blessings of Liberty to ourselves and our Posterity, do ordain and establish this Constitution for the United States of America.

Article I.

Section 1

All legislative Powers herein granted shall be vested in a Congress of the United States, which shall consist of a Senate and House of Representatives.

Section 2

Clause 1: The House of Representatives shall be composed of Members chosen every second Year by the People of the several States, and the Electors in each State shall have the Qualifications requisite for Electors of the most numerous Branch of the State Legislature.

Clause 2: No Person shall be a Representative who shall not have attained to the Age of twenty five Years, and been seven Years a Citizen of the United States, and who shall not, when elected, be an Inhabitant of that State in which he shall be chosen.

Clause 3: Representatives and direct Taxes shall be apportioned among the several States which may be included within this Union, according to their respective Numbers, which shall be determined by adding to the whole Number of free Persons, including those bound to Service for a Term of Years, and excluding Indians not taxed, three fifths of all other Persons. *(See Note 2)* The actual Enumeration shall be made within three Years after the first Meeting of the Congress of the United States, and within every subsequent Term of ten Years, in such Manner as they shall by Law direct. The Number of Representatives shall not exceed one for every thirty Thousand, but each State shall have at Least one Representative; and until such enumeration shall be made, the State of New Hampshire shall be entitled to chuse three, Massachusetts eight, Rhode-Island and Providence Plantations one, Connecticut five, New-York six, New Jersey four, Pennsylvania eight, Delaware one, Maryland six, Virginia ten, North Carolina five, South Carolina five, and Georgia three.

Clause 4: When vacancies happen in the Representation from any State, the Executive Authority thereof shall issue Writs of Election to fill such Vacancies.

Clause 5: The House of Representatives shall chuse their Speaker and other Officers; and shall have the sole Power of Impeachment.

Section 3

Clause 1: The Senate of the United States shall be composed of two Senators from each State, chosen by the Legislature thereof, *(See Note 3)* for six Years; and each Senator shall have one Vote.

Clause 2: Immediately after they shall be assembled in Consequence of the first Election, they shall be divided as equally as may be into three Classes. The Seats of the Senators of the first Class shall be vacated at the Expiration of the second Year, of the second Class at the Expiration of the fourth Year, and of the third Class at the Expiration of the sixth Year, so that one third may be chosen every second Year; and if Vacancies happen by Resignation, or otherwise, during the Recess of the Legislature of any State, the Executive thereof may make temporary Appointments until the next Meeting of the Legislature, which shall then fill such Vacancies. *(See Note 4)*

Clause 3: No Person shall be a Senator who shall not have attained to the Age of thirty Years, and been nine Years a Citizen of the United States, and who shall not, when elected, be an Inhabitant of that State for which he shall be chosen.

Clause 4: The Vice President of the United States shall be President of the Senate, but shall have no Vote, unless they be equally divided.

Clause 5: The Senate shall chuse their other Officers, and also a President pro tempore, in the Absence of the Vice President, or when he shall exercise the Office of President of the United States.

Clause 6: The Senate shall have the sole Power to try all Impeachments. When sitting for that Purpose, they shall be on Oath or Affirmation. When the President of the United States is tried, the Chief Justice shall preside: And no Person shall be convicted without the Concurrence of two thirds of the Members present.

Clause 7: Judgment in Cases of Impeachment shall not extend further than to removal from Office, and disqualification to hold and enjoy any Office of honor, Trust or Profit under the United States: but the Party convicted shall nevertheless be liable and subject to Indictment, Trial, Judgment and Punishment, according to Law.

Section 4

Clause 1: The Times, Places and Manner of holding Elections for Senators and Representatives, shall be prescribed in each State by the Legislature thereof; but the Congress may at any time by Law make or alter such Regulations, except as to the Places of chusing Senators.

Clause 2: The Congress shall assemble at least once in every Year, and such Meeting shall be on the first Monday in December, *(See Note 5)* unless they shall by Law appoint a different Day.

Section 5

Clause 1: Each House shall be the Judge of the Elections, Returns and Qualifications of its own Members, and a Majority of each shall constitute a Quorum to do Business; but a smaller Number may adjourn from day to day, and may be authorized to compel the Attendance of absent Members, in such Manner, and under such Penalties as each House may provide.

Clause 2: Each House may determine the Rules of its Proceedings, punish its Members for disorderly Behaviour, and, with the Concurrence of two thirds, expel a Member.

Clause 3: Each House shall keep a Journal of its Proceedings, and from time to time publish the same, excepting such Parts as may in their Judgment require Secrecy; and the Yeas and Nays of the Members of either House on any question shall, at the Desire of one fifth of those Present, be entered on the Journal.

Clause 4: Neither House, during the Session of Congress, shall, without the Consent of the other, adjourn for more than three days, nor to any other Place than that in which the two Houses shall be sitting.

Section 6

Clause 1: The Senators and Representatives shall receive a Compensation for their Services, to be ascertained by Law, and paid out of the Treasury of the United States. *(See Note 6)* They shall in all Cases, except Treason, Felony and Breach of the Peace, be privileged from Arrest during their Attendance at the Session of their respective Houses, and in going to and returning from the same; and for any Speech or Debate in either House, they shall not be questioned in any other Place.

Clause 2: No Senator or Representative shall, during the Time for which he was elected, be appointed to any civil Office under the Authority of the United States, which shall have been created, or the Emoluments whereof shall have been encreased during such time; and no Person holding any Office under the United States, shall be a Member of either House during his Continuance in Office.

Section 7

Clause 1: All Bills for raising Revenue shall originate in the House of Representatives; but the Senate may propose or concur with Amendments as on other Bills.

Clause 2: Every Bill which shall have passed the House of Representatives and the Senate, shall, before it become a Law, be presented to the President of the United States; If he approve he shall sign it, but if not he shall return it, with his Objections to that House in which it shall have originated, who shall enter the Objections at large on their Journal, and proceed to reconsider it. If after such Reconsideration two thirds of that House shall agree to pass the Bill, it shall be sent, together with the Objections, to the other House, by which it shall likewise be reconsidered, and if approved by two thirds of that House, it shall become a Law. But in all such Cases the Votes of both Houses shall be determined by yeas and Nays, and the Names of the Persons voting for and against the Bill shall be entered on the Journal of each House respectively. If any Bill shall not be returned by the President within ten Days (Sundays excepted) after it shall have been presented to him, the Same shall be a Law, in like Manner as if he had signed it, unless the Congress by their Adjournment prevent its Return, in which Case it shall not be a Law.

Clause 3: Every Order, Resolution, or Vote to which the Concurrence of the Senate and House of Representatives may be necessary (except on a question of Adjournment) shall be presented to the President of the United States; and before the Same shall take Effect, shall be approved by him, or being disapproved by him, shall be repassed by two thirds of the Senate and House of Representatives, according to the Rules and Limitations prescribed in the Case of a Bill.

Section 8

Clause 1: The Congress shall have Power To lay and collect Taxes, Duties, Imposts and Excises, to pay the Debts and provide for the common Defence and general Welfare of the United States; but all Duties, Imposts and Excises shall be uniform throughout the United States;

Clause 2: To borrow Money on the credit of the United States;

Clause 3: To regulate Commerce with foreign Nations, and among the several States, and with the Indian Tribes;

Clause 4: To establish an uniform Rule of Naturalization, and uniform Laws on the subject of Bankruptcies throughout the United States;

Clause 5: To coin Money, regulate the Value thereof, and of foreign Coin, and fix the Standard of Weights and Measures;

Clause 6: To provide for the Punishment of counterfeiting the Securities and current Coin of the United States;

Clause 7: To establish Post Offices and post Roads;

Clause 8: To promote the Progress of Science and useful Arts, by securing for limited Times to Authors and Inventors the exclusive Right to their respective Writings and Discoveries;

Clause 9: To constitute Tribunals inferior to the supreme Court;

Clause 10: To define and punish Piracies and Felonies committed on the high Seas, and Offences against the Law of Nations;

Clause 11: To declare War, grant Letters of Marque and Reprisal, and make Rules concerning Captures on Land and Water;

Clause 12: To raise and support Armies, but no Appropriation of Money to that Use shall be for a longer Term than two Years;

Clause 13: To provide and maintain a Navy;

Clause 14: To make Rules for the Government and Regulation of the land and naval Forces;

Clause 15: To provide for calling forth the Militia to execute the Laws of the Union, suppress Insurrections and repel Invasions;

Clause 16: To provide for organizing, arming, and disciplining, the Militia, and for governing such Part of them as may be employed in the Service of the United States, reserving to the States respectively, the Appointment of the Officers, and the Authority of training the Militia according to the discipline prescribed by Congress;

Clause 17: To exercise exclusive Legislation in all Cases whatsoever, over such District (not exceeding ten Miles square) as may, by Cession of particular States, and the Acceptance of Congress, become the Seat of the Government of the United States, and to exercise like Authority over all Places purchased by the Consent of the Legislature of the State in which the Same shall be, for the Erection of Forts, Magazines, Arsenals, dock-Yards, and other needful Buildings;—And

Clause 18: To make all Laws which shall be necessary and proper for carrying into Execution the foregoing Powers, and all other Powers vested by this Constitution in the Government of the United States, or in any Department or Officer thereof.

Section 9

Clause 1: The Migration or Importation of such Persons as any of the States now existing shall think proper to admit, shall not be prohibited by the Congress prior to the Year one thousand eight hundred and eight, but a Tax or duty may be imposed on such Importation, not exceeding ten dollars for each Person.

Clause 2: The Privilege of the Writ of Habeas Corpus shall not be suspended, unless when in Cases of Rebellion or Invasion the public Safety may require it.

Clause 3: No Bill of Attainder or ex post facto Law shall be passed.

Clause 4: No Capitation, or other direct, Tax shall be laid, unless in Proportion to the Census or Enumeration herein before directed to be taken. *(See Note 7)*

Clause 5: No Tax or Duty shall be laid on Articles exported from any State.

Clause 6: No Preference shall be given by any Regulation of Commerce or Revenue to the Ports of one State over those of another: nor shall Vessels bound to, or from, one State, be obliged to enter, clear, or pay Duties in another.

Clause 7: No Money shall be drawn from the Treasury, but in Consequence of Appropriations made by Law; and a regular Statement and Account of the Receipts and Expenditures of all public Money shall be published from time to time.

Clause 8: No Title of Nobility shall be granted by the United States: And no Person holding any Office of Profit or Trust under them, shall, without the Consent of the Congress, accept of any present, Emolument, Office, or Title, of any kind whatever, from any King, Prince, or foreign State.

Section 10

Clause 1: No State shall enter into any Treaty, Alliance, or Confederation; grant Letters of Marque and Reprisal; coin Money; emit Bills of Credit; make any Thing but gold and silver Coin a Tender in Payment of Debts; pass any Bill of Attainder, ex post facto Law, or Law impairing the Obligation of Contracts, or grant any Title of Nobility.

Clause 2: No State shall, without the Consent of the Congress, lay any Imposts or Duties on Imports or Exports, except what may be absolutely necessary for executing it's inspection Laws: and the net Produce of all Duties and Imposts, laid by any State on Imports or Exports, shall be for the Use of the Treasury of the United States; and all such Laws shall be subject to the Revision and Controul of the Congress.

Clause 3: No State shall, without the Consent of Congress, lay any Duty of Tonnage, keep Troops, or Ships of War in time of Peace, enter into any Agreement or Compact with another State, or with a foreign Power, or engage in War, unless actually invaded, or in such imminent Danger as will not admit of delay.

Article II.

Section 1

Clause 1: The executive Power shall be vested in a President of the United States of America. He shall hold his Office during the Term of four Years, and, together with the Vice President, chosen for the same Term, be elected, as follows

Clause 2: Each State shall appoint, in such Manner as the Legislature thereof may direct, a Number of Electors, equal to the whole Number of Senators and Representatives to which the State may be entitled in the Congress: but no Senator or Representative, or Person holding an Office of Trust or Profit under the United States, shall be appointed an Elector.

Clause 3: The Electors shall meet in their respective States, and vote by Ballot for two Persons, of whom one at least shall not be an Inhabitant of the same State with themselves. And they shall make a List of all the Persons voted for, and of the Number of Votes for each; which List they shall sign and certify, and transmit sealed to the Seat of the Government of the United States, directed to the President of the Senate. The President of the Senate shall, in the Presence of the Senate and House of Representatives, open all the Certificates, and the Votes shall then be counted. The Person having the greatest Number of Votes shall be the President, if such Number be a Majority of the whole Number of Electors appointed; and if there be more than one who have such Majority, and have an equal Number of Votes, then the House of Representatives shall immediately chuse by Ballot one of them for President; and if no Person have a Majority, then from the five highest on the List the said House shall in like Manner chuse the President. But in chusing the President, the Votes shall be taken by States, the Representation from each State having one Vote; A quorum for this Purpose shall consist of a Member or Members from two thirds of the States, and a Majority of all the States shall be necessary to a Choice. In every Case, after the Choice of the President, the Person having the greatest Number of Votes of the Electors shall be the Vice President. But if there should remain two or more who have equal Votes, the Senate shall chuse from them by Ballot the Vice President. *(See Note 8)*

Clause 4: The Congress may determine the Time of chusing the Electors, and the Day on which they shall give their Votes; which Day shall be the same throughout the United States.

Clause 5: No Person except a natural born Citizen, or a Citizen of the United States, at the time of the Adoption of this Constitution, shall be eligible to the Office of President; neither shall any Person be eligible to that Office who shall not have attained to the Age of thirty five Years, and been fourteen Years a Resident within the United States.

Clause 6: In Case of the Removal of the President from Office, or of his Death, Resignation, or Inability to discharge the Powers and Duties of the said Office, *(See Note 9)* the Same shall devolve on the Vice President, and the Congress may by Law provide for the Case of Removal, Death, Resignation or Inability, both of the President and Vice President, declaring what Officer shall then act as President, and such Officer shall act accordingly, until the Disability be removed, or a President shall be elected.

Clause 7: The President shall, at stated Times, receive for his Services, a Compensation, which shall neither be encreased nor diminished during the Period for which he shall have been elected, and he shall not receive within that Period any other Emolument from the United States, or any of them.

Clause 8: Before he enter on the Execution of his Office, he shall take the following Oath or Affirmation:—"I do solemnly swear (or affirm) that I will faithfully execute the Office of President of the United States, and will to the best of my Ability, preserve, protect and defend the Constitution of the United States."

Section 2

Clause 1: The President shall be Commander in Chief of the Army and Navy of the United States, and of the Militia of the several States, when called into the actual Service of the United States; he may require the Opinion, in writing, of the principal Officer in each of the executive Departments, upon any Subject relating to the Duties of their respective Offices, and he shall have Power to grant Reprieves and Pardons for Offences against the United States, except in Cases of Impeachment.

Clause 2: He shall have Power, by and with the Advice and Consent of the Senate, to make Treaties, provided two thirds of the Senators present concur; and he shall nominate, and by and with the Advice and Consent of the Senate, shall appoint Ambassadors, other public Ministers and Consuls, Judges of the supreme Court, and all other Officers of the United States, whose Appointments are not herein otherwise provided for, and which shall be established by Law: but the Congress may by Law vest the Appointment of such inferior Officers, as they think proper, in the President alone, in the Courts of Law, or in the Heads of Departments.

Clause 3: The President shall have Power to fill up all Vacancies that may happen during the Recess of the Senate, by granting Commissions which shall expire at the End of their next Session.

Section 3

He shall from time to time give to the Congress Information of the State of the Union, and recommend to their Consideration such Measures as he shall judge necessary and expedient; he may, on extraordinary Occasions, convene both Houses, or either of them, and in Case of Disagreement between them, with Respect to the Time of Adjournment, he may adjourn them to such Time as he shall think proper; he shall receive Ambassadors and other public Ministers; he shall take Care that the Laws be faithfully executed, and shall Commission all the Officers of the United States.

Section 4

The President, Vice President and all civil Officers of the United States, shall be removed from Office on Impeachment for, and Conviction of, Treason, Bribery, or other high Crimes and Misdemeanors.

Article III

Section 1

The judicial Power of the United States, shall be vested in one supreme Court, and in such inferior Courts as the Congress may from time to time ordain and establish. The Judges, both of the supreme and inferior Courts, shall hold their Offices during good Behaviour, and shall, at stated Times, receive for their Services, a Compensation, which shall not be diminished during their Continuance in Office.

Section 2

Clause 1: The judicial Power shall extend to all Cases, in Law and Equity, arising under this Constitution, the Laws of the United States, and Treaties made, or which shall be made, under their Authority;—to all Cases affecting Ambassadors, other public Ministers and Consuls;—to all Cases of admiralty and maritime Jurisdiction;—to Controversies to which the United States shall be a Party;—to Controversies between two or more States;—between a State and Citizens of another State; *(See Note 10)*—between Citizens of different States,—between Citizens of the same State claiming Lands under Grants of different States, and between a State, or the Citizens thereof, and foreign States, Citizens or Subjects.

Clause 2: In all Cases affecting Ambassadors, other public Ministers and Consuls, and those in which a State shall be Party, the supreme Court shall have original Jurisdiction. In all the other Cases before mentioned, the supreme Court shall have appellate Jurisdiction, both as to Law and Fact, with such Exceptions, and under such Regulations as the Congress shall make.

Clause 3: The Trial of all Crimes, except in Cases of Impeachment, shall be by Jury; and such Trial shall be held in the State where the said Crimes shall have been committed; but when not committed within any State, the Trial shall be at such Place or Places as the Congress may by Law have directed.

Section 3

Clause 1: Treason against the United States, shall consist only in levying War against them, or in adhering to their Enemies, giving them Aid and Comfort. No Person shall be convicted of Treason unless on the Testimony of two Witnesses to the same overt Act, or on Confession in open Court.

Clause 2: The Congress shall have Power to declare the Punishment of Treason, but no Attainder of Treason shall work Corruption of Blood, or Forfeiture except during the Life of the Person attainted.

Article IV

Section 1

Full Faith and Credit shall be given in each State to the public Acts, Records, and judicial Proceedings of every other State. And the Congress may by general Laws prescribe the Manner in which such Acts, Records and Proceedings shall be proved, and the Effect thereof.

Section 2

Clause 1: The Citizens of each State shall be entitled to all Privileges and Immunities of Citizens in the several States.

Clause 2: A Person charged in any State with Treason, Felony, or other Crime, who shall flee from Justice, and be found in another State, shall on Demand of the executive Authority of the State from which he fled, be delivered up, to be removed to the State having Jurisdiction of the Crime.

Clause 3: No Person held to Service or Labour in one State, under the Laws thereof, escaping into another, shall, in Consequence of any Law or Regulation therein, be discharged from such Service or Labour, but shall be delivered up on Claim of the Party to whom such Service or Labour may be due. *(See Note 11)*

Section 3

Clause 1: New States may be admitted by the Congress into this Union; but no new State shall be formed or erected within the Jurisdiction of any other State; nor any State be formed by the Junction of two or more States, or Parts of States, without the Consent of the Legislatures of the States concerned as well as of the Congress.

Clause 2: The Congress shall have Power to dispose of and make all needful Rules and Regulations respecting the Territory or other Property belonging to the United States; and nothing in this Constitution shall be so construed as to Prejudice any Claims of the United States, or of any particular State.

Section 4

The United States shall guarantee to every State in this Union a Republican Form of Government, and shall protect each of them against Invasion; and on Application of the Legislature, or of the Executive (when the Legislature cannot be convened) against domestic Violence.

Article V

The Congress, whenever two thirds of both Houses shall deem it necessary, shall propose Amendments to this Constitution, or, on the Application of the Legislatures of two thirds of the several States, shall call a Convention for proposing Amendments, which, in either Case, shall be valid to all Intents and Purposes, as Part of this Constitution, when ratified by the Legislatures of three fourths of the several States, or by Conventions in three fourths thereof, as the one or the other Mode of Ratification may be proposed by the Congress; Provided that no Amendment which may be made prior to the Year One thousand eight hundred and eight shall in any Manner affect the first and fourth Clauses in the Ninth Section of the first Article; and that no State, without its Consent, shall be deprived of its equal Suffrage in the Senate.

Article VI

Clause 1: All Debts contracted and Engagements entered into, before the Adoption of this Constitution, shall be as valid against the United States under this Constitution, as under the Confederation.

Clause 2: This Constitution, and the Laws of the United States which shall be made in Pursuance thereof; and all Treaties made, or which shall be made, under the Authority of the United States, shall be the supreme Law of the Land; and the Judges in every State shall be bound thereby, any Thing in the Constitution or Laws of any State to the Contrary notwithstanding.

Clause 3: The Senators and Representatives before mentioned, and the Members of the several State Legislatures, and all executive and judicial Officers, both of the United States and of the several States, shall be bound by Oath or Affirmation, to support this Constitution; but no religious Test shall ever be required as a Qualification to any Office or public Trust under the United States.

Article VII

The Ratification of the Conventions of nine States, shall be sufficient for the Establishment of this Constitution between the States so ratifying the Same.

Done in Convention by the Unanimous Consent of the States present the Seventeenth Day of September in the Year of our Lord one thousand seven hundred and Eighty seven and of the Independence of the United States of America the Twelfth In witness whereof We have hereunto subscribed our Names,

GO WASHINGTON—Presidt. and deputy from Virginia
[Signed also by the deputies of twelve States.]

Delaware

George Read
Gunning Bedford Jr.
John Dickinson
Richard Bassett
Jacob Broom

Maryland

James McHenry
Dan of ST Tho. Jenifer
DanL Carroll.

Virginia

John Blair
James Madison Jr.

North Carolina

William Blount
Richard Dobbs Spaight
Hugh Williamson

South Carolina

John Rutledge
Charles Cotesworth Pinckney
Charles Pinckney
Pierce Butler

Georgia

William Few
Abraham Baldwin

New Hampshire

John Langdon
Nicholas Gilman

Massachusetts

Nathaniel Gorham
Rufus King

Connecticut

William Samuel Johnson
Roger Sherman

New York

Alexander Hamilton

New Jersey

William Livingston
David Brearley.
William Paterson
Jonathan Dayton

Pennsylvania

Benjamin Franklin
Thomas Mifflin
Robert Morris
George Clymer
Thomas FitzSimons
Jared Ingersoll
James Wilson
Gouverneur Morris

Attest William Jackson Secretary

The Constitution was ratified
on June 21, 1788.

AMENDMENTS TO THE CONSTITUTION

The first ten amendments were ratified on December 15, 1791.

Amendment I

Congress shall make no law respecting an establishment of religion, or prohibiting the free exercise thereof; or abridging the freedom of speech, or of the press; or the right of the people peaceably to assemble, and to petition the Government for a redress of grievances.

Amendment II

A well regulated Militia, being necessary to the security of a free State, the right of the people to keep and bear Arms, shall not be infringed.

Amendment III

No Soldier shall, in time of peace be quartered in any house, without the consent of the Owner, nor in time of war, but in a manner to be prescribed by law.

Amendment IV

The right of the people to be secure in their persons, houses, papers, and effects, against unreasonable searches and seizures, shall not be violated, and no Warrants shall issue, but upon probable cause, supported by Oath or affirmation, and particularly describing the place to be searched, and the persons or things to be seized.

Amendment V

No person shall be held to answer for a capital, or otherwise infamous crime, unless on a presentment or indictment of a Grand Jury, except in cases arising in the land or naval forces, or in the Militia, when in actual service in time of War or public danger; nor shall any person be subject for the same offence to be twice put in jeopardy of life or limb; nor shall be compelled in any criminal case to be a witness against himself, nor be deprived of life, liberty, or property, without due process of law; nor shall private property be taken for public use, without just compensation.

Amendment VI

In all criminal prosecutions, the accused shall enjoy the right to a speedy and public trial, by an impartial jury of the State and district wherein the crime shall have been committed, which district shall have been previously ascertained by law, and to be informed of the nature and cause of the accusation; to be confronted with the witnesses against him; to have compulsory process for obtaining witnesses in his favor, and to have the Assistance of Counsel for his defence.

Amendment VII

In Suits at common law, where the value in controversy shall exceed twenty dollars, the right of trial by jury shall be preserved, and no fact tried by a jury, shall be otherwise re-examined in any Court of the United States, than according to the rules of the common law.

Amendment VIII

Excessive bail shall not be required, nor excessive fines imposed, nor cruel and unusual punishments inflicted.

Amendment IX

The enumeration in the Constitution, of certain rights, shall not be construed to deny or disparage others retained by the people.

Amendment X

The powers not delegated to the United States by the Constitution, nor prohibited by it to the States, are reserved to the States respectively, or to the people.

Amendment XI (Ratified February 7, 1795)

The Judicial power of the United States shall not be construed to extend to any suit in law or equity, commenced or prosecuted against one of the United States by Citizens of another State, or by Citizens or Subjects of any Foreign State.

Amendment XII (Ratified June 15, 1804)

The Electors shall meet in their respective states, and vote by ballot for President and Vice-President, one of whom, at least, shall not be an inhabitant of the same state with themselves; they shall name in their ballots the person voted for as President, and in distinct ballots the person voted for as Vice-President, and they shall make distinct lists of all persons voted for as President, and of all persons voted for as Vice-President, and of the number of votes for each, which lists they shall sign and certify, and transmit sealed to the seat of the government of the United States, directed to the President of the Senate;—The President of the Senate shall, in the presence of the Senate and House of Representatives, open all the certificates and the votes shall then be counted;—The person having the greatest number of votes for President, shall be the President, if such number be a majority of the whole number of Electors appointed; and if no person have such majority, then from the persons having the highest numbers not exceeding three on the list of those voted for as President, the House of Representatives shall choose immediately, by ballot, the President. But in choosing the President, the votes shall be taken by states, the representation from each state having one vote; a quorum for this purpose shall consist of a member or members from two-thirds of the states, and a majority of all the states shall be necessary to a choice. And if the House of Representatives shall not choose a President whenever the right of choice shall devolve upon them, before the fourth day of March next following, then the Vice-President shall act as President, as in the case of the death or other constitutional disability of the President. *(See Note 14)*—The person having the greatest number of votes as Vice-President, shall be the Vice-President, if such number be a majority of the whole number of Electors appointed, and if no person have a majority, then from the two highest numbers on the list, the Senate shall choose the Vice-President; a quorum for the purpose shall consist of two-thirds of the whole number of Senators, and a majority of the whole number shall be necessary to a choice. But no person constitutionally ineligible to the office of President shall be eligible to that of Vice-President of the United States.

Amendment XIII (Ratified December 6, 1865)

Section 1. Neither slavery nor involuntary servitude, except as a punishment for crime whereof the party shall have been duly convicted, shall exist within the United States, or any place subject to their jurisdiction.

Section 2. Congress shall have power to enforce this article by appropriate legislation.

Amendment XIV (Ratified July 9, 1868)

Section 1. All persons born or naturalized in the United States, and subject to the jurisdiction thereof, are citizens of the United States and of the State wherein they reside. No State shall make or enforce any law which shall abridge the privileges or immunities of citizens of the United States; nor shall any State deprive any person of life, liberty, or property, without due process of law; nor deny to any person within its jurisdiction the equal protection of the laws.

Section 2. Representatives shall be apportioned among the several States according to their respective numbers, counting the whole number of persons in each State, excluding Indians not taxed. But when the right to vote at any election for the choice of electors for President and Vice President of the United States, Representatives in Congress, the Executive and Judicial officers of a State, or the members of the Legislature thereof, is denied to any of the male inhabitants of such State, being twenty-one years of age, *(See Note 15)* and citizens of the United States, or in any way abridged, except for participation in rebellion, or other crime, the basis of representation therein shall be reduced in the proportion which the number of such male citizens shall bear to the whole number of male citizens twenty-one years of age in such State.

Section 3. No person shall be a Senator or Representative in Congress, or elector of President and Vice President, or hold any office, civil or military, under the United States, or under any State, who, having previously taken an oath, as a member of Congress, or as an officer of the United States, or as a member of any State legislature, or as an executive or judicial officer of any State, to support the Constitution of the United States, shall have engaged in insurrection or rebellion against the same, or given aid or comfort to the enemies thereof. But Congress may by a vote of two-thirds of each House, remove such disability.

Section 4. The validity of the public debt of the United States, authorized by law, including debts incurred for payment of pensions and bounties for services in suppressing insurrection or rebellion, shall not be questioned. But neither the United States nor any State shall assume or pay any debt or obligation incurred in aid of insurrection or rebellion against the United States, or any claim for the loss or emancipation of any slave; but all such debts, obligations and claims shall be held illegal and void.

Section 5. The Congress shall have power to enforce, by appropriate legislation, the provisions of this Article.

Amendment XV (Ratified February 3, 1870)

Section 1. The right of citizens of the United States to vote shall not be denied or abridged by the United States or by any State on account of race, color, or previous condition of servitude.

Section 2. The Congress shall have power to enforce this article by appropriate legislation.

Amendment XVI (Ratified February 3, 1913)

The Congress shall have power to lay and collect taxes on incomes, from whatever source derived, without apportionment among the several States, and without regard to any census or enumeration.

Amendment XVII (Ratified April 8, 1913)

The Senate of the United States shall be composed of two Senators from each State, elected by the people thereof, for six years; and each Senator shall have one vote. The electors in each State shall have the qualifications requisite for electors of the most numerous branch of the State legislatures.

When vacancies happen in the representation of any State in the Senate, the executive authority of such State shall issue writs of election to fill such vacancies: Provided, That the legislature of any State may empower the executive thereof to make temporary appointments until the people fill the vacancies by election as the legislature may direct.

This amendment shall not be so construed as to affect the election or term of any Senator chosen before it becomes valid as part of the Constitution.

Amendment XVIII (Ratified January 16, 1919)

Section 1. After one year from the ratification of this article the manufacture, sale, or transportation of intoxicating liquors within, the importation thereof into, or the exportation thereof from the United States and all territory subject to the jurisdiction thereof for beverage purposes is hereby prohibited.

Section 2. The Congress and the several States shall have concurrent power to enforce this article by appropriate legislation.

Section 3. This article shall be inoperative unless it shall have been ratified as an amendment to the Constitution by the legislatures of the several States, as provided in the Constitution, within seven years from the date of the submission hereof to the States by the Congress.

Amendment XIX (Ratified August 18, 1920)

The right of citizens of the United States to vote shall not be denied or abridged by the United States or by any State on account of sex.

Congress shall have power to enforce this article by appropriate legislation.

Amendment XX (Ratified January 23, 1933)

Section 1. The terms of the President and Vice President shall end at noon on the 20th day of January, and the terms of Senators and Representatives at noon on the 3d day of January, of the years in which such terms would have ended if this article had not been ratified; and the terms of their successors shall then begin.

Section 2. The Congress shall assemble at least once in every year, and such meeting shall begin at noon on the 3d day of January, unless they shall by law appoint a different day.

Section 3. If, at the time fixed for the beginning of the term of the President, the President elect shall have died, the Vice President elect shall become President. If a President shall not have been chosen before the time fixed for the beginning of his term, or if the President elect shall have failed to qualify, then the Vice President elect shall act as President until a President shall have qualified; and the Congress may by law provide for the case wherein neither a President elect nor a Vice President elect shall have qualified, declaring who shall then act as President, or the manner in which one who is to act shall be selected, and such person shall act accordingly until a President or Vice President shall have qualified.

Section 4. The Congress may by law provide for the case of the death of any of the persons from whom the House of Representatives may choose a President whenever the right of choice shall have devolved upon them, and for the case of the death of any of the persons from whom the Senate may choose a Vice President whenever the right of choice shall have devolved upon them.

Section 5. Sections 1 and 2 shall take effect on the 15th day of October following the ratification of this Article.

Section 6. This article shall be inoperative unless it shall have been ratified as an amendment to the Constitution by the legislatures of three-fourths of the several States within seven years from the date of its submission.

Amendment XXI (Ratified December 5, 1933)

Section 1. The eighteenth article of amendment to the Constitution of the United States is hereby repealed.

Section 2. The transportation or importation into any State, Territory, or possession of the United States for delivery or use therein of intoxicating liquors, in violation of the laws thereof, is hereby prohibited.

Section 3. This article shall be inoperative unless it shall have been ratified as an amendment to the Constitution by conventions in the several States, as provided in the Constitution, within seven years from the date of the submission hereof to the States by the Congress.

Amendment XXII (Ratified February 27, 1951)

Section 1. No person shall be elected to the office of the President more than twice, and no person who has held the office of President, or acted as President, for more than two years of a term to which some other person was elected President shall be elected to the office of the President more than once. But this article shall not apply to any person holding the office of President when this article was proposed by the Congress, and shall not prevent any person who may be holding the office of President, or acting as President, during the term within which this article becomes operative from holding the office of President or acting as President during the remainder of such term.

Section 2. This article shall be inoperative unless it shall have been ratified as an amendment to the Constitution by the legislatures of three-fourths of the several states within seven years from the date of its submission to the states by the Congress.

Amendment XXIII (Ratified March 29, 1961)

Section 1. The District constituting the seat of government of the United States shall appoint in such manner as the Congress may direct:

A number of electors of President and Vice President equal to the whole number of Senators and Representatives in Congress to which the District would be entitled if it were a state, but in no event more than the least populous state; they shall be in addition to those appointed by the states, but they shall be considered, for the purposes of the election of President and Vice President, to be electors appointed by a state; and they shall meet in the District and perform such duties as provided by the twelfth article of amendment.

Section 2. The Congress shall have power to enforce this article by appropriate legislation.

Amendment XXIV (Ratified January 23, 1964)

Section 1. The right of citizens of the United States to vote in any primary or other election for President or Vice President, for electors for President or Vice President, or for

Senator or Representative in Congress, shall not be denied or abridged by the United States or any state by reason of failure to pay any poll tax or other tax.

Section 2. The Congress shall have power to enforce this article by appropriate legislation.

Amendment XXV (Ratified February 10, 1967)

Section 1. In case of the removal of the President from office or of his death or resignation, the Vice President shall become President.

Section 2. Whenever there is a vacancy in the office of the Vice President, the President shall nominate a Vice President who shall take office upon confirmation by a majority vote of both Houses of Congress.

Section 3. Whenever the President transmits to the President pro tempore of the Senate and the Speaker of the House of Representatives his written declaration that he is unable to discharge the powers and duties of his office, and until he transmits to them a written declaration to the contrary, such powers and duties shall be discharged by the Vice President as Acting President.

Section 4. Whenever the Vice President and a majority of either the principal officers of the executive departments or of such other body as Congress may by law provide, transmit to the President pro tempore of the Senate and the Speaker of the House of Representatives their written declaration that the President is unable to discharge the powers and duties of his office, the Vice President shall immediately assume the powers and duties of the office as Acting President.

Thereafter, when the President transmits to the President pro tempore of the Senate and the Speaker of the House of Representatives his written declaration that no inability exists, he shall resume the powers and duties of his office unless the Vice President and a majority of either the principal officers of the executive department or of such other body as Congress may by law provide, transmit within four days to the President pro tempore of the Senate and the Speaker of the House of Representatives their written declaration that the President is unable to discharge the powers and duties of his office. Thereupon Congress shall decide the issue, assembling within forty-eight hours for that purpose if not in session. If the Congress, within twenty-one days after receipt of the latter written declaration, or, if Congress is not in session, within twenty-one days after Congress is required to assemble, determines by two-thirds vote of both Houses that the President is unable to discharge the powers and duties of his office, the Vice President shall continue to discharge the same as Acting President; otherwise, the President shall resume the powers and duties of his office.

Amendment XXVI (Ratified July 1, 1971)

Section 1. The right of citizens of the United States, who are 18 years of age or older, to vote, shall not be denied or abridged by the United States or any state on account of age.

Section 2. The Congress shall have the power to enforce this article by appropriate legislation.

Amendment XXVII (Ratified May 7, 1992)

No law varying the compensation for the services of the Senators and Representatives shall take effect until an election of Representatives shall have intervened.

INDEX

Note: Page numbers in *italic* type refer to figures or tables.

ABOUT THE AUTHOR

Steven J. Cann is Full Professor, Prelaw Coordinator, and former Chair of the Department of Political Science at Washburn University of Topeka, Kansas. He taught for eight years at Idaho State University before accepting his current position at Washburn. He has published in the area of substantive constitutional law, primarily in civil liberties. He has served on the Board of Directors for the Kansas Chapter of the American Society for Public Administration and was president of this group from 1999 to 2001. Dr. Cann has been certified as an expert witness in Kansas District Court, where he has testified as an expert on public opinion surveys where a survey was used as the basis for a change of venue motion in a first-degree murder case. He is a four-time nominee for Who's Who Among America's Teachers. He is currently a volunteer mediator in a Kansas program for juvenile offenders and victims in mediation, and he also volunteers as a mediator in parent/adolescent conflicts. He coaches the undergraduate mock trial teams at Washburn University.

He received his master's degree from North Dakota State University and his Ph.D. in political science from Purdue University in 1977.